P9-DUC-317

Dreamweaver® MX:
The Complete Reference

About the Authors

Ray West is the Vice President and CIO of Workable Solutions, Inc., an Orlando-based company specializing in the Web-based administration of health care alliances. He has been building data-driven Web applications since 1995 including work for HBO, NBC, and *USAToday*, and is coauthor of the best-selling book *Dreamweaver UltraDev 4: The Complete Reference* (Osborne, 2001). Ray lives in Orlando with his wife and son.

Tom Muck is co-author of four books, including the bestseller *Dreamweaver UltraDev4: The Complete Reference*. He is an extensibility expert focused on the integration of Macromedia products with ColdFusion and other languages, applications, and technologies. Tom has been recognized for this expertise as the 2000 recipient of Macromedia's Best UltraDev Extension Award; he also authors articles and speaks at conferences on this and related subjects. As Senior Applications Developer for Integram in Northern Virginia, Tom develops back-end applications for expedited, electronic communications. Tom runs the Basic-UltraDev site with Ray West and is a founding member of the DW Team (www.dwteam.com).

Dreamweaver® MX: The Complete Reference

Ray West and Tom Muck

McGraw-Hill/Osborne

New York   Chicago   San Francisco
Lisbon   London   Madrid   Mexico City
Milan   New Delhi   San Juan
Seoul   Singapore   Sydney   Toronto

McGraw-Hill/Osborne
2600 Tenth Street
Berkeley, California 94710
U.S.A.

To arrange bulk purchase discounts for sales promotions, premiums, or fund-raisers, please contact **McGraw-Hill/**Osborne at the above address. For information on translations or book distributors outside the U.S.A., please see the International Contact Information page immediately following the index of this book.

Dreamweaver® MX: The Complete Reference

234567890 DOC DOC 0198765432

ISBN 0-07-219514-2

Publisher	**Copy Editor**
Brandon A. Nordin	Darren Meiss
Vice President & Associate Publisher	**Proofreaders**
Scott Rogers	Claire Splan, Mike McGee
Acquisitions Editor	**Indexer**
Jim Schachterle	Claire Splan
Project Editor	**Computer Designers**
Jennifer Malnick	Carie Abrew, Melinda Moore Lytle, Lauren McCarthy
Acquisitions Coordinator	**Illustrators**
Timothy Madrid	Michael Mueller, Lyssa Wald
Technical Editor	**Series Design**
Massimo Foti	Peter F. Hancik

This book was composed with Corel VENTURA™ Publisher.

Contents at a Glance

Part III   An Introduction to Web Scripting

Part IV   Adding Database Features to Your Site

Part V   Advanced Data Integration

Part VI   Getting the Most Out of Dreamweaver MX

Contents

Part I

Getting Started with Dreamweaver MX

Part IV

Adding Database Features to Your Site

Part V

Advanced Data Integration

Part VI

Getting the Most Out of Dreamweaver MX

Foreword

"One Tool." That's the phrase we used around here at Macromedia to define the idea of combining the best of Dreamweaver, UltraDev, ColdFusion Studio, and HomeSite into a single product. The reasoning behind it is pretty clear if you look back to where we were just one year ago. If you took a look at the Web development tool selection from Macromedia after the merger with Allaire, things were a bit confusing, to say the least. We offered nine different stand-alone products and "Studios" for HTML and Web application development.

All of these products made perfect sense given the climate they were developed in, and the customer sets they intended to serve. But it turns out that Web development had changed by the time all these products came under the Macromedia banner, and it was time for Macromedia to build a tool that reacted to that change. In speaking with Web developers about where they saw the future of Web development, three central themes emerged pretty quickly: accessibility, maintainability, and reusability.

Accessibility is not just about building sites to be Section 508, or W3C level 2 compliant; it's about centering Web development efforts around the goals of the user, rather than the goals of the company. The user experience on the Web was stagnating—everything was still too hard, whether accessing the Web with a keyboard and a mouse, or with a screenreader and touch pad. Something had to be done to make Web sites more usable.

Maintainability came through in the cries of Web developers to start building sites in standard ways, using standard technologies. It was no longer about having the hippest, coolest Web site built using whatever quirky coding techniques the nose-pierced, tattooed Web developer decided to implement. Adult supervision has finally come to Web development, and people want sites built in standard ways so that they can be developed in a straightforward manner and passed on to teams who can maintain them without ripping them apart to see what's going on.

The idea of reusable frameworks and components has existed in the world of software development for years, but it has just recently been brought to the Web development arena. When we set out to build a new version of Dreamweaver, for example, we don't throw out the old version and start over, we build on top of what we already have. Most major Web sites fail to do this, however. How many times have you seen a Web site completely rebuilt from the ground up simply because the requirements of the site outgrew the technology with which it was built? Finally, with technologies like J2EE, .NET, and Web services, developers have frameworks around which they can build their sites so that they don't have to start all over every time a new requirement is added, or a new corporate strategy is chosen.

Clearly, Web development is entering a new era, and it is time for a new tool to step up to the plate and provide a complete development environment for building professional sites. Dreamweaver MX is our attempt to do just that. Try as we might, though, we rarely seem to get things correct on the first try, and a lot of credit for Dreamweaver MX has to go to users like Ray and Tom for their patience and help throughout the development cycle. Having a perspective from people like Ray and Tom, who have to both use the product and explain it to all sorts of users, was invaluable to us as we went from planning to beta to the final release you see before you. Ray and Tom should stand up and take a good deal of credit for this release, and I'm sure this volume of the Complete Reference will be a welcome addition to the library of both seasoned veterans and those new to the Dreamweaver world. I welcome all of you to this release of Dreamweaver, and hope that you'll continue to send us your feedback and requests so that the next version will be even better.

David Deming
Product Manager,
Dreamweaver
Macromedia

Acknowledgments

The longer we do this, the longer the list of people we need to thank gets. We are truly appreciative of everyone in the Dreamweaver community who has been so supportive of the things we have done. We hope that we continue to live up to your expectations.

We have received a tremendous amount of support from the folks at Macromedia: Matt Brown, Dave Deming, Tom Hale, Susan Morrow, Susan Marshall, Mike Downey, and, of course, Sho, Randy, Sam, Lori, and the rest of the development team.

At Osborne, we could not do this without Jim Schachterle, Tim Madrid, Jenny Malnick, Wendy Rinaldi, and Sherry Bonelli.

Tom continues to amaze me with how adept he is at learning new things and explaining them clearly. I wish everyone could find such a partner. You could all do great things.

And thank you mostly to my wife, Susan, and our son, Caleb. I hope you are half as proud of me as I am of the two of you.

—*Ray*

The writing process is a collaborative effort and, as such, many hard-working and supportive individuals need to be acknowledged. Thanks to everyone at Osborne for being so helpful in making the book-writing and publishing process go so smoothly, especially Jenny, Jim, and Tim.

My partner Ray provides the perfect complement to my writing. The book you see in front of you is a combined effort that makes this reference complete. Ray's initiative and enthusiasm for new projects keeps us thriving. Thanks, Ray!

Massimo is the man when it comes to Dreamweaver, and he provides excellent technical advice throughout the writing process. He is also a good friend and a guiding light for the Dreamweaver community. Thanks, Massimo!

Everyone at Macromedia has been very supportive of our efforts. The engineers especially deserve a round of applause for delivering the greatest Dreamweaver version to date. As a Web developer, I find the program simply awesome to work with. As an extension developer, I am excited about all of the advances in the foundation of the program, and the integration with other Macromedia programs.

Last, but not least, I have to thank my wife, Janet, who is always a source of inspiration. She provides support and encouragement during my long workdays and often a fresh pair of eyes to edit my chapters. Without her help, none of this would have been possible, and it certainly wouldn't have been as enjoyable. She gets a thank you and a big kiss.

—Tom

Introduction

Welcome to *Dreamweaver MX: The Complete Reference*. Dreamweaver has grown a lot since the last version. In a nod to the ascendancy of the dynamic site, UltraDev's features are included and expanded in the core Dreamweaver product. Macromedia now owns ColdFusion and JRun, making them a true contender in the application server market. As a result, we have a ton of new features to come to grips with and new capabilities to exploit in this version.

There is a learning curve that comes with this much power, though. The new interfaces can be a bit overwhelming, and the server-side functionality can be confusing to a novice. That is why this book is so important. It gives you all of the tools you need to get started and become productive with Dreamweaver MX—in one package. We hope you enjoy it.

Who Should Read This Book

Eighty percent of Web designers use Dreamweaver. If you are in that crowd, you should read this book. There is something in this book that will benefit almost anyone—from beginner to professional—with an interest in Web Development with Macromedia products.

If you are a developer, we can show you how to get the most out of Dreamweaver's tools. If you are not yet a developer, you will do well to become one, as the Web is not standing still, and dynamic, data-driven sites are the future. This book can ease you into that role within the comfort of a product you are used to.

How This Book Should Be Read

The short answer is, however you would like to read it. Chapters certainly do build upon each other, and you might find it less confusing to at least thumb through chapters with familiar content, just so you know where we are in the discussion. But you can safely refer to individual chapters for their specific content on most topics.

We have tried to play a dual role between traditional reference and tutorial by couching many of our explanations within projects and examples. Hopefully, this approach serves a broad audience well.

What Is In This Book

We cover Dreamweaver MX, Fireworks MX, Flash MX, and a bunch of related technologies like ASP, ASP.NET, ColdFusion, SQL, and database design in the pages of this book. It is laid out so that you should be able to locate the parts you are interested in pretty easily, but here is the overview.

Part I in an introduction to the basic concepts that make up Dreamweaver. It takes you through the beginnings of a site's development including much of the graphic layout.

Part II covers the design and construction of an entire Web site, including site design, page design, Fireworks integration, Flash, CSS, and Javascript.

Part III covers Web scripting using the languages supported in Dreamweaver MX.

Part IV picks up with the construction of the Web application and adds data functionality to the site.

Part V covers advanced data-driven topics, including data-driven Flash and eCommerce.

Part VI is for the adventurous, and covers using and creating extensions for Dreamweaver MX.

Conventions Used In This Book

We have used several conventions to make this book easier to read.

You can identify code listings by their typeface. Here is an example:

```
<%
Dim Text
Test = "Hello World"
Response.Write Text
%>
```

If a line of code needs to be split across two lines, you will see the ¬ character.

When you are supposed to press a key or a combination of keys, they will be identified like this:

CTRL-F2

Steps that you need to follow will be presented as a numbered list.

Downloads for Examples

This book demonstrates several examples using a fictitious site named Bettergig.com. The database, template, stylesheet, and other code for the book are available for download at www.dwteam.com/tcr or by going to www.osborne.com and following the links. Also, a working site showing some of the functionality created in the book is at www.bettergig.com.

Support and Errata

We do our best to provide help and errata information at our Web site at www.dwteam.com. Please visit us there and let us know how you liked the book and what else you would like to see. Thanks and enjoy.

The Complete Reference

Dreamweaver MX

Part I

Getting Started with Dreamweaver MX

Dreamweaver
MX

Chapter 1

And Then
There Was One

W e began the last version of this book talking about how fast things move in the Internet world. We had just been hit with a double shot of UltraDev within six months and we were wondering if we could ever write 1,000-page books fast enough for the team at Macromedia.

Well, it took a little longer this time—about 18 months in fact. People have been clamoring for news about a new Dreamweaver release for months. Book publishers even had mystery Dreamweaver and UltraDev 5 releases listed at Amazon long before anything would come out of San Francisco. You are about to find out why Macromedia amended its notoriously aggressive release schedule and exactly how worthwhile the wait was.

On April 29, 2002, Macromedia made one of the most significant announcements in its history. Three new products were revealed that, along with the Flash release of the previous month, form the core of its new product strategy, called MX. The MX products represent the culmination of the integration of Elemental Software and Allaire into Macromedia's toolbox with the best suite of Web development and server software available. In fact, they are so well integrated that we cover portions of Fireworks MX, Flash MX, and ColdFusion MX in this book on Dreamweaver MX. Get some coffee; there is a lot to talk about.

Revising a title like this is difficult. We were tempted to throw everything out and start over with new examples and new ideas. As we review what has happened in the world of Web development in the last year and a half, there have been some tremendous changes. Microsoft's .NET platform has been released, and Dreamweaver MX supports it as a server model. Other technologies such as XML have come into their own and are significant parts of the functionality of the databases that are commonly used. New Windows and Macintosh versions have been released and new browsers make cross-platform development even more challenging.

Perhaps the biggest change is the market for this book. We were the guys out in safe little UltraDev left field until now. But Macromedia's decision to combine Dreamweaver and UltraDev into a single Web application platform has forced us into the mainstream, and will force Dreamweaver users everywhere to reckon with these new features. We encourage you to embrace all of the power of this application even if you can't yet spell PHP.

Still, a lot is the same as it was. SQL (Structured Query Language) and database design concepts are essentially the same as they were. Likewise, the core technologies that control the Internet are still in place and have just as much impact on the work you will do as ever. Netscape 4 is still the bane of the modern designer, and millions of Web sites still run good old traditional ASP.

This is the complete reference to Dreamweaver MX, just as a dictionary is a complete reference to a language. When you grab a copy of Webster's to look up "solipsistic," you may not need the part that defines "cat," but you still expect it to be there; it's the dictionary and somebody will likely need it at some point. Likewise, to truly be worthy of the title "Complete Reference," it is appropriate for us to cover the entire range of Dreamweaver MX and its related technologies. Therefore, we begin at the beginning.

The Internet

If you have been working with the Internet for longer than, say, a week, you have no doubt heard some permutation of the following question: "Oh yeah, the Internet—now, who exactly owns that?" Even worse are those that equate it with sex and danger or those that use the terms Internet and AOL interchangeably. It's easy to roll your eyes and snigger at those less hip than you, but it is often more difficult to clearly articulate exactly what the Internet is and where it came from.

There have been several revolutions in world history that changed the way people lived their lives permanently. But none has occurred as quickly, ubiquitously, and nonchalantly as the Internet revolution. The Internet has affected every corner of our culture in profound ways. At home, at school, and at work, our lives are different, if not better, as we move into the Information Age.

It has been said that information is power; and if that is true, then we are the most powerful we have ever been. From the theme ingredient on the next episode of Iron Chef, to last-minute income tax filing forms, to the complete text of pending legislation, there is almost nothing you can't find with just a little effort and access to the World Wide Web. It is interesting that one of the most exciting uses of twenty-first century technology is the exercise of ideals hundreds of years old. Speech and the flow of ideas have never been more free.

Our businesses have changed. The bookstore isn't necessarily down the street anymore—often it is at the other end of a Uniform Resource Locator (URL) such as www.amazon.com or www.bn.com. People who could never have competed with the "big boys" now have all but equal standing and an unprecedented opportunity to market and sell their products.

We can communicate as never before. Whether it is parents to their kid in a school across the country, constituents to their representative, or a satisfied (or unsatisfied) customer to the CEO, we are more in touch with the world around us. The handwritten family letter of yesterday is today's smartly formatted electronic presentation complete with the latest pictures of the grandkids delivered instantly without a stamp. The Internet makes the world smaller than even Mr. Disney imagined.

But as with any medium with the potential of the Internet, those who choose to fill it with content bear a certain responsibility. Although the Web is full of sites and pages and words of incredible utility, it is also full of poor design, bad programming, and content of dubious validity. This book aims to help you learn how to use one of the most powerful Web design tools available so that you can make a positive contribution.

The History of the Internet

Do you remember Sputnik? The sad fact is, a growing number of computer whizzes weren't around to personally remember the Bicentennial, *This Is Spinal Tap*, or the last episode of *M*A*S*H*, much less the 1957 launch of a little Russian satellite. But that little satellite was the first launched from Earth, and it scared the pants off of the United States military, it being the Cold War and all.

The next year, the Department of Defense formed the Advanced Research Projects Agency (ARPA) to establish and advance U.S. dominance in military science and technology. By 1965, in its effort to establish efficient communications networks, ARPA had developed the concept of a distributed network, and it sponsored a study on networking time-shared computers. "The Experimental Network" was formed between three computers at ARPA, MIT, and System Development Corporation in California communicating over a 1,200 bps phone line. This led to the initial designs of what would become the ARPANET.

Meanwhile, studies were being conducted at several locations regarding a new technology known as *packet switching*. The concept of packet switching involved the routing of information across distributed networks in small chunks called *packets*. This would allow for the efficient transfer and recovery of data with "no single outage point," as Paul Baran put it in 1964.

These two paths began to converge in 1968 when ARPA put its design out to bid. Companies were asked to propose methods by which the ARPANET could be constructed and put to use. Bolt Beranek and Newman, Inc. (BBN) was awarded the contract later that year to build Interface Message Processors (IMPs). Construction began in 1969 with 4 IMP nodes connecting computers over 50 Kbps phone lines.

The 1970s was an exciting decade, with progress being made on several fronts. As the ARPANET grew, other independent networks appeared that would later be connected to it. 1971 saw the first intermachine messaging, which was expanded onto the ARPANET the following year along with the introduction of the @ symbol in the addressing scheme. Larger configurations of up to 40 machines at a time were demonstrated. In addition, other countries began to develop their own versions of the ARPANET. The Telnet specification was developed in 1972.

Two of the most significant events occurred in 1973. The first international connections were made to the ARPANET when the University of London hooked in through NORSAR. And at Harvard, Bob Metcalfe (the eventual founder of 3Com) wrote his Ph.D. thesis describing Ethernet. Ethernet was tested at the Xerox Parc laboratories (eventually responsible for the introduction of the mouse to desktop computing and the inspiration for the LISA, and eventually, the Macintosh interface). Ethernet is still the protocol of choice for thousands of LANs and the Internet in general. The specification for the File Transfer Protocol was developed in 1973.

The next several years saw the expansion of the ARPANET, along with the continued development of technologies that would become central to the Internet. In 1974, the Transmission Control Protocol (TCP) specification was published; and in 1975, the first list server was established with a science fiction lovers' list becoming one of the first mailing lists. Unix to Unix Copy (UUCP) was created in 1976, and 1977 saw the completion of the specification for networked mail. In 1978, TCP was divided into TCP and the Internet Protocol (IP), which remains the communications protocol of today's Internet. The decade was capped off by the invention of USENET (the system of newsgroups) in 1979 and, perhaps most importantly, the introduction of emoticons (the little emotion indicators :-)) that litter our text communications to this day).

The early 1980s can be characterized as a time of rapid network creation. Across the world, networks appeared based on many of the specifications of the prior period. As many new networks developed, some of the earliest began to make a migration from independence to cooperation in what was becoming an international network.

The years 1983 and 1984 were important. Several things happened in succession during this period that spurred the growth of the Internet. First, in 1983, the Name Server concept was developed, which made it possible for computers to communicate without knowing the exact path to one another across the network. This culminated in the introduction of the Domain Name Service (DNS) in 1984. Also in 1983, connectivity extended to the desktop workstation. This led to the number of Internet hosts breaking 1,000 the next year.

In 1987, the number of hosts broke 10,000. In 1988, the communications backbone was upgraded to a T1 (1.544 Mbps) connection, which led to the number of hosts breaking 100,000 in 1989. During the late 1980s, there was some separation between the ARPANET and what was becoming the NSFNET, a commercially supported network. Although TCP/IP was the standard, the Department of Defense decided to go with a competing protocol. By the early 1990s, ARPANET was gone and the Internet was on its way to commercial glory.

What the early 1980s were to the technical development of the Internet, the early 1990s were to its raw growth. In 1990, the first commercial dial-up server provider came online. In 1991, the communications backbone was upgraded to a T3 (45 Mbps); and by 1992, the number of hosts broke 1,000,000.

In 1993, Internic was created to manage Internet services through contracts with AT&T, Network Solutions, and General Atomics. In each of the successive years, more and more countries established connections to the network, making it a truly worldwide network.

The World Wide Web

In 1991, a developer named Tim Berners Lee envisioned a means of going beyond the simple back-and-forth transfer of files over UUCP and FTP connections. He wanted a way to actually view files over remote connections in a formatted way that made scientific and technical papers available to research associates across the network. Mr. Berners Lee developed the concept of the World Wide Web, over which files could be viewed. Those files would basically be text files, but they would be marked up with a tag language (a subset of SGML called *Hypertext Markup Language*, or *HTML*) that enabled their formatting in a hierarchal way that was appropriate for the technical content he wanted to display.

The potential of this new medium was quickly realized. By the next year, the World Bank was online and the term "surfing the Internet" was coined. In 1993, Mosaic (the first real browser) experienced an unbelievable growth rate as more and more people went online for the first time.

The Web continued to expand in 1994. More commercial businesses opened for e-business, the first cyber-bank opened, and the first banner ads appeared—.com became the most popular domain extension, followed by .edu for educational institutions.

Note   *If you were around to view content over the Web on pre-Mosaic browsers, you can truly appreciate the exponential growth graphical browsers has spurred. Although some were awed by the ability to FTP into libraries around the world and view simple HTML files in text-based browsers, it took the eye-candy that the graphics-based browsers allowed to make the medium popular with less technically involved users.*

By 1995, use of the Web surpassed the use of FTP. For the first time, registration authorities began charging to register domain names. One of the most popular technologies became search engines, by which you could find information all over the world.

The last five years have seen a myriad of shifts and changes in the landscape of the Internet and the World Wide Web. Technologies such as Java, .NET, online stock brokerage, online banking, Internet phones, MP3, streaming audio and video, and DSL have made the Internet more accessible and made it more worth accessing. What took 30 years to develop has become ubiquitous and universally useful in just over five years. But the core of the Internet is much like electricity. Although the gadgets that we plug in today are fancier that those of yesteryear, they still plug in with a three-prong plug into a copper wire outlet. The Web is certainly a fancier place today than it was even a short time ago, but it still operates on the infrastructure that was developed and introduced over the first three decades of its use.

TCP/IP

A key component of that infrastructure is the communications protocol over which the Internet operates. Actually a suite of protocols, TCP/IP is the several-tiered method by which data is packaged and sent across the wires that connect the world's computers together. It is made up of the Transmission Control Protocol and the Internet Protocol.

Internet Protocol

Although IP comes after TCP in the name of the protocol, IP is the communications core that makes the Internet work. You have likely heard of IP addresses, those sets of numbers separated by dots that are assigned to each host computer and domain on the Net. The Internet Protocol utilizes that numbering scheme to determine the path that it should take across the routers and hosts that make up the Internet to reach the destination it is intended for. When you make a connection to a computer somewhere out on the Web, you are, in reality, connecting to any number of other computers and routers that forward your request in the most efficient way they can determine, given the millisecond they have to think about it. If you are interested to see how your requests are being routed, you can use the *tracert* utility (for Trace Route) from a command prompt on your computer and see the connections, or *hops*, your request makes as it travels to the destination you provide (see Figure 1-1).

Now, given that this is the way that the Internet works, with each request you make being forwarded through a number of stops, consider what must happen when you download a large Web page, or even a 15MB program from a shareware site. Without

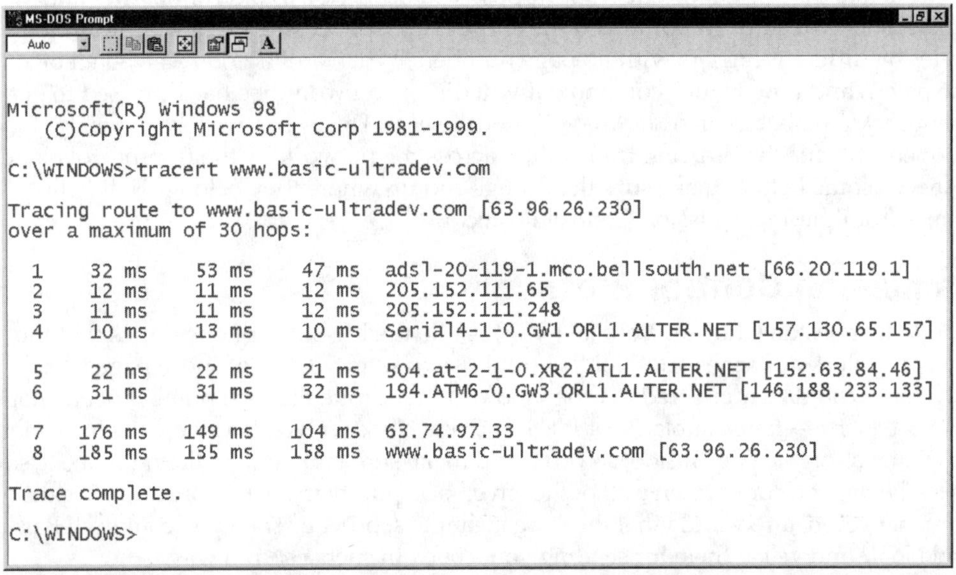

```
MS-DOS Prompt                                                          _ 8 X
 Auto        A

Microsoft(R) Windows 98
   (C)Copyright Microsoft Corp 1981-1999.

C:\WINDOWS>tracert www.basic-ultradev.com

Tracing route to www.basic-ultradev.com [63.96.26.230]
over a maximum of 30 hops:

  1    32 ms    53 ms    47 ms  adsl-20-119-1.mco.bellsouth.net [66.20.119.1]
  2    12 ms    11 ms    12 ms  205.152.111.65
  3    11 ms    11 ms    12 ms  205.152.111.248
  4    10 ms    13 ms    10 ms  Serial4-1-0.GW1.ORL1.ALTER.NET [157.130.65.157]

  5    22 ms    22 ms    21 ms  504.at-2-1-0.XR2.ATL1.ALTER.NET [152.63.84.46]
  6    31 ms    31 ms    32 ms  194.ATM6-0.GW3.ORL1.ALTER.NET [146.188.233.133]

  7   176 ms   149 ms   104 ms  63.74.97.33
  8   185 ms   135 ms   158 ms  www.basic-ultradev.com [63.96.26.230]

Trace complete.

C:\WINDOWS>
```

Figure 1-1. *Running tracert to www.basic-ultradev.com returns a number of stops along the way.*

the IP protocol, it might be necessary for the entire file to be copied to each node along the way until it reached your computer. That could involve as many as 30 or more copies of the same file, depending on where you and your destination site are located. But, thanks to IP, your request and the response for the computer at the other end can be split up into small packets of data that travel easily across the network, following the most efficient path each of them can find.

Note

A number of things can affect the route a packet may take across the Internet, including bottlenecks and outages along the way. The capability of IP to dynamically route around these problems is a key factor in the stability of this kind of distributed network.

So, consider how you might get a group of friends across town to the movies. Unless one of you owned a bus, you would probably split up into two or more cars, and head off for the theater. Perhaps one of the drivers likes the expressway, another knows a "shortcut," and a third doesn't have enough change for the tolls *and* popcorn and takes the normal route. Three cars are all taking different routes to the same destination, and each is liable to encounter things along the way that might speed their travel (such as no line at the toll booth) or slow them down (such as a wreck along the shortcut). Although each car left one after the other, there is no guarantee in what order or in what timeframe they might arrive at the theatre. One car might not even make it at all.

To make the point more clearly, suppose you ordered a book from Barnes and Noble, and instead of shipping you the entire book at once, they sent the individual pages by different carriers with no page numbers. When and if you received all of the pages (and how would you know if you did?), you would be hard-pressed to get them back together in an order that might be useful. This is pretty close to what happens to a file that is being transmitted across the network by the IP protocol alone. IP needs some help to make sure that things end up where they belong. That help comes from the Transmission Control Protocol.

Transmission Control Protocol

The Transmission Control Protocol (TCP) is like the big stack of envelopes that the shipping clerk at Barnes and Noble would use to send you all of those pages. Each envelope would be numbered in order and would indicate the total number of envelopes in the sequence—for example, 36 of 1,008. Each envelope would also give some indication of what was on the page inside, so you could make sure that you got the right one. Using this scheme, you could receive all of the envelopes, put them back in order, and make sure that you had received what the store meant to send you. Then you could call Barnes and Noble and yell at them for sending you a book in such a stupid way.

But that's the way it has to work on the Web. Each packet created by the IP protocol is packaged up, numbered, and labeled so that the receiving computer knows what to do with it. If the receiving computer is missing any packets, it knows to send back for them from the sending computer. And the TCP information indicates what the packet should contain so that the receiving computer can identify corrupted data.

Together, the two protocols within TCP/IP provide the communications basis on which the Internet is built. But it can really only handle the connection between the computers over which the requests and responses of information are sent. Those actual messages are handled by the Hypertext Transfer Protocol.

Hypertext Transfer Protocol

There are basically four parts to any transfer of data over a client/server network (which is really what the Internet is). The first and last of these steps are the connection and disconnection of the two communicating computers, which is handled by TCP/IP. Sandwiched in-between is the work of the HTTP protocol (see Figure 1-2).

You have probably noticed the "http" that begins most Web addresses. Actually, most browsers now assume the HTTP protocol is being used when you type in an address, so the http:// designation is not strictly necessary. But rest assured, that is exactly what the browser is generating when it makes a request.

Note   *Most browsers are also capable of sending ftp and news requests. If that is what is intended, the protocol must be specified, or http will be assumed.*

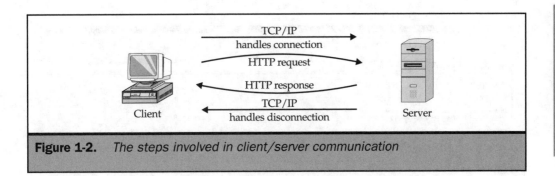

Figure 1-2.   *The steps involved in client/server communication*

Once a connection is made, a request for data is sent in the form of an address. This might be an IP address, or it could be a fully qualified domain name such as http://www.basic-ultradev.com. That request is routed via TCP/IP to the host computer that can fulfill it, and the response is sent back as an HTTP response to the requesting computer. Once it arrives, the TCP/IP protocol again assists in putting the packets of information together so that it can be used or displayed.

How that response is used when it gets back to the requesting computer depends on the content of the information sent. For these discussions, it is assumed that you are requesting the type of content that makes up most of the World Wide Web—HTML content.

Hypertext Markup Language

Hypertext Markup Language (HTML) is the foundation of the World Wide Web. It is this set of tags that describes to the client browser how a file should be displayed, and that is the core purpose of the Web: displaying files of information.

The earliest HTML documents were just text. Often they were the text of scientific or research projects, and the way in which they were formatted was important. HTML provided a hierarchal means of organizing and displaying information so that it could be viewed in a form that emphasized its structure more than its design. It does so by providing a selection of tags that mark up the raw text in ways that the browser can understand.

For instance, you may want to display the raw text file shown in Figure 1-3, so that your fellow scientist can rip you apart for not following standard research guidelines.

This file of simple text does not really allow you to organize your content in a way that will have the maximum effect on your colleague and let him know that you really do know how to write a good outline. HTML allows you to insert indicators such as the

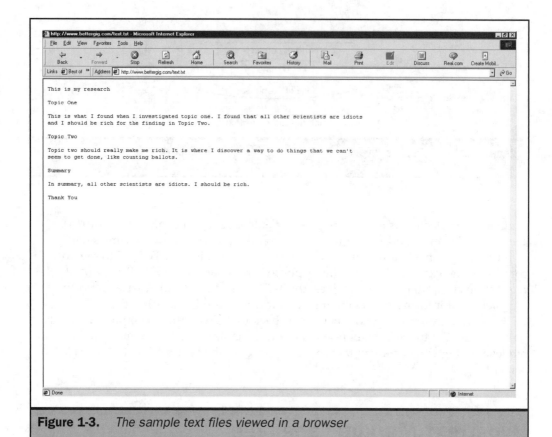

Figure 1-3. *The sample text files viewed in a browser*

following directly into the text that tell the browser on the other end how to display the information:

```
</html>
<head></head>
<body>
<h1>This is my research<br>

</h1>
<h2>Topic One</h2><br>

<p> This is what I found when I investigated topic one. I found that all other
scientists are idiots<br>
and I should be rich for the finding in Topic Two.</p>
```

```
<h2> Topic Two</h2><br>

<p> Topic two should really make me rich. It is where I discover a way to do
things
 that we can't<br>
  seem to get done, like counting ballots.</p>
<h2> Summary</h2><br>

<p> In summary, all other scientists are idiots. I should be rich.</p>
<p> Thank You </p>
</body>
</html>
```

To the end user, these indicators are invisible. They see only the finished product, as shown in Figure 1-4, after the browser interprets your instructions.

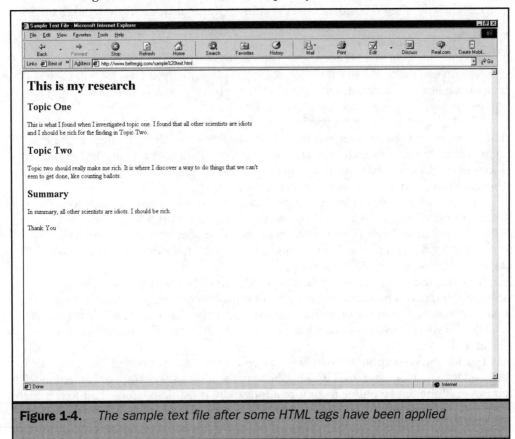

Figure 1-4.   *The sample text file after some HTML tags have been applied*

One of the great strengths of HTML is the ability to create and execute hyperlinks. Hyperlinks are directions built into the content itself that allow users to be sent off to related material with a click of the mouse. For instance, suppose that your document discusses material for which you relied on the writings of another author, whose work is also available on the Internet at its own document address. You could embed a portion of text referring to that work; so that when visitors clicked it, they would be whisked off to that material, where they could properly appreciate how you had interpreted and extended that information in your own research. It is this interconnected structure that led to the coining of the phrase "World Wide Web." The Web is truly a worldwide mesh of interconnected content.

The Web Site

Everything covered so far makes up the component parts of your real interest in this book, which is the Web site. If you understand the standalone HTML document, you can consider the Web site to be a collection of those documents that makes up an interconnected web of information. What the entire Web is on a grand scale, the Web site is in its own little universe.

When you have a lot of content that you need to display, you have a couple of choices you can make. Believe it or not, some people actually choose to make one really long document that scrolls down forever. Although it eventually says everything they wanted to say, there is a more practical solution.

A Web site is formed when you bring together a collection of HTML documents that are related to one another and need to be displayed together. By organizing this content and providing logical ways to navigate it, you are turning your individual documents into a site that users can use to find and access the information they need. There are three common layouts for such a site.

The first is the Table of Contents model that provides a front-end interface to a catalog of material. For instance, if you had a book or a report that was divided into sections, you might have a table of contents page that provided links to each section. As each section is completed, users would return to the table of contents to determine the next section they wanted to access.

Second is the web structure, where content is full of cross-referencing links. On any given page, you might have a number of links to other parts of the site connecting related material. The intent of such a structure is for the user to peruse the content of the site in a sort of stream-of-consciousness way, branching off to related parts of the site at will.

Third is the Web application. In a Web application, the user is typically guided through the site in a structured way by the way the pages are designed. For instance, if you were filling out an online insurance application, it would be important to complete each section of the application in order to be sure that everything was properly filled out. The users would depend on the site designer to guide them through the specific documents that needed to be completed.

The Last Few Years

So, that 30-year history brings you up to the last few years. It is in these last three or four years that a number of concurrent events have occurred that have brought us to the topic of this book: Dreamweaver MX.

WYSIWYG HTML Editors

As HTML matured, more and more designers wanted a way to construct HTML in a fashion more similar to the desktop publishing they were used to. It should come as no surprise that people who were used to dealing in very visual media resisted having to hand-code their HTML in a text editor and run it in a browser every time they wanted to check the layout. The graphical content of HTML documents was becoming more important as the focus of new Web sites became less scientific and more commercial. Designers wanted a What You See Is What You Get (WYSIWYG) method of building Web sites.

One of the earliest applications to offer a means of designing Web pages graphically was Microsoft's FrontPage (see Figures 1-5 and 1-6). FrontPage enables designers of all

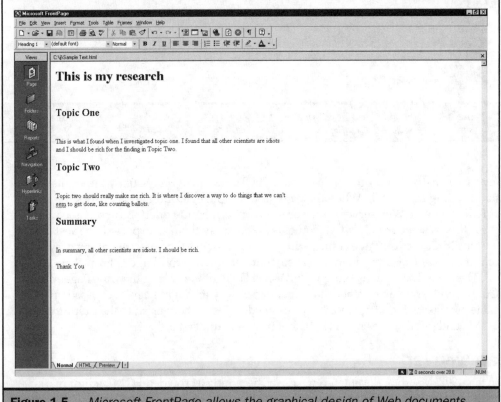

Figure 1-5. *Microsoft FrontPage allows the graphical design of Web documents.*

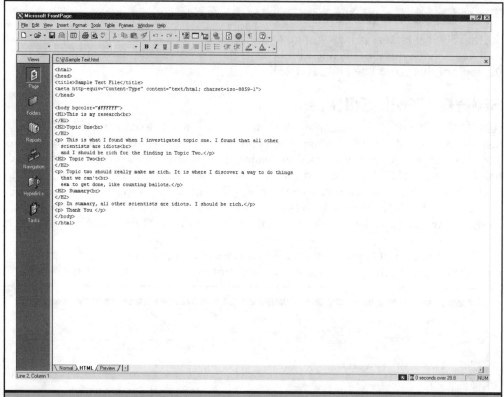

Figure 1-6. *FrontPage allows users to switch back and forth between design view and HTML view.*

levels to construct and publish Web pages by laying them out visually rather than by hand-coding the HTML. When the pages are complete, FrontPage publishes the raw HTML file to the Web server, much as if it had been hand-coded. Browsers recognize these files as standard HTML documents and display them as expected, in most cases.

In addition, FrontPage comes with a set of server extensions that allow easy use of more advanced components. The current version of FrontPage is FrontPage 2002.

There have been many other WYSIWYG HTML editors along the way. Pagemill, GoLive, and a myriad of others have made their way through the market based on the same premise as FrontPage: Visually designed pages are converted to their representative HTML and published as raw HTML that browsers understand.

Dreamweaver

In late 1997, Macromedia entered what was becoming a crowded HTML editor market with Dreamweaver 1. Six months later, version 1.2 was released and Dreamweaver began to gain quite a following. Dreamweaver MX has just been released, and Dreamweaver is now the most popular HTML design tool among professional Web developers, with a user base of over 1,000,000. Several key concepts and features enabled Dreamweaver to make such significant inroads in a competitive market.

Integration with Other Macromedia Products

There are a few companies that can drive markets just because of other product categories they already dominate. Microsoft, for instance, has enjoyed tremendous success because of the functional relationships between their operating systems and their Office suite. Perhaps more relevant is the success of Microsoft's Visual Studio.NET, which enjoys advanced ASP- and COM-related integration (both Microsoft technologies). This success is in spite of the fact that Visual Studio has severely limited design capabilities, forcing its users to perform design work in another product.

Macromedia is certainly enjoying cross-pollination thanks to the development of several excellent design tools. Each of Macromedia's products stands on its own; but when a Fireworks, Freehand, Flash, or Director user goes looking for an HTML tool, the ability to integrate these products with Dreamweaver becomes an important consideration. Macromedia has paid special attention to the ways in which their products work together. This has only been furthered with the announcement of the MX suite of products.

Dreamweaver MX is particularly integrated with Fireworks MX, Flash MX, and the rest of the MX Studio. Some of their functions allow these programs' output to be included in Dreamweaver very easily. Also included are ready-made ways to determine whether a site's visitors have the necessary plug-ins installed to allow them to play special content. Some of the newest of these features are discussed in Chapters 10 and 11.

Integration with Microsoft Office

As we just indicated, Microsoft's Office is a very popular product in the business world. Many times, large portions of content that need to be placed on the Web already exist in business documents created in Microsoft Word. Word has the capability to convert its documents into HTML, but it is not a pretty thing. Word-generated HTML files are bloated, containing extraneous, unnecessary code. Often these files are four or five times larger than necessary and contain code that works properly only in Microsoft's Internet Explorer browser.

Dreamweaver contains a command call, Clean Up Word HTML, which addresses this problem. Within just a few minutes, Word-generated HTML files can be cleaned up and stripped of their Microsoft-specific code, eliminating the need to cut and paste existing content just to get usable files.

In addition, it is often important to publish data that exists in spreadsheet applications or databases to the Web. Dreamweaver contains a special version of an HTML table called Tabular Data. This advanced table allows the developer to identify a data source that is used to populate the table.

Cross-Browser Capabilities

If you have been designing for the Web for very long, you have no doubt experienced the maddening issue of cross-browser compatibility. Because of differing implementations of elements such as Cascading Style Sheets and JavaScript, it can often be a difficult task to get your content to view properly in the browsers that your visitors are likely to use. And it may only get worse, with new browsers coming to market and companies like AOL making changes in the browser engines they ship with their products.

Dreamweaver tries to help you deal with some of these issues by placing some indications of the design tools that are compatible with the popular browser types. For example, one of the most useful features in this regard is a built-in fix that addresses a Netscape issue. When the user resizes a Netscape browser, the page layout is often corrupted unless the page is reloaded. This included piece of script forces the reloading of the page any time the browser is resized. In Dreamweaver, it can be added or removed with one menu selection.

Roundtrip HTML and XML

An important feature to many professional Web designers is the integrity of their code. Many of the popular HTML design applications compromised this integrity by changing code. Dreamweaver was built on the concept that the designer is in charge. The program can certainly help you write HTML from your visual layout, but if you make changes to the code itself, Dreamweaver will leave it alone, representing your changes the best it can. One of the keys to Roundtrip code is that whatever is generated and published by Dreamweaver can be reopened and properly displayed.

Templates

A key design factor for professional Web sites is a consistent look and feel across the site. It is disrupting and incongruent to radically change graphics, colors, layout, frames, and so on, each time a new page is loaded. In this sense, a designer should consider the entire site as one large design rather than a compilation of individually designed pages.

Dreamweaver's templates help you to maintain a consistent look and feel, and save you a lot of work when you add pages to your site. In creating a template in Dreamweaver, you can identify regions that will remain *locked* and, therefore, identical on every page for which the template is used. You can also identify *unlocked* regions of the page, which are the portions that you expect to change for each subsequent use of the template.

Dreamweaver MX has introduced new features to the Dreamweaver template system that give you even more control over the consistency of sections of your site.

History

Professional designers and graphic artists have become used to certain features in packages like Photoshop. One of the most important features is the History function.

The History palette in Dreamweaver MX gives you access to the steps that you took to build your site to its current state. You can use it to repeat a series of steps and even to build an executable command that will repeat those steps at will. It also enables an almost limitless undo capability.

Objects and Behaviors

Objects and behaviors are discussed extensively later in this book, including instructions on how to create your own. But right out of the box, Dreamweaver comes with a host of prebuilt objects and behaviors that encapsulate snippets of code. Need to drop a table onto your page? There is an object that lets you do so, and it will address its properties (number of columns, for example) in one easy step. Need to control a Shockwave or Flash movie? The simple addition of a prebuilt behavior lets you add that functionality quickly and move on to more important things.

In addition to the objects and behaviors that ship with Dreamweaver, there are tons more available for download at sites across the Web. This has become a key to Dreamweaver's popularity.

Extensibility

Closely related to the preloaded objects and behaviors is Dreamweaver's extensibility layer. Based in JavaScript, the extensibility layer provides detailed instructions for interacting with Dreamweaver at an API level. Programmers with a good JavaScript background can easily add complex functionality to Dreamweaver and distribute it to other users, making Dreamweaver a constantly maturing and evolving product.

We look at using and creating Dreamweaver Extensions in Chapters 30 through 32.

Data Access

At the same time the HTML design application revolution was occurring, people were looking for ways to expand the concept of the World Wide Web. Static pages of graphics and text were nice, but there had to be a way to interact with Web pages, to collect information from users, and to communicate with databases of information.

One of the earliest implementations of this concept was the CGI application. Out of this (and because of its inefficiencies) grew HTML Templating—better known as ASP, JSP, and ColdFusion, to name just three examples. You can find extensive discussions of these topics later in the book. Just be aware at this point that there was a crossing of the roads coming, where the users of HTML design applications would require the same ease of use for data-connected Web sites.

UltraDev

In the summer of 1999, two companies had decisions to make. Elemental Software, the creators of Drumbeat, realized that they had scalability issues on their hands. They came to the decision that to take Drumbeat much farther would require a rewrite, a time consuming and stiflingly expensive proposition. At the same time, Macromedia was trying to figure out a way to expand its product line into the world of data connection. Dreamweaver seemed like the place to start.

At quite a remarkably serendipitous moment, Elemental and Macromedia ended up at the table together. What ensued was Macromedia's purchase of Elemental and the migration of much of its development staff to San Francisco to head up a new project. This new project became the marriage of Drumbeat and Dreamweaver into what was known as UltraDev.

UltraDev existed for two versions as a superset of Dreamweaver. It contained all of Dreamweaver's functionality, and added sophisticated support for ASP, JSP, and ColdFusion development.

Summary: And Then There Was One

And now, the integration is all but complete. Dreamweaver MX is the best of Dreamweaver and the best of UltraDev, plus a whole lot more wrapped into one concise package. In addition to the existing functionality, Dreamweaver MX provides support for ASP.NET, PHP, and ColdFusion MX. Its CSS and templates are much improved. And its new interface (or actually choice of interfaces) has finally made a world of developers more comfortable.

In reality, it had to happen. We have spent the last two years preaching the advantages of UltraDev to even the most devoted designers. Because the Web is moving in a more dynamic, data-driven direction, it is important for designers to know at least how to work with data, if not generate it themselves. Dreamweaver MX will put the necessary tools at their fingertips and encourage them to take the leap. And we are here to help.

There is one thing you can be guaranteed of while reading this book. No matter who you are and no matter what your background, there will be content in this book that is either way above your head or very basic to you. One thing to remember about Dreamweaver MX is that it does not exist in a vacuum. Without other significant technologies, Dreamweaver has little purpose.

With that in mind, this book tries to address all of the topics that you need to have a grasp of in order to be productive with Dreamweaver MX quickly. Many volumes have been written on some of these topics, and the chapters here are certainly not comprehensive, but they do represent the most common issues that new users will encounter. We aim to be a complete reference for Dreamweaver and an adequate reference for the related technologies that you need to get going.

At the same time, this book does address some very advanced Dreamweaver topics, such as the extensibility APIs and extension creation and distribution. The chapters on these subjects may include material that some users never need know, but an understanding of the content will certainly make you a more productive Dreamweaver user.

In short, this book attempts to be a one-volume solution for a variety of Dreamweaver MX users. Rather than spending hundreds of dollars for a SQL book, an ASP.NET book, a JavaScript book, and this Dreamweaver book, it is our hope that you will be served well and become proficient very quickly with this single collection of important material.

The Complete Reference

Dreamweaver MX

Chapter 2

Configuring Your Environment

If you are anything like us when you load a new software application, the CD-ROM drive is open before the cellophane is off the box. Manuals are set aside (or worse, left in the box), and you expect the Autorun.inf file to lead you through the setup options. You click the Typical install option and try to make sense of any of the other pop-up options to get the thing running so you can begin realizing an immediate return on the dollars you spent.

That technique may work well with your average piece of software. Standardized interfaces have made it easier to feel your way through new applications with a reasonable expectation of a somewhat productive result. But when we start talking about building something as complex as a data application that will run worldwide across a variety of platforms with an unknown number of users, there are quite a few decisions to make before we can even think of diving in:

- Will you be developing on a PC or a Macintosh?
- What kind of server will you be running, and what operating system is installed?
- Where is your server located? How much control do you have over the software it runs?
- Is it local at your development site, co-located with an ISP, or co-hosted with other sites on a shared server?
- What application servers are available to you? Do you have a choice between ASP, ASP.NET, JSP, PHP, and ColdFusion?
- Do you have access to a staging server?
- Will you be accessing a database, and what database application will you be using with your site?

The answers to some of these questions will dictate the answers to others. For instance, if you will be running some flavor of Unix on your server, it is a pretty safe bet that you won't be running Microsoft's Internet Information Server as your HTTP server. Nor is it likely that you'll be using Microsoft Access as your database.

On the other hand, some answers will raise more questions. Just because you are running a Windows NT or Windows 2000 server does not mean you are limited to IIS and Active Server Pages. Application servers that run Java Server Pages and ColdFusion are available for a selection of operating systems, including Windows.

Let's look at some of the options you have.

Picking Your Team

Although Dreamweaver MX may be the captain of your development effort, you'll need a supporting team to get something done. Seeing as the whole purpose of

Dreamweaver MX is to put information on the Web, you will, at the very least, need a
Web server. An application server and a data store of some kind will be necessary as
soon as you want to add data to your site. And you will also want to seriously consider
a live data server and a staging server.

The Web Server

You are probably familiar with the way the World Wide Web works, but a refresher
never hurts. When you create pages in Dreamweaver, no matter what platform you
choose, you will use some kind of File Transfer Protocol (FTP) program to upload
the pages to a computer that is running a Web server. The Web server program is
responsible for receiving and processing HyperText Transfer Protocol (HTTP) requests
that are generated when users type a Uniform Resource Locator (URL) into their browsers
(see Figure 2-1).

Depending on where your host machine is located and who owns it, you may or
may not have much control over which Web server you use. There are quite a number
available, depending on what kind of hardware and operating system you are using.
Some are free (or at least free with the operating system), like Microsoft's Internet
Information Server or Apache, and others you'll need to purchase. A list of some of
the more popular Web servers and the platforms they support is in Table 2-1.

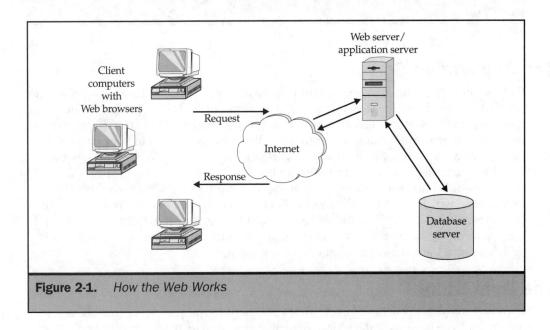

Figure 2-1.   *How the Web Works*

Web Server	Supported Platforms
Internet Information Server	Windows NT, Windows 2000+
Apache	NetBSD, FreeBSD, BSDI, AIX, OS/2, SCO, HPUX, Novell NetWare, Macintosh, Be OS, Windows NT, Linux, Windows 95, Windows 98+, IRIX, Solaris, Digital Unix
Java Server	OS/2, HPUX, Windows NT, Linux, Windows 95+, IRIX, Solaris
Lotus Domino Go Webserver	Digital Unix, AIX, OS/2, HPUX, Windows NT, Windows 95+, IRIX, Solaris
Stronghold Secure Web Server	NetBSD, Digital Unix, BSDI, AIX, SCO, HPUX, Linux, FreeBSD, IRIX, Solaris
Oracle Web Application Server	HPUX, Windows NT, Windows 95+, Solaris
iPlanet	HPUX, AIX, Solaris, IRIX, Windows NT

Table 2-1.   *Popular Web Servers and the Platforms They Support*

The Application Server

Unless you're ignoring the good part of Dreamweaver MX, you will have pages in your site that require more processing than the Web server provides. Pages that connect to databases will have extensions such as .asp, .aspx, .jsp, .php, or .cfm. These pages require the attention of an application server that handles the code or tags in your pages that do the real work. The application server works closely with the Web server, however, to deliver pages that the user's browser can handle.

Some application servers are tightly integrated with a Web server—such as IBM's WebSphere, which can run with its own HTTP server, or with another one such as IIS or Microsoft's asp.dll, which requires IIS to run. Still others, such as ColdFusion, depend on an outside Web server—at least in a production setting. The features that you require will determine the combination that works best for you.

The Data Store

If you are keeping up with the latest in development techniques, it is probably safe to assume that you have some data somewhere that you want to include in your application. Theoretically, that data can reside in a number of different kinds of files, including Excel spreadsheets and delimited text files, but as a practical matter, you will want the flexibility that a Relational Database Management System (RDBMS) provides. There are a number of database applications that qualify, from Microsoft Access, which can be had for a couple of hundred dollars, to enterprise-level server-based systems that cost thousands of dollars and require significant hardware resources.

It is important to select and plan for your database application early in the planning process. Depending on the way you build your site, changing data stores in midstream can be a frustrating, labor-intensive task.

The Staging Server

The Internet is a very public place. When you post something to it, people can and do look at it. When your company or your client depends on what the world reads about them, it is extremely important to get it right before it is made available on a live Web server. The more complex the sites you build, the more important it becomes to make use of a staging server in your development cycle.

A *staging server* is an interim publishing step that allows Web pages to be posted on a nonpublic server for review and quality-control purposes. Depending on the size of your organization, this staging server could be an actual computer set up to serve that purpose on an intranet Web server, or it could be just a folder underneath the root of your Web site to which you can publish a copy of your site and any changes or maintenance items. These items can then be reviewed in a private setting within the context of the entire site. Once approved, the new pages are then copied or replicated to the live Web site.

You don't want to be forced to put your test content up on a live site in order to debug it. Even if you just set up a hidden directory structure within your production domain, do something to allow the testing and review of your work.

Everything from the images you use to the grammar and spelling on your Web site makes a statement about your company or your client. Use of a staging server to allow comprehensive review of the information you intend to post is vital to preserving your reputation.

The Live Data Server

One of the revolutionary parts of Dreamweaver MX is its capability to "bounce" data off a live server and provide an editable design environment using actual data from your data store. Although we will discuss this later, it is important at this point to consider how you will facilitate the use of this feature. For Windows users using the ASP model, it is easiest to use either Personal Web Server or a localized copy of Internet Information Server. Those using other technologies will want to identify a way to take advantage of this valuable design tool by having an application server available on a local machine.

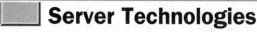

Server Technologies

Dreamweaver ships with five server models on which you can base your site: ASP, ASP.NET, JSP, PHP, and ColdFusion MX.

The decision of which model to use may be guided by several factors and may guide other decisions that you need to make. It is important to make this decision early in your development cycle.

Note   *You need to be careful when choosing your server technology. Once you start generating pages, it is not an easy task to switch to a different technology set. Dreamweaver creates code based on the preferences you set while you were working. At this time, there is no facility for converting that code.*

Active Server Pages

We venture to say that the most common server language selection among Dreamweaver users will be ASP. Microsoft's technology is ubiquitous, easy to learn and use, and available on the many Windows-based servers currently used for Web site hosting. Although some may question its speed, scalability, and capability to keep up with the needs of a growing e-commerce site, it is certainly more than capable of providing tremendous functionality to all but the largest applications.

If you are using a Windows NT or Windows 2000 server running Internet Information Server version 4.0 or 5.0 to host your site, you are all set to include ASP in your pages. IIS4 supports ASP 2. Dreamweaver conforms with the ASP 2 specification. IIS5 (shipped with Windows 2000) supports ASP 3. Although the standard Dreamweaver code will not take advantage of any of the newer features found in version 3.0, you can certainly hand-code portions of your application to do so.

If you are running Windows NT 4.0 and don't have IIS installed, you will need to get a hold of the NT Option Pack. Included are several applications that you will find useful when running Web applications, but the most important at this point are Internet Information Server and Microsoft Transaction Server (both must run ASP). You can purchase an Option Pack CD-ROM or download it for free at www.microsoft.com/ntserver/nts/downloads/recommended/NT4OptPk/default.asp.

ASP on Non-Microsoft Servers

If you need to use a server that runs an operating system other than Windows, or uses a Web server other than IIS, you can still use Active Server Pages for your site, thanks to companies who have ported ASP to other platforms through their proprietary server applications.

Chili!Soft (www.chilisoft.com) makes a program called ChiliASP. ChiliASP provides complete ASP support on AIX, HP-UX, Linux, OS/390, Solaris, and Windows NT. They are willing to consider any other platform and invite visitors to their Web site to make suggestions about the next platforms they should support.

Instant ASP from Halcyon Software (www.halcyonsoft.com) promises to provide ASP support on any Web server, application server, or OS platform. It is a Java-based port of the ASP specification and is designed to allow the ultimate in portability. Instant ASP supports an impressive list of operating systems and Web servers—too many to list here. Complete information is available at their Web site.

The most difficult thing for non-Microsoft solutions is the conversion of the COM components that make ASP so powerful. Most handle this by converting them to some sort of Java or JavaBean implementation.

ASP Scripting Languages

You'll also need to decide which scripting language to use in your ASP code. You will be writing code (or letting Dreamweaver write it for you) that is intended to run at the server (your Web server) and the client (your visitor's browser). Typically, the two choices are Visual Basic Script (VBScript) and JavaScript (or the Microsoft variant JScript). Which language to learn and use is an often-asked question.

VBScript   VBScript is a subset of the Visual Basic programming language. Because ASP is a Microsoft technology, it is not surprising that VBScript is the preferred language for ASP development. Because of this, most ASP tutorials feature VBScript, making example code easy to find. It is relatively easy to learn because its syntax resembles English. There are tons of programmers with Visual Basic experience that find it a comfortable way to use ASP.

The downside of VBScript is that it is not practical as a client-side scripting language. Microsoft's Internet Explorer supports it for browser scripting, but Netscape's Navigator (the other major browser) does not. For this reason, some have concluded that using JavaScript for both the server and the client is a better alternative, especially for newer users who will only need to learn one language.

Note   *If you know that your target audience will be using Internet Explorer, or if you are willing to make that a requirement, VBScript has some definite advantages as a client-side scripting language—for example, event handling is much easier.*

JavaScript   Anyone who does any serious Web programming will need to learn JavaScript. Although you may be most familiar with JavaScript as a client-side language used for things such as form validation and DHTML effects, it is actually a robust language that allows sophisticated object-oriented programming on the server side. Because it can be used for the client side and the server side, it is a logical language choice for the new user, who can then become productive by learning just one language. And, if you plan to write extensions for Dreamweaver, you will need to be intimately familiar with the entire JavaScript language.

However, JavaScript is more difficult to learn than VBScript. It has a less intuitive syntax, and example code is more difficult to find. It is comparable to C or Java in its format, but it must not be confused with either of these; it is its own language. Those coming from a C or Java background may suffer a bit of confusion trying to remember which command goes with which, but having a good reference handy solves this problem quite nicely.

ASP.NET

One of the most exciting parts of Dreamweaver MX is its support for ASP.NET. Microsoft's .NET Framework is the latest in application technologies and borrows heavily from concepts in ColdFusion and JSP. That is to say, Microsoft has paid attention and learned well. ASP.NET is a truly powerful platform and deserves the attention of all ASP developers. Dreamweaver makes the move to .NET easier with its built-in support.

To run ASP.NET, you will need to be using a Windows 2000 server with IIS 5.0 and have the .NET Framework installed. You can find it at www.gotdotnet.com along with a bunch of samples and tutorials. Keep in mind that there is more than one version of the framework. Make sure you get the right version for your purposes, whether it is just the run-time to allow the use of ASP.NET pages, or the SDK that will let you compile and distribute ASP.NET components in languages like C# and VB.NET.

ASP.NET is indeed a paradigm shift in the way ASP programmers think about their page construction. It comes with new languages (C#, VB.NET, and even COBOL.NET), new types of components, and a new server-side processing model. It can be difficult to master because, although it allows the same type of inline scripting found in traditional ASP, this type of programming is discouraged in favor of user controls, components, and something called Code-Behind. We will take a closer look at ASP.NET in Chapter 19.

Java Server Pages

Java Server Pages is Sun Microsystems' answer to ASP, based on its popular Java programming language. Although it provides a scripting environment comparable to ASP, JSP is actually a small part of the Java 2 Enterprise Edition, Sun's enterprise application development framework. Included are the most popular Java technologies such as servlets, Enterprise Java Beans (EJBs), Java Database Connectivity (JDBC), and Java Naming and Directory Interface (JNDI).

One of JSP's claims to fame is its portability. Whereas ASP is generally limited to the Microsoft platform, JSP is available on all major Web platforms. Even better, Web servers and application servers that support JSP are available from a number of manufacturers. A list with contact information follows:

- **Orion**   www.orionserver.com
- **Resin**   www.caucho.com
- **Jrun**   www.allaire.com
- **Tomcat**   jakarta.apache.org
- **WebSphere**   www.ibm.com
- **WebLogic**   www.bea.com

Like ASP, JSP is script-based, which means that your pages are a mix of HTML and script that is prepared at the server and delivered to the browser in a form that it can handle. The scripting in JSP is done in pure Java, so familiarity with the Java programming language and framework is helpful.

An advantage of JSP relates to its roots in the Java servlet framework. The first time a JSP page is called, it is compiled into a servlet that accepts requests from the user and returns a response output stream. The Java Virtual Machine then translates this precompiled code.

By contrast, ASP pages are interpreted every time they are loaded. As big an advantage as this would seem to be, the interpretation of the JSP byte code and the interpretation of the ASP page take about the same amount of time; and, when properly written, ASP and JSP usually run at about the same speed.

ColdFusion

ColdFusion is a proprietary server introduced by Allaire Corporation, which recently merged with Macromedia. Wait, you say, doesn't that mean Macromedia now owns ColdFusion and JRun, two of the most popular application servers around? Yes it does, and look for them to take good advantage of that.

Unlike ASP and JSP, ColdFusion is tag-based, not script-based. This fundamental difference has made ColdFusion extremely popular among Web designers and HTML authors who are used to tag-based programming. However, ColdFusion is no less capable than its competition.

Using its set of built-in tags, ColdFusion can perform any function that you can script ASP or JSP to perform. Some ColdFusion functions are even significantly easier to use because ColdFusion has encapsulated functions that require external components in other languages (such as file upload). It is a compact language that often requires fewer lines of code to accomplish tasks than its counterparts.

ColdFusion MX is the new version released with the rest of the MX product line. ColdFusion MX is built on top of the Java platform and has realized significant advances in its capabilities, including Java Integration, XML support, and Flash Remoting, which is one of the most exciting of all. It has also become a major contender in the creation of new technologies like Web Services.

You will need to obtain ColdFusion Server if you plan to develop ColdFusion applications. It comes in both Professional and Enterprise editions. A complete comparison matrix that helps decide which version is best for a particular implementation is available at the Macromedia Web site. You can download the Enterprise version for free for 30 days. After that time, it reverts to a single user but fully functional version perfect for testing and development.

ColdFusion Server is currently available for Windows, Sun Solaris, and Linux, making it as portable as it is powerful. For those needing to run a non-Microsoft server, ColdFusion presents a popular, scalable, and very capable option. A J2EE version will be released that will run on top of the popular Java platforms like WebSphere and WebLogic.

Popular Web Servers

You are probably coming close to deciding on a combination of applications that will meet your needs. Once you begin to make a few decisions (or have them made for you by your circumstances), other things will start to fall into place. If you can reduce your potential options, your final decision will be easier. There are currently more than 35 Web server programs and, without some direction, it can become confusing.

| Note | *Just for the record, we know that not everyone runs Microsoft servers—indeed, most people don't. However, after careful consideration, it seemed fairly clear that most of the people who will find this section helpful will be setting up and configuring their own Microsoft software. Although we do not wish to appear Microsoft-centric in our approach to Dreamweaver, we have chosen to use Personal Web Server and Internet Information Server as the platform to demonstrate the configuration of new Web sites. For those of you running other setups, we hope that the principles addressed here can be applied to your situation to help you successfully use Dreamweaver with your project.* |

You may well be one of those people who has to do all of the research yourself and make a software choice based on hours of meticulous study. However, the statistics say that there is about a 90 percent chance you will end up running a server from one of three families: Apache, Microsoft, or iPlanet (which includes the Netscape servers). Although you are certainly welcome to find a way to get the most out of Dreamweaver using WebSitePro, WebLogic, or one of the many other servers available, we focus our attention on these three.

Microsoft

The Microsoft family of Web servers includes three applications at this point: Personal Web Server, Internet Information Server 4.0, and Internet Information Server 5.0. Each has a specific purpose or target platform

Personal Web Server

Designed to run on the workstation versions of Windows, Personal Web Server provides a scaled down version of Microsoft's Internet Information Server. It is intended as a development test platform, but it is robust enough to act as a simple low-bandwidth server option for personal Web sites or a small corporate intranet.

| Note | *Personal Web Server will run on Windows NT Workstation, but Peer Web Services, an application that comes with it, offers all of the features of the Personal Web Server application and includes some security services that are useful with the NT file system. If you are using NT Workstation, it is suggested that you use Peer Web Services instead of Personal Web Server.* |

> **Note** *Internet Information Server 5.0 comes with and runs on Windows 2000 Professional and Windows XP Professional It is a limited version, however. It allows only one Web site, one FTP site, and a maximum of ten concurrent connections. In this respect, it is more akin to Peer Web Services than the full-blown IIS server version. Those running Windows 2000 and XP Professional with IIS5 will likely find information in this and the following section useful.*

Personal Web Server is actually a subset of Microsoft's full-fledged Web server application, Internet Information Server. It includes much of the functionality of the full package, including support for Microsoft Transaction Server (MTS), Microsoft Message Queue Server (MSMQ), Active Server Pages (ASP), and ActiveX Data Objects (ADO). Missing, however, is support for some advanced applications such as Index Server, Certificate Server, and Site Server Express, which perform content indexing, security certificate management, and site reporting, respectively.

Personal Web Server is useful under any server model to test the HTML portions of your pages, but if you decide to develop an Active Server Pages application for Internet Information Server, you will definitely want to take advantage of its features. Using Personal Web Server, Dreamweaver allows you to view and test your pages within the design environment.

You will find the installation files you need in various places, depending on which operating system you are running, as shown in Table 2-2.

> **Note** *Neither Windows ME nor Windows XP Home Edition provide support for a Web server. Some people have been able to get Personal Web Server running on them, but bear in mind that it is not officially supported, and the files do not come with these operating systems.*

Operating System	Location of Personal Web Server Setup Files
Windows 95	With the Windows NT 4.0 Option Pack
Windows 98	On the Windows 98 Installation CD
Windows NT Workstation	With the Windows NT 4.0 Option Pack
Windows 2000 Professional	On the Windows 2000 Installation CD
Windows XP Professional	On the Windows XP Installation CD

Table 2-2. *Location of Microsoft Web Server Files for the Different Operating Systems*

Once Personal Web Server is installed and you have rebooted your computer, there are several things to look for on your machine. First, take a look at your hard drive. On the drive on which you installed Personal Web Server, you will find a directory called InetPub and, beneath it, another directory called wwwroot. This is the default path that Personal Web Server uses to hold your Web sites. You can choose to place your pages within this path, or you can set up virtual directories that allow the server to access folders elsewhere on your computer; more about this in a bit.

If you are going to manage your Personal Web Server, you'll need to get to it, and Microsoft has made sure you won't have any problem with that. When Personal Web Server is running, an icon appears in the system tray. Double-clicking it runs the Personal Web Manager. In addition, you can run the manager from the icon on your desktop or from the Start menu. Documentation is provided on the Start menu, as well as access to the Transaction Server Manager and the Front Page Administrator. If you use Front Page extensions or Transaction Server for more than ASP support, you'll need to familiarize yourself with these programs.

The Personal Web Manager is your headquarters for administering Personal Web Server. As you can see in Figure 2-2, the manager provides several screens that help organize the tasks that Personal Web Server does for you. Let's go through them to get your server configured for use with Dreamweaver.

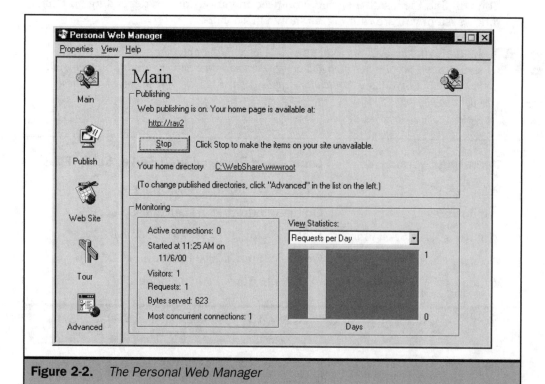

Figure 2-2.   *The Personal Web Manager*

The Main screen shown in Figure 2-2 provides basic information about your server setup and status listed as Publishing and Monitoring. The Publishing information informs you of the location of your home page. This location may look familiar; it is the name of your computer and serves as the default Web site path.

Note *There are actually several ways to access the pages on your local machine. In addition to using your machine's name, you can also use either http://localhost/ or http://127.0.0.1/. 127.0.0.1 is a special reserved IP address that is used to refer only to the local machine. If your computer has a static IP address assigned to it, you can also use that address to refer to the pages housed on your computer.*

The Publishing section of the Personal Web Manager also indicates the status of Personal Web Server, whether it is running or stopped, and lets you start or stop it. Stopping and starting the server allows changes that you make to its configuration to take effect. An additional hyperlink provides quick access to the default Web directory.

The Monitoring section of the Manager gives you basic information about the use of the server, including the capability to graph common metrics. This information is most useful to you if you are actually using Personal Web Server as a server for a small-scale production Web site.

Note *Although Personal Web Server is feature-rich for a freeware application and can adequately serve small sites, it is highly recommended that you use a true server operating system and an industrial-strength Web server such as Internet Information Server to efficiently serve sites on whose reliability your client or your business will depend.*

The next three sections of the Personal Web Manager are of marginal use to the Dreamweaver developer. The Web Site and Publish icons provide access to wizards that help you create and deploy simple HTML pages. Because you will be using Dreamweaver to create and deploy your pages, it is not strictly necessary for you to become familiar with these wizards. If you wish, you may use the Tour section of the Manager to learn more about how these wizards work.

The Advanced tab, however, is very important to the Dreamweaver developer. It is here that you will configure essential information about your sites. In the Virtual Directories list box shown in Figure 2-3, you will see several directories that have already been set up for you. Most of these are related to the way that Microsoft applications structure sites for use with Front Page and Visual InterDev and are not strictly necessary for Dreamweaver development. As a matter of fact, you really should not ever publish files for your sites directly into the site structure you see in this list box. If you do, you will quickly become disorganized. Instead, you should utilize the procedure we cover next.

When you load Personal Web Server, a default home page is created in the wwwroot folder. It is actually just an About Personal Web Server page, but because it is named default.asp and resides directly in the wwwroot folder (which is set as the Personal Web Server home directory), it is the page that appears if you type **http://localhost/** or one of the other local-machine referencing addresses mentioned earlier (unless you

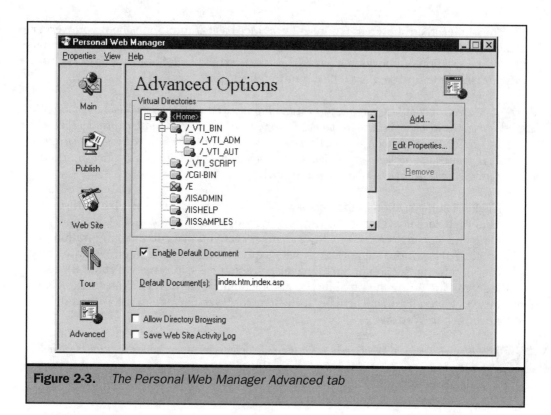

Figure 2-3.   *The Personal Web Manager Advanced tab*

have changed your default documents, which we discuss in a moment). To organize your local development sites, you will want to put each one in its own folder. You can do this by placing uniquely named folders underneath the wwwroot folder. For instance, you could place a folder called \GIG underneath wwwroot, place pages inside it, and reference it from a browser using http://localhost/GIG/.

Better yet, you can use the Personal Web Manager to create a virtual directory. This allows the GIG folder to reside anywhere you choose to place it, rather than being buried within the wwwroot folder. First, create a folder called GIG in Windows Explorer. Place it anywhere you can keep track of it. You will likely amass quite a collection of development folders, and a sense of organization will help you work most efficiently. After creating the folder, return to the Personal Web Manager and click the Add button next to the Virtual Directories list box. In the resulting dialog box, browse to the folder that you created. Then create an alias for this site. The alias can be anything you would like to use to refer to this site—the same as the folder name or something different. You can then refer to this site using the alias—that is, http://localhost/*aliasname*/.

The Default Documents setting will become very important as you begin to set up your site. Default Documents are those page names that will load automatically when a directory is browsed to. For instance, when you type a URL into your browser (such as **http://www.bettergig.com/**), you may not explicitly declare which page in that site you wish to view. In this instance, the Web server refers to the Default Documents list to see if there are any pages in the folder that it can display. In the order that they are listed, the server will compare the page names in your site with the default list and will show the first match it comes to.

Some people use "index" for their default page name. Others use "default," "main," or even "home." In addition, some prefer the .htm extension, whereas others use .html or even one of the application server extensions, such as .asp, .jsp, .cfm, or .php. Create your list of default documents separated by commas.

| Note | *Use any of the page names that you might actually need in your sites, but don't go overboard. The more the server has to search through, the slower its performance will be. And make sure to use the same file extensions that will be used on the server where the site will ultimately be deployed.* |

The final section of the Advanced section of the Personal Web Manager is the permissions setting for the directory. Read and script access is fine for any directories except those such as cgi-bins or others that will house files that need to be executed.

Below the permissions section are two settings that are both disabled by default. Enabling the Allow Directory Browsing setting will let your site visitors see a listing of all of the pages and directories in your site if a default document does not exist—not a good thing. And if you want to save log files, enabling the Save Web Activity Log option will save NCSA formatted log files that can be viewed with a text editor.

Once Personal Web Server is set up, you are ready to test the pages you develop in Dreamweaver or even to deploy them for small-scale use. Personal Web Server will also figure into the use of Dreamweaver's Live Data feature.

Internet Information Server

Microsoft's full-featured professional-level Web server is Internet Information Server. It currently exists in two versions, 4.0 and 5.0, which run on Windows NT Server and Windows 2000, respectively. Because most PC developers are running either Windows 2000 or XP Professional, version 5.0 is probably still most widely used and supports ASP and .NET. We look at its implementation.

If you have Windows 2000 installed, you have a good start, but IIS5 does not install with the basic installation routine You need to install it off of the installation CD using the Windows Configuration features of the operating system.

As with Personal Web Server, there are certain basic functions that we expect the IIS management console to perform, such as setting up sites and starting and stopping Web services. On the Professional versions of the operating system, these functions will be largely the same because of IIS's limited functionality on the desktop operating systems. But on Windows 2000 Server, a production Web server is designed to be used by a number of developers in a production environment. There are a number of additional settings that you will need to consider, including security, IP addresses, Microsoft's Collaborative Data Objects, and FTP access.

To install IIS 5, navigate to your Windows Control Panel and double-click the Add/Remove Programs icon. In the Add/Remove Programs window, select the Add/Remove Windows Components from the choices to the left. The Windows Components panel will open.

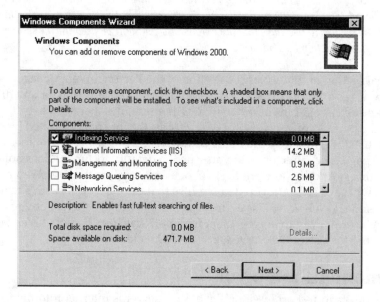

Select the Internet Information Services check box and click Next. Windows will guide you through the installation. The first thing you may want to do after installation is drag a shortcut onto your desktop. You will likely be accessing IIS many times during development, and a convenient link to it is quite helpful.

The Microsoft Management Console looks different from the Personal Web Manager, but you are really being given the same kinds of options in a less wizard-like fashion. Let's look at the highlights of the IIS structure without getting bogged down in services we don't have time to cover. If you have run IIS on your computer, you should be looking at a screen that closely resembles Figure 2-4.

You will see a variety of services listed under Internet Information Server. At this point, we are concerned only with the Default FTP site and the Default Web site.

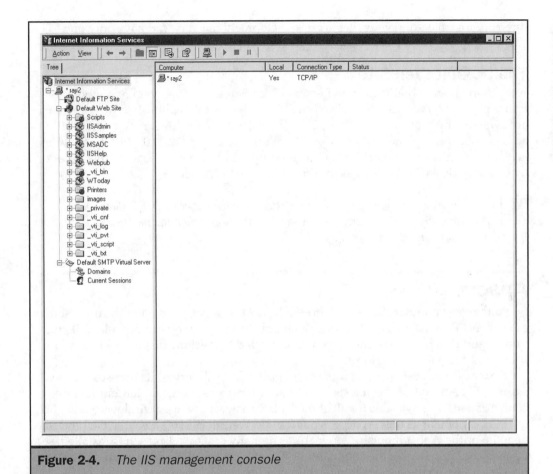

Figure 2-4. *The IIS management console*

The Default FTP Site

As you might guess from its name, File Transfer Protocol (FTP) is the Internet protocol used to transfer files back and forth between machines. It is used when getting a complete file from computer A to computer B is more important than viewing the contents of the file over the Web. For instance, when you create and save Web pages as HTML files on your development computer, they are only accessible once they are placed on a server that is connected to the Internet. If that server is a machine other than your development computer, you will use an FTP program, either within Dreamweaver or from a third party, to transfer those complete files to the appropriate directories on the server. From there, their contents can be viewed over the Web by browsers everywhere.

The Default FTP site is the directory that has been created for this machine. Accessing FTP using this computer's name or using its default IP address will map you to this directory for uploading your files. Your development machine can have only one FTP site, but a server version of the software might have several servicing different Web sites.

The Default Web Site

As with the wwwroot directory in Personal Web Server, your server has a wwwroot folder that can serve as a default Web site. Any sites that you publish to this directory are available by browsing to http://*YourMachineName*/ or this server's default IP address if browsing from a LAN, http://localhost/ or http://127.0.0.1/ (if the browser is actually on the server machine). We can set up additional sites beneath this order or by creating Virtual Directories as we did in Personal Web Server.

> **Note**   *In addition to managing your IIS installation from the server itself, IIS allows you to perform many administrative tasks remotely over the Internet. See the IIS documentation for help setting up this capability.*

Apache

By far the most popular Web server on the Net, Apache is a product of the open source movement. That means that its code is available to anyone who can download it and understand it, and it can be modified and extended to meet the disparate needs of its users. It is currently in version 2.

Apache is unquestionably a robust and powerful Web server. Its huge user base assures that Apache has been tested in a wide variety of settings under innumerable configurations. It is available for all of the Unix variants, as well as Windows 95/98/NT.

But, as popular as it is, Apache is not for everyone. It doesn't have the GUI interface of an IIS or the Web administration features of many other packages. It is installed, set up, and configured from the command line, and is often quite a complicated process to do, depending on the options you wish to employ.

Nonetheless, once you get used to the way it works, you will appreciate the power and flexibility of this package. Although basic features are supported in the core application, additional modules are available to integrate things such as PHP (a popular scripting language) and MySQL (a popular and free database application).

Modules allow these packages to run as processes of Apache itself—a very efficient method, to say the least. And, if you are used to working with Windows, you will be amazed at what you can accomplish remotely through a simple telnet session.

Packages and instructions are available to help you get Apache running on your server. You will need to accomplish the same kinds of tasks in Apache as you did in IIS to get sites set up. You can find directions for completing these tasks in your configuration at the Apache site (www.apache.org).

iPlanet

What was once the Netscape Enterprise Edition Web server has been rolled into the iPlanet Web server. It is a full-featured server ready to play in the big leagues. iPlanet is available for Windows and Unix.

iPlanet is an expensive option (especially compared to Apache and IIS), but upcoming versions will have built-in JSP support, and iPlanet is intended to handle complex Web and data configurations with ease. Installation is straightforward, and a trial version is available to give you a look at it before you pay real money (www.iplanet.com).

Popular Databases

If you think the selection of Web servers is confusing, we are just getting started. Because you are using Dreamweaver MX, it is a safe bet that you want to put some data on the Web, and for that you will need to select a database application. From the free to the expensive and from the simple to the complex, there is a database available to meet any need. The decision regarding which to use is an important one that can be affected by your budget, your server platform, and several other factors. We cover some of the more popular options and mention some others that you might want to take a look at.

Note   *No matter which database application you choose, you will need to spend some time learning a language that the database understands. Most likely this will be Structured Query Language (SQL). It is fairly easy to learn, and Dreamweaver MX will help you through as you get started. We cover more about SQL in Chapter 23.*

Microsoft Access and ISAM

One of the most popular database applications for small sites is Microsoft Access. Access is inexpensive (it is part of Microsoft Office, or you can purchase it separately for just a couple of hundred dollars), widely supported, and has a friendly user interface that makes designing your database a snap, as shown in Figure 2-5.

Access is a member of a file-based family of databases known as ISAM (Indexed Sequential Access Method) databases. These database applications typically create a file (or sometimes a database container) that resides in a folder on your Web server. This self-contained file can be accessed through the proper driver without the actual database application being loaded on the server. For example, Access stores its table in a file with an .mdb extension. This file can be uploaded to your Web server and accessed from your Web application without Microsoft Access being loaded on the server.

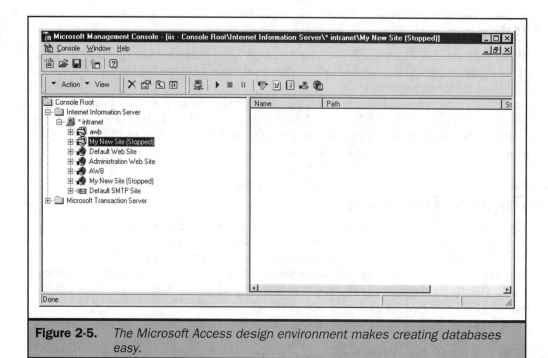

Figure 2-5. The Microsoft Access design environment makes creating databases easy.

Note *ISAM is an older method of file access, but it's a very popular one. Databases such as Lotus Approach, Microsoft Fox Pro, FileMaker Pro, and Paradox are all file-based ISAM databases.*

Databases such as Access are a great way to get you started. They are certainly very powerful and, despite their low cost, they may have all of the features that many sites will ever need. Access can hold up to 2GB of data per table and can support up to 255 concurrent connections.

Note *One of the authors once ran an Access database that had over 40 million records with more than acceptable performance. As a matter of fact, when the database was upsized to SQL Server, single connections did not perform appreciably faster than in Access. Be aware, however, that Access's performance would quickly degrade with multiple connections trying to access such a large amount of data.*

But as a practical matter, these databases are not intended to be enterprise-level solutions. The 255 connections statistic is a theoretical maximum, and you would likely experience significant performance difficulties before you got anywhere near that number. Plus, heavy use with a large amount of data would require constant attention, because the database file would have a tendency to corrupt and would need to be repaired.

Remember that databases such as Access run only on Windows. If you are restricted to an operating system other than Windows, they won't even be an option for you.

Perhaps a greater concern is the security issue surrounding the use of file-based databases. Because these files reside on the Web server machine, if your Web server is compromised, the attacker also has access to your database. This is compounded by the fact that few people bother to implement security on their database files, meaning that anyone who is able to get it off of your server will have ridiculously simple access to credit cards or whatever data you have stored in your database.

There are different schools of thought on whether it is acceptable to store credit card information in a database where there is even a remote chance of it being compromised. No matter how you feel about this, it is absolutely unacceptable to store sensitive data in a file-based database without security implemented. That's just asking for trouble.

Another issue to consider is your need for remote access to your database outside the Web application. With file-based applications such as Access, you must maintain at least two copies of your database, one on your development machine and one on the live site. If you intend to develop on more than one machine, you will need additional copies for those as well, because you will not be able to hit the database with the pages you create until they are uploaded to the live site. This means that if you have to add tables or fields, you need to pull down a copy of the database to do so, so you don't lose data, but while you are making these changes, people could be using your site and entering data that is not in the copy you have—it goes on and on. It's just a mess. It is easy to see why a site with any amount of traffic needs to look to more sophisticated means of data storage.

But there is a reason for the popularity of Microsoft Access. It is easy and inexpensive to develop in, and Microsoft provides a relatively simple upsizing tool that allows you to move your database to SQL Server at any time. SQL Server is an entirely different kind of database application, a true data server that allows enterprise deployment of your data without the performance and security issues of Access and other ISAM databases.

Database Servers

When you are more concerned about performance, security, and advanced data features than just getting your data on the Web quickly, you will need to look to products that provide true data server capabilities. Typically running on their own machines, database servers provide support for things such as record and transactional locking, stored procedures, triggers, and true security.

Record Locking

Record locking is the capability to restrict access to information that is being updated elsewhere. If two people make changes to a record at the same time, the last person to save will end up with his or her changes in the database—but who's to say that this is the most accurate data or that he or she would have made those changes had he or she known that another person was making changes at the same time? Record locking allows a database to lock records so that the first person to access the record has it all to himself or herself until he or she completes the work and releases it.

Most databases support some kind of locking. Some, however, implement their locks at a level that can interfere with users trying to access records other than the one that is actually being edited. Known as page-level locking, these applications restrict up to 4K of data, probably well more than is needed.

Advanced applications will implement locking at a record level, meaning that only the record that is being edited will be locked out. On busy sites, you run the very real risk that users will need to edit records that happen to be in close physical proximity to one another in the database tables. You do not want to risk the usability issue that poor locking methods would impose on your money-making venture.

Transaction Locking

Transactions allow entire sets of instructions to either completely execute or completely fail as a unit. The classic example is an online banking transaction. If you were transferring money from one of your accounts to another, two events would be required: the debiting of the first account and the crediting of the second. If the bank's computer system experienced a problem in-between those two events, you would end up with money taken from one of your accounts and never put in the other. This is not good for you. A transaction guarantees that both of these events will either happen or not happen together. Once begun, a transaction either commits (writes all parts of the transaction to the database from the temporary file where it is held) or rolls back (does not write to the database and clears the temporary file, leaving your data intact as it was before the transaction was run). This is better for your checkbook.

Databases that provide transaction locking ensure that uncommitted changes are not accessible until the transaction is committed.

Stored Procedures

Stored procedures provide a means of embedding complex data manipulation in a program that is stored and run inside the database itself. When stored procedures are used, you make a simple call to the program and pass in any required parameters, rather than forcing the database to deal with your entire SQL statement every time. Stored procedures are precompiled and run quickly, improving site performance. They also provide a significant security boost, because they reduce the ability of an attacker to send malicious SQL commands to your database.

Triggers

Triggers provide the capability to teach your database how to do things that need to happen on a regular basis or when some requisite event (a trigger) occurs. For example, maybe you want to send a quick Happy Birthday e-mail to the customers in your database on their birthdays, which are stored in a field of the database. You could set up a trigger to generate and send e-mails to all customers whose birthday equals today's date, and set it to run every day.

Triggers are very important when you need to respond to the data that is inserted and edited in your database. A key example is *referential integrity*. Maintaining referential integrity is the process of checking on a constant basis to make sure that edits to the database do not result in things like orphaned records. For example, suppose that you have a table with all of your salesmen in it. In another table, those salesmen's customers are listed. If someone were to delete a salesman's record from the first table, the database would be left with orphaned customers. They would exist in the database without a salesman. Reports of all salesmen and their customers would not show those customers, and the company would run the risk of losing them. In order to prevent this, a trigger could be set up to check for customer records whenever someone tried to delete a salesman. It would deny the ability to delete that salesman until all customers had been reassigned, thus maintaining the integrity of the database.

Security

Data servers provide a number of security benefits. For one thing, they typically reside on a separate machine from the Web server, meaning that if the Web server is compromised, the attacker does not automatically have access to the database. Typically, the server is accessed by its IP address or qualified domain name.

 If you are not careful in the way you set up your site, a compromised Web server will provide access to everything on your database server, if only because the attacker can glean addresses and username/password combinations from the code on your pages.

More important, a good database server will provide a method of creating a hierarchy of passwords, accounts, and roles that allow access to certain databases and tables, and allow only certain things to be done by certain users.

Popular Database Servers

A number of excellent database servers are available with very loyal users. Any discussion of these has to include Microsoft's SQL Server. It is an excellent product with a relatively reasonable price tag, but it is limited to the Windows platform. It is a popular choice because many ISPs offer access to a SQL Server account along with your hosting account for just $20 to $25 a month.

Perhaps the granddaddy of Web databases is Oracle's database. It provides a truly enterprise-level database with support for many of the popular operating systems. It also offers an extensive array of development tools. It has a heavy price tag to go with it; but for a large corporation, there are certainly cost of ownership issues that reduce this as a factor.

Less popular, but equally powerful, are offerings from IBM (DB2) and Sybase. It is likely that your choice of which database server to use will be affected by many factors, some of them out of your control. If you have access to any of these excellent products, you should have no problem integrating them into a high-quality Web application.

Open Source

There are also a couple of Open Source options to consider. Open Source is a popular movement lately that calls upon the talents of a product's user base to assist in the improvement of the product through extensive testing and collaborative development. MySQL and PostgreSQL are two such products.

Available for free or for a low cost, these products offer very powerful features. They are both missing features of the commercial applications discussed in the preceding section, but they are nonetheless excellent products that continue to improve with each release. In fact, Dreamweaver MX's PHP depends heavily on PHP's integration with MySQL, making it the most logical choice for this server model.

Summary

Before we dig into Dreamweaver, you need to have a pretty good idea about the operating system, Web server, application server, and database you are going to use, at least during the learning stages. If you have these already chosen and installed, you are ready to discover how Dreamweaver brings these all together into a Web application. We do that in Chapter 3.

The
Complete
Reference

Dreamweaver
MX

Chapter 3

Dreamweaver MX Basics

Dreamweaver MX is the combination of what was Dreamweaver and UltraDev plus a whole lot of new functionality. Because of the integration of these products, it is now possible for the resulting version of Dreamweaver to be developed with the entire product in mind. Where UltraDev seemed, in places, like functionality tacked on to an HTML editor, Dreamweaver MX has been redesigned to be a true application development environment.

You are presented with evidence of the thought that went into this new version from the moment you run the program for the first time. Although the Dreamweaver 4 interface is still available, the PC version of Dreamweaver MX offers two flavors of its new MDI (Multiple Document Interface) environment. In many ways, it is easier to use, especially on single monitor setups, but the sheer volume of it can be intimidating. The good news is that Dreamweaver goes out of its way to allow you to customize your working environment. A little practice will allow you to make good use of whichever interface you choose.

Let's spend some time getting to know the new Dreamweaver MX environment.

Working with Dreamweaver MX

Dreamweaver MX offers what is essentially a three-pronged approach to Web development. Using the tools it provides, you can enter information such as text directly onto the page, have information inserted for you with built-in objects and behaviors, and go behind the scenes to work directly in the underlying code that makes up your page. To construct a site of any substance, you will almost certainly utilize a combination of these methods.

In Chapter 2, we discussed all of the decisions you need to make in preparation to use Dreamweaver. Now that you are ready to start, you will first need to define a site and tell Dreamweaver about the decisions you made. After defining your site, you will begin to develop it by adding pages and then adding content to those pages.

When you first launch Dreamweaver, you are presented with a selection of interfaces. Select the Dreamweaver MX interface for now. We look at changing that choice a little later. Figure 3-1 shows the Dreamweaver MX interface. You can customize this default configuration to meet your needs. We discuss setting your preferences later in the chapter, but for now the defaults will serve us quite nicely as we get started with Dreamweaver.

The Site Panel

In Dreamweaver 4, the Site Manager was the center of much of your activity. In Dreamweaver MX, the Site Manager, although still important, is relegated to its own panel, making it more accessible during page design. It is also easier to get to now that Dreamweaver supports the editing of multiple pages, which you can select with tabs

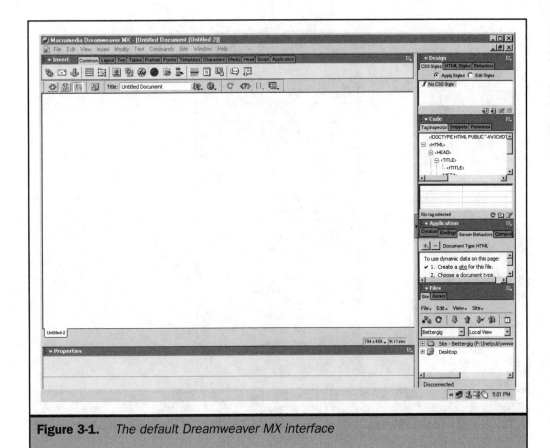

Figure 3-1.   *The default Dreamweaver MX interface*

along the bottom of the design area. But the Site Manager, shown in Figure 3-2, still provides a powerful command center from which to manage all of your Web sites. Using it, you can define the characteristics of each site so that you can administer them efficiently, even if they use different server models and reside on different servers around the Internet. You can use Dreamweaver's built-in FTP program to send and receive files from any of your sites. And you can manage the growth of your site by adding pages, editing pages, and structuring the directories and pages that make it up. But in order to manage a site, you must first define it.

Note   *You can expand the Site Manager to its full size with local files on one side and remote files on the other by clicking the Expand/Collapse button (the far right icon). Click the same icon on the expanded Site Manager to return to the regular design view.*

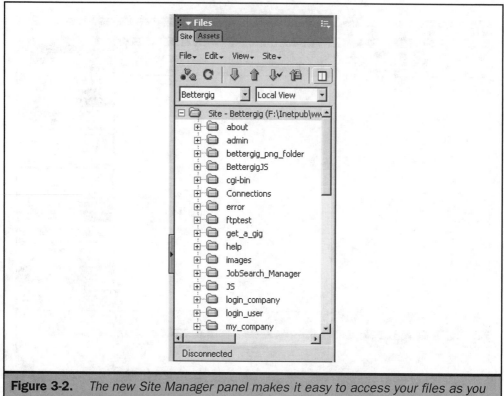

Figure 3-2.   *The new Site Manager panel makes it easy to access your files as you edit pages.*

On the toolbar of the Site Manager is a drop-down list box that lists all of your currently defined sites. If you are using a fresh installation of Dreamweaver, you will have Macromedia tutorial sites in the list. Selecting a site in the list makes that site active. Its directories and pages are then presented in the window below the toolbar.

Next to the site selection drop-down is another drop-down that allows you to select which view is presented in the Site Manager panel. You can select from four options:

- **Local View**   Shows the files that currently exist in the local computer folder that you define as the repository for this site.

- **Remote View**   Shows the files that currently exist on the production server you defined in the site setup.

- **Testing Server**   Shows the files that currently exist on the Testing Server that you defined in the site setup.
- **Map View**   Shows a graphical representation of the site files and their relationships to one another based on the links that Dreamweaver is able to identify.

   Selecting a site and connecting to its remote server will change your Site Manager view to Remote View. This is important to remember as you begin to work. Make sure you are opening and editing the file that you intend to.

We begin by defining a site so that we have something to work with as we continue.

Defining a Site

There are a couple of ways to get to the screens that you will use to define your sites. You can double-click the site displayed in the drop-down list to edit the definition for that site. Or, you can select the Edit Sites option at the bottom of the list and the following screen will appear, allowing you to select a site to edit, create a new site, or delete a site. Follow these steps to define a new site.

1. Select New to define a new site. The Basic tab Site Definition screen will open, as shown here. The Basic Tab is new to Dreamweaver MX and offers a wizard interface that walks you through the creation of your site definition.

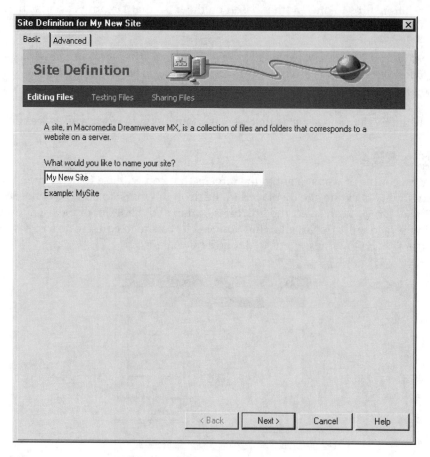

2. Enter a name for your site and click Next.

3. The next screen allows you to select whether this site will use any server-side languages such as ASP or ColdFusion, or whether it will just be browser-based pages like HTML.

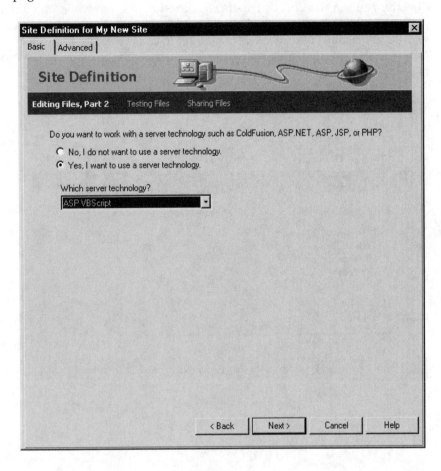

4. On the next screen, you can tell Dreamweaver how you want to work with your files during the development process. You can choose to store the files that you will edit on your local machine, or edit the files on your remote testing server directly. You can also choose whether your testing server resides on your local network or you access it over FTP or RDS. If you have a Web server loaded on your local machine, Dreamweaver will offer to create a folder for your files. You may also specify a file location, which varies with the other options you have chosen.

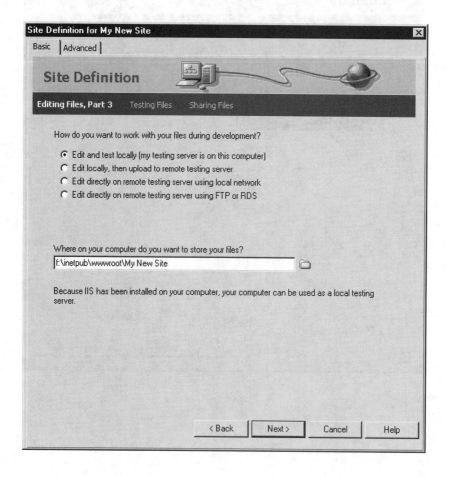

5. Next, specify a URL for the site you are creating. If you are testing locally, the URL may be a virtual directory set up in your Web server. Or you may specify a fully qualified domain name for a remote server. You can test the URL to make sure you have entered it correctly.

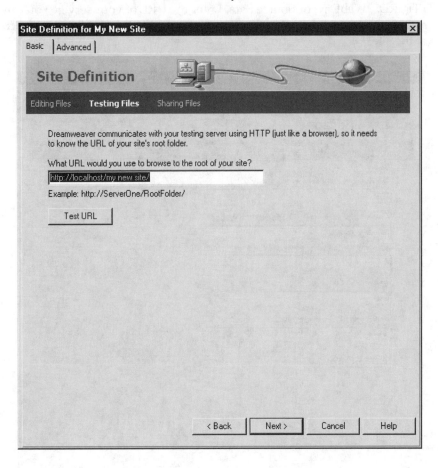

6. Finally, Dreamweaver wants to know whether you will be leaving your files on your local machine, or uploading them to another computer. If you select no, your site definition is complete. If you select yes, the following screen allows you to specify your remote server settings. You may use a local network server, FTP, RDS, WebDav, or Source Safe. Enter the URL of your server. You can also specify a remote directory or simply enter a forward slash (/) to use the root of the site.

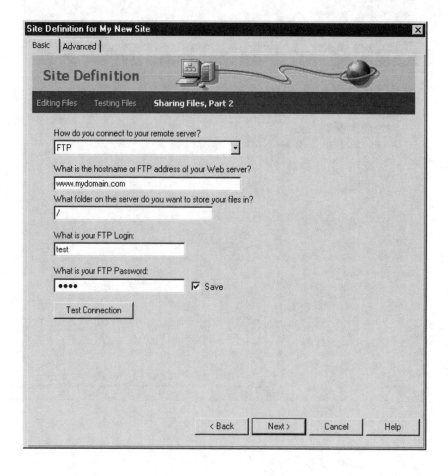

7. If you are using a remote server, you can now specify whether you want to use Dreamweaver's Check In and Check Out features. Check In and Check Out provide a simple locking and markup function that alerts you if you try to open or edit a file that is already checked out by another user. You can specify whether Dreamweaver should check out a file when you open it or just give you a read-only copy and make you explicitly check out the file. You can also provide a name so that others can see who has the file checked out and an e-mail address so they can contact you and bug you about having it tied up too long.

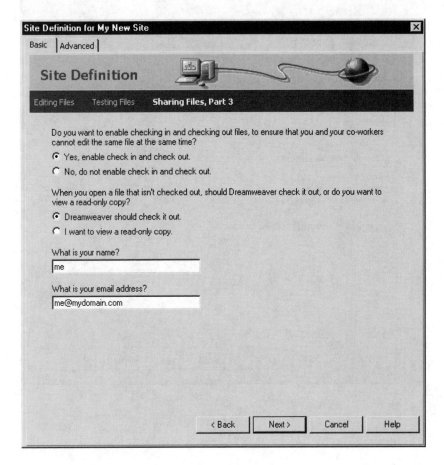

8. The last screen presents you with a summary of the selections you have made. Clicking Done will create your site. You may also switch over at this point and further refine the details of your site with the Advanced tab of the Site Definition window.

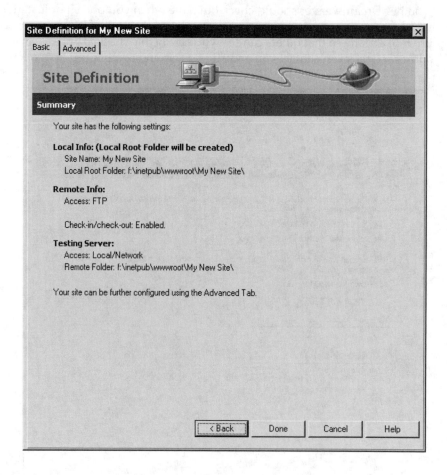

9. The Advanced tab allows you to set further options that offer more control over the development and deployment of your site. If you used the Basic tab, much of this will be input for you. In the Local Info section, you can specify a Default Images Folder. This will specify the folder to which Dreamweaver will save images by default. You may also enter the address of your site so that Dreamweaver can check and report the accuracy of the links you use on your pages. Enabling the cache will save information about your pages and assets in a format that speeds up several of Dreamweaver's file management features.

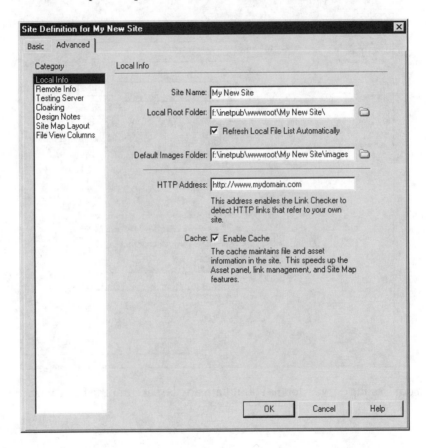

10. Most of the details of the Remote Site sections will have been defined in the Basic wizard. You can set Passive FTP, Firewall, and SSH options here if you need or want to use these options. You can also select to have Dreamweaver automatically upload files when you save them.

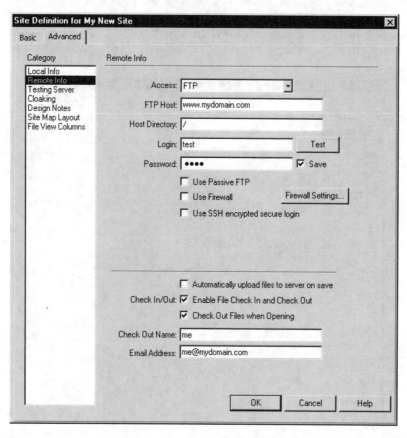

11. Your Testing Server details should already be set from the Basic wizard.

12. Cloaking is a new feature of Dreamweaver MX that allows you to hide certain folders and files from the publishing process. For instance, suppose that you maintain original Fireworks PNG files in your images folder so that Dreamweaver's Integration features can locate and edit them in Fireworks. You may not want those PNG files uploaded to a live server where they could be located and downloaded. You could cloak PNG files so that they are ignored during the publication process.

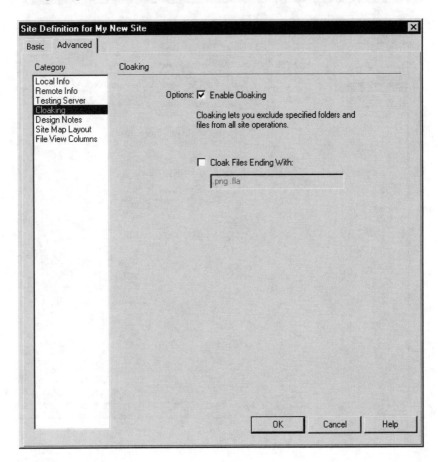

13. Design Notes allow you to save additional information about pages in an associated note. They are used to share information, and can also be used in many of Dreamweaver's integration features with Fireworks and Flash. You can choose whether to maintain Design Notes, as well as whether to upload them so they can be seen by others.

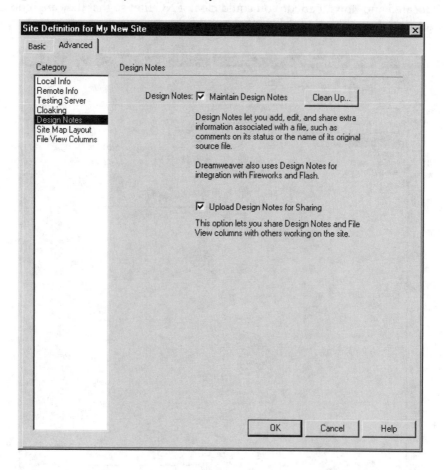

14. The Site Map Layout section allows you to define the structure of the Site Map that is viewable in the Site Manager. To use the Site Map, you must define a home page so that Dreamweaver knows where to start building the map. You can specify how many columns of pages are displayed and whether to display hidden files and dependent files.

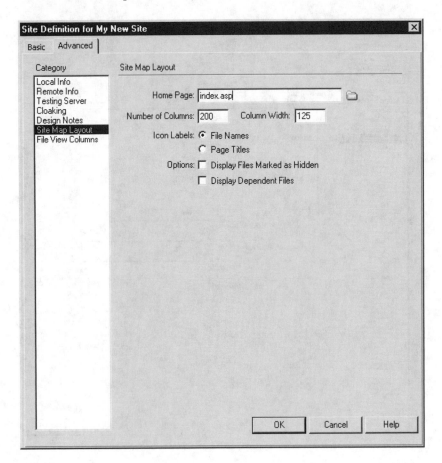

15. The Site Panel has a number of columns of information that you can view. The File View Columns section of the Advanced tab allows you to select which columns are important and in which order you would like to see them. You can also set display properties so that the Site Panel shows you information the way you need to see it.

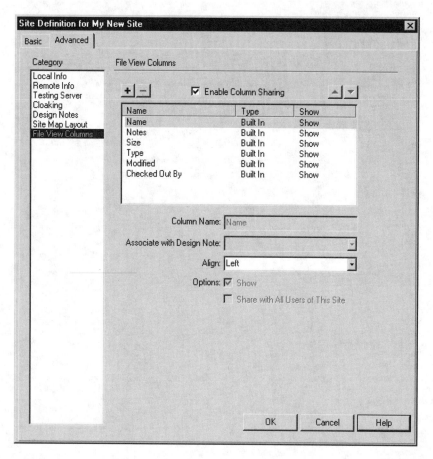

16. Click OK to complete your site definition. You will be returned to the main Dreamweaver interface.

Now that you have described your preferences to Dreamweaver, you are ready to begin constructing your site.

Managing Site Files

You can control many high-level aspects of your site using the Site Panel. With menu options, buttons, and keyboard shortcuts you can:

- Add new pages to your site
- Manage and synchronize files and folders between your local machine and your remote server
- Control changes to your site files by using Dreamweaver's Check In and Check Out features
- Check links
- View a graphical representation of your site using the Site Map Layout

Adding New Pages to Your Site

Dreamweaver offers several methods of adding pages to your site:

- From the main File menu, select the New option. A New Document window will appear. In the New Document window, you may select from a number of different types of documents, from basic HTML and JavaScript pages to a variety of server-side dynamic pages, templates, and framesets. Dreamweaver supplies a wide selection of page types so that your page is created with the proper structure rather than requiring you to add the pieces that are common to a certain page type. You can also create a new page from existing Dreamweaver Templates using the Templates tab of this window.

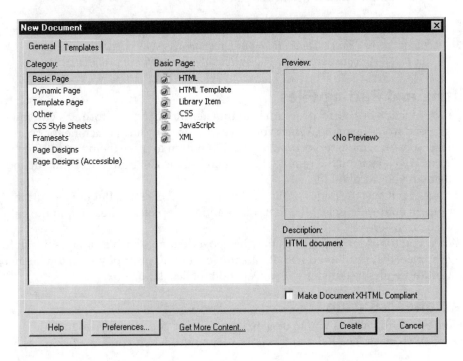

- From the Site Panel File menu, select the New File option. A new file will appear in either the local or remote side of your site, depending on which was selected when the menu option was selected. This new filename will be highlighted, ready for you to give it a unique name.

- In either the Local or Remote side of the Site window, right-click to display the pop-up menu. Select the New File option from the menu. This option works just like the New File option in the File menu.

Managing Your Site

In the Site Panel view, the Site Manager is divided into four sections, each of which is represented in the Views drop-down menu. Be careful to keep track of where you are at all times. You could end up editing the wrong file if you think you are selecting a local file but have the Site Panel set to a remote server.

The Connect and Disconnect Buttons

When you have created pages and are ready to upload them to your remote server, you will need to establish an FTP (File Transfer Protocol) connection. Use the Connect button to initiate a connection to the FTP server that you designated in your site definition. Once an FTP session is started, the Connect button becomes a Disconnect button that allows you to end the session whenever you wish.

You can monitor the activity in your FTP session by using the Site FTP Log in the View menu of the Site Panel. The FTP Log in Dreamweaver MX appears in the Results Panel at the bottom of your screen along with a lot of other useful information.

Getting and Putting Files

The main function of an FTP program is to transfer files back and forth, as you might have guessed from the name. When you have files on your local machine that you need to transfer to your remote server, you use the Put button to place them there. When you need to receive files from the remote server, you use the Get button to get them and save them in your local folder.

To get or put specific pages or files, select them and click the Put or Get button. To get or put an entire site, select the root folder and the top of the file list, and the entire site will be transferred.

When you transfer a page, there may be dependent files such as images, Flash files, or Java applets that need to go with it. Dreamweaver will prompt you as to whether you want those files to transfer with a Dependent Files dialog box.

The Refresh Button

The Refresh button allows you to update your view of your site files to include the most recent changes. The Refresh button is very useful when you are working as a part of a design team. When others make changes to files, or add or delete pages to the site you are working on, you may not have the most up-to-date list in your remote view. Refreshing on a regular basis ensures that you are always aware of the changes that are happening as you work.

Synchronizing Your Site Files

If you do any work offline, or if you are away from a site while others are working on it, you will end up with copies of files in your local window that are out of synch with the versions on your remote server. You may need to place newer versions that you have created offline onto the server, or you may need to bring your local copies up to date.

To synchronize specific files, select them in the local or remote pane of the Site Manager and select the Synchronize option from the Site menu.

When you select the Synchronize menu, the dialog box in Figure 3-3 is displayed, allowing you to choose how your files are synchronized.

In this box, you can select whether to synchronize the entire site or only the files you have selected. You can also choose whether to put newer files from your local folder into the remote server, get newer files from the remote server, or do both, which generates up-to-date versions of the site in both locations.

If you have deleted files on your local machine, you can enable the Delete Remote Files Not On Local Drive option, and they will be deleted on the remote server also.

 Be very careful when setting the Delete Remote Files Not On Local Drive option. If you are working with other developers, it is likely that someone will create a new page that would then be deleted by your synchronization because it does not yet exist on your machine.

Check In and Check Out

There is hardly anything more exciting than working on a big project with several developers. And there is hardly anything more frustrating than having your work overwritten by a careless coworker. Dreamweaver allows you to work safely in a collaborative environment with its Check In and Check Out features.

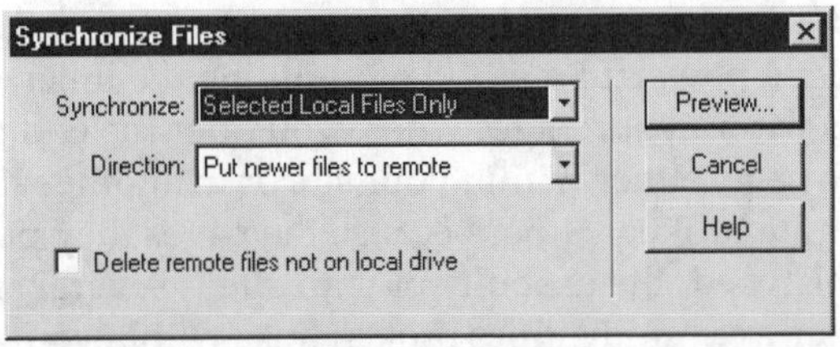

Figure 3-3. *The Synchronize Files Dialog*

Checking files out is Dreamweaver's way of letting other developers on your team know that a file is in use and is likely being edited. It is a warning that, should they decide to edit it as well, someone's changes will get overwritten. Consider the amount of work that could be lost if you were to open a page, and while you were making major revisions to it, a coworker opened the same page to make a simple typo correction. If you saved your file, and then your coworker saved the old version on top of it, your changes would be lost and the site would be left with an old, albeit correctly spelled, version of the page.

When you check out a page, a check mark is placed next to the page name on the remote server; and your name, or whatever identifying name you entered in the Check In/Out category of your site definition, is placed to the right of the filename. A green check mark indicates a file that you have checked out, and a red check mark indicates a file that someone else has checked out.

Note *You can also use Dreamweaver's Check In/Out feature when you are the sole developer on a project. Many developers work from more than one computer, such as a home PC and a work PC. By selecting a name that identifies the computer that opened a file rather than the person, you can always track down the machine on which the file is opened.*

Dreamweaver uses a small text file with an .lck extension to lock a file that is checked out. When this file is present on the server, that file is not available for others to access and edit until you check it back in. Once you have edited a file and checked it in, that file is made read-only on your local machine, forcing you to get the file from the server in order to edit it. This will keep you from editing a local copy of the file and inadvertently uploading it over a newer version of the file.

Note *You can turn this read-only setting off in the File menu or the right-click pop-up menu by selecting the Turn Off Read-Only option. You should carefully consider the consequences of doing this, however, and be careful not to overwrite newer versions of the page on your remote server.*

Caution *This method of locking the remote file is not foolproof. Applications other than Dreamweaver will not realize the significance of the LCK file and will allow these pages to be overwritten.*

Checking Links

Dreamweaver provides a powerful method of verifying the links within your sites. Links are those places within your pages where you offer the end user an opportunity to navigate to another page, either within your site or in another site somewhere on the Internet. If those links are broken, either because the pages they point to no longer exist or because they are mistyped, the usability of your site is severely impacted. Checking your links within Dreamweaver identifies broken links within your site, reports external links so you can verify them manually, and finds orphaned files.

Dreamweaver can verify links that point to other pages in your site. If the pages that are represented in these links do not exist or cannot be found, Dreamweaver reports them as broken.

 In order for Dreamweaver to be able to identify links as internal, it is important that you set the URL of your site under HTTP Address in the Local Info category of your site definition. If this value is not set, Dreamweaver will likely report a large number of your internal links as external links and will not verify them.

If links to external Web sites exist on your pages, they will be reported to you so that you can verify them manually; Dreamweaver has no facility for verifying external links and depends on you to do it.

Orphaned files are pages within your site that have no other pages pointing links to them. Because the Web is a hyperlink environment, it is unlikely that a visitor would ever find the way to a page within your site without following a link there. Orphaned pages serve little purpose, because users will probably never see them.

You can check links in a specific page, a set of pages, or your whole site. To check a page or several pages, select them in the Site Panel and right-click to display the pop-up menu. The Check Links selection in the menu has two options: Selected Files/Folders and Entire Site. You may also check the entire site by selecting the Check Links Sitewide option from the Site menu.

After Dreamweaver verifies your links, the results will appear in a tab of the Results panel. You can use the drop-down list to filter the results that you need to view, and you can even save the report information so it is easier to refer to when making changes to the site to fix broken links and orphaned files.

The Site Map

Dreamweaver's Site Map offers a graphical view of your site in which you can add pages, open pages for editing, create links between pages, and change page titles. The Site Map allows you to perform many Dreamweaver functions in a visual manner, such as selecting a group of pages by dragging across them and adding pages to your site by dragging them from Windows Explorer. Lines between files indicate link relationships, and icons represent things such as broken links within pages. You can view the Site Map in the Map View of the Site Panel, but it is much better used in the expanded Site Manager shown in Figure 3-4.

As discussed earlier, you can adjust the way the Site Map is displayed by altering the number of columns and column width in your site definition.

The Document Window

Dreamweaver is a WYSIWYG (What You See Is What You Get) development tool. Although you can certainly build a Web page in a text editor such as Notepad and view the results after you have finished, the Web is, at its core, a presentational medium, and it's nice to actually see what you are doing while you're designing it.

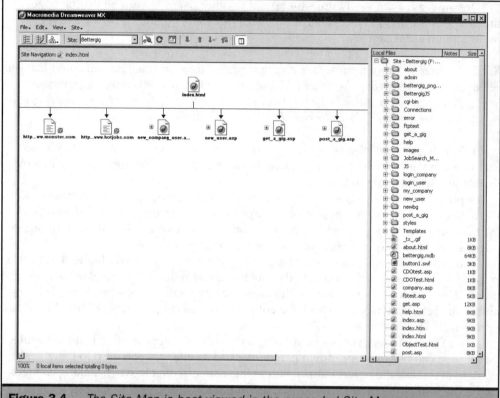

Figure 3-4.   *The Site Map is best viewed in the expanded Site Manager.*

Development in Dreamweaver centers on the Document window, as shown in Figure 3-5.

The Document window is the graphical palette on which you will build your site. When first opened, a new window offers only a white background onto which you will place the text, images, and other elements that make up your site.

Underneath the design area is a status bar region that provides access to information and properties about the page you are working on.

The Tag Selector

At the left side of the status bar, just above the Property inspector, is the Tag Selector. HTML files are made up of tags that describe the hierarchy of the content on the page. The Tag Selector provides a way to view and select that hierarchy as you edit your pages.

When a new page is created, the <body> tag is all that appears in the Tag Selector. As you add content, additional tags appear. If you place a table on the page, a <table>

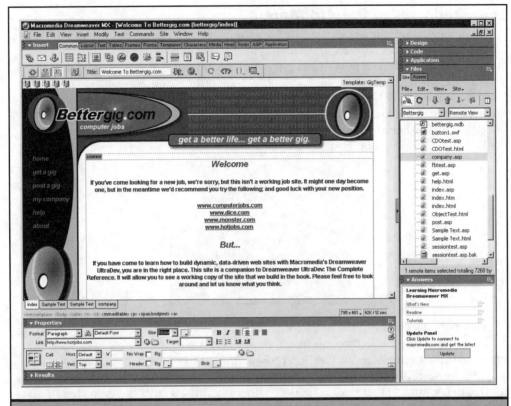

Figure 3-5.   *Several Documents open in the Design Space. You can choose between them using the tabs at the bottom.*

tag is generated. As you add rows and cells to that table, <tr> and <td> tags appear to represent those portions of the page. You can select an element on the page, and the appropriate tag becomes bold to indicate what is selected. You can also select a specific tag in the Tag Selector and that portion of the page becomes selected. Once a tag is selected, it can be easily edited or deleted. This method of selecting specific portions of a page comes in especially handy when pages grow very complex and selecting the proper portion in Design view is difficult.

Note   *The Tag Selector is dynamic, depending on what you have selected on the page. While nothing is selected, you will see only high-level tags, such as the <body> and <table> tags. As you select these tags or their graphical representations on the screen, their system of child tags will appear in the Tag Selector. This method of isolating portions of the page as you navigate it makes for a very elegant way to manage complex pages.*

The Window Size Pop-Up Menu

When you are developing sites for public consumption (as opposed to a captive audience, as with a corporate intranet) you must be constantly aware of the variety of client hardware and software your pages will encounter. Some users will have the latest processor with a high-resolution 21+-inch monitor that does justice to their graphical masterpieces. Others, whose attention may be just as important to you or your client, may not know how to set their video cards to a resolution greater than 640×480 with 256 colors. Dreamweaver helps you develop a variety of settings with the Window Size pop-up menu.

```
592w
536 x 196   (640 x 480, Default)
600 x 300   (640 x 480, Maximized)
760 x 420   (800 x 600, Maximized)
795 x 470   (832 x 624, Maximized)
955 x 600   (1024 x 768, Maximized)
544 x 378   (WebTV)

Edit Sizes...
```

This menu lists some of the more common dimensions available to users, depending on what screen resolution they are using. By selecting an option, you can resize your screen to those dimensions and see a representation of the content area that your users will see. Some developers set their screens to a target dimension and design all of their content to conform to that size restriction. Others simply use this menu to check that their content scales gracefully on a variety of platforms.

Dreamweaver comes configured with several popular screen sizes. The first time you try them, you may feel quite closed in, especially in the vertical setting. Remember, though, that most browsers have chrome that you need to deal with. *Chrome* consists of the menu, button and address bars, and any advertising that may appear at the top of the interface, robbing you of screen real estate in which to place content. Although these default sizes do represent a reasonable selection of the circumstances you are likely to encounter, an Edit Sizes option is available in the menu, which allows you to add, delete, or edit screen sizes to suit your needs.

 The Window Size Menu works only when your page is not maximized in the design area. Maximized pages allow the tab system to work to switch between pages, but because use of the Window Size menu changes the dimensions of the page, it will work only when pages are "undocked" into the design area.

The Download Indicator

Just as you will encounter a variety of screen sizes and resolutions, you will also encounter a variety of bandwidth issues, including the connection speed over which your visitors view your pages. From the home user with the 28.8K modem to the corporate users with a T1 or faster connection, you need to be prepared to serve content in a manner that keeps your audience's attention. On the Web, that generally means optimizing your content to load as quickly as possible over slower connection speeds.

Tools like this are not perfect, because they cannot take into consideration things such as line quality, bandwidth saturation, and bottlenecks in the Internet backbone itself, but the download indicator can give you a pretty good idea of the average download time your users will experience. By taking the size of all of the elements represented on your page and dividing it by the number of bits per second in the connection speed you select, the status bar gives you an indication of how long this particular configuration will take to load. Thoughts on the proper download time of the average page vary, but you should certainly keep pages with normal content within a 10- to 15-second window if you can help it. Much longer, and your visitors are going to go looking for speedier pastures.

You can alter the download speed indicated in the status bar in your Preferences, which we cover shortly.

Note *The download speed indicator on the status bar takes into account only the size of the actual text file you are working on. If you have images or include files that make up your page, the resulting file may be much larger than is indicated to you here. Also, because the HTML that results from a processed ASP, JSP, or CFM page is often much smaller than the actual code file, your resulting page could be smaller and load even faster than the Status Bar shows.*

The Panels

To the side of your design area (or surrounding it, depending on where you choose to put them) are panels and toolbars that provide access to some of Dreamweaver's most powerful features. The objects, behaviors, commands, and other extensions that make up the core of Dreamweaver's functionality are primary reasons for its popularity in the Web development world.

Note *Extensions are add-in pieces of code that allow Dreamweaver to perform certain tasks. An important feature of the product is that the extensibility model is documented. This allows anyone with the requisite programming skills to build extensions and distribute them to others, which makes Dreamweaver more powerful all the time. We cover the various types of extensions and how to create them in later chapters.*

By default, Dreamweaver presents you with the panels shown in Figure 3-6. Additional panels are available in the Window menu.

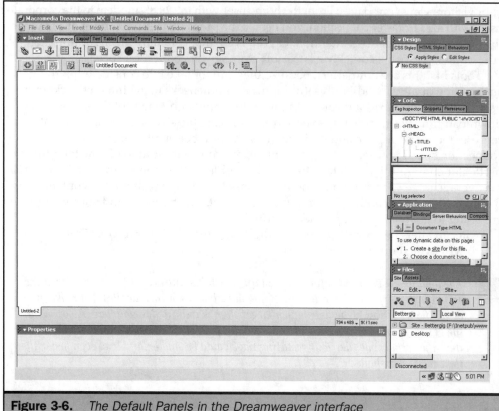

Figure 3-6.   *The Default Panels in the Dreamweaver interface*

Following is a list of the default Panel Groups and Toolbars.

Insert toolbar   Objects are generally snippets of HTML code that are applied to your page. Many objects provide a user interface that allows you to set properties of the tags themselves, such as the number of rows or columns in a table. Others are simple HTML inserts, such as the Horizontal Rule object. New to Dreamweaver MX are the Application Objects, which provide functionality that is specific to each of the server models. The Insert Toolbar is dynamic and changes what is offered to you depending on what kind of page you are editing.

Properties   Property inspectors are windows into the settings that make up objects and Behaviors. When an object is selected, the Property inspector changes to display the appropriate information about the selected item and to allow you to change properties and tag values without entering the HTML code itself. You can do this with many Server Behaviors as well.

Results The Results Panel is new to Dreamweaver MX and consolidates much of the information that Dreamweaver outputs about your site into one convenient area. A number of tabs are available to display search results, validation reports, browser and link checks, and other log information.

Design The Design Panel contains tabs that affect the design, or client side of your site, such as CSS styles, HTML styles, and Behaviors.

Code The Code Panel holds the Tag Inspector, Snippets, and Reference panels. The Tag Inspector shows an overview of the structure of your site by displaying the HTML tags that make it up. You can use it to add tags and edit the properties of the tags on the page. Many of the tag properties can access dynamic elements like recordset fields so that they can be set on the fly by your application.

Snippets are reusable chunks of code that you can add to your page. They are useful for storing lines of code that are used over and over again in your sites. You can add your own snippets to those provided with Dreamweaver.

The Reference tab holds language references so that you can easily check syntax or usage in several popular coding languages.

Application The Application Panel Group holds four panels that are important to the building of dynamic applications. The Database panel contains information about the databases that are connected to your site. It is an easy reference to review table, views, and stored procedure structures.

The Bindings Panel lists the specific recordsets that have been designated for the current page. It can also hold server-specific dynamic elements, such as ASP request and response objects. You can drag and drop elements from the Bindings Panel onto your pages.

The Server Behaviors Panel allows you to add, remove, and edit Server Behaviors, such as repeat regions and dynamic navigation. Server Behaviors are chunks of server-side code that take parameters from the developer and use them to perform common server-side operations.

Files The Files Panel Group houses the Site Panel and the Assets Panel. We have been working with the Site Panel extensively. The Assets Panel is a list of the various types of assets, such as images, templates, movies, and scripts, that exist in your site folder. Dreamweaver searches the entire folder and caches the location of these support files for easy access.

Answers The Answers Panel is Macromedia's attempt to make Dreamweaver a truly self-supporting development environment. From within the Answers Panel you can search the Macromedia support site, get new tutorials, and even download extensions, all without leaving Dreamweaver.

A number of other panels are available in the Window menu and can be selected and displayed wherever you like in the interface.

Remember that you are not locked in to the default panel configuration. You can edit, move, dock, float, and create panels at will. In fact, some of the best new third-party extensions coming out for Dreamweaver MX are new toolbars and panels that you can add to your environment.

You can dock and undock Panel Groups by dragging them around the screen. There is a little five-dot gripper in the upper left-hand corner of each Panel Group that you can use to grab the Panel Group with your mouse and reposition it on the screen. You can also use the right-click context menu to rename, maximize, and close Panel Groups.

You cannot drag and drop panels. Instead, Macromedia has added a menu-based grouping function to the context menu of the panels. Right-clicking any panel tab and selecting the Group With menu item lets you select an active Panel Group to add this panel to. The panel will be added to the tight end of the panels in that Panel Group. A little manipulation is necessary to get things in a specific order.

From the Group With menu, you can also create and name a new Panel Group, which the selected panel will be added to. This is actually the only way to close and remove a particular panel from a Panel Group. You must create a new Panel Group and then use the context menu to close that Panel Group.

Make sure to take notice of the button on the Panel Group divider to the right of the design area. This rectangle button with the arrow on it collapses all of the Panel Groups and re-expands them with one click—a great feature when you need extra screen space.

Dreamweaver's Menus

As you work in the Document window, you will access many features through the status bar and Dreamweaver's system of panels. The main Dreamweaver set of menus duplicates much of this functionality, but some features you can access only through menu and shortcut options. Following is a description of Dreamweaver's default menus.

The File Menu

The File menu contains menu items that relate to file management and page-level features. Table 3-1 describes the menu choices available in the File menu.

Menu Selection	Description
New	Opens the New Document window from which you may select the type of document that you want to open
Open	Allows you to browse to and open a file

Table 3-1. *File Menu Selections*

Menu Selection	Description
Open in Frame	Opens a selected file into the current frame
Close	Closes the current window
Save	Saves the page with the current filename replacing the currently saved version
Save As	Displays a Save As dialog box
Save As Template	Saves the current page as a template file in the Templates folder for future use
Save All	Saves all of the currently open pages
Revert	Disregards current changes and reloads the most recently saved version of the current file
Print Code	Prints the code from the Code View of the current page
Import—Import XML into Template	Creates a new page with XML data inserted inside a template
Import—Import Word HTML	Opens an HTML file generated in Word and cleans up the code
Import—Import Table Data	Imports delimited data to form a new table
Export—Export Template Data as XML	Saves the editable regions in the current template as an XML file
Export—Export CSS Styles	Uses the current page's style sheets to create an external style sheet file
Export—Export Table	Exports table data as a delimited file
Convert—3.0 Browser-Compatible	Converts the current page to a format that is compatible with version 3.0 browsers
Convert—XHTML	Converts the current page to XHTML-compliant tags
Preview in Browser—Edit Browser List	Allows you to add, subtract, and configure the list of browsers loaded on your machine
Preview in Browser—Browser List	Lists the current loaded browsers that Dreamweaver can use as preview browsers

Table 3-1. *File Menu Selections* (continued)

Menu Selection	Description
Debug in Browser	Enables you to debug JavaScript within a local browser session, using any breakpoints you may have set
Check Page	Provides a variety of page checks, such as Accessibility, links, target browsers, and validation
Design Notes	Displays the Design Notes dialog box in which you may enter notes for the current page
Previous Files List	Displays up to four recently opened files for easy access
Exit	Closes open files and exits Dreamweaver

Table 3-1.   *File Menu Selections* (continued)

The Edit Menu

The Edit menu provides you with commands that make page editing easier and allow you to recover from mistakes, as shown in Table 3-2.

Menu Selection	Description
Undo	Reverses the last action taken
Redo	Re-executes a reversed action
Cut	Removes the current selection and places it on the system keyboard for use elsewhere
Copy	Copies the current selection to the system clipboard for use elsewhere
Paste	Inserts clipboard data at the current cursor position
Clear	Removes the current selection
Copy HTML	Copies the current selection onto the system clipboard with the HTML tags

Table 3-2.   *Edit Menu Selections*

Menu Selection	Description
Paste HTML	Pastes the clipboard data to the page with the HTML tags
Select All	Highlights all of the tags and elements on the current page
Select Parent Tag	Selects the tag that surrounds the current selection
Select Child	Selects the first tag within the current selection
Find and Replace	Displays a dialog box in which you can enter the text you want to find on the page, and lets you enter text with which to replace the found instances
Find Next	Finds the next occurrence of the search string
Go to Line	Allows you to jump to a particular line in Code View
Show Code Hints	Turns on the Code Hints window in Code View
Indent Code	Indents a selected line of code
Outdent Code	Outdents a selected line of code
Balance Braces	Checks to see that the braces that surround sections of JavaScript are balanced, that is, that each opening brace has a closing brace
Set Breakpoint	Sets a point at which execution of code will pause for debugging purposes
Remove All Breakpoints	Removes any breakpoints you have set
Repeating Entries	Options for editing repeating regions
Edit with External Editor	Launches an instance of the text editor you have configured in your preferences
Keyboard Shortcuts	Enables you to set, remove, and edit keyboard shortcuts that perform menu operations
Tag Libraries	Opens the Tag Library Editor where you can review and edit the various tags in all of the Dreamweaver-supported languages
Preferences	Displays the Preferences dialog box in which you can set numerous Dreamweaver properties

Table 3-2.   *Edit Menu Selections* (continued)

The View Menu

The View menu controls what you see on the page in the design environment, as you can see in Table 3-3. These menu items toggle page elements to allow you to customize your work environment.

Menu Selection	Description
Code	Switches your working window to Code view, where you can view your pages' underlying code
Design	Switches your working window to Design view, where you can view your page's visual layout
Code and Design	Divides your working window into two sections containing the Code view and the Design view onscreen at once
Switch Views	Switches whichever view you are currently in (Code or Design) to the other available view
Refresh Design View	Reloads the page to properly display any changes you have made
Design View on Top	When using the Code and Design option, enables you to choose whether the Code view or Design view is in the top frame of the split screen
Server Debug	Allows you to debug ColdFusion MX pages from within Dreamweaver
Live Data	Toggles live data on and off
Live Data Settings	Displays the Live Data Server Configuration dialog box
Head Content	Displays categories of information inserted into the head of the current page
Table View	Enables you to switch between Standard view and Layout view
Visual Aids	Provides a selection of layout and design aids, including whether borders are displayed on tables and layers, and whether image map overlays are visible

Table 3-3. *View Menu Selections*

Menu Selection	Description
Code View Options	Provides a selection of Code view options, such as Word Wrap and Line Numbers
Rulers—Show	Toggles the visibility of page rulers
Rulers—Reset Origin	Resets the 0,0 coordinates to the upper left of the page
Rulers—Increments	Controls the measurement that the rulers are incremented by
Grid—Show	Toggles the visibility of the design grid on the current page
Grid—Snap To	Controls whether design elements placed on the page snap to the grid lines
Grid—Edit	Displays the Grid Settings dialog box
Tracing Image—Show	Toggles the visibility of a tracing image
Tracing Image—Align with Selection	Aligns the top-left corner of a tracing image with the top-left corner of the current selection
Tracing Image—Adjust Position	Allows a tracing image to be positioned with the cursor keys
Tracing Image—Reset Position	Places the tracing image in the upper left of the current page
Tracing Image—Load	Allows the selection of a tracing image to be placed on the page
Plug-ins—Play	Plays the currently selected plug-in
Plug-ins—Stop	Stops the currently playing plug-in
Plug-ins—Play All	Plays all plug-ins on the current page
Plug-ins—Stop All	Stops all plug-ins from playing
Hide Panels	Hides all panels and palettes except for the Design window
Toolbar	Toggles the visibility of the Document and Standard toolbars

Table 3-3. *View Menu Selections* (continued)

The Insert Menu

The Insert menu provides easy access to the wide variety of objects that are available to you in Dreamweaver. These objects automate the inclusion of HTML into your page using predefined modules of code. See Table 3-4 for menu choices.

Menu Selection	Description
Tag	Opens the Tag Chooser to allow the selection of any available tag
Image	Allows the selection of an image that will be placed on the page
Image Placeholder	Inserts an Image Placeholder for early design purposes
Interactive Images	Provides a selection of interactive images, such as Flash buttons, rollover images, and Fireworks HTML that you can insert in the current page
Media	Provides a selection of media, such as Flash files and Java applets that you can insert in the current page
Table	Inserts an HTML table with the selected properties
Table Objects	Inserts objects that are a part of tables, such as TR and TD tags
Layer	Inserts a layer
Frames	Provides a selection of frame configurations to be added to the current page
Template Objects	Insert objects that are a part of templates, such as editable and repeating regions
Form	Inserts a form tag
Form Objects	Provides a selection of form elements, such as edit boxes and Submit buttons, that you can add to the current form
E-Mail Link	Inserts an e-mail link at the current selection
Hyperlink	Inserts a hyperlink
Named Anchor	Inserts a named bookmark
Date	Inserts a static client-side date at the current selection

Table 3-4. *Insert Menu Selections*

Menu Selection	Description
Horizontal Rule	Inserts an HTML <hr> tag
Text Objects	Text Objects allow you to apply formatting to text, such as list parameters, HTML text markup, and comments
Script Objects	Script objects let you include blocks of script and server side includes in your code
Head Tags	Inserts head tags, such as Meta and Keywords tags
Special Characters	Inserts special characters, such as foreign currency, trademark and copyright symbols, and nonbreaking spaces
Application Objects	This entire section contains server-side objects that are specific to the different server models supported by Dreamweaver
Get More Objects	Takes you to the Macromedia Exchange where you can download additional objects

Table 3-4.   *Insert Menu Selections* (continued)

The Modify Menu

The Modify menu allows you to make changes to the properties of selected elements on your pages, as you can see in Table 3-5.

Menu Selection	Description
Page Properties	Displays properties of the current page, such as Page Title, Background Image, or Link Colors
Template Properties	Displays the properties of a template
Selection Properties	Toggles the visibility of the Property inspector
Edit Tag	Displays a dialog box with the available properties of the selected tag

Table 3-5.   *Modify Menu Selections*

Menu Selection	Description
Quick Tag Editor	Toggles the visibility of the Quick Tag Editor
Make Link	Displays the file browser for selecting a file to link to
Remove Link	Deletes the currently selected link
Open Linked Page	Opens the linked page
Link Target	Sets the target of a link to the current window, a new window, or a particular frame
Table	Provides a variety of edits and properties for a selected table
Frameset	Provides a variety of edits and properties for a selected frameset
Navigation Bar	Modifies properties of a Navigation bar
Arrange	Sets the z-order of a layer in relation to other layers
Align	Aligns selected layers to one another
Convert	Allows you to convert tables to layers and layers to tables
Library	Adds and updates library items
Templates	Adds, updates, and modifies template files
Timeline	Adds, updates, and modifies timelines on the current page

Table 3-5.   *Modify Menu Selections* (continued)

The Text Menu

The Text menu provides a variety of ways to control the display of one of the most important parts of your site, as you can see in Table 3-6.

Menu Selection	Description
Indent	Indents the current selection using the <blockquote> tag
Outdent	Removes the <dir> or <blockquote> tag to cancel indentation

Table 3-6.   *Text Menu Selections*

Menu Selection	Description
Paragraph Format	Provides a variety of text-formatting options
Align	Provides a variety of text-alignment options
List	Provides a variety of list options, such as numbered list and unordered list
Font	Provides a variety of text-formatting options
Style	Provides text style options, such as bold and italic
HTML Styles	Provides a variety of HTML styles
CSS Styles	Provides a variety of CSS styles
Size	Allows the specific sizing of text
Size Change	Allows for relative sizing of text using + and −
Color	Allows you to choose the color of the currently selected text
Check Spelling	Runs a spell checker

Table 3-6. *Text Menu Selections* (continued)

The Commands Menu

Commands provide streamlined ways to traverse and alter code in your site.
The Commands menu provides access to loaded commands and allows you to
record your own commands in a macro-like fashion, as you can see in Table 3-7.

Menu Selection	Description
Start Recording	Records a series of steps to be saved as a command
Play Recorded Command	Plays the recorded command
Edit Command List	Edits the list of existing commands
Get More Commands	Navigates to the Macromedia Exchange, where you can obtain additional commands

Table 3-7. *Commands Menu Selections*

Menu Selection	Description
Manage Extensions	Runs the Extension Manager
Apply Source Formatting	Uses the Source Formatting Profile to structure the current page
Apply Source Formatting to Selection	Uses the Source Formatting Profile to structure the currently selected chunk of code
Clean Up HTML	Removes HTML that does not conform to the options you select
Clean Up Word HTML	Removes HTML that does not conform to the options you select, with special emphasis on HTML added by Word
Add/Remove Netscape Resize Fix	Adds a function that forces the page to reload when a Netscape browser is resized, fixing a bug in Navigator with pages that contain layers
Optimize Image in Fireworks	Displays the Optimize Image dialog box using Fireworks
Create Web Photo Album	Creates a photo album site using a directory of images
Set Color Scheme	Allows you to select a color scheme for the current page
Format Table	Enables you to apply a table format to the current table
Sort Table	Displays table sorting options

Table 3-7.   *Commands Menu Selections* (continued)

The Site Menu

The Site menu provides access to features that control site-level aspects of your site, such as the Site Manager, site definitions, and FTP commands, as shown in Table 3-8.

The Window Menu

The Window menu provides show and hide access to all of the panels that make up the Dreamweaver design environment. It is unnecessary to list them all here, but any window or palette in the program can be made visible or invisible by selecting it in this menu.

Menu Selection	Description
Site Files	Displays the Site window
Site Map	Displays the Site window with the Site Map enabled
New Site	Opens the Site Definition window for creating a new site
Define Sites	Opens the Site Definition window where you can create a new site or edit existing sites
Get	Gets a file or files from a remote server
Check Out	Checks out a file for editing
Put	Places a file on the remote server
Check In	Checks in a file after editing
Undo Check Out	Reverses a file check-out
Locate in Site	Selects the current document in the site file list
Reports	Provides a series of workflow and HTML reports that contain information about your site
Deploy Supporting Files	Uploads Data Connection support files for the ASP.NET server model

Table 3-8.   *Site Menu Selections*

The Help Menu

The Help menu provides access to Dreamweaver help files and a variety of online support services at Macromedia.

Preferences

As alluded to previously, Dreamweaver goes out of its way to allow you to customize your work environment. Selecting the Preferences option from the Edit menu presents you with 20 categories, covering everything from color schemes to style formats to which tag is used when you insert a layer. The preference settings are fairly self-explanatory, so we don't cover them all here. Just keep in mind that any time you wish something could work a little differently in Dreamweaver, you can probably change it in the Preferences menu. Spend some time here when you first begin using the program. It will acquaint you with what Dreamweaver can do for you to make your development experience go more smoothly, from customizing the way code is displayed to adding browsers to the preview list.

One preference of note is the capability to change the Dreamweaver environment in which you are working. On the General tab, you will notice a button called Change Workspace. Clicking that button displays the same dialog box that you used to select your interface when Dreamweaver ran the first time. You can use it anytime to select between the three environments. Once you restart Dreamweaver, your new selection will be implemented.

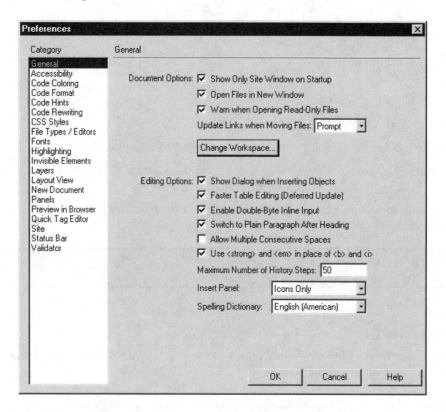

Summary

There is a lot to the Dreamweaver Interface. An incredible amount of thought has gone into its design and layout, especially considering all of the advanced tools that are now integrated into the program. The consolidation of Panels into Panel Groups, and extremely useful additions such as the Results Panel, allows Macromedia to end up with a very concise and useful interface that is efficient for both designers and programmers. In Chapter 4, we put these tools to good use as we begin building pages in Dreamweaver MX.

The
Complete
Reference

Dreamweaver
MX

Chapter 4

Building Your First Site

N ow that we have some of the basics out of the way, it's time to start building something with Dreamweaver. There is good news and there is good news. The good news is that Dreamweaver's page creation tools make it easy to become productive in a very short amount of time. The good (better) news is that this ease of use does not come at the expense of a very powerful environment. In this chapter, we will begin the process of creating pages in Dremweaver and move toward its advanced features over the next several chapters.

Constructing Web Pages in Dreamweaver

One of Dreamweaver's key features is that it deals with HTML on HTML's terms. Simply put, this means that Dreamweaver allows HTML to be HTML; it does not try to turn it into a desktop publishing application.

Several years ago, when HTML began to gain popularity, many designers had difficulty coming to grips with the way it worked. The desktop publishing boom had accustomed computer graphics professionals to sophisticated software, such as PageMaker and Ventura Publisher, that allowed a true WYSIWYG design environment. When you placed things on a page, they went where you wanted them and they stayed there. Design was expressed in pixels, and precision was expected.

But HTML is not desktop publishing. HTML was designed to express the hierarchy of information, not its presentation. Remember that the first browsers were text-based, and the thoughts and words themselves were the focus, not how they looked.

Much like a word processing document, HTML pages begin at the upper left of the page. To illustrate, open a project in Dreamweaver, select File | New and create a basic HTML page. Notice that the cursor is at the upper-left corner of the page. Click anywhere on the page to try and reposition it and it will not respond. Although there are ways around this, discussed later, it is important to see that basic HTML pages are generally constructed from the top down.

Type a sentence into the page. Press ENTER and type another line, and then hold down the SHIFT key and press ENTER. Type a third line on the page. Now, click the HTML Source option on the launcher, and you will begin to see how Dreamweaver works.

The following code is generated by Dreamweaver after you type the text into the document window; don't worry if the words you type are different—the HTML tags are what you are interested in:

```
<html>
<head>

<title>Untitled Document</title>
```

```
<meta http-equiv="Content-Type" content="text/html; charset=iso-8859-1">

</head>

<body bgcolor="#FFFFFF">

<p>This is line one</p>

<p>This is line two<br>

  This is line three</p>

</body>

</html
```

By default, Dreamweaver has created the basic framework of your HTML page, including the HTML tags, some meta information, head tags, a place to put a title, and a default background color. When you began typing on the page, Dreamweaver placed the words as HTML paragraph text within the <body> tags of the page (note the <p> tags). Pressing ENTER generated a new paragraph. Pressing ENTER combined with the SHIFT key inserted a break tag (<br>) and placed line three within the same paragraph.

This is the crux of how Dreamweaver works. The entire goal of the package is to generate an HTML file, which is really just a text file with tags that describe the information inside it. This can be accomplished in a number of ways. The simplest is what you have just caused to happen—the interpretation of keyboard input into HTML format. More complex pieces of code require other methods, such as the use of objects or Behaviors.

Objects

The previous section gave a simple example of how Dreamweaver interprets your input into a format that HTML can handle and display. By turning your keyboard strokes into HTML tags, Dreamweaver can translate the things that you are used to doing (typing on a keyboard) into things you might not be used to doing (writing HTML tags).

Note   *Even if you are an HTML whiz, you have to admit that letting Dreamweaver handle the details for you is a real time saver.*

But, creating Web pages involves a lot more than just entering text. If this is going to be a true visual-design tool, it has to handle the more complex things that people are used to using HTML to do—things such as tables, layers, image tags, and form elements, or even inserting Flash and Shockwave files. Fortunately, Dreamweaver provides a feature that does those things.

It should not be a surprise to you that making Dreamweaver do the things listed is a bit more complicated than the simple keyboard translation reviewed earlier. To accomplish this task, Dreamweaver includes a method of collecting user input and turning it into HTML. This method is represented in Dreamweaver's objects.

When you start Dreamweaver, you should notice the Insert toolbar at the top of the interface. The Insert toolbar contains several tabs, each of which contains several icons representing the various things you can do, as shown next. These tabs represent categories that enable you to keep objects organized by functionality or by their source, or by any other method that makes them easy for you to use. Chapter 21 looks at how you can create your own categories and move objects around within them.

In concept, objects are fairly simple. Their main purpose is to accept input from the user and place it as HTML code in the body of the page they are applied to. Every object works a little differently. With practice, you will learn what to expect from each of them. The following sections look at three objects that vary in the way they are implemented.

The *Horizontal Rule* Object

The simplest type of object is represented by the *Horizontal Rule* object on the Common tab of the Insert toolbar. A horizontal rule is simply a line that rules horizontally across the page. Although it does have properties that can be assigned to it, a *Horizontal Rule* object can be represented with nothing more than an <hr> tag. At the point on the page where that tag appears, a line will be placed on the page. Place your cursor at the desired location on the page, locate the *Horizontal Rule* object on the Insert toolbar, and click it. The horizontal rule will appear on the page.

After your object is placed on the page, you may want to edit its properties to change— in the case of the *Horizontal Rule* object, the height or width, the color, or the alignment. When you select the *Horizontal Rule* object, its details appear in the Property inspector Panel. The Property inspector displays the standard properties that apply to the object that is selected. For instance, when the *Horizontal Rule* object is selected, the Property inspector looks like the following:

On the Property inspector for the *Horizontal Rule* object, you can set the name of the *Horizontal Rule* object, the width in pixels or percent, the height, the alignment, and whether the line is shaded or not. Those are the basic settings and represent the most-used attributes for this object. You can access a complete list of attributes in the Tag Inspector Panel in the Code Panel Group.

The Tag Inspector provides a high level look at the tag structure of your site. You can use it to review your page's tags, add tags, and most importantly, set the attributes of the tags in the complete properties list provided. If you select the horizontal rule on your page with the Tag Inspector open, the inspector will jump to and highlight the <hr> tag. You can use the list in the bottom portion of the panel to view and set properties.

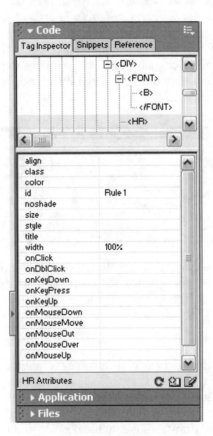

The *Horizontal Rule* is the simplest kind of object. It asks for no input from the user to place the basic object, and then enables you to set properties afterward.

Note   *The* Horizontal Rule *object and the* Table *object (discussed next) are both dependent on your cursor position. They will place the object at your cursor's position.*

The *Table* Object

If you have spent any time at all with HTML, you are familiar with the *Table* object. Originally designed to allow the display of information in columns, *Table* objects have evolved into a primary means of allowing more complex visual designs on HTML pages. The Dreamweaver *Table* object enables you to build complex table structures to accommodate your design.

> **Note** *Tables have become a popular method of display because they are lightweight and are supported by the earlier browser versions. The technically preferred method of creating pixel-perfect designs is the use of layers. Layers, however, are not supported prior to the Version 4 browsers, and then not even consistently across brands. Additionally, old habits die hard, and many designers still prefer to use tables.*

The *Table* object is much like the *Horizontal Rule* object in that it is dependent on your cursor's position. It will place a table on your page consistent with the properties you set, but in this case, you are asked by the Insert Table dialog box to set some of the properties upfront.

After the table is on the page, you can alter not only the properties that you set originally, but also many others by using the Property inspector that is made available when you select the table. Selecting a particular row or cell also exposes properties such as backgrounds and fonts for those particular portions of the table.

The *Layer* Object

Whereas the *Horizontal Rule* and *Table* objects are dependent on the position of your cursor within the current HTML, the *Layer* object is a part of the newer Cascading Style Sheets (CSS) specification that allows absolute positioning of items on your page. When you select the Layer icon on the Objects palette, your cursor changes to cross hairs. Using your mouse, you may draw the layer at the position and to the size that you desire.

> **Note** *Actually, drawing a layer in this fashion is only one of three ways to insert a layer into your page. You may also select Layer from the Insert menu and set it precisely using numeric settings. Or, you may use a CSS definition to set the properties of a new Layer object.*

After your layer is on the page, you can use the Property inspector to alter any of the available Layer properties, including positioning and the HTML tag that is used to create the layer.

Note   *Four tags are available for creating layers. The <div> and <span> tags are the most commonly used, and conform to the latest specifications. Netscape Navigator 4 supported the <layer> tag for absolute positioning and the <ilayer> tag for relative positioning, but they have been abandoned in version 6 for the <div> and <span> tags. It is important to know your target browser so that you use the correct tags. This will ensure that your content is presented as you intended.*

These three examples represent the diverse ways that you may be asked to interact with objects. Just remember that objects are intended to save you work by taking your input and turning it into HTML. Each object may ask for your input in a slightly different way, but you will get used to it with a little practice.

Table 4-1 lists the groups of objects available in the Insert bar.

Insert Bar Tab	Contains
Common	The most common of the HTML elements, such as hyperlinks, images, tables, and layers. The Common tab also contains objects such as Fireworks HTML and Flash files.
Layout	Elements from the Layout View option in version 4 of Dreamweaver. These objects allow you to draw layers on the screen as you might in a desktop publishing environment. You can then convert them to layers, and Dreamweaver will attempt to build a very complex table structure that preserves your layout.
Text	A number of objects related to text markup. The objects here are divided between the font-based and the HTML-based manipulation of text. You will learn in Chapter 12 that it is wise to utilize the HTML elements and control their appearance with style sheets, but both options are available to you here.
Tables	The *Table* object (as on the Common tab) and each of the individual elements that make up tables, such as the <tr> and <td> tags.

Table 4-1.   *Objects Available in the Insert Bar*

Insert Bar Tab	Contains
Frames	A selection of common framesets that you can drag onto the page.
Forms	The *Form* object itself and all of the elements that are used to construct forms, such as buttons, text field, menus, and radio buttons.
Templates	A collection of objects to create templates and nested templates and to create editable regions, optional regions, and repeating regions.
Characters	A host of special characters, including line breaks, copyright, and foreign currency characters.
Media	Flash, Shockwave, Java, and ActiveX elements.
Head	Elements that are common to the Head of an HTML document, such as MetaTags, keywords, and descriptions.
Script	*Script*, *NoScript*, and *Server Side Include* objects.
Application	Server-side objects common to the server models, such as recordsets, repeat regions, recordset navigation, and master-detail pagesets.
Server Specific	Each Server Model has its own set of unique objects. Depending on which server model you have chosen for the current page, a dynamic tab will appear presenting you with a selection of objects applicable to your page.

Table 4-1.   *Objects Available in the Insert Bar* (continued)

Behaviors

Objects are designed to place code within the body of your HTML page, usually as HTML tags with a series of attributes. But, sometimes you need to do more-complex things on your page. Often, your desired effect requires the use of JavaScript functions triggered by events on the page. Behaviors are Dreamweaver's way of handling these issues.

The Behaviors Panel resides in the Design Panel Group by default. Behaviors are used for client-side events. Because of this, and because different browser brands and versions implement client-side code differently, it is important to apply Behaviors that are meant to work in your target browser.

A successful Behavior has three parts: an object, an event, and an action. The object is the part of your page that the event will occur against. For instance, you may have a button that will trigger an action when it is clicked. The button is the object, the click is the event, and the response is the action.

To illustrate, follow this example. On a new Dreamweaver page, place a Form button from the Forms tab of the Insert bar. Make sure the Behaviors Panel is visible, and select the button. The title bar of the panel will indicate the object to which you are about to apply your Behavior. This indication actually shows the tag that is selected. By default, the Form button is created as a Submit button, so you will notice that the Behaviors Panel title says <submit> actions. If you change the button type to Reset, the title bar will read <reset> actions, and if you change it to None, it will read <button> actions.

Click the plus (+) button on the Behaviors palette to view a list of available Behaviors. Select the Go To URL Behavior. In the resulting dialog box, set the URL that you want to go to. Now, whenever this button is selected, your Go To URL Behavior will appear in the list of Behaviors on the palette.

Next, select an event in the list and click the down arrow. A list of available events is presented. Select the *onClick* event to cause your action to be followed when the button is clicked.

Now, take a look at the HTML source window to see what this Behavior did in your code:

```html
<html>

<head>

<title>Untitled Document</title>

<meta http-equiv="Content-Type" content="text/html; charset=iso-8859-1">

<script language="JavaScript">

<!--

function MM_goToURL() { //v3.0

  var i, args=MM_goToURL.arguments; document.MM_returnValue = false; _

  for (i=0; i<(args.length-1); i+=2) eval(args[i]+".location='"+args[i+1]+"'");

}

//-->

</script>

</head>
```

```
<body bgcolor="#FFFFFF">

<form name="form1" method="post" action="">

  <input type="button" name="Submit" value="Submit"
onClick="MM_goToURL('parent','www.bettergig.com');return document.MM_¬
returnValue">

</form>

</body>

</html>
```

Note that the Behavior did two things in the preceding code, one in the body of the page and one above the body. To the basic button tag, the Behavior added the *onClick* event and the parameters you set within a call to a function called *MM_goToURL*. That function was also inserted above the body, ready to be called by clicking the Submit button.

Table 4-2 lists the Behaviors available in Dreamweaver.

Behavior	Associated Action
Call JavaScript	Enables you to define a JavaScript routine that will be run when the associated event occurs
Change Property	Enables you to dynamically alter the properties of several high-level HTML tags, such as Span, Form, and Layer
Check Browser	Allows the determination of a visitor's browser type and subsequent redirection to suitable content
Check Plugin	Checks for the existence of a required plug-in (such as a Flash Player) on a visitor's computer
Control Shockwave or Flash	Supplies external controls to allow the control of Flash and Shockwave files
Drag Layer	Allows the creation of a variety of effects based on a user dragging and dropping layers and their content

Table 4-2.   *Behaviors Available in Dreamweaver MX*

Behavior	Associated Action
Go To URL	Allows the variety of events available to trigger redirection to a URL
Hide Pop-Up Menu	Allows you to set an element on your page to hide a Dreamweaver- or Fireworks-created pop-up menu
Jump Menu	Enables you to edit an existing jump menu
Jump Menu Go	Adds a Go button to an existing jump menu
Open Browser Window	Opens a new, customized browser window when the associated event is triggered
Play Sound	Plays a sound file of a variety of types when the associated event is triggered
Popup Message	Triggers a JavaScript alert (a pop-up message box) to display a message to your user
Preload Images	Causes all images to be preloaded when the page loads; especially useful for rollover buttons and images that are initially hidden
Set Nav Bar Image	Enables you to edit an existing navigation bar
Show-Hide Layers	Gives you control over the visibility of layers based on the triggering of certain events
Swap Image Restore	Restores an image to its original state after an event has triggered a Swap Image
Swap Image	Swaps an original image for another image when an event occurs
Validate Form	Validates contents of form fields before submission
Set Text	Sets the text property of the status bar, a layer, a text field, or a frame
Show Pop-Up Menu	Allows the editing and creation of Dreamweaver and Fireworks pop-up menus and the assignment of the *Show* method to an element on your page.
Timeline	Provides a variety of controls to manipulate an existing timeline

Table 4-2. *Behaviors Available in Dreamweaver MX* (continued)

You now have reviewed the basics of creating Web pages in Dreamweaver. By using a combination of keyboard input, objects, and Behaviors, your actions construct a file of HTML suitable for display in your local browser. But no matter what the history of HTML, today's Web is all about design and presentation, which is where Dreamweaver shines.

The Home Page

Armed with some basic information about your site and some good design rules to follow, you're prepared to turn to the creation of your home page. By reviewing the description of the Bettergig site from earlier, you can get a pretty good idea of the structure the home page needs to take, including what links it needs to provide.

Because this is a simple site, you don't have a whole lot to link to, but the following links are pretty important:

- **Home**   This will become a template for the rest of the site, and you always want a link back to the home page.
- **Get a Gig**   A place for job seekers to search for jobs and post their resumes.
- **Post a Gig**   A place for employers to post new job opportunities.
- **My Company**   A place for employers to manage the jobs they have posted.
- **Help**   Provides assistance with the site.
- **About**   Provides company information and sales contacts for Bettergig.com.

You also need a logo, a design theme, and a place to put content. You'll handle these items in your actual design session, which you can complete using Macromedia Fireworks.

Fireworks

Although you can do your site layout and data integration with Dreamweaver, you need a means of creating and editing the graphical elements that will make up your pages. Macromedia has developed the Fireworks MX application for high-end graphics manipulation. As with the entire Studio MX suite, it is integrated tightly with the rest of the product line.

One of the great things about designing Web sites with Dreamweaver is the way in which you can integrate Fireworks with them to produce high-quality graphics. Fireworks has whole books written about it, and whole sections of those books describe all the things you can do with Dreamweaver and Fireworks together. This section focuses on creating a design, slicing it, and exporting it to be used in your Dreamweaver site.

The actual design that you use is up to you. The design chosen for this book is shown in Figure 4-1. Notice that, just as described in the previous section, this design includes a logo, a links section, a design theme, and space to place content. A 750×500-pixel palette was used to work on, to target an 800×600 screen resolution. That may work for you, or you or your client may feel that it is important to capture 640×480 users. Either way, use your best design skills to create a page that looks professional, incorporates the required features, and presents the site in the manner you desire.

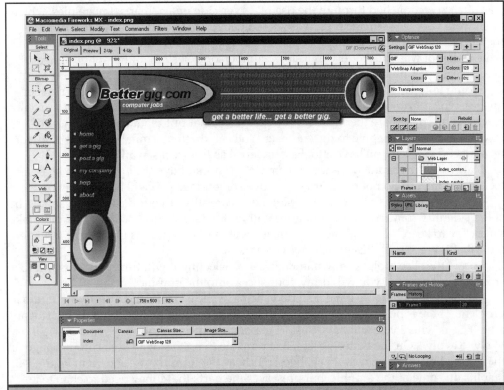

Figure 4-1. *The Bettergig.com site design*

Using the layers feature of Fireworks to build your site from the background up is suggested. Any background graphics, or anything that you are sure will remain static, should go on the bottom layer. When you are through with that layer, lock it in the Layers palette and create a new layer from the Insert | Layer menu. This second layer should contain things like text, button text, or graphics, or anything that may change as the site evolves. Later, you will see how to use this configuration to allow the replacement of portions of the graphic without having to replace the whole thing on your page. When the initial components of this second layer are complete, lock it also, to make sure that nothing gets moved. Then, create a third layer on which you will build your slices and prepare the page for export to Dreamweaver.

Slicing the Image

Depending on your background, slicing graphics may or may not be familiar to you. The concept is simple, and is, in some fashion, an outgrowth of the very earliest use of HTML. Back even before the introduction of tables to the HTML specification, navigation was often accomplished through the use of server-side image maps. Image files, which often were very large image files, were downloaded along with hotspot coordinates that identified areas of the image to the server. The server would redirect based on which hotspot was clicked. It was a slow, cumbersome system, but it got designers used to using graphics files as navigation.

Slicing takes advantage of HTML tables to allow an image to be split into smaller images, which load faster. Instead of one big image, the graphic is divided into several pieces. Those pieces are then loaded into table cells that put them back together so that they appear as one graphic to the end user. You can do this manually, but I would not recommend it when you have a tool as powerful as Fireworks available.

Start with the graphic you have created. You should have the bottom two layers locked so that you do not inadvertently move something. You will be working on the top layer (WebLayer, in the example file). Look carefully at your design. You should be able to identify some natural boundaries within it where slicing the image would make sense. Try to keep logos and message areas together. Be as neat as possible or else the table that is created by this process will be a mess.

Locate the slice tool, as shown in Figure 4-2. Selecting it will turn your cursor into a cross hair with which you will draw your slices onto the graphic.

On the Bettergig home page, I started slicing at the top left, and already I ran into a problem. There is no way to capture the entire logo without encroaching on the slogan area. This is where you will have to start making decisions about how your site is most likely to evolve. On the Bettergig site, it is possible that the slogan area could change or that the tagline in the logo could change, so I chose the compromise shown in Figure 4-3. It splits up some of the graphic, but preserves the parts that I may need to change in the future. You will see how important this is a little later. Use these same ideas to guide you through the slicing of the remainder of your graphic.

The next area you need to pay special attention to is the text that will become your navigational links. After you get your graphic into Dreamweaver, you'll want to turn these text links into *rollover buttons*. Rollover buttons are areas that react visually when the user's mouse interacts with them. They can have up to four states, with a different look for when there is no mouse activity, for when the mouse hovers over them, for when the button is depressed, and for when the mouse hovers over a depressed button. The present example will use a simpler form that just uses the up state (no mouse interaction) and the over state (when a mouse hovers over the button). This means that you need two graphics for each of these buttons, each with a slightly different appearance. For now, just make sure that the slices that make up each text area are as equal as possible. Make liberal use of the magnifier to make sure your slices' lines are exactly where you intend them to be. You can even select a slice and use the Modify menu to transform its dimensions numerically or by a percentage. These topics are covered in a moment.

Complete your slices so that the entire graphic is included. Make sure that you include a slice that encompasses the content area of your page. This ensures that this area will be included as a cell in the table. You can set that cell as an editable region in the template that you will create later.

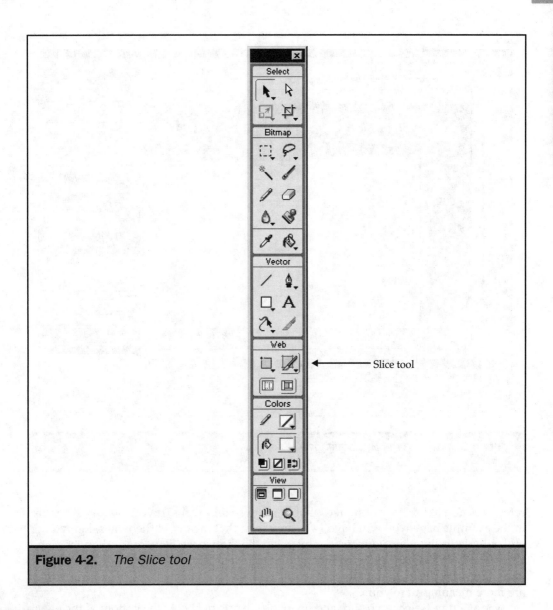

Slice tool

Figure 4-2.   *The Slice tool*

Note *This procedure has an awful lot of overlap. You really have to plan ahead as you work so that the decisions you make work with the steps you take later. I hope you are able to follow this description. It will make sense the first time you try it, or maybe the second time.*

Hopefully, you are starting to understand what is going to happen when you move this graphic to Dreamweaver. When you export the graphic in the next step, Fireworks will actually create an HTML page with a table on it that mirrors the slices you created, with a table cell for each slice. So, you will end up with a table with a bunch of image

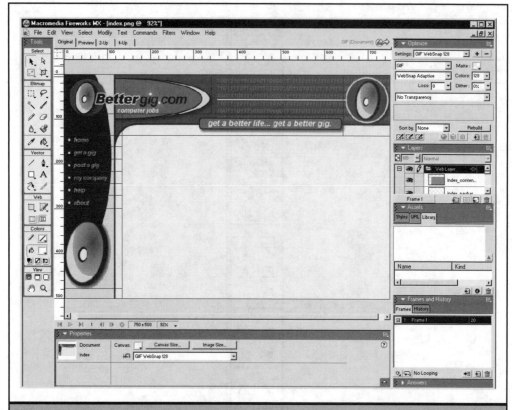

Figure 4-3. *Slicing the Bettergig logo*

references and a directory of images that fit in those table cells. If you have 14 slices, as in the example page, you will have 14 images, and that means 14 filenames. Fireworks will automatically name your images by using the Fireworks filename and appending a number to it. That is very convenient, but makes later identification of the parts of your page very difficult. Luckily, Fireworks will let you rename the slices to names that are more meaningful to you.

One at a time, select each slice and go to the Objects panel. At the bottom of the panel, deselect the Auto-Name Slices check box and type a new name into the text box that appears. For the text images that will become your buttons, use "up" in the name to indicate that these are the up-state images. Later, you will create your over-state buttons and name them with "over" in the name so that you may easily identify them.

Exporting the Fireworks Graphic

After you have all of your slices in place and have renamed them, it is time to export the graphic so that you can use it in Dreamweaver. Select File | Export. In the Export dialog box, shown in Figure 4-4, select a directory in which to save your HTML page and image files. Set the base name of the export. If left as the default, the base filename will be the name of the Fireworks file, as will the name of your HTML page. You can leave it that way or change it to "index" or "default" or any other name you choose. In the Slices drop-down list, select Use Slices.

In the HTML section of the dialog box, you can choose the Style you wish to export. Choose Dreamweaver 3, select the Same Directory option of the Location drop-down list, and click Save.

Note   *You can set many of the options that control how slices are exported by clicking the Setup button in the HTML section of the Export dialog box.*

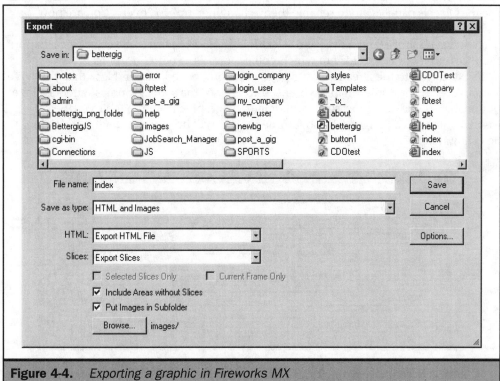

Figure 4-4.   *Exporting a graphic in Fireworks MX*

Go to Dreamweaver and open the HTML file that was just created during your export. You should see your graphic reappear, formatted in a table on the Dreamweaver page. It doesn't get much easier than that, but those buttons still need to be addressed.

Creating Rollover Buttons

You are getting ready to see the real power of handling your graphics in this fashion. Return to your file in Fireworks. You should be looking at a picture that is obscured by the green glow of your slices. It is very important that those slices do not get moved or resized. Lock the WebLayer in the Layers panel. Then, click the eye next to the lock to make the WebLayer, and the green glow, invisible.

You can now make any changes you would like to the graphic by unlocking the layer on which you want to work. Because, for this example, you want to work on the text links, unlock Layer 2. I made two changes to the text. First, I selected it, and went to the Effects panel and altered the bevel slightly. I then placed a dot next to each word.

After those changes are made, relock Layer 2 so that nothing gets changed by accident. Now, turn the WebLayer back on, making the slices visible. Select each of the slices and use the Objects panel again to rename them, changing "up" to "over." You are now going to export just the slices that have changed.

Select each slice one at a time and select File | Export Special | Selected Slice. Export the slice to the same directory in which you exported the entire graphic.

Next, return to the Dreamweaver page that you opened earlier. Now that you have your over-state button available, you need to replace the static graphics with a rollover button. Select one of the text links and delete the graphic from the table cell. Select Insert | Interactive Images | Rollover Image. You will be presented with the dialog box shown here.

Choose a descriptive name for this image, in case you need to reference it in your code. In the Original Image box, select the up-state button graphic. In the Rollover Image box, select the over-state button graphic. Leave the Preload option checked and set the URL hyperlink to follow when this button is clicked.

The Preload Rollover Image option causes both graphics to load when the page initially opens. If you deselect it, your users will likely notice a slight delay the first time they move over the link as the over-state image loads from the server.

This procedure represents only a fraction of the power you have available when using Dreamweaver with Fireworks. We further investigate the integration of these two products in Chapter 10. You now have a home page with rollover buttons ready to use in your site.

Templates

Because you decided earlier that your site would utilize a consistent design that is represented in the home page, it makes sense to use a Dreamweaver template to build your pages. *Templates* are files that maintain specific portions of a page to which you can add content. By using a template in this case, your graphics and navigational links will remain consistent across your pages while the information in the content section of the page changes.

Dreamweaver templates work by locking the regions of the site that you want to remain consistent. Actually, all the areas of a template file are locked except for the areas that you mark as editable regions. On your page, you want everything but the content area to remain locked.

Select the content area of the page. The Fireworks export routine has placed a filler object that you don't need. Press DELETE to remove the graphic. You will be left with an empty table cell the size of the original content area. Right-click the content area and choose Templates | New Editable Region. Name it **Content**. Dreamweaver will place text filler with the name of the region.

Select File | Save As Template. Select the site that you wish to save the template in and then name the file. You have created a template that you will use to build the remainder of your pages.

Templates in Dreamweaver MX have a great deal of new functionality. We look at the new features of Dreamweaver Templates more closely in Chapter 9.

Now that you have designed your site and built a template on which to base your pages, you are ready to begin the actual construction of the site by adding the pages you decided on earlier. Using the information in this chapter, you should be able to begin the very important task of designing your site by identifying its purpose, its audience, and an outline of its content. By using other tools that integrate with Dreamweaver, you can begin the graphic construction of your site and use templates to define its look and feel. Chapter 5 shows you how to use your template file to build HTML pages that will lead you toward your data-driven site.

Summary

Dreamweaver is a very powerful program. Until you begin working with it and its features, you will not realize just now much you can do with it. In this chapter, you have begun to use some of Dreamweaver's basic features to build a Web site. In the upcoming chapters, we will spend more time learning about the concepts and tools that you have seen as you learn more about Web application construction using Dreamweaver MX.

The Complete Reference

Dreamweaver MX

Chapter 5

Adding Pages to Your Site

Chapter 4 looked at basic site design and created a template that you can use to add pages to your site while maintaining an overall graphic and navigational theme. Most of the functionality of the Bettergig site is built in later chapters where database connectivity is discussed, but there is no telling what design elements you may want to use in your site, so this chapter covers page design using many of Dreamweaver's most popular features. We cover these tools, and some that are new to Dreamweaver MX, in more depth in Chapter 9.

Creating Pages from Templates

Once you have one or more templates defined and saved as a part of your site, creating new pages based on them is simple. From the File menu, select New. In the New File dialog box, select the Templates tab. All of your defined sites will be displayed in the left section of the screen. Selecting any one of them will show you the templates defined for that site.

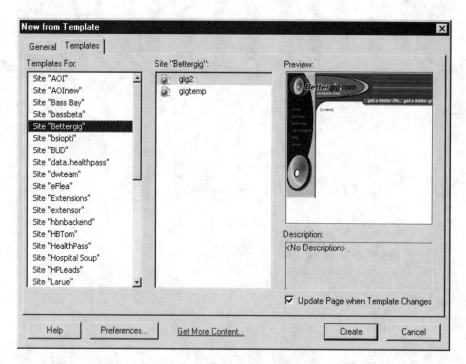

You may, of course, have more than one template in any particular site, and sets of pages can be based on those templates to give areas of your site a different look and navigational content.

Click Create and a new page is created based on the template you selected. It is an unsaved document and must be saved into your current site.

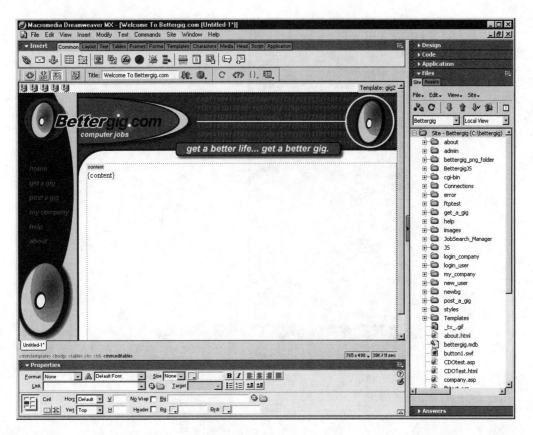

Once you select a template for your new page, a new document window is opened. That new document is an instance of the template you chose, and contains the same locked regions and editable regions as the template. Locked regions are those parts of the page that you want to remain untouched. The only place that you can add new content to the page is in those areas that you have defined as editable.

When the page first opens, you can identify those editable regions by the default text that is placed in each one when the template is created. You can see the one page-level editable region in the Bettergig template, called Content.

The small tag in the upper-right corner of the page indicates the template that this page is based on. This tag will appear only at design time.

The content region is not really the only editable region on the page, though. To see all of a page's editable regions listed by name, select Modify | Templates from the menu bar (see Figure 5-1). The bottom portion of the Templates submenu lists all the editable regions on the page. The check mark indicates the active region, and you can select the region that you want to make active by selecting one from this menu.

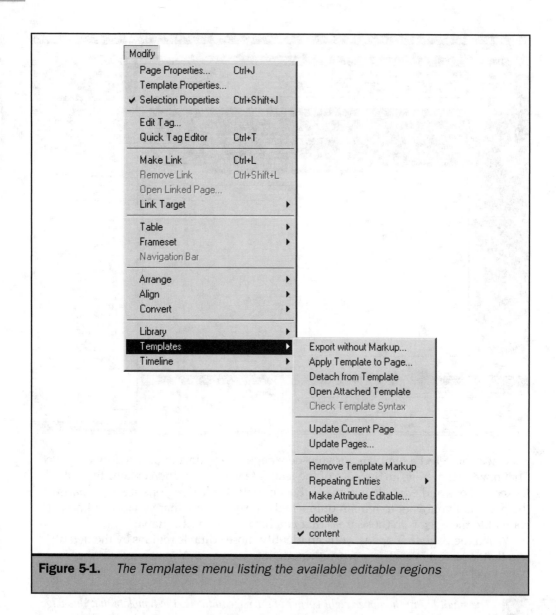

Figure 5-1. *The Templates menu listing the available editable regions*

In addition to the content region, this page has an editable region called doctitle. This is a default region that allows the title of each page that is based on a template to be unique. A look at the code behind a templated page will help you understand why this is important.

Take a look at line 5 of the code in Figure 5-2. This line is the comment tag that signals the beginning of a Dreamweaver template. From that point on, this page is considered locked. Only by explicitly unlocking an area can you make a region editable. For example, look at line 47 of the code in Figure 5-3. Two tags are used here to identify an area of the page that is editable. The BeginEditable tag also contains the name of the editable region ("content" in this case). The EndEditable tag signals the end of the editable region. Within those tags is that area to which you can add new content. Notice that the default text is all that is there right now.

Now look back at Figure 5-3 and notice that the <title> HTML tag comes after the BeginTemplate tag. By the rules previously described, that would mean that the title of each page would remain locked and, therefore, the same for every page based on the template. Making this section of the code an editable region by default ensures that you will always have access to the Title tag of your pages.

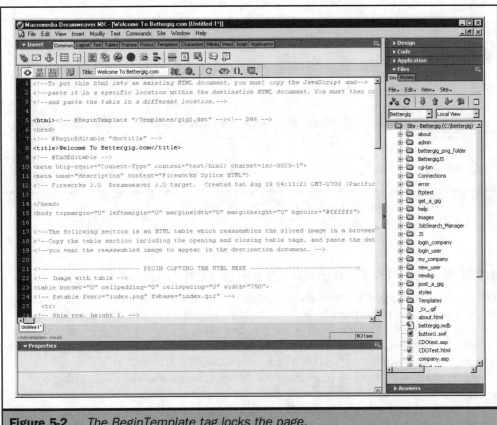

Figure 5-2.   *The BeginTemplate tag locks the page.*

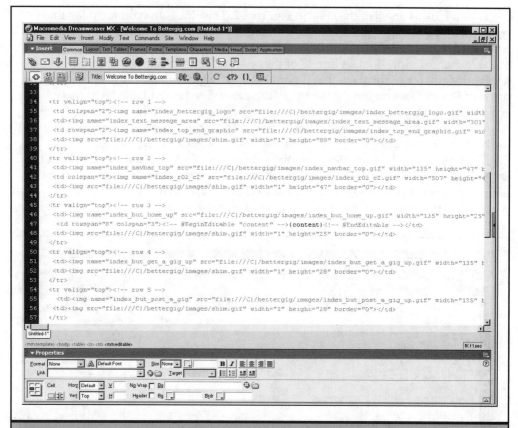

Figure 5-3.   *The BeginEditable tag allows a section to be edited.*

Using the Assets Panel to Create Templated Pages

You can also create pages based on templates by using the Templates section of the Assets panel. The Assets panel is a centralized place where pieces of content, or *assets*, are available to you. These might be images, or templates, or specialized content such as Flash and Director files. The Assets panel is covered in more detail later in this chapter, but you will get a good idea of how it works right here.

Applying a template to a page from the Assets panel is as easy as dragging and dropping the template. With any new document window open, you can simply select a template file from the Templates section of the Assets panel, shown in Figure 5-4, and drag it onto the document window. That template is immediately applied to the page just as if you had used the New Document dialog box.

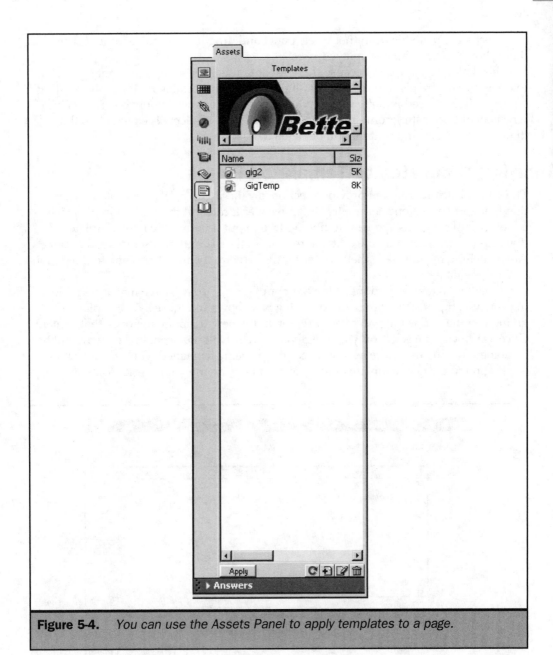

Figure 5-4.   *You can use the Assets Panel to apply templates to a page.*

Adding Templates to Existing Pages

You can add a template to an existing page, even if there is already content on the page.

Select a template file from the Assets panel and drag it onto the document. The dialog box in Figure 5-5 is displayed.

This dialog box appears because there is content that the template is not sure what to do with. You are given the choice of all the page-level editable regions. The existing content will be placed into the region you choose. You can select only one region into which all of the existing content will be combined. If you select Nowhere from the dialog box, the existing content will be deleted.

Applying Templates to Templated Pages

The same principle from the previous section is valid if you apply a template to a page that is already based on a template. Dreamweaver locates all the content in the existing page's editable regions and tries to find a place to put it within the new template. It does this by first matching the editable regions in the old and new templates by name. Any matching regions have their content transferred to the new template, to the region of the same name.

If there is content in regions of the old template that do not have matching regions in the new template, the same kind of dialog box shown in Figure 5-5 is displayed, giving you the opportunity to select a region in the new template to house that content. Once again, you can select only one region into which all the orphaned content will be combined. If you are unsure as to why content is being orphaned, you can cancel the application of the new template at this point and reexamine your work. You may find

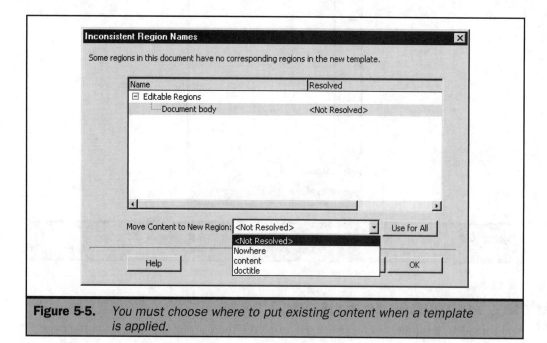

Figure 5-5. *You must choose where to put existing content when a template is applied.*

that a region you meant to include in the new template is missing or misnamed. Selecting Nowhere from the dialog box causes the orphaned content to be deleted from the page.

Managing Templates

Looking back at Figure 5-1, you will see many of the functions that you can perform to manage your templates and the pages that are based on them. In addition to applying templates from this page, you can also detach a page from its template. Doing this will cause the link to the template to be broken, but the existing content of the page will remain in place. The primary effect of detaching a template from a page is that the page will no longer be updated when changes are made to the template.

Updating Templates

So what do you do when you have a whole site full of pages built on a template and then one of the links changes, or a logo changes, or pages are added that need navigational presence on the home page? Luckily, that is one of the beauties of templates, and is the reason you went to the trouble of creating one in the first place. When you edit a template, either by opening the template file directly or from the Modify | Templates menu (refer to Figure 5-1) with the Open Attached Template command, any changes you make can be cascaded down through all the pages that are based on the template. When your changes are saved, you will be prompted to cascade the changes. You can also update your attached pages either one at a time or sitewide with the Modify | Templates menu selections.

Templates can be a powerful way to manage the look and feel of your site. They can also make maintenance of your site much easier by cascading changes down throughout all the pages that are attached to them.

Basic Page Elements

When it comes down to it, constructing pages is just the process of combining page elements in a fashion that meets your design goals. Once you know what you want your page to do and how you want it to look, it's simply a matter of choosing the right combination of elements. This section provides instruction on the use of the basic page elements available in Dreamweaver. Some page elements will be demonstrated within the content region of the Bettergig page; others are better shown on their own on a blank document.

Tables

Because you are likely to want to use other page elements along with tables, we cover tables first. Tables are a lightweight, widely supported means of positioning elements on the page. Dreamweaver supports the creation of everything from simple tables to complex row and column spans that permit precise positioning of your layout.

Simple Tables

A *simple* table is defined as one that is created by selecting a number of rows and columns, without any fancy alteration of the basic table structure. These tables generally have a number of columns that extend the entire length of the table, and a number of rows that span its entire width. These tables are useful for displaying text or images in a columnar format.

To place a table on your page, select the table object from the Common or Tables tab of the Insert bar. When you click the Table Object button, the dialog box in Figure 5-6 is displayed.

In this dialog box, you can select the number of rows and columns you want the table to start out with. You are not limited to the choices that you make here, because you can always add or subtract rows and columns at any time. It simply provides a starting point for your new table.

Also in this dialog box, you can set the width of the overall table in pixels or percent, the border width, cell spacing, and cell padding. Figure 5-7 shows the content region of the Bettergig template with a table inserted that is 3 rows by 10 rows. This table has no border, meaning that the individual cells will not be separated by lines when the page is viewed in a browser. In the design window, dashed lines indicate where the cells are so that you can identify your position within the table.

After you insert your table into the page, you still have access to all of its properties through the Property inspector, a panel that adjusts dynamically to the element that is active on the page. Selecting the table you inserted will cause the Property inspector for tables to appear (shown next) with the particular data of that table populating its field. You can change the properties of the table in the Property inspector, and the table on the page will immediately respond to your changes.

More Complex Table Structures

Using the Property inspector, you can manipulate the cells in your table to create more complex table structures. Use your mouse to select any adjacent rows or columns. Click the Merge Selected Cells button in the Table Property inspector. A span will be created that combines the selected cells into a single cell.

By starting with a simple table and combining cells, you can create structures that allow even more precise placement of your content.

Layout View

All the tables you have been creating up to this point have been done in Standard view. Standard view is the default working mode, but there is also a mode called Layout

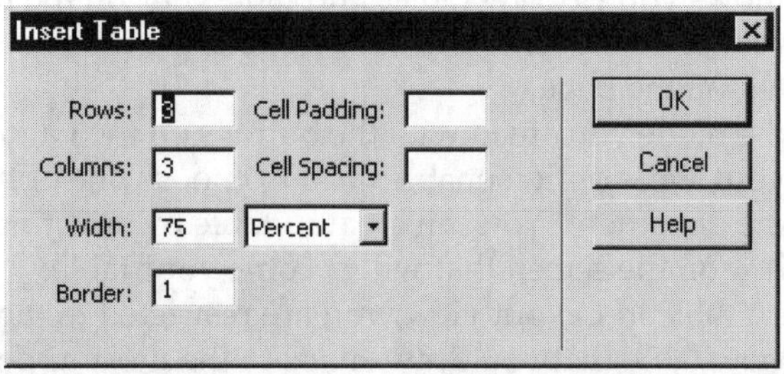

Figure 5-6.   *The Insert Table dialog box*

Figure 5-7.   *A new table inserted in the content area of a page*

view. Layout view allows you to draw tables and table cells on the page anywhere you want them. Dreamweaver then creates the table structure that is necessary to house what you have created on the page.

You can control the mode you are in with the buttons on the Layout tab of the insert bar. Clicking the Layout View option enables you to choose one of the two Layout tools to draw regions on the document. You can create a table by selecting the Layout Table tool and drawing a box on the screen that will become your table.

When you create a table in Layout view, you are restricted to the rules of HTML, which means that a new table that you draw snaps to the most upper-left section of the page that is available. You can then draw cells within the table with the Layout Cells tool. To create multiple cells at once, hold down the CTRL key while you draw the cells; otherwise, you will need to reselect the tool for each cell you create. A cell drawn in a layout table causes Dreamweaver to create a table structure around the cell to permit its placement to remain where you specified. The result can be a convoluted arrangement of table cells that is too complex for practical use.

You don't need to create a layout table before you create layout cells. You can draw cells on the page at any position, and a layout table of sufficient size to contain them will be created at the most upper-left position available. Inside the table will be your cells and sufficient additional structure to maintain the positioning of those cells.

As long as you remain in Layout view, your cells are highlighted within the structure created to contain them. You can place content in your cells, but not in the Dreamweaver-created cells. They remain "locked" because they are really just there to accommodate the cells you created. If you find yourself needing to place something in a grayed-out structure cell, you can just create a new layout cell with the Cell tool at that position.

Once you return to Standard view, your cells are still there and available to you, but the structure cells are no longer locked and you can fill them with content. You can go back and forth between the two views "locking" and "unlocking" the structure cells. If you place content in a structure cell while in Standard view, that cell will become a layout cell when you return to Layout view, "unlocked" and available for content. But, if you delete that content, the cell will return to "locked" status.

Layers

Although tables have become a popular way to position content on your pages, there is another method that is actually more in line with an important principle of Web design, that of the separation of content from design structure. Although tables and other HTML tricks are effective to a degree, the elements of Cascading Style Sheets (CSS) allow precise control over the display of your content without littering it with display instructions.

Layers are the CSS method for allowing precise content placement on your pages. Rather than treating a page like a top-down word processor page, as HTML does, CSS treats the page as an X–Y grid on which elements can be placed. A *layer* is defined as an area of some number of pixels across and some number of pixels down that begins at a certain X–Y coordinate. This allows a more "desktop publishing" style of page layout.

> **Note** *Even though CSS is gaining better cross-browser support and is technically the superior choice for page layout, tables are so popular that Macromedia went to great efforts to incorporate the Layout view discussed in the previous section. Even those who use layers to design their pages will often utilize the Dreamweaver command that converts layers to tables for their final output.*

Placing a layer on a page is as simple as choosing the layer tool from the Insert bar and drawing the layer where you want it. Unlike the tables and layout tables in the previous section, layer placement is not dependent on HTML rules that force content up and to the left.

> **Note** *You must be in Standard view for layers to work. Once you draw layers, you can switch to layout view and draw tables, but your layer will be ignored in the construction of the table structure. When you return to Standard view, you will have a z-order situation with your layer and table cells overlaying one another.*

Once you have layers on your page, each one acts as its own little HTML page, meaning that within a layer, the rules of top-left HTML apply. For instance, if you place an image within a layer, it will snap to the upper-left of the layer. To place content within a layer more precisely, you can build a table (not in Layout view) within the layer and place content within the cells of the table.

Many times, designers need to precisely place their content but need to target version 3 browsers (or have some other reason that they are reluctant to publish with layers). You could spend the time to meticulously create a table structure that meets your needs, or you can let Dreamweaver do that for you. Once you create your site using layers, you can tell Dreamweaver to convert those layers to tables. The Modify | Convert menu offers two options: Layers to Tables, and Tables to Layers. The Tables to Layers option allows you to switch back to layers if you find that you need to make changes after you have converted to tables.

Once you have either tables or layers on your page, you have the structure that will allow your content to be displayed with the look you have designed. You need only to begin placing that content using the other available tools.

Images

Images are a key part of the modern Web site, whether they are a part of your page design, pictures of products you are selling, or even pictures of your kids on your personal Web page. Images and graphics are, in large part, what differentiates modern sites from the text-laden sites of a few years ago.

As with most things, adding images to your site is a simple matter. Once you have the structure of the site completed, as discussed in the previous section, placing images on the page is just a matter of inserting or dropping them on the page in the correct table cell or layer.

Locate your cursor at the spot where you want to place an image. This could be within a table cell or a layer or in the regular flow of your page. Click the image button on the Insert bar or select Insert | Image.

A dialog box will appear asking you to locate the image that you want to use. Browse to the location on your computer where the file resides and select it. You can see a preview of the file you have selected to the right of the box.

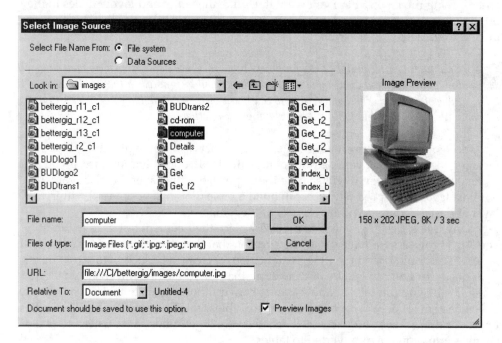

If you are working in a brand new page that has not been saved, you will be warned that a relative path cannot be used until you save the page. Also, if the file you have chosen resides outside the file structure of the current site, you will be notified and given the opportunity to copy it into the current site so that it will be available when the site is published. If you choose Yes, you will be asked to choose the directory you want the file saved to. Choose whichever directory you are saving your images to.

When you have finished, the image is a part of your page.

Rollover Images

Rollover images operate under the same principle as regular images, except that they are made up of more than one image so that they are able to react to mouse activity.

Basic Dreamweaver rollover images have two states: an *out* state that is visible when a mouse pointer is not over the image, and an *over* state that is visible when a mouse pointer is hovering over the image. Thus, you have to create two images in advance to fulfill these two states. At this point, you are just adding them to the page. A way to create these images with Fireworks and Dreamweaver was covered in Chapter 4.

Rollover buttons can have up to four states: the two states previously mentioned, as well as an up and down state indicating whether or not a button has been pressed. To create these kinds of buttons, you will need to use a program such as Fireworks and import the packaged button into Dreamweaver as Fireworks HTML.

Select the spot where you want to insert a rollover image and click the Rollover Image button on the Insert bar. The following dialog box appears:

Insert Rollover Image			✕
Image Name:	Home		OK
Original Image:	Image1.gif	Browse...	Cancel
Rollover Image:	Image2.gif	Browse...	Help
	☑ Preload Rollover Image		
Alternate Text:	Got to the Home Page		
When Clicked, Go To URL:	home.asp	Browse...	

Because you will be using more than one image, each with its own name, to build this rollover, name the rollover so that you can refer to it if need be. You will need to browse to your images twice to select the out state image and the over state image.

Note *Make sure when you create images to be used for rollovers that you name them in such a way that they are easily identified. For instance, name the out state image with the image name plus "_out" and the over state image with the image name plus "_over."*

The two additional settings for a rollover image are the URL and Preload options. Selecting the Preload Rollover Image checkbox will cause all of the images that make up the various image states to load into the browser when the page loads. It takes a fraction longer for the page to load when this option is selected, but that is better than the browser having to make additional trips to the server each time one of the images is engaged for the first time.

The URL setting allows you to select a URL to send the user to when he or she clicks the image.

When you have finished with the dialog box, the new image displays in your page.

Forms

So far, there has been a lot of discussion about providing an interactive experience for your site's visitors. One of the more basic ways for a user to communicate with a Web application is through forms. A form is an HTML element that uses a variety of field types to collect information from a user and pass it along, usually to a CGI application or ASP, JSP, or CF page that takes the data and does something with it. There will be a lot of discussion of forms in the later database chapters, but this section covers the basics of adding forms and form fields to your pages.

A form is kind of a self-enclosed element that contains the pieces that collect information. Everything that makes up the form is housed within the HTML form tags <form> and </form>. Whatever form elements you choose to place within those tags are affected by the form's buttons.

There are typically two form buttons associated with a form. One is a Submit button that is responsible for taking the information that has been entered and sending it off to the destination you have specified for the form. The second button is a Reset button that clears all of the form fields.

To place a form on your page, switch to the Forms tab of the Insert bar.

With your cursor positioned where you want the form inserted, click the form button on the Insert Bar. A form will be inserted on the page. The base form is invisible, and is indicated in the design window by broken lines.

When you select the form by clicking it, the form's Property inspector is displayed.

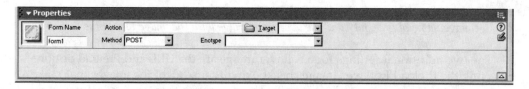

In the Property inspector, you will see three important properties that you need to set for your form:

- **Name** The form name is a means of referring to the entire form. It is especially important to name your form if you will be using more than one form on a page.

- **Method** There are two options for the Method parameter. The *Get* method attaches the form information to the URL. There are size limitations associated with the use of the *Get* method that make it less practical to use than the other method, *Post*. The *Post* method passes the form's information behind the scenes directly to the target pages or application. There is no size restriction on the Post method.

- **Action** The action of a form is the target to which the form will be posted. The action could be a Perl script, a CGI application, or an ASP page. It could even be the same page that the form resides on.

- **Target** Dreamweaver MX adds the target property to the Forms Property inspector. Just like the target in a regular link, this allows you to post your form to a page in a new window or in a specific frame of your page.

- **Enctype** Enctype determines how form data is encoded, or represented. Most times this will be set to application/x-www-form-urlencoded to pass regular text. If, however, you are using a form to upload a file, you can set it to multipart/form-data.

Form Elements

There are nine basic form elements available on the Insert Bar, which we discuss in the following sections.

Text Field

The text field is used to collect text information, such as names and addresses. It has several properties that you can set in the Property inspector.

It is important to set a name for the field so you have a way of referring to the field in the application or on the page that handles its data. Dreamweaver sets a default value for the name, but you will be well served to assign meaningful names to these fields so that you can refer to them easily.

There are three choices for the format of the field. Single Line is the standard one-line text box. Multi Line allows you to set the box up as a memo field. When you choose Multi Line, you can also set how text within the field wraps. The Password option causes asterisks to be displayed for the characters that are entered in the field so that they cannot be viewed by casual observers.

You can also set a width in characters for the box, a maximum length to do some data validation, and an initial value that can serve as a default.

Button

You can use the Form button for three different purposes, as well as set its properties in the Property inspector.

Set a Name for the button so that you can refer to it in your code. You can set a Label that is separate from its name. "Submit" is the default, but you could use "Go!"

or "Send" or anything you would like. The three Actions that you can set are Submit, which submits the form; Reset, which resets the form; and None, which creates a disconnected button that you can reference in your code to call a piece of code or perform any other action that can be assigned to a button's click event.

Check box

Use the check box when there is a list of selections from which a user may need to choose more than one. Each check box passes a supplied value when the box is checked.

The checkbox has three properties that you can set from the Property inspector.

You can use the name of the check box to refer to it. You can also set a checked value, which is the value that is passed when the box is in a Checked state, and select whether or not the box is checked when the page loads.

Radio Button

Use radio buttons when there is a list of selections from which a user can select only one.

You can set the radio button's properties in the Property inspector.

You can make a set of radio buttons by setting the name of more than one button to the same name. Then set the checked value of each to a distinct value. Then check the value of the base radio button name for which checked value was passed. You can also set the initial position of each button to Checked or Unchecked.

List/Menu

The list/menu field provides a drop-down list or menu list of selections that the user can select from.

You can set several properties in the Property inspector. In addition to the name of the field, you can select whether it will be a drop-down list or a menu box. If you choose a menu box, you can set the height in rows and whether multiple selections are allowed. Use the List Values button to display the List Values dialog box.

In the List Values dialog box, you can set the display values that will appear in the menu, and the associated values that will be passed when each of the display values is selected. Back in the main Property inspector, you can select which of these values is initially selected.

File Field

The file field provides the functionality to browse for a file on the local client computer. You can use this field in conjunction with file upload code to collect a file from your user, such as an image or a resume.

The properties for the file field are very simple. Set a name, a character width for the field, and a maximum number of characters.

Image Field

The image field provides a means for placing images within a form. When you select the image fields, you are prompted to select an image from the directories on your

computer, much like the insertion of a regular image. From the Property inspector, you
can name the image field and edit the source of the image that fills it.

Hidden Field

A hidden field is a text field that posts with the form but is not displayed on the page.
You can set the value of a hidden field programmatically and use it to pass information
that you don't want seen. Keep in mind, though, that the value of a hidden form field
can be seen in the source of the page, which is viewable in most browsers.

Jump Menu

A jump menu is a drop-down box that provides navigation for a user. By selecting a
topic in the menu, the user is immediately redirected to an associated URL. When you
select the jump menu button on the Insert Bar, you are presented with the following
dialog box:

In this dialog box, you can set display items for your jump menu, and for each
display item, you can set a URL to which users will be directed when they choose that
menu item. You can also select a target for the new page to open into.

Frames

You don't need to have just one HTML page on a Web page. A method known as *framing*
allows you to put two, three, or more totally independent pages within a frameset.
Although these independent pages, called *frames*, can work together, they are really
separate pages that are constructed and tied together in the frameset.

Dreamweaver takes a lot of the complexity out of creating frames by providing prebuilt framesets that you can drag onto your page. Once you add the frameset, you can construct each of the frame pages in the design window.

Dreamweaver Features

In addition to the basic page elements, Dreamweaver provides other features that you can use to make your pages more interesting and functional.

Behaviors

Behaviors are page-level JavaScript that have been prewritten and packaged for use within Dreamweaver. Behaviors are typically made up of an event and an action. In other words, to make use of a behavior, you first identify an event, such as a button click, that will trigger an action, such as the calling of a piece of code or the playing of a Flash file. Dreamweaver's built-in behaviors are available on the Behaviors panel.

Note *Behaviors are different than Server Behaviors. Server Behaviors typically involve server-side code that does things such as interact with databases and send e-mail. Behaviors, on the other hand, are limited to client-side code for things such as DHTML effects.*

To illustrate, the following example creates a button that displays a message when it is clicked:

1. Drag a form button to the page. When Dreamweaver asks if you want to create a form tag, select No.
2. Change the name of the button to Message in the Property inspector.
3. Change the Action of the button to None.
4. Select the button by clicking it.
5. From the (+) button on the Behaviors panel, select the Popup Message behavior.

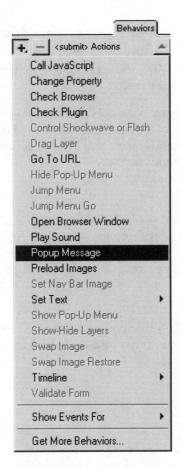

6. A dialog box is displayed in which you can type the message you want displayed.

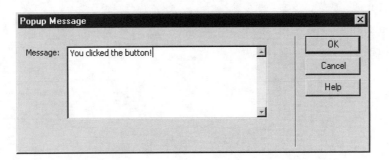

7. When the behavior is applied, it appears in the Behaviors panel. You can edit it by double-clicking the listing in the palette.

8. When the page is published and a visitor clicks the button, a JavaScript pop-up menu appears with your message.

You can apply many different behaviors to different events involving a variety of elements on your page. Many of the best behaviors have been written by third-party authors and do ship with Dreamweaver. You can get information about these at the Macromedia Exchange or around the Web.

Reference Materials

Dreamweaver ships with several references built in. You can also download extensions from the Macromedia Web site that provide additional references, which can be accessed from the References panel. They provide a convenient way to search for information on the languages you are using to build your site.

The Assets Panel

The Assets panel contains things that you have prepared for use in your site, such as images, script, and Flash movies. It has nine categories represented by the icons to the left of the panel:

- Images
- Colors
- Links
- Flash content
- Shockwave content
- Movie files
- Scripts
- Templates
- Library

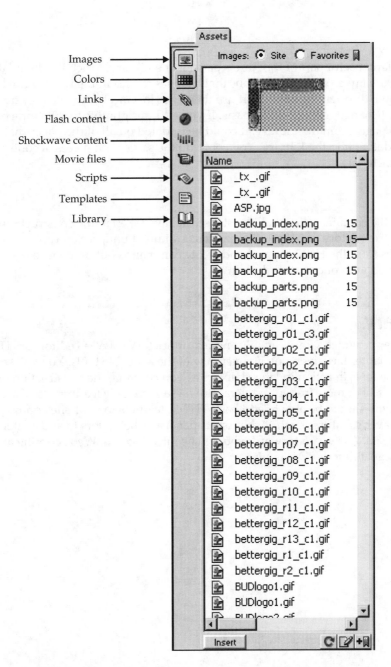

Images
Colors
Links
Flash content
Shockwave content
Movie files
Scripts
Templates
Library

Not a lot can be said about the Assets panel except that it makes the management of site content extremely easy. Any content that is placed within the directory structure of the site is automatically available—you can add content to your site by dragging and dropping it straight from the palette. This makes the continual browsing for files unnecessary and saves time by making your actions more accurate and purposeful.

Library

One particularly useful part of the Assets panel is the Library. Much like templates, Library files are linked files. That means that changes to files in the Library can be cascaded down through the pages that use them. For instance, your site may utilize a graphic that changes on a periodic basis. If you add this graphic to the Library and place it onto pages from the Library, it could be updated on all of the pages that use it just by updating it in the Library. You could do the same with pieces of code or server-side includes.

History

The History file contains a list of all the steps you have taken in the construction of your pages. The History panel provides almost unlimited undos. You can also select a series of steps from the History panel and create commands out of them so that they can be repeated with one menu selection.

Summary

Dreamweaver provides a very capable and feature-rich WYSIWYG editor for HTML pages. This chapter has given you an overview of the available tools. You will see many of these tools in action in later chapters as you continue the construction of your data-driven site. For more in-depth coverage of these client-side features, see Chapter 9.

By now, you should be able to add basic HTML features to your site and use some of Dreamweaver's features such as the Assets panel and behaviors to add content and code to your site. As you go forward, you will be introduced to Web scripting and the data-driven capabilities of Dreamweaver MX.

The Complete Reference

Dreamweaver MX

Chapter 6

Publishing Your Site to the Internet

Now that you have completed the beginnings of your site, you will likely turn your attention to getting it published to the Internet. After all, as cool as your site may be, no one else will know about it, much less praise it or nominate you for designer of the year, until they can see it in their browsers. You likely have a domain name, or at least an IP address, attached to a set of directories on a Web server, as discussed in Chapter 2. In order to make your site available on the Web, you will need to transfer the files from your local development computer to that set of directories.

You have some options as to how you accomplish this. Dreamweaver has the built-in capability to publish your files, but several third-party options are available, if you prefer. Let's look at the technologies involved in publishing your site to the Internet and some of the options you have.

FTP

One of the oldest Internet protocols is still one of the most popular for publishing Web sites to your remote server. File Transfer Protocol (FTP) is a well-named protocol. Its purpose is just that, to transfer files from one place to another. As a means of viewing and interacting with content, it is very limited, which is why HTTP replaced it as the protocol of the Web. But as a means of moving files around, it remains an efficient tool.

Remember that your Web application is really just a collection of individual files. They may be HTML pages, ASP pages, CFM pages, GIF images, or any of a number of file types. But they are still just a series of files that work together as they call each other and pass data back and forth. Publishing a site to the Web involves the transfer of that collection of files to an Internet-connected server. Once you do that, you can maintain your application by editing and replacing only those files that require changes.

Note *In order to use an FTP program on your computer (called an FTP client) to upload files to a remote computer, that remote machine must be running an FTP server program that allows you to connect and deposit files in its directories.*

Many FTP programs are available; for example, you can access FTP from the command line in Unix or Windows. For our purposes, let's look at FTP from the Windows command line. The greater understanding you gain of FTP's commands and capabilities, the easier it will be to master whichever FTP client you choose to use.

Note *Although the following examples use the Windows command prompt to illustrate the use of FTP, you may use the command-line functionality of whichever operating system you use on your development computer.*

FTP from the Command Line

Although as many as 60 FTP commands are available, the core of what you will want to accomplish can be summed up in the following list:

1. Connect to an FTP server.

2. Use a username and password to log in.

3. Figure out where you are in the directory structure.

4. Change to the remote directory you want to communicate with (after creating it, if necessary).

5. Get a listing of the files in that directory.

6. Upload or download files.

7. Disconnect from the FTP server.

To begin the preceding process, open a DOS prompt on your Windows computer by selecting MS-DOS Prompt from your Start menu.

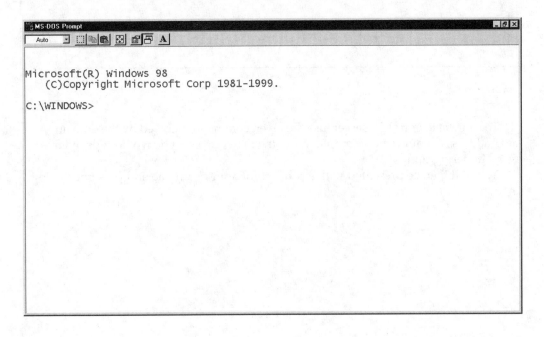

Type **FTP** to start the FTP client. You will be presented with an FTP prompt at which you will enter your FTP commands.

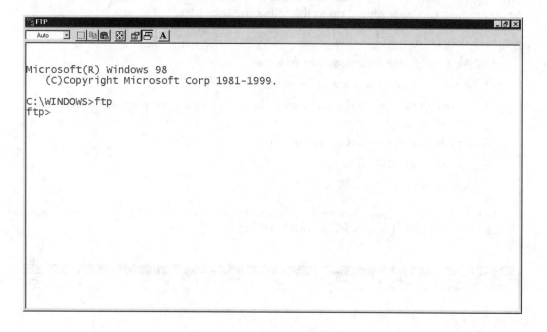

To connect to your FTP server, use the Open command followed by the domain or IP address of your remote computer. For the Bettergig site, you would type **open www.bettergig.com**.

You will then be presented with a prompt for your username and password to log in to the site.

```
FTP                                                                    _ □ X
Auto   ▼  □ ▣ ▣ ⊠ ☞ ⯊ A

Microsoft(R) Windows 98
   (C)Copyright Microsoft Corp 1981-1999.

C:\WINDOWS>ftp
ftp> open www.bettergig.com
Connected to www.bettergig.com.
220 www Microsoft FTP Service (Version 4.0).
User (www.bettergig.com:(none)):
```

Once logged in, you are still only at an FTP prompt. To see where you are in the directory structure, use the *pwd* command to print the working directory. You may be deposited in the root of the site (the highest directory in the structure), or your administrator may have assigned your login a default directory in which you will begin. Depending on your security settings, you may or may not be able to see and navigate to directories about your default location. The *dir* command will show you the files and directories that are immediately available to you.

```
FTP                                                                    _ □ X
Auto   ▼  □ ▣ ▣ ⊠ ☞ ⯊ A
Password:
230 User ray logged in.
ftp> pwd
257 "/" is current directory.
ftp> dir
200 PORT command successful.
150 Opening ASCII mode data connection for /bin/ls.
drwxrwxrwx   1 owner    group              0 Nov  5 15:27 about
drwxrwxrwx   1 owner    group              0 Sep 18 10:05 bettergig_png_folder
-rwxrwxrwx   1 owner    group            686 Jul 16  2001 CDOtest.asp
-rwxrwxrwx   1 owner    group             41 Nov  5 15:23 CDOtest.asp.LCK
-rwxrwxrwx   1 owner    group          11257 Aug 23 18:32 get.asp
-rwxrwxrwx   1 owner    group              9 Aug 22 22:17 get.asp.LCK
drwxrwxrwx   1 owner    group              0 Nov  1 22:24 get_a_gig
drwxrwxrwx   1 owner    group              0 Nov  1 22:24 help
drwxrwxrwx   1 owner    group              0 Nov  5 15:39 images
-rwxrwxrwx   1 owner    group           8641 Sep 20 14:22 index.htm
drwxrwxrwx   1 owner    group              0 Nov  1 22:24 JS
drwxrwxrwx   1 owner    group              0 Nov  1 22:23 my_company
-rwxrwxrwx   1 owner    group            279 Jul 11  2001 ObjectTest.html
drwxrwxrwx   1 owner    group              0 Nov  1 22:23 post_a_gig
drwxrwxrwx   1 owner    group              0 Sep 18 10:05 Templates
226 Transfer complete.
ftp: 1058 bytes received in 0.06Seconds 17.63Kbytes/sec.
ftp>
```

You may want to work in this default directory, or you may need access to another directory, which may or may not exist at this point. To create a new directory inside the directory in which you currently reside, use the *mkdir* command followed by the name of the directory you want to create.

```
drwxrwxrwx   1 owner     group            0 Sep 18 10:05 bettergig_png_folder
-rwxrwxrwx   1 owner     group          686 Jul 16  2001 CDOtest.asp
-rwxrwxrwx   1 owner     group           41 Nov  5 15:23 CDOtest.asp.LCK
-rwxrwxrwx   1 owner     group        11257 Aug 23 18:32 get.asp
-rwxrwxrwx   1 owner     group            9 Aug 22 22:17 get.asp.LCK
drwxrwxrwx   1 owner     group            0 Nov  1 22:24 get_a_gig
drwxrwxrwx   1 owner     group            0 Nov  1 22:24 help
drwxrwxrwx   1 owner     group            0 Nov  5 15:39 images
-rwxrwxrwx   1 owner     group         8641 Sep 20 14:22 index.htm
drwxrwxrwx   1 owner     group            0 Nov  1 22:24 JS
drwxrwxrwx   1 owner     group            0 Nov  1 22:23 my_company
-rwxrwxrwx   1 owner     group          279 Jul 11  2001 ObjectTest.html
drwxrwxrwx   1 owner     group            0 Nov  1 22:23 post_a_gig
drwxrwxrwx   1 owner     group            0 Sep 18 10:05 Templates
226 Transfer complete.
ftp: 1058 bytes received in 0.06Seconds 17.63Kbytes/sec.
ftp> mkdir ftptest
257 MKD command successful.
ftp> cd ftptest
250 CWD command successful.
ftp> dir
200 PORT command successful.
150 Opening ASCII mode data connection for /bin/ls.
226 Transfer complete.
ftp> _
```

This example created an ftptest directory. The server responded that the command was successful. The *cd* command was then used to change to the new directory, and the *dir* command listed the files within the directory (none, of course, because it was just created).

As in the example, you can use the *mkdir* and the *rmdir* commands to make and remove directories, and the *cd* command to move around within the directory structure you have created.

Once you have created or moved to the directory in which you need to place or download files, you can use the *get* and *put* commands to do just that. The *put* command enables you to specify a directory and file on your local machine to be uploaded. The *get* command enables you to specify which file in the current remote working directory you want to download to your local computer.

```
FTP                                                                _ 8 X
Auto  ___  [  ] [  ] [  ]  [  ] [  ][  ]  A
226 Transfer complete.
ftp: 1058 bytes received in 0.06Seconds 17.63Kbytes/sec.
ftp> mkdir ftptest
257 MKD command successful.
ftp> cd ftptest
250 CWD command successful.
ftp> dir
200 PORT command successful.
150 Opening ASCII mode data connection for /bin/ls.
226 Transfer complete.
ftp> put c:\mydocu~1\ftptest.txt
200 PORT command successful.
150 Opening ASCII mode data connection for ftptest.txt.
226 Transfer complete.
ftp> dir
200 PORT command successful.
150 Opening ASCII mode data connection for /bin/ls.
-rwxrwxrwx   1 owner     group                 0 Nov 14 23:12 ftptest.txt
226 Transfer complete.
ftp: 72 bytes received in 0.00Seconds 72000.00Kbytes/sec.
ftp> get ftptest.txt
200 PORT command successful.
150 Opening ASCII mode data connection for ftptest.txt(0 bytes).
226 Transfer complete.
ftp>
```

The *close* command will close the connection; the *bye* command closes the connection and exits FTP.

This is certainly not the easiest way to use FTP; but it is good to know, because it works great in a pinch and should help you understand a bit about the mechanics of the protocol. Table 6-1 contains a more complete listing of the available FTP commands (some on Windows and some on Unix) and their meanings.

Good FTP clients are readily available, including the one in Dreamweaver, which allows you to interact with your FTP server in a more visual way.

FTP Command	Meaning
!	Escape to shell
ascii	Set the file transfer mode to ASCII
bell	Sound a beep when complete
binary	Set the file transfer mode to binary
bye	Close the FTP connection and exit the FTP program
cd	Change to a specified directory
cdup	Move up one directory in the current structure
close	Close the FTP connection
delete	Delete a file
dir	List the files in the current directory
disconnect	Terminate the FTP session
get	Get a file from the remote computer
help	Get help on a listed command
lcd	Change the local current directory
ls	List the file in the current directory
mdelete	Delete multiple files
mdir	List the contents of multiple remote directories
mget	Get multiple files
mkdir	Create a new directory
mls	List the contents of multiple remote directories
mput	Put multiple files
open	Open an FTP connection
prompt	Force interactive prompting on multiple commands
put	Put a file on the remote computer
pwd	Print working directory
quit	Close the connection and exit FTP
recv	Receive a file

Table 6-1.   *FTP Commands*

FTP Command	Meaning
rename	Rename a file
rmdir	Remove a directory
send	Send one file
status	Show current status
?	Print local help information

Table 6-1.   *FTP Commands* (continued)

FTP in Dreamweaver

FTP in Dreamweaver offers this functionality in a visual interface that makes it easy to use and navigate. For almost every command in Table 6-1, there is a corresponding Dreamweaver action that accomplishes the same thing. FTP is accessed directly in the Site Panel, as shown in Figure 6-1.

If you set up your FTP access in Dreamweaver as discussed in Chapter 3, you have already told Dreamweaver how to contact and log in to your FTP server. Just as in the earlier example, there is a set of goals to accomplish with Dreamweaver's FTP client implementation. You need to connect to the site, log in, move around, and upload and download files. To connect to your FTP server, click the Connect button in the Site window. Because you have identified your server, the remote directory, and your username and password in your site definition, a lot of work is done for you when you press the Connect button. The server is located, initial contact is made, the request for a username and password is received and responded to automatically, and you are deposited into the remote directory that you have requested. You have already selected your site on your local computer, and it has a local working directory assigned to it. So, one button press has taken the place of at least five manual commands. Once connected, your site structure is displayed in the Site Panel with the remote files on the Remote Site tab and the Local Files on the Local Site tab.

Now, instead of having to type in commands to navigate your directory structure, you can treat the two site structures just as you work the Windows Explorer, selecting and opening directories by clicking and double-clicking them.

Getting and Putting Files

Once you are connected and can navigate around the site, you can begin to publish your site. If you have developed your site completely within Dreamweaver, publishing can be as easy as the click of a button. If, however, you have files and images scattered

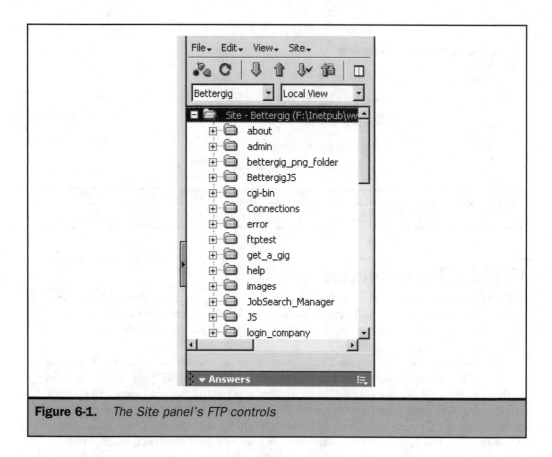

Figure 6-1. *The Site panel's FTP controls*

throughout the hard drive on your development computer, you may need to publish by piecemeal to get all of the files in the correct place.

If you have been following along, you probably have a single directory on your hard drive that contains your entire site, including images, templates, and any additional support files that you may need for the site to operate. The first time you log in to your FTP server to publish your site, you will likely encounter an empty directory that you, your system administrator, or ISP created and tied to your domain name. This directory will serve as the repository for your site files.

During this first visit, you may need to publish the entirety of your site (or at least what you have completed up to this point). To do so, highlight the root directory in your local site tree, as shown in Figure 6-1.

With the root highlighted, click the Put button indicated (the up arrow). Dreamweaver will ask you to confirm that you want to upload the entire site. When you acknowledge that you do, it will upload the site to the remote server.

You can follow the same procedure to upload a single directory of files or a single file. Just keep in mind that whatever you select, as well as anything beneath it in the file structure (meaning any files with a selected directory), will be uploaded. Navigate to and highlight whatever it is that you want to move, click the Put button, and the procedure will be complete.

As a shortcut, you can often double-click the file that you want to transfer. If you do so on the local side, the file will be uploaded; if you do so on the remote side, the file will be downloaded to your local machine.

Getting files from the remote location works just as easily. Highlight a file or directory on the remote side of the Site window and click the Get button (the down arrow). The items you have selected will be downloaded to your local computer.

Synchronizing Files

If you are working on more than one development computer, you may get into a situation in which you have site files spread over more locations than just a development machine and your server. In these cases, keeping all of the site files synchronized is very important. Imagine the wasted effort if you spend hours on modifications at your office computer and then overwrite them with an older file on your home computer.

Dreamweaver has a Synchronize function that you can access from the Site | Synchronize menu to help you keep your files up to date. When you select this menu option, you are presented with the dialog box shown in Figure 6-2.

In the dialog box, you can choose to synchronize the entire site you are working on or only the files you have selected. You can also choose how you want to synchronize by filling in the Direction text box with one of the following:

- Put newer files to remote
- Get newer files from remote
- Get and put newer files

The last of these options (Get and put newer files) ensures that both locations have the newest and most updated files.

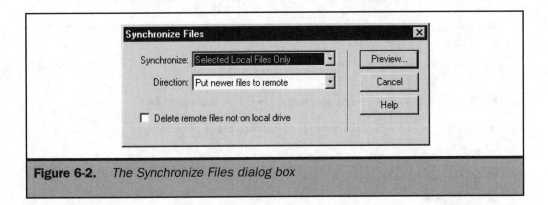

Figure 6-2. *The Synchronize Files dialog box*

The last option in the dialog box asks if you want to delete files from the remote site that have been deleted locally. Although this can keep your remote site clean and free of extraneous files, make sure you use it only when your local site contains a full and complete copy of the site as it should exist.

RDS

Dreamweaver MX integrates tightly with ColdFusion MX. As a result, RDS support has been added to Dreamweaver to allow file management on a ColdFusion server. But Remote Development Services (RDS) provides more than just file transfer for ColdFusion.

RDS provides two levels of security, basic and advanced. Basic security requires that users log in with a password. Once authenticated, users gain access to the file and database assets of the site. Advanced Security allows users to be assigned security levels. Once a user is authenticated using advanced security, he is allowed access to the site assets that are appropriate for his security level.

In addition, RDS provides data source browsing, SQL query building, and CFML debugging.

To enable RDS for your ColdFusion site, select RDS in the Remote Info section of the Site Definition Dialog. Click the Settings button and enter the URL or IP of your ColdFusion server and your login information.

Versioning and Source Control

Two facts regarding Web development are indisputable:

- Sites are getting larger and more complex.
- Because of this, they are increasingly developed and maintained by teams of programmers and designers rather than lone-person operations.

These facts raise a number of issues for the development team:

- How to make sure that files are not edited by more than one programmer at a time
- How to make sure the latest, most accurate versions of your files are published to the Web
- How to allow centralized access to files by all team members

Dreamweaver MX offers three ways to answer these questions:

- Check in/check out
- Microsoft SourceSafe
- WebDAV

Check In/Check Out

When you define your site in Dreamweaver, you have the opportunity to enable its check in/check out functionality. Checking files in and out protects their integrity by making sure that only one person can edit them at a time. A file that is checked into the system is available to be opened, edited, and saved by any developer with access to the site. A checked out file is locked from other developers until the person who checked it out is finished and checks it back in. When you consider the disaster that would occur if two people were editing a file at the same time and overwriting each other's changes, the benefit of being able to check out files is obvious.

To enable File Check In and Check Out, check the appropriate box at the bottom of the Remote Info tab of the Site Definition window, shown in Figure 6-3.

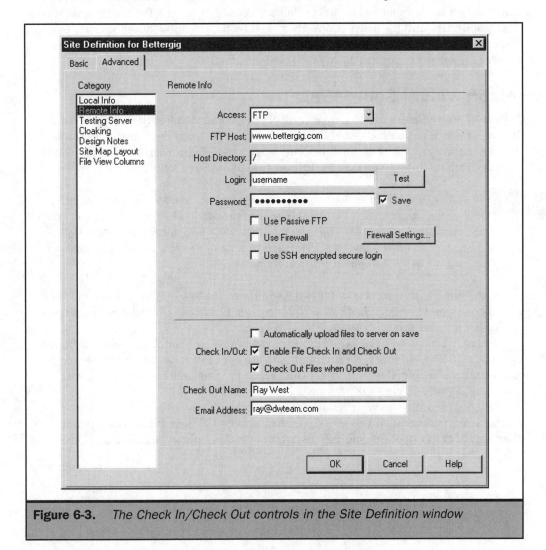

Figure 6-3. *The Check In/Check Out controls in the Site Definition window*

You will be asked to enter a name and an e-mail address. The name will be attached to any files you have checked out so that other users can identify who is working on the file. The e-mail address is also indicated next to the checked-out file and can be used to contact you regarding the file.

When File Check In/Out is enabled, the status of the remote file is checked each time you try to open a file. Rather than simply opening the file from the local site, Dreamweaver connects to the remote server and checks the availability of the file. If it is not being edited by another user, you will be able to open the file and the remote file will be marked with a lock file that indicates who has it checked out. When you've finished working with the file, you can check it back in and it will be available to other users.

Note that Dreamweaver does not make the remote file read-only in any real, universal sense. Another FTP application could easily overwrite the file because it does not understand the instructions given to it by the Dreamweaver lock file. To implement more stringent source control, you must migrate to a product designed to enforce file integrity, such as Microsoft's SourceSafe.

Microsoft Visual SourceSafe

Microsoft SourceSafe is a true source control environment that ships with Microsoft Visual Studio. It has both client and server components that manage user accounts and enforce file integrity during the development process. Dreamweaver MX integrates with SourceSafe through its Remote Info section of the Site Definition window.

In order to use Microsoft SourceSafe, you must have its components installed on a server and your client machine. The SourceSafe administrator will set up a working directory, username, and password so that you can access and utilize the features of the system. Make sure that this is done and that you have that information available to you before attempting to set Dreamweaver to use SourceSafe.

In the Remote Info section of the Site Definition window, where you set FTP as your access point before, you can select Sourcesafe Database. Click the Settings button to display the dialog box shown in Figure 6-4.

You may browse your network to locate the SourceSafe database you wish to use. Ask your system administrator if you are unsure about its location. Enter the project name that was assigned in SourceSafe, and the username and password that was assigned to you, and click OK to save.

When you connect to your remote site at this point, you are connecting to the SourceSafe project that you specified, not to a remote FTP site. When you open files, they are checked out of the SourceSafe database and are not available to any other

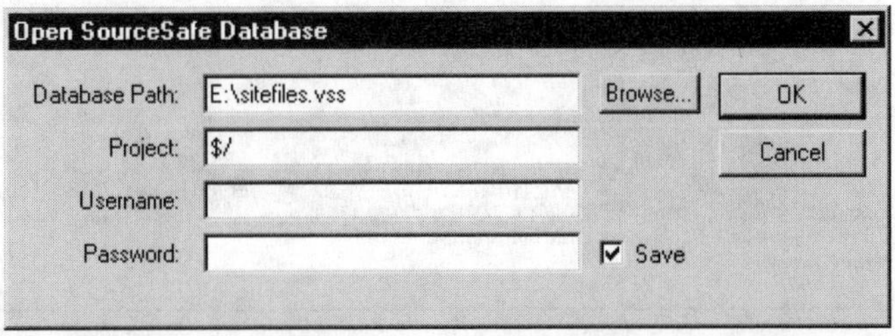

Open SourceSafe Database

Database Path: E:\sitefiles.vss   Browse...   OK

Project: $/   Cancel

Username:

Password: ☑ Save

Figure 6-4. *SourceSafe settings*

users until you check them back in. When you are ready to publish your site to the FTP server, you will need to change your settings to allow FTP access or use a third-party FTP client application.

WebDAV

WebDAV stands for Web-based Distributed Authoring and Versioning. It is a set of HTTP extensions that allows you to establish a source control directory that is available from anywhere over the Web. Open-source WebDAV implementations are available at www.webdav.org.

Once you (or an administrator) have established a WebDAV site, and you have been assigned a username and password, setup is much like the SourceSafe setup covered earlier. Select WebDAV in the Access portion of the Remote Info section of the Site Definition window. Click Settings and enter the URL of the WebDAV server, your username and password, and an e-mail address. This e-mail address will be displayed in conjunction with your checked-out files so that you can be contacted by other users.

Other FTP Clients

Although Dreamweaver's FTP access is convenient and powerful, some people prefer to use a third-party FTP application for any number of personal reasons. You have several choices, many of which you can see and evaluate at sites like www.tucows.com. A couple of popular options include WSFTP and CuteFTP, as shown in Figure 6-5.

Most of these work in a very similar fashion to Dreamweaver's FTP client, and you should have no trouble getting up to speed with whatever you select.

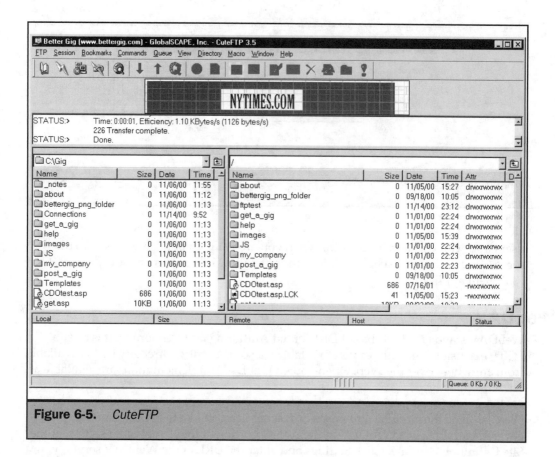

Figure 6-5. *CuteFTP*

Summary

In this chapter, we covered many options related to site management and publishing, including the basics of FTP, the Dreamweaver FTP client functionality, and source and versioning control. By now, you have completed the basic design of your site and a few of the pages that will make up your site. As we move forward, we discuss the addition of data access to the work that you have completed, and guide you through the languages and technologies you have selected to use for your site.

The Complete Reference

Dreamweaver MX

Part II

Web Site Design and Construction

The
Complete
Reference

Dreamweaver MX

Chapter 7

Designing and Planning Your Site

149

Building Web sites is a big business, and new sites are being launched at an alarming rate. Because some HTML software is available for free or only a few dollars, casual observers may conclude that it doesn't take a whole lot to be a Web page designer. However, in truth, designing and building quality Web applications is a difficult, time-consuming task. Tools like Dreamweaver make the job easier, but there are some things that no software can ever do for you. This chapter considers the importance of taking time to properly design and plan your site, and you will begin the construction of a data-driven Web application.

Note *In the real world, Web sites cost money. Although there are—and will continue to be—many people who put up sites for their own use or to promote and support their small business, the Web is becoming an increasingly important place to do business, and the sites that support this are not built in a matter of hours. A recent survey indicates that an average site with modest database interaction costs more than $100,000 to build.*

Planning and Designing Your Site

When you begin to build data-driven sites, taking the time to plan and design your site becomes more important than ever. Too many people jump right into the construction of pages without properly considering the details of what they are doing. Not only will a lack of planning significantly impact the quality of your final product, it may also get you into a sticky situation with a client whose ideas about the site are different than yours.

Note *Not only is it important that you plan your site in cooperation with your client, you should also get your client to sign off on that design before you begin work. Taking this extra step will help ensure that you and your client are on the same page and will help to eliminate feature creep (those persistent phone calls with neat things to add to the site while you go). Some of the things you need to consider when planning your site are the following:*

- *Purpose and goal of the site*
- *Target audience*
- *Tools and platforms available to you and your client*
- *Site's design*
- *Navigation scheme*
- *Development time and cost*

The Purpose and Goal of the Site

It should go without saying that you need to understand the purpose and goal of the site you are designing; yet, too little attention is paid to this basic element of Web site creation. The following are several questions that you must answer to truly understand the purpose of the site you are creating:

- Is this an information, education, entertainment, or commerce site?
- Is the site intended to display cutting-edge technique, or to reach a broad audience?
- Will the site service a company, regional, or global community of users?
- How will the site be used?
- How will traffic be driven to the site?
- What competition is there for the niche this site will service?

If you can answer these questions, you will be well on your way to developing an understanding of the work you are about to undertake. However, it is important that your answers to these questions are the same answers as your client's. Too often, a designer has spent hours on a snazzy Flash introduction only to find that the client doesn't like Flash. Work with your client to discover the answers to these questions.

The Focus of the Site

The focus of your site will cross the lines between information, education, entertainment, and commerce. Many sites, like Pepsi's at www.pepsi.com, seek to entertain while also educating its visitors about its products and generating sales. Still, whether your site will have a single focus or a combination of purposes, you should be able to produce a statement or two that will serve as the "mission statement" under which you will work.

For instance, consider the sample site that we have created in this book. The site is for an organization called Bettergig.com, a service that enables job seekers to search for jobs that have been posted by employers in the computer industry. It also enables them to post their résumés so that employers can search them out based on the company's needs. Employers can post jobs that are available at their company or search the résumés at the site based on the requirements needed to accomplish the tasks that they have at hand.

Bettergig.com's slogan is "Get a Better Life . . . Get a Better Gig." From that slogan, you can see that this company's focus is helping its customers improve their standards of living by providing them with opportunities to improve the jobs that they perform and the compensation they receive.

You can also make some assumptions about the site. Because this will be a corporate presence for Bettergig.com, you can assume that it should be a professional presentation. "Professional" in this context refers not to quality (everything you do should be of professional quality), but rather that the presentation should not be artsy, cutting edge, or cutesy (using handwriting fonts, and so on). The demeanor of the site should be consistent with an appearance of experience and knowledge doing business as a job service. You may need the help of your client and some research to determine exactly what look is consistent with those things, but by making sure the presentation is "professional," you at least are on the right track.

So, to tie all of this together, the following "mission statement" might be used to guide you through the development of this site:

> The Bettergig.com Web site will be a place where our company can evolve its experience as a job placement service into a professional online meeting place for workers and the employers who need their services. It will enable employers to post jobs and search résumés, and will enable job seekers to search posted jobs and post their résumés, encouraging the ongoing involvement of both sides of the job market.

This statement may change as the site progresses, but it is a good place to start, and it provides a cogent picture of the site.

Site Content and User Community

At the same time, the mission statement tells you what the site will not be. For example, job seekers will be coming to this site to investigate opportunities for the advancement of their careers. They don't care that you have the new beta of Flash that does cool new compression and that they can download your presentation three seconds faster than with the old version. It just gets in the way of their new, bigger paycheck.

This site will not be an opportunity to display cutting-edge design technique or the latest development tools. Although sites like that are great, and there is some truly impressive talent out there, the fact remains that most of those sites are done for the benefit of the designer and the design community. Few clients pay for content like that.

This site will seek to attract the broadest audience possible within the geographic regions that it serves. Anyone who is looking for a job in the computer industry will be welcome and will be provided unfettered access to information about the jobs and opportunities that are available to them.

How Will the Site Be Used?

Just as different sites have different purposes, different sites are used differently by their visitors. Some sites are free flowing, allowing navigation to any page from any other page. Others guide the user through a series of steps toward a goal, and allowing deviation from that series of steps would interrupt its effective use.

The Bettergig site, as with many sites, is a combination of these purposes. While the casual visitor may jump from place to place investigating the services that are available to them, a user who decides to participate will need to be walked through the steps necessary to create an online job résumé or job posting.

How Will Traffic Be Driven to the Site?

You need to consider how your audience will hear about your business and get to your site in the mangle that the Web is becoming. If your visitors will simply type in your URL or link to the home page from some outside site, your job is pretty simple. But, if you will be running promotions or targeted advertising that makes it important to track your users and where they come from, you may need to have a variety of entry points to your application that can make the design of your navigation more complex.

Competition

Unless you are one of the rare few who creates an industry, your site will likely have competition, and you are well advised to pay attention to it. It is entirely acceptable to offer services in a different way than your competition, but it is not acceptable to do so without a clear purpose. Learn everything you can about what is happening in your industry. It can only help you service your customer base better.

Your Target Audience

The need to understand your target audience cannot be stressed enough. In the big world of the Web, it is likely that any one site will appeal to only a small percentage of users. If you do not know who is in your percentage, you have no hope of finding them and getting them to your site. You need to know several things about your target audience before you can figure out how to reach them over the Internet:

- Does my audience have computers?
- How much time do they spend on the Web?
- What browsers do they use?
- How do they hear about new Web sites?
- How computer-savvy are they?

Two issues are especially important to the actual design of your site: the browsers your visitors use and how computer-savvy they are. A critical consideration is whether you will construct your site so that version 4 browsers (Internet Explorer and especially Netscape Navigator) are supported. There are different schools of thought on this issue.

One school of thought insists that sites must support version 4 browsers either in their general construction or through redirection. For the site designer, this involves constructing a site without the use of the dynamic HTML elements that have become popular. For some applications, this presents no problem, but it can make for a less-interactive experience for your users. Although you have already established that the purpose for this site is something other than the entertainment of your visitors, providing an enjoyable, interactive experience is certainly acceptable.

The point of those who hold this position is that version 4 browsers are still in use by many Web users; even though surveys show a much higher distribution of version 5 and higher versions, the people who use version 4 browsers are not exactly the ones who find themselves in a position to take those kinds of surveys. Although newer browsers are available for free download, a few factors can hinder certain users from upgrading:

- Casual and less-knowledgeable users typically use whatever browser is preinstalled on their computers (or whatever browser their technically competent nephew loaded for them last time he visited).

- Even those who might otherwise brave the upgrade often have only 56K or even 28K connections, and 18MB downloads just aren't feasible.

The other school of thought is just as compelling. In the desktop application world, Windows 3.1 users (and even Windows 95) generally are no longer considered. Setting your program's baseline as Windows 98 or above has certainly become acceptable. Given that fact, and the fact that version 5 browsers come with the operating systems above Windows ME, it is fairly safe to assume that most users have at least one version 5 browser available to them.

You will need to make decisions about the platforms you will support before you begin construction of your site. You would not want to get halfway through a site using fancy invisible-layers techniques, only to find out that your client insists on compatibility with legacy browsers.

The Tools and Platforms Available to You

When you are working on sites for your own use, you are free to use your choice of development tools and platforms. This consideration becomes more important when you begin constructing sites for clients who already have ideas about the way they want things done. Often, you will be called upon to maintain or add to existing architecture. Convincing a client who has a considerable amount of work done in, say, ColdFusion that they should allow you to do your part in ASP is a tough sell; and even if you can sell it, the client is often dissatisfied with the final product. Although many developers work quite successfully in a number of languages, you will certainly want to build some space into your design plan if you will be working on a platform that is less than familiar to you.

The Site's Design

Although you will likely begin to formulate the actual look and feel of the site only after you sit down at the computer and start fiddling with the design, the following are some decisions that you can make at this point in the process that will help you when your design comes together.

Will the Site Be Based in HTML or in Graphics?   Sites based in HTML are typically made up of HTML text over a colored background or a tile or image background. This technique can be used very effectively, and it gives a very slim, no-nonsense interface when the information is the most important thing.

Sites based in graphics often use a more intricate interface, often designed and imported from a graphics program such as Fireworks or Photoshop. The links are often graphic text rather than text anchors.

Will You Use Frames?   Whereas frames were all the rage for a while, they seem to have fallen into some disfavor of late. Opportunities to make good use of frames certainly exist, but you will typically find it cleaner to avoid them and the temptations they afford. Too many sites end up framing in other sites, which frame in other sites, and the result is just a big mess. That said, used properly, frames can allow you some impressive design possibilities, but learn to use them well.

Which of the Common Layouts Will You Use?   Several basic page layouts seem to work best on the Web. Although designers are forever looking for ways to differentiate their pages, the most usable pages seem to adhere to two or three basic layouts: the left-hand navigation bar, the top navigation bar, and the page of links where the entire page is made up of columns that house links to other places. A few sites use a right-hand navigation bar, but users seem to have grown accustomed to the other three layouts and find them the most easy to navigate.

Commit to Avoiding the Design No-Nos.   Although you probably don't need to hear this, it is such an annoying problem that we need to mention it. Text is unreadable when placed over a tiled image of your pet dog, and light-yellow text is unreadable on anything except a solid-black background. Similarly, although I'm sure the '60s were a lot of fun, tie-dyed page backgrounds are annoying.

Take care that you do not spend your time creating something that is unusable or annoying to your visitors. A quick tour around the Web will provide you with a great many examples of this. If you need help to determine an appropriate design, seek out help on the many great newsgroups or from a knowledgeable colleague.

Your Navigation Scheme

The design of your navigation scheme goes hand in hand with the site-design considerations previously discussed. But, as you begin to consider your site's navigation, it is appropriate to start sketching out the pages that you will need to create for the site. Start with the home page, and begin adding pages in your drawing and indicating links, as shown in Figure 7-1. Tools such as Microsoft's Visio and Rational Software's Rational Rose can assist in this process. You will be amazed how much more quickly your site will come together when you have planned the pages that make it up and how they connect to one another.

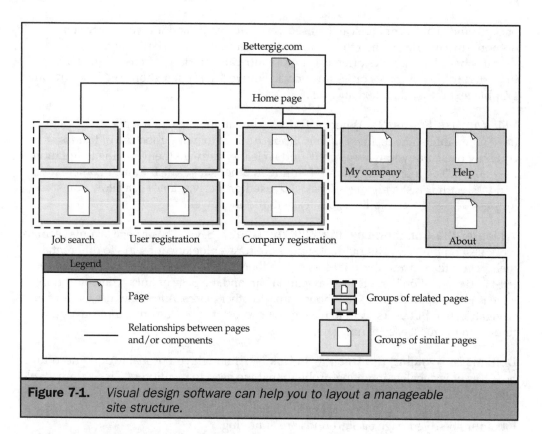

Figure 7-1. *Visual design software can help you to layout a manageable site structure.*

Development Time and Cost

You need to carefully consider the amount of time it will take to construct a site. Only by knowing this important piece of information can you determine a fair price to charge for your work. Unfortunately, everyone works at a different pace, and no formula exists to help with this calculation. You will gain the ability to judge construction time through the experience of building sites.

Developers charge for site development three main ways: per page, per hour, and per project. Each has its benefits.

Newer developers or those accustomed to building very small sites tend to offer a per-page pricing model. When a customer wants a simple five- or six-page presence for their small business, it is easy to budget using this method, and developers can often churn out these small sites rather quickly. This pricing model is an unwieldy method for larger sites, though.

There are two compelling reasons to insist on the per-hour method, from a developer's perspective. If you are unable to get the client to commit to a design specification and are afraid that you may be embarking on a wandering design adventure, charge a per-hour rate. As long as they are paying you per hour, you should care very little that they change their mind every couple of days. Also, if the project will entail a great deal of site maintenance, such as content rotation, an hourly rate ensures that you are fairly compensated for your work.

If, on the other hand, the client is very clear about what they want, and the project has a definable beginning and ending, a per-project rate enables both you and the client to better budget from a time and money standpoint. Just make sure that the client signs off on what work is to be done for the price agreed upon.

If you can do this much planning before you sit down to construct your first page, you will have done far more than most developers, and you will be well on your way to a well-organized, usable site. The effort spent up front on this kind of exercise will return great dividends during the actual construction process.

Design Concepts

It's all about packaging really. The days of single-color or tiled backgrounds with simple text on them are not gone, as a quick tour around the Web will show, but they are on their way out. Your competition has great-looking sites, and if you want to be competitive, you need a great-looking site, too.

If I could teach you in a few paragraphs how to become a world-class graphic artist, I would be rich, and this book would be worth its weight in gold. However, this book can teach you a few things that will be very valuable to you as you design Web sites.

Navigation

Navigation is the means by which you enable users to get around your site. As stated earlier, sometimes you will want to allow users to move freely to and from any page that strikes their fancy; other times you'll need them to remain on a set path in order to complete the task they have set about. Both forms of navigation will be used in the Bettergig Web site.

The basic motto that applies to navigation in general is to keep it clear, keep it simple, and don't overdo it.

Keep It Clear

When users look at your site, they should be able to tell two things rather quickly: where the navigation links are (how to get around) and where those links will take them. There is a trend in Web development that has been dubbed "mystery meat navigation," which refers to sites where the designer presents you with image-based links with little if any indication of where they lead. At best, you can hover over the image link (if you can find it) and get a tooltip with a hint as to where you might end up if you were to click on it. Although this kind of navigation might lend itself to the look and feel of the art you are trying to create, it is frustrating to the user and is more likely to prompt visitors to move on to a site that clearly presents the information they are seeking than to stay and fawn over your design sense.

Keep in mind that most Web sites are for the purpose of communicating with visitors. Use links that are text based (either HTML or graphic text) or images along with text that identify the links. Although it may offend your design sense, it will keep visitors at your site longer because they can clearly see how to get around.

Keep It Simple

Your site may be 200 pages. Each and every page may contain something very interesting that you are excited about sharing with everyone who drops by. But 200 links on your home page is going to overwhelm them and drive them away in frustration.

Keep your navigation simple. Design a hierarchy of concepts within your site that leads visitors to areas of interest, and then offer additional pages that fall within that area. Keep the number of links on your home page reasonable. What is reasonable? That is for you to decide. But if you are feeling the need to put much more than 10 navigational links on the home page, you may want to rethink your site structure. If every one of those pages is so unrelated to the other pages around it that it has to have its own link from the home page, then you have a maze on your hands that few people will want to wade through.

These "rules" are generalizations. They are good generalizations, but they may not apply to your specific circumstance. If you are designing a site—perhaps a portal site like www.yahoo.com or www.cnet.com—there may be a good reason to make your home page a mass of links. As always, rules are made to be broken, but you must know what rules you are breaking and why.

Don't Overdo It

Another disturbing trend in page design is repeating links. Almost as a means of filling space, designers will put identical links in the left-hand navigation bar, as an image in the body of the page or at the top, and as a text link at the bottom of the page. Unless your pages are extremely long and you are concerned that users will get lost in them, you don't need to provide duplicate links all over the place.

Usability

We can't say it enough: Web sites are for the communication of information to your visitors. It does not matter whether you are tired of making sites with left-hand navigation, if that is what your visitors expect to see; if that is what will keep them at your site, then that is what you need to give them.

The following are a few more rules that are fairly accepted usability practices:

- Keep your page load times to 15–20 seconds on a 56K modem.
- Don't pop up new windows on your visitors.
- Frames are not the best idea. If you do use them, don't frame in other sites. It is annoying to your users and to the people whose site you are framing in.

- Always provide a link back to your home page.
- Make sure that your site's features work in the available browsers. Make sure you know going into a project what browsers you are targeting so that you can test for degradation, especially if you plan to use CSS styles.

Media

Media is a pretty broad term. It can relate to anything from the images on your site, to sound files, to extravagant Flash files. Here is a list of things to remember when choosing and using media on your site:

- **Use the appropriate file type for images.**   JPEG files are often preferred for photographs, but they are *lossy*—meaning that the compression used to make the file smaller can affect the quality of the resulting image, and the files can be larger if you are not careful. GIFs are good for graphics and graphic text.

- **Only use transparency when it is needed.**   Don't make part of an image transparent and then stick it on a white background. It bloats the file unnecessarily.

- **Use an appropriate number of colors in your image files.**   A product like Fireworks enables you to optimize your files by selecting different numbers of colors and observing how the change affects the picture quality.

- **Size your images properly before putting them on your page.**   Resizing in HTML takes a long time and produces questionable quality.

- **Use Flash cautiously.**   Although the Flash player is becoming ubiquitous, bandwidth that can handle the files is not. If you do use it, give your visitors a way out—a way to skip the file or never start viewing it in the first place.

- **Do not load with your home page MIDI files that start playing as soon as the page loads.**   They usually sound terrible. If you are forced to use one, provide a prominent Off button.

Summary

You can readily see that a lot of time goes into designing a web application, and we have not even begun to discuss the data structure that will support the HTML pages. The best advice you can get is to develop a method of communicating with your client (whether it be a local business or another department in your organization) and stick to it with every job that you do. You will quickly learn the pitfalls and how to judge the time and effort it will take to complete the work that is requested of you. That leads to a more profitable experience for both you and your client.

In the next chapter, we investigate the wide variety of data options provided by Dreamweaver MX and show you how to define your site so that making a connection to your database is easy.

The
Complete
Reference

Dreamweaver
MX

Chapter 8

Defining Your Site

Past versions of Dreamweaver allowed you to build Web pages. Dreamweaver MX can build Web pages too, but it's a much more capable program that can build Web applications better than any other tool out there. Web applications are simply a series of Web pages that are linked together to perform some function defined by the end user, which could be as simple as displaying text, or as complex as a dedicated e-store selling a product or a series of products. Whatever your requirements may be, Dreamweaver MX is up to the task. The page-design tools and back-end tools of Dreamweaver are second to none in the arena of Web-design software.

Building a Web page is easy, but building a Web application with a database back end is no trivial task, and proper planning is a necessity. From the server type to the database type to the language you are going to use—these are all considerations when planning your Web site. You might have a background in Visual Basic but decide that the features of a ColdFusion site make it more cost-effective. Or, maybe you have access to JSP and MySQL but know only ASP. Dreamweaver MX makes the transition from one server model to another much easier. This one tool works with many different server models, and makes the transition between them almost invisible. Applying a Server Behavior to a JSP page is identical to applying the same Server Behavior to an ASP page or a ColdFusion page or a PHP page.

After you decide on a course of action, however, you can't change midstream easily. Dreamweaver MX doesn't have any built-in functionality for changing or converting from one server model to another or from one language to another while constructing the site. Planning your site in minute detail before actually committing yourself with the pages that you've built is always a good idea. Although the techniques for building the pages are the same, the code that's used in creating the functionality is completely different.

Choosing the Server Model

Dreamweaver MX works with five major server models and two choices of language, in the case of ASP and ASP.NET. This may or may not be a consideration for you, but you shouldn't make the decision without a little background information. There isn't a "better" or "best" server model in the world of Web development. Each server model has strengths and weaknesses, and often the one you may be most familiar with isn't the best choice for the task at hand.

ColdFusion

ColdFusion has a definite advantage with Web developers who already know HTML. It is a tag-based language, and offers a substantial set of tags and functions to handle everything from database interaction to file manipulation. Pop e-mail retrieval and sending e-mail through an SMTP server are also powerful options. Things like Java-based grids for data display and tags for registry manipulation make it an extremely flexible and powerful environment. There's even a built-in scripting language—CFScript—that's similar to JavaScript.

ColdFusion is available for various flavors of Linux , HP UX, and Sun Solaris servers in addition to Windows servers, so you have a little flexibility in the OSs and databases that ColdFusion will work with. Also, ColdFusion will work with a variety of databases on each of the platforms. Also, the latest version of ColdFusion— ColdFusion MX— will be available for J2EE servers as well.

One of the disadvantages of ColdFusion is the relatively high cost of a dedicated server. If you're planning to set up your Web site with a Web host somewhere, this isn't an issue, unless the Web host happens to charge more on a per-month basis for use of the ColdFusion server. Many of them do, but many also offer ColdFusion at the same price as ASP. It's important to find out all the costs of a Web host before deciding which route to take.

Macromedia offers 30-day trials of all of its products, so a test-drive of ColdFusion is within everyone's reach. A complete tutorial on how to use ColdFusion and how to program in the tag-based language is included with the trial, and may be a real eye-opening experience. You can access many of the most powerful features with just a few lines of code. Chapter 17 offers a brief introduction to the ColdFusion language.

Dreamweaver MX makes a lot of the language-specific advantages irrelevant, but learning the underlying language of your Web application should be one of your prime concerns. ColdFusion is certainly the easiest of the server models to learn.

ColdFusion, like HTML, is a tag-based language. So many HTML developers feel right at home with its syntax and make the transition easily.

ASP

The popularity of ASP has a lot to do with the mass popularity of Microsoft Windows, and the fact that anyone with Windows can set up a Web server that runs ASP for free. Even Windows 95 users have access to the Personal Web Server, which is capable of deploying ASP pages. If you have a cable modem or DSL line, you can have a Web site running from your basement in no time.

Also, ASP pages in Dreamweaver MX can be written in either JScript or VBScript, so if you have knowledge of either language, learning ASP is a snap. JScript is Microsoft's version of ECMAScript, which is a standardized form of JavaScript that was implemented in 1997. The terms JScript and JavaScript are used interchangeably in the book, but when referring to server-side ASP code, JScript is the language being used. Many Web developers have a basic knowledge of JavaScript, so following the Dreamweaver MX–generated code in JavaScript flattens the learning curve. Also, VBScript has a basis in Visual Basic, which many programmers learn in school or use in corporations all over the world. With a little knowledge of either language, ASP might be right up your alley.

Note   *The VBScript programmer has a distinct advantage over the JavaScript programmer in ASP. If you look at the various books, magazine articles, and Web sites devoted to ASP, most of them show you the examples in VBScript. Also, VBScript has a lot of built-in language features that make it a good choice for developing your site.*

WEB SITE DESIGN
AND CONSTRUCTION

Of course, if your site isn't on a Windows server, ASP might not even be an option. You can run ASP on Unix, Solaris, HP, and other servers using a third-party ASP product such as Chili!Soft, but you always risk incompatibilities when you use third-party components. These are things to consider, and a full test of the environment should be performed before committing to it. Chili!Soft offers trial versions of its software for the various configurations of servers that it supports.

One of the disadvantages of using ASP is that it doesn't support some of the advanced features, such as e-mail and file manipulation, without configuring server components or purchasing third-party server components. Most Web-hosting companies have one of the popular server components installed, but you should find out all the details and specifications for what's provided. For instance, to send an e-mail, you could use CDONTS, ASPMail, JMail, or SA-SMTPMail. Whichever component your ISP is using, you will have to learn the syntax for hand-coding the necessary code, or find a Server Behavior that works with the component, if you want to use such a feature.

| Note | *Many Web hosts won't set up special third-party components for you, so make sure you find out what the Web host is using before you commit yourself to that particular host. E-mail components and file-upload components are a necessity in today's Web applications.* |

JSP

JSP may be the most powerful and versatile of the server models, but it is also the most difficult to use and program for. The language for JSP is Java, and it is much more complex than the tag-based ColdFusion Markup Language or the scripting languages (VBScript and JavaScript). JSP developers have at their disposal the whole of the Java language. With the added complexity of the language comes added power, but not without a cost: JSP pages also need proprietary servers to run them. Tag libraries, however, greatly reduce the complexity for the page designer, much the way that ColdFusion tags make it easy for a Web designer to work with server side functionality.

JSP servers come in various shapes and sizes, from Macromedia's JRun to IBM's WebSphere to Apache Tomcat. Each one has different requirements, so you're going to need to do some research to find out the advantages and disadvantages of each. Most JSP servers are available as trial versions, so a test-drive of the server environment is always an option. Configuring a JSP server can be something of a nightmare, so it's not something that you should take lightly. Also, JSP-based Web hosts are a little harder to find and generally don't come cheaply.

In addition to the server, most databases need specific drivers in order to be accessible to the JSP server, so you're going to need to find a driver that meets your needs. Many drivers are available, and all are of varying degrees of quality and cost. Again, trial versions of most of these are available as well. Dreamweaver MX ships with the Sun JDBC:ODBC Bridge, but you should use it in a test environment only and not on a production server.

PHP

PHP is a great option for a Unix or Linux server, and is a viable option for a Windows server as well. The server is freely available as a download, and the language is not difficult to learn. The syntax is similar to JavaScript, and it also has many powerful built-in features for e-mail, file manipulation, and database manipulation.

PHP is one of the new server models available in Dreamweaver MX—UltraDev did not have support for PHP, but a third-party extension allowed UltraDev users to work with PHP Web sites.

The server is easily installed and configured for a variety of Web servers, but works best with Apache. Also, PHP will work with many leading databases, but it works best with MySQL and PostgreSQL. One of the disadvantages of PHP development with Dreamweaver is that it supports only the MySQL database. Most PHP sites are built with that database, however. Learning MySQL is a little tricky for the beginner, so third-party front ends are available that ease the pain. Also, third-party extensions are available that allow you to use Dreamweaver MX with other databases.

ASP.NET

This is Microsoft's latest technology, and it is a very powerful technology to use. Much of the syntax and framework of the server technology is based on JSP, but it takes the concepts several steps further. ASP.NET server controls are powerful and easy to use, similar in concept to JSP's taglibs and ColdFusion's CFML language.

ASP.NET also allows you to program in many different languages. Dreamweaver MX features support for VB.NET and C#. VB.NET is similar in syntax to VBScript of classic ASP, but is far more powerful. C# is a mixture of Java, C++, and JavaScript, and is Microsoft's own language.

ASP.NET is easier to use in many ways than classic ASP. For one, server components had to be registered on the server in ASP, which frequently required a server restart. Many hosts simply won't install your component. ASP.NET allows you to add components on the fly, making it easy to build and utilize custom components.

Like JSP, ASP.NET is compiled on the fly, so you can create your pages in Dreamweaver MX or any text editor and save them. When the page is hit the first time, the page is compiled. Subsequent hits to the page are much faster because the pages are compiled.

Choosing Your Database

Each of the server models that you can work with in Dreamweaver MX—ASP, JSP, PHP, ASP.NET, and ColdFusion—has specific databases that it works well with. Although you may be fully committed to one database or another in your day-to-day workflow, putting that same data up on the Web is another matter entirely. Most databases have an export facility of some sort, so changing databases in many cases may be a viable option. The following sections cover some of the pluses and minuses of the different databases available to you.

Microsoft Access

Access is one of the cornerstones of Web development because of its ease of use and universal appeal. Databases can be designed easily on Access, and can be integrated into your Web site easily as well. It is almost certainly the best database for the job of a design-time connection because it will run on Windows and exist even without having Access installed on the system. All you need is the MDB file that contains the data, and you will be able to connect to it via ODBC or an ADO Connection String, or even through the Sun ODBC:JDBC driver if you are using JSP.

Access comes as part of Microsoft Office Professional or Premium versions, and is also available as a stand-alone product. You can get a special competitive upgrade price on Access from a variety of different databases. Having Access installed on your system is considered a "must" for the Web developer, because it allows easy manipulation of tables and queries in the design environment, before actually deploying your data to the server. You can also use Access on a Macintosh, if you have FWB SoftWindows or Connectix Virtual PC installed on the system. For a Macintosh user, it's a much more suitable alternative to the various Macintosh-only databases. Keep in mind, however, that you can't use the Access database within Dreamweaver MX from the SoftWindows or Virtual PC environment. The database has to reside on an actual Windows server to be able to access it from Dreamweaver MX. The advantage to using SoftWindows or Virtual PC is that you can design and configure your database on the Mac before deploying it to a server.

In addition, Access contains a query builder that enables you to test your queries in a controlled environment before deploying them from your Web page. You can copy/paste an Access query into the Dreamweaver MX environment with minor changes. Access databases also contain a *Compact* command that decreases the size of the data, and also optimizes the data for quicker access. The *Compact* command can be accessed right from the ODBC administrator as well.

If Access sounds too good to be true, it is. Although we wholeheartedly recommend Access for use in the design environment, we can't recommend its use on a live Web site, unless you expect that your Web site will never have more than a few simultaneous users. Although the specifications of Access claim more users, many people have found that slow access and data corruption can result when used in a real-world environment. Also, if the machine that hosts your Web site isn't a Windows machine, Access might not even be an option.

| Tip | *Microsoft Access 2000 or 2002 can be used as a front end to a Microsoft SQL Server–like database by using Microsoft Data Engine (MSDE). MSDE is an actual client/server data engine, which makes it much more scalable than the Jet engine of a typical file-based Access database. Access 97 doesn't have this option. Access also works as a front end to a SQL Server database as well.* |

Microsoft SQL Server

If you plan to deploy your Web site from a Windows-based server, Microsoft SQL Server would have to be the number one choice for the database. Beginning with SQL Server 7, Microsoft began implementing some of the ease-of-use features of Access. Enterprise Manager allows quick access to tables, views, and stored procedures that make using SQL Server a snap. In addition, upsizing from Microsoft Access is a simple process.

Whereas Microsoft Access is a file-based database, SQL Server is a full-fledged server. Making simultaneous connections in SQL Server is no problem, and SQL Server can maintain hundreds of connections without corruption of data. In addition, SQL Server has more security than the file-based Access.

SQL Server also offers the use of stored procedures and triggers, which not only speed up the data transfer, but also allow the use of *transactions*, which enable you to execute several queries at once, thereby making it possible to do batch updates or deletes from your Web site.

Note   *One possible scenario to illustrate stored procedures and transactions is a bank transfer. In that scenario, the first account is debited and the second account credited. When using a transaction, the two actions always occur together. If you were to execute them as separate queries, the possibility would always exist that one would execute and the other one would have some sort of error, which would have serious consequences.*

In addition, stored procedures give you the capability to retrieve return values from your database. Suppose you are adding a new customer to an e-store, and the user has entered all of his personal information. Some sort of *primary key* in the database would be necessary to enable you to access that particular user in the future. When the data is being inserted, the primary key could be returned via the stored procedure to enable you to continue to access the database from within the Web application.

Microsoft SQL Server is an expensive proposition if you are deploying your site from a dedicated server. On the other hand, if you are deploying your Web application from an ISP, it's certainly a viable option. Most ISPs charge a small surcharge of $20 to $40 a month for the use of SQL Server, but it's well worth it if you plan to run a professional Web site.

If you have a Windows server, 120-day trial versions of SQL Server are available from Microsoft that will give you an opportunity to try out the advanced features of this database.

Oracle

Oracle is an option for a Windows-based server, and also is available for most other servers, making it the best choice for a Web site deployed from a non-Windows-based server. Many would argue that it is the best choice for a Windows-based server as well. Oracle has all the advanced features of Microsoft SQL Server, and many more, and it also runs on a Linux or Sun Solaris server.

WEB SITE DESIGN AND CONSTRUCTION

Oracle also has advanced security and encryption features for maintaining secure access to sensitive data. Also, auditing features enable you to track users and the way that the data is accessed, for even greater security.

Oracle has a tight integration with JSP servers, and has native drivers available for OLE DB using ColdFusion 5 or ASP. ColdFusion 5 also allows native connections to the Oracle server, making the connection faster and more reliable than an ODBC connection. You can order trial versions of Oracle databases from the Oracle Web site at www.oracle .com, and a Lite version is also available for download.

MySQL

MySQL has become immensely popular in this day of open-source software. Despite being lightweight, it is a sophisticated, efficient, and powerful database application. On top of that, the price can't be beat, because you can download it from various sources for free or for a small licensing fee.

MySQL is available in many shapes and sizes, and is available for most config-urations of servers. Whether you decide on a JSP, ASP, PHP, or ColdFusion site, you can probably find a MySQL implementation to meet your needs. You can usually find the latest builds on the MySQL Web site, at www.mysql.com. In addition, ODBC drivers are generally available for MySQL, to make connections quick and painless in the design-time environment. The MyODBC driver also is available from the MySQL Web site. For JSP, several JDBC drivers are available for MySQL.

One of the disadvantages of the open source databases is that they lack an "administrator" or GUI, thus making the design and implementation of the database a little tricky for beginners. An option here is to design your database in Microsoft Access and then convert your data to MySQL format using one of the utilities that are freely available from the Web. Also, front ends for MySQL are becoming more commonplace. One of the best of the GUIs for MySQL is the *urSQL* utility, available at www.urbanresearch.com/software/utils/urbsql/.

MySQL is highly optimized for Web applications, and is one of the fastest and most lightweight databases around. Reading from the database is very fast with MySQL, although it's slower with insert, modify, and delete tasks. Also, it doesn't offer some of the advanced features of its rivals, such as stored procedures and nested *Select* statements.

DB2

DB2 is IBM's answer to Oracle and SQL Server. It is an enterprise-level database, much like Oracle and SQL Server, and is very well integrated with IBM's WebSphere JSP server. If you plan to implement a JSP site on a WebSphere server, DB2 certainly is a good choice for the database. It also has ODBC drivers for simple connections, and even has a native OLE DB driver, if you happen to be using ASP. ColdFusion Enterprise Server contains native database drivers for DB2. DB2 will run on a variety of systems, such as Windows, OS/2, Linux, Sun Solaris, and HP-UX.

The DB2 Control Center is reminiscent of SQL Server Enterprise Manager. Databases can be created here from scratch or from built-in templates. Database creation is a simple process with the Control Center. Views and stored procedures can also be created easily.

In addition, DB2 has a highly optimized in-memory search engine, making text searching one of its strong points. It was designed from the ground up with the Internet in mind, according to in-house blurbs.

IBM usually has free downloads of this enterprise-level database for developers available from its Web site, but the commercial version is pricey. Still, in terms of functionality, it's right up there with Oracle and SQL Server.

PostgreSQL

PostgreSQL is one of the best open source databases around, and much more powerful and feature-rich than MySQL. It is starting to rise in popularity as an alternative to MySQL for PHP-based Web sites. PostgreSQL can be run easily in a Linux environment, and even comes pre-installed with some flavors of Linux, like Red Hat.

PostgreSQL is also available for Macintosh OS X, making it one of the most attractive database servers to run on the Mac platform. The Macintosh has not been a popular platform for applications that utilize database servers until OS X came out. Now there are several good candidates for a Mac application server and database server solution.

Other Databases

Although this chapter has covered the major databases, several others are available that you might be tempted to use. Filemaker Pro, for example, is a popular Macintosh database, but it's not a popular option for a Dreamweaver MX Web site. Other possibilities include dBASE, FoxPro, and Paradox, but these databases don't offer the robust environment of Microsoft SQL Server, Oracle, Sybase, Interbase, or IBM's DB2. Above all, real-world testing will give you the best indication of whether one of these other databases will do the job for you and your planned site. You can even use a text or CSV file for a database, using Microsoft's text ODBC driver, as long as you are aware of the limitations.

The Site

Now that you understand the basic elements that will make up your Web pages, and you know the background on some of the technologies available, it is time to learn about how Dreamweaver MX organizes and handles all of the individual files that make up a Web site. Rather than forcing you to deal with the parts of your site individually, Dreamweaver MX allows you to define a site structure that allows the sharing of assets and connections so that your pages work together as an efficient application.

The modern Web site is more than a collection of static pages. Today's sites contain pages that work together and are dependent on one another. Dreamweaver MX allows you to define Web applications that organize your files and assets and allow you to treat them as a whole for development, deployment, and synchronization.

The Site panel is the central organization point for your site in Dreamweaver MX. From here you can define sites, each with their own unique properties, and easily switch between sites, even if they use different server models and reside on different servers around the Internet. You can use Dreamweaver MX's built-in FTP program to send and receive files from any of your sites. And you can manage the growth of your site by adding pages, editing pages, and structuring the directories and pages that make it up. But in order to manage a site, you must first define it.

The Site panel in Dreamweaver MX by default will be docked in the Files panel group (shown in Figure 8-1). The Files group also includes the Assets panel, which contains all assets for your site and favorites from other sites as well. The Site panel is

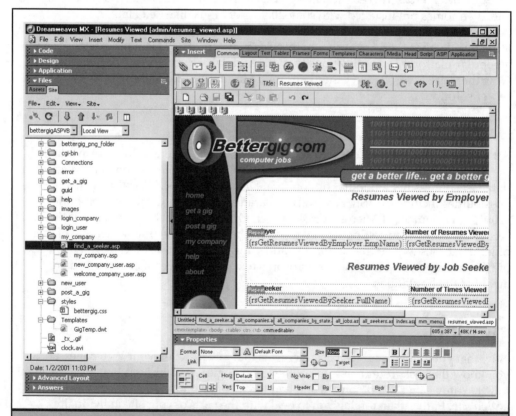

Figure 8-1.   The Site Panel in Dreamweaver MX occupies a small panel on the left or right (shown here on the left) grouped with your other tools.

where all site-related activity takes place, such as creating, copying, moving, and deleting files and directories. Files can be dragged from here into the main editing window or double-clicked to open. Also, the contextual menu contains many helpful commands that relate directly to file and site management.

The Site panel can also be expanded. The expanded Site window in Dreamweaver MX allows you to see the site laid out in a Windows Explorer–like view (see Figure 8-2).

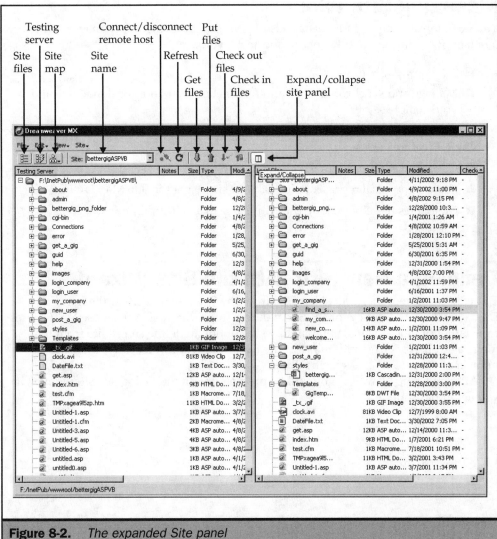

Figure 8-2.   *The expanded Site panel*

By default, your Testing Server pages are on the left-hand side and the local pages are on the right-hand side. This can be changed through a Preference menu item.

The Site window is also the FTP interface to the remote server, acting as an effective FTP program that allows you to keep track of all of your sites and keep site notes and even individual page notes. Indeed, you can even "check out" and "check in" pages in a team environment, so that two people aren't working on a page at the same time.

Managing Site Files

You can control many high-level aspects of your site using the Site Manager. With menu options, buttons, and keyboard shortcuts, you can:

- Add new pages to your site.
- Manage and synchronize files and folders between your local machine and your remote server.
- Control changes to your site files by using Dreamweaver's Check In and Check Out features.
- Check links.
- View a graphical representation of your site using the Site Map Layout.
- Cloak files thereby making them invisible to all site operations, such as *get* or *put*.

Defining a New Site with the Site Wizard

To define your new site, select New Site from the Site menu in either the main Dreamweaver MX window or the Site window. In addition, if you choose Define Sites from either of those menus, you will have the option to define a new site from that menu as well. As is true with many of the Dreamweaver MX features, there are a number of ways to do this specific thing.

After choosing New Site, you will be presented with the dialog box shown next if you are in Basic mode.

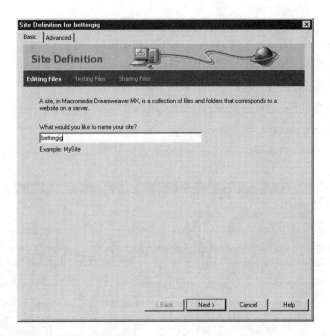

This is the Site Wizard. The Site Wizard is the easiest way to get your new site set up and running. You have to fill out six dialog screens for the site; each one deals with one aspect of the site definition. The first screen asks you for a site name. Next, you are asked to choose a server technology for the site. If ColdFusion is on your machine, the Site Wizard will detect it and tell you:

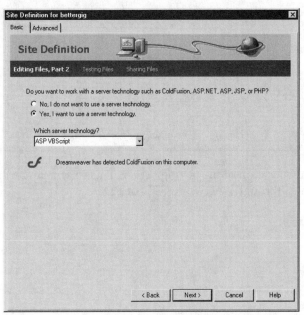

Next, you are asked where you want to work with the files. If you are working with an application server, you need to have your application server installed and running so that you can test your pages. The options are:

- Edit and test locally (my testing server is on this computer).
- Edit locally, then upload to a remote testing server.
- Edit directly on remote testing server using local network.
- Edit directly on remote testing server using FTP or RDS.

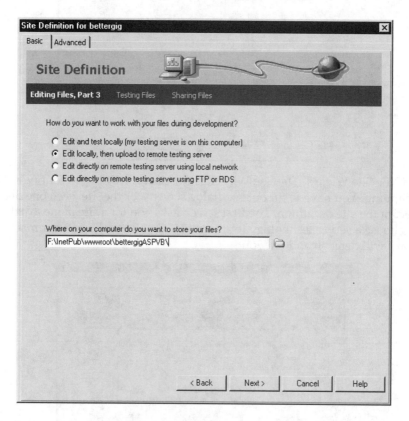

Next, choose the location of the testing server. This server can be local or remote, and you can connect through a network, FTP, or RDS.

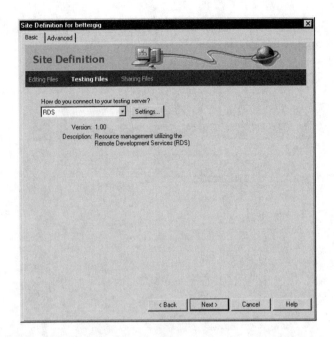

If you have an FTP or RDS connection, you'll have to set up the username, password, and directory info for that connection:

Next, you have to set up the URL for your testing server. If this is on your local machine, it is probably http://localhost/mysite or some variation of that. If you are testing on a remote server, the IP address can go here, as in http://192.168.0.72/mysite. The Test URL button on the interface enables you to test the setting:

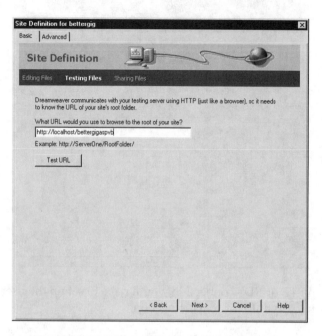

This one setting is the most important setting of the whole procedure. If this test URL is not correct, your database connections won't work, and your pages won't preview. A common mistake is to leave off the "http://" or forget to include the folder that your site is in. This setting is critical to all operations inside of a dynamic site.

 Some people coming from a static site background sometimes don't realize that every page in a dynamic site has to go through the application server rather than be browsed with a file path. Make sure you set up the URL prefix properly so that if you use dynamic pages you'll be able to browse them through the Web server rather than directly through the file system and browser.

Next, you can set up Dreamweaver MX's check-in/check-out feature. With this feature enabled, anyone on your team working with Dreamweaver can communicate about the site via site notes and can check out pages so that others will know that the page is being worked on. This prevents two people from working on a page at the same time, as shown next.

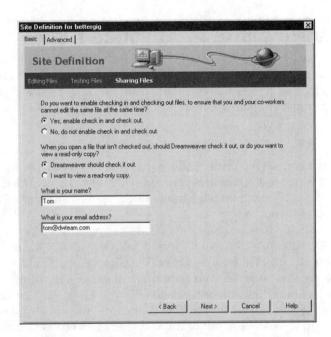

Finally, the information you've entered is shown in a summary page. You can click Back to edit the information, or click Done if you are satisfied that your site is set up properly. You can always go back and edit the information using the Advanced tab if you need to make any changes:

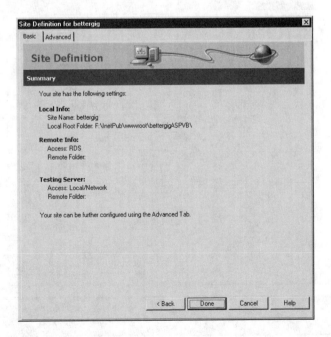

WEB SITE DESIGN
AND CONSTRUCTION

Defining a New Site in Advanced View

The Site Wizard takes you through the complexities of setting up a site, but you can set up the site manually as well. In addition, if you need to go back and make changes in your site settings, you can do so more easily from the Advanced view of the Site Definition dialog box, if you know exactly where everything is.

Local Info

The first screen that you see (Figure 8-3) allows you to enter the basic information for your site. The Site Name text box allows you to give the site a name. The name should follow general naming conventions (alphanumeric characters) and should be descriptive of the site that you are about to work on.

The Local Root Folder text box allows you to either type in the local path to your site (for example, **c:\inetpub\wwwroot\myrootfolder**) or click the folder icon, which brings up the Choose Local Folder dialog box. The Choose Local Folder dialog box will allow you to browse to a folder on your hard drive or create a new folder, if necessary.

Underneath the Local Root Folder box is the Refresh Local File List Automatically check box. Checking it will cause the site files in the local window to be refreshed if any changes are made to the site. Whether or not you check this box is personal preference,

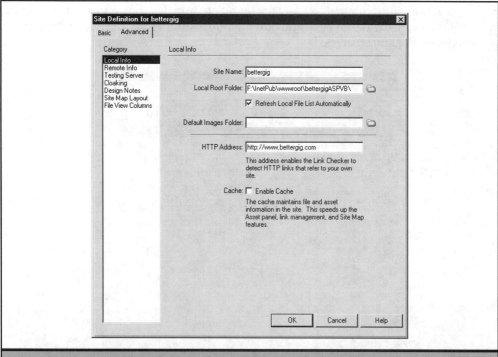

Figure 8-3.   *Local Info page of the Advanced tab of the Site Definition dialog box*

because you may find that it slows down the program if your site tree is refreshed too often. You can refresh files manually by clicking the Refresh icon in the taskbar of the Site window.

Fill out the HTTP Address text box with the actual Web address of your site. This is optional and is only there to help the Link Checker detect links in your site that might reference pages by the full URL, rather than a relative file path.

Checking the Enable Cache check box causes Dreamweaver MX to write a cache file to the hard drive that allows most link management, Asset Panel, and Site Map features. The cache file is stored in the SiteCache folder under Configuration.

Remote Info

The Remote Info dialog screen (Figure 8-4) is where you enter information about the remote Web server if it differs from the local environment. The choices for the Access drop-down box are listed in the following sections.

None

No other user input is required for this option. This assumes that the local and remote hosts are the same.

WEB SITE DESIGN AND CONSTRUCTION

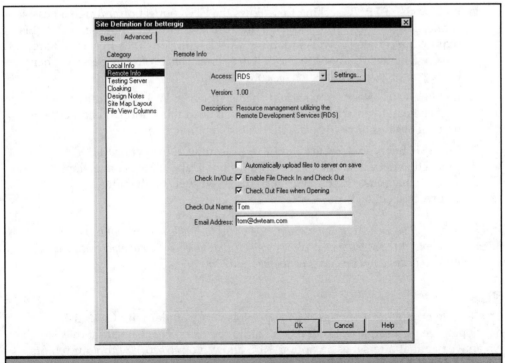

Figure 8-4. The Remote Info dialog screen of the Advanced tab of the Site Definition dialog box

FTP

This option assumes that you will have FTP access to your remote host. With this option, you will have to input the following information:

- **FTP Host** This is the actual address of your FTP site, such as ftp.bettergig.com or 192.168.0.4. A common mistake here is to use the protocol name as a prefix, such as ftp://www.bettergig.com or ftp://192.168.0.4. It's not needed and will cause errors.

- **Host Directory** This is the physical directory on the server where your files are located. If, for example, you log in and have to browse to the bettergig directory to get to your site, you would enter **bettergig/** in the box. If you log in directly to your site root, all you need in this box is a forward slash (/).

- **Login** This is your FTP username.

- **Password** This is your FTP password, which is shown as asterisks for security. You can check the Save check box next to the password so that you don't have to enter the password each time, or you can leave it unchecked.

In addition to the preceding information, you will also need to decide whether you want to check the following check boxes:

- **Use Passive FTP** Checking this allows the FTP connection through a passive connection (through your local software rather than the remote server) that is required in certain firewall situations. Check with your Web host if you are unsure whether you need to check this option. This is often necessary when using personal firewalls, such as Zone Alarm.

- **Use Firewall** Again, you should check with your Web site administrator or Web host if you are unsure whether you need this option. If checked, the firewall options have to be defined in the Preferences menu.

- **Use SSH Encrypted Secure Login** This setting allows your FTP connection to be encrypted. There is a technote about SSH connections at www.macromedia.com/support/dreamweaver/ts/documents/secure_connection.htm.

Macintosh users need to download a SSH client to enable a SSH connection. There is a technote at the Macromedia Web site about the subject at www.macromedia.com/support/dreamweaver/ts/ documents/mac_ssh.htm.

RDS

The Remote Deployment Service (RDS) option is very popular with ColdFusion developers, being a staple of ColdFusion Studio for years. This is the first release of Dreamweaver that offers it as an option. RDS allows you to work with your remote files as if they were on your local hard drive.

For RDS to work you have to be using a ColdFusion server (or have a ColdFusion server installed on your remote host.) You don't have to be building a ColdFusion site, but the server has to be running.

To set up RDS you need the server name, RDS username, RDS password, and the directory of the Web site on the machine running RDS.

Local/Network

This option can be used if your Web server resides on the same physical network as your local machine. You can type in the path to the folder on the network drive, or you can click the folder icon to browse to the folder. The path will show up as a network path, as in \\machine2\inetpub\wwwroot\bettergig.

There is also a check box to allow the remote file list to be refreshed automatically, which occurs if you make any changes in the site.

SourceSafe Database

This feature was introduced in UltraDev 4 and allows you to use Microsoft's Visual SourceSafe 6 on a Windows machine or MetroWerks Visual SourceSafe version 1.1.0 on a Macintosh to allow for version control of your files. The options available when you click the Settings button are as follows:

- **Database Path**   This is the SourceSafe database name that you are using. This can be set up in the Visual SourceSafe Administrator interface.

- **Project**   This is the name of the project as it is set up in the Visual SourceSafe Explorer.

- **Username**   This is the username that is set up for you by the SourceSafe Administrator.

- **Password**   Your SourceSafe password, which is also set up from the SourceSafe Administrator.

- **Check Out Files When Opening**   This option allows you to check out the files so that others can't access them while you work on them.

To use the SourceSafe Database option, you must have Microsoft's Visual SourceSafe 6.0 installed on the server and a SourceSafe client such as MetroWerks Visual SourceSafe 1.1.0 (Macintosh) or Microsoft Visual SourceSafe 6.0 (Windows PC).

If you try to check out a page that's been checked out by another user when using SourceSafe, you'll get an error message. You will also be able to use the built-in features of SourceSafe for version control, allowing you to track and view different versions of your pages so that you can see all the changes that were made on each version (see Figure 8-5).

WebDAV

WebDAV is the Web-based Distributed Authoring and Versioning standard and is a set of extensions to the HTTP protocol. It was developed as an easy way for developers

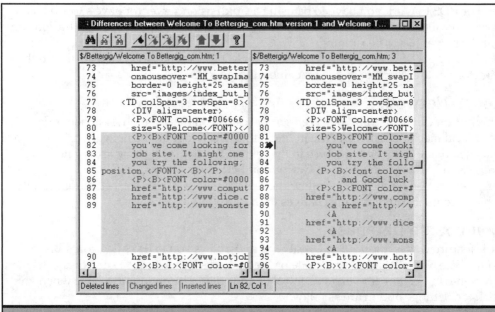

Figure 8-5. Microsoft's Visual SourceSafe allows you to view changes made between different versions of a file.

to share files. When a Web folder is set up with WebDAV, it acts as a virtual drive that you can access via HTTP. You can check out files and lock them to keep others from making changes while you are working on the file. You can find more information about WebDAV at www.Webdav.org. Currently, several open source WebDAV servers are available.

To connect to your remote site through a WebDAV server, choose the WebDAV option, and then click Settings, which will bring up a dialog box for the following attributes:

- **URL**   This is the URL that you will use to access the remote server.
- **Username**   Your WebDAV username.
- **Password**   Your WebDAV password.
- **E-mail**   Your e-mail address to identify you to other WebDAV users of your site.

Check-in/Check-out

Also from the Remote Info page you can set up your check-in/check-out features:

- **Enable File Check In and Check Out**   Check this option if you want to be able to use Dreamweaver MX's built-in check-in/check-out features for accessing pages. If you decide to check the box, you need to fill in a few other items: the check box for Check Out Files When Opening and Check Out Name and E-mail

Address fields. These items are to identify you to your coworkers as the person who has checked out a given page.

- **Automatically Upload Files to Server on Save**   This option will cause Dreamweaver MX to upload the files automatically without any intervention.

- **Check Out Files When Opening**   This option will cause the file to be automatically checked out when you double-click the file in the Site panel.

Testing Server

The third page of Site Definition options allows you to define the settings for the Testing server (shown in Figure 8-6). This page was labeled App Server Info in UltraDev 1.0, and Application Server in UltraDev 4. The settings that are defined are a little different, but the functionality remains the same. In UltraDev 1.0, there was a Live Data Server that could be set to Local Web Server or Remote Web Server. In addition, there was a Live Data Prefix option that confused many people. Macromedia changed these features to avoid potential confusion.

The Testing server is generally either your local machine or a remote staging server. This is where the temporary files are stored when you browse a page using the Preview

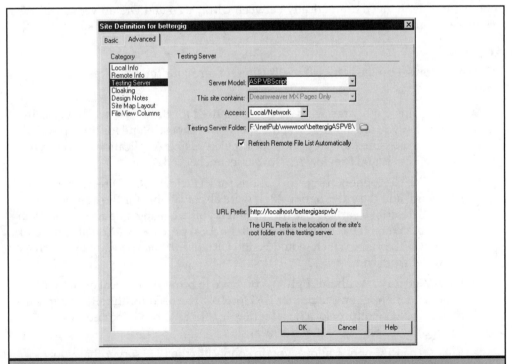

Figure 8-6.   *The Testing server is where your application server is running and your pages are tested from.*

In Browser functionality. The application server that your site is going to use needs to be running on this machine.

The new settings allow you to define the testing server and specify whether it's a local/network drive, FTP site, RDS server, or no access, which effectively shuts off the Live Data and Preview in Browser features. The parameters that you need to enter for the Testing Server are listed in the following sections.

Server Model

This can be one of several choices: ASP VBScript, ASP JavaScript, ASP.NET C#, ASP.NET VB, ColdFusion, JSP, PHP MySQL, and None. If you choose None, you will only be able to edit and browse HTML and other nondynamic files. In the future, these choices can be extended to include other server models.

 The First server model developed by a third party was released in December 2000 by Unify Corporation for J2EE 1.2 for UltraDev 1. InterAKT, a company in Romania, later offered a complete PHP server model for UltraDev 4.

This Site Contains

For ColdFusion, you can specify whether the site contains Dreamweaver MX pages only, UltraDev 4 pages only, or a combination of the two. This is because the underlying code changed dramatically between UltraDev 4 and Dreamweaver MX, so both server models were kept to maintain compatibility with existing sites.

Access

This is how you set up the access to the Testing server. Your three choices are as follows:

- **None**   This option means no server is required for the pages, which basically means that you are defining a static site. If you choose None for this option, you have to make sure that the option for Preview Using Application Server in the preferences section Preview In Browser is unchecked.

- **FTP**   The FTP option brings up options for FTP Host, Host Directory, Login, Password, and the other options that were also available for the Remote Info page, as described earlier. Use this option if you are using a database and Web pages located on the remote server with no local previewing. You also have to set up a URL prefix, which would be the URL used to access your site, such as www.bettergig.com.

- **Local/Network**   With this option, you have to browse to a local or network folder and then set up the proper URL prefix to be used for the site. A typical prefix would be http://localhost/bettergig/ for a Web site located in the bettergig folder at the root of the local site.

- **RDS**   The RDS option allows you to connect to the RDS server that you specified in the Remote tab.

Cloaking

This feature allows you to turn off certain operations of Site panel to certain file types or folders. The operations affected are:

- Put and Get
- Check In and Check Out
- Reports
- Select newer local
- Select newer remote
- Sitewide operations (such as search/replace)
- Synchronize
- Asset panel contents
- Template and library updating
- Automatic link updating

Cloaking cannot be done to individual files, but only to file types and folders. For example, if you want to exclude PNG files from these operations, you can enable cloaking and put the PNG extension in the list of cloaked files. Folders can be cloaked directly from the Site panel, not from this configuration screen. To cloak an individual folder, right-click a folder in the Site panel and choose Cloaking | Cloak.

Design Notes

One way to communicate with others on your team is by using "sticky notes." These notes are typically pasted to the desktop or monitor of the person that the note is intended for. Dreamweaver MX has its own version of the sticky note, called a *design note*. Design notes can be attached to any page in the site by using the Site window or Site Map.

This page (see Figure 8-7) allows you to use Design Notes in the site, which are stored in the _notes folder under your site root. The actual Note file is an XML file with an *.mno extension that Dreamweaver MX will read internally. Each page that has a note attached to it will cause a file to be generated in the _notes folder on the remote site (and the local site). A typical note is shown in Figure 8-8.

The dialog box has two check box options:

- **Maintain Design Notes** This option effectively turns the feature on.
- **Upload Design Notes for Sharing** This feature will cause your notes to be uploaded to the remote server so that other people working on the site can have access to them.

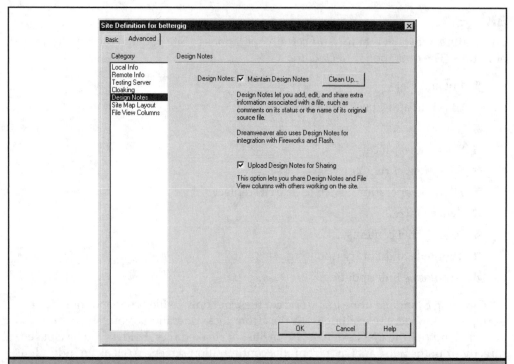

Figure 8-7. The Design Notes dialog box allows you to maintain notes about your pages and gives the option to upload them to the server.

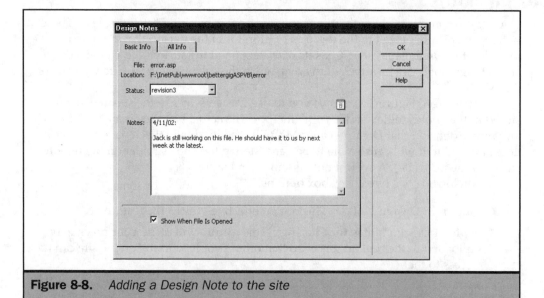

Figure 8-8. Adding a Design Note to the site

Design Notes are a great way to log changes to a page so that other people working on the site can follow what is going on. If everyone is religious about adding notes every time they make a change, the design process can be a lot smoother.

In addition, the Clean Up button will cause all orphan notes (notes not associated with a file) to be deleted.

Design notes can be set to open automatically when you open a file. This is especially handy when working in a collaborative environment. If your teammate has made a change to the file, he or she can leave a design note attached to the page. You will be able to see the note the next time you open the page. This way, it is less likely that another person will overwrite any changes in the page.

Site Map Layout

The site map is a visual representation of the linking in your site. For instance, if you have a home page with links to six pages, the site map will show the home page with six arrows pointing to the six files that the home page links to. Each link in those six pages will have a corresponding arrow pointing to pages that the link points to. The Site Map Layout dialog box contains the following attributes to help define the site map:

- **Home Page**   This is your site's home page. You can either fill in the complete path or browse to it by clicking the folder icon.

- **Number of Columns**   This is the number of columns in the top level of the site map. For instance, if you have a home page that links to five pages under it, you might set up the number 5 for Number of Columns.

- **Column Width**   This is a number between 70 and 1,000 to define the width of each column in the site map. If you make your columns wider, you will be able to fit more items in each group, but you may have to scroll left and right to see the whole map.

- **Icon Labels**   These two radio buttons are labeled File Names and Page Titles. You can choose one or the other for the label of the page on the site map.

- **Options**   These two check boxes allow the following:

  - **Display Files Marked as Hidden**   Allows you to display pages such as template files, which are generally hidden from view.

  - **Display Dependent Files**   These are files that may not be linked to a page, but they are dependent on the page via a form action or some other means. This box allows these pages to be shown as well.

File View Columns

The last dialog box in the Site Definition window allows you to configure the look of the site panel by allowing you to pick, choose, and even define the columns that you are going to show (see Figure 8-9). For instance, you could have a Programmer column to show the name of the person responsible for a given page, or you could have a Date

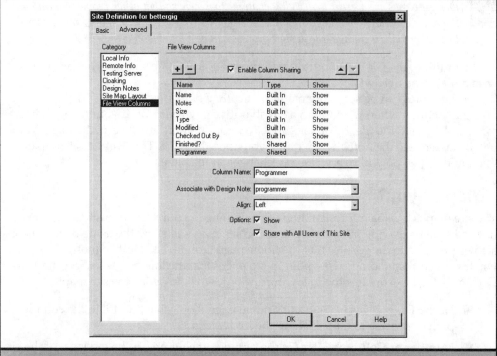

Figure 8-9.   *The File View Columns dialog box allows you to create custom columns that appear in the Site panel.*

Due column listing specific due dates for pages. An Important Message column could allow you to place a short message that will be seen by everyone on your team when they open up the site. You can use your imagination and create columns that pertain to your own situation and add the appropriate design notes to each page. The way this is done is to define your column with a column name and then associate it with a design note. When you create a design note, you can give the note a name/value pair that will cause it to show up in the column.

   You can add a new column by clicking the plus (+) button above the column list, or you can take one away by clicking the minus (–) button. The up arrow and down arrow buttons allow you to arrange the columns in a particular order. The attributes associated with the File View Columns window are as follows:

- **Enable Column Sharing**   This check box enables the columns to be shared between users. In other words, the columns that you see are the same columns that the rest of your design team will see.

- **Column Name**   A unique name that will be the column heading in the Site window.

- **Associate with Design Note**   The name of the design note that the column will get its information from. For instance, if you have a design note named Important

Message, every page that has an Important Message note attached to it will show the actual contents of the message in the column whenever someone opens up the Site window.

- **Align**   The alignment of the data in the column (left, right, or center).
- **Options**   There are two check box options:
  - **Show**   Allows you to turn off certain columns if you don't want them to show in the Site window.
  - **Share with All Users of This Site**   Determines whether the column is something that will be stored on the server for all users to see, or if it's only to be seen on your particular computer.

Preplanning

Preplanning your site is the most important aspect of the creation of your site. This holds true for any site, but is especially true with sites created in Dreamweaver MX. By planning the site out beforehand, you can save yourself a lot of work in the long run by taking advantage of features like templates, library items, the Asset center, and site-wide link checking.

Proper preplanning also enables you to keep better track of your files. A typical Web site could have thousands of files in it—from graphics to hit counters to the actual Web pages themselves. An organizational folder structure is something to decide on early on in the process. The Bettergig site has folders for each of the main navigation links on the home page. Each folder contains the files that are required for the specific page that the link points to. For example, the Get a Gig link has a corresponding get_a_gig folder name containing the get_a_gig.asp file and other files that are required by that page.

Images typically will have their own folder as well—depending on the size of your site, you may decide that you need subfolders for different categories of images. Perhaps you have a graphical menu that has a set of images that go with it—this could have its own folder. However you decide to organize your site, it's important that the organization is easy for you and your fellow developers to follow. In addition, the folder structure should be identical on your local site and the remote site.

Site Reporting

The site reporting functionality is accessed by using the Site menu in the Site window and clicking Reports. You'll see the dialog box shown in Figure 8-10. The options are as follows:

- Current Document
- Entire Local Site
- Selected Files in Site
- Folder

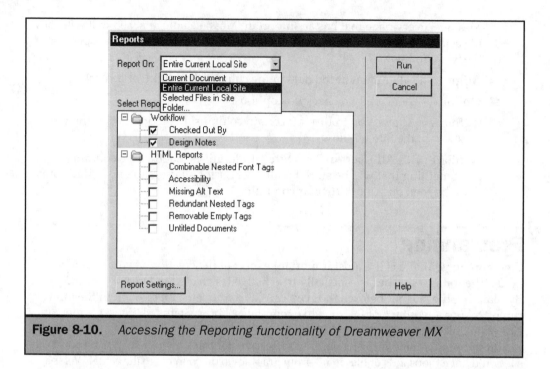

Figure 8-10.   *Accessing the Reporting functionality of Dreamweaver MX*

The report will tell you the current state of the site—who has the files checked out and all the design notes of the site. In addition, it will allow you to check for certain HTML aspects, such as font tag nesting, untitled documents, and removable empty tags. The report can be viewed or saved to an XML file. In addition, the Open File button allows you to open the file in question and edit the line in question. For example, if your file has a default title (Untitled Document), clicking the Open Document button will open up the document in question, and the title tag of the file will be selected in HTML source view.

Synchronizing the Site

When more than one person works on a site, there is often a need to make sure you have the most recent files on your own machine. That's where the Synchronize feature comes into play. Clicking Synchronize in the Site menu of the Site window updates the site with the most recent files. This feature works with selected files or an entire site. There are three options to choose from when you are ready to synchronize:

- Put Newer Files to Remote
- Get Newer Files from Remote
- Get and Put Newer Files

After clicking the Preview button, the synchronization begins, and a list of files is built. You can then choose which files you want updated, or choose to update all of them.

Adding New Pages to Your Site

Dreamweaver MX offers several methods of adding pages to your site.

■ From the File menu, select the New option. This will bring up the new file dialog box, allowing you to choose a document type. After choosing one, a new document window will appear. This new document window is not strictly related to your site at this point. You must select Save As from the File menu and save it in your site folder with a unique file name.

■ From the Site panel File menu, select the New option. A new file will appear in either the local or remote side of your site, depending on which was selected when the menu option was selected. This new file's name will be highlighted, ready for you to give it a unique name.

■ In either the Local or Remote side of the Site window, right-click (or COMMAND-click on the Macintosh) to display the pop-up menu. Select the New File option from the menu. This option works just like the New File option in the File menu on the Site panel.

■ Press the keyboard shortcut CTRL-N. Depending on the way you have your preferences set up, this will either open a new document immediately, or it will open the New Document dialog box.

■ Use the Standard toolbar and click the new file icon. This will also bring up the New Document dialog box.

No matter which method you choose, you will create a new page onto which you will need to add content. If you chose to create a new page from a template, you will have a page with some elements on it, and you will need to fill in only the content area that was defined when the template was created. If you chose any of the other methods, you will have only a blank page and you will need to add all of the content that will make up the page.

Once a new page is created, you can use any combination of the available Dreamweaver methods to add content to it.

Adding a Database to the Site

Obviously, if you are using a server-based database such as IBM's DB2 or Microsoft SQL Server, the choice of database location won't be necessary. However, if you're using a file-based database, such as Microsoft Access, you'll have to decide where to put it.

The database should always be stored in a location that is inaccessible to the Web browser. A location outside of the site root is preferable, but you can store it in a protected folder within the site also. The best possible location would be in a folder that is not even accessible to the Web server.

In many cases, such as a situation in which a hosting company hosts your site, you may have access only to the site root. If this is the case, you might be able to put your database in a protected folder on the root and place your site in another folder within the root, as well. For instance, if your site root were located at the location e:\inetpub\wwwroot\yoursite, you could place the database in the folder e:\inetpub\wwwroot\yoursite\cgi-bin, and put your actual Web site into the folder e:\inetpub\wwwroot\yoursite\sitefiles.

Obviously, if the file-based database is stored somewhere other than your site root folder, you will need to set up a way to get the database uploaded to the server. You could use a third-party FTP program, or you could use Dreamweaver MX's FTP capabilities and simply set up a new "site" that would contain only the database. The purpose of this dummy site is only to get your database to and from the server. Obviously, if you are testing your site, you should be working with a duplicate of the live database. Never use the actual live data for testing purposes.

Database Permissions

If you've stored your database on the server, the folder that it is in must have certain permissions set up for it, or you may not be able to write to the database. On a Windows server, simply setting the permissions to Everyone within Windows NT is not good enough. The folder needs to have the *IUSR_machinename* permissions set for full control (or read/write) so that the Web server can access the database. Then, within IIS or the Web server of your choice, you can set up the permissions so that the Read permission is turned off for the folder (see Figure 8-11). Browsing the folder won't be permitted, but the Web pages will be able to access the database through scripting.

You should also check to make sure that the database itself has IUSR permissions set up for it. If you happen to be copying the database from another location, the database might not automatically pick up the permissions from the folder that you are putting it in. Many times you'll have to explicitly set up the permissions for the database itself within Windows NT. Again, this applies only to the file-based databases such as Microsoft Access.

Setting Up Data Sources for the Site

We know that the database is the key data source for the site, and Chapter 20 is going to describe the various connection methods for the database. Once a connection is made to the database by defining the connection within Dreamweaver MX, it is available to all pages in the site. Beginning with UltraDev 4, the connection information is stored in a

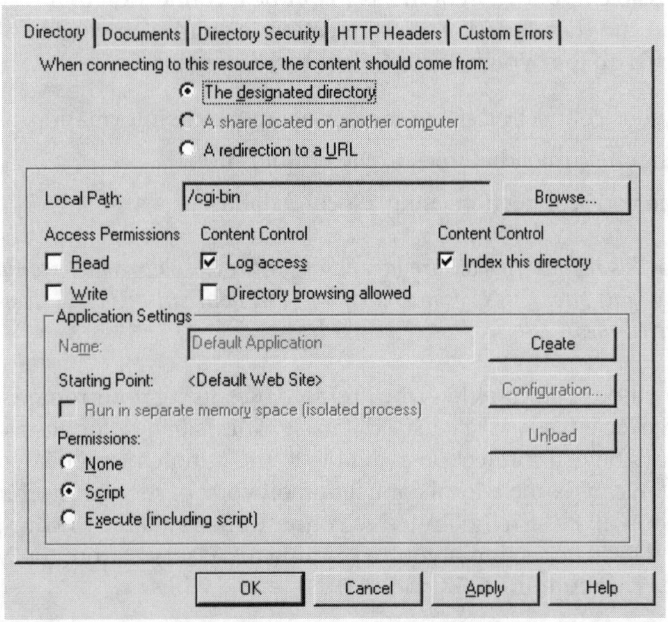

Figure 8-11.   *The Microsoft Internet Information Server properties dialog box allows you to set permissions for folders.*

central Connections folder within your site. All pages have access to and can include this one file to get the connection information. Also, by changing this one connection file, the connection is effectively changed on all pages that use the connection.

The database connection information is stored in a file that is named after your connection. For example, if you named your connection "connBettergig" in a ColdFusion site, your connection file would be connBettergig.cfm. The file is kept in the Connections folder in your site root. Every connection that you define for your site will be stored in this folder. Also, when you first install Dreamweaver MX, you might find that all of your connections from UltraDev 1 (which were machine-wide connections) are migrated to the Connections folders for each site.

The pages that you use the connection on will use an include file that will dynamically include the connection file when a user browses the page. Having the connection stored in an external file like this allows you to make site-wide connection changes and have the changes reflected on every page.

Note   *The ColdFusion server model doesn't utilize a connection file like this, but you are free to use one if you desire, because of the flexibility of the ColdFusion Bindings panel.*

Another possible application of this is to define a connection that resides on your remote machine and then redefine the connection to store it on your local machine for a local database. To do this, you have to follow these steps:

1. Define your connection using the remote database information.

2. "Put" the site (upload all files to the remote site).

3. Redefine your connection using a local database.

If you use this method, make sure you don't write over your remote connection file when uploading your site. This is easy to do if you Put your entire site. Always choose to Put only selected files.

With this method, you can view your remote files using your remote database; you can also view the local files using a local database. This is handy for people with laptops who don't always have a connection available to the remote machine. Note that this works only if you can define a local connection on your particular machine. If you have a Macintosh, you will be strictly limited to connections available to your particular Mac, such as a JDBC connection if you're running a JSP server from the Mac or a PHP connection if you are running OSX and PHP.

Other Data Sources

One thing that you may not realize is that other data sources, such as Session or Application variables, can be set up and accessed by all pages in the site. By defining a Session variable on one page, it will appear in the Bindings panel in other pages in your site. By planning out your session variable usage at the beginning, you can save yourself some time by having the variable available when you need it. There is also less margin for error when you drag and drop a data source on the page rather than typing it in by hand each time you need it. This is especially true of JSP pages, in which upper- and lowercase letters are treated as different entities. To define a site-wide Session or Application variable, follow these steps:

1. Open up the Bindings panel.

2. Click the plus (+) sign to create a new data source.

3. Click Session Variable (or Application Variable).

4. Give the variable a name and click OK.

5. The variable is now available as a data source on all pages in the site.

Defining data sources in this way allows you to easily display variables, but there is no built-in method to assign values to variables. You can do this by hand or with a Server Behavior.

Site-Wide Find/Replace

One feature that you may find very handy is the site-wide Find and Replace dialog box. Find/Replace has become a standard feature in most computer programs—and it's one of the most often used features, as well. One thing that you might not be aware of, however, is that in Dreamweaver MX you can do the searches on a site-wide or directory-wide basis. This makes it especially handy for changing something that is on every page in the site, such as a color.

The Find and Replace dialog box (Figure 8-12) has several unique features that are worth mentioning.

Find In

This drop-down list gives you several options for finding text and code within your site:

- **Current Document**   This is a standard search in the currently opened document.
- **Entire Local Site**   This allows you to do a site-wide search and replace.
- **Selected Files in Site**   This allows you to multiselect files in the Site window and restrict your search to certain files.
- **Folder**   This allows you to do searches on any folder on your hard drive. In effect, it turns Dreamweaver MX into a powerful search-and-replace tool that you can use outside of Dreamweaver MX.

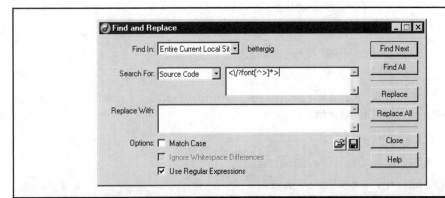

Figure 8-12.   *The Find and Replace feature of Dreamweaver MX is very powerful, especially when using regular expressions or tags.*

Search For

This is a drop-down list that gives you four search options:

- **Source Code**   Allows you to search through the source code of your page—scripting, server-side code, tags, and actual text all fall under this category. In short, if it's in the document in any form, you can find it with this option.

- **Text**   Narrows the search to the actual text that is viewable on the page. For instance, if you want to search for the word *color*, but you don't want to match the instances of the word in the HTML, then you could use the Text option.

- **Text (Advanced)**   Allows you to refine your search to text that is contained within or outside of certain tags. You can access further refinements and several other options by clicking the plus (+) button.

- **Specific Tag**   Allows you to not only search for specific tags, but also to search for attributes within those tags and even set the attributes for a tag site-wide. For example, if you wanted all <td> tags to have a mouseover attribute set to a certain function, you could do it here. Or, if you wanted all <font> tags with a size of 2 to have their size attribute changed to 3, you could do it with this feature.

Specific Tag: Using the Tag Replace Functionality

One of the most powerful aspects of the find/replace dialog is the tag functionality. For example, if you wanted to replace all <th> tags with <td> tags, simply set it up as follows:

Find In	Current Document
Search For	Specific Tag th
+ –	(click – to remove all choices)
Action	Change Tag
To	td

Changing a tag is just one of the many types of functionalities available for working with tags. Some of the others include:

- Search for Specific Tag:
  - With attribute (attribute name)
  - Without attribute (attribute name)
  - Containing (text)
  - Not Containing (text)
  - Inside tag (tag name)
  - Not inside tag (tag name)

You can also group these together, such as:

- Search for:
  - Specific tag: font
  - With attribute: size
  - Without attribute: color
- Action:
  - Set Attribute: color
  - To: #000066

Some of the other actions available for tag matches are as follows:

- Replace tag and contents
- Replace contents only
- Remove tag and contents
- Strip tag
- Change tag
- Set attribute
- Remove attribute
- Add before start tag
- Add after end tag
- Add after start tag
- Add before end tag

Options

The Options for the Find/Replace dialog box are shown as check boxes, and are as follows:

- **Match Case**   This allows you to match only those words that match the case exactly. For example, *font* wouldn't match *Font*.

- **Ignore Whitespace Differences**   This allows you to do searches in which spaces, line feeds, and tabs have no effect on the outcome of the search.

- **Use Regular Expressions**   If you know how to use Regular Expressions, you can take advantage of the powerful RegExp features of the Find/Replace dialog. For example, to search for all instances of things contained within quotes, you could use the following RegExp:

```
\"[^\"]*\"
```

This RegExp searches for a quote, and then gets all characters up to and including the next quote character that it finds. The next RegExp will search for all opening and closing layer tags.

```
<\/?layer[^>]*>
```

Find/Replace Source Example

What if you want to find all references to "Copyright © 2001" in the site? This is a simple case of scanning the source code for the following string:

```
Copyright &copy; 2001
```

For the settings, you'll want to choose the following:

Find In	Entire Local Site
Search For	Source Code
Find	Copyright © 2001
Replace With	Copyright © 2002
Match Case	unchecked
Ignore Whitespace Differences	checked
Use Regular Expressions	unchecked

That was almost too easy, but the one key thing to remember about this query is that you have to check Ignore Whitespace Differences. When Dreamweaver formats the HTML in your document, there may be times when line breaks are inserted in places you wouldn't expect. The preceding example might appear like this in your document:

```
Copyright
&copy; 2001
```

If you hadn't checked the box, this occurrence would not have been replaced. What happens if your copyright notice looks like this in the source code?

```
Copyright &copy; <b>2001</b>
```

Now, the same query won't work. You might think that you can search Text instead of Source, but when you do that, you have to use actual unencoded text, such as the copyright symbol instead of the HTML equivalent:

Find In	Entire Local Site
Search For	Text
Find	Copyright © 2001
Replace With	Copyright © 2002
Match Case	unchecked
Ignore Whitespace Differences	checked
Use Regular Expressions	unchecked

One concern here is that when you replace the text, the bold tags will be lost on the replace as well. What can you do? This is one area where regular expressions can come into play:

Find In	Entire Local Site
Search For	Source code
Find	(copyright[^&]*©[^2]*)(2001)
Replace With	$1 2002
Match Case	unchecked
Use Regular Expressions	checked

If you are unfamiliar with regular expressions, this one needs some explanation. Regular expressions use pattern matching, much like when you perform a Find Files function on your computer using an asterisk (such as *.txt) only much more powerful. For a full set of regular expression patterns, consult a JavaScript book, such as *JavaScript: The Complete Reference* (Powell and Schneider, Osborne/McGraw-Hill, 2001). For now, here's an explanation of the regular expression in the preceding example:

- ◾ (copyright[^&]*©[^2]*)(2001)

The first thing you should take note of is that there are two groups:

- ◾ (copyright[^&]*©[^2]*) is the first group.
- ◾ (2001) is the second group.

The first group is the part of the code that will stay the same. You can represent this as $1 in the Replace dialog. When you have groupings in regular expressions, you refer to the groups as $1, $2, $3, $4, and so on. This way, you can retain sections of your code while replacing others. The code is broken down as follows:

- **copyright** Self-explanatory. This will be an exact match of the word.
- **[^&]*** Anything and everything up to a & character.
- **©** Again, this is an exact match of the HTML representation of the copyright sign.
- **[^2]*** Anything up to a 2 character.

The second grouping consists of the number 2001. This will be replaced in the query by using the first saved group ($1) and substituting the number 2002 for the remainder. By doing this, you are effectively replacing all occurrences of the copyright statement, and keeping any existing tags in place. On a huge site, this could be a timesaver.

Open and Save Buttons

The Open and Save buttons are the folder and disk icons in the dialog box. If you can't figure out what these buttons have to do with searching and replacing, consider this: A search that consists of complex search criteria may be useful in other sites, and you can save it and reopen it for reuse. After you have gone through the trouble of defining search criteria, such as removing all Netscape <layer> tags from the site, you may decide that the search was worth saving so that you don't have to type it in again. You can also save a complex RegExp that requires testing and retesting until you get the exact expression that you need.

The search criterion is saved in the Queries folder under the Configuration folder in Dreamweaver MX. The file is saved with a .dwr extension and is an XML file that Dreamweaver and Dreamweaver MX can translate the next time you want to use the same search criteria.

When you save a query (a find/replace expression with a .dwr extension), you can move these queries from machine to machine and even share them with other people. The files are located in the Queries folder.

Summary

The Site features of Dreamweaver MX will make your life easier if you know how to take advantage of them. Whether you are a single developer or a member of a team, proper planning and utilization of the time-saving features of Dreamweaver MX will help you deliver a well-organized site in a fraction of the time that it once took.

Chapter 9

Advanced Page
Design Tools

E ven as just a basic HTML editor, Dreamweaver is a powerful environment. It makes simple HTML easier to work with because of its visual representations of the site you are building. But Dreamweaver is much more than that. It contains advanced tools to help you build and polish your site. Dreamweaver MX builds upon existing features and adds more of its own, some of which whole books could be written about.

In this chapter, we cover seven tools included in Dreamweaver that assist with advanced page design. They are:

- Advanced template features
- Snippets
- The Tag Inspector
- Code view features
- Validation
- Target Browser Check
- The link checker

Advanced Template Features

We covered some basic template functionality in Chapter 4. Now let's look at the new things that templates can do in Dreamweaver MX. The general purpose of a template is to provide a consistent design to groups of pages. Basic templates provide a way to lock down documents and protect them from changes, except for certain areas, called editable regions, that will hold the information unique to each page. As your sites get larger, however, you will likely have times when the basic template does not allow you the proper balance of protection and design freedom. Dreamweaver MX has added a wealth of features to its templates that should allow you a greater degree of flexibility when designing templated pages.

One of the things that Dreamweaver's new template structure kind of supposes is that there will be template authors who design templates and page authors that use those templates. Rather than thinking of templates as time savers that maintain consistent design elements in your sites, these new features encourage you to think of templates as ways to restrict what page authors can do within the regions they are assigned to manage. What you end up with is an odd marriage of content management and pseudo-dynamic content that is a useful, if not ideal, way to control page design.

Nested Templates

One of the most useful new features in Dreamweaver MX's templates is nested templates. Nested templates enable you to create templates with specific portions of your site in mind. For instance, a company site might have a basic template for the main part of its site, which has content on it that remains consistent throughout the site. A particular section of that site, the products section for instance, might need to contain all of that basic information, plus additional content that is consistent on every product page. The support section of the site might have its own content, but not need the product content on its pages.

Using nested templates, you can create a base template for this kind of site. Then, you can create a new page based on that base template, add new content and editable regions for the products portion of the site, and save that page as another template. When basing a new products page on that second template, all of the content from the base template and the products template remains locked, and only the editable regions defined in the products template are available for new content.

Need to define an even more specific set of consistent design content for a specific subsection of products? You can define another template based on the products template, include new design elements and editable regions, and save that document as an additional nested template. Pretty soon you won't have any room left to put anything new, but you can see that nesting templates allows you to take advantage of site-wide or section-wide design elements while creating templates for specific areas of your site. We build some nested templates in the example a little later in this chapter.

Optional Regions

Optional regions are regions of a template that depend on some variable factor. It could be a setting that your page designer makes or something that occurs in the code on your page, but optional regions determine what content to display based on some decision that is made after the template has already been created.

Optional regions use a subset of the JavaScript language to build expressions that can be evaluated at run-time. The results of these expressions determine what content is displayed and what is hidden. You can use the following operators within your expressions:

- **Literals**   Numeric literals, string literals (double-quote syntax only), Boolean literals (true or false)
- **Variable references**
- **Field references**   the "dot" operator
- **Unary operators**   + (positive), – (negative), ~ (bitwise not), ! (not)
- **Binary operators**   +(addition), – (subtraction), * (multiplication), /(division), % (modulus), & (bitwise and), | (bitwise or), ^ (bitwise XOR), && (Boolean and), | | (Boolean or), < (less than), <= (less than or equal to), > (greater than), >= (greater than or equal to), == (comparison), != (not equal), << (left shift), >> (right shift)
- **Conditional (ternary) operator**   ?:
- **Parentheses**   ()

You can access the objects that are defined as a part of the Expression Object model, which are only two. The *_document* object contains the document-level template data. You can access the title of the document (and each of the other template parameters) with *_document.title*.

The *_repeat* object offers information about a repeat region in a template. You can acccess the following:

- **_index**   The numerical index (starting at 0) of the current entry.
- **_numRows**   The total number of entries in this repeating region.
- **_isFirst**   Evaluates true if the current entry is the first in the repeating region.
- **_isLast**   Evaluates true if the current entry is the last in the repeating region.
- **_previousRecord**   The *_repeat* object for the previous entry. Evaluates to an error if you access this property from the first record in the region.
- **_nextRecord**   The *_repeat* object for the next entry. Evaluates to an error if you access this property from the last entry in the region.
- **_parent**   Gives the *_repeat* object reference for the parent repeating region in a nested repeating region.

Note   *You can access the properties of the _document and _repeat object implicitly by typing "title" instead of "_document.title," for instance. If there are conflicting properties, the _repeat object is referenced. If you know that conflicts exist with the names of parameters in the document and the repeating region, reference them explicitly.*

Repeating Regions and Repeating Tables

Repeating regions and repeating tables are used when the template designer knows that a page needs a certain kind of content, he or she just doesn't know how much of it. For instance, a products page on a Web site might include a region for inserting a picture and a description of a product. The template designer knows that there will be products on that page, just not how many and if that number will change. The product region can be made into a repeating region so that the page designer can add and remove the region and insert picture and product descriptions as the catalog changes. The example later in this chapter shows how to use these features.

Editable Tags

Editable tags allow even finer control over page design elements by allowing the page designer to edit only certain types of tags. For instance, a template designer may know that an image needs to go in a certain place, but not what image it should be. The template designer can make the <src> tag of the image editable, allowing the page designer to alter the image that is included on the page.

1. On your template page, insert an image.

2. Save the page so that the reference to the image file is relative and not a path to your hard drive.

3. Select the image, and choose Modify | Templates | Make Attribute Editable from your menus.

4. A dialog box will appear so that you can choose which attributes to make editable. You can select only those attributes that currently exist as a part of the tag. You can use the Add button to add additional attributes that were not included with the default tag, such as an alignment tag if you aren't sure where to position the image.

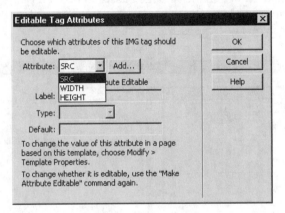

5. Click the Make Attribute Editable option, which makes additional settings available to you.

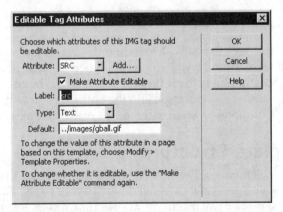

6. You can select a label for the tag, like Image Source, so that the page designer knows what to provide. This is especially important if you will have multiple

images on the page for which a source will be set. The label will let the designer know what he is editing. You can also choose what type of entry is to be made so that the page designer is given the proper interface to make his or her choice. Finally, you can select a default value.

7. You should also make the WIDTH and HEIGHT attributes of an image tag editable, unless you know for sure that every image the designer may pick from is the same size. If you don't, the WIDTH and HEIGHT will remain that of the original image, and the page designer's selection may get stretched or squashed with no way to fix it.

8. Click OK.

9. When a page designer creates a page based on this template, your default image will appear. He or she can select Modify | Template Properties and edit the attributes you have exposed.

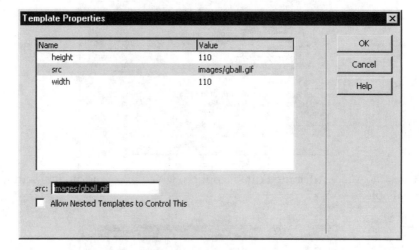

You can use editable tags to restrict access to only certain properties of a page's design, down to the tag attribute level. The combination of these new template features gives template designers the ability to create structures that can be customized and reused by page designers or clients without exposing the entire design to the ravages of the unaware novice. Let's use some of them together to create a template structure for a site.

Creating a Template Structure

You can use all of the elements of Dreamweaver's new templates to construct complex templates that control all aspects of the overall design of your pages. Each of the templates you build can then be made available to the appropriate designers who will use them to customize the individual pages in your site. In this section, we build a set of templates that uses many of the features we have just discussed.

A Basic Template

Create a base template for your site. All of the other templates will be based on this template. This site is for Big Harry's Sporting Goods and will provide templates to display the different sections of the site and the products and services in those sections.

1. Create a new document. Place a one-column, two-row table with a width of 500 pixels centered on the page. Insert the main header graphic for your site in the top row of that table.

2. In the second row, right-click and select Templates | New Editable Region. This will create an editable region with the name you specify in the second row. If you created a regular document instead of a template document, you will get a message that says your document will be converted to a template. Select File | Save As Template and give your template a name. You have created the basic template.

A Nested Template

3. Use File | New menu to create a new document. Select the Templates tab in the New Document dialog box. You can select which site's templates you want to

create a document from and then select which template to base the document on. Choose the template you just created and click Create.

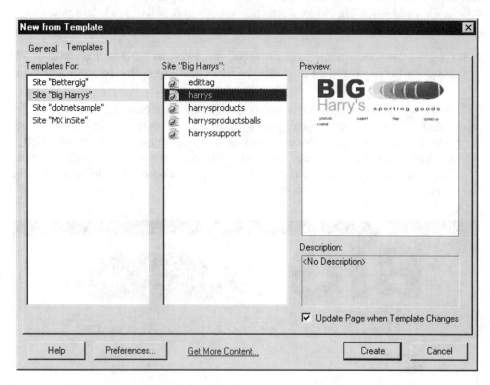

4. Because the second row of the table is editable, you can put whatever you would like there. Insert a two-column, one-row table with a width of 100 percent. Give the left cell a colored background and type **Products** in it. This will be the template for the products section of the Web site.

5. This side of the table will be locked and the page designer will not be able to change it, but you may want to let them change the background color you chose for the cell. Choose the left table cell and select Modify | Template | Make Attribute Editable from your menus. Select the BGCOLOR attribute for the <td> tag. Click the Make Attribute Editable option and provide a label, type, and default settings. Click OK.

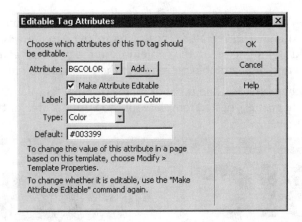

6. Insert a New Editable Region in the right-hand cell of the table.

7. Select Save As Template from the File menu and specify a name for your template. You have just created a nested template. Any new documents created based on this template retain the content from the original template plus the editable tag and new editable region from the nested template.

8. Create another new document based on the original template and perform the same steps to create a nested template for the Support area of the site.

Adding Optional Regions

9. Create a new document based on the Products template you just created. We are going to continue refining the template by adding Optional Regions to the Product Content editable region. But first, we need to pass through the editable tag we created to the next level of templates. Select Modify | Template Properties. You will see the Product Background Color tag that we made editable. Select it and check the Allow Nested Templates To Control This option. This will pass the editable tag through to the next layer of templates.

10. Insert a one-column, three-row table with a width of 100 percent in the editable region of the template.

11. Insert a product image in the top row of the table. In fact, enter three images of different products side by side in the table cell. Then insert a fourth graphic with the word "Sale" to be displayed when a product that is on sale is shown.

12. We are going to create optional regions so that the page designer can choose which of these images should show for the page he or she is working on. He or she can then create pages for each of the products by using the images the template designer has provided.

Note

You may be wondering why someone would go to all this work when Dreamweaver can so easily provide product information from a database. Well, the fact is that not everyone will have that option, and these template features provide some of the same functionality to those that need an HTML-based site. A data-driven application would be preferable due in large part to the maintenance issues that these types of templates raise as products come and go.

13. Right-click your first image and select Templates | New Optional Region. A New Optional Region dialog box will appear. In the Basic tab, name the region and select whether to show the image by default. Click OK.

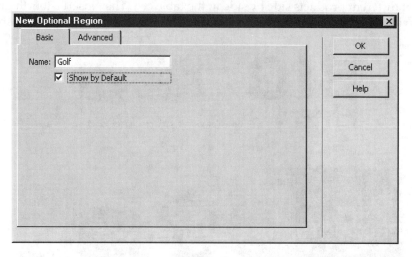

14. You will notice a little blue If tag on the image. It says "If Golf," indicating that if the *Golf* parameter is true, this image will show. Your page designer will be able to set whether the parameter *Golf* is true or not. Do the same for the other two product images, giving them unique names.

15. The Sale image needs to show only if the product being viewed is on sale. Select it and make it a New Optional Region. If only one product is on sale, you can

simply use the Advanced tab of the New Optional Region dialog box to select the appropriate parameter.

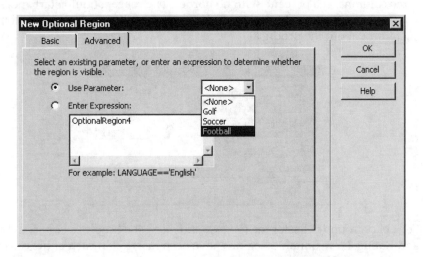

16. You can also create an expression to determine when the Sale image shows, perhaps because two products are on sale. Check the Enter Expression button and type **Golf | | Football**. This equates to Golf OR Football. If the page designer sets either the golf image or the football image to true, the Sale image will show.

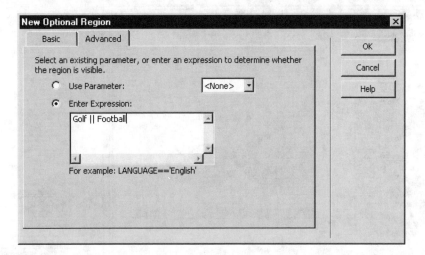

17. In the second row of your table, insert an Editable Region that will hold the Product description.

18. Place your cursor in the third row of your table. Select Insert | Template Objects | Repeat Table. In the dialog box, set the repeat table to two rows, three columns, 100 percent, with no border. The repeat should start and end on row 2 and be named Comments. This section will hold comments from customers about the product.

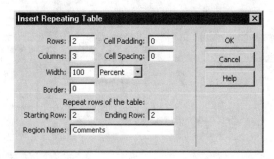

19. Set a background color for the top row and insert the headings Name, Comment, and Rating. New Editable Regions have been inserted in each of the cells in the second row so that content can be entered there.

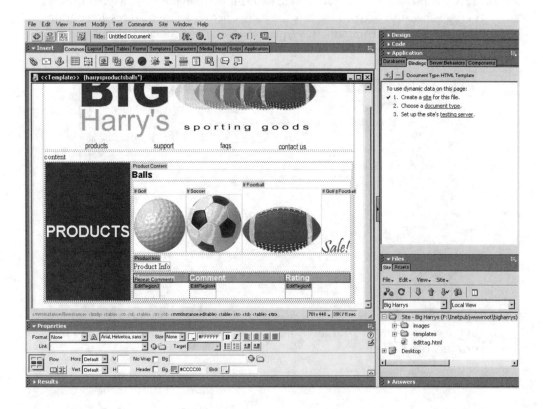

20. Save your file as a template. You have now created a third-level nested template using repeating regions, editable tags, and optional regions. Now let's look at putting this monster to use.

Using Your Template

21. Create a new page based on this latest template. Select Modify | Template Properties. The following dialog box will appear, allowing you to set the values of all of the template properties that you have built into the templates. Select each of the images and use the Show <image name> check box to determine whether that parameter is true, and whether the associated image should show on the page. The Sale image will be controlled by which images you set to true. Also, select the Product Template Background and use the color picker to select a background color for the table cell.

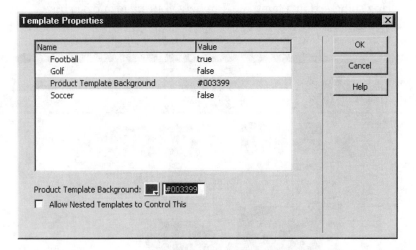

22. The repeating table provides a set of controls with which you can add a new row, subtract an existing row, or move the current row up or down.

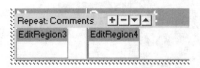

23. Enter name, comment, and rating information into the cells for each customer comment that applies to the product image you selected. Use the (+) button on the repeating table controls to add rows, the (–) button to delete rows, and the up and down arrows to move rows up and down in the order.

24. Finally, enter a product description in the second row editable region. After the text of the description, select Insert | Image Placeholder. In the resulting dialog

box, name the placeholder **Buy**, set it to 150×50, and select a color and Alternate Text. This will create a place where we will eventually place a Buy Now graphic button. We create that in Chapter 10.

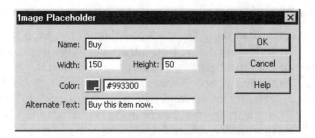

25. You have now created a product page by making some selections and entering some text in a template. Preview your page and see how everything works together.

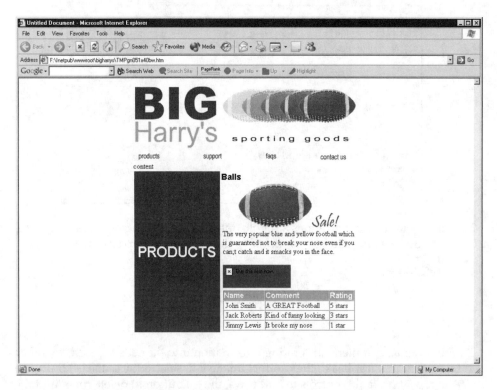

Templates in Dreamweaver MX are very powerful and very complex. They are a radical improvement over the one-layer templates that have been available in Dreamweaver for several versions. They can take some time to get your head around, but offer amazing flexibility and control for the template designer.

Snippets

Snippets are simple. And it is their simplicity that makes them so incredibly useful, as well as easy to use and easy to make. They are Dreamweaver extensions in the most basic sense, without the complexity of the extensibility layer. They will save you time and improve the consistency of your code. And you can begin using them in just minutes.

Snippets are new to Dreamweaver MX. They were an integral part of Homesite and ColdFusion Studio and have finally found their way into Dreamweaver. They can be used with HTML, JavaScript, server-side code—pretty much anything that you can include in your page.

Snippets were available in Dreamweaver and UltraDev 4 through a third-party extension from Massimo Foti. The native snippets of Dreamweaver MX work a bit differently, but there are sure to be additional snippets tools available from Massimo and team, like the snippets converter available at www.dwfaq.com/Snippets/converter.asp.

Using Snippets

Take a few minutes and browse through the large number of snippets that come with Dreamweaver MX. By default, you will find them in the Snippets Panel on the Code Panel Group, shown in Figure 9-1. Snippets are organized in folders that go several deep. High-level folders include Accessibility, Comments, Content Tables, Form Elements, and several others. Beneath those folders are subcategories.

Inside these folders are pieces of code. Some of it is design-time code such as form elements, including simple table structures to quickly create a login form to accept a username and password, for instance. Some of it is JavaScript or other "behind the scenes" code designed to do things like detect the user's browser or perform simple math functions. These pieces of code represent things that you are likely to use quite often in the course of building Web pages and provide you with a way of accessing them that is quicker and more consistent than looking it up and typing it in.

Using a snippet is as simple as placing your cursor, locating the proper snippet in the Snippets Panel, and double-clicking it. For example, imagine you want to create a login page with a form to accept a username and password. On a blank page, locate your cursor in the design view and then go to the Content Tables folder of the Snippets Panel. In Content Tables, you will see four subfolders. In these subfolders are four versions of the same basic concepts in tables with no border, with a one-pixel border, with an icon placeholder, and with a tabbed interface.

As convenient as snippets are, you will begin to notice some inefficiencies. For instance, were you to implement these content tables as objects instead of snippets, an interface would be available to ask you exactly how much of a border, if any, you wanted on the table, meaning that one object would serve a variety of needs rather than needing several almost identical versions of the same basic snippet.

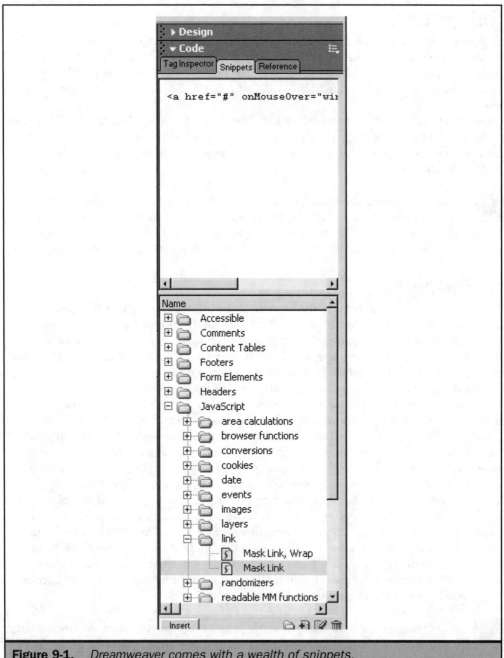

Figure 9-1. *Dreamweaver comes with a wealth of snippets.*

Select the one-pixel-border folder and click the Form: 2 Fields snippet. In the Snippets preview, you will see a representation of the code that will appear on your page, as shown in Figure 9-2.

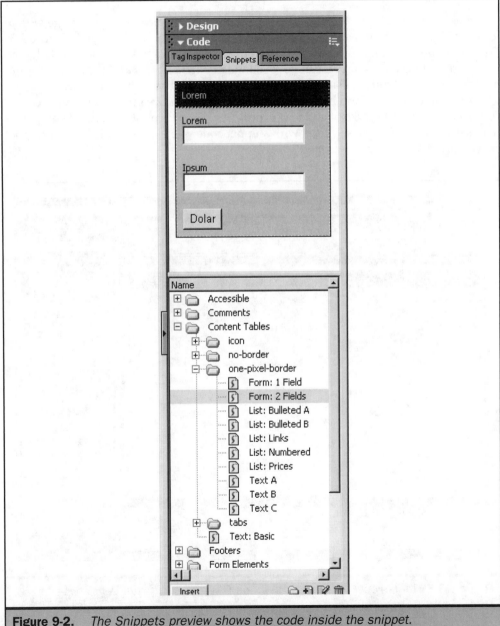

Figure 9-2. *The Snippets preview shows the code inside the snippet.*

The Snippets preview will show a graphic representation of the snippet code if it is available. You may also see actual lines of code. The snippet author can choose whether the preview shows design or code. The preview allows you to inspect the snippet you have selected before committing it to your page.

Double-click the Form: 2 Fields snippet. A table will be placed on your page with a form inside it. In that form are two form fields and a submit button, shown in Figure 9-3. The text is "greeked," meaning that standard nonsense verbiage is used as placeholders for where text needs to go. You can now change that default text and the properties of the form fields and button using the design view and the Property inspector.

This kind of snippet, and most of them that come with Dreamweaver, are block snippets. They insert blocks of code into your page. There is another kind of snippet that is designed to wrap a selection with snippet code. We examine this kind of snippet as we learn to create a new snippet.

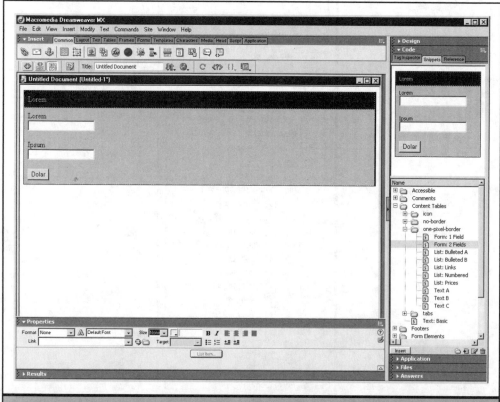

Figure 9-3. *The snippet places a form in the Design view of your page.*

Creating Snippets

There are some very useful snippets that come with Dreamweaver, but as we discovered with the Content Table Snippets, you may want versions that are slightly different to better serve your purposes. You can create snippets of your own to do anything that you find repetitive about your site development.

As an example, let's assume that you have some text that mentions your company several times. You may want to make each mention a hyperlink that takes the user to your home page. Let's create a snippet that wraps some selected text with an anchor tag.

First, place some sample text in the design view of a document. We are going to use Dreamweaver's built-in tools to generate the code we will use to build our snippet. Any text will be fine. Select a word in the text and use the Property inspector to add a link to your home page, as in Figure 9-4.

Open Code view and identify the two pieces of code that make up the hyperlink before and after the sample text you entered. Figure 9-5 shows the code.

The two bits of code are:

```
<a href="http://www.dwteam.com">
```

and

```
</a>
```

These are the bits of code that will be used to create our snippet.

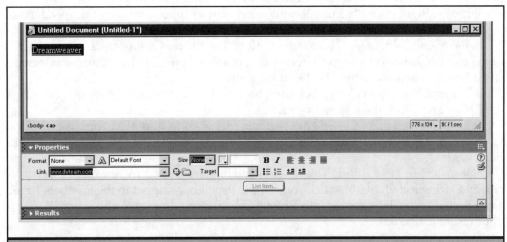

Figure 9-4.   *Add a link to your sample text in the Property inspector.*

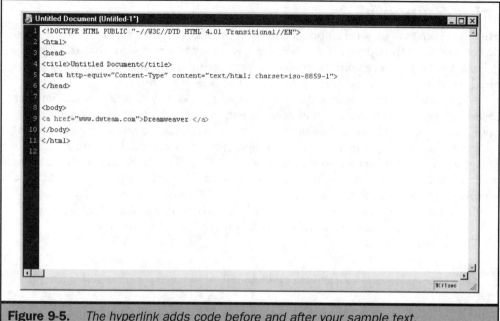

Figure 9-5.   *The hyperlink adds code before and after your sample text.*

In the Snippets Panel, right-click and choose New Folder from the menu. Make sure you are not pointing at an existing folder when you right-click (CMD-click on a Mac), or the new folder will be created inside the selected folder. Name your new folder MySnippets. Right-click MySnippets and select New Snippet. The New Snippet dialog box will open, shown in Figure 9-6.

In the Name field, enter **Home Page Link** to identify this snippet as a link to your home page. In Description, type a description of this snippet, such as **Turns a selected word into a hyperlink to the DWTeam Web site.**

In Snippet Type, select Wrap Selection because this snippet will place two bits of code before and after the selected word.

In Insert Before, place the first piece of our anchor code, and place the closing </a> tag in Insert After. And, because this is a code snippet, select Code in the Preview Type field. Click OK.

Now in any text in the design view, select and highlight one or more words with your cursor. Once selected, double-click your Home Page Link snippet in the Snippets Panel. The selected text will be turned into a hyperlink to your home page and you will see your results immediately.

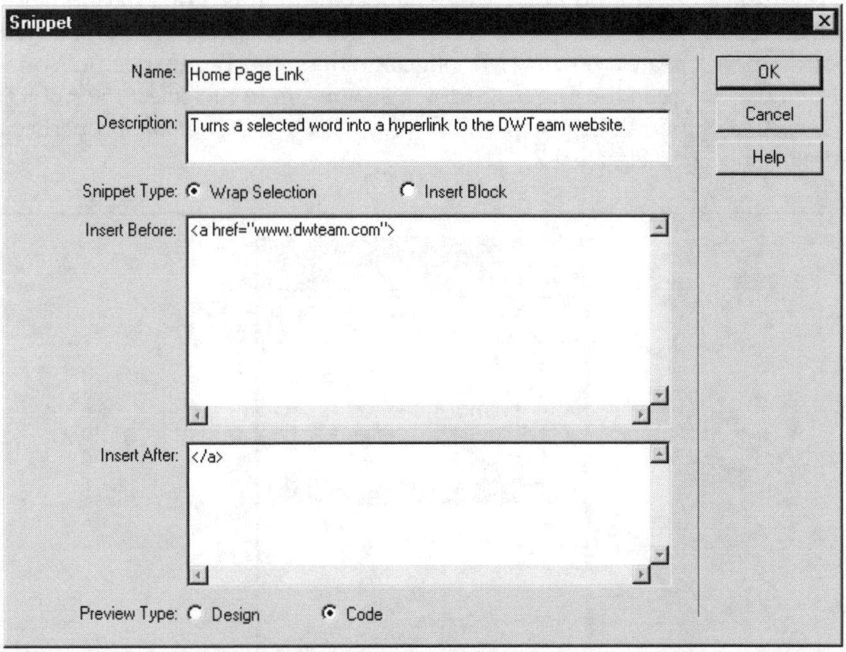

Figure 9-6.   *The new Snippet dialog box*

Note	*You can also begin the creation of a new snippet by selecting a bit of code and selecting Create New Snippet from the right-click context menu. The highlighted code will be inserted in the new Snippet dialog box.*

Snippets are a powerful and easy to use addition to Dreamweaver MX. You will find more snippets available at the Snippets exchange at www.dwfaq.com, and you can quickly learn to create your own. They can hold both client-side and server-side code, so anything you find yourself doing repeatedly is a great candidate.

The Tag Inspector

Web pages are made up of a series of tags. These tags are the component parts of the HTML language. Most HTML pages will have at least Head, Title, HTML, and Body tags. Those tags often have properties that define how the tags display or behave. An entire Web page has what is described as a structure of tags that make it up. You can view and edit this structure, including the tags and their properties, in the Tag Inspector.

The Tag Inspector is found in the Code Panel Group. It is a two-part panel with the tag structure in the top and the list of properties associated with the selected tag in the bottom part. Create a new HTML page and open the Tag Inspector. You will see a basic HTML structure in the Tag Inspector. Use your mouse to select the <BODY> tag. The lower section of the Tag Inspector will display a list of the available properties for the <BODY> tag, shown in Figure 9-7.

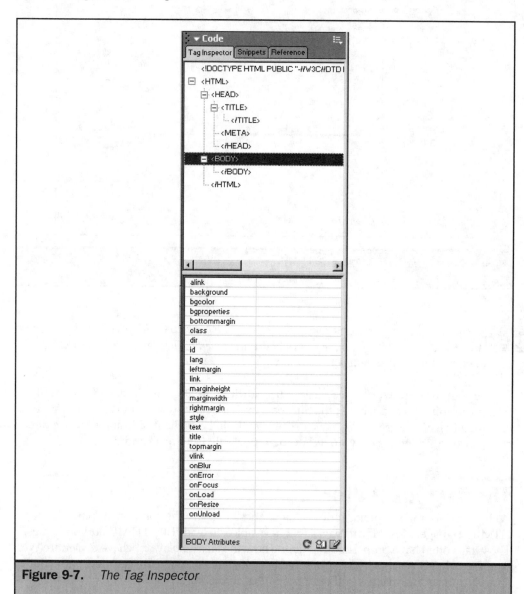

Figure 9-7.   *The Tag Inspector*

You can edit each of the properties for each tag here in the Tag Inspector. Select the *alink* property, for instance, and you will be presented with a color picker and a lightning bolt. You can enter a value for this property by typing in a hex value for a color, using the color picker to select a color, or using the lightning bolt to identify a dynamic source for the property. This makes it easy to define HTML tag attributes based on information gleaned from a database recordset.

You can also use the Tag Inspector to add and delete tags. Right-click any tag to display the context menu. From there you can delete a tag, or add a new tag before, after, or inside the selected tag.

When adding a new tag, you can add either an empty tag or a regular tag. An empty tag is a tag that does not require a closing tag, such as <br> for line break. There is no </br> tag to close the break, and using one is not allowed according to the latest HTML specification. A regular tag has both an open and a close tag, such as <table> and </table>. Even if you select the wrong menu choice, Dreamweaver is smart enough to know whether most common tags require a closing tag.

The Tag Inspector is a great way to review the structure of your site, identify a certain place with its structure, and quickly edit properties of the tags that make up your page.

Code View Features

It has been Macromedia's goal to encourage users of its HomeSite and Cold Fusion Studio products to make the move to Dreamweaver MX as their primary coding environment. That goal meant that Macromedia had to address some serious deficiencies in the program's code editor. Dreamweaver ships with HomeSite+, which is a hybrid of HomeSite and ColdFusion Studio, so Macromedia realizes the remaining value of those products, but they have made some significant advances in Dreamweaver's coding tools.

The first improvement is extensive and customizable code coloring. The spectrum of code types, from HTML tags to server-side language code, can be assigned particular colors in the Preferences dialog box. This makes comments, HTML tags, properties, and values easy to identify in chunks of code.

One of the best new features in all of Dreamweaver MX is its code completion. Code completion in Dreamweaver is context-sensitive, meaning that Dreamweaver knows what kind of page you are working on and displays the appropriate code possibilities for each page type. For instance, in an HTML page, start typing a new HTML tag by typing < in code view, and code completion will appear giving you a choice of tags. As you continue to type, the listing adjusts to display the tags that match what you have entered so far. So type **<im** and Dreamweaver jumps to the <img> tag. Press ENTER or TAB to select the highlighted tag and continue.

In an ASP page, code completion works much like Microsoft's Intellisense. Type **Response** and Dreamweaver will display the appropriate *Response* object selections, such as *Write, Cookie,* and *Redirect.* Select the code you want and Dreamweaver completes the line and gives you the proper structure for the parameters that are expected by the code you have entered. The section that needs completion is highlighted so that you can simply type in the variable portion of the command.

The Tag Editor provides a powerful way to manage the events and methods assigned to your tags. You can access the Tag Editor, shown in Figure 9-8, by right-clicking a tag in design view and selecting Edit Tag or by using the Input bar in code view to insert a new object.

The Tag Editor lets you set several types of properties for your tags. The General section is basically a duplicate of the Property inspector and allows you to set basic properties for the particular tag you have selected.

The Style Sheet/Accessibility section lets you assign CSS classes and Accessibility properties to your tags.

Note   *Accessibility is an important consideration for new sites, especially because new government regulations mandate accessibility standards for sites it contracts for. But Accessibility is more than a law; it is a necessity for certain people to make reasonable use of your site using special equipment such as Braille and voice browsers.*

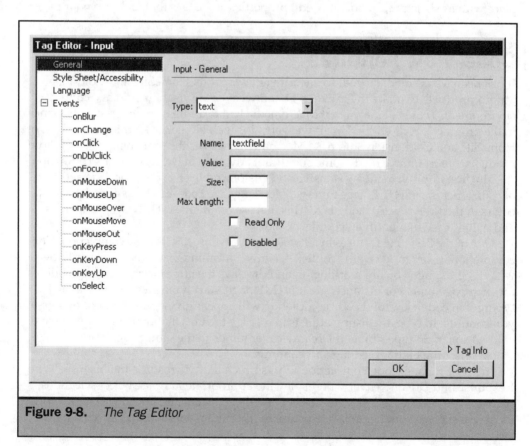

Figure 9-8.   *The Tag Editor*

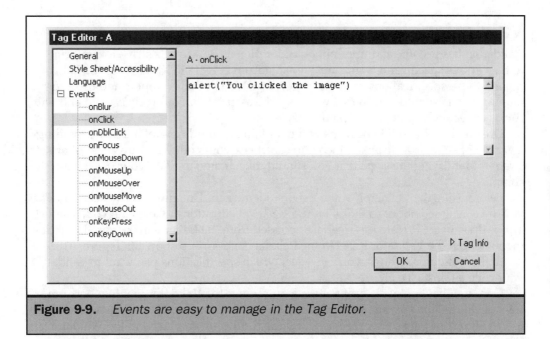

Figure 9-9. *Events are easy to manage in the Tag Editor.*

Some tags, such as the <image> tag, will also have a Dynamic section with indications of which browsers the various properties are supported in. Use these features carefully if you are concerned about browser support.

One of the best parts of the Tag Editor is the Events section, which lists the available events for a selected tag and allows you to enter code for each of them in the editor. This makes management of the events for your tags much easier. See Figure 9-9 for an example.

Finally, the lower section of the Tag Editor provides reference information about the selected tag, shown in Figure 9-10, which includes available properties and suitability in the various browsers.

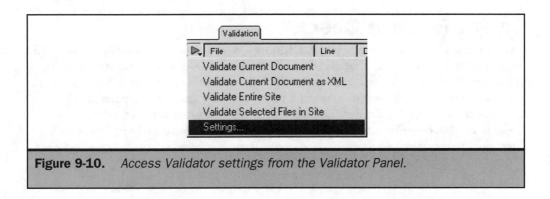

Figure 9-10. *Access Validator settings from the Validator Panel.*

Validation

Validation has become an important consideration as developers strive to conform to the various specifications that are available from HTML, to XHTML, to XML. In theory, these specifications provide targets at which both developers and browser manufacturers should aim so that we can all be assured that our code is valid and will run as expected on a variety of platforms.

Dreamweaver's Validator helps you maintain standards compliance by providing a variety of standards against which you can check your code. Dreamweaver offers a report identifying the steps that you should take, if any, to bring your pages into compliance.

Before using the Validator, you must first identify for Dreamweaver which standards you are concerned about so that it knows what specifications to test your code against. This is done in the Preferences interface accessed from the Edit menu or from the Settings menu item in the Validator Panel in the Results Panel Group shown in Figure 9-10.

In the Validator settings, you can select which specifications you want to validate your code against (see Figure 9-11).

Once you have set your preferences, you can use the Validator menu to perform several validations on a single page or an entire site. Once you choose what you want to validate, your pages are processed, and the results are displayed in the Validator Panel. You are provided with an icon that indicates the severity of the issue, the name of the offending file, the line number where the problem exists, and a description of the problem. Double-clicking any item in the report opens the appropriate file and takes you to the referenced line number.

You can right-click any item in the report and select More Info to see if more information about the issue is available. You can also use the icons at the right of the panel to save the report or to browse it in report format, as shown in Figure 9-12.

Although you can get away with nonvalidating pages for many simple HTML jobs, as you move into more strictly regulated file types, such as XML and XHTML, it will become more important for you to ensure that your code meets the requirements of the standard. Dreamweaver's new validators are a great help in that effort.

Target Browser Check

One of the decisions to be made when planning a new site is which browsers you plan to support. Once you make that decision and settle on a target browser, you need to make sure that your code will render successfully in it. Dreamweaver MX has a Target Browser Check that allows you to select a target browser and check a page or set of pages against a stored definition. Dreamweaver will then report to you whether your code meets that definition, which should be a pretty good clue as to whether it will display as you expect.

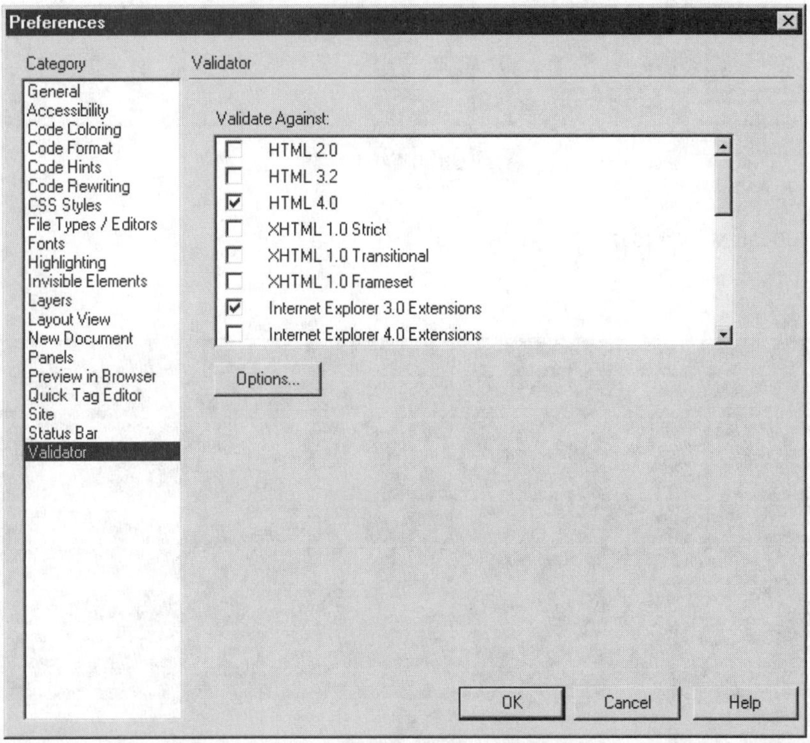

Figure 9-11.   *Validate your code against a selection of standards.*

In the Results Panel Group, locate the Target Browser Check Panel. The controls are similar to the Validator Panel. Clicking the green arrow will allow you to choose whether you want to check the current page, all pages in the site, or selected pages. Select Check Target Browsers. A dialog box will appear for you to select which browser or browsers you want to check your page against. Select a browser, then use the SHIFT key to select another browser and all those in between, or use the CTRL key (CMD on a Mac) to select or deselect individual browsers, as shown in Figure 9-13.

Click OK and your page will be checked against the selected browsers. The Target Browser Check Panel will display the results of the check. Double-clicking any reported issue will take you to the appropriate page and line number so you can address the issue. You can also save the results and print a formatted report, just as you can with the Validator Panel.

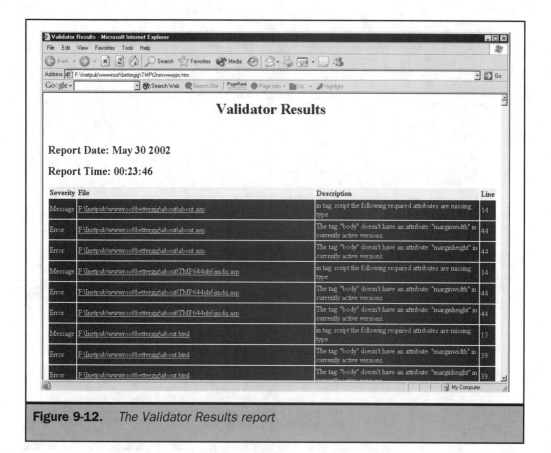

Figure 9-12.   *The Validator Results report*

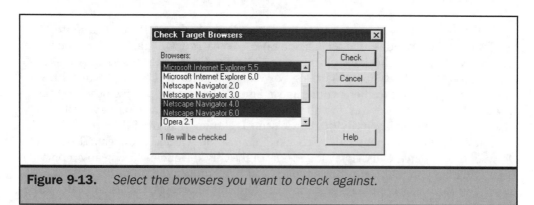

Figure 9-13.   *Select the browsers you want to check against.*

The Link Checker

As your site grows, you will no doubt amass a series of links to other pages and other sites. Making sure that these links are valid can be a time-consuming job. Fortunately, Dreamweaver includes a Link Checker Panel that validates your links for you in one easy step. Unfortunately, it doesn't do the entire job for you.

The link checker will report on three kinds of link issues: broken links, external links, and orphaned files. Broken links are links in your pages to other pages in your site where the page you have linked to is not present on your local disk. The link checker will identify the page on which the link exists and the link that is broken.

External links are links on your pages that point to pages outside your domain. These are provided to you for reference, but they are not checked. You will need to validate external links yourself.

Orphaned files are pages within your site that do have not other pages pointing to them. There are certainly cases where you might have files like this on purpose, but in general, people get to your pages through links on other pages beginning with the index page. Your visitors will have a difficult time guessing the name of a page that you do not provide a link to.

Use the green arrow in the Link Checker Panel to select which pages you want to check. The results will display in the panel. You can use the drop-down list at the top of the panel to select which of the three file types you would like to see in the results.

Summary

Dreamweaver provides a number of very powerful tools to aid you in the design and maintenance of your pages. Its coding environment is finally becoming robust enough to compete with standalone editors, and the variety of reports available to you helps to automate many of the tedious tasks associated with troubleshooting your site. From advanced coding tools to detailed site reports, you can build pages faster and more accurately with these features.

Dreamweaver
MX

Chapter 10

Fireworks MX
Integration

One of the great things about Macromedia's Studio MX focus is the way in which the products are designed to work together. Instead of disjointed applications, Macromedia has built a suite of programs that, to a great degree, look the same and act the same, making them easy to use together to build complex projects. Graphics have become an integral part of well-designed Web sites, and Macromedia has made sure that Dreamweaver MX and Fireworks MX work well together.

In the early chapters of this book, we looked at some of the ways that you can use Fireworks graphics in your Web pages. Let's look at a few of the ways that Dreamweaver and Fireworks work even more closely together.

Quick Export

Fireworks' Quick Export is a convenient way to export graphics to Dreamweaver, Flash, and Freehand. It provides a selection of options for each program that represents things that you will commonly do when working with the programs together. Quick Export is located in the upper right-hand corner of the document window in Fireworks, shown in Figure 10-1.

In Figure 10-1, you can see the header graphic used in the Big Harry's sporting goods site in Chapter 9. The graphic has been sliced for exporting and includes separate slices for each of the navigation items. From the Dreamweaver menu of Quick Export, you can do the following:

- **Export HTML**   This option exports the current document as an HTML file and associated graphics. Each slice is exported according to the optimization settings you have assigned it.

- **Update HTML**   If you make changes to the HTML, the images, or the slices in your Fireworks file, you will want to update the HTML that you exported. You can do this quickly and easily by selecting the Update HTML option from the Quick Export menu. Fireworks will examine the previous export and make corrections to the HTML files, the image, or both in order to bring the export up to date with the current state of the image and its slices.

- **Copy HTML to Clipboard**   Already have a file that you want to use Fireworks HTML in? Fireworks will let you copy the export to the clipboard. You can then go to the page where you want to use it and simply paste it in; no more time-consuming middle steps.

- **Launch Dreamweaver**   You can also launch Dreamweaver independent of Fireworks.

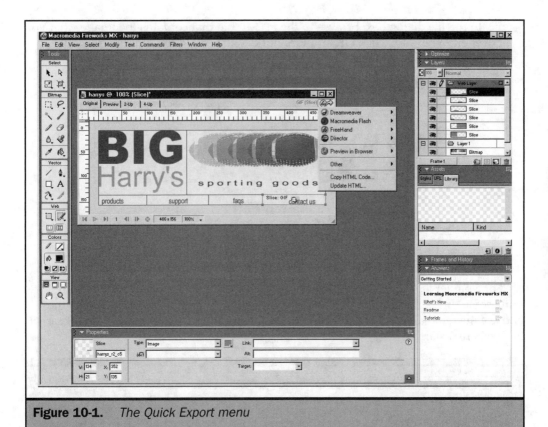

Figure 10-1. *The Quick Export menu*

The Quick Launch menu provides quick and easy ways to get your graphics exported and into Dreamweaver. You can also use Fireworks to pull images in from Dreamweaver files.

Reconstitute Tables

There may well come a time when you need to rebuild a Fireworks image, but the original files do not exist. Perhaps you are taking over a site and you do not have access to the original files, or they never existed in the first place. Fireworks can help you rebuild a PNG file from the exported HTML files.

You can test this with the Big Harry's files we just exported.

1. Select File | Reconstitute Table.

WEB SITE DESIGN
AND CONSTRUCTION

2. In the file dialog box, browse to the HTML file that contains the images that you want to rebuild. Click OK and Fireworks will rebuild the graphic from the component parts, slices and all, as shown here:

For a bigger test, I pointed Fireworks at the Bettergig index page that was built quite some time ago. Although it did not quite know what to do with the text in the body of the template, it did faithfully rebuild the graphic. A little clean up and it can be back where it started.

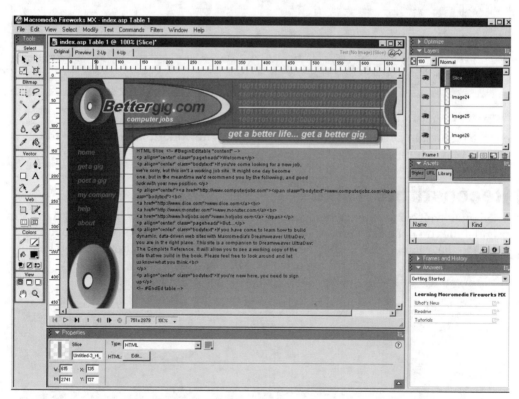

Image Placeholders

In Chapter 9, we used an image placeholder to design a spot where a Buy Now button will go, without needing to have the graphic on hand. From that page within Dreamweaver, we can jump out to Fireworks, create the button and return to Dreamweaver with a minimum of fuss.

1. Select the image placeholder in the HTML page in Dreamweaver.

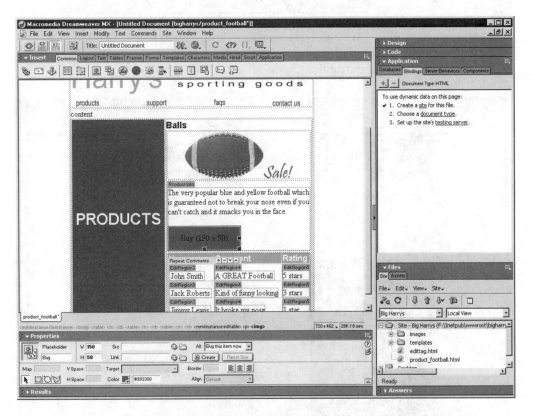

2. On the Property inspector for the image placeholder, click Create. Fireworks will launch with a canvas appropriate for the size of your graphic.

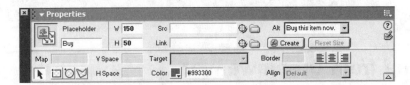

3. Create your button using Fireworks' graphics tools, set its Optimization properties so that Fireworks knows how to export it, and click Done.

4. Fireworks will save a PNG version of the file and an exported version of the file. When you return to Dreamweaver, the newly created graphic will now fill the space where you originally used an image placeholder.

Editing from Dreamweaver

Once your graphic is created and placed in Dreamweaver, you can still use Fireworks to make any changes that you need. Where there was a Create button on the property inspector, there is now an Edit button.

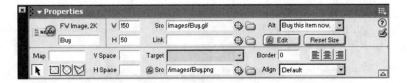

When you click Edit, Fireworks locates the original PNG file and loads it for editing. You can make any necessary changes and click Done. The changes will be saved and the image returned to Dreamweaver.

Fireworks will try to locate the original of the file you are editing. If it cannot find it, you will be prompted for the original. If it is not available, you can edit the GIF or JPG file itself, but you are limited in what you can edit because the image is flattened, and things like text you cannot easily change. Also keep in mind that the more times you export a file, especially a JPG, the more image quality you lose.

Pop-Up Menus

It is easier than ever to create text-based pop-up menus in Fireworks and export them to Dreamweaver. And you can even edit them in Dreamweaver now. If you end up needing to add, subtract, or change items in your pop-up menus, you don't need to leave Dreamweaver to accomplish your changes.

1. To create a pop-up menu in Fireworks, select the Products slice on the Big Harry's graphic. Select Modify | Pop Up Menu | Add Pop-Up Menu.

2. The Add Pop-Up Menu Editor will appear.

3. Add text for the pop-up, a URL, and a target for each menu item. This example adds "Football," "Golf Ball," and "Soccer Ball" items to the Products menu and provides links to those three pages.

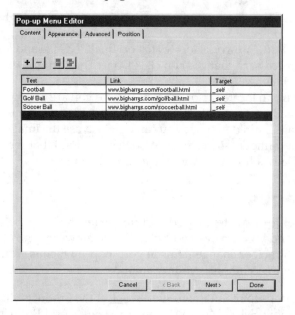

4. On the Position tab, select where you want your menu items to appear in relation to the graphic they are attached to. I have chosen the second option, below the graphic.

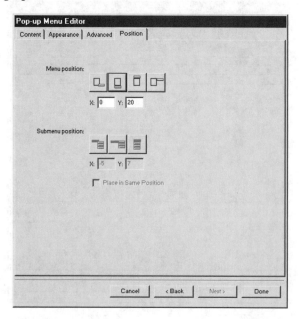

5. Click Done and use the Quick Export menu to export your file to Dreamweaver HTML. Fireworks creates the HTML and the necessary JavaScript files to make your pop-up menu work. Open the exported page in Dreamweaver and preview it in a browser to see your menu work.

6. If you need to make edits to your pop-up menu, you can do so in the Behaviors Panel of Dreamweaver. Select the graphic that has the pop-up menu attached to it. In the Behaviors Panel, you will see the mouse events that show and hide the pop-up menu.

Note   *Dreamweaver can only edit text-based pop-up menus. Menus created with images will need to be edited in Fireworks.*

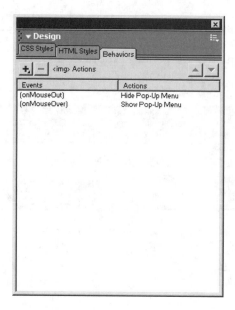

7. Double-click an event in the Behaviors Panel and you will be presented with a Show Pop-Up Menu editor that resembles the one in Fireworks. From here, you can edit all aspects of your text-based pop-up menu and save your changes right in Dreamweaver—no need to return to Fireworks at all.

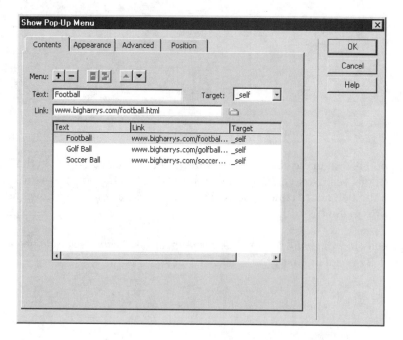

Optimizing Graphics for the Web

Broadband connections are slowly making their way into more and more homes around the world. But they are far from ubiquitous yet. Even in areas where DSL and cable connections are available, many users see no need for the extra expense to enable their e-mail to arrive one second faster.

Size remains an important consideration in the development of Web pages. It is critical to deliver engaging content as quickly as possible to keep your potential visitors from clicking the Stop button and moving on to another site. In general, you should try to keep your page load times under 10 seconds, which translates to something under 40K of total content per page. You can go about achieving this in several ways, from dividing content appropriately and avoiding over-long pages to strictly controlling the number and size of the graphic images you use.

Controlling the size of your graphics is known as *optimization*. Optimization involves taking into consideration which file formats and compression techniques you use to prepare your graphics for the Web so that they are delivered efficiently while retaining the look that you want. This process is part technique and part subjective and involves a few trade-offs.

File Formats for the Web

A ton of different image formats are available, each with their own advantages and disadvantages. BMP, EPS, TIFF, WMF, SVG, GIF, JPG, and PNG are just a few of the popular file formats used to save image files for use in a number of applications. Of these, three are most popular for the Web, and only two have universal acceptance in the available browsers.

GIF

GIF (pronounced jif or gif with a hard *g*) stands for Graphic Interchange Format. It is a lossless compression, meaning that no image quality is lost in the compression itself, but it is limited to 256 colors. Images with 256 colors or fewer will experience no loss in quality when converted to GIF files. But images with more colors will experience color shifts in an attempt to represent the current data in 256 colors. This results in the loss of detail in blended areas, and areas that require continuous tone, like photographs.

GIF files are best for line art and images with large areas of flat color. Images that are made up of only a few colors can also be converted into GIFs with good results. GIFs also allow certain color regions to be designated as transparent.

GIF files are usually smaller than decent quality versions of other formats, so using them can save file size and page size. They do not always produce the best aesthetic result, however. More complex images and photographs can benefit from JPG compression.

JPG

JPG (or JPEG, pronounced jay-peg) stands for Joint Photographic Expert Group. JPG is a lossy compression, meaning that information is lost from the base file in the compression process, but can display millions of colors, making it excellent for processing photographs and other complex image types. You can control just how lossy your compression is (how much information is lost) when you configure Fireworks to create a JPG file. Image quality is controlled by setting a quality value to a number between 1 and 100; 100 being the maximum quality available from the compression scheme.

Note *Keep in mind that JPG compression is cumulative. If you compress an original image with an 80 quality setting, and then edit that JPG and save it again with an 80 quality setting, you are further degrading the image quality. Try to make edits to the original file to keep your compressed image a first-generation product. Also keep in mind that a 100-JPG setting just means the best of JPG compression. The image will still be compressed, and you will still lose some quality.*

JPG images are typically larger because they retain a more accurate selection of the colors used in the original file. This means that, although you get a more realistic representation of your original image, the file size can make JPGs difficult to use in a Web setting without some attention to how the image is prepared. JPGs do not allow transparency.

PNG

PNG (often pronounced ping) stands for Portable Network Graphic. It is the native file format of Fireworks. PNG files are actually metafiles that contain descriptive information about the bitmaps, vectors, and text that make up the image itself. They are very high quality, but can also be very large depending on the nature of the components that make them up.

PNG files are gaining acceptance as a standard graphic format. Many print and design programs, such as Adobe's inDesign, allow you to link PNG files directly into your publications. They are not, however, universally supported in the popular Web browsers. Unless you know what platforms your clients will be using and can be confident of their support, you should avoid using PNG files at this point.

Slicing Graphics

We have talked about slicing graphics in Fireworks in a couple of contexts: to create complex layouts and to allow for the insertion of rollover navigation images. You can also use slicing to prepare an image for use on the Web, even when the image will simply be reconstituted in the browser. There are a couple of reasons for this.

First, multiple small files will often download faster than one large file. In theory, it doesn't seem that it should be true, bandwidth being a fixed quantity, but in practice, two 50K images downloading at the same time will often complete before one 100K image.

Second, even if the total download time of the split and full images is the same in the end, with a sliced graphic, certain portions will become available in the browser and provide your visitor with some visual feedback that all is going well. It is often more comforting to see pieces of images appearing than to have to wait while a full file downloads before anything is seen on the screen.

Third, and quite importantly for complex images, is the capability in Fireworks to separately optimize each slice of a graphic to the setting that is best for the content of that slice. That means that you can save areas of text or flat color in your image as smaller GIF files, and you can set the more color-intense portions to JPG so that their quality is maintained. Let's look at doing just that.

Optimizing a Complex Image in Fireworks

In this section, we look at slicing and optimizing a fairly complex image in Fireworks. This particular image was supplied by Japi Honoo, an exceptionally talented designer and a good friend. You can see more of her work and learn about Fireworks at her Web site, www.escogitando.it.

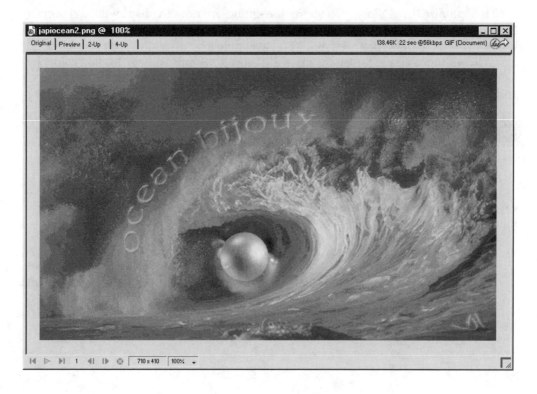

The original image is a little over 1.1MB; way too large to consider using on the Web. We can begin to investigate how it might export by using the Optimize Panel in Fireworks MX.

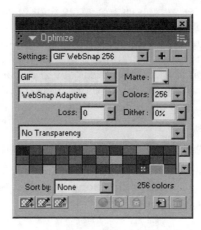

The Optimize Panel allows you to provide settings for how an image will be exported. It makes no changes to the original image itself, it just allows you to preview what the image will look like at certain settings. You have quite a bit of control. You can select from GIF settings that use transparency, or dither colors (approximate missing colors by using a mix of available ones). You can also select how many colors your GIF will use and what numerical quality you want for a JPG.

Fireworks also allows the exporting of several other file formats, such as TIFFs and BMPs. Although these aren't useful for Web work, you may find them handy when supplying Fireworks images to other sources.

Our first step is to get a general feel for how the image is going to look when it is exported as a GIF or a JPG. In the Optimize Panel, select GIF WebSnap 128. This is a good place to start.

GIF files come in three flavors in Fireworks:

■ **WebSnap Adaptive** This format evaluates the colors in an image and snaps each color to its nearest Web safe color, plus or minus seven values. This means that not every color is guaranteed to be Web safe, but they will be close to those that are. This is the default setting for Fireworks.

Note *Web safe colors are a special set of 216 colors that are guaranteed to be available on any 256-color PC or Macintosh system. The 216 colors were arrived at by comparing the PC and Mac 256-color palettes and selecting only those colors that were in both.*

- **Adaptive** This setting locates the 256 most prominent colors in your image, and converts all other colors to one of those. These colors need not be in the Web safe palette; they can be any 256 colors. This method often presents a truer representation of your image, but is not guaranteed Web safe.

- **Web 216** This setting snaps all colors to Web safe colors.

Note *At one time, it was important to use only Web safe colors in your pages because most computers were still using 256-color video cards, and some wild dithering would occur if you strayed outside the lines. These days, it is less critical because the vast majority of computers have significantly larger palettes available to them. The biggest concern today is those users who have a capable system set to 256 colors and are neither aware of that nor know how to change it. They may just think your page is screwed up.*

1. With your Optimize Panel set to GIF WebSnap Adaptive, click the Preview Panel at the top of the image canvas. This will allow you to view the image as it will look when exported with the current settings.

2. At the top, between the Preview Tabs and the Quick Export button, you will see a size setting. This tells you how large a file this setting will produce and about how long it will take to download over a 56K connection. This setting produces a file that is about 118K. Still a little large for our purposes, even though this isn't really a Web page, but people may be willing to wait a little longer to see a specific image. We still want the best combination of size and quality we can get.

3. But the size is not our biggest problem. Looking at the pearl in the middle of the image, the quality is unacceptable. There are obviously color variations in the detail of the pearl that cannot be represented in a 128-color palette. Select some of the other settings, such as WebSnap 256 and Adaptive. What you will notice is there are no GIF settings that get that pearl looking its best.

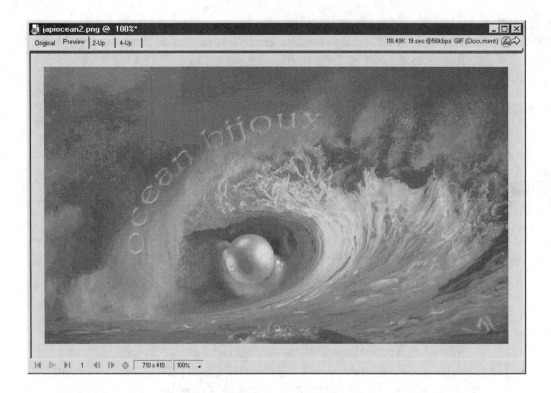

4. Try one of the JPG settings, either Better Quality or Smaller File. The size is much better, fantastic with the Smaller File Setting, and the pearl looks quite good now, though some detail is lost in the lower quality setting. But a careful look will reveal that we have lost a lot of details in the surrounding waves. Switch back and forth between the Original and Preview tabs, or better yet, use the 2-Up tab to see the original and your optimized Preview side by side.

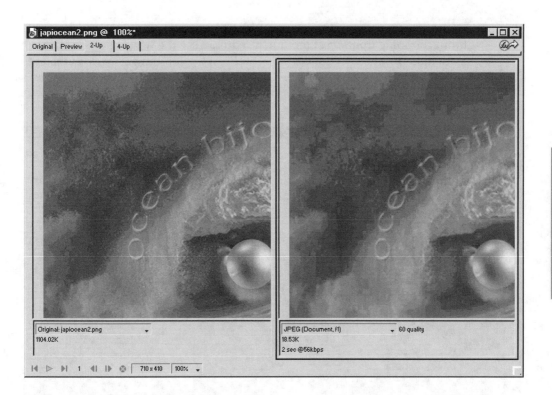

5. Set the Quality of the JPG setting to 100 using the slider in the Optimize Panel. This produces a great quality image, but with a hefty file size. It would be nice to find a mix that retains the detail in the GIF image and the color of the pearl in the JPG. You can do just that by slicing the image.

6. You can slice the image however you like. The goal here is to isolate the pearl without chopping up the rest too much. You can see the way I chose to slice it. This method produces five slices, about the fewest you can get away with, and avoids splitting up letters in the text by slicing in-between the words. Use the Slice tool in the Tools Panel and draw your slices on the canvas.

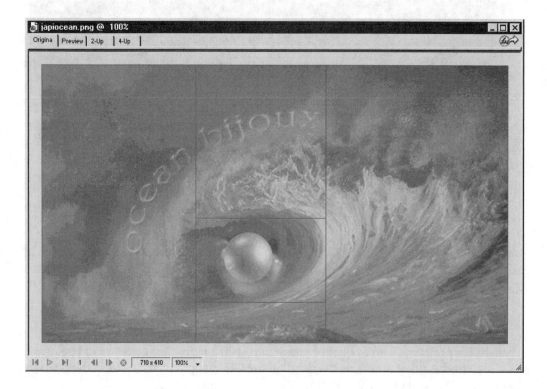

7. Your goal now is to deal with these five slices as five individual images and set them to optimize the look of their contents. To compare settings, use the 4-Up setting to see the original and three other settings. Click each of the views and

use the Optimize Panel to configure the settings for that view. You can closely compare the quality of each selection against the original. Use the hand tools, found at the bottom of the Tool Panel, to drag your image around and see all of its parts in the small preview screens.

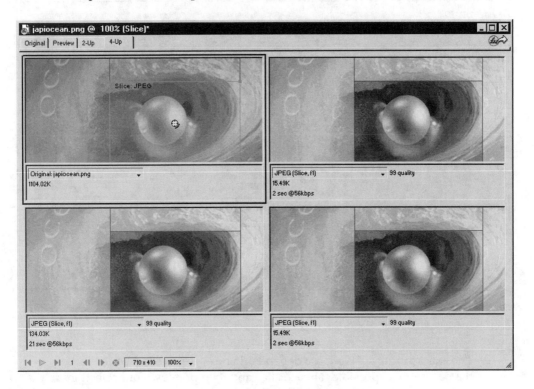

8. At any time, you can see exactly what the current setting will produce in a browser by using the Quick Export button at the top of the canvas to Preview In Browser. This will create an ad hoc table structure and display the slices in a browser using the image settings you have currently selected.

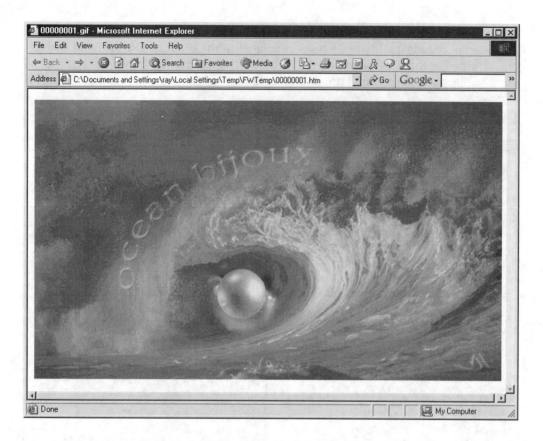

9. The exact settings you choose depend on your purpose and your eye. Select the best settings possible for each slice and then preview your selections in the browser. I selected the same GIF settings for the four outer slices because their content was similar and the level of detail needed to be maintained. A JPG setting of 70–80 produces a good quality pearl without too much smoothing, but you may choose a 100 setting for it in order to have it stand out in great detail. Once you have a group of settings that meet both your file size and quality specifications, you can export your slices to be used in Dreamweaver.

Summary

You can see that, after learning a few buttons and procedures, it is easier than ever to work with graphics in Dreamweaver and Fireworks. Macromedia has made it possible to round-trip your graphics and even re-create graphics that you no longer have access to. Fireworks is an extremely powerful program that deserves your attention. It will take some time before you are comfortable with all of the available tools. But the ease with which you can move between these two programs makes Fireworks an appealing choice as your main Web graphics editor.

The Complete Reference

Dreamweaver MX

Chapter 11

Flash Integration Basics

In a few short years, the Internet has gone from a drab, research-oriented place where you could view documents to a multimedia, multisensory experience. Imagine if Hollywood had gone from producing silent films with Charlie Chaplin to producing a film like *The Matrix* in a few short years and you will appreciate the technological advances that have occurred in the area of Web technology. Macromedia's Flash is at the forefront of the emerging Web technologies that enable multimedia content to be accessible to anyone with a Web browser and a Flash player plug-in.

When you are dealing with HTML and JavaScript, you are constantly fighting numerous cross-browser and cross-platform issues. What looks good in Internet Explorer 6 on a Windows machine might look completely different on Netscape 4.7 on the Mac or Netscape 6 on a Linux box. In contrast to that, a Flash movie will look the same on any browser that has the Flash plug-in installed. According to statistics from Macromedia, the Flash player is installed on about 98 percent of the browsers in the Web world. You can't get much better penetration than that.

For Flash penetration statistics, go to www.macromedia.com/software/player_census/ flashplayer/.

Flash can be used for many things. Many people think of a Flash movie as a splash page with the skip intro button. Although it is true that many of the cool site introductions were done in this manner with Flash, that is just one of the many uses of this versatile tool. With the latest generation of the Flash authoring environment, Flash MX, many of the same functions can be performed as with HTML and JavaScript, but in a more flexible environment. HTML is limited to a few standard controls that can be enhanced with DHTML and CSS, but Flash is limited only by the imagination. Flash content can contain video, images, sounds, and animation, and can deliver feature-rich user interfaces that use sophisticated controls. The new MX family of products from Macromedia has Flash as its centerpiece—an authoring environment with unlimited potential.

To learn Macromedia's Flash MX, there are several good books available on the subject. One of the best books about Flash MX is Macromedia Flash MX: The Complete Reference, by Brian Underdahl, also published by McGraw-Hill/Osborne (2002).

Flash has achieved its current popularity because of the rich content that it provides and because it is able to deliver the content utilizing minimum bandwidth. A Flash animation does not have to be stored as separate images; its files use *vector graphics*, which means that the graphics are stored as coordinates, colors, and mathematical formulas rather than bitmaps. Thus, the Flash graphic is drawn in real time when it reaches the user. This explains why you can zoom or resize a Flash movie with no noticeable loss in quality. If you were to do that with a bitmap graphic, you would see jagged edges on your graphics because of the change in resolution. In addition, because a bitmap graphic is stored with the complete pixel information, the file sizes are very large compared to a Flash movie.

SWF Files in Dreamweaver

Flash files have a SWF (<u>S</u>hock<u>w</u>ave <u>f</u>ile) extension and are playable with a standalone Flash player or inside a browser with a Flash plug-in. They can be embedded in a Web page with a few lines of HTML code, like so:

```
<object classid="clsid:D27CDB6E-AE6D-11cf-96B8-444553540000"
codebase="http://download.macromedia.com/pub/shockwave/cabs/
flash/swflash.cab#version=6,0,29,0" width="502" height="400">
  <param name="movie" value="Paycheck_calculator.swf">
  <param name="quality" value="high">
  <embed src="Paycheck_calculator.swf" quality="high"
  pluginspage="http://www.macromedia.com/go/getflashplayer"
  type="application/x-shockwave-flash"
  width="502" height="400"></embed>
</object>
```

The Flash file is embedded using two tags: <object> and <embed>. The <object> tag works in Internet Explorer. The Flash player in Internet Explorer is an ActiveX control. The <embed> tag works in Netscape, using the Netscape plug-in technology. Because of the differences in implementation of the Flash player, the plug-in page is different for both tags. You can see that the <param> tags that go along with the <object> tag contain the same attribute names and values as the <embed> tag.

> **Note**   *The Opera browser uses the <embed> tag and acts in a similar fashion to Netscape when dealing with plug-ins.*

When working in Dreamweaver MX, this code will be generated automatically for you. Simply click the Flash icon on the Common tab of the Insert bar (shown in Figure 11-1) or click Insert | Media | Flash to add your Flash file to the Web page that you are currently editing. This will show the Select Flash Source File dialog box. After choosing the .swf file, you are given an option to copy the file to your site if it isn't there already.

> **Tip**   *There are several other ways to get a Flash file into your document. The easiest way is to drag it from the site panel into Design view. You can also drag it from the Assets panel into Design or Code view, or right-click from the Assets panel and select Insert. The Flash icon on the Insert bar is also in two places: the Common tab and the Media tab. Also, you can drag the Flash file directly from your file system (such as your desktop) to the Dreamweaver MX design environment.*

The Flash file shows up in the Dreamweaver MX environment as a gray placeholder with a Flash icon in the center, but you can preview the Flash content within Dreamweaver MX by clicking the Play button on the Property Inspector.

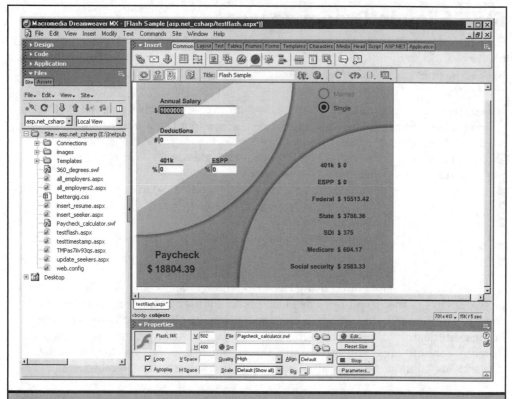

Figure 11-1.   *You can insert a Flash object from the Insert bar Common tab.*

You can also play all Flash content that is on the page in the design environment by pressing CTRL-ALT-SHIFT-P on Windows or SHIFT-OPT-CMD-P on the Macintosh.

 Dreamweaver MX comes with its own Flash player plug-in to allow you to play the movies in the design environment.

Flash Properties and the Property Inspector

Property inspectors are the best place to access properties and attributes of most items in a document within Dreamweaver. Its interface is so useful that Macromedia has incorporated it into the user interfaces for Fireworks MX and Flash MX as well. The Property inspector is based on context—wherever your cursor is located on the document, the relevant Property inspector will appear at the bottom of the screen. In other words, if the cursor is on a table, the Property inspector for a table will appear. For Flash objects (shown in Figure 11-2), the Property inspector contains several unique features, including the capability to play a Flash movie within the Dreamweaver MX design environment.

> **Tip** *Setting the properties from the Property inspector ensures that both the Object and the Embed tag will be updated with the new values.*

The *W* and *H* (width and height) boxes allow you to specify the size of the Flash movie. Your Flash movie was created in a default size, but you can change that for the Web page by setting the size here. Also, the Reset Size button will reset the size of your movie to the default and fill in the width and height boxes automatically.

A Flash movie, like an image, has an *aspect ratio*. The aspect ratio is the relationship of width to height. Changes made to width and height can affect the aspect ratio of the Flash movie.

By setting the width and height dimensions to a percentage rather than a fixed pixel size, your Flash movie will resize with the browser, without any loss in quality. If you decide to use percentage values for the width and height, be aware that the aspect ratio of the movie can be distorted as well.

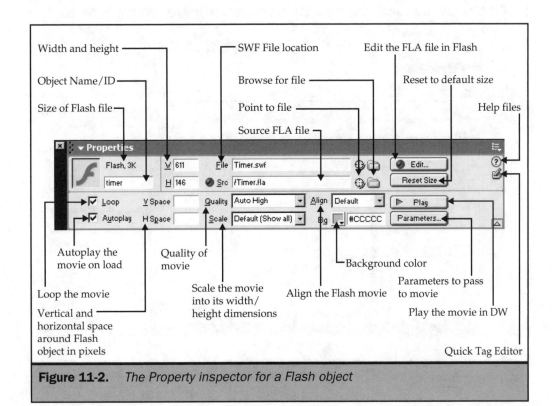

Figure 11-2. *The Property inspector for a Flash object*

You can resize the Flash movie visually as well. To do this, select the movie in the design environment and drag the handles to the desired size. The settings for width and height in the Property inspector will be updated automatically. If you want the aspect ratio to be accurate when you are resizing in this way, you can hold down the SHIFT key while you resize the movie, which will keep the width and height in proportion.

If you have Flash MX installed on your computer, you will see a *Src* option in the Property inspector. This allows you to specify the source FLA file for your Flash movie. You can edit the Flash movie from within Dreamweaver MX by clicking the Edit button on the Property inspector—this will cause Flash to open up. An indicator in the Flash environment shows that you are editing from Dreamweaver (shown in Figure 11-3). Any changes made in Flash MX will be made automatically to the FLA file and the SWF file.

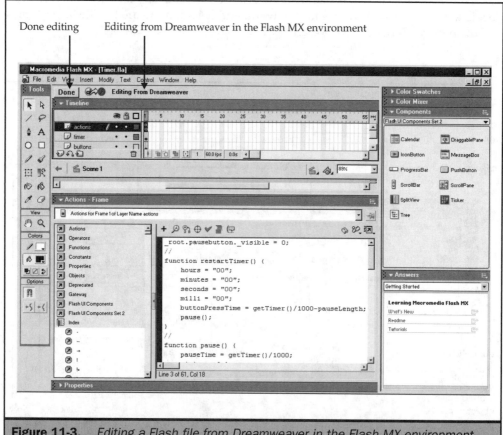

Figure 11-3. *Editing a Flash file from Dreamweaver in the Flash MX environment*

You can also edit a Flash file from within Dreamweaver by holding down the CTRL key in Windows, or the COMMAND key on the Macintosh, and double-clicking the movie in the design environment. There is also a context-menu item that enables you to edit the file. If Dreamweaver MX can't find the FLA file, you will be prompted for the location of the file.

The Quality box has four different settings: Low, High, Auto Low, and Auto High. The Flash movies depend on the quality and speed of the end user's computer, so if you have a complex movie that you want to be accessible to older machines, you can set the quality level to Low. The best possible option in most cases is to allow the Flash player to auto-detect the speed of the user's computer. By setting it to Auto Low, the movie will start out at a low quality setting and increase quality if possible. By setting it to Auto High, the movie will start out with the best possible quality, but make speed adjustments if the computer is too slow to process the movie.

The Loop property will cause the movie to loop over and over without stopping. The Autoplay property, meanwhile, will cause the movie to start playing upon loading the page.

Set the Scale property to Default if you have the size of the movie set accurately. If you have resized the movie, you have a couple of options. You can set the Scale property to Exact Fit, which will disregard the aspect ratio and distort the movie. This may be what you want, but there is another option as well: No Border. This option maintains the original size and aspect ratio of the movie, but will show only the portion of the movie that fits into the sized area while still maintaining the aspect ratio. In other words, if you have made the object width smaller than it really is, the sides will be cut off in the display. If you have made the object height smaller, the top and bottom of the movie will be chopped off.

The BG property sets the background color of the Flash file. This is used not only when the Flash file is playing, but also to keep the background color consistent when the file is loading—the BG color will be seen by the end user rather than the white color of a Flash file with no background color specified.

You can enter *parameters* (Flash variables) from the Property inspector as well. Using parameters is the easiest way to add dynamic content to your Flash movie. In Dreamweaver MX, you can easily assign server-side content to these parameters by using the lightning bolt icon in the Property inspector (shown in Figure 11-4). You can code the Flash movie in such a way that it will use the parameters that are sent to it from the page on which it resides.

Flash Assets

One of the features of Dreamweaver MX is the capability to keep a list of your favorite assets. Buttons in the Assets panel allow you to access different categories within Assets, such as images, scripts, links, and Flash files. The Flash category makes it easy to work with the SWF files contained in your site, or from your own personal favorites list.

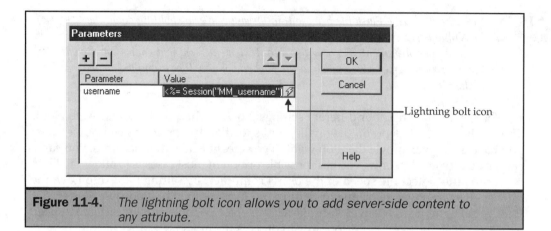

Figure 11-4. *The lightning bolt icon allows you to add server-side content to any attribute.*

The Assets panel has two views—Site and Favorites—accessible from the radio buttons on the top of the panel. When in the Site view, your panel may appear blank until you hit the refresh button, which will cause the Assets panel to reload. Dreamweaver will search your site for all Flash files and add them to the Assets panel.

The Favorites panel allows you to group frequently used assets into a panel that will be accessible from all of your sites. This can be handy for your Flash files if you have certain logos, banners, or interface elements that you use from site to site.

The contextual menu of the Assets panel (shown in Figure 11-5) allows you to insert a Flash file into your document. This is the equivalent of using the Insert bar and clicking the Flash button. There is also an option to copy your Flash file to another site. This option will add the Flash file to the Favorites panel of another site, and also copy the file to the root level of that site.

The Assets panel also contains a Play button that allows you to preview the Flash file within the Assets panel. Note that this is off by default to avoid any unnecessary use of processing power while working within Dreamweaver MX.

Flash Generation

Macromedia Generator is another program that works in conjunction with Flash. Generator can create Flash files on the fly by using a template that is able to accept parameters. The Generator server supplies parameters to the template as it is served. Beginning with version 4 of Dreamweaver, simple Flash generation became part of Dreamweaver. Dreamweaver can utilize simple text and button templates using a built-in version of Generator.

You can create Generator templates by using Flash 5 and the Generator Authoring Environment. When you install Flash 5, you can also install the Generator Objects, which allow you to create templates that can interact with the Generator server. Flash MX will

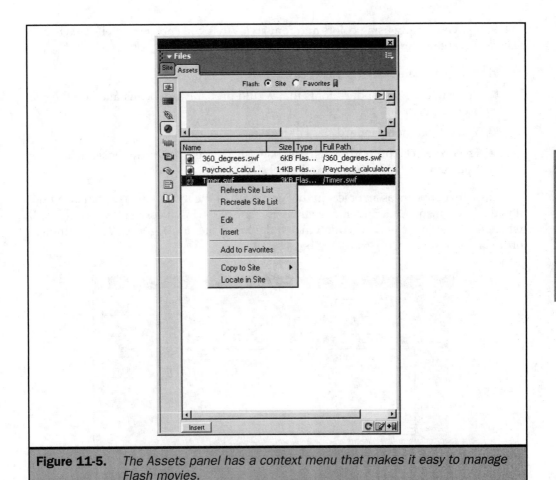

Figure 11-5. *The Assets panel has a context menu that makes it easy to manage Flash movies.*

not create Generator templates—if you want to utilize that functionality, you have to work with Flash 5. Flash 5 and Flash MX can co-exist on the same computer.

Now that Macromedia has acquired Allaire, they have discontinued Generator. The technology of Generator is being completely supplanted by a new architecture, beginning with the new Flash MX. Flash MX introduces new methods of communication with ColdFusion MX, JRun 4, Web Services, ASP.NET, Websphere, and other server platforms and technologies. Server-side Flash integration is covered in Chapter 28.

Flash Text

The Flash Text object utilizes Generator templates to allow Dreamweaver MX to insert a customized Flash movie into your page. The Flash movie is a static movie, but it consists of text that you supply using colors and font styles that you choose as well. This has several advantages over standard text in certain situations:

- You can create rollover effects easily.
- You can use nonstandard fonts that would probably not be installed on the end user's system.
- You can use nonstandard sizes of text.
- The text can be proportional to the page size by setting the dimensions to a percentage rather than a fixed pixel size.

Flash Text appears as an object in the Media tab of the Insert bar. You can also find it in the Insert menu under Interactive Images—one of the instances in Dreamweaver MX where the Insert bar categories don't match the Insert menu categories. Both methods bring up the Insert Flash Text dialog box:

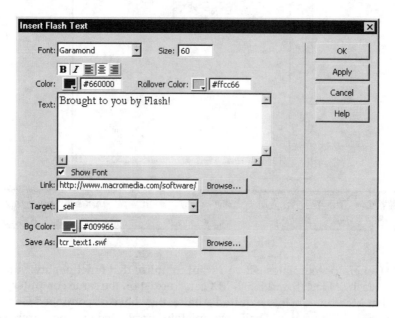

This dialog box has many options for your Flash Text object. You can choose the font style, size, color, rollover color, and background color for the object, as well as the style of the text (bold and italic) and the position (left, right, center). In addition, you can assign a hyperlink and target to the text. Once you finish with the Flash object, you must save it in your site. The file saves as a SWF file (Flash movie).

You can edit the text objects as well, by simply double-clicking the text in the design environment. Doing so will bring up the Insert Flash Text dialog box once again.

The Flash Text object has a Property inspector that functions in the exact same way as the Flash Property inspector, with one minor exception: the Edit button will bring up the Insert Flash Text dialog box rather than Flash MX.

Flash Buttons

If you're looking for a quick and easy way to get some rollover buttons on a page, you can choose from the Flash Buttons that come with Dreamweaver MX, or you can download new buttons from the Macromedia Exchange. The buttons are easy to use and are easily configurable.

Flash Buttons are built out of Generator templates, like the Flash Text objects. Once again, they are static Flash movies that are generated by Dreamweaver to conform to your custom specifications. Unlike the Flash Text object, which only allows you to format text, buttons require that you make many different design choices.

The Flash Button object is accessible from the Media tab of the Insert bar. You can find it in the Insert menu under Interactive Images as well. Both options will bring up the Insert Flash Button dialog box:

There are many button styles to choose from, and each button style has its own rollover style. In addition, you can download new buttons from the Macromedia Exchange. The Get More Styles button on the Insert Flash Button dialog box opens up a browser directly to the Exchange home page. Some of the most popular extensions on the Exchange are the Flash button extensions. Extensions and the Exchange are covered in Chapter 30.

You can configure the text on the button by choosing your font style and size. You can set a link and a target as well.

 Standard Behaviors do not work with the Flash Text and Flash Button objects. Because these are Flash-oriented, any behavioral changes to the objects need to be made with Flash and not with Dreamweaver.

Figure 11-6 shows some of the Flash button objects that are part of Dreamweaver MX.

Generator Templates

If you look inside the Configuration | Flash Objects | Flash Buttons folder, you'll see a bunch of files with a .swt extension. Flash MX can't open up these files, but they can be created in Flash 5 using the Generator objects. These templates are used by the built-in Generator functionality of Dreamweaver MX when it generates the Flash Buttons for your pages.

You can create your own Generator templates in the Flash 5 authoring environment. A technote on the Macromedia Web site at www.macromedia.com/support/

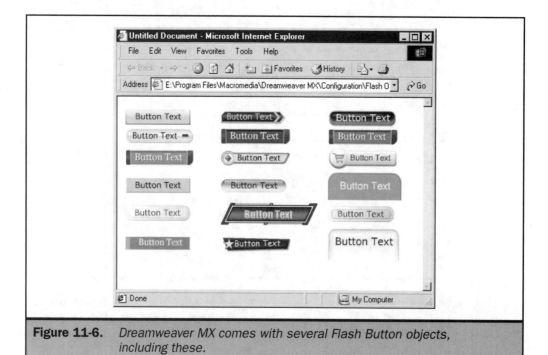

Figure 11-6.   *Dreamweaver MX comes with several Flash Button objects, including these.*

dreamweaver/assets/flashbutton/describes the process. If you create your own templates, you can store them in the Flash Buttons folder and they will show up in your list of choices for Flash buttons.

ActionScript

ActionScript is the language of Flash. It is true that you can work in the Flash environment not knowing or caring about ActionScript. For that matter, you can work on an HTML page without knowing HTML or JavaScript from within Dreamweaver MX. Still, knowing ActionScript and being able to apply it to your Flash movies can greatly enhance the types of functionality you are able to achieve with Flash. Programming with ActionScript allows you to add new levels of interactivity to your Flash movies.

Editing ActionScript

If you've ever tried to edit ActionScript in Flash, you know that the program is not really set up to be a dedicated code editor. The code-editing window is small, and there is no easy and manageable way to make it larger while maintaining the ability to work on your Flash movies visually as well. Even though ActionScript programming is a core part of creating Flash movies, the code-editing environment is very hard to work with.

Luckily, Dreamweaver MX can edit ActionScript using its built-in code editing capabilities. Dreamweaver MX also has syntax coloring and code hints for ActionScript (as shown in Figure 11-7). The ability to use Dreamweaver MX for ActionScript coding opens up a lot of options for you, the Flash programmer. For example, you can create ActionScript snippets to use with the Snippets panel. Also, viewing and editing the code is more convenient in a larger window.

Tip *Windows users can also take advantage of the coding features of Homesite+, which is on the Dreamweaver MX CD-ROM.*

ActionScript coding is necessary if you plan to do any work with server-side code integration with Flash, which is covered in Chapter 28.

Shockwave

Shockwave, which many people confuse with Flash, is Macromedia's other animation technology that goes a few steps beyond Flash in complexity. A Flash movie typically has a "cartoony" look to it, whereas a Shockwave movie can get really complex and offer some very sophisticated and interactive Web content.

Shockwave files are created with Macromedia's Director product. The latest version, Director 8.5, allows the Web developer to create complex 3-D interactive movies. You can create a Shockwave movie as a standalone application (for CD-ROM content) or for a Web browser using a Shockwave plug-in. A Shockwave file for the Web has a .dcr file extension.

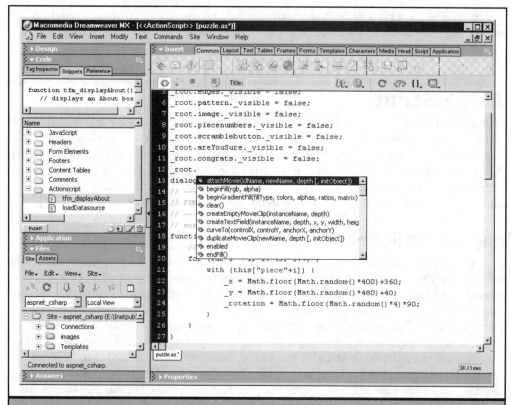

Figure 11-7. *Editing ActionScript in Dreamweaver is enhanced with code hints, syntax highlighting, and code completion.*

Note   *Shockwave plug-ins are not nearly as prevalent on the Web as Flash plug-ins. For that reason, a site that uses Shockwave probably has in mind a target audience of people who would have the Shockwave plug-in, such as gamers.*

You can insert Shockwave files from the Media tab of the Insert bar by clicking the Shockwave icon (fourth icon from the left) or by clicking Insert | Media | Shockwave. Also, like Flash files, you can drag them from the Site panel or from the Shockwave section of the Assets panel.

Controlling a Flash or Shockwave Movie

Dreamweaver contains several Behaviors that allow you to control a Flash or Shockwave movie from HTML elements, such as an image or a button. This gives your HTML elements more control over your Flash or Shockwave files. Behaviors are covered in greater depth in Chapter 13, but we discuss the basics of the integration here.

Built-In Dreamweaver Behavior

The Behavior called Control Shockwave or Flash is available in the Behaviors panel of the Design group. The Behavior will be grayed out if you don't have any Flash or Shockwave files on the page, or if you don't have a selection on the page that the Behavior can be applied to. Typically, you will apply this Behavior to an image, and it is usually applied to the *onClick* event.

To enable the JavaScript functionality of the Behavior, you must name your Flash or Shockwave object on the page. It is named so that JavaScript will know how to address the movie. If you think of your HTML objects as a crowd of people, and if you yell "Hey You!" into the crowd, you might not get a response. But, if you yell "Hey Mr. Jack Robinson" you will likely get a response from Mr. Jack Robinson if he is present. JavaScript works the same way—if it knows the name of the object, it can communicate with it. If the movie is unnamed, an alert box will tell you to cancel the dialog box and name your movie.

The options in the Control Shockwave or Flash dialog box (shown in Figure 11-8) allow you to play a movie, stop a movie, rewind a movie, or move to a specific frame. To apply the Behavior, select an image, button, or other element on your page that you want to control the movie, and choose one of the options in the Behavior.

 The Control Shockwave or Flash Behavior doesn't work in IE on the Mac or NN 6. This is because of problems with the browsers, not because of any fault in the Behavior code.

The JavaScript Integration Kit for Flash 5

The JavaScript Integration Kit for Flash is a Macromedia-authored extension that is a must if you want to work with Flash within the Dreamweaver environment. The extension contains several important JavaScript (and VBScript) Behaviors and scripts that make working with Flash files much easier.

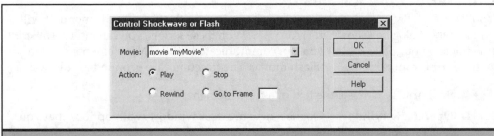

Figure 11-8. *The Control Shockwave or Flash Behavior allows you to control Flash and Shockwave movies from HTML elements.*

WEB SITE DESIGN AND CONSTRUCTION

Macromedia Flash Player Controls

This set of controls goes beyond the standard Dreamweaver MX Behaviors, which offer only limited capabilities to control Flash movies. These Behaviors can be applied to the *onClick* event of an image, button, link, or other HTML object. The Flash Player Controls offer the following Behaviors:

- **Fast Forward Flash** Moves forward to a specific frame or through a specified percentage of the movie
- **Go to Flash Frame** Goes to a specific frame of the movie
- **Go to Flash Frame Based on Cookie** Goes to a specific frame based on the value in a cookie on the user's machine
- **Load Flash Movie** Loads in a movie in place of a movie that is already loaded. This Behavior doesn't work in Netscape
- **Pan Flash** Pans a Flash movie, but only if it has been sized over 100 percent
- **Play Flash** Plays a Flash movie
- **Rewind Flash** Rewinds a Flash movie to the beginning
- **Set Flash by List** Provides a list from which the user selects one Flash movie to play
- **Stop Flash** Stops the Flash movie
- **Zoom Flash** Zooms in on a movie by a percentage

Advanced Form Validations

JavaScript is a rich language that you can use for many things, but one of the most popular features is the capability to validate a form element before the values are submitted to the server. Dreamweaver MX comes with a small supply of JavaScript validations. The JavaScript Integration Kit for Flash contains 18 different form validations that you can use with or without Flash—you can use these Behaviors by themselves strictly as form validations, or you can use them with Flash form elements.

Browser Scripts for Flash

You'll find the Browser Scripts For Flash menu item in the Commands menu. It will bring up the dialog box shown in Figure 11-9. With these scripts, you can insert JavaScript functions in your page so that you can communicate with HTML elements by using ActionScript from within your Flash movie. The functions are grouped as follows:

- **Set Form Text** Sets the text of a form element
- **Open New Window** Opens a new browser window, with options that you select (menus, scrollbars, etc.)

- **Set Cookie**   Stores name/value pairs on the client machine
- **Edit Form Lists**   Four functions that allow you to work with <select> elements from your Flash movies
- **Control Images**   Image functions, such as Swap Image and Preload Images

These functions are called from your ActionScript using *getURL()* within the Flash movie, such as the following call to the *FDK_newWindow()* function from the release event of a button:

```
on (release) {
 getURL ("javascript:FDK_newWindow('about.aspx','about','320','240',
 '','','','','','','')");
}
```

Macromedia Flash Dispatcher Behavior

The Flash Dispatcher Behavior (shown in Figure 11-10) puts some JavaScript code into your page that will detect the Flash version that the user is running. There are several options available in the Behavior that allow you to redirect the user; they could be sent to an alternate page if they don't have the Flash plug-in, or to the Macromedia site to download the latest version. An updated version of the Flash Dispatcher Behavior is available as part of the Flash Deployment Kit at www.macromedia.com/software/flash/download/deployment_kit/.

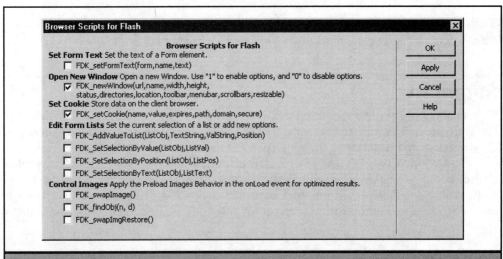

Figure 11-9.   *The Browser Scripts for Flash item allows communication between a Flash movie and HTML elements.*

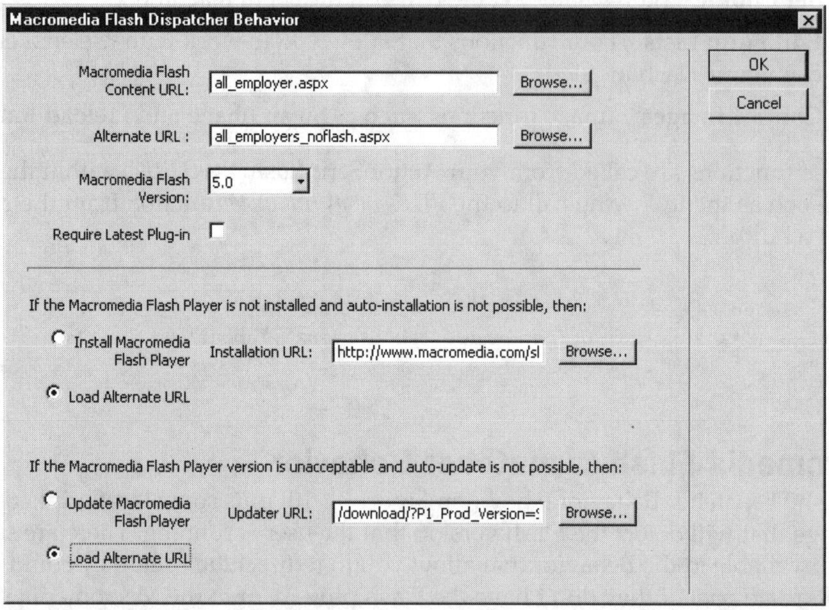

Figure 11-10. *The Flash Dispatcher Behavior allows you to specify an alternate page if your users don't have the correct Flash plug-in.*

Caution *If the user has JavaScript turned off, the Flash Dispatcher Behavior won't work. It also doesn't work in some browsers, such as Internet Explorer 4.5 for the Macintosh.*

Summary

Flash enables your Web pages to offer a wide variety of functionality and interactivity that were previously unheard of using HTML and JavaScript. Flash MX is Macromedia's latest version, and it stands as the centerpiece of the new Studio MX. The integration between Dreamweaver MX and Flash MX is evident in the workspace design as well as the functionality. Also, you can edit Flash ActionScript in Dreamweaver MX much more easily than in the Flash environment. Chapter 28 covers some of the more advanced uses of Flash MX communicating with server-side code created in Dreamweaver MX.

The
Complete
Reference

Dreamweaver
MX

Chapter 12

Cascading Style Sheets

When the Web was young, it didn't matter much how individual browsers displayed HTML data. One could think that H1 and H2 tags should be 35 and 25 pixels, respectively, and another could believe that 40 and 30 pixels was easier to read. The important point, in the beginning, was that the structure of the document was maintained to allow for the rendering of an outline of information. Tags were more important relative to each other in a particular browser, rather than relative to some standardized definition of how those tags should look.

The introduction of graphical browsers to replace the old text ones brought an element of design to Web documents. In addition to structure and outline, users became interested in how their information was presented. As a result, new tags were created to allow more control over the visual appeal of an HTML page. Designers were now able to use the Web as they might a word processor, adding tags like <font> and <b> and <i> to mark up the characteristics of their type. In addition, they began experimenting with tables to allow more precise positioning of page elements.

Soon, though, the Web was littered with the extra weight caused by these new tags. Consider that HTML pages are basically text files that are downloaded and rendered in a browser. Each character in that text file, whether it is actual page content or HTML markup, adds size to the page and to the download. Over limited bandwidth where you are trying to squeeze efficiency out of your pages, those extra bytes can be important, and rampant use of presentation tags can become a problem. In addition, making changes to the look and feel of your pages becomes a nightmare when you must manually locate and alter numerous instances of tags that affect only small portions of content.

There has been a return to the concept of using HTML pages to define content and structure by separating the presentation layer. This makes for smaller, more maintainable HTML pages that can be easily adapted to a number of designs. This separate presentation layer is called Cascading Style Sheets.

Cascading Style Sheets

Cascading Style Sheets (or CSS) define how HTML looks. Rather than depending on defaults, or browser implementations, CSS allows the designer to specify at a granular level exactly how each of his or her page elements will appear when a user sees it. A style sheet can be embedded in a specific HTML page, or it can be housed in a separate file that is linked to one or more pages. This means that a single style sheet can be used to define the design elements of large numbers of pages, and those design elements can be altered in an instant, changing the entire look of the site, with changes to that one linked file. Lighter weight code, greater control, and easier maintenance. These are the goals of CSS.

As with any new technology, the use of CSS is still limited by certain browser constraints. Older browsers may not implement CSS at all and will ignore your style sheets. Version 4 browsers offered incomplete, and often buggy, support that is still the bane of many designers. The newer browsers have more complete support for CSS on a more consistent basis, and that is spurring the advance of this extremely powerful technology.

Using CSS

Cascading Style Sheets define the visual properties of HTML elements. They do this in one of two ways: by redefining the base element so that every time it is used the new visual properties are applied, or by defining a class that can be explicitly applied at the discretion of the designer. These style sheet definitions are made up of rules.

A rule is made up of two main components:

- **Selector**   The selector is the page element that you want your formatting to be applied to. For instance, if you want the text contained in paragraphs (<p> tags) to be red, the selector that you are defining is the <p> tag.
- **Declaration**   The declaration is the property/value pair that identifies which property of the element you want to define, and what value that property will have. So to define your paragraph text as red, you would define the color property of the <p> tag with a value of red.

So, a complete rule defining the paragraph tag to contain red text would look like this:

```
p {color: #FF0000;}
```

The declaration is enclosed in braces and ends with a semicolon. Using this syntax, you can declare several declarations for a single selector:

```
p {color: #FF0000; font-size: 18pt; text-align: center;}
```

Use semicolons to separate the declarations in your rule. The closing semicolon is technically optional, but you should use it because its absence may cause trouble in some browsers.

You can also define several selectors with one rule. This can be useful when using some older versions of Netscape that require the definition of additional tags to render consistently. For instance, you might expect a browser to render all paragraph text according to a <p> tag rule, but once table rows and cells become involved, you can have troubles. To get a font rendered consistently, for example, you might define several selectors like this:

```
p, tr, td {color: #333333; font-family: Arial; text-align: left;}
```

Nested Tags

Selectors can also be nested inside one another to allow further control over how page elements display. Suppose that you want all of your paragraph text to be gray, except for text inside a table row, which should be red to make it stand out. You can define that in your rule by nesting the tags as follows:

```
p {color: #333333;}
td p {color: #FF0000;}
```

Nesting begins to display the power of Cascading Style Sheets. They allow a great deal of control over the appearance of your pages in a format that allows for consistent and simple maintenance.

CSS Classes

In addition to redefining HTML tags, you can define multiple rules for a particular selector, or even define rules completely independent of a selector by using CSS classes.

Standalone Classes

Standalone classes are defined independent of a particular selector. They can be used to modify any appropriate tag on a page by selecting the tag and applying the class. For instance, you could define a standalone class that declares italic text. You could use that class to modify a <p> tag or a <span> tag or a <tr> tag at your discretion by selecting the tag and applying the class.

Standalone tags are defined much as other classes are, except that they are not tied to a selector. Following is the italic standalone class rule:

```
.italics {font-style: italic}
```

Notice that the period is still used to identify the rule as a class, but it is not assigned to any particular selector and can be used in a variety of circumstances.

CSS can also be used to define things such as borders on tables and table cells. The following class defines a blank, medium, solid line as a top border, but does not define which selector it is to be attached to. This makes it possible to use this class to add a top border to an entire table, a table row, or just one cell.

```
.border {
    border-top-width: medium;
    border-top-style: solid;
    border-top-color: #000000; }
```

Multiple Rules

Suppose that you want to post an interview on your Web site that consists of questions and answers. To make the interview more readable, you might choose to display the questions in one color and the answers in another, or the questions in bold, and the answers in regular type, or the questions in one typeface and the answers in another. To make matters more complicated, you might even want to change your mind at some point about how the questions and answers are displayed. Defining CSS classes can solve your display problems and your indecision.

You can define certain instances of a tag by creating classes. For instance, we will define the <p> tag to be bold for questions and normal weight and italic for answers.

```
p.questions {font-weight: bold;}
p.answers {font-style: italic;}
```

A class rule applied to a selector is separated from the selector by a period. The questions and answers classes are subsets of the <p> tag in this case and will not modify normal text within a <p> tag unless the page designer selects a particular class to apply to a certain paragraph.

Applying Cascading Style Sheets

There are three ways that you can apply style sheets to an HTML document:

- External style sheets
- Embedded style sheets
- Inline styles

External Style Sheets

An external style sheet is merely a text document saved with a .css file extension that contains the rules that you want to apply to your page. Because it is a separate document, linked to the pages in your site, maintaining the design of your site is as simple as altering and saving the style sheet file. All of the pages that are linked to that file will automatically reflect the changes that you make.

To link an external style sheet to an HTML document, place the following in the head of the page:

```
<link rel=stylesheet href="mystylesheet.css" type="text/css">
```

This will link a style sheet called mystylesheet.css that exists in the same directory as the HTML page to the page in question. You must add this link to every page to which you want the style sheet to apply. But once it is linked, all changes to the styles will be reflected in your pages.

Embedded Style Sheets

Style sheets can be applied to a single HTML page by embedding the rules of the style directly into the head of the document. Place your rules within a <style> tag, as shown here:

```
<head>
<title>My Test Page</title>
```

```
<style>
!--
p {color: #333333; font-face: Arial;}
-->
</style>
</head>
```

Notice that the actual text of the rules is enclosed in a pair of HTML comment tags. This keeps the rules from rendering as text in some older browsers that do not recognize the <style> tag.

Embedded style sheets can be handy to define a particular page, but they nullify a great number of the powerful maintenance advantages of CSS. Style changes would have to be manually applied to each individual page when embedded styles are used. Although they are better than using deprecated <font> tags, it is better to link your CSS files if possible. Embedded style sheets are most useful to invoke the cascading feature of CSS, as shown later in this chapter in the section "Cascading Your Style Sheets."

Inline Styles

Inline styles are styles that are defined directly in the body of an HTML page when the tag you want to modify appears. This can give you complete control of a specific tag instance without requiring that you modify a linked style sheet. But it will not affect any other tags on the page or on any other pages.

```
<p style="font-weight: bold;">This is my heading</p>
```

Applying CSS Classes

CSS classes are not applied to page elements by default. The designer must select the tags to which he or she wants them applied. This allows for the use of multiple rules for a particular selector, as shown earlier. For instance, you may have a series of <p> tags that contain questions and answers in your interview. You can apply the *p.questions* class to the questions and the *p.answers* class to the answers and have your page formatted properly. The resulting code would look like this:

```
<p class="questions">So, how does it feel to be a rich rock and roll
star?</p>
<p class="answers">What do you mean how does it feel? Better than your lame
reporter lifestyle I bet!</p>
```

Cascading Your Style Sheets

So far, we have talked about styles and style sheets, but not much about the cascading part. Understanding how CSS cascades is important to its effective use.

CSS cascades in the same order that we have discussed its application. That means that external style sheets affect all of your linked pages. Embedded style sheets affect only the page on which they exist, and they override settings in the external sheet. Inline styles affect only the tag to which they are applied and override settings from both external and embedded style sheets.

This arrangement allows you to set rules and then amend them for page-level or element-level requirements. A <p> tag that is set to red in an external sheet could be set to blue for a particular page in an embedded sheet and then to green, or even back to red in an inline style. This allows a tremendous level of control over the individual elements of your pages, while still allowing you to separate the rules of presentation into a separate layer to a great degree.

Note   *We cannot cover the entire topic of CSS in the space available. As you migrate your pages to more strict validation schemes, such as XHTML, you will find that you will be required to separate more and more of your presentation-level elements into style sheets and out of your HTML code. A good reference to the details of CSS, such as Eric Meyer's* Cascading Style Sheets: The Definitive Guide *(O'Reilly & Associates, 2000) or* Cascading Style Sheets 2.0 Programmer's Reference *(Osborne, 2001), will become a much-used reference.*

Cascading Style Sheets in Dreamweaver MX

Dreamweaver MX provides an interface with which you can create, manage, and apply style sheets for your site. The CSS Styles Panel is found in the Design Panel Group by default and provides access to the editors you need to add CSS to your pages. With the previous sections in mind, let's look at creating a new style sheet in Dreamweaver.

Creating a New Style Sheet

In the CSS Styles Panel, right-click and select New CSS Style from the menu.

WEB SITE DESIGN AND CONSTRUCTION

You will be presented with a New CSS Style dialog box.

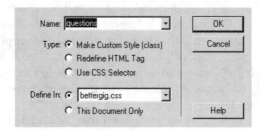

Choose one of the following style types:

- **Make Custom Style (class)**   Creates a class style. You will need to provide a name for the class in the Name box above the radio button.

- **Redefine HTML Tag**   Applies the style to the HTML tag that you select from the drop-down box that appears when you select this option. These style settings will be automatically applied to the selectors you choose.

- **Use CSS Selector**   Applies your style to one of the four defined links that appear in the drop-down box. This allows you to define how your links appear in your pages.

Choose where your style will be defined:

- To create an external style sheet that you can link to your pages, select the (New Style Sheet File) option from the drop-down list. Dreamweaver will prompt you for the name of the new CSS file and where you would like to save it. A folder called css within the root folder of your site is usually a good idea.

- To add this style to an existing style sheet associated with this site, select that style sheet from the drop-down list.

- To create an embedded style sheet that will be placed in the head of this document, select the This Document Only radio button.

Click OK to continue.

As mentioned earlier, style sheets are really just text files. Rather than creating a new file in Dreamweaver, you can simply link to a file that you created at another time by clicking the Attach Style Sheet icon, which is the first icon at the bottom of the CSS Styles Panel. That file could have been created for another site in Dreamweaver, or created in a more complete style sheet editor like BradSoft's TopStyle (www.bradsoft.com). TopStyle Lite ships along with HomeSite+, which ships with Dreamweaver MX.

At this point, you are creating a style. Dreamweaver has either created a style sheet for you or will insert this style into an existing file. Keep in mind that you are working on one style at a time, not several styles within the sheet. Whatever rules you apply during this process will be applied to the selector or class you have chosen.

The Style Sheet Definition editor in Dreamweaver has eight categories. Each category combines several properties that are related to each other. You can pick and choose which properties you want to apply to your style and Dreamweaver will build the rule for you. The following sections outline the available options.

Type

The Type category contains properties related to the display of your text. You can make simple rules applied to all of the text in your site by setting a font, size, and color for the <p> tag, for instance, or you can set only specific properties in a class, such as Weight, that can be applied to a specific selection of text. So, your base text might be Arial, 12 point, and gray. A separate style definition creating a class called *bold* might have only one rule set: a Weight of bold. That class applied to text on your page would result in Arial, 12 point, gray, bold text. The class would cascade on top of the selector rule adding the bold property to the existing properties.

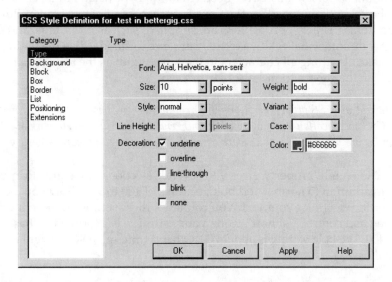

Font   Font provides a list of font families you can select for your text. Font families allow a greater chance that the font you select, or one reasonably similar to it, exists on the user's computer. Remember that the font used to display in a browser must reside on the end user's computer. Just because a fancy font is loaded on your computer and displays properly in your browser does not mean that everyone else will have it. If you need to display text in nonstandard fonts, use graphics. Most base text should be restricted to the Arial, Times, and Verdana families.

The browser will attempt to use the first font in the list and will move to the next if it is not available, until all choices are exhausted and the browser's default font is used. You may select from one of the font families provided, or select the Edit Font List option and create your own.

Size Size is an important consideration. HTML text sizes are relative, meaning that you really only set (+) and (–) sizes in relation to a default font size, which is controlled by the browser settings. If you encounter an odd browser setting, your page is suddenly not what you expected it to be. CSS allows you to precisely control font sizes so that you can control your design.

You can make a size setting either explicitly or relatively (basically the same thing as HTML font sizes). Select one of the text settings, such as small, medium, large and x-large, to create relative sizing.

You can also create a more precise setting by selecting or typing a number in the Size box. When you do, the increment drop-down will enable. It is not enough to say that text should be 10. Dreamweaver needs to know 10 of what. Points is the most common choice, but you can also select pixels, inches, centimeters, and millimeters. In addition, some printer specifications are supplied, such as picas, ems, and exs. Ems and exs are somewhat relative terms, but serve to standardize the widths that characters take by setting all characters to the same width as the *m* or *x* characters respectively in the chosen font.

> **Caution** *Note that the CSS property options in Dreamweaver are based on what is available in the CSS specification and not on what will render properly or even work at all in the popular browsers. Check your work carefully when using the more esoteric CSS settings.*

Weight The Weight property gives you several selections of weights to apply to your text. In addition to normal and bold, settings of 100 to 900 allow you a progressive control over the weight of your text. You could use these settings to redefine the HTML <strong> tag and control just how strong your <strong> is. Normal text has a weight of around 400. The bold setting is about 700. Other settings give you weights in between or outside those.

Style Style allows you to select normal, italics, or oblique. Italic and oblique are similar, but not exactly the same. Exactly how they are displayed is related to the font itself, and whether a specific oblique version is available. Often, oblique will display as a slanted normal font, or in its italic version. A greater difference is seen in serif fonts, where the look of the serifs is styled in the italic version so that they look different than a slanted version of the normal font.

Variant   Variant allows you to set your text to small caps, which is a downsized version of capital letters.

Line Height   Line height allows you to set the leading before a line of text. This affects the space between lines in a paragraph.

Case   Case sets your text to display in uppercase, lowercase, or with initial capitals.

Decoration   Decoration allows you to set additional text properties, such as underline, overline (a line over the text), or line-through. Just forget that the blink option is even there.

Color   Color lets you pick a color for your text using the standard color picker.

Background

The background category allows you to control background colors and images in your site, as well as how they repeat and scroll.

Background Color   Background color allows you to set the background color for an element. You can use it with the \<body\> tag to set the background for a page, or with a table cell, a paragraph, or a link to set it apart from its surroundings.

Background Image   Background image allows you to select an image to be used as the background—most often a page or table cell.

Repeat   Repeat sets whether a background image will repeat if the area it is to fill is larger than the image itself.

Attachment   Attachment sets whether a background image should scroll with the rest of the page. A fixed setting causes the text to scroll over the top of the image, allowing a logo, for instance, to remain in place as the page is scrolled.

Horizontal Position   Horizontal position sets the initial horizontal position of a background image, either numerically or in relation to the element in question.

Vertical Position   Vertical position sets the initial vertical position of a background image, either numerically or in relation to the element in question.

Block

The Block settings control the alignment and spacing of blocks of text.

Word Spacing   Word spacing defines the space between words using the normal size increments discussed earlier. The default value is ems, which is the width taken by the character *m* in the font being used. Positive values increase the space relative to normal, whereas negative values decrease the space.

Letter Spacing   Letter spacing defines the spacing between individual letters.

Vertical Alignment   Vertical alignment sets text alignment relative to its associated elements, such as within a table cell.

Text Align   Text align aligns text relative to its associated elements, such as left, right, center, or justified within a table cell.

Text Indent   Text indent indents or outdents the first line of text in a block by the chosen setting. Use a negative number to outdent.

Whitespace   Whitespace controls how spaces and tabs are displayed within elements. Normal causes extra whitespace within your HTML to be ignored. Pre causes extra whitespace to be rendered. Nowrap causes text to continue in a line until a <br> tag is encountered, ignoring the restriction of the browser window.

Display   Display controls whether the element it is applied to displays, and, if so, how. Setting display to none will turn off the display of the element.

Box

Box styles control spacing and positioning of elements, much like tables. They provide a CSS method of controlling layout, in conjunction with Positioning properties.

Width   Width sets the width of the element it is applied to.

Height   Height sets the height of the element it is applied to.

Float   Float sets the positioning of an element against the left or right margin.

Clear   Clear clears the left, right, or both areas around the element so that text does not flow around it.

Padding   Padding sets the amount of space between the element it is applied to and the element's border or margin.

Margin   Margin sets the margin between the element it is applied to at surrounding elements.

Border

Border styles set borders around elements. Each side of the element can have its own style, width, and color. Check boxes are provided for convenience if you want to have all four set the same for each property.

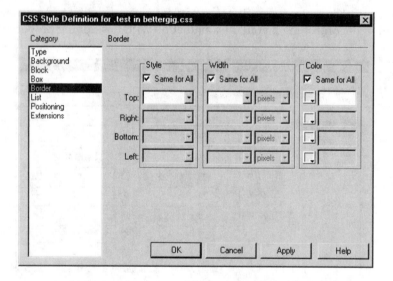

Style   Style sets the style of line to be used for the border to a selection of line styles.

Width   Width sets the width of the line in the standard size increments.

Color   Color sets the color for the line using the standard color picker.

List

List styles control the way that text lists are displayed.

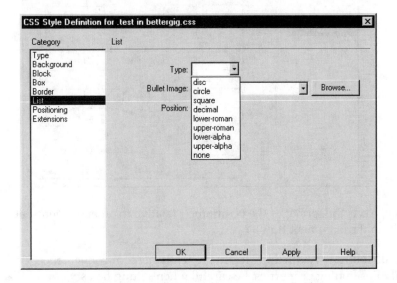

Type   Type allows you to select from a list of standard styles that control the appearance of bullets in unordered lists.

Bullet Image   Bullet image allows you to select an image to use as a custom bullet for unordered lists.

Position   Position sets wrapping for the list. Outside wraps the text to the indent of the list. Inside wraps the text to the page margin.

Positioning

Positioning styles control the exact positions of elements on a page. In fact, what we commonly call *layers* are really precisely positioned block-level elements.

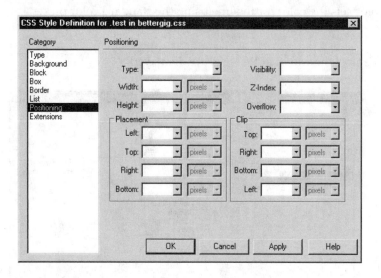

Type   Type sets the format of the positioning relative to other elements, absolute or static (within the document flow).

Width and Height   Width and Height are really here for convenience. They are not strictly Positioning properties. Be careful when setting Box styles and Positioning styles in the same class. The two categories do not always properly synchronize to your desired settings, and your results could be unpredictable. The Box settings should override the Positioning settings.

Visibility   Visibility sets the visibility of the element.

Z-index   Z-index sets the stacking order of the element, providing for elements to exist on top of each other.

Overflow   Overflow controls how an element's contents are handled when they are too large for the size you have defined. You can set it so that the overflowing content is hidden, so that scroll bars are provided, or so that the scroll bars are used only when they are needed.

Placement   Placement sets the actual placement of the element on the page.

Clip   Clip specifies which part of the element is to be visible. You can access clip settings to create DHTML effects using JavaScript.

Extensions

Extensions are properties that control a few special settings.

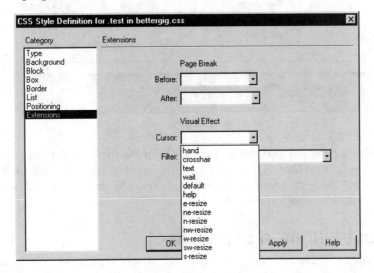

Page Breaks   Page breaks help to control the printing of a Web page by setting page breaks in long documents.

Cursor   Cursor controls how the user's cursor is displayed while at your site.

Filter   Filter provides some filter effects, such as opacity, glow, and masking.

Attaching a Style Sheet

If you are working on a page and pause to create a style sheet, the style sheet will be attached to the page. But when you create additional pages to which you want those styles to apply, you will need to attach the style sheet using the menu selection in the CSS Styles Panel, shown in Figure 12-1.

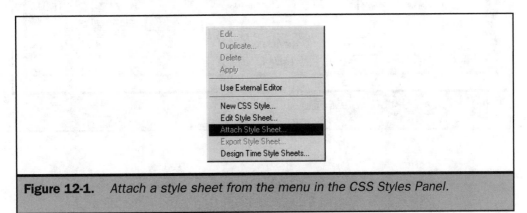

Figure 12-1.   *Attach a style sheet from the menu in the CSS Styles Panel.*

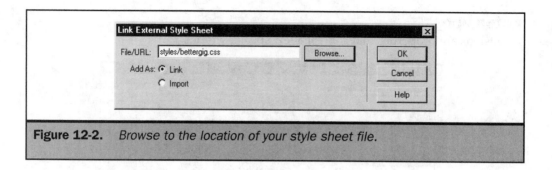

Figure 12-2.   *Browse to the location of your style sheet file.*

You will be prompted to select a file or URL for the location of your style sheet. Use the Browse button shown in Figure 12-2 to locate the file you want to attach. Any styles that affect elements that you have already used on your page will be reflected immediately, such as <p> tag properties.

Applying and Editing a Style Sheet

Dreamweaver's CSS Styles Panel has two views: Apply Styles and Edit Styles. Clicking a style in the Apply view applies that style to the selected element. Double-clicking will open the editor, but the style will have been applied on the first click. That can be a little confusing.

A great new way to apply styles is in Dreamweaver's Property inspector. Notice Figures 12-3 and 12-4. Figure 12-3 shows the default Property inspector view with regular HTML settings.

Click the yellow A. The Property inspector will change to CSS mode. Instead of allowing you to set HTML properties, you can now select from your available styles to display your elements.

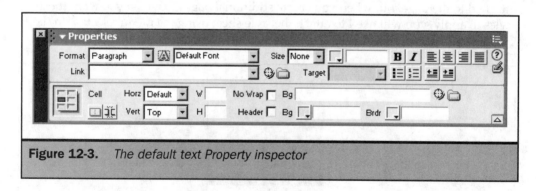

Figure 12-3.   *The default text Property inspector*

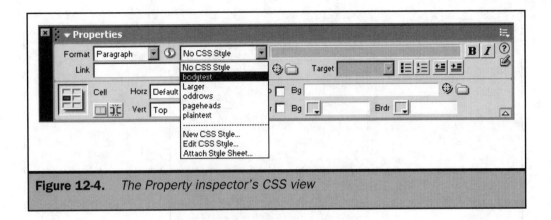

Figure 12-4.   *The Property inspector's CSS view*

From the Edit Styles view, shown in Figure 12-5, you can see the properties that make up each of your classes. Double-clicking a class in this view will open the editor for that class and allow you to edit it.

You can also select Edit from the right-click menu, and the dialog box in Figure 12-6 will allow you to select which class you want to edit.

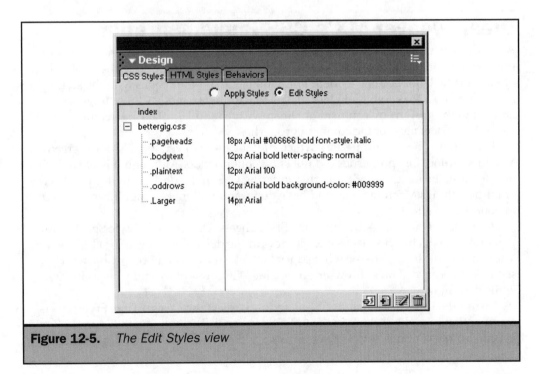

Figure 12-5.   *The Edit Styles view*

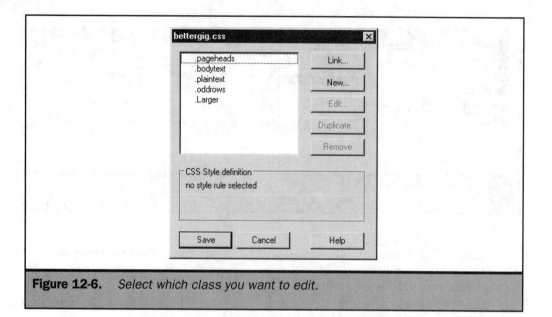

Figure 12-6.   *Select which class you want to edit.*

Dreamweaver MX's CSS Implementation

A lot of work has been done in Dreamweaver's CSS implementation since version 4. But you may not recognize it when you are creating and editing style sheets. The bulk of the work will not become evident until you begin to build pages with the styles you have created. At that point, you will realize that although many CSS settings were ignored in the design environment of Dreamweaver and UltraDev4, Dreamweaver MX correctly renders most of the common properties.

For instance, border properties, which did not show in version 4, show correctly in MX. In addition, List properties did not show, but now do. Although it is not a flashy new feature, the inclusion of properly rendering CSS in the design environment is one of the best things Macromedia could have done, and will make a significant difference in your design efforts.

Another new feature is Design Time Style Sheets. Design Time Style Sheets allow you to select which style sheet's effects show in the design window and which do not. You can use this feature to see what pages look like if CSS is ignored by browser settings or because of older browsers, or to hide Windows- or Macintosh-specific styles while designing.

To use the Design Time Style Sheets settings, select the Design Time Style Sheets menu option by right-clicking in the CSS Styles Panel. The window in Figure 12-7 will appear, allowing you to select which sheets are shown and hidden at design time.

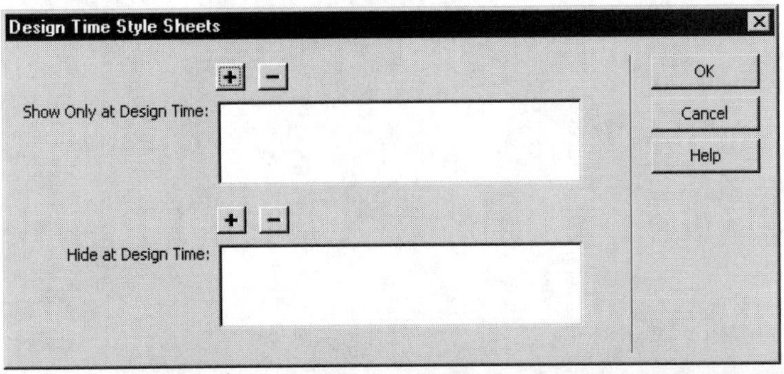

Figure 12-7. *Design Time Style Sheets settings*

> **Caution**   *When your page is viewed in a browser, the actual styles associated with it will appear regardless of your Design Time Style Sheets settings. These settings affect only the Dreamweaver design environment.*

Summary

Cascading Style Sheets is a huge topic. Many older browsers did not properly support them, which has bred a class of designers that does not understand their power. The rise of XHTML will push more and more people towards CSS, however. To be strictly compliant, all display code must be removed from the HTML of your pages, and that means moving even simple things such as table cell alignment to a style sheet.

You may have noticed several properties that resemble things that you can set in Dreamweaver's Property inspector, but resist that urge. Setting a font in a style sheet and setting a font using the <font> tag in HTML are not the same thing. Switch your Property inspector to CSS view and get used to defining those properties in style sheets. You will have more control over your designs, and you can more easily generate standards-compliant code.

The
Complete
Reference

Dreamweaver MX

Chapter 13

JavaScript and DHTML

JavaScript and DHTML are core parts of the Dreamweaver MX experience. In Dreamweaver lingo, a Behavior is what you will be applying to the page to accomplish the task of adding JavaScript or DHTML to a page. Using a Dreamweaver MX Behavior, you can add things such as rollovers, form-field validation, and dynamic menus. Adding a Behavior to a page is a matter of knowing three simple things:

- What do you want to do?
- With which object do you want to accomplish it?
- When do you want it to occur?

If the built-in Dreamweaver MX Behaviors can't do what you need to do, you can download third-party Behaviors, third-party scripts, or you can delve into the world of hand-coding. Either way, you will need to know the basics of DHTML and JavaScript. Before proceeding to Dreamweaver Behaviors, the chapter gives a brief introduction to DHTML.

HTML, CSS, JavaScript, and the DOM

The language of a Web page is HTML, or *hypertext markup language*. With HTML you can have text, images, forms, and hyperlinks, but a markup language is very limited. It can't actually *do* much. You can think of HTML as the *noun* of the Web page whereas JavaScript is the *verb*. JavaScript enables your Web page to have an action of some variety, all enabled from within the browser. If the browser is JavaScript enabled, a whole world of possibilities opens up to you. JavaScript came about for exactly this reason.

HTML at its core is supposed to be a markup language—it is there to form the skeleton of the page, to enable content to be displayed. The formatting of that content should be handled by *cascading stylesheets*, or CSS, which was discussed in the last chapter. The interaction between HTML, CSS, and JavaScript is what makes up *dynamic HTML*, or DHTML. Although the term "dynamic" might make you think of server-side programming or delivering content from a database, when we speak of DHTML, we are referring to the client-side interaction of HTML, CSS, and JavaScript.

The Web browser is enabled with a *document object model*, or DOM. You can think of the DOM as an internal table of contents for your page. A quick look at the table of contents will point you to the part of the DOM that you need. The DOM, however, works behind the scenes to allow other behind-the-scenes players like CSS and JavaScript to find the HTML elements that they need and allows them to interact. If you give your HTML elements names or IDs, your JavaScript can find them more easily.

This DOM can be accessed with JavaScript using *events* of the various HTML elements that make up a page. Different HTML elements have different events associated with them. For example, if you click a button, that button has an associated *onClick* event that fires. This event can be captured by your client-side JavaScript to perform an action on the page. An image has an *onMouseOver* event that can be captured, among others. Knowing what the events of each HTML element are and what can be done with them is the first step. Most DHTML works as the result of an event being fired. Table 13-1 contains a list of some of the more useful events. Actually, many more

Event	Occurs When
onBlur	When an element loses focus
onFocus	When an element gains focus
onClick	When an element is clicked
onLoad	When an element loads
onUnload	When an element is unloaded
onMouseOver	When an element is moused over by the user
onMouseOut	When the mouse is no longer over an object
onMouseDown	When the mouse button is held down (one half of *onClick*)
onMouseUp	When the mouse button is released (the other half of *onClick*)

Table 13-1.   *Some Popular Browser Events*

events are available, but not all events work with all browsers, and indeed some of the listed events work differently in different browsers.

You can also consider the DOM as a container—a container that contains other containers, such as <p> tags, <h1>, <h2>, and <h3> tags, and <table> tags, among others. With DHTML, you perform actions on these containers, such as move them around, make them visible or invisible, or even move them completely off the screen.

History of JavaScript

JavaScript, contrary to popular belief, has nothing to do with Java. It was originally called LiveScript when it first became known, but the name was changed shortly thereafter to JavaScript. The confusion began almost immediately, but despite the fact that the language has a similar syntax, it's not related in any way to Java. Netscape included an early version of JavaScript in its 2.0 browser, and most browsers from that point on have been supporting it. Microsoft's Internet Explorer has a language built into it called JScript, but it is essentially JavaScript.

JavaScript is intended as a general-purpose language that can be used to control many different things. It is built into browsers primarily as a method to control HTML and CSS. It is also built into other programs, such as Dreamweaver and Fireworks, to allow communication with the built-in objects of those programs as well. Flash MX also uses a language called ActionScript, which is very similar to JavaScript.

JavaScript, as its name implies, is a *scripting* language. A scripting language is so named because it is created as a text file that is never compiled—it is executed in the same manner as it is read. Because it is a scripting language, many people don't realize that it can be a powerful multipurpose language that is capable of far more than its name leads you to believe. JavaScript is at its heart a complex object-based language that can perform a multitude of tasks, from moving layers around on your page to generating complete Web sites from the Dreamweaver environment.

Although JavaScript can have many forms, such as server-side ASP, JavaScript Server Pages, or even the JavaScript API of Dreamweaver MX, this chapter discusses client-side JavaScript in a Web browser.

Basic Language Structures

If you are familiar with C++ or Java, learning JavaScript is a breeze, since the syntax is very similar to those languages. If you aren't familiar with a programming language of any variety, you can learn the basics of JavaScript pretty easily; however, JavaScript is far from being a simple language. Depending how deep you want to delve into the intricacies of the language, JavaScript can be a very complex and challenging language.

The most basic part of the language is the concept of the variable. A variable is a container as well. It can contain a number, a string of characters, or an entire object such as a Web page. A variable name can consist of letters, numbers, and underscores, and shouldn't conflict with any built-in JavaScript objects. Variables are also case-sensitive. In fact, JavaScript is completely case-sensitive, so you have to be careful about your case when you are coding. These two variables are completely different:

```
var myvariable = 1;
var myVariable = 10;
```

If you were to display the value of *myvariable*, it would display the value 1.

The keyword *var*, shown in the preceding code, is important in JavaScript. It allows you to create an instance of the variable by declaring it. Even though using it is not strictly necessary, it is important for variable scope. A variable used in a function without a *var* declaration can possibly cause harm by assuming a global scope and possibly overwriting other variables of the same name in other places. It is good practice to always use the *var* keyword the first time you reference a variable.

Some basic things to keep in mind about JavaScript as you proceed through the chapter:

- JavaScript lines have an optional semicolon at the end. If a line break occurs at the end of a line, a semicolon is optional, but using it is good practice—we recommend always using the semicolon.

- JavaScript can contain several statements on one line if they are separated with semicolons.

- You can greatly enhance readability and manageability by utilizing strict coding practices of indentation and naming conventions.

- You can separate commonly used functionality from your page and place it into separate files that are included as JS files.

- Comments are very important, because they allow you to document your code for yourself and for others. A JavaScript one-line comment uses two slashes //, whereas a multiline comment is surrounded by /* */.

Conditional Statements

Conditionals are also a big part of a programming language. In JavaScript, the *if/else* conditional is expressed like this:

```
if (condition ) { //statements }else{//other statements }
```

The *if* statement is followed by a parenthetical statement that is evaluated to true or false. Depending on the result, the statement within the first set of curly brackets could be executed. The *else* statement is optional. If the condition is evaluated to false, the statement within the curly brackets after the *else* keyword would be executed. An *if/else* construct is more properly indented like this:

```
if(condition) {
     //statements;
} else {
     // other statements;
}
```

Some programmers prefer to put their curly brackets on separate lines:

```
if(condition)
{
     //statements;
}
else
}
     //other statements;
}
```

Keep in mind when you code JavaScript that whitespace (spaces, tabs, linebreaks) doesn't hinder performance, and can dramatically improve the readability of your code.

Control Structures and Loops

The main control structures in JavaScript—or any other programming language, for that matter—are the loops and the conditional statements. You can create several types of loops in JavaScript. The most basic type is the *for* loop:

```
for (var i = 0; i < 10; i++) {
     //code to execute
}
```

This loop will cycle 10 times. Because the variable *i* starts at 0, it will cycle through until *i* is no longer less than 10; in other words, 0 through 9. This is one of the fundamental principles of loops that is most confusing for a beginner—the concept of a starting index number of 0.

The *for* loop consists of three optional expressions. The first expression (the *initial* expression) usually sets an index variable to be used in the loop. This variable can be set to 0 or any other number. The next expression is the *condition*. If this condition is evaluated to true, the loop continues. Again, this condition usually compares the index variable to a number, but is entirely optional. If the condition is omitted, it is always assumed to be true. The third statement (known as the *update* expression) is usually an incremental operator (as shown in the example). An example of a *for* loop that never ends can be written like this:

```
for (;;) {
     //never ending loop
}
```

There is no initial expression, a conditional expression is always true when omitted, and there is no update expression. Loops like this can be used with a *break* statement that can terminate a loop.

Another type of looping construct is a *while* loop:

```
while (i < 10) {
     alert(i);
     i = i + 2;
}
```

Lastly, a *for...in* loop can iterate through the properties of an object. JavaScript can reference objects as variables, which is one of the most powerful aspects of the language. This is extremely useful in DHTML where you are frequently working with objects. An example of a *for...in* loop that iterates over every object and property of the body of a document before displaying the result in an alert box is shown here:

```
var theBody = document.body;
var result = "", i = "";
for (i in theBody){
    result += "body" + "." + i + " = " + theBody[i] + "\n";
}
alert(result);
```

Arrays, Functions, and Objects

Arrays are important in JavaScript. An array is nothing more than a variable that has multiple elements. For example, if your page contains several images, you can access these images as an array and reference them by index number or by reference.

Functions are declared using a *function* keyword, and return values can be created by using the *return* keyword. A simple example of a function that capitalizes the first letter of a word and returns the result is shown here:

```
function firstLetterCap(theWord) {
    var theFirstLetter = theWord.charAt(0);
    theFirstLetter = theFirstLetter.toUpperCase();
    var theRest = theWord.substr(1).toLowerCase();
    var theNewWord = theFirstLetter + theRest;
    return theNewWord
}
```

Objects and dot notation are at the core of the way that DHTML works, and is the focus of the next section. JavaScript is an object-based language, and as such objects play a very important part of the language. Whereas integer or boolean variables are examples of simple data types, objects are complex datatypes that can contain other variables, arrays, functions, and objects.

Another important concept of JavaScript is the keyword *this*. When you refer to *this*, it refers to the current object, and you can then access all properties, methods, and events of that object through the keyword. To see the keyword in action, look at the following section of code:

```
<input type="text" name="textfield"
 onblur="this.value = this.value.toLowerCase()">
```

This is a simple text field HTML element that has an *onblur* event with some inline JavaScript. The JavaScript uses this to reference the text field element itself, and therefore has full access to all of its properties, methods, and events. The code here is causing any text in the text field to be converted to lowercase, immediately upon the user leaving the text field.

Dreamweaver MX comes with a JavaScript reference book that is accessible from the Reference panel (see Figure 13-1). Simply choose O'Reilly JavaScript Reference from the Book drop-down menu.

The keyboard shortcut for the Reference panel is SHIFT-F1 and is easy to remember because the basic Help system is F1—adding the SHIFT key allows you to access this "alternative" help system of the Reference Books.

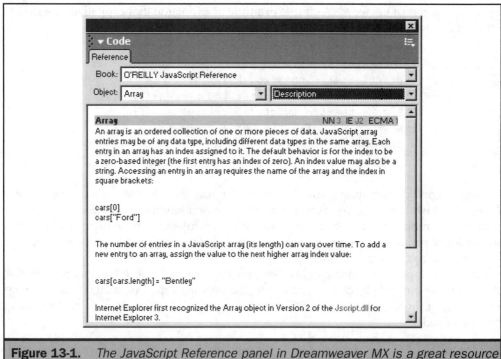

Figure 13-1.   *The JavaScript Reference panel in Dreamweaver MX is a great resource for looking up JavaScript keywords.*

The DOM

The DOM of your Web page has a root level of *document*. This document can be considered everything in between and including the <html> </html> tags. If you look at a basic Web page, the concept will become clearer:

```
1   <html>
2       <head>
3           <title>Home Page</title>
4       </head>
5       <body>
6           <h1>Welcome</h1>
7           <p>If you've come looking for a new job, we're sorry, but this isn't
8               a working job site. It might one day become one, but in the
9               meantime we'd recommend you try the following; and good luck with
10              your new position.</p>
11          <ul>
12              <li><a href="http://www.computerjobs.com">www.computerjobs.com</a></li>
13              <li><a href="http://www.dice.com">www.dice.com</a></li>
14              <li><a href="http://www.monster.com">www.monster.com</a></li>
15              <li><a href="http://www.hotjobs.com">www.hotjobs.com</a> </li>
16          </ul>
17          <p>But...</p>
18          <p>If you have come to learn how to build dynamic, data-driven web
19              sites with Macromedia's Dreamweaver MX, you are in the right
20              place.</p>
21      </body>
22  </html>
23
```

As you can see, the <html> tags are the outermost tags on the page. Also, you should be able to tell from the indentation levels of the code which tags are the direct children of the <html> tags—these are the <head> and <body> tags. They are said to be the children of the <html> tags because they are one level beneath the <html> tags in the hierarchy. The <html> tags are considered the parents of the <head> and <body> tags as well. In fact, *children* is a property of DOM objects that you can access using JavaScript.

These children have children of their own—the <title> tag is a child of the <head> tag, and the <body> tag has several children—<h1>, 3 <p> tags, and a <ul> tag. The <ul> tag, in turn, has children: the <li> tags.

You can refer to the elements using dot notation. If you've never seen dot notation, it is a little like the breadcrumb navigation systems that you find in a Web site. You can access children of an object using a dot, in a hierarchical fashion:

```
document.body
```

This gives you the body object, or the <body> tags of the document. As you recall, the body had several children, so you can access them as an array, as such:

```
document.body.children[0]
```

This gives you the first element of the array—in this case the <h1> tag in the sample page. You can check the length of the *children* property of the body tag like this:

```
document.body.children.length
```

For this sample document, the length property would be 5, because the body tag has five children. The <ul> tag would be the third element of that array (*document.body.children[2]*), so you can find how many <li> tags are under the <ul> tag like this:

```
document.body.children[2].children.length
```

Another property of a tag is *tagName*. You can find the *tagName* of each element of the <body> by using JavaScript to cycle through the array, as in this example for Internet Explorer:

```
var theChildren = document.body.children;
for (var i=0; i < theChildren.length; i++) {
    alert(theChildren[i].tagName);
}
```

As you can see, the script takes advantage of JavaScript's capability to reference any object as a variable. The *children* property of the body object was set to the variable named *theChildren* for easy access in the loop. Now the script can reference *theChildren* object without having to worry about the hierarchy each time it references it. Then the script forms a loop using the length property of *theChildren*, and simply fires an alert box with the *tagName* of each child tag.

Each of these examples will do the same thing. JavaScript is insensitive to whitespace at the end of an expression.

JavaScript also has great text-handling (or, more appropriately, *string*-handling) capabilities as well. A string in JavaScript can be pulled apart, changed to different cases, concatenated, or examined a letter at a time. Because of the case-sensitivity of JavaScript, one of the things you have to remember is that two strings have to be *exact* matches in order to match each other in comparison statements.

You can easily manipulate and calculate numbers in JavaScript as well. All of the standard mathematical operators that you expect to find are there, shown in Table 13-2.

Math plays an important part in DHTML. Not only is it important for looping and examining lengths of arrays in JavaScript, but it is also important because screen coordinates need to be examined, calculated, and plotted for your HTML elements. This is all done with JavaScript. To move an object from point A to point B, you need to know where point A is (the x and y coordinates), where point B is, and how to get from point A to point B.

With that background, we can discuss Behaviors.

Operator	Type	Function
+	Arithmetic	Add
–	Arithmetic	Subtract
*	Arithmetic	Multiply
/	Arithmetic	Divide
<	Relational	Less than
>	Relational	Greater than
<=	Relational	Less than or equal to
>=	Relational	Greater than or equal to
==	Relational	Equal to
!=	Relational	Not equal to
+=,–=, *=, and so on	Compound assignment	Uses the right-hand expression double-duty as the first operand
++	Incremental	Increment a number by 1
--	Decremental	Decrement a number by 1

Table 13-2.   *Operators in JavaScript*

Behaviors

Dreamweaver Behaviors are to JavaScript what Dreamweaver Objects are to HTML. A Behavior consists of JavaScript functions and event handlers. The JavaScript functions are known as *actions* in Dreamweaver terminology. All of the actions respond to *events*. Like most aspects of Dreamweaver MX, Behaviors have a panel of their own. The Behaviors of Dreamweaver are designed to be cross-browser compatible, easy-to-use, and configurable. The Dreamweaver engineers have taken the complexity out of adding JavaScript to your pages and put the functionality into a point-and-click interface.

The Behavior Panel

The Behaviors panel is typically docked in the Design panel group along with CSS Styles and HTML Styles (see Figure 13-2). The panel works in conjunction with the currently selected tag or object. For example, as you open your page, the <body> tag is the current

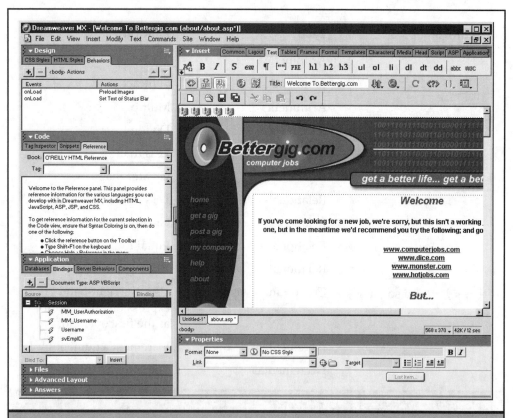

Figure 13-2.   *The Behaviors panel is docked in the Design panel group by default, shown here in Homesite/coder style interface.*

tag. As such, the Behaviors panel (or *Behavior Inspector*) is context-sensitive and displays the Behaviors that are currently applied to the currently selected item.

Figure 13-3 shows a breakdown of the different areas of the Behaviors panel. The plus button (+) and minus button (–) allow you to add a Behavior to the currently selected object. You can see which object is selected by looking at the current tag selection indicator next to the plus/minus buttons. You can also use the tag selector of the document (see Figure 13-4) to select a tag. After selecting the tag, the Behaviors that are available to that tag will be shown in the drop-down menu after clicking the plus sign.

The Behaviors panel is also context-sensitive to the type of browser that you are targeting. You can set up the panel to work with any one of the following browser configurations:

- 3.0 and later browsers

- 4.0 and later browsers

- IE 3.0

- IE 4.0

- IE 5.0

- IE 5.5

- IE 6.0

- Netscape 3.0

- Netscape 4.0

- Netscape 6.0

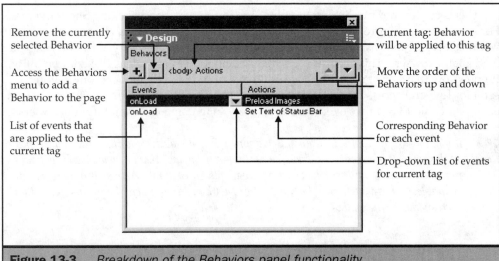

Figure 13-3.   *Breakdown of the Behaviors panel functionality*

Figure 13-4.   *Tag selector for the document makes it easy to select tags to apply Behaviors to.*

This is configured by clicking the plus sign in the panel and clicking Show Events For (as shown in Figure 13-5). This brings up a menu that lets you choose your own functionality. For the vast majority of sites, you are probably better served by choosing 4.0 And Later Browsers. This ensures Netscape 4 compatibility as well as IE 4 compatibility. If you know that your target audience will have only IE 5 and above, though, you can set it for IE 5 and access many events that are not available to IE 4 or Netscape 4. As an example, Table 13-3 shows events for the <body> tag using different target browsers.

If you look in the Configuration | Behaviors | Events folder, you'll see files that contain all the different browser types. Each file contains a list of tags that are available for Behaviors in those browsers, and which events are available for each tag. As new browsers become available, you can customize Dreamweaver MX by adding a new file in this folder that corresponds to the new browser.

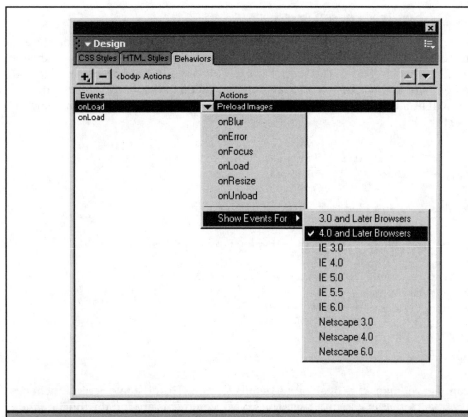

Figure 13-5. *Choosing which browser or browsers to target*

3.0 and Above	4.0 and Above	IE 5.0	Netscape 6.0
onLoad, onUnload	onBlur, onError, onFocus, onLoad, onUnload, onResize	onAfterUpdate, onBeforeUpdate, onBlur, onClick, onDblClick, onDrag, onDragEnd, onDragEnter, onDragLeave, onDragOver, onDrop, onFinish, onFocus, onHelp, onKeyDown, onKeyPress, onKeyUp, onLoad, onLoseCapture, onMouseDown, onMouseMove, onMouseOut, onMouseOver, onMouseUp, onPropertyChange, onResize, onScroll, onStart, onUnload, onAfterPrint, onBeforePrint, onStop, onContextMenu	onBlur, onError, onFocus, onLoad, onMove, onResize, onUnload

Table 13-3. *Events for the <body> Tag in Different Browsers*

Adding a Behavior to a Page

A Dreamweaver Behavior is nothing more than a small JavaScript function (or more than one function) that is added to the page, along with a reference to call that function in the event of an object (an HTML tag). For example, if you open up a blank page and apply a Behavior named Set Text of Status Bar and type in the word "Hello!", the Behavior will be added to the *onLoad* event of the <body> tag. The <body> tag now looks like this:

```
<body onLoad="MM_displayStatusMsg('Hello!');
return document.MM_returnValue">
```

Also, this script is added to the head of the document:

```
<script language="JavaScript" type="text/JavaScript">
<!--
function MM_displayStatusMsg(msgStr) { //v1.0
  status=msgStr;
  document.MM_returnValue = true;
}
//-->
</script>
```

Dreamweaver takes care of all of the details for you. To add a JavaScript function, you have to enclose it in <script> tags. The HTML comments around the function hide the function from older browsers, or other browsers that might not recognize JavaScript. The JavaScript comment, in turn, hides the closing HTML comment (//-->). Dreamweaver puts this script block into the page for you when you first add a Behavior. Upon adding subsequent Behaviors, Dreamweaver will automatically use this same script block each time and continue to add functions to it. If a function already exists, Dreamweaver is smart enough not to add it a second time. If an updated function exists, Dreamweaver will add the updated function in place of the older version. Dreamweaver knows the version number of the function by the JavaScript comment next to the function declaration (*//v1.0* for the previous function).

Other things of note include the *MM_* prefix that Macromedia uses in its JavaScript (and indeed its server-side script as well.) This is not just a marketing ploy to get their initials into your pages. This is to differentiate the scripts from any custom scripts that you might develop. For example, the variable *MM_returnValue* is unique. If you were to have a variable named *returnValue*, which is entirely possible, a conflict would have occurred if it hadn't been for the *MM_* initials. If you are planning to write your own JavaScript functions, consider a naming convention like this to avoid any potential conflicts.

When you add extensions to Dreamweaver MX, you'll notice that many of the developers of those extensions use a prefix for their function names and variable names.

The other thing you should notice is that Dreamweaver automatically chose the default event of the body to apply the Behavior to. The default event of the <body> tag is *onLoad*, so that's what Dreamweaver MX added to the <body> tag. Other HTML elements have different default events. For example, the default event of a button is *onClick*. The default event of an image is *onMouseOver*. You can apply Behaviors to other events as well, and you can even edit the default events to events of your own liking, if you prefer to work with other default events (such as the *onClick* event of an image, for example.)

Changing the default event for a tag is easy to do. For example, if you wanted to change the default event for an <a> tag for 4.0 browsers, simply open up the Configuration | Behaviors | Events | 4.0 Browsers.htm and change the location of the asterisk by taking it out of one event and putting it in another. The asterisk always denotes the default event. The event list for an <a> tag looks like this:

```
<A onClick="*" onDblClick="" onKeyDown="" onKeyPress="" onKeyUp=""
  onMouseDown="" onMouseOut="" onMouseOver="" onMouseUp="">
```

To change the default event from *onClick* to *onMouseOver*, change the code to this and save the file:

```
<A onClick="" onDblClick="" onKeyDown="" onKeyPress="" onKeyUp=""
  onMouseDown="" onMouseOut="" onMouseOver="*" onMouseUp="">
```

The next sections cover all of the built-in Dreamweaver Behaviors.

Call JavaScript

This Behavior allows you to add a custom JavaScript to an event. The dialog box is rather small for this (shown in Figure 13-6), so it's limited to short sections of JavaScript. You can also use this to call functions of your own design as well.

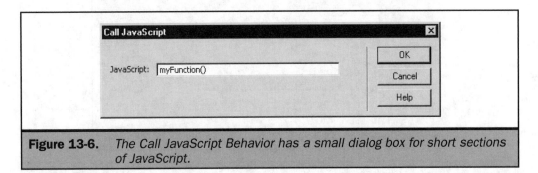

Figure 13-6.   *The Call JavaScript Behavior has a small dialog box for short sections of JavaScript.*

This Behavior is great for adding short sections of JavaScript and not worrying about hand-coding all the details or worrying about which events are available to a particular object. Because Dreamweaver MX automatically assigns the Behavior to the default event, it can be a quick method of adding the JavaScript to your page.

 This Behavior is also great for adding quick debugging information to a specific event. Suppose you want to check the vertical position of a specific element. You could temporarily add an alert box displaying the property that you want to examine using this Behavior, and then remove it just as quickly by removing it from the Behaviors panel.

Change Property

This Behavior changes any property of any object. The Behavior is shown in Figure 13-7, and is limited to the items in the drop-down box for Type of Object. These types are layer, div, span, img, form, input/check box, input/radio, input/text, textarea, input/ password, and select. In addition, you'll notice the Property box has a drop-down list next to it that limits the properties to different browser types. These are IE 3, Netscape 3, IE 4, and Netscape 4.

This Behavior is useful for many things, such as changing the background color of a <div> when an image is moused over, or adding a CSS style to a specific element when that element is moused over. For this Behavior to work properly, your elements have to be named.

You can apply Change Property to any of the available events of various elements, but it is usually used in conjunction with the *onMouseOver* event or the *onClick* event of an element.

Check Browser

This Behavior will check which version of browser the user has and allows you to send the user to another page if they are browsing with a specific browser. The dialog box (shown in Figure 13-8) is quite versatile, allowing you to choose a minimum

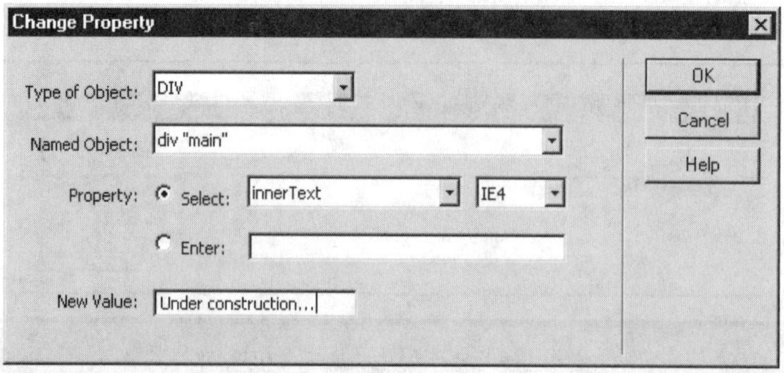

Figure 13-7. *The Change Property Behavior*

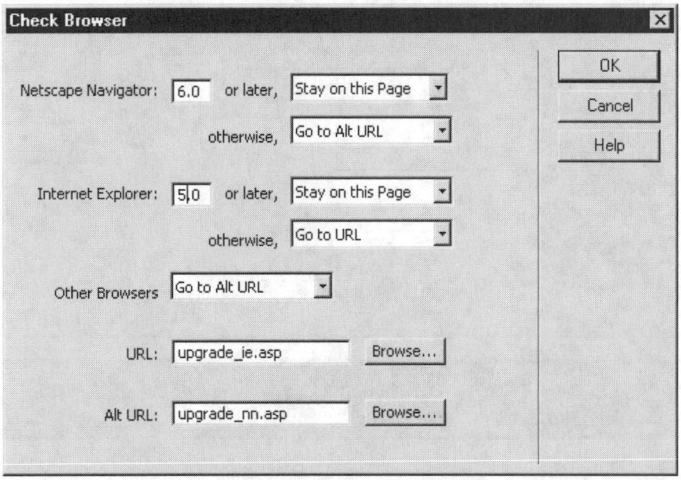

Figure 13-8. *The Check Browser Behavior has several options for redirection.*

Internet Explorer version and a minimum Netscape Navigator version. Also, there is a third box that allows you to target "any other" browser. You have three options for each browser type:

- Stay on this page
- Go to URL
- Go to Alt URL

The URL and Alt URL are set up near the bottom of the dialog box. This way, you can have 1, 2, or 3 separate pages that are set up for different browsers. The alternative page might just be a page that shows upgrade links for the different browser versions, or it can be a similar page that has functionality that works for a particular browser. Many times you will want to accomplish something with DHTML that isn't possible with Netscape 4, so an alternative page can have an alternative form of DHTML that works well with Netscape. Of course, with a little effort there are ways to make DHTML work across different browsers and platforms as well.

Check Browser is usually applied to the <body> *onLoad* event.

Check Plugin

This Behavior allows you to check the browser of the end user for a specific plug-in and act accordingly. Plug-in detection is not 100 percent accurate in different browsers. IE on Windows is usually pretty accurate when detecting plug-ins, but other browsers like IE on the Macintosh cannot always detect plug-ins accurately. For this reason, the Behavior has a check box that allows you to send the user to the default page if plug-in detection isn't possible. Figure 13-9 shows the dialog box for the Check Plugin Behavior.

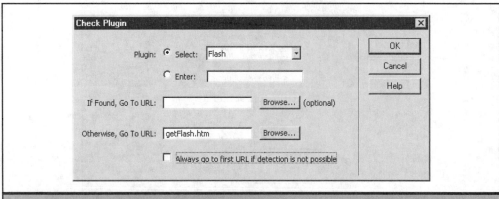

Figure 13-9. *The dialog box for Check Plugin allows you to choose from a predefined list of plug-ins or type in your own.*

You should always put a statement on a page that requires a plug-in giving information to users that a plug-in is required on that page, and also give users a URL to go to if they want to download the plug-in. This way users are not left in the dark as to why the page might not be working—especially if the plug-in detection isn't working properly or if they have JavaScript disabled on their browsers.

The drop-down box for selecting the plug-in contains the following plug-in types:

- Flash
- Shockwave
- LiveAudio
- QuickTime
- Windows Media Player

If you want to check for a different type of plug-in, you can enter the name in the Enter box directly below the Select box.

The Check Plugin Behavior is usually applied to the *onLoad* event of the <body> tag, allowing quick detection before the page is loaded in.

Control Shockwave or Flash

If you have a Flash or Shockwave file on the page, you can control it from another object, such as starting a movie from the click of an image. This gives your HTML elements more control over your Flash or Shockwave files. The Behavior will be grayed out in the menu if you don't have any Flash or Shockwave movies on your page.

The Flash or Shockwave embedded movie has to be named in order for the Behavior to work. If the movie is unnamed, an alert will tell you to cancel the dialog box and go back and name your movie.

The options in the Control Shockwave or Flash dialog box (shown next) allow you to play a movie, stop a movie, rewind a movie, or move to a specific frame.

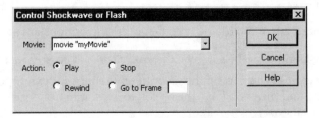

The Control Shockwave or Flash Behavior is usually applied to the *onClick* event of buttons or images.

 The Control Shockwave or Flash Behavior doesn't work in certain browsers, such as versions of Internet Explorer on the Mac and Netscape 6. This is because of problems with the browsers, not because of any fault in the Behavior code.

Drag Layer

This Behavior allows a visitor to your site to drag a layer around on the screen. This is useful for games, menus, puzzles, or other special effects. This Behavior is best applied to the *onLoad* event of the body, allowing the functionality to be activated upon loading the page. It can also be activated by some custom JavaScript. For example, if you have an online quiz that the user can answer questions to, a correct answer could trigger an area to become movable. This Behavior is one of those Behaviors that are limited only by your imagination.

Many options are available to this Behavior. There is a Basic tab (shown next) and an Advanced tab. In the Basic tab, you have the following options:

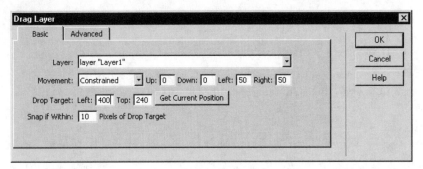

- Choose the layer you want the user to be able to drag.

- The movement can be unconstrained, or it can be limited in any direction (up, down, left, right).

- You can set the Drop Target left and top positions. A handy button allows you to get the current top and left positions of the layer, so that you can make an informed decision about where to set these.

■ You can also set the snap accuracy. If the layer is within a specified number of pixels, code will be written that will allow the layer to "snap" to the drop target coordinates.

In the Advanced tab of the dialog box, the following options are available:

■ The Drag Handle can be set to be the entire layer of an area inside the layer.

■ When dragging, you can set the layer to ignore its z-index property and always be in front, and then you have the option to leave it in front or restore its original z-index position.

■ You can fire a JavaScript function while dragging.

■ You can also fire a JavaScript function after the layer is dropped. There is an additional option that will check to see if the layer was snapped to the drop area. The JavaScript function can be set to go off only if the layer was dropped in the drop area.

The Drag Layer Behavior offers a wide variety of interesting functionality that can be appreciated only by experimenting with it. The following is a simple example of the Drag Layer functionality. The example will also take advantage of the Change Property Behavior described earlier.

1. Add the following code to a page:

```
<div id="jobsearch" style="position:absolute; left:0px; top:0px;
 width:250px; height:80px; z-index:1; background-color: #FFFFFF;
layer-background-color: #FFFFFF; border: 1px solid #000000;">
<form name="form1" method="post" action="job_search.asp">
      <table width="100%">
      <tr>
        <td>Drag Layer Demo</td>
      </tr>
      <tr>
        <td><input type="text" name="textfield">
<input type="submit" name="Submit" value="Submit"></td>
      </tr>
      <tr>
        <td>Enter Search criteria or <a href="#">close</a></td>
      </tr>
    </table>
</form>
</div>
```

2. Select the <body> tag using the tag selector of the document.

3. Add a Drag Layer Behavior to the page. Leave everything set to the default values. This will allow the layer to be activated upon page load, with unconstrained movement, no drop target, no JavaScript functions executed, and using the entire layer as the drag handle.

4. Add a Change Property Behavior to the <a> tag around the text "close." In that Behavior, choose the following options:

- **Type of Object**   div
- **Named Object**   div jobsearch
- **Property**   Enter **style.visibility**
- **New Value**   hidden

Browse the page to test it out. The layer should be draggable over the entire page, and clicking the link on the text "close" will cause the layer to be hidden and unusable. Figure 13-10 shows the effect on an existing page. Notice how the layer sits on top of the entire page, allowing the end user to reposition it anywhere. You could also add some text to your page that would also cause the layer to become visible again using the Change Property Behavior as well.

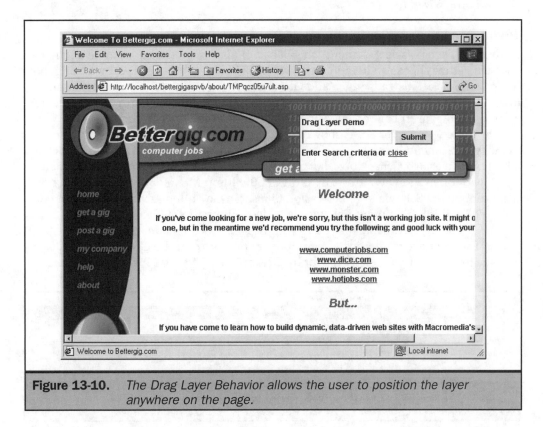

Figure 13-10.   *The Drag Layer Behavior allows the user to position the layer anywhere on the page.*

Go To URL

This Behavior redirects a visitor to another Web page in the main window or in a frame. It is especially handy when dealing with frames, because you can add redirection to each frame element. This is what separates this Behavior from a standard <a> link. The Behavior is shown here:

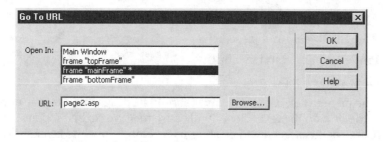

Hide Pop-Up Menu

Hides a pop-up menu that's been shown. Pop-up menus are covered in the section "Show Pop-Up Menu."

Jump Menu

Added to a list box (select element), this Behavior allows a visitor to jump to another URL when they choose an item in the box. The Behavior is best applied by adding the Jump Menu object instead, which adds the <select> tag and the Behavior at the same time. The Jump Menu can be added to the page from the Insert | Form Objects menu, or by using the Insert bar and choosing the Forms tab (shown in Figure 13-11).

The Jump Menu interface is shown in Figure 13-12. The interface allows you to add as many static menu items as you need, with separate boxes to fill in for a text label and a URL. There is also a check box that allows you to specify whether to use the main window or open a new window. In addition, the Jump Menu object has a check box that is not on the Behavior—it allows you to insert a Go button next to the jump menu. If you check this box, another Behavior is added—Jump Menu Go.

The Behavior is available for you to edit the choices you made in the Jump Menu object. The interface is identical except for the check box for the Go button. This is actually treated as a separate Behavior by Dreamweaver because it is applied to the

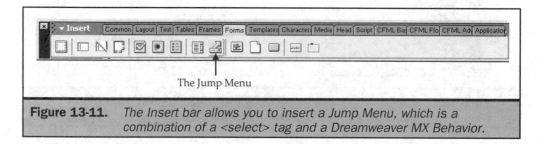

The Jump Menu

Figure 13-11. *The Insert bar allows you to insert a Jump Menu, which is a combination of a <select> tag and a Dreamweaver MX Behavior.*

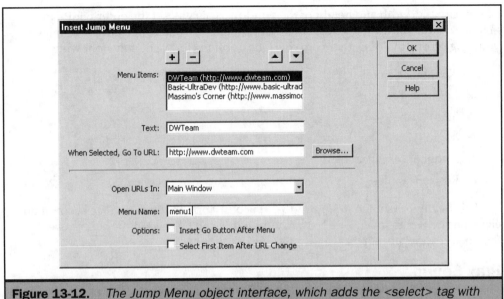

Figure 13-12.   *The Jump Menu object interface, which adds the <select> tag with a Jump Menu Behavior already attached to it*

button and not to the menu itself. It is available as Jump Menu Go from the Behaviors menu, and is covered next.

Jump Menu Go

This Behavior associates a Go button with a Jump Menu. If you added a Go button directly from the Jump Menu object interface, this Behavior allows you to edit or remove the Behavior. The only parameter that you can edit is which Jump Menu the button is attached to (shown next). Also, you may notice that the Jump Menu continues to work in the *onChange* event of the menu itself. The Go button is mostly used to allow the user to be redirected to the site that is currently showing in the Jump Menu without changing the selection.

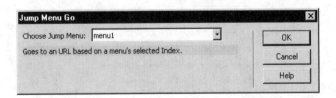

Open Browser Window

This Behavior allows you to open another browser window with a specific URL. This Behavior also allows you to specify exactly how you want that window to appear. You can specify the width and height of the window. This will set the outer width and height, so you will want to make sure that different browsers are going to display your page correctly. Also, there are check box options for each of the following:

- Navigation Toolbar
- Location Toolbar
- Status Bar
- Menu Bar
- Scrollbars as Needed
- Resize Handles

This Behavior (shown in Figure 13-13) is best applied to the *onClick* event of an element, such as an image or a button, although it can be used in the *onLoad* event of the <body> as a "pop-up."

Play Sound

This Behavior allows you to choose a sound file to be played on an event. The sound can be any valid sound file, such as a WAV or MP3 file. The only parameter for this Behavior is the name of the sound file that you want to play. You can choose a file outside of your site and Dreamweaver MX will automatically prompt you to save it into your local site.

This Behavior is typically applied to the *onClick* event of a button or image, but it can be applied to almost any event that makes sense. For example, to have a sound play upon loading the page (such as a background music file), you can apply it to the *onLoad* event of the <body> tag. You can also create special effects, such as enhancing your rollovers with sound effects. Keep in mind, however, that sound files can increase the load time of your page dramatically. Also, compatibility with different players is not always guaranteed.

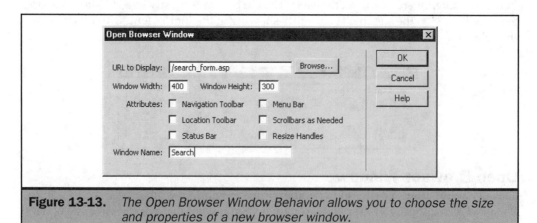

Figure 13-13.   *The Open Browser Window Behavior allows you to choose the size and properties of a new browser window.*

Pop-Up Message

This Behavior pops up a JavaScript alert box with a message. This is perhaps the simplest Behavior available. One advanced feature isn't apparent from the interface: You can include JavaScript in the message if you enclose it in curly braces, like this:

```
The year is {new Date().getFullYear()}
```

Preload Images

This is one of those "behind the scenes" Behaviors that can enhance the end user's experience at your site. This Behavior allows your page to load all images needed before the page loads, to make rollover effects more natural. Some of the other built-in Behaviors will add this Behavior to the page. Also, when you export HTML from Fireworks, this Behavior is added as well.

It allows you to browse to each image file individually to allow them to preload. You can preload as many images as your page needs, but you should also be aware that this Behavior will cause the page load time to increase as well. It is, however, a great way to get your rollover images to load with the page rather than after the user rolls over the image for the first time. Figure 13-14 shows all of the "down" images for the rollovers on a page loaded into this Behavior.

The Preload Images Behavior can also be attached at the same time as the Swap Image Behavior for rollovers. A check box on that Behavior allows you to attach both Behaviors at the same time. It is also an option in the Insert Navigation Bar and Insert Rollover Image objects as well.

Set Nav Bar Image

The Navigation Bar is an interactive object from the Insert menu and toolbar. This Behavior allows you to set an image on that bar if it's on your page already.

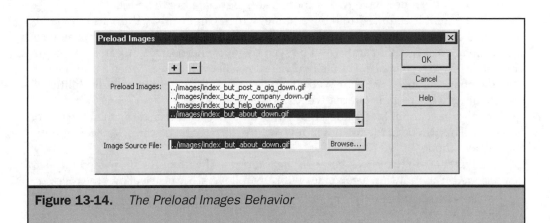

Figure 13-14.   *The Preload Images Behavior*

To insert a Navigation Bar object, locate the Navigation Bar on the Common tab of the Insert bar, or choose Navigation Bar from the Insert | Interactive Images menu. This brings up the following dialog box:

From this box you can create and customize the Navigation Bar. Before starting, however, you need to have all your ducks in a row and have all of your images ready that are going to be used in the bar. Each bar element can use one, two, three, or four separate images—Up Image, Down Image, Over Image, and Over While Down Image. This object is most useful when you have two or more states associated with an image.

Each element is required to have a name, which can be any valid variable name. No spaces or special characters are allowed, but you can use underscores. This name is for the JavaScript function and won't be seen by your end users. You can also assign alternative text to each image. The alternative text is what will be seen when a user hovers over the image. If you want your Web site to be accessible to people with disabilities, you should always include alternative text for your images.

You also have to set the location that you want the user directed to when the button is clicked. This can be in the main window, or if your page has frames, you can assign the link to a frame.

Finally, there are two check boxes in the interface. The first is to allow the images to be preloaded. This is always a good idea with any rollovers, because it allows the rollover effect to be preloaded with all of the images that it needs, instead of loading them in the first time the user attempts the rollover. The second check box is to allow the Down image to be used as the default rather than the Up image.

With all of that information filled out for each set of images you are using, you can click OK, and the object will be inserted into the page, along with all of the Behaviors necessary to make the object work. The object will insert a table into your page, with each default image in its own table cell. Also, a Behavior is applied to each image for each event that you have chosen in the object interface. For example, if you have an Over image, there is an *onMouseOver* event that calls the *MM_nbGroup* function. This function is called for each aspect of each effect.

Later, if you try to add another Navigation Bar to the same page, you won't be able to but will instead be prompted to edit the existing Navigation Bar. You can re-edit the Navigation Bar from the same interface as you used to create it, or you can edit the individual Behaviors that are attached to each image by using the Behaviors panel.

To edit the individual Behaviors, you have to select the image inside of the Navigation Bar. This will cause the Behaviors panel to list any Behaviors that are associated with each image. There should be three Behaviors associated with each button—*onClick*, *onMouseOver*, and *onMouseDown*. The Set Nav Bar Image Behavior looks like this:

As you can see, it looks almost like the Navigation Bar object interface except for two key things: You can work with only one image at a time, and there is an Advanced tab.

The Basic tab has the exact same functionality as the Navigation Bar object. The Advanced tab, on the other hand, allows you to control other images, as shown here:

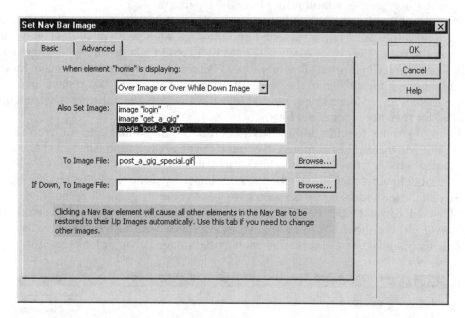

You can utilize this to achieve interesting effects with your navigation bar by having up to six different images associated with each button.

Set Text

This menu item in the Behaviors menu supplies four different Behaviors to set the text of a Layer, Frame, Text field, or the Status Bar. Each one works similarly, with the exception of the Status bar. The Behaviors allow you to choose the element that you want to set the text for, and then choose the text or html that you want to be placed inside the element. The Set Text Of Status Bar Behavior is even simpler because the only option is for the actual text that you want placed in the status bar. The Set Text Of Text Field Behavior is shown here:

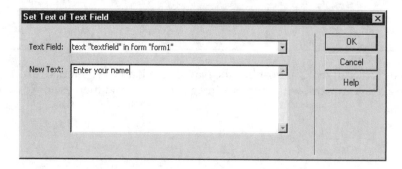

These Behaviors become activated only if there is an element on the page that they can be applied to. For example, if there is no text field on the page, the Set Text of Text Field Behavior will be grayed out in the menu.

These Behaviors can be applied almost anywhere, such as the *onChange* of a <select> element, or the *onClick* of a button, or the *onFocus* of the element itself.

These Behaviors have another useful feature that is not apparent from the interface: you can use JavaScript within the text by enclosing it inside of curly braces, like this:

```
Today is {new Date()}
```

Show Pop-Up Menu

This Behavior allows a user to edit or create pop-up menus, or edit menus imported from Fireworks. If the menu has been imported from Fireworks, it most likely contains images. The pop-up menus created in Dreamweaver MX contain text only, but images created in Fireworks can be directly edited from Dreamweaver MX.

To create a new menu, open the Show Pop-Up Menu Behavior. Your page must be saved before the menu can be applied to it, because a JavaScript include file is going to be written to the site to the same directory as your page. If your page isn't saved, a dialog box will pop up telling you to save the page first.

The pop-up menu should be applied to an HTML element, such as an image or a button. You'll see the dialog box shown here:

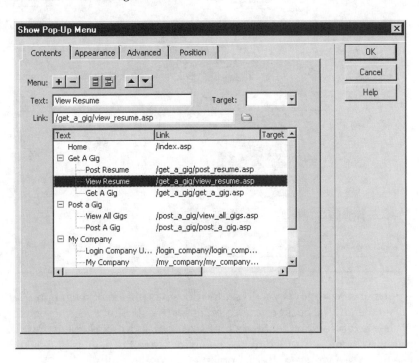

The names and locations for each menu item need to be completely spelled out in this interface. Again, like the Navigation Bar, you have to be completely ready with all of the information you are going to need before applying this Behavior. You should have the design of the menu plotted out beforehand. What is each button going to say? What is going to be in the submenus? Are the submenus going to have submenus? What colors are you going to use?

With all of that information in hand, you can begin creating your menu. Like all of the Dreamweaver MX Behaviors, you don't need to know JavaScript to apply this Behavior, yet it will insert some very sophisticated DHTML effects into your pages through the point-and-click interface.

On the first page of the interface, labeled Contents, you can insert all of the text and links for your menu. Upper-level menus don't require a link, because they will open up submenus. You can indent the text by clicking the indent button on the interface to create the submenu. By indenting the text, the structure of the menu is defined. Each level of indentation provides another submenu. You can create many levels of submenus by simply indenting the text in the interface. After your menu structure is complete, you can switch to the Appearance tab, shown here:

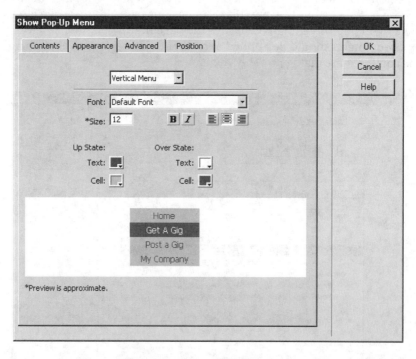

The Appearance tab allows you to set the design elements of the menu. Here is where you set the *up state* background color, *up state* text color, *over state* background color, *over state* text color, text font face, font size, font styles, and orientation. This style information is dynamically added by the Behavior when the page is browsed. You can also choose to make a vertical or horizontal menu from this tab.

After you've completed the appearance of the menu, you can switch to the next tab, which is the Advanced tab, shown here:

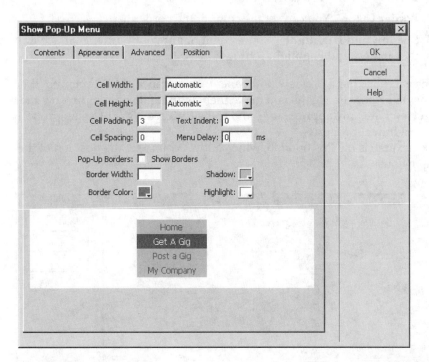

The Advanced tab is really not "advanced," but instead allows you to edit properties of the cells that contain your menu items. From this tab, you can control the following properties of the menu items:

- **Cell Width** Actual pixel width of the cell. The default is Automatic, which will cause the menu to be slightly larger than your largest text item in each menu.

- **Cell Height** Actual pixel height of the cell. The default for this is Automatic as well.

- **Cell Padding** This setting allows you to pad your cells with space (in pixels) so that the text doesn't feel cramped in the menu.

- **Cell Spacing** This setting allows you to pad the spacing between the outer edge of the border and the outer edge of the actual cell. Padding and spacing were both described in Chapter 12.

- **Text Indent** This setting is for the left indentation of the text. If you choose to center your text, you shouldn't need to use this setting, but if you set your text to the left edge, you can use this to put a little bit of space between the outer edge and the text. Again, this is measured in pixels.

- **Menu Delay** You can specify the number of milliseconds before your menu opens up. For quick-response menus, you can leave this set to 0.

- **Show Borders**   This check box allows you to have borders in your menus.
- **Border Width**   You can set the width of the border here.
- **Border Color**   You can set the color of the border here.
- **Shadow and Highlight**   Your can highlight your borders with color by using the Shadow and Highlight settings.

This page also has a preview of the menu appearance at the bottom of the tab, so you can view your changes as you make them without having to preview the page. The previews are only approximate, and some features don't preview properly (such as the Text Indent property).

The next tab is the Position tab, which allows you to set the position of the pop-up menus:

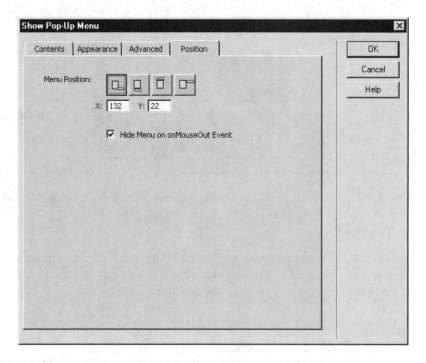

There are four preset buttons in this tab that have predefined x and y positions. You can also write in your own x and y positions if the presets don't work for you. The last option on this page is the check box for Hide Menu On onMouseOut Event. This should always be checked, unless you have a specific reason for leaving the menu open after a user has moused off of the menu.

With all of the items filled in, you can click OK, and the menu will be applied to the page. Also, a JavaScript include file is written to your site to the directory of your page. If you need to edit the Behavior at a later date, you can go back to the Behaviors panel and double-click on the Behavior. The same dialog box will pop up. It takes a few seconds to load in because of all of the information that it contains, but all of your original menu settings will be preserved. This is handy when you want to test out your menus and then go back and make changes later.

Show-Hide Layers

This useful Behavior allows you to turn layers on and off. This Behavior and others like it are at the core of DHTML in the Dreamweaver MX environment. The key to utilizing these Behaviors is to understand the workflow among the Layers panel (shown in Figure 13-15), Property Inspector (shown in Figure 13-16), and Behaviors panel. The Layers panel is not shown by default, but can be shown by clicking Window | Others | Layers.

When you insert layers on the page (usually <div> tags), they are given ID attributes like "Layer1," "Layer2," and so on. The first thing you should do when you apply a layer to the page is to give it a meaningful name, which will be added as an ID attribute to the layer. You can do this from the Property Inspector or from the Layers panel. All layers should have a unique ID value.

Note *When you change the name of the layer from the Layers panel, you are actually changing the layer ID attribute.*

Layers are very flexible in that you can have many layers on your page and they can overlap, be stacked as a set, or exist side by side. The trick to working with them— especially layers that are stacked or overlap—is to hide them while in design view and display the layer you are currently working on. You can do this easily from the Layers panel by clicking the icon in the *eyeball* column. An open eyeball means the layer can be seen, and the shut eyeball means the layer is hidden.

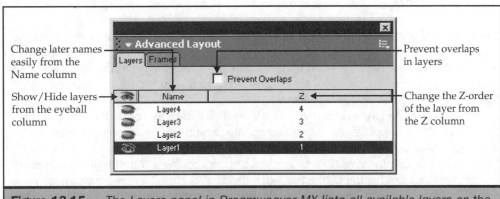

Figure 13-15. *The Layers panel in Dreamweaver MX lists all available layers on the page, and allows layers to be shown/hidden easily.*

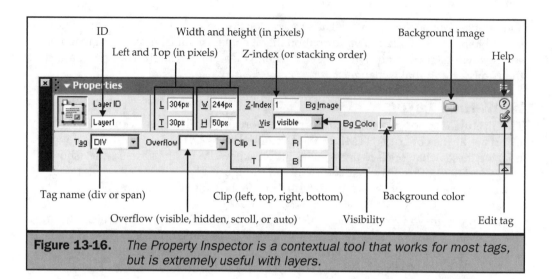

Figure 13-16. *The Property Inspector is a contextual tool that works for most tags, but is extremely useful with layers.*

You can manipulate layers one by one, or you can SHIFT-select multiple layers in the Layers panel or in design view and do one of two things:

■ Change properties of multiple layers by changing the values in the Property Inspector while multiple layers are selected

■ Align left, align right, align tops, align bottoms, make widths the same, or make heights the same by accessing the Modify | Align menu while multiple layers are selected.

Tip *You can set the visibility of multiple layers at once by using the same method: Select all layers in the Layers panel and click the eyeball icon. This is a quick and dirty way to turn off all layers so that you can concentrate on an individual layer.*

You can adjust the z-index, or *stacking order*, of layers by using the Layers panel as well. The layers in the panel are in the correct stacking order, so they will automatically arrange themselves as you reposition them. Simply select a layer in the panel and drag it to a new position. You can also set z-indexes manually by typing the number into the Layers panel or the Property Inspector.

The Show/Hide Layers Behavior (shown next) is generally applied to elements other than layers. For example, a mouseover on an image might show a description in a hidden layer right next to the image. Upon mousing off the image, the layer can be hidden again. Or you can display an image in a larger layer upon clicking a thumbnail version of the image. You can create effects like this with the Show/Hide Layers Behavior. Simply apply the Behavior to an element, click the Show button for each layer that should be shown, click the Hide button for each element that should be hidden, and leave the other layers set to default (or leave them set to nothing).

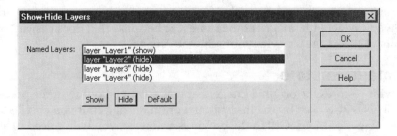

Swap Image

You can apply this Behavior by itself to swap one image for another. The Insert Rollover image object also adds this Behavior to the page. It is the basis of image rollover techniques in Dreamweaver MX.

To use it, select the image that you want the rollover to apply to. You should already have the alternate image picked out and located in your images directory in your Web folder. Choose Swap Image from the Behaviors menu. This will bring up the dialog box shown here:

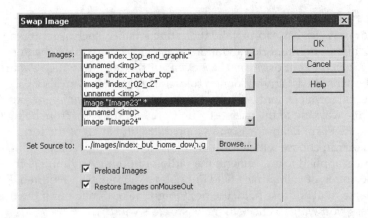

The dialog box will show all images on the page. To utilize this Behavior properly, you should have your images named, so that they are easily distinguishable by the Behavior. Pick your image from the list (it should be preselected if you applied the Behavior directly to it). Next, pick an image to Set Source To by using the Browse button to bring up the Web directory to pick your image file. You can repeat this for as many images as you need to swap—more than one image can be swapped by this Behavior at any one time, and this Behavior can also be applied as many times as needed on your page.

You should also check the box to preload the images. This will ensure that your DHTML effects are smooth. Also, you should check the box to restore the image on mouse out. This will add the Swap Image Restore Behavior to the page, and will ensure that your images are returned when the user moves his or her mouse off the image.

Use Swap Image with images of the same size because all it does is swap out the *src* attribute of the image tag with your alternate image.

Swap Image Restore

This Behavior restores the original image that was swapped out with the preceding Behavior. This is also used by the Insert Rollover Image object. If you checked the box to Restore Images onMouseOut in the previous Behavior, you won't need to apply this one. They are kept separated, however, in case you want them to act separately or if you want the image to remain on the screen after the mouseover.

Timeline

These Behaviors (Go To Timeline Frame, Play Timeline, and Stop Timeline) work together with the Timeline (Window | Others | Timeline). The Timeline is one of the DHTML marvels of Dreamweaver MX. The timeline, however, inserts a lot of code into your document and should be used only where special effects are the reason for the page—don't apply it as a casual effect to an informational page.

Validate Form

This Behavior provides basic form validation functionality, such as required field, e-mail address validation, and numeric validation. You should place this Behavior on a <form> tag in the *onSubmit* event or the *onClick* event of the button, which ensures that the form won't be submitted if any validation rules are broken. You can also place the Behavior on an individual form element, such as a textfield, on the *onBlur* event, but this serves only as a gentle warning to the user—it won't prevent the form from being submitted.

The Validate Form Behavior is shown next. It will list all of the form elements on your page. You can choose which form elements to apply individual validations to. If no validation is applied to an element, the radio button for Anything is checked. You also have the option of validating a field but not making the field required. For example, if you have an e-mail address field, the field might be optional, but if the user enters an e-mail address, you want to check to make sure it's valid.

This Behavior also allows you to validate for a range of numbers, like between 1 and 10.

 As with all critical data, if you are validating a form field for storage in a database, you should always back up the client-side validation with server-side validation as well. Some users disable JavaScript in the browser, and if they do, the validation won't work.

Third-Party Behaviors

The Behaviors that ship with Dreamweaver MX will give you a core set of DHTML effects and JavaScript functionality, but the Behaviors panel is best exploited by third-party developers such as Project Seven, Massimo Foti, Jaro von Flocken, and other talented developers around the world. Extensions are available from the Macromedia Exchange (www.macromedia.com/exchange) and from other developer sites.

Third-party Behaviors and other extensions are covered in Chapter 30.

Timelines

Timelines are Dreamweaver's one-stop shopping store for DHTML. Timelines consist of frames, like a movie, and each frame is spelled out with the locations and actions of each element. With a timeline you can animate a layer, play sounds and movies, or fire off other Behaviors from frames within the Timeline. Timelines have become somewhat outdated with the arrival of Flash, but for a quick DHTML page with a minimum of effort, a timeline might be just what your page needs.

Timelines have a panel of their own that is accessible from the Window | Others menu. Timelines are programmable from the Modify | Timelines menu. The Behaviors panel offers the controls for the timelines—Go To Timeline Frame, Play Timeline, and Stop Timeline. Between these three areas you can find all of the timeline functionality.

The timeline represents a length of time, which is denoted by the frame numbers in the playback bar. If your frame rate is 15 frames per second, for every second of time you must plot out 15 frames. You can quickly plot out animations by knowing your starting points and your ending points and letting Dreamweaver plot the points in between.

Inserting a Timeline in Your Page

To add a timeline to your page, open up your Timeline Inspector by clicking Windows | Others | Timelines. This will bring up the timeline window to allow you to begin adding elements to the timeline. At this point, the timeline is not actually on your page. As soon as you add an element to the timeline, the timeline will be added to the page. You can add elements to a timeline by clicking Modify | Timeline | Add Object To Timeline (or Add Behavior To Timeline). This will start the process.

Add an element by right-clicking on the timeline on the frame that you want the element to start at and choose Add Object. This will add the object to the timeline at that frame.

WEB SITE DESIGN AND CONSTRUCTION

With the timeline panel open, you can select your layer in design view and then open up the Property Inspector for that layer to change the properties. Keep in mind that you can specify negative values for the left and top attributes to have your element appear from offscreen to move onscreen or vice versa. Also, you need to keep in mind that your Property Inspector is showing the properties for the layer *at that particular point in the timeline*. If you move the head across the frames, then in design view, your objects will actually move, and the Property Inspector will show the values of the current position of that object.

Adding a Behavior to a Timeline

You can apply Behaviors to timelines as well. For example, you might want to show a particular layer at a specified time in relation to the timeline. You can right-click a frame and Add Behavior to add the Behavior to that particular frame. A dialog box will pop up and ask you to choose the Behavior. After choosing one, your timeline will show a placeholder in the Behaviors Channel of the Timeline Inspector.

Because Behaviors are so flexible, you can use this technique to add your own custom JavaScript to the timeline as well. For example, you could have a quiz site that only allows a specified amount of time to answer a question. After the time is up, your timeline could cause a JavaScript form submit to take place.

Starting and Stopping Timelines

The Timeline Inspector has two check boxes—Autoplay and Loop. The Autoplay check box will actually cause a Start Timeline Behavior to be applied to the page in the *onLoad* event of the <body> tag. This Behavior will show up in the Behaviors panel as well as showing up on the Timeline Inspector as a check. You can manually apply the Behavior to the <body> *onLoad* event, or to other events of other objects, such as the *onClick* event of an image, to allow the timeline to start upon a click.

The other check box will allow the timeline to continuously play over and over if checked. You can also apply a Stop Timeline Behavior to objects as well, which will cause the specified timeline, or all timelines, to stop at that moment.

Automating Path Creation

One of the neat features of the timeline is the automatic path creation. This takes a little practice to get right, but can produce some interesting effects. The way to use this feature is to select an object that you want to animate and then choose Record Path Of Layer from the contextual menu of the Timeline Inspector or from the Modify | Timelines menu. This puts you in *record* mode. As you move the object, the path on which you move the object is recorded. When you let go of the object, the recording stops.

Timeline Hints

A few things you should consider when building timelines:

- The timeline animates layers. All objects must be within layers to be usable with a timeline. Otherwise, they won't work in the timeline.

- The more complex the timeline becomes, the slower it will be on the screen for the end user. You can make up for this by speeding up the frame rate.

- You can use timelines for things besides simple animations as well, such as showing layers at different times by animating the Show-Hide Layers Behavior, or executing custom JavaScripts at specified moments of time on the timeline.

- You should preload images used in a timeline to avoid any delays or jerky movements. Do this by manually adding a Preload Images Behavior to the page.

- Multiple timelines can and should be used for complex interactions. Doing so makes it easier to keep track of your interactions if disparate elements are separated into their own timelines.

- A timeline's speed and smoothness basically depends on CPU and graphic card speed. Sometimes finding the right compromise for frame rate across different hardware is a matter of trial and error.

WEB SITE DESIGN AND CONSTRUCTION

JavaScript Debugger

Dreamweaver comes complete with an integrated JavaScript debugger that can be used to debug your client-side JavaScript in either Internet Explorer (Windows version 4 or above) or Netscape (version 4.5–4.*x*). To use the debugger, your browser needs to have both Java and JavaScript enabled.

The debugger works on JavaScript that is embedded in your page, or on external JavaScript files. You have to debug from a Web page, however. You can't debug a .js file by itself. Assuming you have a page opened that has some JavaScript in it, you can use the debugger by following these steps:

1. Click the globe icon on the Document toolbar to show the context menu.

2. Choose Debug in Internet Explorer or Debug in Netscape.

3. The debugger is a Java applet, so you will get a warning message. Click OK.

4. Another box will pop up that says Click OK to Start Debugging. If you don't see this box, it may be hiding behind the browser window. Click OK (or Grant on Netscape, as shown next).

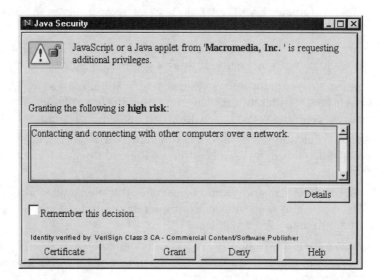

5. The debugger will start. If you've previously set up breakpoints, the page will stop at the first breakpoint. If not, the page will be executed fully, awaiting any input from the user.

6. Buttons on the debugger for Step Into, Step Out, and Step Over allow you to control the actions of the debugger. You can also type in any variables that you want to watch, and also change the values of these to test the reaction of your scripts.

Breakpoints can be set from the debugger, or from within Code view of Dreamweaver MX. Breakpoints are the most important part of debugging, because they allow you to interact with your scripts. You can set a breakpoint and then examine variables to see if they actually contain what they are supposed to contain (as shown in Figure 13-17), and also to test the flow of statements. Is your conditional statement being followed? Does your variable contain 0 or 1? Is the loop executing 10 times or only 9 times? The debugger can answer these types of questions.

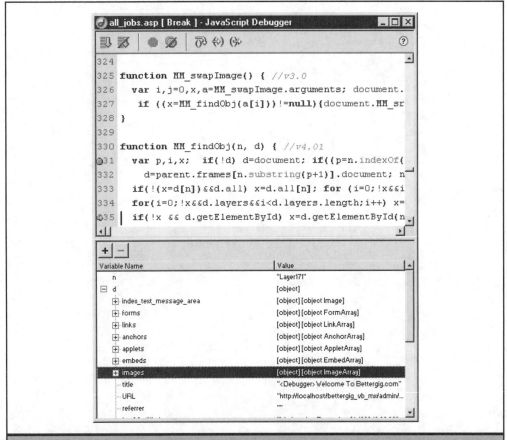

Figure 13-17. *The JavaScript debugger of Dreamweaver allows you to examine variables.*

Summary

DHTML has become more and more sophisticated over the past few years, and with the release of newer browsers such as Internet Explorer 6 and Netscape 6, it's easier than ever to create dynamic pages strictly with HTML, CSS, and JavaScript. With Dreamweaver MX, you don't need to be a JavaScript whiz to add sophisticated rollovers, menus, and animations to your Web pages.

The
Complete
Reference

Dreamweaver
MX

Part III

An Introduction to Web Scripting

The Complete Reference

Dreamweaver MX

Chapter 14

Developing a
Web Application

U p to this point, you've been able to do some rather powerful things without a lot of programming. Even without knowing much HTML, you can use the objects and Behaviors in Dreamweaver MX to build sophisticated Web sites. But static HTML is not the state of the Web today.

Today's Internet is a dynamic, interactive, happening place to be. On the Web, you can plan and book your next vacation, download and listen to music, buy gifts for your favorite Dreamweaver author, and get information about just about anything you need to know. Try sitting in front of the television with your laptop in your lap, acting like you're working, while your favorite game show is on. Your family will be quite impressed when you correctly answer each and every question thanks to a quick search on Google.

But the Web was not always such a dynamic place. The earliest uses were really just for information sharing between workers and researchers, and were based around protocols such as UNIX to UNIX Copy (UUCP) and File Transfer Protocol (FTP). The idea was simply to get a file of information from one place to another so that someone else could open and use it and then send it back to you.

HTML

Eventually, the idea of actually being able to display the information upon request led to the development of the HTML tag language. HTML was intended as a hierarchical organization method, which explains the entire <H1> <H2> structure. This is an important point to grasp. HTML was never intended to be a display language capable of the intricate graphical product that Web users have grown used to. Its purpose was to allow the viewing of information in an outline form based on the hierarchy that was described in the tags.

Note   *Consider the importance of this point as the Web stretches its boundaries into appliances and platforms that are not strictly display-based. For instance, how do you imagine that a Web browser that converts the text of a Web site into speech for a visually impaired user would handle a <bold> or <italics> tag? The original HTML specifications, as primitive as they may seem, are actually better suited to these applications. The <strong> directive of the earlier specifications likely would be more meaningful to a speech converter than would <bold>. Although you could certainly program your new-age application to respond to the <bold> tag however you would like, the word "bold" has a specific connotation in the publishing world—that of a heavier typeface. The word "strong," on the other hand, has a more universal connotation—that of additional emphasis that could be handled by a color change on a simple terminal or increased volume on a speech interpreter.*

Remember that the birth of HTML was coming about at a time when desktop publishing was gaining popularity. Programs such as PageMaker and Ventura Publisher made it possible to create pixel-perfect designs for advertising or publishing. While the Web offered a tremendous opportunity for distributing content to a wide audience, HTML just didn't provide the control that many designers required.

For a long time, the graphical wizards of Web design were forced to find workarounds to enable them the design control they needed to make the Internet interesting to look at. Perhaps the most popular "hack" that gave them that control was the way in which tables have been used over the past several years.

Tables were originally intended as a means of viewing related data in a logical columnar format. Using the <table> tags, you can define a table and its properties, such as the width of the border and whether it takes up a set number of pixels in width or takes up a certain percentage of the screen. Within the table, the <tr> (table row) tag controls the creation of rows, and the <td> tag controls the creation and population of table cells within a row. The following code sets up a table that lists the positions within a company, and the people who fill those positions:

```html
<html>
<head>

<title>Table Example</title>
<meta http-equiv="Content-Type" content="text/html; charset=iso-8859-1">

</head>

<body bgcolor="#FFFFFF">

<table width="75%" border="1">

  <tr>
    <td>President</td>
    <td>Jim Wagner</td>
  </tr>

  <tr>
    <td>Vice President</td>
    <td>Jane Grier</td>
  </tr>

  <tr>
    <td>Secretary</td>
    <td>Albert Luffman</td>
  </tr>
```

```
<tr>
  <td>Treasurer</td>
  <td>Roy Thompson</td>
</tr>

<tr>
  <td>Manager</td>
  <td>Theresa Franklin</td>
</tr>

</table>

</body>

</html>
```

When displayed in a browser, the previous code looks like this:

President	Jim Wagner
Vice President	Jane Grier
Secretary	Albert Luffman
Treasurer	Roy Thompson
Manager	Theresa Franklin

Not very exciting, but certainly functional. You can, of course, set additional properties within the tags of the table to adjust for background colors, fonts, typefaces, and so forth. You can even set specific widths for cells within the table, which prompted the idea that if you could set specific pixel widths, you could use tables to approximate a page's layout—especially because you can set the border attribute to 0, making the table's borders invisible. Use of tables as a layout tool grew from there. More recent HTML specifications have included such tags as <colspan> and <rowspan> to allow individual cells to spread out over multiple rows and columns.

Even with the advent of Cascading Style Sheets (CSS) as a presentation language, HTML tables remain a popular method of designing a page layout because they are supported by earlier browser implementations and are relatively lightweight in the bytes they add to a file. Dreamweaver enables you to either develop in tables or do your layout in CSS layers and then convert it to tables. But these fancy uses make for quite convoluted table layouts, which are nothing like the simple example provided earlier.

Cascading Style Sheets

Everything that HTML is not from a presentation standpoint, CSS tries to be. CSS gives the designer the power to control design in a manner that is impossible using just HTML. From precise margins to pixel-perfect spacing to fonts and typefaces, CSS is becoming the layout method of choice for today's designers.

As important as the power that CSSs provide is the fact that they separate the organization of Web content from its presentation. Instead of having to embed presentational commands within the actual HTML script, the CSS commands that control the layout of the content exist more as wrappers, allowing content developers and designers to work independently, and allowing the same content to be displayed differently in different contexts.

Note *The concept of separating content from presentation is an important one. It is the same idea that spawned the separation of static content from data and led developers out of the difficult world of CGI scripts. More on that shortly.*

CSSs also restore some control over the final display of pages, which developers had lost with HTML. Often, the final output of a page was dependent on settings in the end user's browser, including the type size selection and available fonts. The fact that CSSs "cascade" is an important aspect of their power. You can set CSSs as "global" to a site, meaning that they cascade down the site tree to the pages below. Those pages can, however, have local style sheets that override the global settings. Also, in certain circumstances, a developer's settings can override the end user's preferences, allowing for a more faithful presentation of the intended look and feel of the site. For a more complete look at CSSs, see Chapter 12.

As powerful as all of this technology is, though, it's still only static Web content. The real excitement is dynamic content—specifically, content that responds to a user's actions and involves content fed by databases. As with the presentational side of the Web, the generation of dynamic content has undergone an evolution that began with the CGI script.

CGI Scripts

One of the first attempts to make Web content dynamic came in the form of CGI programming. CGI stands for *Common Gateway Interface* and describes a method by which a browser can request information from an executed program rather than a simple HTML text file. Typically, a Web server has a directory usually called cgi-bin, which means that the directory holds CGI programs. Its permissions are set so that programs within the directory can be executed. You can write these programs in a number of different languages.

For instance, consider a very simple example that outputs a message to the screen. In HTML, it might be as simple as the following:

```html
<html>

<body>

<h1>The browser sees this as HTML.</h1>

</body>

</html>
```

If you wanted to re-create this output from a CGI script, you might use one of several languages, discussed in the following sections.

The C Language

One of the earliest CGI programming languages was C. It is powerful and widely used, and is a compiled language, which adds to its speed of execution. To get the same output from a C program, the code might look like this:

```c
#include <stdio.h>

int main()
{

  printf("Content-type: text/html\n\n");

  printf("<html>\n");

  printf("<body>\n");

  printf("<h1>The browser sees this as HTML</h1>\n");

  printf("</body>\n");

  printf("</html>\n");

  return 0;

}
```

That is too complicated a way to do simple HTML output, but remember that this is just an example. What it does illustrate clearly is how wrapped up in logic the content becomes when you program this way. Any change to the text would require the editing and recompiling of the C program. As quick as C is, that is a lot of maintenance overhead. The search for an easier way led to script languages that can also be executed from a CGI directory.

Perl

One of the first scripting languages used in CGI programming was Perl. Perl was developed by a man named Larry Wall, whose goal was to include everything from other languages that was cool, and to exclude everything that was not. The same script in Perl looks like this:

```
#! /usr/bin/perl

print "Content-type: text/html\n\n";

print "<html><body><h1>The browser sees this as HTML.";

print "</h1></body></html>\n";
```

Easier to write, edit, and maintain, Perl improves upon the CGI concept. Perl, however, is an interpreted language. Notice the first line of the script, which is a pointer to the Perl interpreter that resides on the server. What Perl gains in manageability, it gives up in processing speed compared to a compiled C program. Still, it is a worthwhile tradeoff when the name of the game is keeping your code up to date in the simplest way possible.

Other Scripting Languages

Since the introduction of Perl, other scripting languages have emerged as popular CGI scripting languages, such as Tcl and Python. Although the syntax is often different, the concept of the easily maintained script at the core of the CGI program remains intact with these other implementations.

The real usefulness of CGI scripting is seen in its capability to handle all the dynamic things that you might want a site to do: handling forms, sending e-mail, and interacting with databases. CGI was one of the first ways that these things became possible. But CGI has its limitations.

The Problem with CGI

CGI programs are executed in response to a request by a browser. They do their work and then go away. Each time a new request comes in, a new program is spawned, and then it goes away when its job is completed. What's more, a CGI program's definition of "its job" is much narrower than you would like it to be. For instance, regular CGI scripts have no way to maintain the state of a visitor. So, if you are using CGI to implement a shopping cart, the program does not know from page to page what the shopper has done or seen or purchased earlier in the visit, without some help. Usually, the script uses information stored in a database or text table of some sort to keep track of visitors. By placing a cookie on the user's computer, the script can track that user as he or she moves through the system. The overhead of this continuous database access is stifling, though, and can easily impact your Web server.

Attempts have been made to improve on CGI, specifically through a process known as *Fast CGI.* Fast CGI overcame some of the issues discussed by creating programs that run continuously (more like a service responding to multiple requests), rather than shutting down after every job. Fast CGI is more difficult to maintain, however, because the program has to be shut down and restarted to implement any changes.

One of the most pressing problems with CGI was mentioned a bit earlier. Examine the previous script examples and notice how the actual HTML is embedded within the program code. Now, think about how most Web teams work. Very often, a team is made up of programmers and designers, each of whom has a task to perform that is complementary to, but very different from, one another. In most shops, designers complete the look and feel of sites and then pass them on for inclusion of the code that makes them work by the programmers. In real life, the transfer is not quite that clean, but in concept, it is an efficient way to work. How would a designer and a programmer work together if they were required to construct a program like these CGI examples? The programmer would have to sit down and type until he or she came to a design part, and then would have to trade off while the designer added some lines, and this process would continue back and forth until they finished the page—not very efficient.

An easier way was needed, one that provides for the power of CGI with the flexibility of scripting and the separation of content from design seen in the relationship of CSS to HTML. HTML templating provides just such a method.

HTML Templating

Consider what is meant by a "template." If you need to fill out some legal paperwork, such as a simple will or a bill of sale, you might go to the office-supply store and buy a book of legal templates. These forms contain the basic language of the page, with blanks for you to fill in the specific details that pertain to your situation. HTML pages that use a templating method are very much the same.

From user to user, most of an HTML page remains the same. The basic content, the menus, the graphics—all of these elements are preset by the designer so that all visitors have a uniform experience. It is the details that differ from user to user, such as the specific account information, the package shipment detail, or the merchandise order. Given this situation, you can see how a designer might build the structure of a page and then pass it to the programmer to implement the details.

For instance, if the designer wants to greet a user by name on a certain page, the designer might enter the following:

```
Hello <enter name here>
```

The programmer would then be instructed to look for all the bracketed references inserted by the designer and to implement the requested data. So, depending on the languages and methods of data access in use on the particular site, the programmer would enter the code necessary to obtain and display that user's name at that point on the page. Everything on the page remains the same for every user, except for their names. That is an HTML template.

Several languages allow for the implementation of HTML templates, and five of them that make up the core of Dreamweaver MX are discussed in the upcoming sections.

ASP

Microsoft's Active Server Pages (ASP) was one of the first implementations of the templating concept. ASP uses VBScript and JavaScript (or JScript, as Microsoft's implementation is known) as its scripting languages. ASP has gained wide popularity as a result of the large existing Visual Basic user base. ASP's true power is seen in its integration with Microsoft's COM architecture. ASP is covered in detail in Chapter 15.

JSP

A newer templating implementation is Sun's Java Server Pages (JSP). JSP is built upon the Java programming language. As such, it is very secure, because its components are intended to run in *sandboxes* (secure memory spaces separated from the core of the computer so that they cannot affect its internal workings). Integral to JSP are all the components of the Java 2 Enterprise architecture, including servlets and beans. JSP is covered in depth in Chapter 16.

ColdFusion

Although ColdFusion is not strictly a scripting language, it takes advantage of the same concepts being discussed here. ColdFusion is really more of a tag language. Its custom tag structure defines functions that take developers many lines of code to implement in other languages. Its tag-based nature has made it extremely popular with HTML authors who are accustomed to using tags to develop. The newest version, ColdFusion MX, promises to be a truly powerful and efficient environment with its new Java engine and support for Web Services. ColdFusion is covered in Chapter 17.

PHP

As open source software such as Linux grows in popularity, open source implementations of technologies other than OSs are appearing. PHP is an open source implementation of a hypertext preprocessor that fulfills the same role as these other languages. It is available for free and is extremely popular among users of Linux, Apache, and MySQL, which has spawned the term *LAMP*—meaning a computer configured with Linux, Apache, MySQL, and PHP. Dreamweaver MX expands on UltraDev by providing native support for PHP and MySQL. PHP is covered in Chapter 18.

ASP.Net

Microsoft's latest and greatest is its .Net (dot-net) framework and ASP.Net. In reality, you can use the .Net framework to develop any kind of application for the Web or desktop using tools like Visual Studio .Net as a development environment. It utilizes a new language called C# (c-sharp) and updated versions of Visual Basic and JScript as its core languages, and those are equally applicable to Web development, taking ASP.Net out of the interpreted scripting environment and into the realm of faster, more efficient compiled code. In many ways, ASP.Net is a product of its forerunners. It has learned a lot from Java and JSP and is a remarkable platform. More about ASP.Net in Chapter 19.

Summary

The Web has come a long way in its structure, both from a presentation perspective and a dynamic content perspective. As with any technology, it began with methods that were useful for their time, and that have been improved upon as the medium has evolved. The early roots of CGI programming have largely been supplanted by the more modern techniques, such as ASP, JSP, ColdFusion, PHP, and .Net. But without that history based in CGI, Web design would not be where it is today, and advances undoubtedly are around the corner that will make these techniques appear primitive. But you can do a lot with the languages that already are available. The next chapters examine the details of these languages and how you can use them to create and manage dynamic content on your sites.

The
Complete
Reference

Dreamweaver
MX

Chapter 15

Active Server Pages

B ecause you have decided to learn how to use Dreamweaver MX, chances are you will want to learn about the incredible benefits of server-side processing. Although you have several options for doing so, one of the most popular is certainly Microsoft's Active Server Pages (ASP).

For some time, Web designers have recognized the benefits of dynamically altering their pages. For Web pages to take into account the input of a user or the data from a database table, there must be some means of changing the static HTML that makes them up. One of the first methods of doing so involved the use of Common Gateway Interface (CGI) applications. Often known as CGI scripts, these programs were written in languages such as Perl or C, and were stored in directories within your site and invoked from the URL. But, there were limitations, especially performance limitations, because of the way that CGI scripts were run.

Active Server Pages

Active Server Pages are part of a newer breed of methodologies known as *HTML templating*. An HTML template actually embeds the dynamic portions of the page within the static HTML. The static portions make up a template that is then customized by the embedded code. For instance, consider the following:

```
<html>
<head>
<title>Hello</title>
<meta http-equiv="Content-Type" content="text/html; charset=iso-8859-1">
</head>

<body bgcolor="#FFFFFF">

Hello George

</body>
</html>
```

This very simple ASP page will print "Hello George" in the browser when run from a Web server. You can begin to make this page dynamic by removing the name "George" that is hard-coded into the page. Suppose that you want to address your visitor at several places throughout the page. Chances are good that only a very few of the visitors will actually be named "George," so you need to prepare to handle other names as well. Your first attempt might look something like this:

```
<html>

<%
```

```
Dim name

name = "George"

%>
<head>
<title>Hello</title>
<meta http-equiv="Content-Type" content="text/html; charset=iso-8859-1">
</head>

<body bgcolor="#FFFFFF">

Hello <%Response.Write name%>

</body>
</html>
```

This file will result in exactly the same browser output as the previous one. If you were to view the source of each of these pages, they would be identical. But, more certainly is going on in the second version.

The first thing you may notice is little bits of code that don't make any sense as far as HTML is concerned. What makes them work is the fact that they are enclosed in pairs of tags like these: <% %>. These tags notify the server that it has some work to do before it can send this page to the browser.

Client/Server Architecture

Everything that happens on the Web is based on a client/server architecture. The process begins when a browser (the client) requests a page from a Web server (the server). The server then returns a block of text that is interpreted and displayed by the browser. When the page is simple HTML, the contents are returned to the browser, which knows how to handle the commands and functions contained in it. When the page contains extra code like the preceding second example file, the server must perform some additional processing before the file can be returned to the browser.

Your Microsoft Web server includes a file called asp.dll, which is a dynamic link library that handles the processing of the dynamic portions of an Active Server Page. Whenever the Web server is parsing a page and comes across the <% %> tags in a file with a .asp extension, it calls the asp.dll file to help it interpret the enclosed code. The code enclosed in the ASP tags can do anything from complex database manipulation to the simple text handling in the previous example.

Note *The code within the ASP tags can be a combination of ASP objects, Visual Basic Script (VBScript), and JScript. Each of these is covered in turn later in this chapter.*

So, when your page loads, the Web server takes a look at the page before sending it to the requesting browser. When it notices the ASP tags, it calls the asp.dll file to help it interpret portions of the page that the browser will not understand. Within the first pair of tags, the server comes across these directives:

```
dim name

name = "George"
```

Dim is a VBScript command that causes the dimensioning of a variable; in this case, a variable called *name*. The next line sets the string value "George" to that variable. At this point, the page has set a variable and assigned it a value, and is holding it to see what it will be asked to do with it.

Note   *In ASP, all variables are set as* variants. *A variant is a data type that can hold any type of value and manipulate it in the most logical way based on your instructions. For instance, if you were to set two variables, i and j, to the values 1 and 2, those values are stored not as integers or as strings, but as variants. If you then try to concatenate the two variables as strings (i & j), the result will be consistent with string concatenation (the string 12). If you then try to add them as integers (i + j), you would get the result that you expect (3). Variants can be very convenient to use, but can also cause trouble when dealing with databases, and whenever the specific data type and format are important to your procedure.*

The next few lines of the file won't cause any trouble for the browser, so they are sent as is in the response stream. Then, after the word "Hello," another set of tags surrounds this line:

```
Response.Write name
```

Response is an ASP object that is responsible for sending things out in the response stream. It has a *Write* method that causes HTML to be written to the browser. That HTML can be defined literally as a string or expression result, or it can be defined as a variable, as it is here in the example code. The variable name holds the string value "George", so this line of code will result in the text "Hello George." The rest of the file is just HTML that the browser can parse itself, so it is sent in the response stream as is.

Note   *Response is just one of several objects in the ASP object model, all of which are discussed later in this chapter.*

Getting User Input

The page discussed in the preceding section was a little fancier, but it could still cause a problem for any site except onlygeorgesallowed.com. At the very least, you will probably want to ask your user what his name is and then address him by it. You might place a form on your page with a place for your user to enter his name, and then post that form to the following page:

```
<html
<%
Dim name

name = Request.Form("name")
%>
<head>
<title>Hello</title>
<meta http-equiv="Content-Type" content="text/html; charset=iso-8859-1">
</head>

<body bgcolor="#FFFFFF">

Hello <%Response.Write name%>

</body>
</html>
```

Notice the one small change where the value of the variable name is set. Instead of setting a literal string value, the page looks for a form element called *"name"* in the form that is posted to it. The value of that form element is set to the variable and is then returned later in the code.

Note

This time, another of the ASP objects was used, called Request. *Whereas the* Response *object sends things out, the* Request *object is responsible for taking things in from a form, query string, cookie, or some other source. The* Response *object is discussed at greater length later in this chapter in the section "The Response Object."*

Although ASP is often spoken of as an entity unto itself, it is actually a combination of technologies that work together to deliver dynamic page content. At the base is the HTML that serves as the static framework of the page. To that is added a series of ASP objects that can be manipulated by scripting languages such as VBScript and JScript. Finally, ASP can include a number of Active Server Components from Microsoft's ActiveX Data Objects (ADO) for data access to custom COM components that you develop in-house or get from third parties.

The ASP Object Model

Integral to the process are the ASP objects that tie together the client and the server. The following are the six ASP objects:

- *Request*
- *Response*
- *Session*
- *Application*
- *Server*
- *ObjectContext*

Note   *Because Dreamweaver MX technically supports the ASP 2 specification, this discussion focuses on that version. Version 3 of ASP is available with Internet Information Server on Windows 2000 Server. We cover a couple of items that are unique to version 3 because you can certainly use these elements in your pages. The defining factor is that the code generated by Dreamweaver complies with the object model of ASP version 2. Almost all of the ASP improvements in this version of Dreamweaver focused on the ASP.NET implementation, which we cover in Chapter 19.*

The *Request* Object

When a browser makes a call to a server to retrieve a Web page, it is making a *request*. In addition to the name of the page it wants, the browser sends a variety of other information to the server. The added information may be intentional, such as a form post or a query string, or it may be the standard information that is passed in by the browser behind the scenes whenever it communicates with a server. Either way, the ASP *Request* object grabs all of that information and makes it readily available to the server.

The *Request* object has five collections from which it gathers all of this information:

- The *QueryString* collection
- The *Form* collection
- The *ServerVariables* collection
- The *Cookies* collection
- The *ClientCertificate* collection

The *QueryString* Collection

You are no doubt familiar with the Uniform Resource Locator (URL) used to direct your browser to the site you wish to visit. A URL contains a protocol (such as http://)

and a fully qualified domain name (for example, www.macromedia.com). It may also contain a reference to the specific page that you are looking for.

A *QueryString* is additional information that is passed to the page you request. The information is passed in name/value pairs following a question mark. For example, a page called login.asp at the Dreamweaver Team site might be accessed with the following URL:

http://www.dwteam.com/login.asp

That page might expect a username and password to be passed in so that your visit can be validated. That username and password could be passed in a QueryString like this:

http://www.dwteam.com/login.asp?name=jim&pass=huffy

Notice the extra information in this version of the URL. Following the ? are two name/value pairs. The parameter names "name" and "pass" are assigned the values "jim" and "huffy", respectively. Each pair is separated by an ampersand (&).

You can pass parameters into any page like this. If the page doesn't expect them, they are ignored. But if the page knows what to do with this information (or even requires it to work properly), it can make use of it within the page's code. The *Request* object enables you to retrieve and manipulate these parameters.

To retrieve the value of a name/value pair, you can simply place the following line within ASP tags on your page:

```
Request.QueryString("name")
```

This creates a direct reference to the value for "name" ("jim," in this case). You can set this to a variable to use later, like this:

```
dim user

user = Request.QueryString("name")
```

> **Tip**   *It is not strictly necessary to use the .QueryString indication in the previous example. The* Request *object will search through its collections to find the parameter name that you ask for. If only one instance of that parameter name exists (meaning that a form doesn't try to post a duplicate value or there is not a cookie with the same name), a simple* Request("name") *will do just fine. If a duplicate value exists, the* QueryString *is searched first and will be used. Although not required, explicitly declaring where you expect your page to find its parameter is still more accurate and a better practice.*

You can also set multiple values to a *QueryString* parameter, as follows:

```
?name="jim","bob","billy"
```

You can then get a count of parameter values

```
Request.QueryString("name").Count
```

and reference them by index:

```
Request.QueryString("name")(2)
```

The *QueryString* is a convenient way to pass information between pages. It enables you to use a single page destination for multiple purposes by passing in a parameter that indicates where a user came from or where the user wants to go. Remember, though, that the *QueryString* is available to users in the address bar of their browsers. They can see what you are passing, and can even fiddle with it by changing parameter values and resubmitting the page. This can cause a security nightmare if you do not consider ways to make sure that visitors see only information that should be available to them.

Note | *There are ways to hide the* QueryString *from your user by passing it in an internal page of a frameset or by opening a custom browser with no address bar. A savvy user can circumvent these efforts, though, and you shouldn't consider these techniques to be a substitute for adequate security planning.*

The *Form* Collection

The *Form* collection works much like the *QueryString* collection, except that its name/value pairs come from the elements of a form that is posted to the ASP page. While the *QueryString* is a great way to pass parameters that you can control, a form is much more suited to collecting input from your user and capturing it for manipulation within your code.

The form in the following illustration will be posted to a page that expects to receive values for each of its fields.

On the resulting page, you can capture all of this information into variables, as follows:

```
Dim name, address, city, state, zip, email

name = Request.Form("name")

address = Request.Form("address")

city = Request.Form("city")
```

```
state = Request.Form("state")

zip = Request.Form("zip")

email = Request.Form("email")
```

Note
Bear in mind that the parameter names you will reference in the Forms *collection refer to the names of the actual form elements on the previous page, not to the field labels. For example, you may choose to label a text field "Street Address" for your users' benefit, but name the actual text field associated with that label "StAddress." To reference this value, you would use* Request.Form("StAddress").

The *ServerVariables* Collection

Each time a request is sent by a client to your Web site, a wealth of information is sent along with it. You can think of this information as freebies, because you don't have to do anything extra to get it; it comes by default each time someone views one of your pages. Some of the information is supplied by the client, and some of it is supplied by the server on which the application is running. Server variables contain information about things such as the client's browser, the page that referred to your page, and even the location of your pages on the server. You can access all of this information through the *Request* object; and although some of it is of dubious use to the average user, some can be quite helpful to you.

Table 15-1 lists the available server variables and a description of each one.

Server Variable	Description
ALL_HTTP	All the HTTP headers sent by the client request formatted with HTTP_ in front of each capitalized header name
ALL_RAW	All of the HTTP headers sent by the client in raw form, exactly as they are sent
APPL_MD_PATH	Retrieves the metabase path for the application for the ISAPI DLL
APPL_PHYSICAL_PATH	Retrieves the actual physical path of the application by converting the metabase path to the physical directory where the application resides

Table 15-1. *The* ServerVariables *Collection*

Server Variable	Description
AUTH_PASSWORD	The value entered into the client's authorization dialog box if Basic Authentication is used
AUTH_TYPE	The authentication type used by the client when accessing a protected area
AUTH_USER	The raw authenticated username
CERT_COOKIE	The unique ID of the client certificate
CERT_FLAGS	A 2-bit header that indicates the presence and validity of a client certificate: bit 0 set to 1 if the client certificate is present, and bit 1 set to 1 if the client certificate's certificate authority (CA) is not in the list of recognized CAs on the server (indicating that it may be invalid)
CERT_ISSUER	Issuer of the client certificate
CERT_KEYSIZE	Number of bits in the Secure Sockets Layer key, e.g., 128 for 128-bit encryption
CERT_SECRETKEYSIZE	Number of bits in the server certificate private key
CERT_SERIALNUMBER	The serial number of the client certificate
CERT_SERVER_ISSUER	Issuer of the server certificate
CERT_SERVER_SUBJECT	Subject of the server certificate
CERT_SUBJECT	Subject of the client certificate
CONTENT_LENGTH	The content length as given by the client
CONTENT_TYPE	The type of data that makes up the content, such as GET, POST, or PUT
GATEWAY_INTERFACE	The revision of the CGI specification used by the server
HTTP_ACCEPT	The value of the ACCEPT header
HTTP_ACCEPT_LANGUAGE	The language used for displaying content
HTTP_USER_AGENT	Information concerning the browser that sent the request

Table 15-1. *The* ServerVariables *Collection* (continued)

Server Variable	Description
HTTP_COOKIE	The cookie string that was sent with the request
HTTP_REFERER	The URL of the original request when a redirect has occurred
HTTPS	ON if the request came through SSL (a secure channel) or OFF if it came through a nonsecure channel
HTTPS_KEYSIZE	Number of bits in the SSL layer connection key
HTTPS_SECRETKEYSIZE	Number of bits in the server certificate private key
HTTPS_SERVER_ISSUER	Issuer of the server certificate
HTTPS_SERVER_SUBJECT	Subject field of the server certificate
INSTANCE_ID	The ID of the IIS instance to which the request belongs
INSTANCE_META_PATH	The metabase path of the IIS instance that will respond to the request
LOCAL_ADDR	The server address to which the request came
LOGON_USER	The Windows account that the user is logged in to
PATH_INFO	Any extra path information sent by the client
PATH_TRANSLATED	The translated path after any virtual-to-physical mapping is completed
QUERY_STRING	Information following the ? in the HTTP request
REMOTE_ADDR	The IP address of the remote host that sent the request
REMOTE_HOST	The name of the remote host that sent the request
REMOTE_USER	The username string sent by the user unmodified by authentication filters
REQUEST_METHOD	The method used to make the request, i.e., GET, HEAD, or POST
SCRIPT_NAME	The virtual path to the script being executed
SERVER_NAME	The server's name or IP address used in self-referencing URLs

Table 15-1.   *The* ServerVariables *Collection* (continued)

Server Variable	Description
SERVER_PORT	The port number to which the request was sent
SERVER_PORT_SECURE	Returns 1 if the request is being handled on a secure port, or 0 if being handled on a nonsecure port
SERVER_PROTOCOL	The name and revision of the request information protocol
SERVER_SOFTWARE	The name and version number of the server software that answers the request
URL	The base portion of the URL

Table 15-1. *The* ServerVariables *Collection* (continued)

Perhaps it would be useful if you could view a listing of the actual HTTP headers that are generated by a request to one of your pages. You can save the following script as an ASP page and load it onto your server. Open a browser and navigate to the page, and you will see a list of server variables and the values they hold live from your site.

```
<! DOCTYPE HTML PUBLIC "-//W3C/DTD HTML 4.0 Transitional//EN">

<HTML>
<HEAD>
<TITLE> The ServerVariables Collection </TITLE>
</HEAD>

<BODY BGCOLOR="#FFFFFF#>

<TABLE BORDER = 1>
<TR><TD><B>Variable Name</B></TD><TD><B>Value</B></TD></TR>
<% For each key in Request.ServerVariables %>
<TR>
<TD><%= key %></TD>
</TD>

<% If Request.ServerVariables(key) = " " then
    Response.Write "No Information"
    else
    Response.Write Request.ServerVariables(key)
```

```
end if
%>

</TD>

</TR>

<% next %>

</BODY>
</HTML>
```

Similar to the way in which you access information with other collections, you can access *ServerVariable* collection information as follows:

```
Request.ServerVariables("header")
```

where "header" is the name of the variable you want to access. Some server variables just supply you with information. It may even be information you already know. For instance, you could access the *SERVER_SOFTWARE* variable like this:

```
Request.ServerVariables("SERVER_SOFTWARE")
```

This would return information about the name and version of the software on the server that was receiving the request. For instance, IIS 5 might return "Microsoft-IIS/5.0." But, you probably already knew what software your server was running; and even if you didn't, you could easily find out without checking the server variables each time.

Your visitor's browser, however, is something that is likely to change with each new user. Depending on what features your site uses, you may need to be aware of the capabilities of the browser that is trying to view your site. Information like this enables you to redirect visitors with browsers that do not conform to certain specifications either to a site that is friendly to their browsers or to a message informing them that their visit will be hampered by the software they are using.

The information you need to do this is in the *USER_AGENT* variable, which you access like this:

```
Request.ServerVariables("USER_AGENT")
```

This will return information like the following:

Mozilla/4.0 (compatible; MSIE 5.0; Windows 98; DigExt)

indicating that Microsoft Internet Explorer is being used on a Windows 98 computer. By checking the contents of this variable in your server-side code, your initial page can make decisions about how to handle requests coming from a variety of browsers.

For now, you mainly need to understand what kind of information is available to you in the *ServerVariables* collection. As you become a proficient ASP programmer, you will come across uses for this information, and it will be good that you are aware of what is available to you.

The *Cookies* Collection

The use of cookies has created much hoopla over the past several years. Apparently, people want a highly interactive Web experience, but object to the tiny files called "cookies" that help make that possible. However, cookies play an important role in a site's ability to offer a personalized experience for its users. They make the Web more interesting and more convenient for most users. The risk of a security breach is overblown, which becomes obvious when you understand how cookies work.

Cookies are nothing but small text files that reside in a directory on your user's computer. Each browser has a special directory in which it keeps cookies. As a result, a computer may have more than one directory of files, each associated with a particular brand of browser. These files store information about a user that relates to the site that creates the cookie. It could be a username and password, or the user's choice of a colored background when visiting the site. Anything that can be expressed as a name/value pair in a small text file can be written to a cookie by an application and later retrieved.

Note *You may have seen sites with a "Remember Me" check box near the username and password entry fields. If you select this box when you log in, you will likely not need to use your password to gain access next time. Your user information is written to a cookie on your computer, and the site simply queries for your identity the next time you visit. This is very convenient, but it can also risk revealing information or allowing access to private information if others use your computer. If they were to visit the same site, the cookie information would still be read and they would be permitted to use the site as if they were you. This concern is addressed in later versions of Windows, such as 2000 and XP. These versions make better use of the Windows login to separate user files. Each user on these operating systems has his or her own temporary Internet files directory, which includes his or her own cookies folder. The cookies that are used by a particular site depend on which user is logged in to the client computer, making them more secure.*

The number and size of cookies on a user's computer have limits. An individual cookie cannot be larger than 4K, and no more than 300 cookies can be on the computer at a time. Each cookie over 300 knocks one off the list at the other end, so that you end up with a rolling directory of the most recently set cookies. A little math will tell you that the most space cookies can take is a little over a megabyte, but it is extremely rare that a single cookie reaches anywhere near the 4K limit, so the actual impact is much smaller.

Note *The fact that cookies are stored on a user's computer, and are stored separately for each browser that the user may use, means that cookies are not universal to a visitor's use of your site. If he or she uses a different computer or even a different browser, the information you store about him or her will not be accessible to your application. It is important that you consider how you can gracefully handle a user's visit regardless of whether information is available about them.*

An important point to remember is that a Web application can read only the cookies that it wrote itself. So, a rogue application cannot read the information on the user's computer and glean password information for another site.

Cookies are read using the *Request* object, much like the other collections. Use the following format to read a cookie that was set previously:

```
Request.Cookies("cookiename")
```

The upcoming section called "The *Response* Object" looks at how to set cookies.

The *ClientCertificate* Collection

You may have heard of Secure Sockets Layer (SSL), the protocol that allows for secure, encrypted communication across the Internet. SSL uses certificates to verify the legitimacy of the client and the server and to encrypt and decrypt information as it is sent back and forth. For the client computer to identify itself to a secure server application, it sends a client certificate along with its ASP page request. The particulars of this certificate can be accessed with the *Request* object.

Table 15-2 lists information that is sent with each client certificate.

You can access portions of the *ClientCertificates* collection in the same manner as you access the other collections. For instance,

```
Request.ClientCertificate("SerialNumber")
```

would return the serial number of the certificate sent with the *Request* object.

An interactive Web site is all about communication with the users. The *Request* object helps make that communication effective by giving you a means of retrieving information from their computers, their input, and their requests. But good communication must be two-way. The *Response* object helps you complete the loop by providing ways to talk back to your users that make for a satisfying experience.

The *Response* Object

What the *Request* object is to receiving information, the *Response* object is to sending it out. Whether you simply need to write information into the user's browser or direct them off to another location, you can send information and commands back to your

Field	Description
Certificate	The entire set of certificate information in one stream
Flags	Additional information about the certificate, such as whether the issuer is recognized
Issuer	A string of values about the issuer listed in subfields— primarily, names and locations of the certificate issuers
SerialNumber	A string representation of the certificate's serial number
Subject	A string of subfields that lists information about the subject of a certificate
ValidFrom	A date that the certificate becomes valid
ValidUntil	A date until which the certificate is valid

Table 15-2.   *The* ClientCertificates *Collection*

visitor's browser by using the *Response* object. This section covers four main methods of the *Response* object:

- *Buffer*
- *Write*
- *Redirect*
- Content Expiration (*Expires* and *ExpiresAbsolute*)

The *Buffer* Method

The *Buffer* method of the *Response* object controls how content is sent back to the browser. You can think of the data that is sent by a Web server in response to a request by a browser as a stream of information. Like a stream of water, the information that is sent out first reaches the destination before information that is sent after it; often just milliseconds before, but still before. After some data has been sent back to the browser and a page has begun construction, you no longer can do some things. For instance, consider the following code:

```
<!DOCTYPE HTML PUBLIC "-//W3C//DTD HTML 4.0 Transitional//EN">
<HTML>
<%
```

```
Dim X

X=53

%>

<HEAD>
<TITLE> Buffer Example </TITLE>
</HEAD>

<BODY BGCOLOR="#FFFFFF">

This is a test page to show how the HTML stream can be affected by your
  ASP code

<%

If x = 53 Then

Response.Redirect ("SomeOtherPage.asp")

End If

%>

</BODY>
</HTML>
```

Note *The* Redirect *method of the* Response *object and the* If ...Then *constructor are covered later in this chapter in the section "Conditional Statements."*

This code will cause your application to fail with an error to the user that headers have already been written to the page. Basically, this means that because some information has already been sent out the HTML stream to the browser, the page is no longer able to obey the *Response.Redirect* directive, which tells it to send the user to another Web page altogether as long as X = 53. After a page has been started, a command like that is not allowed.

The problem is that you may well encounter times when you need to get into the processing of the ASP page itself before you will know whether a condition exists that requires the user to be redirected. The key is to complete all the necessary processing before sending the HTML stream to the browser. You can accomplish this by the use of the *Buffer* property of the *Response* object.

The following is the same code with one minor alteration:

```
<!DOCTYPE HTML PUBLIC "-//W3C//DTD HTML 4.0 Transitional//EN">
<html>
<%
Response.Buffer = true
Dim X

X=53

%>

<head>
<title> Buffer Example </title>
</head>

<body bgcolor="#FFFFFF">

This is a test page to show how the HTML stream can be affected by your
  ASP code

<%

If x = 53 Then

Response.Redirect ("SomeOtherPage.asp")

End If

%>

</body>
</html>
```

Notice the following line (two lines after the <HTML> tag):

```
Response.Buffer = true
```

This line tells the ASP page that no information should be sent to the browser until the entire page has been processed. It holds the entire HTML stream in a buffer until all the code is run and all the decisions have been made. Then, it sends the entire thing at once. This allows for the interruption of processing by things such as a *Redirect* command that causes the early parts of the response to be ignored in favor of sending the user to an alternate page for some reason.

Under normal circumstances, the pages would then be buffered until the code was completed, and then the result would be released to the browser and displayed. Sometimes, however, you may want portions of the buffer released prior to the completion of the code. If, for instance, a particular operation is time-consuming, you may want to first send a message to the browser indicating that code is running and that the user should stand by. Then, the intensive portion will be processed into the buffer so that it will be delivered all at once, and not piecemeal. You can precisely control at what points during your page's processing buffered information is released to the browser by using the *Flush* method, as follows:

```
Response.Flush
```

When this command is encountered, all buffered information is sent out the HTML stream and subsequent processing is buffered until the page completes or another *Flush* is encountered. If you want to flush the buffer and stop processing the page at that point, you can use the following:

```
Response.End
```

The only difference is that the page ceases processing at the point at which the *End* method is called.

You may also have occasion to clear a portion of the buffer if, for example, some condition exists that means a subset of a page's processing should not be released to the browser. *Response.Clear* will clear any portion of the buffer since the last flush was called, but it will clear body information only, not header information.

The *Write* Method

Now that you know how the HTML stream works, you will be interested to know how you can use ASP to insert items into it based on the processing of your page. You can use the *Write* method of the *Response* object to insert information into your pages. For instance,

```
Response.Write variable
```

will write the value of the variable into the text stream wherever it occurs. The following is a slight alteration of the example previously used:

```
<!DOCTYPE HTML PUBLIC "-//W3C//DTD HTML 4.0 Transitional//EN">
<html>
<%
```

```
Dim X

X=53

%>

<head>
<title> Write Example </title>
</head>

<body bgcolor="#FFFFFF">

This is a test page to show how the Write method works.
<br><br>

<%

Response.Write "The value of X is " & x

%>

</body>
</html>
```

This code shows four ways to get information written back to the browser. The first is the straight HTML at the beginning of the <body> tag. You should be familiar with HTML text at this point.

The other three ways are within the *Response.Write* just before the closing </body> tag. You can use the *Write* method to return a literal string by enclosing that string in double quotes. You can also get the *Write* method to return the value of a variable by referencing that variable's name, as was done with the variable X in the preceding code. Last, you can concatenate the two methods as the following does to end up with an actual line of text:

```
The value of X is 53
```

In this method, any portion of the string that is a literal value or that you want interpreted as HTML must be enclosed in strings. For example,

```
Response.Write <br>
```

would return an error. To get an HTML break within a *Response.Write* call, the <br> tag must be in quotes, like this:

```
Response.Write "<br>"
```

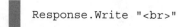

Because VBScript is being used here, the & character is used to concatenate the strings. In JScript or JavaScript, you can do the same thing by using the + operator.

You can also use a shortcut method to write the value of a variable, like this:

```
<% = X %>
```

This line would simply write "53" to the browser. This method is best used when the data you are writing is self-explanatory, such as <% = Now %> to write the time, or when it is in conjunction with other formatting that makes the values that you are displaying meaningful.

The *Redirect* Method

Often, you'll need to send users to other pages within your application based on their input or the processing of the data they submit. The *Redirect* method of the *Response* object enables you to do server-side redirection to the page of your choice.

A good example of this would be a username and password verification that you might use to secure portions of your site. Consider the following code:

```
<!DOCTYPE HTML PUBLIC "-//W3C//DTD HTML 4.0 Transitional//EN">
<html>
<%

Dim username, password

username = Request.Form("user")
password = Request.Form("pass")

If username = "tommy" AND password = "3245" Then

Response.Redirect ("success.asp")

Else

Response.Redirect ("fail.asp")
```

```
%>

<head>
<title> Redirect Example </title>
</head>

<body bgcolor="#FFFFFF">

</body>
</html>
```

This is a very simple login routine insofar as it does not even rely on a database; it simply checks that the values entered on the preceding page match the hard-coded values selected. The point is that if they do match, the user is sent to a "Success" page called success.asp, and if they do not match, they are sent to a "Fail" page called fail.asp.

Anything that happens on the pages after a redirect occurs is abandoned. The user is gone and is no longer available to accept output from the page that redirected him. Make sure that no critical information processing occurs after your user has been redirected.

Content Expiration

If you have spent any time at all on the Web, you know what a cache is. Intended as a means to save strain on servers and to speed up the surfing experience, a browser's cache saves recently viewed pages and graphics so that they can be viewed again quickly. That is great when the page's content is static. When it is dynamic, however, you need a way to make sure that each time a visitor tries to view a page, the user gets it directly from the server. That way, you can make sure that the user is viewing the latest data.

The *Response* object provides two properties that enable you to limit the amount of time that a page is cached in your visitor's browser. The *Expires* property enables you to set a number of minutes for which the existing content is valid. After that time passes, subsequent views must come from the server. A value of 0 ensures that each page view comes from a hit to the server. You can set the Expires property for a page as follows:

```
Response.Expires = minutes
```

You can also set an absolute day and time at which content will expire. This is helpful if content is updated on your site on a periodic schedule, and you want to make sure that any page view after the next update cycle comes from the server itself, and not from the cache. You can set the *ExpiresAbsolute* property like this:

```
Response.ExpiresAbsolute = #DateTime#
```

The *Session* Object

Essentially, the Internet operates on what are known as *stateless* protocols. This means that the basic HTTP protocol does not maintain a record of who is currently connected to it. Each request is handled by the server as if it were the only time that particular client had asked for something.

Contrast that to the way in which LANs work. If you have ever rebooted your computer in a networked setting, you may have seen a warning message stating that a certain number of computers are currently connected to your computer and that shutting down will disconnect them. Your local network protocols are maintaining the state of those users connected to your computer.

Your Web server, however, treats each request it receives as totally independent of other requests. That means that the server must have some way of reconstructing where the user is in the flow of the application each time it responds. It is especially important for a secure application to keep track of the following pieces of information:

- Who is making the request
- Whether they have been validated
- Whether they have placed anything in their shopping cart

You can pass a lot of this kind of information in the *QueryString*. As discussed earlier, you can then use the *Request* object to access that information on each page. This method has several problems, though:

- It makes for long, confusing *QueryStrings*.
- It is insecure, because all the information in the *QueryString* is open for examination and alteration by a user who has only a little knowledge about how they work.
- Complicated *QueryStrings* must be reconstructed each time a user changes pages, to pass the correct information to the next page.

You can also keep a lot of this kind of information in cookies. Again, though, an experienced user could open the cookie's text file and play around with the name/value pairs that make it up.

ASP provides a quite elegant solution to the problem of maintaining state in Web applications. The *Session* object can hold information about your user in a way that is unique, secure, and easy to use. The *Session* object is actually a set of variables that you define that are stored on the server. As long as your visitor remains connected to your site (meaning that he or she continues to make requests without pausing longer than the timeout value set for the *Session* object), those variables persist and can be used to identify and track them.

> **Note**
>
> *The* Session *object uses a unique session ID for each user. This ID is written to a cookie on the client computer and serves to identify which set of session variables should be associated with that user. So, if the user has cookies disabled in his or her browser, the* Session *object will fail.*

A session variable can have just about any name you choose, and can hold any type of data in a variant data type. For instance, to create a session variable called ID and assign a value of 25 to it, you would simply use the following:

```
<%Session("ID") = 25 %>
```

To recall the value of the session variable, simply call it by name, like so:

```
<% = Session("ID") %>
```

or

```
<% Response.Write Session("ID") %>
```

or

```
<%
Dim userid
userid = Session("ID")
Response.Write userid
%>
```

> **Note**
>
> *Technically, the correct way to write these references is Session.Content("ID"), but it is regularly abbreviated Session("ID").*

Because session variables are stored on the server, you have total control over how they are set and what values are allowed in them. This is a much more secure way of maintaining sensitive pieces of data away from the access of your users.

You need to consider some issues as your sites start to scale up in size. Sessions are dependent on the server on which they were created. In a load-balancing scenario in which several servers are used to serve identical content while spreading the user load over several CPUs, there is no way to guarantee that each hit to the server will reach the server where that user's session information is stored. Special third-party software is necessary for session management in these situations.

Session Properties

The *Session* object has several properties that you can read and set. The two most important to you will be the *SessionID* property and the *Timeout* property.

The *SessionID* property will return the unique session ID that is assigned to visitors when they first begin using your application. You can access it as follows:

```
<% = Session.SessionID %>
```

The *Timeout* property is used to set the length of time that a session persists without activity from the user. For instance, you can set the timeout value to 30 minutes like this:

```
<% Session.Timeout = 30 %>
```

The trick is coming up with the correct value for your site. Too short a session timeout value will abandon the information you are storing on users too often, perhaps while they take the time to read information that is presented to them on the site. They will be constantly required to log back in, which will hamper their use of the site. Too long a value opens the security risk of someone coming up behind a user and gaining access to the user's session, and also ties up server resources longer than necessary.

Session Variables

Much debate has occurred about the expediency of session variables because of the drain they place on server resources. Each time a session is begun (when a user hits an ASP page in your application), a session is created to service that user. That takes 2K of server memory right off the bat. The only way around that is to turn off sessions on the server, in a global.asa file or at the page level. Most people don't do that, especially in a cohosted environment, so each user has 2K set aside for them. If you then store an integer UserID in the session, that takes 8 more bytes, for a total of around 2,008 bytes; 2,000 bytes if you don't use session variables, and 2,008 bytes if you do. At this point, the difference between using and not using session variables is really all about the delta; the 8-byte difference between 2,000 and 2,008. For the incredible convenience they provide, and the relatively low server resources they take, session variables are a tremendous asset to the Web developer. Passing around recordsets in them isn't recommended; but for storing IDs and user group settings that facilitate site security, session variables are ideal.

Session Methods

The one method of the *Session* object is the *Abandon* method, which releases all the variables in a session ID and frees the server resources associated with them. Calling *Session.Abandon* when your user logs out destroys that user's session variables, requiring the user to log in again if he or she wishes to continue using the site; and it frees the related server resources immediately when your visitor has completed the application, rather than waiting for the timeout period to elapse.

The *Application* Object

What the *Session* object does for the individual user, the *Application* object does for the entire site. Variables can be set in much the same way:

```
Application("users")+1 %>
```

The difference is that this variable is accessible by any user at any time. Any page within your application can then access the "users" variable and display the number of people currently logged in.

Note *A script that you can use to track users is discussed later in this chapter in the section "global.asa."*

Because any user can access the application variables and modify them, you need to manage your users' access with the *Lock* and *Unlock* methods of the *Application* object. Calling *Application.Lock* before allowing the manipulation of a variable ensures that two concurrent applications will not affect one another. *Application.Unlock* will then release the variable to other users within the site.

The *Server* Object

The *Server* object is a low-level object that you can use to perform several tasks within ASP. The most common use is to create instances of server-side components using the following syntax:

```
Set InstanceName = Server.CreateObject("ClassName.ComponentName")
```

So, to create an instance of the CDO *Newmail* object to send e-mail from your page, you might use the following:

```
Set Email = Server.CreateObject("CDONTS.NewMail")
```

The object reference *Email* can then be manipulated as the class itself, adding properties and calling methods.

The *Server* object has a couple of useful methods that are new to version 3 of ASP and work only on IIS5.

Server.Execute

Server.Execute is used to dynamically execute externalized ASP scripts from within an ASP page. When you can *Server.Execute* and provide a file name, the code in that external file is executed and the ASP code within it is evaluated. Control is then passed back to the calling page. All ASP objects are passed to the called page in the process, which means that the *Forms* and *QueryString* collections are available in the called script. This is an excellent method of carving out pieces of code that must be run from several locations or code that is run conditionally based on decisions made in the calling script. It allows you to dynamically include script files in a manner that is not available with a regular server-side include file

Server.Transfer

A related method is the *Server.Transfer* method. *Server.Transfer* redirects the user to the provided page and sends the ASP objects along as well. But control is not ever returned to the calling page. The transfer is final and the user now resides on the called page. This is equivalent to using *Response.Redirect* except that the forms and *querystrings* and other ASP object collections are sent along and are available to be manipulated in the called page's script.

The *ObjectContext* Object

The *ObjectContext* object relates to ASP's use of Microsoft Transaction Server. It enables you to access the MTS component management system from within ASP. For more information on this object, see a reference on programming using MTS.

global.asa

This is a file, core to the ASP Object model, that is left out of the basic Dreamweaver implementation. Although it is not strictly necessary to have this file in your application, it can be a powerful addition, enabling you to do things on a site-wide basis that make your site more responsive to your user's needs and your own. The global.asa file is a site-wide file that lives in the root directory of your domain. It contains just four functions by default:

- *Application_OnStart*
- *Application_OnEnd*
- *Session_OnStart*
- *Session_OnEnd*

You will recognize the names of these functions from the previous discussion of *Application* and *Session* objects. The functions in the global.asa file take advantage of ASP's ability to know when sessions and applications begin and end, and they can react to those events with code that you specify.

You can do anything from setting up recordset connections to tracking users with the global.asa file, and that's what you will do here. After you launch your new site, you will no doubt be sitting back waiting for the thousands of concurrent connections that forced you to shell out the big bucks for SQL Server. Sitting there looking at your home page, you will wonder who else is looking at it right that minute. Will it look different while experiencing the adoring stares of users across the globe? How can you tell how many people have visited?

Some people like those speedometer-looking graphic numbers that pronounce the number of times your home page has been visited since some date in the past. Prominent hit counters too often just confirm the fact that, in the scheme of things, no one has visited your site much at all in the months since it was last updated (and if you're not going to update it, don't put a date on there that proves it); and, other than the occasional snicker, no one really much cares anyway. Except for you. That's why you need an accurate, discreet way to track how many people have visited your site and how many are there right now. The following is global.asa code to allow you to do just that:

```
Sub Application_OnStart
Application("visits") = 0
Application("Active") = 0
End Sub


Sub Application_OnEnd


End Sub


Sub Session_OnStart
Application.lock
Application("visits") = Application("visits") + 1
Application.unlock
Application.lock
Application("Active") = Application("Active") + 1
Application.unlock
End Sub


Sub Session_OnEnd
Application.lock
Application("Active") = Application("active") - 1
Application.unlock
End Sub
```

Understanding the use of the *Application* and *Session* objects in the global.asa file is helpful, and thus is the focus of the rest of this section. The *Application* object is accessible and writable from your entire site, meaning that all the users of your site can read and write to the same variables. The *Session* object is unique to each user and is accessible only by that user.

As is implied by their names, these functions are triggered when your application begins or ends, and when an individual session begins or ends. The global.asa file sees these events automatically, so you don't need to anything extra to cause the events that you place in these functions to occur.

The *Application_OnStart* function will really trigger only once, unless you shut down your site or have some special functionality that restarts the application. You will use it to initialize and store variables that are available to everyone at the site. This allows the beginning of each session to increment your visits counter and your active counter and allows a counter page to display these figures for you. The following is the code:

```
Sub Application_OnStart
Application("visits") = 0
Application("Active") = 0
End Sub
```

That's all you need. Because the site starts only once, you initialize the two variables you are interested in: how many total visits have you had and how many active users are there.

The *Application_OnEnd* function has no code in this context. You are not explicitly calling the end of the application; and an accidental crash of the site would not allow *OnEnd* code to run anyway, so there is no need for it.

The *Session_OnStart* function triggers each time a new user visits your site. This function increments both counters to add a visit and a new active user to your application variables. Here is the code:

```
Sub Session_OnStart
Application.lock
Application("visits") = Application("visits") + 1
Application.unlock

Application.lock
Application("Active") = Application("Active") + 1
Application.unlock
End Sub
```

Notice that you call an *Application.Lock* and *Application.Unlock* each time you write to a variable. This ensures that two users don't try to overwrite each other and mess things up. Each variable that you initialized in the *Application_OnStart* function is incremented to update the counters with this current user.

All that is left is the *Session_OnEnd* function:

```
Sub Session_OnEnd
Application.lock
Application("Active") = Application("active") - 1
Application.unlock
End Sub
```

When a session ends (either explicitly, by calling the *Session.Abandon* event, or by timing out), this code runs and decrements the active users variable. Notice that the *visits* variable is not decremented and contains a complete history of the number of sessions ever started in the application.

Keep in mind that few sites even try to coax users into logging out of a site, and even fewer are successful. Therefore, most sessions end with a timeout. Remember, too, that your count of active users will be off slightly, because some users who have left your site still have active sessions as far as the server is concerned. But, over time, you will receive an accurate average of the momentary usage of your site.

Now, all you need is code in an ASP page to read the application variables and present your counters to you:

```
<%
Response.Write Application("Active") & " active users<BR>"
Response.Write Application("visits") & " total visits"

%>
```

As you become more comfortable with the way ASP works, you will recognize the power of the global.asa. file. Although Dreamweaver currently focuses on development at the session level, you can certainly add site-wide code that extends the abilities of your site.

The Languages

All the intricacies of languages as powerful as VBScript and JScript (or JavaScript) cannot be covered in this space, but a review of the following few things will help you with some light-duty scripting:

- Variables
- Conditional statements
- Loops

Variables

Variables are simply representations of other things to your computer program. You no doubt can remember a time when you grabbed a few rocks to draw out the battle plan for storming the neighbor kids' tree fort, or even when you played Monopoly and each chose a die-cast token to represent you on the board. You didn't actually become the car or the shoe, but everyone knew what space you occupied on the board by locating the token you had selected. Every time they saw your playing piece, they saw you within the scope of the game. The next time the game was played, someone else might have chosen the same token, and thus it represented them that time around. The tokens are variable in their representation, taking on the value of whomever selected it in the minds of the players.

Program variables are the same, except you are not limited to 8 or 10 little pieces of metal to hold your values. You can make up pretty much whatever character combination you'd like to represent other things to the computer. For instance, you could select the letter *i* to represent the age of your user. A 25-year-old user who visited your site would then have the value 25 assigned to the letter *i*. Then, every time the computer came across the letter *i* in your code, it would really see the number 25. You could add 1 to *i* and the computer would respond with 26. Or you could add *i* to another *i* and get the answer 50.

But, if a new user were to come along who is 40 years old, his or her instance of the application would assign the number 40 to *i* and all of his or her calculations would be altered accordingly. That is the power of variables. One set of code can be reused regardless of the actual values that need to be manipulated, because the representation, the variable itself, is always the same. You just tell the computer what to see when it comes across the variable by assigning a value to it.

This concept is consistent in both VBScript and JavaScript, but the implementation is slightly different.

VBScript

Here is a sample VBScript that you can examine:

```
<%
Dim name
Dim address, city, state, zip
name = "Joe"
address = Request.Form("address")
city = "Florida"
zip = 32811
Response.Write "Your name is " & name & ".<BR>"
Response.Write "You live in " & city & ", " & state & ".<br>"
%>
```

The first two lines take care of a process known as *declaring* variables. Although declaring your variables is not absolutely necessary, it is a good practice that will save innumerable debugging headaches down the road. Get into the habit of declaring your variables.

In VBScript, this is known as *dimensioning* variables and uses the *Dim* keyword. The previous example does this on two lines to illustrates the ways that it can be done. The first line dims one variable, and the second line dims three separate variables. The commas indicate that you are describing three different variables that you will be using, and VBScript treats these just as if you had dimmed them on three separate lines.

Because all variables in ASP are variants (meaning that they can hold any data type), you don't need to specify that one is an integer or another is a string. VBScript assigns the variable the most logical way that it can and manipulates it according to its best interpretation of the instruction you give it.

The rules for variable names are as follows:

- They must begin with an alpha character.
- They cannot contain embedded periods.
- They should be unique within the page or function in which they are used (or you risk overwriting information unintentionally).
- They cannot be more than 255 characters long.

Next, you assign values to the variables. The previous example assigned hard-coded string values to some and used a *Request* for another. You likely won't have such a combination on your page, but it illustrates the point that you can assign variables from a number of places. Notice also that VBScript accepts both string values and numerical values into the variable because all variables in ASP are variants.

When you are ready to output your variable values, it is most meaningful to the end user if they are displayed within the context of how they are being used. You can concatenate (string together) literal string output without variable values by using the & operator. When used with string values, the & operator tells VBScript to put the values together into the output string.

JavaScript

The script for JavaScript is much the same. Only slight differences exist in how the variables are declared and then concatenated with the string output:

```
<%
var name
var address, city, state, zip
name = "Joe"
address = Request.Form("address")
city = "Florida"
```

```
zip = 32811
Response.Write "Your name is " + name + ".<br>"
Response.Write "You live in " + city + ", " + state + ".<br>"
%>
```

You will notice two changes. First, the keyword *var* is used to declare the variables instead of *Dim*. Second, the + operator is used to concatenate the string values. Otherwise, the VBScript code and the JScript code are the same.

 The + operator has different uses in JavaScript. When used with numerical values, it does addition, as you would expect. If any of the values are strings, however, it concatenates instead.

Conditional Statements

Conditional statements are ways of testing what is going on in your application, and responding differently to the variety of situations you may encounter. For instance, you may want to send your visitors to one site if they live in the North, to another if they are from the South, and yet another if they are from the West. You could use a conditional statement to gather information and determine what action to take. Consider this VBScript code:

```
<%
Dim region
region = Request.Form("region")

If region = "North" Then
     Response.Redirect("North.asp")
ElseIf region = "South" Then
     Response.Redirect("South.asp")
Else Response.Redirect("West.asp")
End If

%>
```

In this script, a variable is dimensioned to hold the region, and then a value is assigned to it that is gleaned from a form submitted by the user. A conditional statement is then entered that tests the value of the region variable and sends the user off accordingly.

The *If* keyword begins by checking to see whether the value is "North". If it is, then the redirect to the North.asp page occurs. If it is not, the next line is invoked, which asks again whether the value is "South" by using *Else If*. *Else If* begins another test for the value of region. If the value is neither "North" nor "South", your script assumes it must be "West" and uses the *Else* keyword to invoke the only remaining option, which is to send the user to the West.asp page. The *End If* statement is required to demarcate the entire conditional statement so that the script knows when to stop testing conditions and return to regular code.

The JavaScript version of this script is somewhat different:

```
<%
var region
region = Request.Form("region")

If (region = "North") {
    Response.Redirect("North.asp")}
Else if (region = "South") {
    Response.Redirect("South.asp")}
Else {
    Response.Redirect("West.asp") }

%>
```

Each *If* conditional in JavaScript is contained within parentheses, and the response to a true response for that condition is then enclosed in brackets beneath it. This is really just a syntactical difference, and the concept of conditionals remains the same in the two languages.

Loops

Loops are places in your code where you will want to run a set of instructions a number of times. It may be a set number of times, such as 100; or it may depend on some criteria that you won't even determine until the program runs, such as once for every record in a recordset. Although several different ways to manipulate a *For. . . Next* loop are available, the basic idea is that you determine a starting number, an ending number, and an increment.

So, suppose that you want to perform an operation on all the even numbers from 1 to 100. The first even number is 2, so the starting number is 2. The last even number is 100, so the ending number is 100. Even numbers occur every two numbers, so you want to increment by two at each pass. Consider the following VBScript code:

```
<%
Dim I
For I = 2 to 100 step 2
Response.Write I * I
Next
%>
```

Here, the variable *I* is dimensioned to hold where you are in your loop. You then begin the loop in the next line, which says that you want to run the code that is coming up once for each value of *I* that is between 2 and 100, stepping up two each time. The code then outputs the current value of *I* times itself and calls the *Next* keyword to begin the process again with the next value of *I*.

The concept is the same in JavaScript, with a bit of a syntactical difference:

```
<%
var I
for (I=2;I<=100;I=I+2){
    Response.Write I * I
}
```

The JavaScript code in this case uses the same parentheses and bracket construct that you saw earlier. After the *for* statement, the three portions of the statement in parentheses establish the starting, ending, and incremental value of the variable, and then the code within the brackets runs until the ending conditional is no longer true.

Summary

Thus concludes a quick overview of Active Server Pages as they are used in Dreamweaver. With this information, you should have a better handle on how Dreamweaver uses ASP to do the following:

- Get user input with the *Request* object.
- Output information and browser commands with the *Response* object.
- Maintain state with the *Application* and *Session* objects.
- Script logic with VBScript and JavaScript.

The limited space devoted here to ASP cannot do justice to all of its features and associated technologies. Hopefully, the information presented will help you be more productive with Dreamweaver as you begin learning your way around the details of what the program does. Numerous excellent tutorials, both in book form and on the Web, are available that can teach you more advanced features of ASP, when you are ready.

Chapter 16

Java Server Pages in the Dreamweaver MX Environment

One of the most popular programming languages that emerged from the Web era of the late 1990s is Java. Although Java has been around for several years, it is only in the last few years that Java Server Pages (JSP) has come into prominence. JSP was built upon some of the same ideas as its predecessor, ASP, but was able to avoid some of its shortcomings by taking the "best" ideas of ASP one step further.

JSP is a mixture of Java code within the constructs of an HTML page. The Java code is enclosed in <% %> server tags, like ASP code, but the code is compiled into *servlets* on the Web server when the page is browsed for the first time. Upon each successive hit, the code doesn't have to be compiled again—the compiled version remains on the server. In fact, the entire page is compiled, not merely the code that is between the server tags.

Java is a language that is based in part on the C language. It started as a small language that could be used in a wide variety of appliance hardware. It quickly grew, however, into a robust, platform-independent language that enabled Web developers to include *applets* in their Web pages. Applets are mini applications that exist client side and can be executed from a browser by invoking the Java of that browser. Applets can exist server side as well.

From applets to servlets to JSPs and Enterprise JavaBeans (EJBs), Java has steadily evolved over its short lifetime. Applets have been considered somewhat of a failure to most Web developers, because the technology never really took off as anticipated. JSP, however, now has a solid foundation and a large user base.

The JSP Server

Although Java was developed by Sun Microsystems, JSP is not strictly a Sun technology. Indeed, JSP servers are produced by some of the top names in the computer software industry today—IBM, Macromedia, Sun, and Apache all have implementations of a JSP server. Some, like IBM's Websphere and Macromedia's JRun, are available in Enterprise editions at a substantial cost. Others, like Apache Tomcat, are available as downloads from the Internet. Whichever implementation you choose, there are enough similarities among them to allow a general discussion of JSP. You can find a list of JSP application servers at java.sun.com/products/jsp/industry.html. Nearly all of the companies that market a JSP server have a development version that you can use for little or no charge. These versions are typically scaled-down versions of the full server, which may limit simultaneous connections. Macromedia's JRun is an excellent choice for a JSP server. JRun is one of the easiest JSP servers to implement because of the easy-to-use installer and its Web-based administration interface. JRun Enterprise Server also comes with its own set of JDBC drivers to make it easy to connect to most databases, and it also comes with a standard set of powerful tag libraries to make many common tasks easy to incorporate into your Web application. JRun is also at the crest of the latest technology, making it easy to implement such growing technologies as Web services and Enterprise JavaBeans.

JSP servers aren't limited to Windows and are available for most of the major operating systems. Versions of Tomcat and JRun for Linux are extremely popular. Web sites designed on Dreamweaver MX, on the PC or on the Mac, should be compatible with most of the major JSP servers and operating systems.

The Java Programming Language in JSP

The underlying language of JSP is Java. If you are familiar with Java, you should have no trouble transferring your skills to the arena of Web programming with JSP. If you have a C, C++, or JavaScript background, much of the syntax will be familiar to you.

Java offers many advantages compared to other programming languages. For starters, it's an object-oriented programming language, and it offers a full set of standard classes for most tasks. Java is also portable, having the capability to run on most platforms using the same code. One advantage it has over C++ is automatic garbage collection. C++ programmers have to take care of their own memory management. In addition, Java is multithreaded, which allows the programmer to run different tasks at the same time.

JSP pages are HTML pages with a .jsp file extension and Java server-side code mixed in. JSP pages contain three types of scripting—scriptlets, expressions, and declarations. Java snippets, called *scriptlets*, are contained inside <% and %> tags. The code inside the tags is compiled and run on the server, and the resulting HTML code is sent to the browser. A Java scriptlet in a JSP page might look like this:

```
<% out.println("Greetings " + request.getParameter("firstname"));%>
```

Another type of JSP expression is called, simply, an *expression*. A JSP expression looks like the shorthand *Response.Write* expression in ASP but is, in fact, a member of the *out* object rather than the *response* object. The *out* object is another name for the JSPWriter, which writes directly to the output stream. For instance, the following code displays the session variable *Username*:

```
<%=(session.getValue("Username"))%>
```

When the JSP server sees the =, it's telling the server that the following expression is to be evaluated and sent to the browser as text to be displayed. Additionally, if the parameter inside the expression isn't a string, the JSP server converts it to a string to allow it to be displayed. If you look at the code that Dreamweaver MX generates for the same type of expression, it looks something like this (all on one line):

```
<%=((session.getValue("Username")!=null)?
        session.getValue("Username"):"")%>
```

Dreamweaver MX adds error checking to most of the code it generates to prevent the occurrence of error messages. Dreamweaver MX uses the *ternary* expression in the preceding expression, which you can consider as a shorthand *if/else* statement (explained in more detail in the section "Control Structures in Java," later in this chapter). If the session variable is not null, the server will pass the value to the browser. If it is null, the server will pass an empty string to the browser. This prevents unwanted errors and allows the user to concentrate on the functionality of the site and spend less time on "bullet-proofing" the code.

Another type of JSP tag that you might see is the *declaration.* The declaration is used to declare a method, variable, or field. A declaration tag will have *page* scope, meaning that anything declared within the tag will be available to the whole page. A JSP declaration looks like this:

```
<%! int i = 1000; %>
```

One thing that you must be mindful of when writing Java code is that everything is case-sensitive. The following might look the same to someone not familiar with Java, but the first is correct and the second will cause an error:

```
<%=(session.getValue("Username"))%>
<%=(session.GetValue("Username"))%>
```

The latter code snippet will cause the JSP server to throw an error message that "No method named GetValue was found." Java developers must pay strict attention to the case of the code they write. This applies to functions, variables, properties, methods, events—in short, the whole of the language has to be thought of as being 100 percent case-sensitive.

Variables in Java

Java is strictly *typed* when it comes to variables. Type, in the case of variables, refers to the kind of data that the variable will contain. In ASP—both JavaScript and VBScript— you can get away with declaring variables without worrying about the type. The ASP variable type is a *variant*, which can hold any kind of data. In Java—and in JSP—you have to declare the variable type when you declare its name, as in these examples:

```
<%
boolean myFlag = (session.getValue("Username")!=null);
String myFirstName = "Tom";
int myCounter = 0;
%>
```

Note   String *is a special Java class, and not a variable type per se.*

If you try to use a variable before it's declared, the JSP server will throw an error. Also, if you try to put a value into a variable of the wrong type, the JSP server will throw an error. This forces the programmer to maintain strict coding practices. Java developers consider the nontyped ASP languages to be "lazy" languages, allowing the programmer to develop bad programming habits by not typing the variables.

In addition to declaring the variables with the proper type, you can't change types or mix two variables of different types in the same expression without first *casting* the variable. Casting refers to "changing" the variable type for the expression. The actual variable isn't changed, but the way that the server "sees" the variable is changed. For instance, to cast a session variable as an integer, you might use an expression like this:

```
<% int myUserID = (int)session.getValue("UserID");%>
```

The rules for casting variables are described in the Java API or any good Java reference. For example, a Boolean value can't be cast into another type. If you are planning to do any JSP development, you should have a good Java reference handy at all times. Table 16-1 shows the different variable types that are available to the Java developer.

Type	Range of Values	Description
byte	−128 to 127	Byte-length integer (8-bit)
short	−32768 to 32767	Short integer (16-bit)
int	−2147483648 to 2147483647	Integer (32-bit)
long	−9223372036854775808 to 9223372036854775807	Long integer (64-bit)
float	+/−3.40282347e38 to +/−1.40239846e−45	Single-precision floating-point number (32-bit)
double	+/−1.79769313486231570e308 to +/−4.94065645841246544e−324	Double-precision floating-point number (64-bit)
char	Single character	A single 16-bit Unicode character
boolean	True or false	A true/false value

Table 16-1.   *Variable Types and Their Ranges in Java*

You can also declare more than one variable on a line of code, as in this example:

```
<%
int i=1, j=100, k=1000;
boolean isAllowed, isNewUser, isAdmin = false;
char newLine = '\n', answerYes = 'y', quoteChar = '\u0022';
%>
```

Variables must be named according to Java conventions, which also apply to functions, classes, and packages. They may contain upper- or lowercase letters, digits, underscore characters, and the $ character. Although upper- and lowercase letters are allowed, Java is case-sensitive. For instance, the variables *myCounter* and *MyCounter* would be completely different variables.

Expressions

Java is an expression-based language, like C. Java expressions represent computations, declarations, and flow of control. The simplest of Java expressions is a variable declaration, as in the following:

```
int i = 0;
```

A more complicated expression would be a computation, which can use any of the Java operators listed in Table 16-2.

Operator	Type	Function
+	Arithmetic	Add
−	Arithmetic	Subtract
*	Arithmetic	Multiply
/	Arithmetic	Divide
<	Relational	Less than
>	Relational	Greater than
<=	Relational	Less than or equal to
>=	Relational	Greater than or equal to

Table 16-2.   *Operators in Java*

Operator	Type	Function
==	Relational	Equal to
!=	Relational	Not equal to
+=,−=, *=, and so on	Compound assignment	Uses the right-hand expression double-duty as the first operand

Table 16-2.   *Operators in Java* (continued)

The following statements are examples of legal expressions in Java:

```
int a = 1 + 2;
total += subtotal;
boolean c;
c = a > b;
```

This example illustrates a Boolean value being assigned to the boolean variable *c* as the result of a comparison between *a* and *b*. In Java, unlike some other languages such as C and JavaScript, a comparison yields a true or false (Boolean) value, rather than a one or a zero.

Integers have another set of operators available to them, outlined in Table 16-3.

Operator	Function
+	Arithmetic constant
−	Arithmetic negation
~	Bitwise complement
++	Increment
− −	Decrement
%	Modulus (remainder)
&, | , ^	Bitwise *AND*, *OR*, and *XOR*

Table 16-3.   *Integer Operators*

AN INTRODUCTION TO WEB SCRIPTING

Operator	Function
<<	Left bit shift
>>	Right bit shift with sign fill
>>>	Right bit shift with zero fill

Table 16-3. *Integer Operators* (continued)

In addition to the integer operators shown in Table 16-3, the binary operators can be used as compound operators. Also, the integer types (*int*, *long*, *short*, and *byte*) can be operated on in combinations—type casting is automatic, and the result is always type-cast into the higher of the values. For instance, if you add a *byte* variable to an *int* type variable, the result would be an *int* type. This allows you to work with different integer data types without worrying about casting the variables into the same type beforehand.

Strings can also be operated on with a plus sign (+), which effectively concatenates the variables, as in this example:

```
<%
String myFirst = "Fred";
String myLast = "Periwinkle";
String myName = myFirst + ' ' + myLast;
out.println(myName);//the result would be "Fred Periwinkle"
%>
```

Strings also allow the use of compound concatenation, as in this example:

```
theCode += '\n';  //add a line feed to the end of the code
```

Control Structures in Java

Java uses control structures that are similar to C or JavaScript. The most common control structure would have to be the *if/else* structure, but there are others that may be more suitable for certain tasks. The basic structures are outlined next. Note that some of the control structures evaluate an expression inside a set of parentheses that returns a Boolean value, and then act upon the result of the value.

if/else

```
<%
if (username == "Jim") {
    out.println("Hello, Jim");
    }else{
    out.println("Hello");
    }
%>
```

switch/case

```
<%
switch (whichPage) {
    case 1:
        response.sendRedirect("Page1.jsp");
        break;
    case 2:
        response.sendRedirect("Page2.jsp");
        break;
    default:
        response.sendRedirect("Home.jsp");
}
%>
```

AN INTRODUCTION
TO WEB SCRIPTING

The Ternary Operator: Shorthand *if/else*

```
<%
(userid!=null)?out.println("Goodbye"):out.println("Welcome")
%>
//The ternary operator deserves a little explanation.  The first
//expression is evaluated (userid!=null) to true or false.
//If true, the next expression is executed and if false, the third
//expression is executed. The statement above could have been //written as:
<%
if(userid!=null) {
    out.println("Goodbye");
}else{
    out.println("Welcome");
}
%>
```

Note	*Dreamweaver MX uses the shorthand version of the if/else construct in code that displays a data source on the page.*

Looping Construct Using *for*

```
<%
for(int i=0; i<totalRows; i++) {
    out.println("<tr><td>" + cookies[i].getName() + "</td></tr>");
}
%>
```

while Statements

```
<%
while (i<10) {
    spaceString += ' ';
    i++;
}
%>
```

do/while Statements

```
<%
do {
    out.println("<li>" + myList[i] + "</li>");
    i++;
}
while (i < 10);
%>
```

JSP Objects

If you're an ASP programmer looking to expand your knowledge by learning Java, learning JSP is an excellent way to start. If you are new to the language and server-side technologies in general, JSP is a good, but difficult, way to learn this complex technology. JSP contains many of the same server-side features and objects that an ASP developer might be familiar with. If you've skipped the ASP chapter, you are advised to go back and read it, because it contains explanations of most of the basic server-side functionality that is common to ASP and JSP.

This section provides a brief rundown of the eight built-in variables, or *implicit objects*, that a JSP developer can use. They are *request, response, out, session, application, config, page, pageContext,* and *exception.*

The *request* Object

This object gives the Web developer access to the incoming HTTP headers, request parameters, and request types (*GET, POST,* and so on). Similar to ASP and ColdFusion, these request objects can be any of the following types (also called *collections*):

- *Form*
- *QueryString*
- *Cookies*
- *ServerVariables*

The *Form* and *QueryString* parameters can be retrieved from the client by using the following syntax:

```
request.getParameter("myFormElement")
```

or

```
request.getParameter("queryStringVariable")
```

Because Java is case-sensitive, it expects the request object to be in lowercase. The *getParameter()* method covers both *GET* and *POST* processes of form submission. To display the contents of a *Form* or *QueryString* variable, you can use the shorthand version of JSP expression evaluation, which displays the result in the browser, similar to the *Response.Write* object in ASP:

```
<%=request.getParameter("myVariable")%>
```

Cookies in JSP

JSP has its own method for retrieving cookies that differs considerably from the other server environments. You can't retrieve a cookie by name in JSP. You have to retrieve the entire *Cookies* collection and loop through the results looking for your particular cookie. First, you create a new *Cookie* object, and then you retrieve the *Cookies* collection by using the *request* object:

```
Cookie[] myCookies = request.getCookies();
```

Then, you must loop through the collection to look for the cookie that you are interested in (in this case, a cookie named *username*):

```
for (int i=0; i<myCookies.length; i++) {
    if (myCookies[i].getName().equals("username")) {
        String strUsername = myCookies[i].getValue();
        break;
    }
}
```

Looping through the Cookies *collection is a frequently used method and could be made into an Enterprise JavaBean (EJB) for reuse.*

The *ServerVariables* Collection

The *request* object can also retrieve the *ServerVariables* collection, as in ASP and ColdFusion. The server variables are retrieved one by one, by using methods of the *request* object that roughly correspond to the names of the server variables. The list of available methods for retrieving server variables is as follows:

- *request.getAuthType()*   The authentication type (generally not used)
- *request.getContentLength()*   Indicates the number of bytes in the response
- *request.getContentType()*   MIME type of the response document
- *request.getHeader("User-Agent")*   The client browser being used
- *request.getMethod()*   The method of the response, usually *GET* or *POST*
- *request.getPathInfo()*   Path from the site root
- *request.getPathTranslated()*   Full physical path to the page
- *request.getProtocol()*   The HTTP protocol being used
- *request.getQueryString()*   The entire *QueryString* following the question mark
- *request.getRemoteAddr()*   The IP address of the client
- *request.getRemoteHost()*   If remote user has DNS entry, might be returned in this value
- *request.getRemoteUser()*   Possibly contains username of user, but generally not used
- *request.getRequestURI()*   Section of the path to the page, usually from the site root
- *request.getServerName()*   Name of the server, useful for building links
- *request.getServerPort()*   Port number of the JSP server, usually 80
- *request.getServletPath()*   Path to the page, usually from site root

The *response* Object

This object is the *HTTPServletResponse* for sending responses back to the client, such as status codes and response headers. As in ASP, the response is buffered and is not legal to send to the browser once the HTML headers have been sent.

The following sections outline the various methods of the *response* object.

response.setHeader(), response.setDateHeader(), and *response.setIntHeader()*

These methods are useful for setting the header of the Web page, as in the following statement, which instructs the user's browser to never cache the page:

```
response.setHeader("Cache-Control","no-cache");
```

response.sendRedirect()

This statement is similar to the *Response.Redirect* in ASP or the *CFLOCATION* in ColdFusion. Provided the headers haven't been sent to the browser yet, this method will redirect the user to a page specified in the string, as in this example:

```
String strErrorMessage = "Unknown%20user";
response.sendRedirect("error.jsp?error=" + strErrorMessage);
```

response.setContentType()

This is a widely used method to set the content type of the response output sent to the browser. The *type* attribute is a standard MIME type that the browser recognizes, such as text/html or image/jpeg. For example, to display the contents of a shopping cart variable in the browser, you could use something like this:

```
<%
response.setContentType("text/html");
out.println("<table>");
for (int i=0;i<cart.length;i++) {
    out.println("<tr><td>" + cart.productName[i] + "</td></tr>");
}
out.println("</table>");
%>
```

response.setContentLength()

This method is useful for setting up persistent connections to the browser, among other things. Rather than open and close connections for a large number of items, such as text files or images, you can use this method to set the content length and then use the output stream to send the files as one large stream.

response.addCookie()

Use this method for adding a new cookie to the client's machine. Generally, when you set a cookie, you'll want to give it a name, a value, and an expiration time, as in the following example:

```
<%
String strUsername = request.getParameter("username");
Cookie ckUsername = new Cookie("ckUsername",strUsername);
response.addCookie(ckUsername);
ckUsername.setMaxAge(24*60*60*30);//set age to thirty days
%>
```

The out Object

Also known as the JSPWriter (the buffered form of the PrintWriter), this object sends a stream of output to the client's browser. This object is used in scriptlets and is usually accessed by using the *println* method, as in the following example:

```
<%
out.println("Your book is " + request.getParameter("title"));
%>
```

Note   *The JSP expression syntax (<% = %>) rarely uses the* out *object, because the equal sign (=) automatically places the expression in the output stream.*

The session Object

The session object enables you to store *state* information regarding a client/server session, and is created even if you don't explicitly reference the *session* object. Because the Web is a stateless environment, Web servers must use other methods to maintain state in an application. Creating a unique session ID number for every user is one way. The session ID is stored on the user's computer in a cookie. Each time the user requests another page, the cookie is read and the value of the session ID is compared against the active sessions to determine whether the user has an active session. Just like ASP, if the client has cookies turned off, you can't use the *session* object. The only way the *session* object isn't created is if you specifically turn sessions off with the following:

```
<%@ page session="false" %>
```

To access the *session* object, you have to set a name and a value to a variable. In JSP, the session variable name is referred to as a session *attribute.* You have to explicitly set the attribute and the value when you create a session variable, as in this example that uses the *setAttribute()* method of the *session* object:

```
<%
session.setAttribute("Username",request.getParameter("Username"));
%>
```

In the example, you are setting a session variable named *Username* to the value retrieved in either a *QueryString* or a *Form* variable (recall that the *getParameter* method of the *request* object can take either type). You could also have used the *putValue* method of the *session* object, as in this example:

```
<%
session.putValue("Password",request.getParameter("Password"));
%>
```

You can retrieve the values by using the *getAttribute (*variable name*)* method of the *session* object, as in the following:

```
<input type="text" value="<%=session.getAttribute("Username")%>">
```

The previous example combines HTML with a JSP expression that will put the value of the session variable named *Username* into the text field before it is sent to the browser.

Caution   *Although simple expressions are being used to demonstrate some of the methods of JSP, you should check all variables for their existence before using them in an expression, as was demonstrated earlier, to avoid compiler errors.*

To remove a session variable from the *session* object, you can use the following method:

```
<%
session.removeAttribute("Username");
%>
```

The *removeAttribute* method effectively removes not only the value, but also the reference to the session variable.

To list all session variable names (attributes) in the *session* object and their corresponding values, you can use the following method:

```
<%
Enumeration mySession = session.getAttributeNames();
while(mySession.hasMoreElements()) {
    String mySessionVarName = (String)mySession.nextElement();
    String myValue = (String)session.getValue(mySessionVarName);
    out.println(mySessionVarName + "=" + myValue + "<br>");
}
%>
```

AN INTRODUCTION
TO WEB SCRIPTING

The previous example will display all current session variables and their values. To use this scriptlet, you need to include the *java.util.** library to be able to use the *Enumeration* class. The object returned by the *getAttributeNames()* method of the session is an *Enumeration* object. The *Enumeration* class has two methods—*hasMoreElements()* and *nextElement()*. These methods should be self-explanatory. One of the nice features of Java is the plain-language syntax of many of the classes. The *Enumeration* type has to be converted explicitly to a *String* type upon each iteration of the loop, as you can see in the example. You then use the *out* object to print the session variable name and value to the browser.

> **Note**   *The* session *object will be created only if you have session tracking enabled. It is enabled by default, but you can turn it off with a page directive of* session="false"*. Also, a session object is maintained only if the user has cookies enabled on his or her system.*

The application Object

The same way you can track a variable in the session of one individual user, you can track a variable that is available to all users in the application. These application variables can be defined and retrieved anywhere in the site, but are usually placed somewhere at the entry point of your application, such as in the Home.jsp or Index.jsp file. Most of the methods that are available for the session are also available for the application object, such as *getAttribute(*string name*)* for the retrieval of a variable, and *setAttribute(*string name, value*)* for setting the variable's value.

The following code will count the hits to the page and store the count in an application variable named *counter*:

```
<%
Integer hits = (Integer)application.getAttribute("counter");
if(hits==null) {
     hits = new Integer(0);
}else{
     hits = new Integer(hits.intValue() + 1);
}
application.setAttribute("counter",hits);
%>
```

Then, you can display the result on the page with this expression:

```
<% =application.getAttribute("counter")%>
```

Note that this is a page-hit counter, not an application-hit counter.

If you are familiar with ASP, you may have used the global.asa file in your ASP applications. Some JSP servers have adopted a global.jsa file that works in a similar fashion, with application start and end events, as well as session start and end events. As of this writing, it's a nonstandard file, so we don't examine its details here. Macromedia's JRun allows the use of the global.jsa file.

The *config* Object

This is an instance of the *javax.servlet.ServletConfig* class and represents the *servlet* configuration. This object is not typically used, but it will give you information about the configuration, such as the current servlet name, with the *getServletName()* method, as in this example:

```
<% = config.getServletName()%>
```

The *page* Object

The *page* object is also a rarely used object, and we mention it here for the sake of completeness. It has page scope and can be accessed as *this*.

The *pageContext* Object

The *pageContext* object was created for JSP as an easy way to get information about the page. Each JSP page has a *pageContext* object that is created when a user visits the page, and it is destroyed after the page is executed. Some of the methods of the *pageContext* object are as follows:

- *findAttribute(String name)*
- *getAttribute(String name)*
- *getAttributesScope(String name)*
- *setAttribute(String name, Object obj, int scope)*
- *findAttribute(String name)*
- *removeAttribute(String name)*

The *exception* Object

The *exception* object will allow the programmer to have access to the errors that are thrown on a JSP page. The *exception* object has three methods that are available to the programmer:

- *getMessage()*   Returns the error message
- *printStackTrace()*   Returns the entire stack trace
- *toString()*   Returns a string that describes the *exception* object

You would generally use the *exception* object on an error page, which you can define with the *page* directive

```
<%@ page isErrorPage="true"%>
```

 Caution   *The* exception *object is enabled only if you have defined an error page with the method just outlined.*

The Directives

Directives are used in JSP to set certain properties of the page, scripting language, tag libraries, and include files for the page. The three possible directives are *page*, *include*, and *taglib*. Some directives are placed at the beginning of the file, and occur before any processing is done on the page; but they can be placed where needed. The JSP server parses the page before any evaluation of expressions on the page. As such, the directives can't contain variables or expressions. The directives also don't produce any output for the client, because they aren't evaluated—they are simply there to give instructions to the server.

The *page* Directive

The *page* directive has several possible attributes to tell the server various things about the current JSP page. These attributes are discussed next.

The *language* Attribute

By default, the language of the page will be Java, using the *language* attribute of the *page* directive, as shown in this example:

```
<%@ page language="java" %>
```

You'll find in Dreamweaver MX-generated pages that the program will insert this directive by default into your page when you add server-side code in the form of data sources or Server Behaviors. You could conceivably set the language to be something other than Java, such as JavaScript, as in this example:

```
<%@ page language="javascript" %>
```

When working with a JavaScript page, all of the standard objects of JSP will be available to your server-side JavaScript. The following example shows the use of JavaScript in a JSP page:

```
<%
var a=1;
var b = "Hello, World";
```

```
session.setAttribute("c",2 + a + b);
%>
<%=a%>              <!--prints "1.0" to the screen-->
<%=b%>              <!--prints "Hello, World" -->
<%=session.getAttribute("c")%> <!--   prints "3Hello, World" -->
```

As you can see, in JavaScript, the variables are all treated as variants, and type-casting isn't an issue. The session variable *c* contains the addition of the literal value 2 to the value of variable *a*, which is 1.0, and the result is concatenated as a string to the contents of variable *b*, "Hello, World". Not all servers support languages other than Java. Macromedia's JRun 3.0 supported JavaScript as well as Java. In the future, other servers may support JavaScript or other languages, although JRun 4.0 dropped the support for the use of JavaScript.

The *import* Attribute

This attribute will tell the JSP server which class packages it needs to include on the page. Generally, several packages are included by default (if the language is Java) and don't need to be explicitly declared:

- *java.lang.**
- *java.servlet.**
- *java.servlet.jsp.**
- *java.servlet.http.**

You can explicitly declare other packages that your page might need by adding an *import* attribute to the page directive, or by including a comma-delimited list of packages if the *import* attribute already exists, as in this example:

```
<%@ page import = "java.io.*, java.sql.*, java.util.*"%>
```

> **Note** *When you use the built-in Dreamweaver MX Server Behaviors and data sources, the page directives are included as needed and don't need to be added by hand. For instance, when you add a recordset to the page, the* java.sql.* *package is included in the* import *attribute.*

The *contentType* Attribute

This attribute specifies the MIME type and character set (*charset*) of the page. The default MIME type is text/html unless you specify a different MIME type with this attribute, as in this example:

```
<%@ page contentType = "text/plain; charset=us-ascii" %>
```

The *contentType* attribute can be used to your advantage for allowing the dynamic generation of different file types. For instance, a content type of "application/unknown" will cause the output stream to be downloadable as an unknown file. A content type of "application/vnd.ms-excel" will cause the resulting page to be output to Microsoft Excel, if the user has it on his or her computer.

The contentType *can also be specified using the* setContentType() *method of the* response *object, as in* <%response.setContentType("text/plain");%>.

The *session* Attribute

The *session* attribute is true by default—allowing the use of session tracking and session variables. You can turn off sessions by specifying "false," as in this example:

```
<%@ page session="false" %>
```

The *buffer* Attribute

The *buffer* attribute is the size of the buffer before it is flushed to the client. If you specify a size, you have to use "kb" in the string, as in this example:

```
<%@ page buffer ="32kb" %>
```

The default buffer size is 8K unless specified otherwise. You can also specify *buffer="none"*, which will cause the output stream to go right to the browser instead of being buffered.

The *autoFlush* Attribute

By default, the buffer will flush automatically when it fills up. You can override this behavior by specifying the following:

```
<%@ page autoFlush = "false" %>
```

This setting will cause an exception to be thrown when the buffer reaches capacity. Note that you can't set the *autoFlush* attribute to "false" when the buffer is set to "none," because there is no buffer to flush.

The *isThreadSafe* Attribute

This attribute sets the thread safety level of the page and will cause the server to create multiple instances of the page if the attribute is set to "false." This will cause the servlet to use the *SingleThreadModel*. By default, the *isThreadSafe* attribute is set to "true."

Generally, when the user accesses a page, multiple threads can access a single instance of the servlet, sometimes causing overlap. In most cases, this isn't a problem; but if you have critical or private data, such as user information or ID numbers that you don't want to be accessed by more than one person, you should set this attribute to "false," as in the following example:

```
<%@ page isThreadSafe = "false" %>
```

The *info* Attribute

The *info* attribute defines a string that can be retrieved later with the *getServletInfo()* method. It's used like this:

```
<%@ page info="Some info about this page, last updated 10-20-00" %>
```

You can display the *info* attribute at some point by using the following:

```
<%=getServletInfo()%>
```

The *errorPage* Attribute

This attribute will allow you to set an error page to catch any exceptions that are thrown on the current page. The *exception* object of the current page will be available to the error page specified. The attribute is used like this:

```
<%@ page errorPage="error.jsp" %>
```

The *isErrorPage* Attribute

For the *errorPage* attribute to work, you need to have an error page set up in your application. This is accomplished with the *isErrorPage* attribute of the page directive. The attribute is placed on the error page itself, as in the following:

```
<%@ page isErrorPage = "true" %>
```

After the error page is defined, you can use the *exception* object to report the error of the page that caused the error, or use it to perform some predefined action depending upon what type of error is encountered.

The *extends* Attribute

This attribute allows you to specify a fully qualified class name that the servlet produced by the JSP page extends. The attribute is usually not used. The servlet engine generally has a specific class that adds functionality to the server that would be circumvented by using this attribute. Avoid it, unless you have a specific reason for using it. It is implemented like this:

```
<%@ page extends = "com.myCustomClass.MyServletImplementation" %>
```

The *include* Directive

Just as in ASP and ColdFusion, in JSP you can include files at translation time that will be inserted directly into the place where the *include* directive is placed in the page. For instance, if you have a page footer that is on every page, it makes sense to make an include file out of it, so that if it changes, you have to change it in only one place. The directive is used like this:

```
<%@ include file="myfooter.jsp" %>
```

The file path is considered to be relative to the current page unless it has a leading /, in which case the file path is relative to the application.

The *taglib* Directive

You can use this directive to declare a *tag library* to be used in the JSP page. Tag libraries, also referred to as *custom actions*, enable you to create your own custom tags that can be called within the JSP page. One of the main reasons for building tag libraries is to allow complex functionality to be coded by Java developers and abstracted into an easy-to-use tag. This way, Web content developers and Web designers can use the tags in their pages without having to learn a complex language like Java. The tag library is called with the *taglib* directive like this:

```
<%@ taglib uri="/myTagLib" prefix="myTagLib" %>
```

After adding the directive to the page, you can call your custom tags with XML syntax, using a prefix for the name of the tag library, the tag name, and attributes, like this:

```
<myTagLib:tagname  id="obj1" attribute="value" />
```

Tag libraries are implemented inside of custom Java classes called *tag handlers*. These classes are similar in concept to Java beans in that they abstract the details of the functionality from the page content developer. The tag library developer creates an interface to the functionality and leaves the Web page developer with a simple tag that can be used in a similar fashion to an HTML tag.

UltraDev added JavaBean support in UltraDev 4, but tag libraries were left behind. Dreamweaver MX added support for tag libraries, allowing you to import and use tag libraries in your application.

Tag libraries are an important part of JSP development and are something you should learn if you intend to pursue a path as a JSP developer. Building tag libraries requires skill in the Java language, but using them requires only a knowledge of how the interface of the custom tag works. You can find details on how to create your own tag libraries in the Servlet 2.3 API at java.sun.com/products/servlet.

Serving the JSP Page

When a JSP page is browsed for the first time, the JSP server will compile the Java and HTML code into servlets that are then stored in the default servlet directory for the server. The first time the page is visited, there is additional overhead to the compile time; but after that, the pages will execute more quickly because the code is already translated into Java bytecode. You can avoid this delay by always testing the page one time after the page is deployed. Depending on which JSP server you are using, the actual source code of the servlet can be accessed as well. The following is a typical JSP page, which is followed by the servlet source code that is generated by the server in the next section:

```
<%@page language="java" %>
<html>
<head>
<title>Test JSP</title>
<meta http-equiv="Content-Type" content="text/html;¬
charset=iso-8859-1">
</head>
<body bgcolor="#FFFFFF">
<table>
<%
int x = 10;
while (x > 0){
%>
  <tr>
    <td><%= x-- %></td>
  </tr>
 <% } %>
</table>
</body>
</html>
```

AN INTRODUCTION
TO WEB SCRIPTING

This simple page sets a variable x to the value of 10, and then counts down to 1 using a *while* loop and displaying the countdown in a table. Note that the variable declaration is inside a scriptlet. The JSP tags are closed to allow the table row tags, <tr>, and the table cell tags, <td>, to be sent to the browser, after which a JSP expression of <%= x—%> is placed in the page. This expression displays the variable and also decrements the value by one. Then, the table cell and table row tags are closed, and once again a JSP scriptlet is used to close out the *while* loop with a simple bracket. Then, the <table>, <body>, and <html> tags are closed.

In ASP, when you open and close the server-side tags like this, the server executes each tag set individually, so you actually lose a little bit of execution time by opening and closing the tags. In JSP, as you'll soon see, the entire page is translated into Java as the page is executed for the first time. If you open the *.java file that is generated by the JSP server (in this case, it's a JRun 3 server), you'll see the actual Java code:

```java
// Generated by JRun, do not edit
import javax.servlet.*;
import javax.servlet.http.*;
import javax.servlet.jsp.*;
import javax.servlet.jsp.tagext.*;
import allaire.jrun.jsp.JRunJSPStaticHelpers;
public class jrun__TestJSP2ejspc extends allaire.jrun.jsp.HttpJSPServlet
implements allaire.jrun.jsp.JRunJspPage
{
    private ServletConfig config;
    private ServletContext application;
    private Object page = this;
    private JspFactory __jspFactory =
JspFactory.getDefaultFactory();
    public void _jspService(HttpServletRequest request,
HttpServletResponse response)
        throws ServletException, java.io.IOException
    {
        if(config == null) {
            config = getServletConfig();
            application = config.getServletContext();
        }
        response.setContentType("text/html; charset=ISO-8859-1");
        PageContext pageContext = __jspFactory.getPageContext(this,
request, response, null, true, 8192, true);
        JspWriter out = pageContext.getOut();
        HttpSession session = pageContext.getSession();
        try {
    out.print(" \r\n<html>\r\n<head>\r\n<title>Test JSP</title>
\r\n<meta http-equiv=\"Content-Type\" content=\"text/html;
charset=iso-8859-1\">\r\n</head>\r\n<body bgcolor=\"#FFFFFF\">\r\n
<table>\r\n");
int x = 10;
while (x > 0){
    out.print(" \r\n  <tr> \r\n    <td>");
out.print(x--);
out.print("</td>\r\n  </tr>\r\n ");
}
    out.print(" \r\n</table>\r\n</body>\r\n</html>\r\n\r\n");
    } catch(Throwable t) {
        if(t instanceof ServletException)
            throw (ServletException) t;
          if(t instanceof java.io.IOException)
              throw (java.io.IOException) t;
          if(t instanceof RuntimeException)
              throw (RuntimeException) t;
```

```
            throw JRunJSPStaticHelpers.handleException(t, pageContext);
        } finally {
            __jspFactory.releasePageContext(pageContext);
        }
    }
    private static final String[] __dependencies__ =
{"/TestJSP.jsp",null};
    private static final long[] __times__ = {972008391139L,0L};
    public String[] __getDependencies()
    {
        return __dependencies__;
    }
    public long[] __getLastModifiedTimes()
    {
        return __times__;
    }
    public int __getTranslationVersion()
    {
        return 14;
    }
}
```

Several things should be immediately apparent from the code:

■ The JSP server has translated everything into Java—the JSP tags are gone.

■ The HTML code is enclosed in quotes inside of *out.println* statements.

■ The entire *while* loop is enclosed in a *try/catch* block to catch any errors that might occur.

■ Carriage return and line feed characters are explicitly written to the out stream.

■ All servlet classes and helper classes that are needed by the page are included.

■ It's a lot of code!

If you happen to be using the JRun server, these Java files are located in the Allaire\ JRun\servers\default\default-app\WEB-INF\jrun folder. In the Tomcat 3 server, you have to specifically set the *isWorkDirPersistent* attribute in the Install_dir/ server.xml file to "true" (it's set to "false" by default). The files are located in the install_dir/ work/ port-number directory. If you have another JSP server, consult your documentation to locate the source files.

These files should never be edited, but looking at them can give you some insight into what's going on behind the scenes in the JSP server. Along with the *.java files, which are the source code, the compiled files that the JSP server uses when a page is served are stored. As long as the original page isn't edited, it won't be translated again, and serves simply as a "pointer" to the actual compiled code. The first time the page is browsed, the code is translated into a servlet. You'll notice a definite speed improvement the second time you browse the page, because the servlet has already been compiled.

Using JSP with Dreamweaver MX

Dreamweaver MX supports ASP, JSP, PHP, ASP.Net, and ColdFusion using the same interface. This is previously unheard of in the world of Web development. As the first-generation product, UltraDev 1 came up a little short in its JSP implementation. The original release in June of 2000 had many problems with JSP. A patch was soon released that fixed a few of the issues, but many features were still lacking, such as EJB and tag library support. If you are using UltraDev 1 with JSP, make sure you have the patch installed as well.

You can download the JSP patch for UltraDev 1 from the Macromedia site at http:// download.macromedia.com/pub/ultradev/jsp_update.mxp. UltraDev 4 and Dreamweaver MX don't need the patch.

UltraDev 4 increased the support for JSP, adding support for beans. Dreamweaver MX has become a robust environment for the JSP developer, adding support for tag libraries. The following sections go through some of the key features of Dreamweaver MX that relate to the JSP implementation.

The JSP Insert Bar

The Insert bar was covered earlier in the book, but this chapter on JSP wouldn't be complete without showing you the JSP objects that are available from the bar. Figure 16-1 shows the JSP bar.

Some of the items will insert a generic code block in your page to give you a starting point to hand-code your own functionality (such as the *include* directive), whereas other

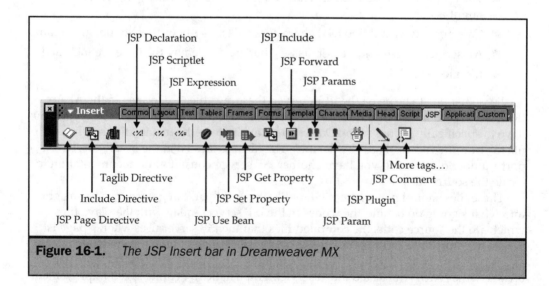

Figure 16-1. *The JSP Insert bar in Dreamweaver MX*

objects will pop up a Tag Editor to allow you to input parameters before the code is actually inserted into the page (such as the JSP Include, shown in Figure 16-2.)

The Bindings Panel

Dreamweaver MX uses an MDI interface with dockable menus called *panels*. The server-side functionality of Dreamweaver MX is in the Databases panel, Bindings panel, Server Behavior panel, and the Components panel. Bindings are so called because they "bind" the data on your page to a server-side construct, such as a recordset or a variable. The elements that reside on the Bindings panel are called *data sources*, and they vary in complexity from the simple (sessions and requests) to the complex (stored procedures and recordsets).

The Recordset Data Source

Recordsets (or resultsets) are the key element to the dynamic Web page—the back-end database gives the static HTML page dynamic content. To create a new recordset, you need to first define a JDBC connection (connections are described in Chapter 20). In UltraDev 1, the connection was defined right on the page; but in UltraDev 4, the connection was placed into an include file, and the connection information was placed into variables that are then used on the page. Dreamweaver MX follows this tradition for the JSP server model.

After the connection exists, you can name your recordset and then write a SQL statement to retrieve data from the database (see Figure 16-3).

To define a basic SQL statement, you can use the Simple dialog box or the Advanced dialog box. For most SQL statements, you'll probably want to stay with the Advanced

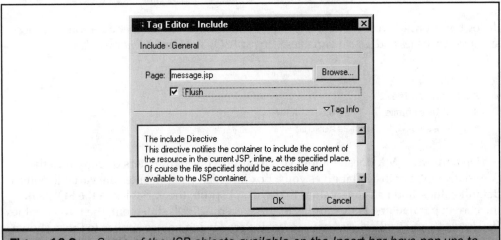

Figure 16-2. *Some of the JSP objects available on the Insert bar have pop-ups to allow you to enter parameters.*

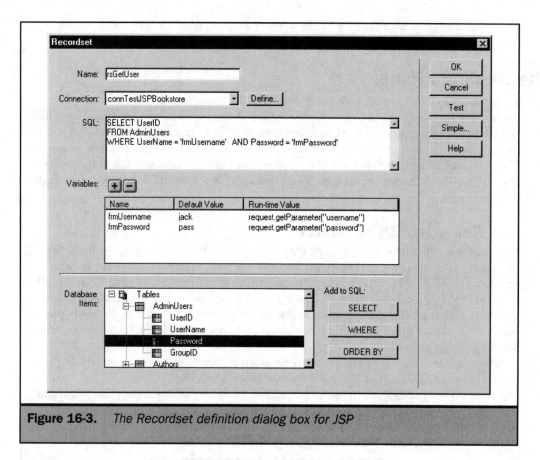

Figure 16-3.   *The Recordset definition dialog box for JSP*

dialog box, in which you can define variables and attach them to other data sources, such as *request* variables and *session* variables. *A typical SQL statement might read like this:*

```
SELECT UserID
FROM AdminUsers
WHERE Username = 'frmUsername'
AND Password = 'frmPassword'
```

Dreamweaver MX doesn't allow you to insert your parameters directly into the SQL statement, but instead it gives you a box in which you can enter the variable names, default values, and run-time values that will substitute the variables in the SQL with the correct parameters. For example, in the preceding SQL statement, the two variables *frmUsername* and *frmPassword* have to be declared using values similar to those shown in Table 16-4.

Name	Default Value	Run-Time Value
frmUsername	jack	*request.getParameter("username")*
frmPassword	pass	*request.getParameter("password")*

Table 16-4. *Declaring Variables in the Recordset Definition Dialog Box*

Note that the default value is a value that will be inserted in the page as a default in the event there is no incoming value. In a testing situation, you might want to include a default value that is in your database so that you can see the data on the finished page; but in a real-world situation, the default value should always be something that won't appear in your database, such as a special character or sequence of characters.

The SQL statement that you define will get passed directly to the database—both in the Dreamweaver MX environment and in the deployed Web application. The syntax of the statement should be legal to your particular database. Also note that the SQL builder in Dreamweaver MX will build only simple SQL statements. Anything but the most basic SQL will have to be coded by hand.

The JavaBean and JavaBean Collection Data Sources

JavaBeans are reusable classes that bring portability to JSP applications. The JavaBean API allows beans to be created that conform to a standard interface. The basic structure of the bean is this:

- It must contain a constructor that names the bean and has no parameters or attributes.

- Private variables in the bean can be made accessible to the programmer through the *getMyBeanProperty* and *setMyBeanProperty* methods, where *myBeanProperty* is the name of the property.

- The bean should have no public variables.

UltraDev 4 added JavaBean support, much to the delight of JSP programmers. The JavaBean data source that appears in both the Bindings panel and the Server Behaviors panel allows the programmer to access the methods of the bean through a visual interface, with Dreamweaver MX generating the appropriate code in the background. The Components panel also allows the JSP programmer to introspect all properties and methods of the bean, which is a new feature to Dreamweaver MX. Using these panels, you can inspect the bean and also drag/drop the methods onto the page from the Bindings panel to generate the JSP tags necessary to call your bean.

To get Dreamweaver MX to recognize your bean, you have to first put the compiled bean CLASS file, or the archived JAR or ZIP file, into the Classes folder under the

Configuration folder in the Dreamweaver MX root program folder. The class has to be accessible to Dreamweaver MX using the same structure of the package. In other words, if the JavaBean has the structure of *com.MyPackage.MyBean*, you can put the MyBean.class file into the Configuration | Classes | com | MyPackage folder or put your package directly into the Classes folder. After doing this, Dreamweaver MX will be able to recognize the bean for use in the program.

The following is an example of a very simple bean that accepts a message and then returns it. First, you need to create the bean in your Java IDE and create a class file. The bean class is called *MessageBean*, and the Java class file is called MessageBean.class. Here's the MessageBean.java file before compilation:

```java
public class MessageBean {
    private String message = "No message";
    public MessageBean(){
    }
    public String getMessage() {
        return(message);
    }
    public void setMessage(String newMessage) {
        this.message = newMessage;
    }
}
```

The *MessageBean* class constructor is empty, as required, and there is a *getMessage* method that returns a property named message, and a method for setting the message, named *setMessage*, which has a *String* parameter named *newMessage*. This is the complete bean, and it can be compiled into a class file and dropped into the Classes folder in Dreamweaver MX. In addition, it will have to be copied to the appropriate directory for your JSP server to be able to access it.

The following page has been created in Dreamweaver MX:

```html
<%@page language="java"%>
<html>
<head>
<title>Message Bean</title>
</head>
<body bgcolor="#FFFFFF" text="#000000">
<div align="center">
  <table border="2">
    <tr>
      <td align="center" bgcolor="#FF9900">
          <strong>Type a message to try out the Bean</strong>
      </td>
    </tr>
```

```
  <form method="post" name="theForm" id="theForm">
    <tr>
      <td align="center">
        <input type="text" name="message" style="width:300px">
      </td>
    </tr>
    <tr>
      <td align="center">
        <input type="submit">
      </td>
    </tr>
  </form>
</table>
<h1>Message: (bean goes here)</h1>
</div>
</body>
</html>
```

The page has a heading that states "Type a message to try out the Bean," a text field to accept the message that the user types in, and a Submit button. To apply the bean to the page, you have to choose the JavaBean data source from the Bindings panel and bring up the Java Bean dialog box (see Figure 16-4). If you've placed your CLASS, JAR, or ZIP file in the Classes folder, the bean should appear on the drop-down list. Check the box at the bottom of the dialog box that says Set Properties Using Values From

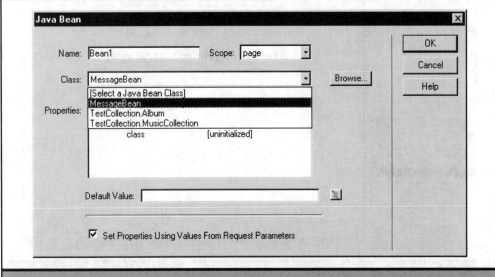

Figure 16-4.   *The Java Bean dialog box in Dreamweaver MX*

Request Parameters. Leave the Scope attribute set to Page for this particular example; the other possible values in the drop-down list are Request, Session, and Application.

After clicking OK, the bean class should appear in the Bindings panel, with the properties of the class accessible by clicking the plus sign (+) next to the JavaBean in the window. You can highlight the "(bean goes here)" placeholder text and drag the message property from the Bindings panel to the placeholder and drop it. Your screen should now look like Figure 16-5.

The code inserted by Dreamweaver MX is XML scripting, which the JSP server recognizes. The code looks like this:

```
<jsp:setProperty name="Bean1" id="Bean1" class="MessageBean"
scope="page"/> <jsp:setProperty name="Bean1" property="*"/>
```

That's the code for the bean instantiation, and the code to set the *Bean* property to the incoming request variable. The code that allows the bean to be viewed on the page is this:

```
<jsp:getProperty name="Bean1" property="message"/>
```

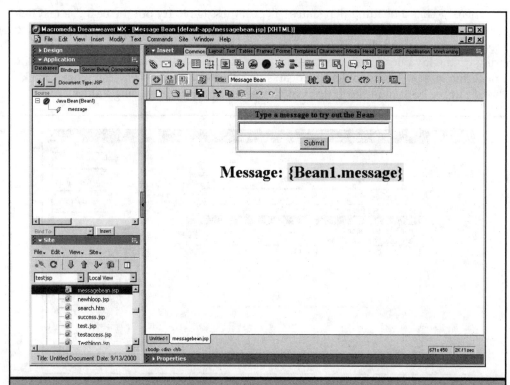

Figure 16-5.   *The Bindings panel has a newly registered bean. The message method has also been placed on the page by dragging and dropping it.*

AN INTRODUCTION TO WEB SCRIPTING

Note *The use of the asterisk allows for the bean properties to assume all of the incoming form fields with form field names that match the properties. For example, if form fields named* firstname, lastname, *and* message *were submitted to the page, the bean would attempt to match up each of the incoming form field names as bean properties. By checking the Set Properties Using Values From Request Parameters box in the Java Bean dialog box, Dreamweaver MX automatically writes this shorthand version.*

Beans are also available from the Components panel, which is grouped with Server Behaviors, Databases, and Bindings in the Application Building panel group. In the Components panel, you can access all methods and properties of the bean (shown in Figure 16-6.)

Callable (Stored Procedure) Data Source

The Callable data source enables you to insert a callable statement to access a stored procedure from your database. Stored procedures will be addressed in Chapter 26.

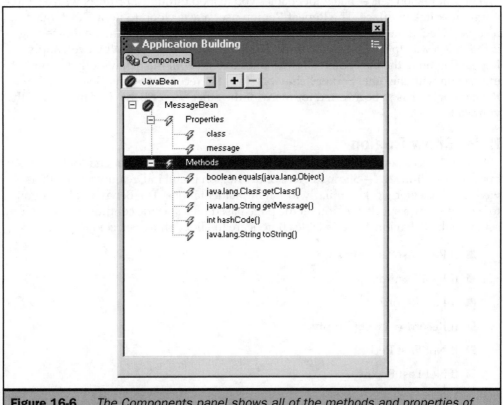

Figure 16-6.   *The Components panel shows all of the methods and properties of a bean.*

Session and Request Variables

The session and request data sources give you a place to store the names of session and request variables that you might use on your page. You simply insert a name for the variable, and it will show up on the Data Sources panel. Once it's in the panel, you can drag it to the page or use it in Java beans, form elements, Server Behaviors, or other constructs. Session variables that are set up in this way on one page will be available for use in the entire site.

The Server Behaviors Panel

Server Behaviors are the main server-side code generators of Dreamweaver MX. These Server Behaviors insert code into your documents to perform a variety of functions. Most of these functions are related to the display of the resultset on the page and navigation through the resultset. The use of Server Behaviors will be covered in Chapters 24 through 26, but here's a brief introduction to some of the Server Behaviors.

Repeat Region

The Repeat Region Server Behavior enables you to loop through a resultset with a simple point-and-click interface. The Repeat Region uses a *while* loop to iterate through a resultset. One of the advantages to using the Repeat Region rather than hand-coding is that it is a way to set up the Recordset Paging Server Behaviors. When you apply a Repeat Region to the page, there are variables that go with the Behavior that allow interaction with the other Server Behaviors. Like the recordset Server Behavior, the Repeat Region has to be inserted for many of the other Server Behaviors to work with your code.

Hide/Show Region

UltraDev 1 had a Server Behavior called Hide Region. This was changed to the exact opposite in UltraDev 4—Show Region. Show Region is still in Dreamweaver MX as well. The Behavior works similarly for all implementations. The Behavior allows you to hide or show a specific region on the page based on a specific condition that you can set up in the Behavior. The available choices are to Hide/Show Selected Region:

- If Recordset is Empty
- If First Record
- If Last Record
- If Recordset Is Not Empty
- If Not First Record
- If Not Last Record

Recordset Paging

This is a group of Server Behaviors that interact with a recordset and a Repeat Region Server Behavior. They allow you to move to the First, Previous, Next, Last, and Specific records. These Server Behaviors were grouped under the heading of Move To in UltraDev.

Dynamic Elements

The Bindings panel allows you to apply dynamic text items to the page and also allows you to insert values into other objects, such as form objects. Another way to do this is to use the Dynamic Elements menu entry in the Server Behaviors panel and click one of the five items:

- **Dynamic Text**   A text item, such as a recordset column or a session variable that's on the page

- **Dynamic List/Menu**   A list/menu form element that gets its values from a data source

- **Dynamic Text Field**   A text field form element that gets its value from a data source

- **Dynamic Check Box**   A checkbox form element that gets its checked value based on a data source

- **Dynamic Radio Buttons**   A set of radio buttons that get their value from a data source

The Components Panel

The Components panel allows you to introspect Java beans (covered earlier in the chapter) and also find and utilize Web services through the interface in the panel (shown in Figure 16-7). Basically, a Web service is a component that is created to communicate using standard XML formats to any application that knows how to talk to it. The component can be created in any language, including Java. The Web service will have an interface written in Web Service Description Language (WSDL), which describes what the Web service does and how to communicate with it. The actual communication is done with XML. Since XML is basically just text, an application that can read text can read, interpret, and interact with a Web service. Because of this, Web services can be created by one type of server and utilized by anyone who can read the XML. This type of universal communication between disparate operating systems and languages has really made Web services one of the fastest rising technologies ever to grace the Web.

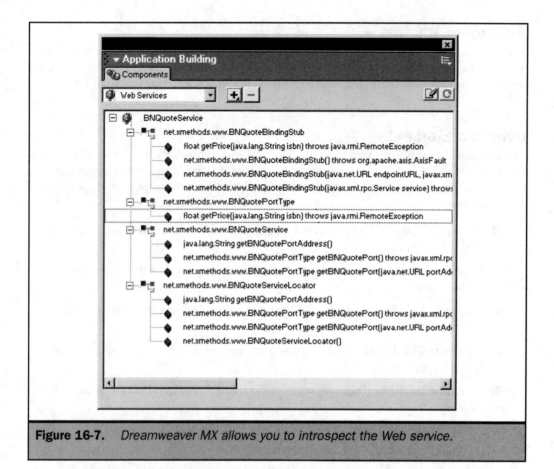

Figure 16-7. *Dreamweaver MX allows you to introspect the Web service.*

Web services can provide information as an answer to a question, a response to a call, or simply act as an information service. Dreamweaver MX can introspect these Web services, and also make it easier to use within the JSP environment by allowing you to drag/ drop the methods and properties of the Web service as Java code from the Component panel to the page.

To locate a public Web service, you can use one of the lists that are available from within the Dreamweaver MX environment. Dreamweaver MX can use the link to the WSDL page to communicate with the Web service and create the interface that will be used in the Dreamweaver MX environment. The Web service then appears with its methods and variables broken down into the Components panel, much like your data sources appear in the Bindings panel.

Using Tag Libraries in Dreamweaver MX

Dreamweaver MX allows you to import your tag libraries by accessing the Edit | Tag Libraries menu. By clicking the plus sign (+) in the dialog box (shown in Figure 16-8), you can import tag libraries from a TLD, JAR, or ZIP file, import JRun Server tags from a folder, or import from a server web.xml file, and then browse for the file.

After retrieving the tag library definitions, you can then view them in the Tag Editor, allowing you to browse the tags, along with their properties or attributes (shown in Figure 16-9). The Tag Editor allows you to specify how the tags will be inserted into your pages. You can control how the line breaks, capitalization, and indentation will apply to each and every tag. This allows a great deal of flexibility for building pages and formatting them to your own specifications.

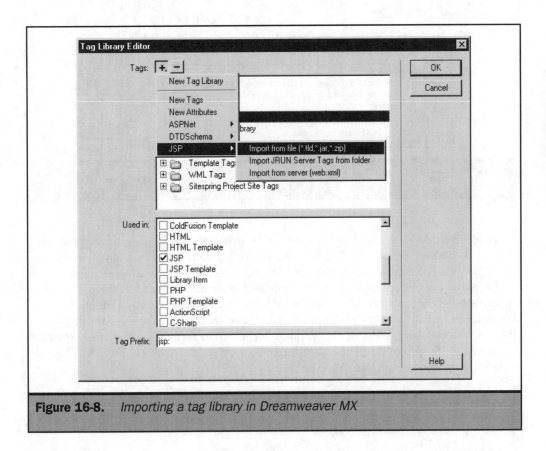

Figure 16-8. *Importing a tag library in Dreamweaver MX*

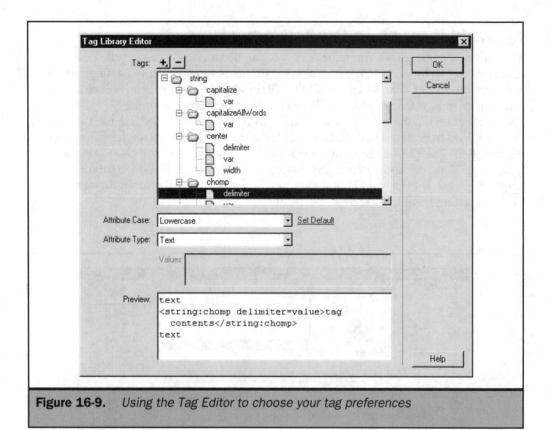

Figure 16-9.   *Using the Tag Editor to choose your tag preferences*

While in Code View, the Tag Chooser can be invoked by accessing the contextual menu and choosing Insert Tag. This will bring up the dialog box allowing you to choose any tag from all of your available tag libraries. The Tag Chooser is shown in Figure 16-10.

Dreamweaver MX also comes with the JRun tag libraries already defined and available from the interface. JRun tag libraries contain a lot of everyday functionality that you can utilize in your own applications. There are tags to ease the handling of database queries, send e-mails, and validate form elements. Tag libraries bring the ease of use of ColdFusion to JSP. This example of a `<jrun:sendmail>` tag will send off an e-mail to a recipient from your Web page:

```
<jrun:sendmail
 host="mail.myserver.com"
 sender="tom@myserver.com"
 recipient="ray@basic-ultradev.com"
 subject="Your check is in the mail">
</jrun:sendmail>
```

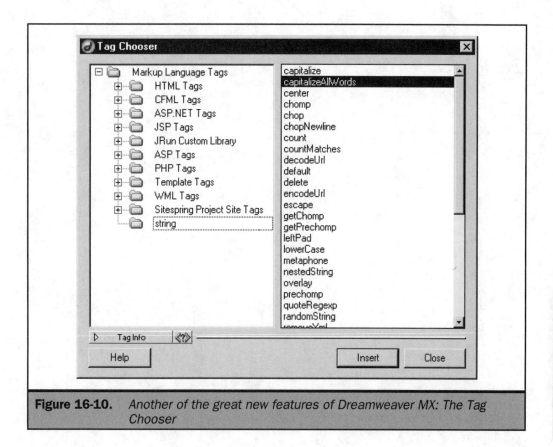

Figure 16-10.   *Another of the great new features of Dreamweaver MX: The Tag Chooser*

JRun's Java Server Tags (JST) are also easily used within the Dreamweaver MX environment. JSTs are easy to develop for a JSP programmer because they can be created using JSP syntax instead of the custom tag API.

Summary

This chapter was intended as a general introduction to JSP and the Java language. The Java language is a vast and powerful language with a rich history of cross-platform compatibility. Also, Java beans allow you to encapsulate code for reuse and move your business logic out of the pages and into the beans. Dreamweaver UltraDev started off slowly with its JSP support in UltraDev 1.0, but became a full-fledged JSP power tool with UltraDev 4.0. Dreamweaver MX adds even more power to the JSP developer's arsenal with tag libraries and Web services support. With the acquisition of Allaire, Macromedia has also become one of the top suppliers of an enterprise-level application server with JRun.

Chapter 17

ColdFusion

Dreamweaver MX accomodates many different server models, including Macromedia's own server, ColdFusion. The other server models available to Dreamweaver MX are Active ServerPages (ASP, which was discussed in Chapter 15); PHP (Personal Home Page, discussed in Chapter 18); Java Server Pages (JSP, which was discussed in Chapter 16); and ASP.NET (discussed in Chapter 19). ASP offers unparalleled support, compatibility, and ease of use for a Microsoft-based solution. JSP, on the other hand, offers tremendous power for a variety of server types and operating systems. PHP is free and popular for Linux environments. Finally, ASP.NET, the new kid on the block, is powerful and extensible. ColdFusion offers the best qualities of JSP and ASP, has a free version like PHP, has the extensibility of ASP.NET and JSP, but also offers the accessibility of HTML.

Macromedia began supporting ColdFusion with UltraDev 1, but the support was far from adequate. There were many problems with rendering of pages that were constructed anywhere but inside of the UltraDev environment. UltraDev 4 provided better support for ColdFusion code, but with the release of Dreamweaver MX, Macromedia has finally built a first-class environment for creating ColdFusion applications. Dreamweaver MX actually has two modes of operation for ColdFusion: CF-UD4 mode, which allows backward compatibility with code that was generated by UltraDev 4, and ColdFusion mode, which contains much better code generation.

ColdFusion is a tag-based language, like HTML, but offers a rich set of over 70 tags that are executed on the server—unlike HTML, which is executed on the client. When you execute the CFQUERY tag, for example, the server interprets the tag and executes a connection to the database and a return of information from the database. A single CFQUERY tag offers the same functionality as 8 to 10 lines of ASP or JSP code.

Note *ColdFusion tags use name/value pairs, just as HTML tags do. The tags, however, should be thought of as server-side script blocks.*

In addition, ColdFusion has just about everything you need built right into the language, including such functionality as database manipulation, e-mail distribution and retrieval, file manipulation, directory manipulation, and anything else you might need to get your site up and running. In ASP and JSP, much of this functionality involves add-on components or hand-coding of complex scripts, beans, applets, and objects. ColdFusion programmers can realize the complexity of a data-driven site by implementing tags that are similar in style to HTML tags.

A ColdFusion page is called a *template*. This is not to be confused with the Dreamweaver template, which is a design-time element. The ColdFusion template is an HTML page with ColdFusion tags mixed in that are executed and replaced on the server.

The ColdFusion Server

In addition to the ease of programming, ColdFusion offers a powerful server that is able to scale to the most demanding of Web applications. It offers load balancing, just-in-time compiling, security, dynamic caching, and failover. The server is robust and capable of high volume using multithreaded processing. Also, it is easily integrated with other programming technologies—such as ASP, XML, COM, CORBA, EJB, Java, and C++—and with application technologies, such as databases, mail servers, file systems, and a host of others. The server is also easily clustered and offers unparalleled server administration features that enable you to administer the server remotely—including your database connections.

Note   *The latest version of CF server is called ColdFusion MX. It works well together with Dreamweaver MX and Flash MX. Most examples in this book will work with ColdFusion 5.0 just as well as with ColdFusion MX, except where noted. New features of ColdFusion MX are noted in this chapter, as well as features of ColdFusion 5 that are no longer in ColdFusion MX.*

In addition to its Windows functionality, ColdFusion can be deployed on Solaris, HP-UX, and Linux, making it quite versatile as an option for a non-Windows system. The Linux version of ColdFusion has become quite popular since its release in late 2000.

Dreamweaver MX is shipped with a single-user license of the ColdFusion Server Enterprise version. The server will run on Windows 98, NT, and 2000. Different levels of the ColdFusion server are available, with the Enterprise version being the top of the line. The version that ships with Dreamweaver MX contains all the advanced features of the Enterprise edition, but can be accessed only locally—that is, through http://localhost or through the default 127.0.0.1 IP address.

The Enterprise version has all the features that a high-end Web application demands—clustering, load balancing, and server failover, to name a few. In addition, the security features are top- notch, including the "sandbox" security, which allows multiple applications to have their own security features.

The Professional version of ColdFusion is a much–lower-cost alternative to the Enterprise version, and has most of the key features. It doesn't offer the load balancing or server failover that the Enterprise version offers. If you don't specifically need this functionality, you might well consider this version, which is available at a substantially lower cost than the Enterprise version. This is the ideal application server to run in a one-server environment where you might need a database connection to a SQL Server database.

AN INTRODUCTION
TO WEB SCRIPTING

ColdFusion also comes as a free version—ColdFusion Express version 4.5.1. ColdFusion Express has 19 of the most popular tags, including CFQUERY and CFOUTPUT. Although Express is certainly a viable option to run your data-driven site, it doesn't contain certain key features to make it usable with Dreamweaver MX-generated code. Dreamweaver MX uses CFScript occasionally in its Server Behaviors, and CFScript isn't included with the ColdFusion Express server. The Express version also doesn't include CFMAIL, CFFILE, or CFPOP, among other tags. Nonetheless, an application developed to run on ColdFusion Express will be 100 percent compatible with the Professional or Enterprise versions.

Note   *ColdFusion Express can be found on the Macromedia Web site at www.macromedia.com/software/coldfusion/trial/cf_server_express.html.*

CFML: The ColdFusion Programming Language

ColdFusion Markup Language (CFML) isn't a traditional programming language, per se. CFML is a tag-based language, which is somewhat different than the script-based ASP languages and the object-oriented Java language. ColdFusion has a script language built into it—CFScript—but the majority of ColdFusion programming involves the use of tags. A page that contains CFML is saved with a .cfm or .cfml file extension. Any page with a .cfm or .cfml extension that is requested from the Web server will be parsed by the ColdFusion server before being sent to the browser.

A tag is nothing more than a command that is flanked by the < > symbols, like the HTML tags that Web developers are accustomed to seeing. A typical ColdFusion statement might look like this:

```
<cfoutput>#form1.Username#</cfoutput>
```

The CFOUTPUT statement is similar to *Response.Write()* in ASP or *out.print()* in JSP. The pound signs (#) are signals to the ColdFusion server that the code contained within the signs is to be evaluated by the server. In this particular case, a Form variable named *Username* will be evaluated and directed to the browser. Specific rules apply to using the pound signs, and these are covered in an upcoming section; but in general, the pound signs imply that the code contained within is a variable or an expression. Also, they must exist inside of a ColdFusion tag or tag set. In other words, the server won't interpret the pound signs if they aren't contained within a valid ColdFusion tag.

ColdFusion tags all begin with the <CF prefix. Those three characters act as a signal to the server that the current tag is to be executed by the ColdFusion server. It's similar to the <% prefix found in ASP and JSP or the <? prefix found in PHP. Some of these tags come as a "set," with an open tag and a close tag, such as the preceding CFOUTPUT tag. Others, such as the CFFILE tag, exist as one tag. A complete list of the available ColdFusion tags is shown in Table 17-1. Generally speaking, a ColdFusion tag

contains a series of name/value pairs that provide the server with the information needed to execute the tag. The following CFFILE tag is an example:

```
<cffile action="Delete"
 file="c:\inetpub\wwwroot\images\#form.filename#">
```

The ACTION attribute of the tag is set to "Delete," the FILE attribute is set to the c:\inetpub\wwwroot\images directory, and the filename is set to an incoming Form variable named "filename." When the ColdFusion server reads this tag, it will execute the tag—which, in this case, will cause a file named in the form element to be deleted from the server. Using the same CFFILE tag, you can create a file upload by setting the ACTION attribute to "Upload":

```
<cffile action="Upload"
 filefield="Filename"
 destination="c:\inetpub\wwwroot\images\"
 nameconflict="Overwrite">
```

In this case, a FILEFIELD attribute of Filename is specified, which will be the name of the incoming Form variable. The DESTINATION attribute is the folder on the server in which the file will be stored, and the NAMECONFLICT attribute instructs the server what to do if the name happens to conflict with a file that already exists on the server.

As with most ColdFusion tags, the CFFILE tag has some required attributes and some optional attributes. The NAMECONFLICT attribute in the preceding CFFILE tag is optional. Whenever an optional attribute is included, the server follows a default behavior if the attribute isn't contained in the tag. In this case, if the NAMECONFLICT attribute isn't defined, the default behavior is to throw an error if a file already exists. See Table 17-1 for a list of available tags.

ColdFusion tags all behave differently and all have different degrees of complexity. For instance, a CFABORT tag exists by itself, and has an optional attribute of SHOWERROR. You can put it on the page like this:

```
<cfabort>
```

If the ColdFusion server encounters this tag, it will simply stop processing the page. If you give it a SHOWERROR attribute, as in this example,

```
<cfabort showerror="You have to be more careful!!!">
```

the page will execute and the error page will display the message (see Figure 17-1). A CFABORT tag is useful in a conditional statement to stop processing the page if a certain condition exists.

CFABORT	CFAPPLET	CFAPPLICATION
CFASSOCIATE	CFAUTHENTICATE	CFBREAK
CFCACHE	CFCOL	CFCOLLECTION
CFCONTENT	CFCOOKIE	CFDIRECTORY
CFERROR	CFEXECUTE	CFEXIT
CFFILE	CFFORM	CFFTP
CFGRID	CFGRIDCOLUMN	CFGRIDROW
CFGRIDUPDATE	CFHEADER	CFHTMLHEAD
CFHTTP	CFHTTPPARAM	CFIF/CFELSEIF/CFELSE
CFIMPERSONATE	CFINCLUDE	CFINDEX
CFINPUT	CFINSERT	CFLDAP
CFLOCATION	CFLOCK	CFLOOP
CFMAIL	CFMAILPARAM	CFMODULE
CFOBJECT	CFOUTPUT	CFPARAM
CFPOP	CFPROCESSINGDIRECTIVE	CFPROCPARAM
CFPROCRESULT	CFQUERY	CFQUERYPARAM
CFREGISTRY	CFREPORT	CFRETHROW
CFSCHEDULE	CFSCRIPT	CFSEARCH
CFSELECT	CFSERVLET	CFSERVLETPARAM
CFSET	CFSETTING	CFSILENT
CFSLIDER	CFSTOREDPROC	CFSWITCH/CFCASE/ CFDEFAULTCASE
CFTABLE	CFTEXTINPUT	CFTHROW
CFTRANSACTION	CFTREE	CFTREEITEM
CFTRY/CFCATCH	CFUPDATE	CFWDDX
CFGRAPH*	CFGRAPHDATA*	CFFLUSH*
CFLOG*	CFSAVECONTENT*	CFDUMP*
CFIMPORT**	CFTRACE**	CFXML**
CFINVOKE**	CFCOMPONENT**	CFPROPERTY**
CFFUNCTION**	CFARGUMENT**	CFRETURN**
CFLOGIN**	CFLOGINUSER**	CFLOGOUT**
CFCHART**	CFCHARTDATA**	CFCHARTSERIES**

Table 17-1. *Complete List of ColdFusion Tags Available in ColdFusion (* denotes functionality added in CF 5.0; ** denotes new CF MX functionality)*

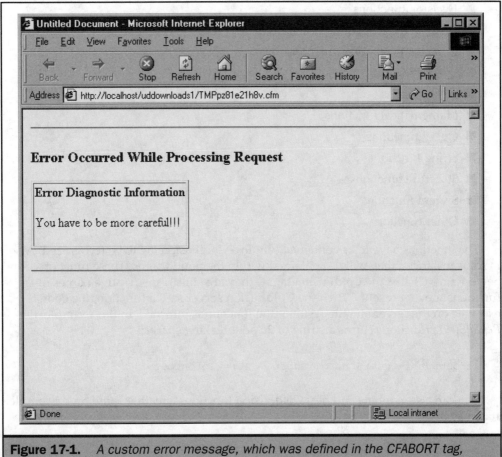

Figure 17-1.   *A custom error message, which was defined in the CFABORT tag, is displayed.*

ColdFusion Functions

In addition to the many available ColdFusion tags, over 200 built-in functions are available. These functions consist of everything from basic string-handling functions—such as *Len(string)*, which returns the length of a string—to complex functions, such as *QuotedValueList*, which will convert a column returned from a database into a comma-separated list with the values enclosed in single quotes. The functions are grouped into these categories:

- Array functions
- Authentication functions
- Date and time functions

- Decision functions
- Display and formatting functions
- Dynamic evaluation functions
- International functions
- List functions
- Mathematical functions
- Query functions
- String functions
- Structure functions
- System functions
- Other functions

The functions have to be contained within a ColdFusion tag to be recognized. Also, in some instances, they will be contained within the pound signs. These functions don't begin with <CF like the ColdFusion tags—they are simply descriptive names of the functions they represent. When the ColdFusion server sees a function, the code is executed on the server and the result of the function is returned. In this example, the *RepeatString* function returns a string of 20 nonbreaking spaces:

```
<cfoutput>#RepeatString(" ",20)#</cfoutput>
```

You can also combine and nest ColdFusion functions, creating some pretty complex statements:

```
<cflocation url="#IIF(ListFind(ValueList(
    myquery.username),form.username),'Page1.cfm','Page2.cfm')#
</cflocation>
```

This statement uses a query named *myquery*, which contains a *resultset*. The resultset is transformed into a list with the *ValueList* function; then the *form.username* is checked against that list with the *ListFind* function. Finally, the IIF function performs an *if/else* statement, depending on whether the username is found in the list returned by the query. The CFLOCATION tag sees only the result of the function—either Page1.cfm or Page2.cfm.

Tip *All the ColdFusion functions are available to the built-in scripting language as well—CFScript. User-defined functions are also available in CF 5.0 and later.*

ColdFusion contains some truly powerful functions that make the development process much quicker by offering native functionality for commonly used features. For instance, some list and array functions are available that make working with lists and variable arrays much easier. Some system functions also are available, such as the *DirectoryExists* function, which determines whether a given directory exists on the server; and the *GetCurrentTemplatePath* function, which returns the path on the server to the current page that's being served.

ColdFusion Variable Types

Like other languages, ColdFusion uses some specific types of variables, and each type has its own unique uses. Variables can be named with alphanumeric characters or underscores, and must begin with a letter. The type, or *scope*, of the variable is generally appended to the beginning of the variable with dot notation, as in *form.username*. However, you can address a variable without using the prefix. The following statement, for instance, is legal:

```
<cfoutput>Hello #username#</cfoutput>
```

Whenever a variable doesn't have its variable scope specified, the ColdFusion server checks all possible scopes for the existence of the variable. Obviously, this is going to slow the execution time, because the server will run through each possible scope; but in some cases, the vague reference to the variable is desirable, as in the case in which a username could be coming from a form, a database, or a cookie. In this case, if you were to specify *form.username*, the page wouldn't work with a URL variable named *username*.

The following is a list of variables used in ColdFusion:

- **Local**   A variable that has page scope and that doesn't use a prefix. You can also use the name *LocalVariable* or *Variables* as a prefix.

- **Session**   A variable that's available for the entire session of the user. Session variables rely on cookies being set on a user's machine, but can be utilized without access to cookies by using special ColdFusion built-in variables as well. Session variables need an Application.cfm file to be defined in the site.

- **Application**   A variable that is available to all users of an application. Application variables need an Application.cfm file to be defined in the site.

- **Client**   Special variables that are stored in a cookie on the client's machine, and also in the Registry or an ODBC data source on the server, used to identify the user to the server.

- **Form**   A form element from the previous page that has been submitted to the current page is treated as a variable with Form scope. The form has to be submitted with the *post* method.

- **URL** A variable that is attached to the URL from the previous page or from a link. This is also known as a query string variable, and can also be a form variable that was submitted using the *get* method.

- **Server** Variables used by the server, such as the ColdFusion version and other information.

- **Cookie** Variables written to the client's machine as cookies.

- **CGI** Server variables that hold information about various aspects of the current HTTP session.

- **Request** Special page-level variable that is available to the page, but can also be accessed by custom tags.

Note *ColdFusion expects a variable to be defined before it is used, and it will throw an error if it finds a variable that hasn't been defined. Always set a default value with a CFPARAM tag if a variable is expected but not defined with a CFSET, like a Form, Session, or URL variable.*

ColdFusion also has many tags that have their own variables for use by the programmer, such as the CFDIRECTORY, CFERROR, CFPOP, and CFQUERY tags. For example, a CFQUERY tag has a *queryname.RecordCount* variable available for use.

ColdFusion allows the use of arrays and lists, as well, and has a whole slew of functions for dealing with them and converting between the two types. A *list* is simply a comma-separated list (or a list separated by a user-defined character) of values that can be stored in a single variable and manipulated with the various list functions that are available.

Table 17-2 shows a list of the different object and variable types that are permitted in ColdFusion. In general, these types can be assigned to variables and passed in any of the variable types previously described.

The Pound Signs in ColdFusion

If you're unfamiliar with the CFML language, then you're probably wondering about the use of the pound signs (#) around certain expressions. A lot of rules apply to the use of pound signs; but in general, they are used when something is to be evaluated before being sent to the browser, and they are placed around an expression that the ColdFusion server is to differentiate from regular text. For instance, in the following expression, the pound signs signify to the server that the name "username" should be replaced by the value that's stored in the variable named "username":

```
<cfoutput>Welcome #username#</cfoutput>
```

Object Type	Object Description
Arrays	Arrays of values or objects.
Boolean	The result of an expression—true or false; converting to numerical gives you 1 and 0, and converting to a string gives you "yes" and "no."
COM	Component Object Model objects can be assigned to variables; the properties, methods, and events can be addressed with DOT notation.
Date	Date and time values.
Integers	Numbers with no decimal point.
Lists	Strings consisting of any number of elements separated by a delimiter, such as a comma.
Queries	Any resultsets returned from a CFQUERY tag can be treated as an object.
Real Numbers	Floating-point numbers (numbers with a decimal point).
Strings	Text values enclosed by single or double quotes.
Structures	A grouping of elements that enables you to refer to them by name (as in *Employee.LastName*, if the structure were named *Employee*).

Table 17-2. *Object Types in ColdFusion*

The pound signs aren't limited to use in text that is to be written to the Web page, however. They can be used inside of any ColdFusion tag to allow a value to be replaced by the current value of the variable:

```
<cfquery name="myQuery" maxrows="#maxrows#" datasource="#myDSN#">
```

In this case, assume that two variables have been set up in advance: *maxrows* and *myDSN*. The *maxrows* variable holds the data that the MAXROWS attribute of the CFQUERY tag needs in order to process the tag. The *myDSN* variable holds the name of a data source name that was set up in advance as a variable. What the ColdFusion server is doing, in essence, is evaluating the areas in between the pound signs first, then substituting the results of the evaluation in the expression, and then evaluating the expression.

If you are using a function, you have to place the pound signs around the entire expression, as in this example—which simply converts the value in the variable *username* to uppercase:

```
<cfoutput>Welcome <b>#Ucase(username)#<b></cfoutput>
```

This example also shows that you can put HTML tags inside of a CFOUTPUT statement. Whatever is inside of the CFOUTPUT statement will be sent to the browser.

The pound signs aren't always used, however, which may be confusing to some people. In this expression, for instance, the variable name is enclosed in quotes:

```
<cfif IsDefined("Form.username")>
```

Here, you are verifying that the Form variable named *username* exists—you aren't interested in the value. In general, when you are using the variable itself in the expression, and not the value, you don't use the pound signs.

Installing the ColdFusion Server

The ColdFusion server shipped with Dreamweaver MX is a trial version of the ColdFusion MX Enterprise version, which can be installed on a Windows 98, Me, NT, 2000, or XP machine. On the Windows NT, 2000, and XP OSs, the CF server will run as a service. On the Windows 98 and Me OSs, the CF server will start as an application and remain running in the background, using a small amount of the system's resources. Note that on Windows 98 and Me, the ColdFusion Server can only be used with the built-in standalone Web server that installs along with ColdFusion MX.

Having the server installed on your local machine enables you to test CFM pages locally. You will also have access to the ColdFusion Administrator and the ability to administer your sites and database connections, as well as debug your pages with CF's debugging options.

The installation requires that you have a Web server running on the machine— ColdFusion requires a Web server to operate. That server can be Microsoft Internet Information Server (IIS), the Apache Web server, or Netscape Enterprise Server, among others. New to ColdFusion MX is a built-in Web server that you can use if you don't have another Web server installed. The built-in Web server is not recommended for production.

To install the ColdFusion server, you'll need to follow these steps:

1. If you're on a Windows NT, 2000, or XP machine, you should install from an account with full administrator privileges. Double-click the Installer icon to run the installer. The installer will first check to make sure that you have the required components. Click Next. If you were missing any of the components, the installer will install them for you, after which you may need to reboot the machine.

2. Next, the installer will check for an existing ColdFusion installation. If you have a previous version of ColdFusion installed, you are given the option to run them both simultaneously using the built-in server for the new ColdFusion MX installation. If you do this, ColdFusion MX will run on port 8500, leaving your old ColdFusion server intact. If you choose to upgrade your existing ColdFusion server installation, however, the installer will remove your old server but keep all the settings.

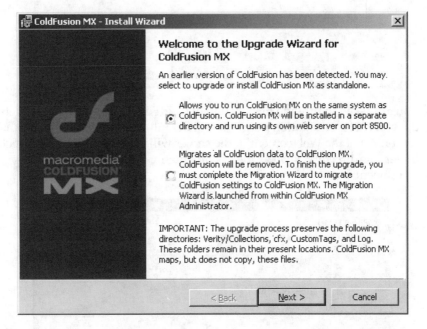

3. You will be asked to agree to the license agreement—click Yes to continue.

4. Enter your name, company name, and serial number, if you have one. The Trial edition of ColdFusion Server works with no serial number and defaults to the Developer edition after 30 days.

AN INTRODUCTION TO WEB SCRIPTING

5. The wizard will ask you for your Web server type. On a Windows machine, this most likely is the default IIS server. The installer will automatically configure some Web servers, such as IIS. You also have the option for the standalone server.

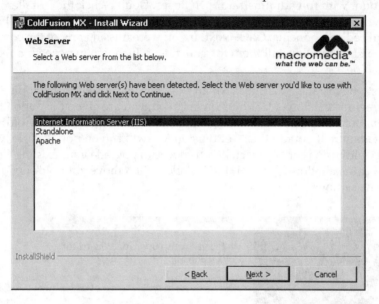

6. You are asked to provide the location of ColdFusion and the default Web server directory. The installation program will default to the root folder of your Web server. All of the Web content of the server will be unpacked to subdirectories under this directory, such as the documentation, examples, and HTML components.

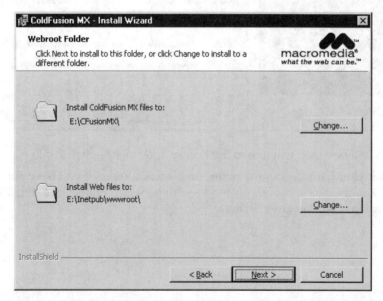

7. Next, you have to choose the password for the CF Administrator, and for CF Studio as well, which can be the same password. Note that Dreamweaver MX will use this ColdFusion Studio password as well.

8. A confirmation screen shows the selected settings, which you can print for your records. You have the option of going back and making changes if you so desire, or clicking Next to proceed with the installation.

9. The installation program proceeds to copy the files and folders to the hard drive, and make the necessary changes in the system Registry. After the

installation is completed, you are asked to restart the computer. When you restart, you will have a fully functional ColdFusion server on your machine.

10. If you are installing ColdFusion MX over an existing ColdFusion 5 installation, your settings will be migrated to the new version of ColdFusion. This mainly involves saving your preferences from the previous version, but also involves changing all of your data sources to the new JDBC data sources of ColdFusion MX.

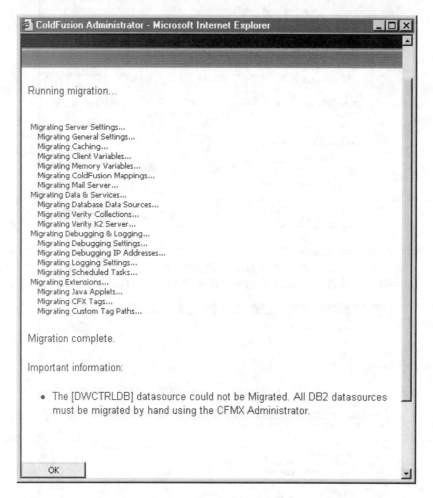

After the migration takes place, you can view the various help documents that are available for ColdFusion server, or you can log into the CF Administrator.

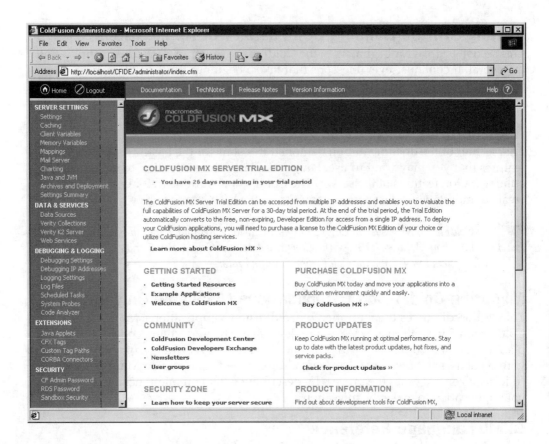

ColdFusion Documentation

The best place to start with the server is the ColdFusion Documentation item in the ColdFusion Administrator. Computer program documentation in general is not very good, but the documentation that comes with ColdFusion is fairly extensive and offers examples of each function and tag that is available with the server. In addition, an easy-to-follow tutorial on programming ColdFusion is included.

The documentation has several sections, and each is broken down into chapters, which are outlined in the following sections.

Installing ColdFusion MX

This section discusses the requirements and installation procedures for the ColdFusion server. If you've already installed the server and can see this documentation, you probably don't need it, but it can help you to determine a strategy for installation on another server, or an installation procedure using different parameters than those you used when you installed the server.

Getting Started Building ColdFusion MX Applications

This section is great for beginners to the ColdFusion server or data-driven applications in general. It contains several lessons that take a beginner through many of the basic features of a Web application, such as how to interact with a database and the basics of the ColdFusion language.

Administering ColdFusion MX

This section of the documentation demonstrates some of the basic administration features that you may want to use. Pay particularly close attention to the database administration features of the server. The ColdFusion Administrator enables you to create or modify your data source names from the Web interface.

 In ColdFusion MX, system ODBC DSNs are no longer editable from the CF Administrator. ColdFusion MX uses JDBC connections to a database. ColdFusion 5 and earlier allow you to edit system DSNs from the ColdFusion Administrator.

Migrating ColdFusion 5 Applications (Available Only in CF MX)

This section discusses the migration of ColdFusion 5 applications. Moving from ColdFusion 5 to ColdFusion MX is a major move. The underlying code of the entire platform has shifted from C++ to Java, and that affects everything from how you access your databases to how e-mails are sent and retrieved. ColdFusion MX ships with a code analyzer that eases the process by describing what you might need to change in your application to make the migration.

CFML Language Reference

This section of the documentation is the reference that you'll be using most: every tag, function, and expression that is available in ColdFusion is described in detail (see Figure 17-2) within this section. In addition, each tag and function has a corresponding example that runs from the live server using sample databases that are installed with the ColdFusion server. You'll find that you can copy and paste code from the Language Reference into your programs to give you an extra boost when you don't understand a particular syntax.

Developing ColdFusion MX Applications with CFML

This section of the documentation describes the language and demonstrates how to create Web applications in CFML using step-by-step tutorials. This language is very robust, and the tutorial starts off with the basics and ends up with more advanced topics, such as accessing the Registry through ColdFusion. There is a section dealing with the CFAPPLICATION tag, which enables you to create an Application.cfm file that acts as a "global" file in your Web application.

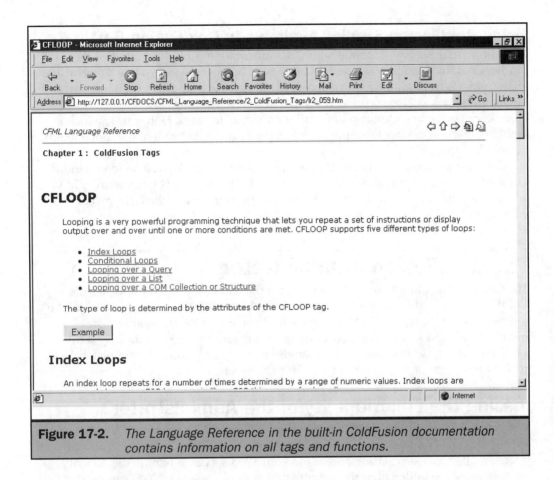

Figure 17-2.   *The Language Reference in the built-in ColdFusion documentation contains information on all tags and functions.*

Using Server-Side Actionscript in ColdFusion MX

One of the great new features of ColdFusion MX is the communication with Flash and the new server-side Actionscript you can use to enable your Flash applications to communicate with the ColdFusion server.

Using Clustercats

Clustercats is the load-balancing technology that ColdFusion server utilizes to enable server clusters. Configuration and maintenance of a clustered server are discussed here.

Working with Verity Tools

ColdFusion server comes complete with a Verity K2 Server search engine to allow you to enable complex searches on your site across databases, Web pages, or other documents that reside on your site. The Verity tools are fully documented here, including the server configuration and how to manage your collections.

Using ColdFusion Studio (Available in ColdFusion 5.0)

In addition to the server documentation, documentation is provided for ColdFusion Studio. ColdFusion Studio is based on Homesite; however, it goes a few steps further. With ColdFusion Studio, you have access to the Remote Data Services, which enables you to access any database connections that you have residing on a remote server. Also, it contains complete support for all the ColdFusion tags. Homesite+, which is included in the Windows Dreamweaver MX package, contains all of the functionality of ColdFusion Studio.

ColdFusion Studio (or Homesite+) is a program that works well hand in hand with Dreamweaver MX. You can set it up as your default editor for Dreamweaver MX and use it to tweak your code after you design the pages inside the Dreamweaver MX environment.

The ColdFusion Administrator

The ColdFusion Administrator is the interface that enables you to administer the ColdFusion application server (see Figure 17-3). In the Administrator, you'll find the functionality to change security settings, add database connections, administer log files, schedule tasks, and set up debugging, among other things. If you have a full version of the server installed (not the single-user version), you can administer the server from a remote location through a Web browser.

Accessing the Functionality of the Administrator

When you first install the ColdFusion server, you provide a password for the Administrator. This password is needed to log in to the Administrator. You can override this password setting and allow your Web server to handle the security by protecting the folders that the Administrator pages reside in. You can do this from the Basic Security settings in the Administrator interface.

The server functionality is provided through links in a navigation bar in the left frame of the Administrator interface. This section goes through the various pages that the links point to and gives a short description of some of the things that they do. The following sections describe some of the functionality of the ColdFusion Administrator.

The Server Settings

Several functions are listed under the Server heading. The Settings page enables you to assign various server settings. You can set up the limits of simultaneous requests, among other things, which will improve your system's performance. Also, this is where you can define a site-wide error page, and also a site-wide missing template handler, which would be a default page to go to if the user requests a page that doesn't exist. By creating a site-wide error-handling page, you can define how an error will appear to an end user.

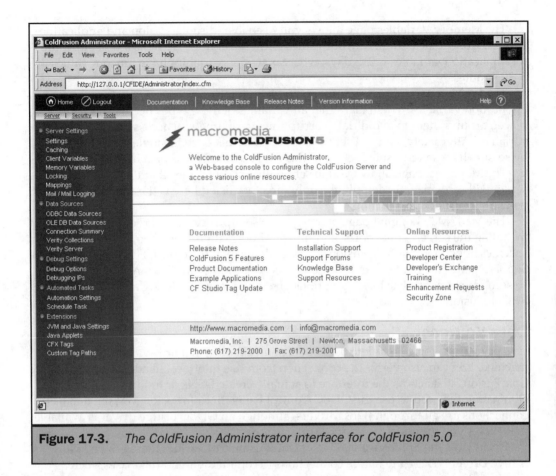

Figure 17-3.   *The ColdFusion Administrator interface for ColdFusion 5.0*

The Caching page is where you can set up the size of the Template cache for your machine. If you have plentiful memory, this figure can be set to a fairly high level to allow for faster execution of pages. The pages are stored in cache as they execute, and get removed from cache in a last-in, first-out scenario. Obviously, if the pages are in memory and don't have to be accessed on the hard drive, they will execute more quickly. Also on this page, you can set up the query cache maximum. ColdFusion gives you the opportunity to cache a query in memory, which means that the entire resultset of a query remains in memory. This can be overused if you're not careful, but it has definite advantages in certain situations.

The Client Variables page enables you to specify where you want to store your client variables. These are special variables that enable you to keep track of users through ID numbers, and that are stored in cookies on a user's machine. By default, these variables are stored in the Registry; but you can store them in an ODBC data source if you specify a data source here. If you are going to use client variables, you should specify a data source so that the server does not overuse the Registry.

The Memory Variables page allows you to enable/disable session and application variables, or set the default timeout values of these variables. A typical timeout value for application variables is 2–5 days, whereas session variables have timeout values of 5–20 minutes.

The Locking page allows you to specify default locking of session, server, and application variables. You'll learn that all variables of these types need a special lock placed around them to avoid data corruption every time you access one of these variables. Alternately, you can set the check box in this page to single-thread sessions by session ID to avoid using locks, but this isn't recommended on a high-traffic server.

The Mappings page allows you to set up virtual directories that the ColdFusion server will recognize. By default, the only directory listed here is the root directory that you specified upon installation.

The Mail/Mail Logging page allows you to set up your mail server information, including the server name, ports, and timeout information. The spool interval setting specifies how often the ColdFusion server delivers mail from the CFusion | Mail | Spool folder to the mail server. The default is 60 seconds, but you can set it down to 15 seconds in CF 5.0. The logging options give you the option to log all messages sent by ColdFusion.

Data Sources

This page gives you a complete list of data source names that are available on the machine. You can also verify the connection from this interface. In addition, in ColdFusion 5.0 it acts as the interface to actually create DSNs or modify existing DSNs, eliminating the need to use the ODBC Control Panel. In ColdFusion MX, the database connections are all through JDBC drivers, although an ODBC bridge driver is available that allows you to connect to an ODBC datasource.

If you have the Enterprise version of ColdFusion 5 or earlier, there is a page for Native Drivers. These are native connections to certain high-end databases, such as Oracle, DB2, Informix, and Sybase. You can add, modify, or delete native connections from this page.

In the ColdFusion 5 Administrator, there is an OLE DB page that enables you to create OLE DB connections. By default, it has settings for SQLOLEDB and Microsoft.Jet.OLEDB.3.51. On this page, you can add, modify, or delete OLE DB connections. ColdFusion MX doesn't have an option for OLE DB connections.

Verity

The Verity section is broken into two pages. The Verity Collections page lists all collections available to ColdFusion, with the capability to add new collections. The Verity Servers page allows you to set up connections to your Verity K2 Server. A Verity server allows you to conduct searches of databases and documents stored on your server, such as word processing documents, desktop publishing documents, spreadsheets, and presentations.

One Verity collection is already set up when you install the server—the *cfdocumentation* collection, which allows fast searches of the ColdFusion documentation that resides on your Web server.

Web Services

A new addition to ColdFusion MX is a Web Services page. On this page, you can map names to your ColdFusion MX Web services. ColdFusion MX makes it very easy to create your own Web Services using simple ColdFusion tags and code, and then map your WSDL URL here.

Debug Settings   The Debugging pages enable you to set up debugging for your ColdFusion development. By default, debugging is disabled; but you can allow debugging information to be accessible to certain IP addresses. The debugging information available includes such things as processing time; variable names and values; query record count, time, and SQL statement; and all server variables. Enabling server-side debugging helps when you are tracking down errors in your site, and also allows you to display useful information, such as query execution times and all variables used on the page:

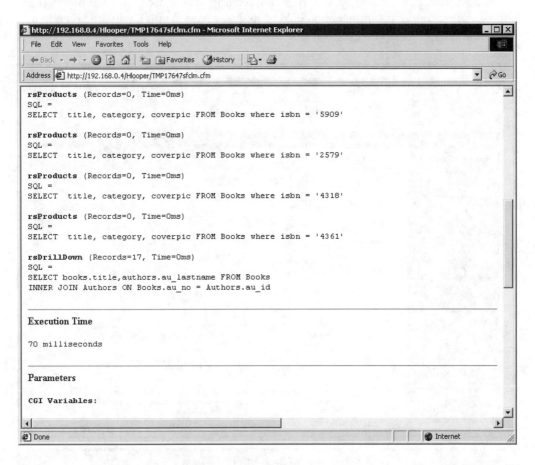

Automated or Scheduled Tasks The Settings page enables you to specify how often to check for new scheduled tasks; also, it allows you to enable the logging of scheduled tasks.

Scheduled tasks can be a great timesaver for repetitive tasks, and they have the full arsenal of ColdFusion tags available to them, such as CFFILE and CFMAIL.

The Scheduled Tasks page enables you to automatically execute a ColdFusion page. You could, for instance, schedule a page to automate creation of reports for logging or click-through information (see Figure 17-4).

Extensions The JVM and Java Settings page allows configuration of the Java settings that might be used by ColdFusion. For instance, if you have custom CF tags written in Java, you can store the classpath here so that CF will have a way to access it.

The Applets page enables you to register Java applets for use by the ColdFusion server. After naming the applet and clicking Register New Applet, you are taken to a form in which you can enter all of its parameters.

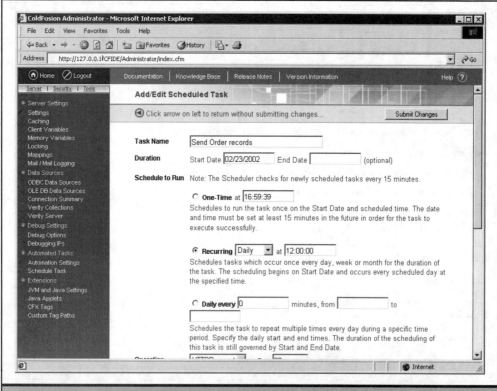

Figure 17-4. *Creating a scheduled task in the ColdFusion Administrator*

ColdFusion is extensible through C++ or Java and the use of CFX_ tags. These tags can be registered on the machine through the CFX Tags page. Custom tags can be an extremely powerful addition to the server, and you can find them on the Macromedia site or on many other ColdFusion support sites all over the Internet.

Security

Security is always a concern, and the CF Administrator allows you to configure the server to conform to your own security preferences, by allowing you to access the Security section of the Administrator. This is where you can change the passwords for the Administrator, and also for RDS. Users of ColdFusion Studio or Dreamweaver MX can access the Administrator if they have the password that is defined here. Also on this page, you'll find the capability to restrict access to certain powerful tags. At times, in a shared environment, certain tags should be disabled because of the power behind them. These particular ColdFusion tags should be used only by responsible individuals, to prevent any server meltdowns. The CFREGISTRY and CFFILE tags are especially powerful, and can give a user the ability to take down the server. The tags and options that can be turned off are

- CFCONTENT tag
- CFDIRECTORY tag
- CFFILE tag
- CFOBJECT tag
- CFREGISTRY tag
- CFADMINSECURITY tag
- CFEXECUTE tag
- CFFTP tag
- CFLOG tag
- CFMAIL tag
- DBTYPE=DYNAMIC tag attribute
- CONNECTSTRING tag attribute

There is also an Unsecured Tags directory that you can set up here to allow access to the forbidden tags by a trusted user. Any pages placed in this directory can have full access to all tags within ColdFusion.

Advanced Security   In the Enterprise version of ColdFusion 5, there is also a page for Advanced Security. These settings override the Basic Security settings and allow more advanced security settings to be implemented. Security Contexts, which act as "access groups" to allow access to certain pages to certain individuals, can be set up here.

Logging Settings

On the Settings page, you can define a default directory for all ColdFusion logs. Also, the system administrator's e-mail address is stored on this page. If you insert an e-mail address here, it will appear on error pages. There's also a handy option here to log which pages take longer than a specified number of seconds to execute, to help you pinpoint where bottlenecks exist. If you set this to 30 seconds, for example, a log entry will be generated for any page that takes longer than 30 seconds.

You also have the option to use the operating system logging facilities. Log files will still be generated by ColdFusion and maintained in the directory that you specify, but the log entries will also appear in your system's logging facility (EventLog in Windows NT and the syslog facility for UNIX.)

Log Files

The Log Files page provides a handy access to the log files through hyperlinks to the actual log files on your server. You can use this page to search, view, download, schedule, archive, and delete log files. A new log format starting with ColdFusion 5 allows you to view each entry in a Web-based format (see Figure 17-5).

Learning the CFML Language

It is not required that the ColdFusion server be installed on your local machine to use Dreamweaver MX with ColdFusion, but it makes life easier. In general, you'll be able to debug your pages more quickly locally than through a remote server. Also, it is a wise move to use your local machine as a development server with a similar configuration to your remote server. This way you aren't testing and debugging on your production server— a dangerous thing to do.

You don't have to know the language of ColdFusion to use Dreamweaver MX—but it surely helps. This section goes through some of the basic (and later through some of the advanced) functionality of ColdFusion and how it relates in the Dreamweaver MX environment. This discussion assumes the reader has a little general programming knowledge.

The Core ColdFusion Tags

These are the tags that are considered "required" for any ColdFusion developer, and they are included in the free ColdFusion Express package.

CFSET and CFPARAM

These two tags enable you to set variables and parameters in ColdFusion. What's the difference between them? With a CFSET tag, you are simply assigning a value to a variable. In the following expression, you are assigning the *UserID* value from a query to the session variable *UserID*:

```
<cfset Session.UserID = myQuery.userID>
```

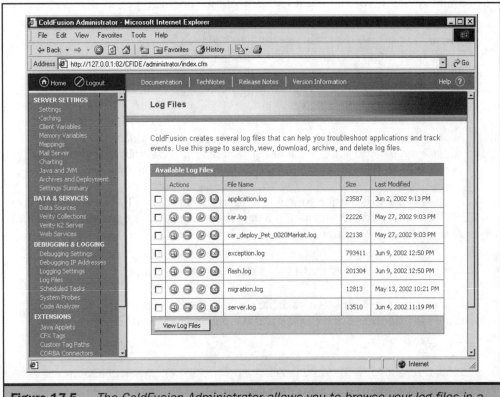

Figure 17-5. The ColdFusion Administrator allows you to browse your log files in a structured format from a browser.

With CFPARAM, you have three usage choices. You can check for a parameter's existence by using the NAME attribute, check to make sure that a variable is of a specific type by using the TYPE attribute, or set a DEFAULT value for a possible variable:

```
<cfparam name="form.username" default="newuser">
```

In this example, you have a Form variable of *username* that is expected on the page. But what if the user types in the link by hand and doesn't use the login form? In that case, there is a risk of errors on the page, because your ColdFusion functions are expecting a Form variable named *username*. With this statement in place, if the Form variable doesn't exist, it's given a default value. If the variable *does* exist, the CFPARAM statement doesn't do anything. It exists as a safeguard to give a value to a parameter that may or may not exist. You can use it with any of the variable types, as in this statement:

```
<cfparam name="url.userid" default="baddata">
```

In this case, your page is expecting a URL variable named *userid*. If, for some reason, the URL variable doesn't come through, the default value of "baddata" is assigned to the URL variable.

When addressing variables on the ColdFusion page, an error will be thrown if the variable is referred to and it doesn't exist. You can either check for the variable's existence before using it, or you can set up a CFPARAM to give it a default value.

You can also use ColdFusion functions within a CFSET or CFPARAM declaration. The CFSET in that statement will assign a date that is seven days ago from the current server date to the variable named *Lastweek*:

```
<cfset Lastweek=DateFormat((Now()) - 7)>
```

The following statement sets a variable equal to the filename of the current page without the file extension, such as *mypage* if the path was c:/inetpub/wwwroot /bettergig/mypage.cfm:

```
<cfset CurrentPage = GetFileFromPath(GetCurrentTemplatePath())>
<cfset CurrentPage = Left(CurrentPage,Len(CurrentPage)-4)>
```

You can also declare variables in CFSCRIPT, which is discussed in the "CFSCRIPT and Its Use in Dreamweaver MX" section.

CFOUTPUT

The CFOUTPUT tag is the multipurpose bull worker of ColdFusion. It does many things besides display text, which you've seen in a few examples. In general, it's used to interpret ColdFusion functions and expressions so that the result can be output to the browser. It also acts as a loop when you specify the QUERY attribute. The QUERY attribute can be the result of a database query, or it can be the name of a CFPOP, CFDIRECTORY, or other tag. You can use it in the body of the document to display text in the browser, or to dynamically apply a value to an HTML element. Here are a few examples. The following simply displays the current server time in the browser:

```
<cfoutput>The time is now #TimeFormat(Now())#</cfoutput>
```

This example shows the CFOUTPUT tag used to insert a value returned from a query into a hidden form element:

```
<input type="hidden" name="hiddenAccessCode"
value="<cfoutput>#UserAccessQuery.AccessCode#</cfoutput>">
```

The next example populates an unordered list (bulleted list) with the results of a CFQUERY tag, which can be one row or a thousand rows. The results are limited only by the capacity of the browser. In actual practice, you'll break up the queries with the MAXROWS attribute. The CFOUTPUT QUERY acts as a loop by itself and does not need any other programming to construct a loop, such as a *for/next* or *do/while* construct:

```
<ul>
<cfoutput query="myQuery"><li>#FirstName# #LastName#</li>
</cfoutput>
</ul>
```

Caution   *When using the CFOUTPUT QUERY, you have to consider everything that you are looping over. If there is a line break in the code, the line break will be output in the loop as well. In the example, the open <cfoutput> tag was placed on the same line as the <li> tags so as to not introduce an extra line break into the resulting HTML source code.*

The next example dynamically populates the title of the page with the filename of the current file without the path. In other words, the browser will see <title>*mypage*</title>:

```
<title><cfoutput>
#Replace(GetFileFromPath(GetCurrentTemplatePath()),".cfm","")#
</cfoutput></title>
```

CFIF/CFELSE/CFELSEIF

These tags are used in ColdFusion to implement conditional logic. The CFIF tag enables you to check for a condition before executing a statement. The CFIF tag has a corresponding closing tag that you must use. Here's an example:

```
<cfif form.password NEQ rsCustomers.password>
    <cflocation url="FailedLogin.cfm">
</cfif>
```

Note   *The NEQ statement means "not equal to" and is the same as <> in VBScript or != in Java, PHP, and JavaScript. ColdFusion uses EQ for "equal to" in comparisons. In ColdFusion you are also allowed to spell out "not equal to" and "equal to."*

You can use the CFELSE and CFELSEIF tags in the conditional statements to construct more complex conditions. You must use them within a CFIF code block. Here's an example using both:

```
<cfif form.location EQ "Buffalo">
    <cfset session.location = "NY">
<cfelseif form.location EQ "Rochester">
    <cfset session.location = "NY">
<cfelse>
    <cfset session.location = "not valid location">
</cfif>
```

There are many functions available to ColdFusion users that increase the efficiency of the conditional logic. Here are a few examples. The first one uses the ColdFusion function *IsDate* to determine whether the user has entered a date value:

```
<cfif form.dateofbirth EQ "">
    You didn't enter a date!
<cfelseif IsDate(form.dateofbirth) is TRUE>
    You were born <cfoutput>#DateDiff('yyyy',form.dateofbirth,Now())#
    </cfoutput> years ago.
<cfelse>
    Your entry was invalid.  Please go back and try again.
</cfif>
```

The next example checks a variable to make sure it's an array, using the ColdFusion function *IsArray*. If it isn't an array, the user hasn't reached the minimum of two purchases. If it is an array, the shipping cost is set using the number of elements in the *session.ShoppingCart* variable:

```
<cfif Not(IsArray(session.ShoppingCart)) is TRUE>
    <cflocation url="Error.cfm?error=LessThan2Items">
<cfelseif IsArray(session.ShoppingCart,2) is TRUE>
    <cfset session.shipping = 7.50>
<cfelseif IsArray(session.ShoppingCart,3) is TRUE>
    <cfset session.shipping = 8.50>
<cfelse>
    <cfset session.shipping = 9.50>
</cfif>
```

CFQUERY

If you are familiar with ASP or JSP, you know that you must create a recordset object to retrieve a *resultset*. In ColdFusion, you don't create a recordset, per se—you define a CFQUERY tag giving a datasource and a *Select* statement, and the ColdFusion server does the rest. Here's an example that simply retrieves all columns and all records from the Customers table of the Bookstore database:

```
<cfquery name="rsCustomers" datasource="Bookstore">
Select * from Customers
</cfquery>
```

The only two required parameters for the tag are NAME and DATASOURCE. The query needs a name so that it can be referred to on the page when displaying the information. For instance, a FirstName column can be referred to like this:

```
<cfoutput>#rsCustomers.FirstName#</cfoutput>
```

The DATASOURCE parameter is simply a data source name that has been previously established in the ODBC Administrator on the machine (in CF 5 or earlier), or in the ColdFusion Administrator interface.

The CFQUERY tag can pass commands to your database in the form of valid Structured Query Language (SQL). These commands can be simple *Select* statements, as in the previous example, or they can be *Insert*, *Update*, or *Delete* statements—or even stored procedures. You can think of the CFQUERY tag as an interface to the database.

Tip *Although the CFQUERY tag will perform all the required database interactions, other ColdFusion tags are targeted for inserts, updates, and stored procedures and make those tasks easier in some situations.*

Another powerful construct of the CFQUERY tag is that you can use any valid ColdFusion statements within the text of the query. Here's an example that checks for the existence of an optional search attribute; and if it exists, it then checks for a null value before assigning a *Where* clause to the query:

```
<cfquery name="rsProducts" datasource="Orders">
SELECT * from Products
<cfif IsDefined("form.product")>
    <cfif form.product NEQ "">
        WHERE Product Like '%form.product%'
    </cfif>
</cfif>
</cfquery>
```

By using conditional logic inside of a ColdFusion query, you can save server resources by passing to the database only *the statements that are needed for the current task.*

Other attributes are available to CFQUERY, such as MAXROWS, which make it easy to set up pages that show partial resultsets. Consult the ColdFusion documentation for a full explanation of the CFQUERY tag.

CFLOCATION

The CFLOCATION tag is similar to the *Response.Redirect* statement in ASP or the *response.sendRedirect* statement in JSP. When the ColdFusion server finds this tag, the processing of the page stops and the user is redirected to another page. The tag has only two parameters: *URL* and *Addtoken*. The *URL* parameter is simply the location that the user will be redirected to. It can be a relative or an absolute URL. The *Addtoken* parameter adds the user's Client variable information to the URL and takes a "yes" or "no" value (which is assumed to be "no" if it's not specified). In this example, the user is redirected to an error page, with Client variables not being sent:

```
<cfif Not IsDefined("form.username")>
    <cflocation url="error.htm">
</cfif>
```

CFCOOKIE

The CFCOOKIE tag sets a cookie on the user's machine. The parameters are NAME, VALUE, EXPIRES, SECURE, PATH, and DOMAIN. The NAME parameter is the only required parameter of the tag. The VALUE parameter enables you to set a value to the cookie. The EXPIRES parameter can be used with an absolute date, as in 12/31/2000, or a number of days, as in 10, 30, or 100. Two other values can be used in the EXPIRES parameter: "Now" and "Never". If you set the attribute to "Now", you are effectively deleting the cookie from the client's browser. If you set it to "Never", the cookie never expires.

Here's an example of a cookie being set depending on the status of a "Remember Me" check box on the previous page:

```
<cfif IsDefined("chkRememberMe") is TRUE>
    <cfcookie name="RememberMe" value="TRUE" expires="Never">
<cfelse>
    <cfcookie name="RememberMe" expires="Now">
</cfif>
```

For a full explanation of the use of the CFCOOKIE tag, see the Macromedia ColdFusion documentation.

CFINCLUDE

The CFINCLUDE tag takes only one parameter: Template. Recall that a template is the ColdFusion term for a CFM or CFML page.

The CFINCLUDE statement enables the user to insert a separate ColdFusion page into the current page. This is useful for such things as headers, footers, login screens, welcome statements, and a host of other uses. In addition, any variables declared in a ColdFusion page can be referenced from the included file, and vice versa. When you use the CFINCLUDE tag, it's as if the code were directly inserted into your page. Here's an example of a CFINCLUDE tag being used conditionally in a login page:

```
<cflock scope="Session" type="ReadOnly">
<cfif (Not IsDefined("session.login"))
      AND (session.login NEQ "loggedIn")>
    <cfset NotLogged = "true">
</cfif>
</cflock>
<cfif NotLogged EQ "true">
    <cfinclude Template="LoginForm.cfm">
<cfelse>
    <cfinclude Template="WelcomePage.cfm">
</cfif>
```

ColdFusion Comment Tags

You can comment your code in ColdFusion using the special comment tags that look similar to HTML comment tags, except that they have an extra dash character, as in the following example:

```
<!---This is a ColdFusion Comment--->
<!--This is an HTML comment-->
```

The comments that you create using this syntax won't be viewable in the browser—the server strips them out when the page is processed. In the above example, the HTML comment would be viewable in the browser, but the server would have stripped the ColdFusion comment out. They also don't add anything to the processing time, so it's wise to use comments liberally to decipher the code more easily.

CFDUMP

CFDUMP was introduced in ColdFusion 5.0. It allows you to dump variables to the browser while you are debugging, and will even dump complex structures or database queries. It takes one attribute, *var*, which is the variable name that you want to dump to the browser. The tag is very useful when you need to see the results of a query.

A simple call to CFDUMP will output the entire resultset in a nicely formatted table for easy viewing:

```
<cfdump var=#myQueryname#>
```

Similarly, if you need to view the CGI server variables, you can output the entire set of CGI variables to the browser with a single CFDUMP call:

```
<cfdump var=#cgi#>
```

CFScript and Its Use in Dreamweaver MX

CFScript, introduced to ColdFusion in version 4, allows the use of a JavaScript-like syntax to write code on a ColdFusion page. Although CFScript is similar to JavaScript, it's not interchangeable. Many features of JavaScript aren't available to CFScript. One advantage of CFScript over JavaScript is the use of ColdFusion functions within the script language—all ColdFusion functions are available to the script language as well.

Caution *Although ColdFusion functions are available to CFScript, the tags are not.*

UltraDev 4 used CFScript extensively in all of the Server Behaviors that work with ColdFusion. This was done primarily to keep the Server Behaviors consistent between server models, and also because of the way in which the Server Behavior API works. Dreamweaver MX has two modes of ColdFusion use to allow backward compatibility with UltraDev 4. When you start to look at the code that Dreamweaver MX generates in UD 4 mode, you'll notice a large amount of CFScript as opposed to ColdFusion tags. Dreamweaver MX mode uses ColdFusion tags more regularly. If you are starting out a fresh site, it is advisable to use the ColdFusion server model of Dreamweaver MX rather than the CF-UD4 mode.

CFScript has some great features, but also some major limitations:

■ You can't create "local" variables—all variables are accessible to the whole page. The exception to this is inside of user-defined functions, where you can create variables local to the function.

■ It provides no access to the Document Object Model (DOM) of the Web page. This is a client-side technology, and CFScript is executed only on the server.

■ The JavaScript functions, methods, and operators aren't carried over, such as the string manipulation methods and the comparison operators.

Here is an example of a CFScript code block and the equivalent code using ColdFusion tags:

Using CFScript

```
<cfscript>
  Customers = StructNew();
  Customers.Name = form.name;
  Customers.CustID = Session.UserID;
  Customers.email = form.email;
  Customers.state = form.state;
  Customers.LastAccessDate = Now();
  WriteOutput("Hello #Customers.Name#");
</cfscript>
```

Using ColdFusion Tags

```
<cfset Customers = StructNew()>
<cfset Customers.Name = form.name>
<cfset Customers.CustID = Session.UserID>
<cfset Customers.email = form.email>
<cfset Customers.state = form.state>
<cfset Customers.LastAccessDate = Now()>
<cfoutput>Hello #Customers.Name#</cfoutput>
```

The key advantage to using CFScript in this example is to avoid the redundant use of CFSET tags to declare the variables. In general, if you have three or more variables in a row to declare, you might consider enclosing the declarations within a CFScript block. Opening and closing of CF tags have a cost in a ColdFusion application. Another advantage is the ability to define your own user-defined functions (in CF 5 and higher). These functions can be used inside of the script blocks or in any of your ColdFusion tags on the page.

There's not much documentation on CFScript, but you can use what you know about JavaScript and make notes of the changes between JavaScript and CFScript. Table 17-3 shows the comparison operators in JavaScript and the equivalent CFScript operators. Note that the comparison operators are also valid in CFML.

User-Defined Functions

Introduced in ColdFusion 5, user-defined functions (UDFs) have become one of the most popular of ColdFusion's features. You can create a user-defined function to handle any type of programming construct that isn't available with the built-in

Comparison Operators	JavaScript	CFScript
Equal to	==	EQ or IS
Not equal to	!=	NEQ or IS NOT
Greater than	>	GT
Less than	<	LT
Greater than or equal to	>=	GTE
Less than or equal to	<=	LTE
Contains	*indexOf* method	Contains
Doesn't contain	*indexOf* method	Does Not Contain

Table 17-3.   *Comparison Operators in JavaScript and the Equivalent CFScript Operators*

functions or tags. For example, ColdFusion doesn't contain a function to create a random string of letters, so you could create a function to do this:

```
<cfscript>
function getRandomString(theLength) {
    var theString = "";
    var theNum = 0;
    for (var i=0; i LT theLength ; i=i+1) {
        theNum = RandRange(48,90);
        if(theNum LTE 64 AND theNum GTE 58) {
            i=i-1;
        }else{
            theString = theString & chr(theNum);
        }
    }
    return theString;
}
</cfscript>
```

You can then call the function from anywhere on your page:

```
<cfoutput>#getRandomString(10)#</cfoutput>
```

You can also keep your user-defined functions in *include* files. You'll eventually develop libraries of UDFs that you can reuse in all of your applications. With the introduction of user-defined functions, the CFSCRIPT tag has seen an increased use by ColdFusion programmers.

Many handy user-defined functions are available at www.cflib.org, which has become a central repository for user-defined functions.

Advanced ColdFusion Tags

You've seen some of the simple tags and examples that make up ColdFusion, but you may have been wondering how to do more advanced programming using the CFML tags. Some of the more advanced server-side functionality is built right into the ColdFusion language.

Sending E-Mail with ColdFusion

One of the features of ColdFusion that is widely used is the CFMAIL tag, which enables you to send e-mail from the Web page. You need to have access to a mail server to use this feature, but most Web servers nowadays include this functionality. To use the tag, you must put it on the page, define a few parameters, and you're all set. The next example assumes that you've submitted a form from the previous page with text fields named *txtFrom*, *txtTo*, *txtSubject*, and *txtMessage:*

```
<cfmail to="#form.txtTo#"
    from="#form.txtFrom#"
    subject="#form.txtsubject#"
    server="mail.mysite.com">
#form.txtmessage#
</cfmail>
```

The CFMAIL tag also has other optional attributes. You can find the full list in the ColdFusion documentation. An easy method to send bulk e-mail to a list of e-mail addresses in a database is also available. You simply have to use a CFQUERY tag to get the e-mail addresses, like this:

```
<cfquery name="emailQuery" datasource="Customers">
    SELECT email FROM customers
</cfquery>
```

Then you can use this query name in the CFMAIL tag by using the QUERY attribute of the CFMAIL tag:

```
<cfmail to="#emailQuery.email#"
    query="emailQuery"
    from="info@bettergig.com"
    subject="Monthly News from Bettergig"
```

```
      server="mail.mysite.com"
      type="HTML">
<cfinclude template="ThisMonthNewsletter.htm">
</cfmail>
```

Notice that the FROM and SUBJECT attributes were specified this time, and TYPE, which enables you to send HTML e-mail, and QUERY, which causes the CFMAIL tag to loop through all rows returned by the query, were added. Then the *emailQuery.email* column of the database is referenced in the TO attribute to cause the tag to send out an e-mail to everyone in the database. Also, the body of the e-mail wasn't hard-coded—instead, the CFINCLUDE tag was used to include an HTML file as the body of the e-mail.

Retrieving E-Mail with ColdFusion

In addition to the CFMAIL tag for sending e-mail, ColdFusion comes with a tag to retrieve e-mail from a POP e-mail server. The CFPOP tag enables you to get the messages from the server, or the headers only, and also offers the option to delete the messages. Here's a basic CFPOP implementation that checks an e-mail box that a user has specified in a form on the previous page, and returns the messages, displaying them on the page using a CFOUTPUT tag:

```
<cfpop server="#form.servername#"
      username="#form.username#"
      password="#form.password#"
      action="GetAll"
      name="exampleMessages">
<!---at this point, all messages have been retrieved
      The CFOUTPUT tag will display the entire list--->
<cfoutput>
<b>You have #exampleMessages.RecordCount# messages</b><br>
</cfoutput>
<table>
<cfoutput query="exampleMessages">
      <tr><td>#From#</td><td>#subject#</td><td>#date#</td></tr>
      <tr><td colspan="3">#body#</td></tr>
      <tr><td colspan="3"><hr></td></tr>
</cfoutput>
</table>
```

First, the CFPOP tag retrieves all the messages. There are also optional attributes for STARTROW and MAXROWS that make it possible to page through the resultset as if it were a resultset of rows from a query. A CFOUTPUT tag is used to display the number of messages, stored in the *RecordCount* property that is referenced by the name of the CFPOP instance using dot notation. Then a CFOUTPUT tag is used to display the results in a table. The table has three rows, with the From, Subject, and Date fields of the e-mail displayed in the first row, the Body of the e-mail in the second row, and a horizontal rule tag (<hr>) in the third row to act as a divider between rows. You can see the page in Figure 17-6. As you saw in the earlier CFOUTPUT examples, the tag serves as a loop if a QUERY attribute is specified. In this case, the query name is the name of the CFPOP instance, specified by the NAME attribute of the CFPOP tag.

Other attributes for the CFPOP tag make it usable for attachments. Consult the ColdFusion documentation for a full explanation of this powerful tag.

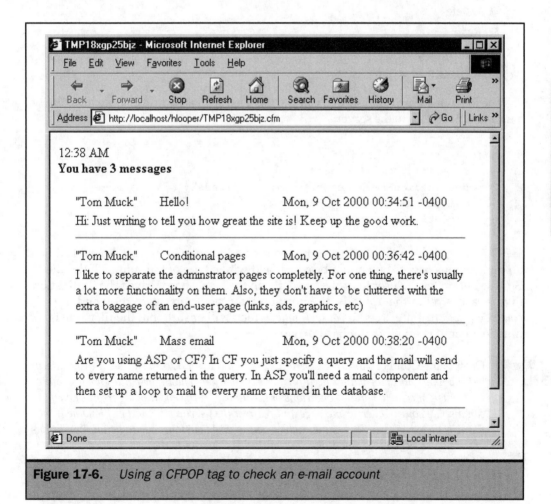

Figure 17-6. *Using a CFPOP tag to check an e-mail account*

File Manipulation in ColdFusion

The CFFILE tag is a multipurpose tag for file manipulation. It's a powerful tag that has access to the entire server, so many Web-hosting companies have the tag disabled in the ColdFusion Administrator. The ACTION attribute specifies the type of action that you want to take with the file, which can be any one of the following parameters:

- Upload
- Move
- Rename
- Copy
- Delete
- Read
- ReadBinary
- Append

The following is an example of a CFFILE tag used with an action of Upload, to allow a user to upload files to the server:

```
<cffile action="Upload"
    filefield="txtFilename"
    destination="c:\inetpub\wwwroot\uploads\"
    nameconflict="MakeUnique"
    accept="image/gif,image/jpg">
```

This example assumes that a user has entered a filename in the *txtFilename* text field on the previous page. This should be a text field with a type of file, and includes the Browse button for the user to browse to a file on the user's hard drive. The destination in this case is set to the uploads directory under c:\inetpub\wwwroot; and the *NameConflict* attribute is set to *MakeUnique*, which will ensure that the filename is unique when it is saved to the hard drive.

> **Tip** *Other NameConflict values are Overwrite, Skip, and Error. Overwrite is self-explanatory, but the Skip and Error values need further explanation. The Error value enables you to write custom code to handle conditions of the upload in the event of an error—i.e., you can display your own error message and redirect the user to try another filename if the file already exists. The Skip value enables you to write custom code to handle conditions of the upload depending upon the value of the FILE attribute that is returned when the CFFILE executes.*

In the next example, a file named GuestBook.txt is written to by the user; the example assumes that the user has filled out a *txtComment* text field on the previous page:

```
<cffile action="Append"
    file="c:\inetpub\wwwroot\comments\GuestBook.txt"
    output="#form.txtComment#">
```

Using CFFILE in Combination with CFDIRECTORY   Finally, the next example
is of a CFFILE tag using an action of Delete. This example also illustrates the use of a
CFDIRECTORY tag, which will display the contents of a given Web directory. This
page will display a list of files in the current directory as a list of links to download
the file, and also display a Delete link that enables you to delete the file from the server
(see Figure 17-7). The file is named Home.cfm. As you can see, the CFFILE tag is capable
of some pretty powerful functions.

```
<!---First, set up a url parameter named "file" --->
<cfparam Name="url.file" default="">
<!---Next, check for a value in url.file, and create a variable
    named DeleteFile containing the path to the file--->
<cfif url.file NEQ "">
    <cfset DeleteFile = ¬
        Replace(GetTemplatePath(),"home.cfm","") & Url.file>
<!---Next, the CFFILE tag has two parameters: Action, and File--->
    <cffile action="Delete"
        file="#DeleteFile#">
</cfif>
<!---Next, the CFDIRECTORY tag displays the whole directory,
    using a filter of *.gif to only display GIF files--->
<cfdirectory directory="c:\inetpub\wwwroot\testingCFFILE"
    name="FileCleanup"
    filter="*.gif"
    sort="name ASC, size DESC">
<!---Lastly, we set up a table using the CFOUTPUT tag to loop thru
    the list of names in the directory by specifying a Query
    attribute.  Variables are defined for "link" and "deletelink"
    upon each iteration of the loop.  The "deletelink" contains
    the URL variable for the current filename--->
<table>
<cfoutput query="FileCleanup">
<cfset link='<a href=' & chr(34) & #FileCleanup.Name# ¬
    & chr(34) & '>#FileCleanup.Name#</a>'>
<cfset deleteLink = '<a href=' & chr(34) & ¬
'home.cfm?file=#FileCleanup.Name#' & chr(34) & '>Delete</a>'>
<tr>
    <td>#link#</td>
    <td>#deleteLink#</td>
```

```
</tr>
</cfoutput>
</table>
```

Using CFTRY and CFCATCH

One of the more powerful features of ColdFusion is the error-handling capability using CFTRY and CFCATCH. The way these tags are utilized is to put a CFTRY tag around a block of code on which you want to enable error handling. For instance, you could place the CFTRY block around a database insert, and then handle any resulting database errors using your custom code rather than by letting ColdFusion display an error message.

CFTRY requires that you have at least one CFCATCH block within the CFTRY block. CFCATCH encloses the code that you want to execute if an error occurs within

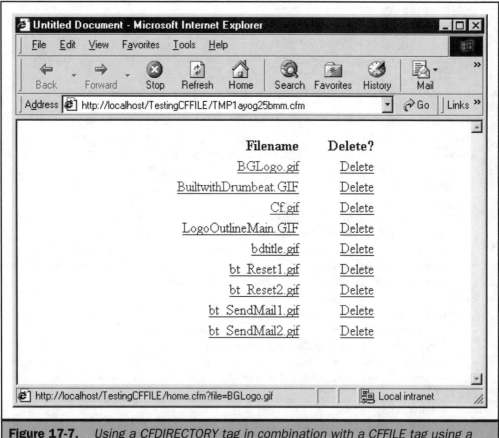

Figure 17-7. *Using a CFDIRECTORY tag in combination with a CFFILE tag using a DELETE action*

the CFTRY block. The CFCATCH tag enables you to use the TYPE attribute to pinpoint the types of errors that are encountered. This way, you can customize the error handling of the page depending upon what type of error is encountered. The types that are allowed are as follows:

- Application (default)
- Database
- Template
- Security
- Object
- MissingInclude
- Expression
- Lock
- Custom_type
- Any (default)

Here's an example of a CFTRY/CFCATCH block that traps the database errors that might occur when the CFQUERY tag executes:

```
<cftry>
    <cfquery name='rsCustomers' datasource='Orders'>
        INSERT into Customers(FirstName, LastName, CurrentDate)
        VALUES ('#form.Firstname#','#form.lastname#',#Now()#)
    </cfquery>
    <cfcatch type='Database'>
        <cflocation url='Error.cfm?error=database'>
    </cfcatch>
    <cfcatch>
        <cflocation url='Home.cfm?error=1'>
    </cfcatch>
</cftry>
```

The example is a CFQUERY using an *Insert* statement inside of a CFTRY block. The first CFCATCH statement checks for database errors and redirects the user to the Error.cfm page with an error parameter set to "Database." The second CFCATCH block catches all other errors and redirects the user to the Home.cfm page, with an error flag set as well.

The use of CFTRY/CFCATCH is useful for debugging, as well, with options for error messages, exception type, stack trace, SQLSTATE from the database, and a host of other informative properties. Check the ColdFusion documentation for a full explanation of the error-handling capabilities of ColdFusion.

Creating a ColdFusion Application with the CFAPPLICATION Tag

The Application.cfm file and the CFAPPLICATION tag that is associated with the page require mention. For those familiar with ASP, the Application.cfm page is similar in concept to the global.asa file. Session and Application variables are enabled in this file (you can't use the variables without first enabling them from this file), and timeout values for the Application and Session variables are set.

When a page is requested with a .cfm extension, the ColdFusion server first checks whether an Application.cfm file exists. If it does, the server executes the Application.cfm page first. The Application.cfm page, in many cases, will contain the authentication code for a user. If the user is logged in, the page that was requested will execute; if the user is not logged in, the login form in the Application.cfm page will be displayed.

The CFAPPLICATION tag is declared on the page as follows:

```
<cfapplication name="myApplication"
    sessionmanagement="Yes"
    clientmanagement="Yes"
    applicationtimeout="#CreateTimeSpan(2,0,0,0)#"
    sessiontimeout="#CreateTimeSpan(0,0,5,0)#">
```

The SESSIONMANAGEMENT attribute assumes a Yes or No value. If the value is Yes, Session variables can be used in the pages of the application. The *CreateTimeSpan* function is a built-in ColdFusion function that enables you to specify days, hours, minutes, and seconds as a comma-delimited list and have the list automatically converted to a date/time object that can be manipulated by the ColdFusion server.

Also, application-level variables can be defined on this page. These are variables that can be used by all users of the application. These variables are usually locked with a CFLOCK tag, as in the following example:

```
<cflock scope="Application" timeout="30" type="Exclusive">
    <cfif Not IsDefined("application.States")>
        <cfquery name="getStates" datasource="Orders">
            SELECT States from StateTable
        </cfquery>
        <cfset application.States = ValueList(getStates.States)>
    </cfif>
</cflock>
```

The example first locks the Application variable from all access. Then it checks whether the Application variable named "States" has been defined. If it has, nothing is executed; but if it hasn't, a CFQUERY tag is executed. The query returns a list of U.S. states, which is then stored as a list in an Application variable named *States*. The access of the variable inside of a CFLOCK ensures that no access is permitted to the variable by any other user while it is being written to by this page. This block of code is executed only once when the page is hit for the first time, and then again after the application times out. Application timeouts are usually set pretty high—several days—whereas Session timeouts are usually set between 5 and 20 minutes.

ColdFusion and Dreamweaver MX

ColdFusion has been around for a while and has developed a core following of loyal users. ColdFusion developers did not have a visual tool for developing Web sites until UltraDev came along. ColdFusion Studio is an impressive package for the programmer, but offers little in the way of a visual design environment. UltraDev, in its first-generation release, was the strong beginning of a powerful visual environment for designers and programmers. Dreamweaver MX takes that a few steps further. Also, because Dreamweaver MX is multiplatform, many of the same techniques can be applied to ASP, JSP, PHP, ASP.NET, and ColdFusion pages from within the same environment.

The ColdFusion Bindings Panel

When you click the Window menu and select Bindings, the Bindings panel pops up, which is side by side with the Server Behaviors panel in a default "out of the box" environment. The panel contains the various data sources that are available to the ColdFusion developer:

- **Recordset**   This is where the CFQUERY tag is generated. It can be a SELECT, INSERT, UPDATE, or DELETE statement, but only SELECT statements are shown in the Bindings panel as a resultset. Other statements turn up in the Server Behaviors panel as a CFQuery Server Behavior.

- **Stored Procedure**   This data source writes a CFSTOREDPROC tag to the page.

- **CFPARAM**   This data source allows you to create a CFPARAM tag. If you create a CFQUERY or CFSTOREDPROC tag using the Bindings panel that contains a variable, that variable will show up here as well.

- **Form Variable**   Gives access to a form variable. These are typically page-level variables that can be posted from a Web page using a form and the *post* method.

- **URL Variable**   Gives access to a URL variable. A URL variable is also known as a query string variable, and can be a form variable that was submitted using a form with the *get* method.

- **Session Variable**   Gives access to a Session variable. A Session variable is available sitewide.

- **Client Variable**   Gives access to a Client variable.

- **Application Variable**   Gives access to an Application variable. These are available sitewide as well.

- **Cookie Variable**   Gives access to a cookie variable.

- **CGI Variable**   Gives access to a CGI variable.
- **Server Variable**   Gives access to a Server variable.
- **Local Variable**   Gives access to a Local variable (as `<cfoutput>#Variables.Variablename#</cfoutput>`).
- **Data Source Name Variable**   You can use a variable as a data source name within the CFQUERY or CFSTOREDPROC tag. That variable can be accessed or defined here as well.

Defining a recordset on a ColdFusion page causes Dreamweaver MX to generate a CFQUERY tag with a DATASOURCE attribute that matches the data source that was established when you defined your connection. If you've coded ColdFusion queries in the past, you may have used a *Select* statement similar to this:

```
SELECT SeekID, SeekUsername, SeekPassword, SeekAccessGroup
FROM Seekers
WHERE SeekUsername = '#form.username#'
AND SeekPassword = '#form.password#'
```

You can use these statements—just as you would have hand-coded them—in the new Dreamweaver MX. In the past, with UltraDev 1 and 4, there were incompatibilities between hand-coding and UD-generated code. With Dreamweaver MX, Macromedia has delivered a product that creates clean ColdFusion code, much like a person would hand-code it.

The advanced recordset dialog box for Dreamweaver MX using ColdFusion is shown in Figure 17-8. You can simply choose your database connection, fill in the username and password if applicable, and write your SQL—either by hand or with the aid of the query builder.

When using parameters (such as *form.username* and *form.password* in the preceding query), you have to define them as page-level parameters from the recordset dialog box (shown next). The default value can be left blank. The generated code for this Dreamweaver MX-generated recordset would look like this:

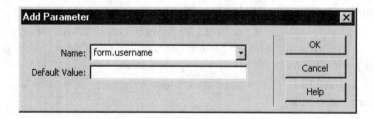

```
<cfparam name="form.username" default="">
<cfparam name="form.password" default="">
```

```
<cfquery name="rsGetSeeker" datasource="Bettergig">
SELECT SeekID, SeekUsername, SeekPassword, SeekAccessGroup
FROM Seekers WHERE
SeekUsername = '#form.username#' AND SeekPassword = '#form.password#'
</cfquery>
```

In contrast to that, in UD4-mode, the runtime values for the query have to be defined as variables before using the query (see Figure 17-9). This is done by defining a variable Name, a Default Value, and a Runtime Value. The Name entry can be any valid variable name, but it's a good idea to use something that won't be mistaken for something else or cause a conflict. It's also a good idea to append a prefix to your variables to distinguish them from other variables. The Default Value entry should be something that won't be in the database, although for testing, you can use a value here that you know *is* in the database. The Runtime Value column is where you put the incoming data that you want in your query—in this case, *form.username* and *form.password*.

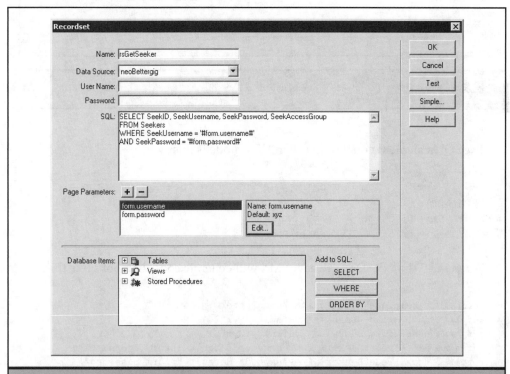

Figure 17-8.   *The dialog box for creating a recordset in Dreamweaver MX using ColdFusion in MX mode*

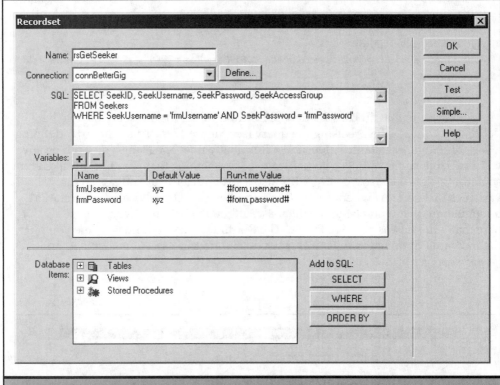

Figure 17-9.   *Building the same recordset in ColdFusion-UD4 mode*

The SQL statement you would use in UD4 mode is this:

```
SELECT SeekID, SeekUsername, SeekPassword, SeekAccessGroup
FROM Seekers
WHERE SeekUsername = 'frmUsername'
AND SeekPassword = 'frmPassword'
```

When in UD4 mode, Dreamweaver MX will generate code that looks like this:

```
<cfinclude template="Connections/connBetterGig.cfm">
<cfparam name="form.username" default="xyz">
<cfparam name="form.password" default="xyz">
<cfparam name="rsGetSeeker__frmUsername" default="#form.username#">
<cfparam name="rsGetSeeker__frmPassword" default="#form.password#">
<cfquery name="rsGetSeeker" datasource=#MM_connBetterGig_DSN#
```

```
username=#MM_connBetterGig_USERNAME# password=#MM_connBetterGig_PASSWORD#>|
SELECT SeekID, SeekUsername, SeekPassword, SeekAccessGroup
FROM Seekers WHERE
SeekUsername = '#rsGetSeeker__frmUsername#'
AND SeekPassword = '#rsGetSeeker__frmPassword#'
</cfquery>
```

Note   *ColdFusion programmers generally like to use uppercase letters when referencing tags. However, Dreamweaver MX generates lowercase tags for most of its ColdFusion code. In the future, lowercase will most likely be the preferred way to reference tags, because of the acceptance of XML and XHTML.*

The code is still fairly clean, but contains an extra set of variables that Dreamweaver MX has generated for the query—*rsGetSeeker__frmUsername* and *rsGetSeeker__frmPassword*. These variables take the place of the runtime values that you inserted when the record-set was created. You can also see from the listing that Dreamweaver MX has set up the CFPARAM statements to assign default values to the variables used. UD4 mode shifts the actual datasource name, username, and password to an external connections file that it includes with a CFINCLUDE tag, and uses variables to reference the connection.

As you can see, there is a bit of redundancy in the variable declaration. For this reason, it is always recommended to stick with Dreamweaver MX mode for ColdFusion code unless you are maintaining compatibility with a site built with UltraDev 4. The Dreamweaver MX–generated code is cleaner, easier to read, and easier to debug.

The Recordset dialog box also enables you to create Insert, Update, and Delete statements by hand-coding the SQL in the dialog box; but the resulting CFQUERY doesn't show up in the Bindings panel, because the query doesn't return a resultset. It will, however, show up in the Server Behaviors panel as a CFQuery Server Behavior. There are also Server Behaviors that enable you to create *Insert*, *Update*, and *Delete* statements in a more "wizard-like" manner. The following SQL statement inserted in the SQL box of the Recordset dialog box will insert the values of two form fields— username and password—into the Employers table.

```
INSERT INTO Employers (EmpUsername, EmpPassword)
VALUES ('#form.username#', '#form.password#')
```

Tip   *Dreamweaver MX also allows you to use variables in place of data source names. This allows greater flexibility because it allows you to declare the data source name inside of an Application.cfm file for use on every page, or inside of a CFINCLUDE file.*

Stored Procedures

You can use stored procedures in ColdFusion with the CFSTOREDPROC tag—they offer significant power over single SQL statements. Stored procedures are available from the Bindings panel. The interface enables you to visually develop your stored procedure code, which is then generated by Dreamweaver MX as a CFSTOREDPROC tag and inserted into the page.

Stored procedures are described in Chapter 26, which deals with more advanced database interactions.

Other Data Sources

The remaining Bindings menu items are the Session, Form, URL, Application, Client, CGI, Server, Cookie, and Local variables. These data sources enable you to specify a name, as shown next, but not a value. To declare variables in your code, you have to hand-code them or find a third-party Server Behavior that writes the code for you. The data sources available here, however, make it easy to drag and drop the variables on the page so that you can edit the visual appearance of the variables on the page. Here's an example of a session variable that's been defined as *Username:*

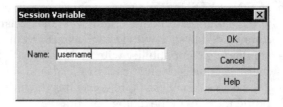

```
<cfoutput>#Session.Username#</cfoutput>
```

After defining the variable in the panel, you can drag it to the page and apply a Server Format to the displayed value by clicking the down-arrow on the selected variable and choosing one from the drop-down menu (see Figure 17-10). Many Server Formats are available to the Dreamweaver MX ColdFusion developer—and most of them insert standard ColdFusion functions "around" your code. For instance, when you choose Trim | Both from the Server Formats menu, the Session variable code from the preceding example now looks like this:

```
<cfoutput># Trim(Session.Username) #</cfoutput>
```

The Server Behaviors Panel

Server Behaviors are the core server-side code builders of Dreamweaver MX. These Behaviors generate code to insert into your documents to perform a variety of server-side functions. Many of these functions are related to the recordset, or CFQUERY tag. The use of Server Behaviors is covered in the coming chapters, but here's a brief introduction to some of these Behaviors.

Figure 17-10.   *Choosing a Server Format to apply to a data source, such as a Session variable, Application variable, or recordset field*

The Repeat Region

The Repeat Region is the granddaddy of Server Behaviors. It enables you to loop through a resultset with a simple point-and-click interface. This is of greater significance to ASP, PHP, and JSP developers, because they have no built-in structure that accomplishes this. However, ColdFusion has the CFOUTPUT statement, which contains automatic looping behavior. The repeat region Server Behavior will insert a *<cfoutput query= "somequery"></cfoutput>* around your code.

One of the advantages of using the Repeat Region rather than hand-coding ColdFusion is that it is a way to set up the Recordset Paging Server Behaviors. When you apply a Repeat Region to the page, you can choose to display all records or limit the resultset to a specific number of records. If you choose to limit the results, variables are written to the page by the Repeat Region that allow interaction with the other Server Behaviors. Like the Recordset behavior, the Repeat Region has to be inserted for many of the other Server Behaviors to work with your code. For example, if you hand-code your own CFOUTPUT statement to loop through a recordset, you can't use the Move To Next Record Server Behavior.

AN INTRODUCTION TO WEB SCRIPTING

Show Region

This Behavior enables you to show a specific region on the page based on a specific condition that you can set up in the Behavior. The available choices for conditions are

- If Recordset Is Empty
- If Recordset Is Not Empty
- If First Page*
- If Not First Page*
- If Last Page*
- If Not Last Page*

* When in UD4-compatibility mode, these Server Behaviors refer to "records" and not "pages."

This Behavior generates code that uses the ColdFusion CFIF tag and tests the values of certain variables. The following example shows the ColdFusion code written by the Show If Recordset Is Not Empty Behavior:

```
<cfif rsProducts.recordCount GT 0>#rsProducts.Name#</cfif>
```

The Show Region Server Behaviors can be applied to a single item or to a whole block of code—HTML or ColdFusion code. For example, you can hide a particular table row by applying it to the entire <tr> tag.

Recordset Paging (Move To Record in UD4-Compatibility Mode)

This is a group of Server Behaviors that interacts with a recordset and a Repeat Region Server Behavior. All of these Behaviors enable you to create your own interactions using the variables that have been predefined by the built-in code.

These Behaviors will be detailed in the coming chapters as you build the Bettergig.com Web site.

Dynamic Elements

The Bindings panel enables you to apply dynamic text items to the page, and also enables you to insert values into other objects, such as form objects. Another way to do this is to use the Dynamic Elements menu entry in the Server Behaviors panel and click one of the five items:

- **Dynamic Text**   A text item, such as a Recordset column or a Session variable that's on the page.
- **Dynamic List/Menu**   A list/menu form element that gets its values from a data source.

- **Dynamic Text Field**   A text field form element that gets its value from a data source.

- **Dynamic Check Box**   A check box form element that gets its checked value based on a data source.

- **Dynamic Radio Buttons**   A set of radio buttons that get their values from a data source.

The Dynamic Elements have to be applied to an existing element on the page. For instance, if you have a basic list/menu on the page, you can apply the Dynamic List/Menu Server Behavior to the page, and define the values for the element (see Figure 17-11). The following is sample code written by the Server Behavior, and it is what you would expect if you had hand-coded a list/menu using ColdFusion:

```
<select name="select">
<option value="0"
<cfif (isDefined("session.userid") AND 0 EQ session.userid)>
selected</cfif>>*none*</option>
  <cfoutput query="rsGetSeekers">
    <option value="#rsGetSeekers.SeekID#"
    <cfif (isDefined("session.userid") AND
     rsGetSeekers.SeekID EQ session.userid)>
     selected</cfif>>#rsGetSeekers.SeekUsername#</option>
  </cfoutput>
</select>
```

AN INTRODUCTION TO WEB SCRIPTING

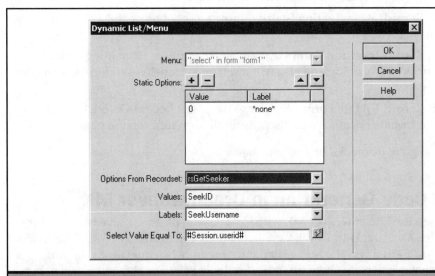

Figure 17-11.   *A dynamic list/menu dialog box prompts for a number of values.*

User Authentication Server Behaviors

Many dynamic sites have a login form to allow the site administrators to maintain information about users. The Login User Server Behavior enables you to check a database for an existing user and redirect the user to a page if the login is successful, and redirect to a "failed" page if the login is unsuccessful.

The Restrict Access To Page Server Behavior enables you to set an access level on the page. This Behavior depends on the Log In User Server Behavior being applied to a login page. In this Server Behavior, you can define access levels that will be available to the site. The access levels can be words (like "admin" or "seeker") or numbers.

The Log Out User Server Behavior enables you to set a link on your page to allow a user to log out from the site and be redirected to another page.

Last, the Check New Username Server Behavior enables you to check the database for an existing username before inserting the user data into the database. This Server Behavior requires that an Insert Server Behavior already exists on the page.

Server Objects

UltraDev 4 introduced some new objects to the Objects panel—Live Objects. Dreamweaver MX renamed them as Server Objects. These objects are combinations of various Objects and Server Behaviors bundled into "wizard-like" forms that enable you to insert several things at once into a page. These Server Objects include the following:

- **Insert Master-Detail Page Set**   Enables you to define a standard Master/Detail page combination.

- **Insert Recordset Navigation Bar**   Inserts a set of recordset navigation links, such as First Previous Next Last, inside a small table.

- **Insert Recordset Navigation Status**   Inserts a set of recordset status numbers, such as Records 1 to 5 of 20.

- **Insert Record Insertion Form**   Automates the process of creating an Insert Record Server Behavior, and also will insert all form fields and form information to the page.

- **Insert Record Update Form**   Similar to the Insert Record Object, but works with an Update Behavior and also inserts all form fields to the page.

Note   *Server Objects are covered in detail in Chapter 24.*

ColdFusion Code Generation in Dreamweaver MX

If you decide to use Dreamweaver MX with ColdFusion, note that several problems existed in UltraDev 1 and UltraDev 4. Certain hand-coding resulted in Server Behaviors showing up as "partial" on the Server Behavior menu. Also, queries containing ColdFusion syntax ceased to show up in the Bindings panel, or showed up there but did not allow you to work with the recordset columns. "Unbalanced" ColdFusion tags showed up as invalid tags.

The good news is that Dreamweaver MX has been completely revamped so that the ColdFusion code is more "fusionesque." Whereas UltraDev used CFSCRIPT tags for most of its operations, Dreamweaver MX uses ColdFusion tags, making the code more readable and more user friendly. Also, the rendering bugs that plagued UltraDev have been eliminated from this release. That is good news for the thousands of ColdFusion developers out there. Dreamweaver MX has come of age, and can be considered a serious tool for rapid application development.

The best thing to do if you find a bug, whether it's a known bug or not, is to notify Macromedia with as much information as possible at www.macromedia.com/support/email/wishform so that the issue can be addressed. Although a large number of bugs were fixed for Dreamweaver MX, no software is ever bug-free.

ColdFusion MX

ColdFusion MX is the latest version of ColdFusion server available from Macromedia. ColdFusion MX was well known in the ColdFusion circles as code-name Neo. ColdFusion MX is the new generation of CF servers based in Java. ColdFusion had to be rebuilt from the ground up for this release. The server sits on top of a Java J2EE-compliant server, and has the full arsenal of ColdFusion tags and functions, as well as the whole of the Java language and the advantages of JSP, such as JSPs and tag libraries. In addition, a substantial number of new features make ColdFusion programming even more enticing.

Also, because ColdFusion MX is radically different in some ways from previous releases, it comes complete with the Code Compatibility Analyzer that will analyze your pre-MX ColdFusion code for compatibility problems (see Figure 17-12).

ColdFusion MX has many great new features that you can take advantage of from within the Dreamweaver MX environment. Web services, CFCs, and XML support bring ColdFusion into the big leagues.

Web Services

Web services are a fairly new technology that has taken the Web by storm. Basically, a Web service is a component that is created to communicate using standard XML formats to any application that knows how to talk to it. The Web service will have an interface written in Web Service Description Language (WSDL). The interface describes what the Web service does and how to communicate with it. The actual communication is done with XML. Because XML is basically just text, an application that can read text can read and interpret a Web service. As a result, Web services can be created by one type of server and utilized by anyone who can read the XML.

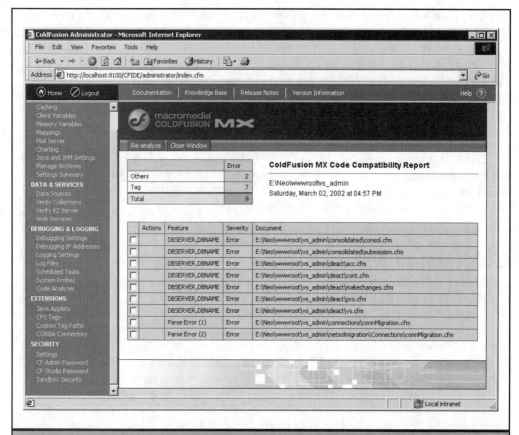

Figure 17-12. The Code Compatibility Analyzer in ColdFusion MX reports any possible compatibility problems with existing ColdFusion applications.

Some examples of Web services are

- **Stock services** Type in a ticker symbol and get a stock quote.
- **Weather service** Type in a ZIP code to get local weather.
- **Currency exchange rates** Type in "currency from," "currency to," and a value.
- **Language translation** Type in a phrase, "language from," and "language to" for a translation.
- **Web search** Type in a search word or words and get Web results.

And there are many more too numerous to mention. Web services, in short, can offer anything that has a question and an answer, a call and a response, or a simple information service. ColdFusion MX has made working with Web services even easier by allowing the developer to interact with Web services by using traditional ColdFusion-style tags. Also, Dreamweaver MX can introspect these services, and it will automatically create the ColdFusion MX code necessary to utilize the services.

To locate a public Web service, you can use one of the lists that are available from within the Dreamweaver MX environment:

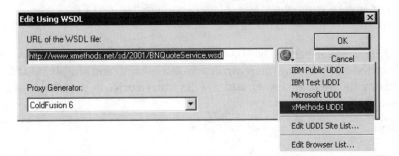

Dreamweaver MX can use the link to the WSDL page to create the interface for the Web service. The Web service appears with its methods and variables broken down into the Components panel, much like your data sources appear in the Bindings panel:

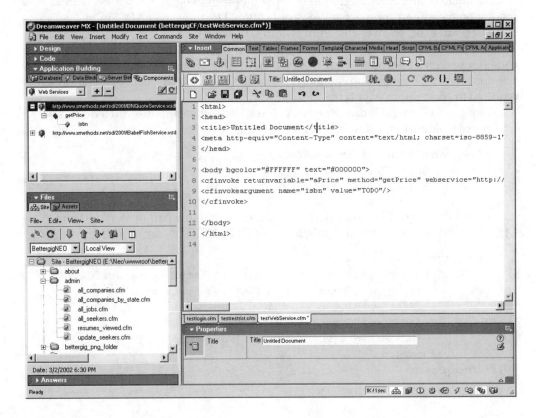

After you've added the Web service to your Components panel, you can drag and drop it onto the page, and Dreamweaver MX will create the code for you, which in this case is a CFINVOKE tag:

```
<cfinvoke returnvariable="aPrice" method="getPrice"
webservice="http://www.xmethods.net/sd/2001/BNQuoteService.wsdl">
    <cfinvokeargument name="isbn" value="TODO"/>
</cfinvoke>
```

This particular Web service is a Barnes and Noble book price quote service. The method is called *getPrice*, and the return variable is *aPrice*. You simply need to pass it an ISBN (using the *value* attribute), and it will return a price in the *aPrice* variable. Then you can simply display the price with

```
<cfoutput>#aPrice#</cfoutput>
```

CFC: ColdFusion Components

CFCs are ColdFusion Components, which greatly simplify the reuse of code by allowing developers an easy way to bundle functionality into a component that can be shared, reused, queried, and even used from within other technologies. They are a truly revolutionary way to approach a Web application. Dreamweaver MX can introspect these CFCs to make them useful from within DW as well.

A CFC is created using traditional ColdFusion tags and attributes, but the resulting code is saved on a page with a .cfc file extension. After doing this, the code becomes self-documenting because you can then browse the page to retrieve all of the information required to communicate with the CFC.

A simple CFC might return a word with the first letter capitalized. To do this in traditional ColdFusion, you might code it like this:

```
<cfset wordToCap = Trim(wordToCap)>
<cfreturn UCase(left(wordToCap,1)) &
 LCase(right(wordToCap,len(wordToCap)-1))>
```

To turn this into a CFC, simply enclose the code within a pair of start and end CFCOMPONENT tags located within a pair of CFFUNCTION tags:

```
<cfcomponent>
    <cffunction name="toCapsFirstLetter" returnType="string">
        <cfargument name="wordToCap" required="true"/>
        <cfset wordToCap = Trim(wordToCap)>
        <cfreturn UCase(left(wordToCap,1)) &
          LCase(right(wordToCap,len(wordToCap)-1))>
    </cffunction>
</cfcomponent>
```

The CFCOMPONENT tag creates the CFC. Inside of that tag, you are creating the function named *toCapsFirstLetter*. This becomes a method of the CFC. A CFC can have many methods, but this is a simple example with only one. One argument is passed to the function—the word that will be capitalized (*wordToCap*). There is also a return value—the word after it has been operated on. You can place this code in a file called toCaps.cfc and place it in your root Web directory.

To invoke this CFC on a ColdFusion page, you use a CFINVOKE tag, just as you do with a Web service:

```
<cfinvoke component="toCaps" method="toCapsFirstLetter"
 wordToCap="jehosephat"  returnvariable ="cappedWord"/>
```

The CFINVOKE tag invokes the *toCaps* CFC using the *toCapsFirstLetter* function (or method). The CFC operates on the word and returns it to the calling page with the first letter capitalized. The value is then stored in the variable *cappedWord*. To display the result, you may use a simple CFOUTPUT tag:

```
<cfoutput>#cappedWord#</cfoutput>
```

To view the description of this CFC you've just created, you can simply browse the CFC file. This will give you an output similar to the following:

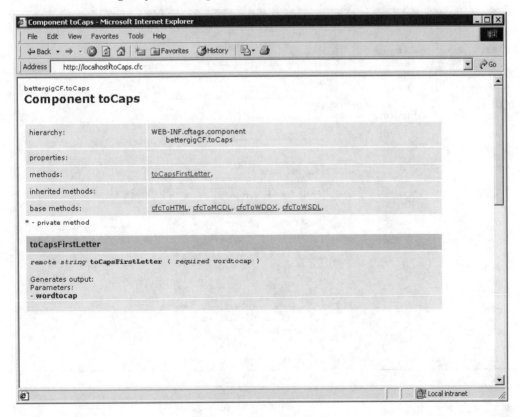

That is pretty cool in and of itself, but what makes CFCs even more powerful is that you can turn them into Web services by adding a simple attribute (*access="remote"*) to the CFFUNCTION tag within the CFC:

```
<cffunction name="toCapsFirstLetter" returnType="string"
 access="remote">
```

After adding the attribute, the CFC is now available as a Web service to anyone using any other technology. ColdFusion MX actually creates the WDSL specifications for you. You can invoke the new Web service like this from within ColdFusion:

```
<cfinvoke webservice="http://localhost/toCaps.cfc?wsdl"
 method="toCapsFirstLetter" returnvariable="cappedWord">
      <cfinvokeargument name="wordToCap" value="jehosephat"/>
</cfinvoke>
```

Dreamweaver MX also simplifies the creation of CFCs with a CFC wizard, which you can access by clicking the plus sign (+) on the Components panel:

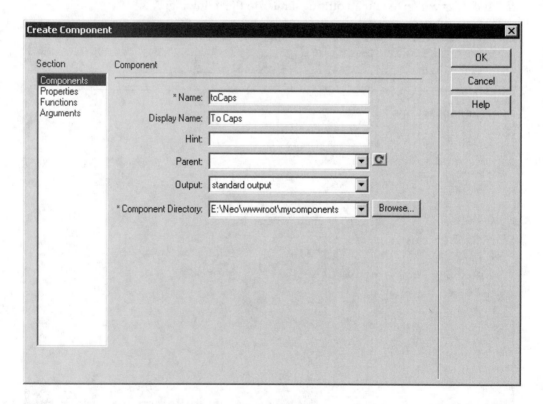

XML Parsing

XML is a standards-based language that makes it easy to create documents that contain data *and* describe the data within the same document. It has always been a problem sharing data between different platforms. XML eases this burden by providing a common language specification that all platforms can use to communicate. It is called *extensible* markup language because the language itself is not fixed like HTML—you can design your own tags to describe your data.

ColdFusion MX contains native support for XML documents, and also includes a built-in parser. Several new tags were created to make dealing with XML documents even easier, including the new CFXML tag for creating XML, and the new *ParseXML* function, which transforms the XML into a ColdFusion struct.

A typical XML construct to describe a customer might look like this:

```
<customers>
    <customer>
        <name>John Jehosephat</name>
        <phone>703-555-3434</phone>
        <email>jj@jehosephatlodge.com</email>
    </customer>
</customers>
```

ColdFusion MX allows you to address the XML construct as a structure, using dot notation. Assuming that the preceding XML is in a string variable named *Orders*, the following code pulls apart the struct created by the XML tags and sets variables to hold the data:

```
<cfset getCustomer = XMLParse(Orders)>
<cfset CustName = getCustomer.customers.customer.name.xmltext>
<cfset CustPhone = getCustomer.customers.customer.phone.xmltext>
<cfset CustEmail = getCustomer.customers.customer.email.xmltext>
```

To display the variables on the page, you can use simple CFOUTPUT tags:

```
<cfoutput>
Customer Name: #CustName#<br>
Phone: #CustPhone#<br>
Email: #CustEmail#
</cfoutput>
```

ColdFusion Resources

A tremendous amount of support is available from the Web and in user groups around the world. The Macromedia Web site is the best place to start when you need assistance. Numerous technical documents and white papers are available, as well as the complete set of documentation that ships with ColdFusion. Also, most of Macromedia's products are available as trial downloads from the site, including ColdFusion server and ColdFusion Studio. The Macromedia Developer Forums (news://forums.macromedia.com/) are also a good place to get your questions answered. In addition, any patches or updates to Macromedia products are available for download from the site.

The Macromedia Partners program is a good way for a developer to get developer versions of Macromedia software. If you are interested in the program, go to the Macromedia site and look for the Partners link.

ColdFusion User Groups (CFUGs) are popping up all over the world, and may number in the hundreds by now. Most of these groups have monthly or bimonthly meetings that you can attend to hear lectures, see demonstrations, or bring some code that you need some help with. The ColdFusion community is a close-knit group of people who are usually willing to help out.

Several ColdFusion books also are available on the market. The most popular of these are *The Macromedia ColdFusion 5 Web Application Construction Kit* and *Advanced ColdFusion 5 Application Development,* both written by Ben Forta (Que Publications), highly regarded as one of the leading ColdFusion experts in the world. Ben Forta also hosts one of the best ColdFusion Web sites, at www.forta.com, with examples, articles, links, and custom tags. Many other books have sprung up since ColdFusion 5 came out, including several excellent books from Osborne, notably *Optimizing ColdFusion 5,* by Chris Cortes.

ColdFusion Developer's Journal is another resource. It is a monthly magazine available from your local newsstand or directly from the publisher, Sys-Con Media. The company also publishes *Java Developer's Journal* and *The XML Journal,* among other magazines. For more information on these periodicals, consult the Sys-Con Web site at www.sys-con.com/coldfusion.

The mailing lists at www.houseoffusion.com have some of the top ColdFusion experts in the country among their members. Literally hundreds of posts per day occur on the various lists. Chances are good that if you have a ColdFusion-related question, you can get it answered here.

Many ColdFusion Server Behaviors are popping up on the Macromedia Exchange, including some by the authors and the technical editor of this book. You can find ColdFusion custom tags there as well.

Summary

This chapter was intended as a general introduction to ColdFusion and the CFML language, and its implementation in Dreamweaver MX. CFML is a robust language, and is relatively easy to use—especially for the Web developer who is already familiar with HTML. The ease of use, however, doesn't imply that the language is any less powerful than ASP or JSP. In fact, many consider it more powerful because of all the built-in functionality. Whatever your background, ColdFusion is a viable way to get your data-driven site to the Web, and Dreamweaver MX is the perfect way to combine the designer-friendly history of Dreamweaver with the server-side functionality of ColdFusion.

The
Complete
Reference

Dreamweaver
MX

Chapter 18

PHP

PHP, Personal Home Page, has come into prominence in the last few years as a low-cost alternative to JSP, ASP, and ColdFusion. The cost of ownership of PHP is generally thought of as being much lower than the other server models because it can run on a free (or minimal cost) server platform such as Linux, whereas ASP requires a high-cost Windows server, and ColdFusion requires the purchase of an application server license. PHP is also an accessible language, much like JavaScript.

PHP was originally conceived as a means for a talented programmer named Rasmus Lerdorf to put his résumé on the Web and to track visitors. It grew from there when Rasmus released the code. PHP quickly became an open source project for independent developers. Now, PHP has come to mean PHP Hypertext Processor. It is a *recursive acronym*, where the first word in the acronym is an acronym itself, like the well-known Unix acronym GNU stands for "GNU's not Unix."

Dreamweaver MX supports only the combination of PHP with a MySQL database in a default installation, but other options are available through third parties.

The PHP Server

PHP can run on Linux, Unix, or Windows operating systems. Also, because Mac OS X is Unix-based, a PHP server can run on a Macintosh as well. If you are using a Linux box, the best way to set up a PHP server is to download the source code and compile the binaries yourself, but for Windows, installers are available from www.php.net (see Figure 18-1) that streamline the installation process.

Installing the Windows CGI

The Windows version of PHP can run as a server API or as a CGI. A CGI program, or Common Gateway Interface, is a standard method for creating modules for Web servers. Typically, the program will be called each time a request is made. For that reason, it runs a little slower than a server API. A server API version is tailored specifically for the server that it's running on. Therefore an ISAPI version is for Internet Information Server, and a NSAPI version is for Netscape server.

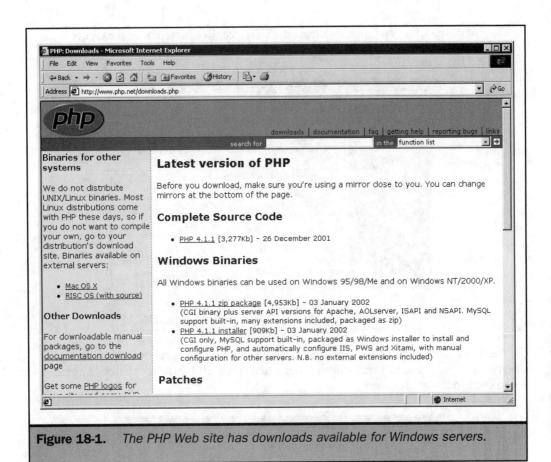

Figure 18-1. *The PHP Web site has downloads available for Windows servers.*

Caution *If you are using Internet Information Server as your Web server, use the CGI version on Windows because of instabilities with the ISAPI module. No such problems exist with the Apache API module.*

To install the CGI version, download the CGI installer program and execute it. You'll see the introductory screen to proceed with the installation:

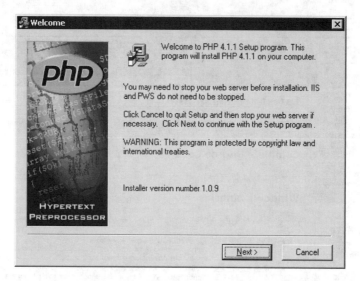

Next, you'll be asked to accept the terms of the licensing agreement. PHP is an open source program, but that doesn't mean licenses aren't attached. Click "I agree" to proceed to the next screen:

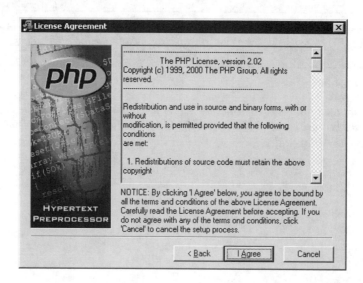

You can choose Standard or Advanced installation options. The Advanced option gives you more choices:

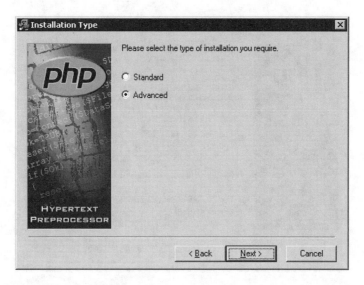

Now, choose your destination folder:

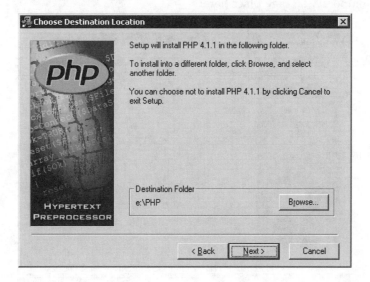

You can make backup copies of files that are changed or deleted during installation by specifying a directory:

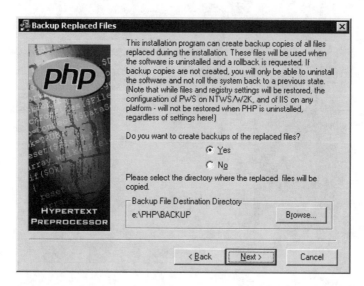

Next, you can choose a temporary upload directory. Any uploads made to your site will have a temporary storage place here:

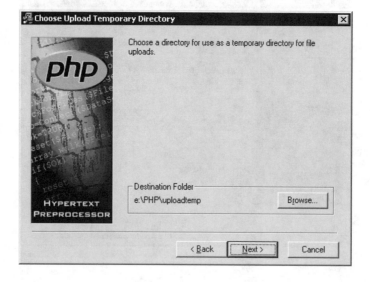

Choose a directory for storage of file-based session information:

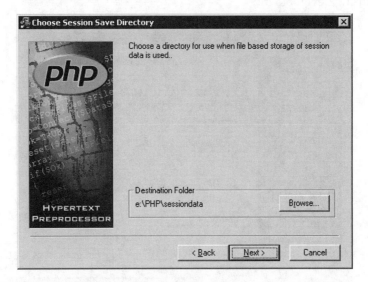

Next, fill in the administrator's e-mail address and the mail server to use for PHP:

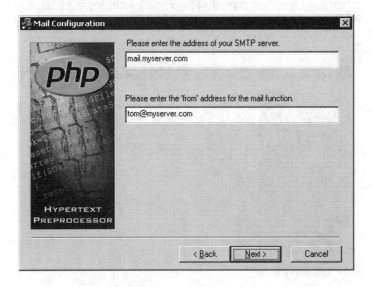

Here, you have an option to show error messages and warning notices, which you should do during development:

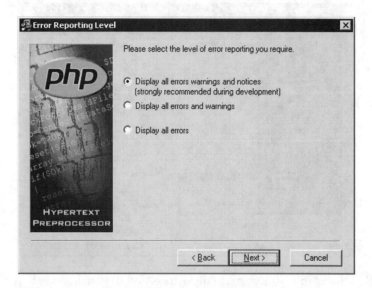

Now, specify the Web server type that you will be deploying PHP pages from. If you are on a Windows 2000 machine, this might be IIS 5.0, but other options are available as well, such as Apache:

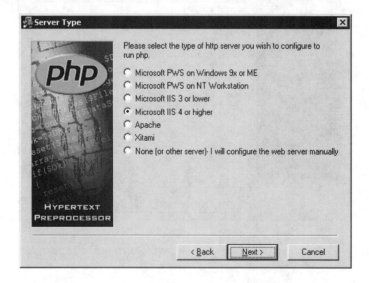

Next, you can choose which file extensions that PHP should handle. By default, the file extension is .php, but you can also serve files with .php3 and .phtml extensions, although these have been deprecated:

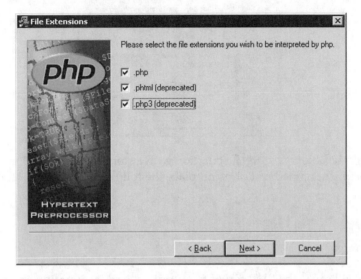

The configuration is complete, so you can click Next to begin the installation:

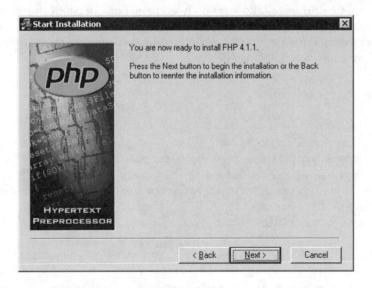

If everything installed correctly, you'll be presented with a success page:

You should be able to test the installation with a sample PHP file. Simply create a new Web document named test.php and place the following inside the <body> tags:

```
<?php
phpinfo();
?>
```

The code will cause the PHP server to output general information about the server (shown in Figure 18-2), the build number of the PHP version, and all configuration information about your installation. If you need to go back to configure any options of the server, you can edit the PHP.ini file located in the system root (Windows or WINNT). If you look at the PHP.ini file, you'll see all the questions that you just answered in the installation program completely spelled out:

```
; php.ini for PEAR tests
include_path=..
[mail function]
SMTP= mail.myserver.com ; for Win32 only
sendmail_from= tom@mail.myserver.com ; for Win32 only
upload_tmp_dir = e:\PHP\uploadtemp  ; temporary directory for HTTP uploaded
files (will use system default if not specified)
[Session]
session.save_path= e:\PHP\sessiondata    ; argument passed to save_handler
[PHP]
error_reporting= E_ALL; display all errors, warnings and notices
```

If you are installing to an Apache server rather than an IIS server, you have to manually configure the httpd.conf file located in Program Files\Apache Group\

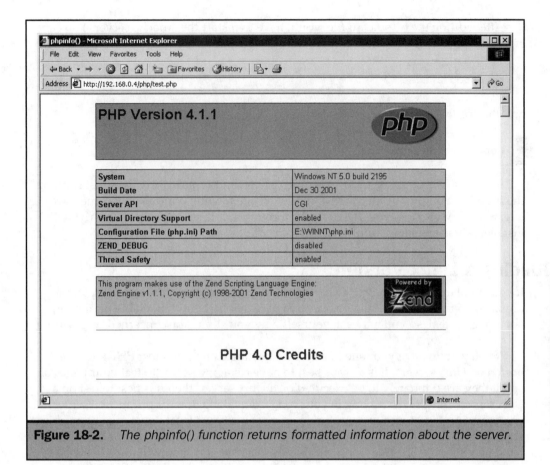

Figure 18-2.   *The phpinfo() function returns formatted information about the server.*

Apache\conf in a default installation of Apache. You can add these lines to the file to allow PHP files to be served by Apache as a CGI (assuming an installation to c:/php):

```
ScriptAlias /php/ "c:/php/"
AddType application/x-httpd-php .php
Action application/x-httpd-php "/php/php.exe"
```

To configure Apache to use PHP as a server API module, copy the php4ts.dll to the winnt/system32 (in Windows NT or 2000). Also, you'll have to copy the php4apache.dll file to the /apache/modules folder and add the following lines to the httpd.conf file:

```
LoadModule php4_module modules/php4apache.dll
AddType application/x-httpd-php .php
```

After editing the httpd.conf file, you'll have to restart the Apache server. You can stop the Apache server from a command line with

```
net stop apache
```

and then restart it with

```
net start apache
```

Installing MySQL on Windows is much easier, and typically involves just running the installer. You can install the MyODBC package to your Windows machine as well, to give your MySQL server ODBC access through a data source name. The MyODBC installer is also available from www.mysql.com.

Building a Linux Version

If you are planning to use PHP to build your dynamic sites, you'll want to set up a Linux box on which to test the pages. Dreamweaver MX is not available for the Linux operating system, so you may ask yourself why you should be concerned with setting up a Linux server?

If you plan to have your site hosted by a hosting company, most PHP sites are hosted on Unix servers. It is always best to have a staging server to test your pages on and if they are ultimately to be executed on a Unix server, then it is best to test on a Unix server. This prevents a bug in your code from taking down a production server. If you are going to test locally on a Windows machine (your local development machine) you can test a PHP/MySQL/Apache program with no problems, but you have to remember that the final environment that the pages will run on will most likely be a Unix environment, and there may be some issues with compatibility. Even if your site runs 99 percent the same way on your Windows machine, the 1 percent that doesn't will give you problems and will likely be difficult to track down and fix.

| Tip | *A staging server can aid in the development process, but it should always be as close a match as possible to your production Web server.* |

Linux comes in many distributions, but the Red Hat distribution has become one of the most popular. A Linux combination typically involves an Apache Web server, a MySQL database server, and the PHP server (using the acronym LAMP for Linux/Apache/MySQL/PHP). Red Hat typically comes with a PostgreSQL database server as well, which is a much more robust solution for a Web application than MySQL. Unfortunately, Dreamweaver MX supports only a MySQL configuration, so we will concentrate on that here.

The best way to install PHP in Unix/Linux is to compile it along with Apache. If you don't have the source code packages, you can download them from the following addresses:

- **Apache** www.apache.org
- **MySQL** www.mysql.com
- **PHP** www.php.net

You should be logged on as root to avoid any permissions issues. The servers will be installed into the following directories:

- /usr/local/apache
- /usr/local/mysql
- /usr/local/php4

Next, it's time to configure and install the binaries of MySQL. To begin the installation, you should have the source files downloaded to a TMP directory, such as /tmp/myfiles. Switch to that directory:

```
#cd /tmp/myfiles
```

Then you can extract the files with the following (your version number may be different):

```
# gunzip -c mysql -3.23.33.tar.gz | tar xvf -
```

The extraction should have created a new directory for you. Switch to that directory now:

```
# cd mysql -3.23.33
```

MySQL has a lot of configuration options, but the most basic is as follows, specifying the directory where the MySQL server will be located:

```
# ./configure --prefix=/usr/local/mysql
```

The configuration takes a few minutes. With that complete, you can make the binaries:

```
# make
```

This process may take a few minutes also, after which you can install the binaries. This is done with the following command, which will install the binaries to the directory that you specified in the *configure* command earlier:

```
# make install
```

The install is complete, but you still need to configure the MySQL server by installing the user tables:

```
# scripts/mysql_install_db
# cd /usr/local/mysql/bin
# ./safe_mysqld &
```

You'll also have to add a user password so that you'll be able to access the server:

```
# ./mysqladmin -u root -p password 'mypassword'
```

If the install was successful, you should be able to perform some tests:

```
# /usr/local/mysql/bin/mysqlshow -p
```

This command should pop up a password prompt, which you should answer with the password you just created. After entering your password, you'll see a list of databases that are already in MySQL:

```
+-----------+
| Databases |
+-----------+
| mysql     |
| test      |
+-----------+
```

To test the server, you can log in using the following command:

```
# /usr/local/mysql/bin/mysql -u root -p
```

You'll be prompted for a password again, after which you should be at the mysql prompt:

```
mysql>
```

You can run a few simple *select* statements to verify that the server is working correctly. First, tell the server to use the mysql database:

```
mysql> use mysql
```

Then perform this *select* statement, which gives you a list of all users of the database server:

```
mysql> select user, host from user;
```

Database commands to MySQL end in a semicolon, so if you have a complicated SQL statement, you can span multiple lines and refrain from executing the statement until a semicolon is encountered. You can use *SELECT * from user* to view the privilege level of each user. After you've played with MySQL, you can exit with the *exit* command:

```
mysql> exit
```

With MySQL installed, configured, and working properly, you should install Apache. You need to configure Apache before you can install PHP. Assuming that you've already downloaded the tar.gz files into a /tmp directory, you should unzip them (your version numbers may be different):

```
# gunzip -c apache_1.3.23.tar.gz | tar xf -
# gunzip -c php-4.0.4pl1.tar.gz | tar xvf -
```

After you've unzipped the servers, two new directories should have been created under /tmp: apache_1.3.23 and php-4.0.4pl1. PHP requires that the Apache server already be configured before installing PHP, so the process is to configure Apache, configure and install PHP, then reconfigure and install Apache. Switch to the Apache directory to configure it:

```
# cd /tmp/apache_1.3.23
# pwd /tmp/apache_1.3.23
# ./configure --prefix=/usr/local/apache
```

Again, the configuration process may take a few minutes. After the process is complete, you can configure PHP and make the PHP binaries. Switch to the PHP directory and begin the process (note that the backslashes in the *configure* command break it up into readable lines, but it is just one command):

```
# cd /tmp/php-4.0.4pl1
# pwd /tmp/php-4.0.4pl1
```

```
# ./configure --with-mysql \
    --with-xml \
    --enable-track-vars \
    --with-apache=../apache_1.3.23 \
```

This will configure PHP for use with Apache as a static library, with MySQL support. If you need to add support for another database, check the documentation for PHP to determine which switches you need to set. For example, to configure PHP for PostgreSQL support, you would use the switch *--with-pgsql*.

Next, build and install PHP:

```
# make
# make install
```

Each one of these steps will take a little time to execute. With PHP installed, it's time to switch back to the Apache directory again to reconfigure and build the Apache server:

```
# cd /tmp/apache_1.3.23
# pwd /tmp/apache_1.3.23
# ./configure --prefix=/usr/local/apache \
    --enable-module=rewrite \
    --activate-module=src/modules/php4/libphp4.a
# make
# make install
```

One last bit of configuring and you should be finished—you need to edit Apache's configuration file (httpd.conf) manually to add PHP support. It should be located at the /usr/local/apache/conf directory. Look for these lines that may or may not be commented out. If they already exist and aren't commented out, you are all set. If they are commented out, remove the comments and save the file:

```
AddType application/x-httpd-php .php
AddType application/x-httpd-php-source .phps
```

A simple configuration test will test out the server and tell you whether things are set up properly:

```
# cd /usr/local/apache/bin
#./apachectl configtest
```

The server should respond with "Syntax OK." If so, you can start the HTTP server:

```
# ./apachectl start
```

You should be able to test the installation with a sample PHP file. Simply create a new Web document named test.php and place the following inside the <body> tags:

```
<?php
phpinfo();
?>
```

Place the file in your default Web folder, which will usually be at /var/www/html in a default Apache installation. The PHP server will intercept and serve all pages in the Web directory with a .php file extension. The *phpinfo()* function in this file will cause the PHP server to output general information about the server, the build number of the PHP version, and all configuration information about your installation.

The PHP Programming Language

If you are familiar with Java, Perl, C, C++, or JavaScript, you should have no trouble transferring your skills to programming with PHP. The language is similar to those, but it also has many noticeable differences, particularly in the way in which you refer to variables.

PHP was designed for ease of use. Many things that are expensive add-ons to other servers, such as e-mailing, file uploading, dynamic PDF creation, image creation, and database access, are built directly into the language or in easy-to-find modules that you can add to PHP. Direct database access is provided for many popular database servers, and add-ons are available that create classes for database access so that you can call databases generically.

PHP Templating

PHP pages are HTML pages with a .php file extension and PHP server-side code mixed in. The code is enclosed in <? ?> server tags, but there are other options as well. PHP can run in ASP mode, whereby you can use the more standard <% %> tags. Also, XML mode allows you to use <?php ?> style. There is also a script style of tags, but that is rarely used, except when you have an HTML editor that has trouble displaying the other standard PHP tags. A typical PHP statement might look like this:

```
<?php echo("Greetings ".$HTTP_POST_VARS["firstname"]);?>
```

In this case, a form variable named *firstname* is evaluated along with a string expression ("Greetings") and then "echoed" to the page, which is much like the *Response.Write* expression in ASP or <cfoutput> in ColdFusion.

The page structure is much like the other server models. HTML tags and PHP tags can be mixed freely on the page. The PHP server (or preprocessor) executes the code within the PHP tags, and the result is an HTML page that can be sent to the browser. The following is a PHP page:

```
<?php if (!isset($firstname)) $firstname="User"; ?>
<html>
<head>
  <title><?php echo $HTTP_POST_VARS["firstname"];?>'s Page</title>
  <meta http-equiv="Content-Type" content="text/html; charset=iso-8859-1">
</head>
<body bgcolor="#FFFFFF" text="#000000">
  <p><?php echo "Hello $HTTP_POST_VARS["firstname"]"; ?></p>
</body>
</html>
```

If that page were processed, the resulting HTML would look like this, if the user were to view source (assuming he filled in a form field named *firstname*):

```
<html>
<head>
  <title>Tom's Page</title>
  <meta http-equiv="Content-Type" content="text/html; charset=iso-8859-1">
</head>
<body bgcolor="#FFFFFF" text="#000000">
  <p>Hello Tom</p>
</body>
</html>
```

You can see that the PHP code blocks have been evaluated and the resulting code from those blocks has been inserted into the places where the blocks originated.

Variables in PHP

Variables in PHP are preceded by a dollar sign. A typical variable in PHP might look like this:

```
$username
```

A letter or underscore, and any combination of letters, numbers, and underscores can follow the dollar sign. To PHP, a letter can be a–z or A–Z or any of the ASC characters between 127 and 255. Variables are also case-sensitive, so the variable name *$UserName* would be a different variable from *$username*. Dollar signs are also permitted within variable names; you should avoid them, however, because of *variable variables*, which we describe later.

Variable names should not conflict with any of the 2,500+ built-in PHP functions. If you have a specific naming convention, such as using your company initials in all variable names, you will be less likely to run into this problem.

Scoping

Variables are not always scoped in PHP the way that other application servers reference variables. In PHP, there is a switch in the PHP.ini file that determines how the variable scope will be utilized. For instance, in ColdFusion, you can refer to a form element like this:

```
form.username
```

In PHP, if the *register_globals* switch is set "on" in the PHP.ini file, you can refer to variables without any scope prefix, like this:

```
$username
```

The *$username* variable could be a form variable, local variable, request variable, or any number of other variable types. The *register_globals* switch is set to "on" by default in PHP servers prior to version 4.2.0, but its practice is discouraged. If the switch is not set, you have to scope your variables with the appropriate collection, such as *$HTTP_POST_VARS* for *post* (form) variables and *$HTTP_GET_VARS* for *get* (form or query string) variables.

PHP variables do have a scope in reference to the page, however:

- Variables used at the page level have a global scope.
- Variables used inside a function are local to the function.
- Variables declared as global inside a function are global to the page.

What this means is that you can have a page-level variable named *$username*, but if you use a variable named *$username* inside of a function, it is a completely different variable.

Accessing Variables by Reference

Low-level languages like C++ allow you to access variables by reference rather than passing or assigning the entire variable. This can speed up programs dramatically when large variables are being passed through functions or assignments, because the variable itself is not moved—only a pointer to that variable is addressed.

You can access a variable by reference by appending an ampersand to the variable:

- **$myvariable**   Standard way to address a variable
- **&$myvariable**   Accessing the variable by reference

When you assign a variable by reference, any changes made to one variable will be made to the other. This is because they both address the same memory space. Assigning a variable by reference is in essence giving an alias to the original variable, because they now both refer to the same area of memory. Take a look at the following:

```php
<?php
$a = "Jake";
$b = &$a;
$a .= " Jehosephat";
?>
```

After running this script, both *$a* and *$b* contain the value "Jake Jehosephat", because they both address the same memory space—the same variable.

Data Types

Variables and data are very loosely typed in PHP, unlike Java. PHP has several variable types, however:

- **integer**   Whole number types (or *int* in PHP 4.2 and above)
- **double**   Real number types (deprecated in PHP 4.2)
- **string**   Strings of characters
- **array**   Multiple elements of any type
- **object**   Store an instance of a class
- **float**   Real number types (PHP 4.2 and above)
- **null**   No value (PHP 4.08 and above)
- **boolean**   True or false value (or *bool* in PHP 4.2 and above)

Being loosely typed has its advantages and disadvantages. You can explicitly set a variable to be a certain type, but there is implicit type conversion while your code is being executed. Because of this, you can easily introduce errors by not being consistent with your variables. Several built-in functions help you determine the types of variables, such as *is_integer*, *is_string*, *is_array*, *is_object*, and *is_double*, among others.

You can explicitly set a type of variable with the following:

```php
$myVar = "18 Legendary Weapons of China";
settype($myVar, "integer");
```

After setting *$myVar* to an integer, the value of *$myVar* becomes 18. A *gettype()* function is available, but we recommend that you use some of the built-in functions that determine type instead (such as *is_integer* or *is_string*):

```
if(is_integer($myVar)) {
    echo "The variable is an integer";
}
```

Strings are treated uniquely in PHP. You can use either single or double quotes around a string when you define it, but the way that the data within the quotes is handled is different. If you use single quotes, the value inside of them is treated literally, whereas if you use double quotes, any variable contained within them will be expanded. For example, this expression

```
$firstname = 'Tom';
$myVar = "Hello $firstname";
```

would result in the variable *$myVar* containing "Hello Tom".

Arrays are available in PHP and are very flexible. You can use indexing, such as *$myArray[1]*, or you can create associative arrays, such as *$myArray["color"]*. Arrays can also be multidimensional, using a combination of associative and indexed arrays, such as *$help_docs["php"][1]*.

Although arrays can be indexed or associative, if you have an array like $myArray[0] *and* $myArray[1], *then create* $myArray[4], *PHP will not create* $myArray[2] *and* $myArray[3] *as empty elements. You may think you have an indexed array with five elements, but instead you have an associative array with three elements. Basically, when you think you are using indexed arrays, your array is just using associative arrays masquerading as indexed because their keys are numbers. This may lead to weird bugs in your code.*

Request Variables

Form and query string variables are indistinguishable from other variables on your page. They are referenced just like local variables or page-level variables. For example, if you had two form elements named *Username* and *Password* on your page, you can use the contents of these form variables on your next page, assuming that the user has submitted the form. Use them just like a regular variable, without any prefix or special mode of addressing the variables:

```
<?php
echo "Your username is $Username and your password is $Password";
?>
```

This is the easiest way to use your request variables, but it can also be confusing on a complicated page. If you use this method, give your form variables a unique naming convention that distinguishes them from other variable types. For example, you could name your text field with a *txt_* prefix, and your check boxes with *chk_* prefixes. This way you can keep track of the different variables in your script, as in this example:

```php
<?php
session_register("sess_username");
$sess_username = $txt_username;
?>
```

In the example above, we set a session variable equal to an incoming form element. Obviously, there can be many instances of a *$username* variable on the page, so if your naming convention keeps the variable types clear, your scripts will be easier to read. This technique will work only if *register_globals* is set to "on" in your PHP.ini file.

Caution *Be aware of some security concerns with having the* register_globals *switch set to "on" in your PHP.ini file. A malicious user could conceivably pass a query string variable to your page and overwrite a session variable, thereby defeating the purpose of any authentication code.*

You can access these variables another way, though. You can access these variables as members of their respective collections. Form and query string variables are stored in two arrays: *HTTP_POST_VARS* and *HTTP_GET_VARS*. You can access those same two form elements like this:

```php
<?php
echo "Your username is $HTTP_POST_VARS["Username"] and your password is
$HTTP_POST_VARS["Password"];
?>
```

This method may seem a bit cumbersome, but in actuality it executes more quickly, and it's easier to understand the code. There is no doubt in this example that the two variables are form elements. Also, beginning with PHP 4.1.0, the short style of referencing these variables is deprecated, meaning it might not be available at some time in the future.

Using that same technique, you can retrieve the query string variables as well:

```php
<?php
echo "You are viewing page $HTTP_GET_VARS["pagenumber"] of
$HTTP_GET_VARS["totalpages"];
?>
```

PHP Cookies

Cookies are the little text files that the browser stores on the computer to allow a Web site to keep track of a user's preferences or other data from visit to visit. Cookies also make it possible to track user sessions and enable application state in an otherwise stateless Web. A cookie variable is stored as a name/value pair on the user's computer, along with an expiration date.

Many users turn cookies off, so using a cookie variable should not be considered a fail-safe method of storing and retrieving information. You can, however, still utilize cookies as a time saver for many types of functionality where the information is not critical, such as "remembering" a user's settings when they return to your page.

In PHP, you can utilize cookies by using some built-in functions. You set a cookie like this:

```php
<?php setcookie("firstname",$HTTP_POST_VARS['firstname'],
 time() + 60*60*24*30);?>
```

The first three arguments of the *setcookie* function are used here: the name of the cookie variable, the value (set to a form element named *firstname* here), and the time in seconds (set to 60 seconds * 60 minutes * 24 hours * 30 days, or 1 month).

The cookie has to be set before any headers are sent to the browser. Also, a cookie that is set on a page will not be available to any server-side scripts on that page—it will only be usable upon each succeeding page visit.

To read the cookie value, you can use one of the following to display it to the page:

```php
<?php echo $firstname;?>
```

or

```php
<?php echo HTTP_COOKIE_VARS["firstname"];?>
```

Cookies are tied closely to sessions, which are described next.

PHP Sessions

As mentioned previously, the Web is a stateless protocol. The Web server sees each visit from a browser as a completely new visit. That's where application servers come in; most of the application servers contain functionality to manage a session for each unique user. Sessions were covered in Chapter 15. You should read that chapter as a general introduction to Web applications, because all of the server platforms have session management of one type or another.

Session information is typically stored in a folder that is specified in the PHP.ini file:

```
session.save_path= e:\PHP\sessiondata
```

This directory should always be outside of your site root so that the session information is safe from other users inside your site.

Caution   *Sometimes PHP.ini files inside distributions for Windows still have Unix-like path information for sessions. Of course, PHP is then unable to set the sessions. To prevent errors, check the path inside the PHP.ini to make sure that the path is correct for your server.*

In PHP, you can start the session in several ways. If you want session management enabled and started by default, you can put this line in your PHP.ini file:

```
session.auto_start=1
```

If you have this line in the file, sessions are started automatically the first time the user hits a page regardless of whether you use session variables. Ordinarily, you would want this set to 0 so that you can control when to start the session.

To start a session manually in your PHP page, use this line:

```
<?php session_start();?>
```

Sessions are useful to keep track of information from page to page, such as a user's userid number or username. To use a session variable in PHP, you have to first register the variable as a session variable, with the following line:

```
session_register("username");
```

Notice that you don't use the $ prefix when you register the session variable, but you need to use the prefix when you use the variable, as in this example, which sets the session variable named *username* to the value of the incoming form element named *username*:

```
$username = $HTTP_POST_VARS['txt_username'];
```

You can also register multiple session variables at once by using comma delimiters:

```
session_register("username","firstname","order_number");
```

You can check session variables for their existence by using one of PHP's built-in functions: *session_is_registered*:

```
if(! session_is_registered("username") {
    header("Location: login.php");
}
```

Just as you can register a session variable, you can unregister it just as easily while still maintaining the session by using the *session_unregister* function:

```
session_unregister("order_number");
```

To completely kill a session and remove all session variables, use this function:

```
session_destroy();
```

Sessions rely on cookies to work, and as such they are not entirely fail-safe, just as cookies are not fail-safe. For that reason, PHP also maintains the session ID in a global constant named *SID* for the user, which you can add to a URL whenever a user changes pages. The typical way to do this is to first check whether the user has cookies enabled, and add it to the URL if the user has cookies disabled. The *SID* constant contains a name/value pair of *PHPSESSID=[session number]* so that it can be added to the URL easily, as in the following example:

```
<?php
if(isset($_COOKIE["PHPSESSID"])) {
    echo "Cookies enabled";
}else{
    echo "Cookies not enabled";
    $myUrl .= "?".SID;
}
?>
```

After executing this code, if the value of *$myUrl* was "home.php", the value would be something like "home.php?PHPSESSID=5ce7d8f9786bdda3b19a7a1088b64c35" if the user had cookies turned off.

New Methods of Referencing Variables

Beginning with PHP 4.1.0, there is a new method for referencing the variable collections:

- *$_GET*
- *$_POST*
- *$_COOKIE*

- *$_SERVER*
- *$_ENV*
- *$_REQUEST*
- *$_SESSION*

In a push to convince programmers to stop using the short method of referencing variables (such as a form element named *$username*), the makers of PHP created these new variable collections, which are much easier to use than the old methods (as in *$HTTP_GET_VARS*). These variables are global in scope. Also, using this new method for referencing session variables actually registers the session variable for you as if you'd called *session_register("variablename")*. To create a session variable using this method, simply use the following:

```
$_SESSION["variablename"] = "tom";
```

Expressions

PHP is an expression-based language, like Java. PHP expressions represent computations, declarations, and flow of control. The simplest of PHP expressions is a variable declaration, as in the following:

```
$i = 0;
```

A more complicated expression would be a computation, which can use any of the PHP operators listed in Table 18-1.

Operator	Type	Function
+	Arithmetic	Add
−	Arithmetic	Subtract
*	Arithmetic	Multiply
/	Arithmetic	Divide
%	Arithmetic	Modulus
.	String	Concatenation
=	Assignment	Set equal to

Table 18-1. *Operators in PHP*

Operator	Type	Function
!	Logical	NOT
&&	Logical	AND
||	Logical	OR
and	Logical	AND with lower precedence
or	Logical	OR with lower precedence
<	Relational	Less than
>	Relational	Greater than
<=	Relational	Less than or equal to
>=	Relational	Greater than or equal to
==	Relational	Equal to
!=	Relational	Not equal to
===	Relational	Identical
+=,−=, *=, /=,%=,.=	Compound assignment	Uses the right-hand expression double-duty as the first operand

Table 18-1.   *Operators in PHP* (continued)

The following statements are examples of legal expressions in PHP:

```
$a = 1 + 2;
$total += $subtotal;
$firstname = 'Tom';
$fullname = "$firstname Muck";
```

Strings can also be operated on with a dot character (.), which concatenates the variables, as in this example:

```
<%
$myFirst = "Fred";
$myLast = "Periwinkle";
$myName = $myFirst.' '.$myLast;
```

```
echo $myName;//the result would be "Fred Periwinkle"
//could also have been written as:
$myName = "$myFirst $myLast";
%>
```

Strings also allow the use of compound concatenation, as in this example:

```
theCode .= "\n";  //add a line feed to the end of the code
```

 The preceding example uses double quotes so that the line feed character is translated into a line feed. If you were to put single quotes around this, the literal backslash and "n" characters would have been output to the page.

Control Structures in PHP

PHP uses control structures that are similar to C or JavaScript. The most common control structure would have to be the *if/else* structure, but others may be more suitable for certain tasks. The basic structures are outlined next. Note that some of the control structures evaluate an expression inside a set of parentheses that returns a Boolean value of true or false, and then act upon the result of the value.

if/else

Just as in Java or JavaScript, the *if* expression in PHP requires that the following statement be enclosed in parentheses. The expression inside the parentheses is evaluated to true or false, and the statement following the expression is executed on the event of a true expression:

```
<?php
if ($username == "Jim") {
  echo "Hello, Jim";
}else{
  echo "Hello";
}
?>
```

switch/case

The *switch/case* construct is also similar to Java or JavaScript; the expression in the *switch* statement is evaluated and the result is then used for comparisons in the *case* statements. The *switch/case* statement allows the code to "fall through" the statements, so a *break* statement is necessary inside of each *case* statement if you don't want the other *case* statements compared.

```php
<?php
switch ($whichPage) {
    case 1:
        header("Location: page1.php");
        break;
    case 2:
        header("Location: page2.php");
        break;
    default: header("Location: home.php");
}
?>
```

The Ternary Operator

The ternary operator is a shorthand version of *if/else*. The construct has three parts: an expression (which evaluates to true or false), a statement that is executed if the expression is true, and a statement that is executed if the expression is false. The entire operation can be expressed as *expression* **?** *statement1* **:** *statement2*, as in the following:

```php
<?php
echo($userid != "")?"Goodbye":"Welcome";
?>
//The statement above could have been //written as:
<?php if($userid != "") {
    echo "Goodbye";
}else{
    echo "Welcome";
}
?>
```

Looping Construct Using *for*

The *for* loop takes on three optional expressions, just like Java and JavaScript. The first expression usually declares the variable and sets it up for the loop. The second expression is the decision maker: Should the loop continue or stop? The third expression is usually a counter or a mathematical expression that moves the loop along:

```php
<?php
for($i=0; $i < 10; $i++) {
    echo "<tr><td>myArray[$i]</td></tr>\n";
    }
?>
```

Because the expressions are all optional, creating an endless loop is possible by leaving all three expressions out:

```
for (;;) {
    // execute some code in an endless loop, until
    break;
}
```

while Statements

The *while* loop is very handy for creating loops when you need to wait for a certain condition to be met, such as reaching the last record in a resultset or waiting for a variable to reach a certain value:

```php
<?php
while ($i < 10) {
    $spaceString .= ' ';
    $i++;
    }
?>
```

do/while Statements

A *do/while* statement is almost the same as a *while* loop, except for one minor thing: The code within the loop is always executed once, whereas in a *while* loop the code won't be executed if the condition is met before the loop is reached:

```php
<?php
do {
?>
    <tr>
        <td><?php echo $row_Recordset1['SeekLastName']; ?></td>
        <td><?php echo $row_Recordset1['SeekFirstName']; ?></td>
    </tr>
<?php
} while ($row_Recordset1 = mysql_fetch_assoc($Recordset1));
?>
```

foreach() Statements

The *foreach* construct is used with arrays. It will allow you to loop through the array and assign a key and a value so that you can work on the individual elements of the array. For example, to loop through and display all of the cookies that have been set, you could use this:

```
<?php
foreach($HTTP_COOKIE_VARS as $key => $value) {
    echo "Cookie name: $key.<br>";
    echo "Value of element: $value.<br>";
}
?>
```

The *foreach* construct is crucial due to the way PHP uses associative arrays. You may use a *for* loop on an array and be in for some nasty surprises if elements are missing in the array, but a *foreach* loop is a 100 percent safe solution.

Built-In Functions in PHP

PHP has a vast number of available built-in functions, and the number is ever increasing as new versions of the server come out. PHP v 4.1.*x* has over 2,500 functions available. You can find a current list of functions at www.php.net/quickref.php. Some of the functions that you may see inside of Dreamweaver MX's generated code, as well as some other general-purpose functions, are shown here.

array_unique(array)

If you pass an array to this function, you can eliminate all duplicates from the array. This function is handy for programmatically building select boxes, among other things.

checkdate(month, day, year)

Checks whether the date is valid or not, given the month, day, and year. The month value can be 1 through 12, and the day value has to be a valid day in that month. Years are valid from 1 to 32767.

Chr(ascii code)

This function returns the ASCII character specified, such as a carriage return for *Chr(13)*.

date(format,[timestamp])

The date function allows you to format a date timestamp (or current timestamp if the second parameter is not given) using a format that you selected. For example, if you want to display a date in the format of "Mar 22, 2002", you can use the function like this:

```
<?php echo "Today is ".date("M j, Y"); ?>
```

In that example, "M" references a three-letter month abbreviation, "j" is a day of month with no leading zeros, and "Y" is a four-digit year. For a complete listing of the date formats available, check the PHP Web site.

die(message)

This function causes the page execution to cease, but also passes a message to the page. It is used frequently as an error-handler, as in the following:

```
$connBettergig = mysql_pconnect("localhost", "Bettergig", "bettergig")
    or die("There was an error connecting to Bettergig");
```

This type of statement works because of *short-circuit evaluation*. The theory behind this is if the first statement before the *OR* operator is executed successfully, the second statement will never be executed. If the first statement fails, because there is an *OR* operator, the PHP application server will attempt to execute the second statement, which is the error handler.

each(array)

This function deserves a bit of explanation, because it is very useful for traversing through request elements or other arrays. The *each()* function returns the key/value (or name/value) pairs that are associated in an array, and it is frequently used with the *list()* function in that scenario. For example, if your form has two form elements named *txt_username* and *txt_password*, you could call the *each* function like this on the page that the form is posted to:

```php
<?php
while(list($key,$val) = each($HTTP_POST_VARS)) {
    echo "Form element: $key is $val<br>";
}
?>
```

The code would print the names and values of the form elements on the page, including the submit button:

```
Form element: txt_username is Tom
Form element: txt_password is mypassword
Form element: Submit is Submit
```

empty(variable)

This function determines if the variable contains a value other than 0 or an empty string.

exit()

Quits execution of the page at that point.

explode(delimiter, string)

This function returns an array that consists of the string split by the delimiter. For example, if your string contains a list of names, you can split the names into an array by using the *explode* function:

```php
<?php
$mystring = "Tom,Ray,Massimo";
$myarray = explode(",",$mystring);
?>
```

The function *split()* performs similar functionality, only it allows the use of regular expressions for the delimiter. If you are using simple string delimiters, always use the *explode* function to avoid the overhead of the regular expression engine.

file(filename)

This is a rather useful function: it reads a file (or Web page from a URL) into an array, with the line breaks of the file as delimiters that split the file into the array. Once the file is in the array, you can use array techniques to access the parts of the file. This is useful for parsing CSV files, Web pages, or log files.

getdate(timestamp)

This function is great for turning a timestamp into a useful array of its component parts. The function returns an associative array of seconds, minutes, hours, mday (day of month), wday (day of week), mon (numeric month), year (numeric year), yday (day of the year), weekday (full text of day of week), month (full text of month).

implode(delimiter, array)

As you can imagine, *implode* is the opposite of *explode*. If you have an array that you want to turn into a delimited string, use *implode*. Using the earlier *explode* example, this turns the array back into a string:

```php
$mystring = implode(",",$myarray);
```

The function *join()* performs the same functionality.

in_array(value, array)

Searches an array for a specific value and returns true if the value is found in the array.

intval(number)

Intval returns the integer part of a number.

isset(variable)

This function tests a variable to see if it has already been defined in order to avoid potential errors. In PHP, depending upon the *error_reporting* setting inside of the PHP.ini file, you can't always use a variable that isn't defined yet. A common programming practice is to use *isset($myVar)* to return a true/false value.

ltrim(string), rtrim(string), and trim(string)

These functions trim the whitespace from a string from the left, right, and both sides, respectively.

nl2br(string)

One of the most often used functions when returning data from a database, this function inserts a `<br>` tag before every new line character (ASCII 10, or \n) so that the text retains its formatting in a Web browser.

rawurlencode(string)

This function encodes a string into a URL-friendly version with special characters replaced by their hexadecimal equivalents, such as %20 for a space, and %40 for an "@" character. You can decode the string with the *rawurldecode()* function.

similar_text(string1, string2, percent)

This function is handy for search pages, because it gives you a percentage value on how close the match to a string is. For example, look at the following string:

```
$string1 = "Dreamweaver MX: The Complete Reference, by Ray West and Tom Muck";
```

The following strings produce the percentages shown:

String	Percentage
West Muck Dreamweaver Complete Reference	57.692307692308%
West Muck Dreamweaver	25.882352941176%
West Muck	24.657534246575%
Complete Reference	43.90243902439%

Pass the third parameter by reference (using *&$variablename*). After calling the function, the variable will contain the percentage value.

size_of(array)

Counts the number of elements in the array and returns an integer.

sort(array [,sort_flags])

Sorts in place the elements in an array. If you use the optional second parameter, you can specify one of the following sort types:

- *SORT_REGULAR*   Compare the items normally
- *SORT_NUMERIC*   Compare the items as numbers
- *SORT_STRING*   Compare the items as strings

Many other sort functions work with arrays as well, such as *rsort()* for sorting in descending order, and *multi_sort()* for sorting multiple-dimension arrays.

split(pattern, string [, limit])

The *split()* function is similar to the *explode* function—it splits a string into an array. The difference is that with the *split* function you can use multiple delimiter characters or patterns through the use of a *regular expression* pattern. Consult www.php.net for information on regular expressions.

stristr(string, string to find) and strstr(string, string to find)

These functions find a string within another string and give you a substring consisting of all characters from the first occurrence of the match to the end of the string. If no match occurs, the function returns false. The *strstr()* function is case-sensitive, whereas the *stristr()* function is case-insensitive.

strip_tags(string [,string of allowable tags])

As the name states, this function strips out all tags, HTML or other, from a given string. This is useful for accepting form input from users and stripping away any HTML put in the form field.

strlen(string)

strlen() simply returns the integer length of a given string.

strpos(string, string to look for)

This function finds the position of a given substring within a larger string and returns an integer position of that substring.

strtolower(string)

This function converts a string to lowercase.

strtoupper(string)

The opposite of *strtolower()*, this function converts a string to all uppercase.

str_replace(string from, string to, string)

This is a very useful function for many applications where you might want to highlight or apply some HTML styling to a given string. What it does is allow you to replace all occurrences of a specific series of characters to another series of characters. For example, look at the following:

```php
<?php
$searchstring = "php";
$myfield = "PHP has become one of the most prevalent technologies on
the Web. PHP version 4.2.0 was recently released, and includes many
new features not available in PHP 4.1.x.";
$myfield = str_replace($searchstring,"<strong>$searchstring</strong>",
$myfield);
echo $myfield;
?>
```

After running this code, the following would be seen in the browser:

> "**PHP** has become one of the most prevalent technologies on the Web. **PHP** version 4.2.0 was recently released, and includes many new features not available in **PHP** 4.1.x."

str_pad(string, pad length [, pad string] [, pad type])

This function allows you to pad your strings with spaces or other characters. The first parameter is the string you want to pad, and the second parameter is the length that you want the string to be *after* the padding is applied. The padding character is assumed to be a space, unless you specify a third parameter. The fourth parameter is the type of pad that you want to apply. This can be any of the following constants:

- *STR_PAD_RIGHT*
- *STR_PAD_LEFT*
- *STR_PAD_BOTH*

The default is to pad on the right.

substr(string, start [, length])

This function returns the portion of the string that you specify with a *start* parameter and an optional *length* parameter. If you don't specify the length, the function returns the portion from the start to the end of the string.

substr_count(string, substring)

This function simply counts how many times a substring appears inside of a string and returns an integer.

unset(variable1, variable2, etc)

Essentially the opposite of setting a variable, this function destroys the variable and its contents. If used inside a function, however, it may not work as you would expect. Only the local copy of the variable inside of the function is destroyed.

wordwrap(string [,width] [,break] [,cut])

This function is useful for formatting e-mail, among other things. It breaks up a long string with line breaks after 75 characters, unless you specify a width. You can also specify another character other than a line break, specified in the third parameter. The *cut* parameter, if set to 1, causes the break to occur in the middle of a word if the word goes past the assigned width.

User-Defined Functions

PHP allows you to declare functions on your page, similarly to JavaScript or Java. You declare a function with the *function* keyword and the name of the function, followed by the list of incoming parameters (if any) inside of parentheses, followed by your function body inside of curly braces:

```
function makeSearchWordsBold($string, $word) {
    $temp = str_replace($word,"<strong>$word</strong>",$string);
    return $temp;
}
```

After declaring the function, you can use it within your code in the same way that you would use any of the built-in functions.

Sending E-Mail with PHP

Sending e-mail is one of the most often-used features in a Web application. You can use this feature to allow users the ability to retrieve lost passwords, send a page to their friends, send greeting cards, or confirm orders in an e-commerce site. PHP has a built-in function that allows you to easily send e-mail from your Web application. The function ties into the sendmail shell command in Linux, or an SMTP mail server in Windows.

Windows users can configure CDONTS as their SMTP mail server. Information on how to set up CDONTS is in Chapter 16.

The function is in the basic format of

```
mail(to, subject, message [, headers])
```

The *to* field is required and is the recipient of the message. This field can also contain a comma-separated list of recipients. The *subject* field is required as well, and is the subject of the e-mail message. The *message* is specified in the third required parameter. The fourth parameter is optional and gives you the opportunity to specify other headers, such as reply-to, from, or content-type (to make attachments.) You must separate the headers specified by a new line character (\n).

This function is primarily used with variables that have been set up beforehand:

```php
<?php
$to = $HTTP_GET_VARS["txt_tofield"];
 // set the to field from an incoming form field
$subject = "Your order confirmation number is: ";
$subject .= $HTTP_SESSION_VARS["order_number"];
$message = "Thank you for your order";
$from = "From: Tom <tom@myserver.com>";
$replyto = "reply-to: administrator@192.168.0.4";
$header = $from; // set the from field in the header
$header .= "\n"; // add a line feed
$header .= $replyto; // add the reply-to header to the header
mail($to, $subject, $message, $header); // send the e-mail
?>
```

Using PHP with MySQL

PHP has a rich tradition of being utilized with the MySQL database server. MySQL has been criticized for not being a true relational database management system. It doesn't have such things as referential integrity that a true RDBMS has. Still, MySQL is very popular and is in fact the most popular database for PHP. It is lightning fast for simple data display.

Dreamweaver MX is configured to work seamlessly with MySQL. All of the generated code that Dreamweaver MX produces uses PHP's built-in MySQL functions. In fact, Dreamweaver MX by default will work only with the MySQL database. This was done to minimize the complexity of building compatibility for PHP into Dreamweaver, but also because the vast majority of PHP Web sites utilize MySQL databases.

MySQL is freely available for most operating systems, including Windows, Linux, and Mac OS X. The product is covered by the GNU license, like PHP. It has a command-line interface, but many third-party programs are available that make the database administration a little easier for the Windows user who is less comfortable in a command-line environment than a point-and-click environment.

After installing MySQL, you need to do a few things:

- Add a password to the root user
- Delete the anonymous user
- Start the service and make sure it's set up to run automatically
- Create a database

Throughout this book, we refer to the Bettergig.com Web site and the Bettergig database. To create the Bettergig database in MySQL, issue a *create database* statement from the command prompt:

```
mysql>create database Bettergig;
```

After doing this, you can run the script file from the Osborne Web site (www.osborne.com) to create your tables and populate the tables with the sample data. You can either copy the file to the bin directory, or simply use the path to the file from the command line, and issue an execute file statement (\.):

```
mysql>\.createbettergigmysql.sql
```

To view the tables in the database, type the following statements into your command prompt:

```
mysql>use Bettergig;
mysql>show tables;
```

After doing that, you can view the properties of any of your tables by using the following statement:

```
mysql>describe categories;
```

This will give you the properties for the Categories table, including the field name and type, whether the column is nullable, whether it's a primary key or not, the default value (if any), and any extra information, such as an *auto_increment* field:

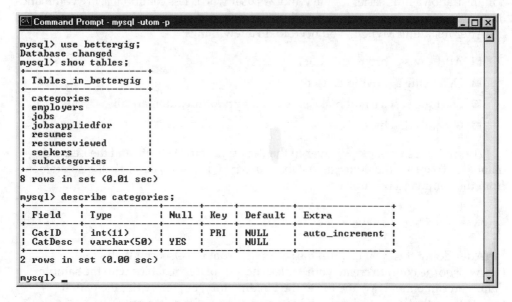

```
mysql> use bettergig;
Database changed
mysql> show tables;
+---------------------+
| Tables_in_bettergig |
+---------------------+
| categories          |
| employers           |
| jobs                |
| jobsappliedfor      |
| resumes             |
| resumesviewed       |
| seekers             |
| subcategories       |
+---------------------+
8 rows in set (0.01 sec)

mysql> describe categories;
+---------+-------------+------+-----+---------+----------------+
| Field   | Type        | Null | Key | Default | Extra          |
+---------+-------------+------+-----+---------+----------------+
| CatID   | int(11)     |      | PRI | NULL    | auto_increment |
| CatDesc | varchar(50) | YES  |     | NULL    |                |
+---------+-------------+------+-----+---------+----------------+
2 rows in set (0.00 sec)

mysql>
```

MySQL has a privilege system that you'll have to learn in order to work with the database. Essentially, all users can have specific privileges on the databases, tables, columns, and SQL statements. You should never use the root user, or an administrative user for your Web application. You should always set up a specific user for each Web application that has permission granted only for the functionality of the database that the Web application is going to use. For example, your Web application would probably never need the *CREATE* statement for databases or tables, so you would be wise not to allow it. Also, you might not need the *DELETE* statement for your Web application. If not, don't allow the user to have *DELETE* privileges. If your Web application displays data only, grant only *SELECT* privileges on the tables needed.

To grant privilege to a user, you can type the following into a command line (from your MySQL prompt):

```
mysql> grant select, insert, update, delete
->on bettergig.*
->to myuser identified by 'myuserpassword';
```

After doing this, you should be able to create a database connection in Dreamweaver MX. Database connections are covered in Chapter 20.

Although you may be able to see all of the available databases in Dreamweaver MX, you will be able to work only with the databases for which you have specifically set up privileges.

You can also use a third-party utility to administer a MySQL database. Some popular utilities are available from www.urbanresearch.com/software/utils/urbsql, dbtools.vila.bol.com.br, and phpmyadmin.sourceforge.net. These utilities provide a graphical user interface to make it easy to administer the database.

Using PHP with Dreamweaver MX

Dreamweaver MX supports ASP, JSP, ASP.Net, and ColdFusion out of the box using the same interface, in addition to PHP. If you have worked with Dreamweaver or UltraDev in any of these other languages, it's easy to transfer your knowledge to PHP development using the same tool. That is one of the major advantages of Dreamweaver MX—you have an almost limitless compatibility with most of the existing server technologies. Learning the development environment is often half the battle, and with Dreamweaver, you need only learn it once. The techniques you learn apply to all of the languages and technologies.

History of PHP in Dreamweaver

PHP has had a history with Dreamweaver and UltraDev, even though Dreamweaver MX is the first release that supports PHP out of the box. The extensibility mechanism of Dreamweaver and UltraDev enabled a group of enterprising programmers in Romania to deliver a complete server model for UltraDev as an extension that could be downloaded for free. The company is InterAKT and the extension was called PHAkt. With this server model extension, it was possible to build PHP applications using UltraDev using the exact same techniques that were available to the other server models.

PHAkt grew out of the php4ud project of Dan Radigan, who turned the project over to InterAKT. InterAKT completed the server model and released several updates to the extension. It is still available and is a good place to start if you are still working with UltraDev and haven't upgraded to Dreamweaver MX yet.

   InterAKT also has a commercial version of the PHP extension named ImpAKT that contains more refined code for greater speed and stability. The InterAKT extensions are available from www.interakt.ro.

What made PHAkt unique (and some consider even more versatile than the Dreamweaver MX implementation of PHP) is that it used a database abstraction layer called ADODB. ADODB solves one of the major problems of PHP: The language treats each database differently, and as a result, building an application that can easily migrate to another database server is very hard. With this abstraction layer in place, you can write code that works across many different database servers. Other database abstraction layers are available for PHP in addition to ADODB.

InterAKT continues to produce high-quality software and extensions for Dreamweaver MX that enhances the PHP ability of the program, including a new version of PHAkt for Dreamweaver MX.

With Dreamweaver MX, Macromedia has implemented its own version of a PHP 4 server model, allowing database connectivity to a MySQL database. With that limitation, however, comes the speed and compatibility of a rich history of PHP/MySQL applications. The Dreamweaver extensibility mechanism is even more open than it ever was to new server models. With the release of Dreamweaver MX, Macromedia has made it extremely easy to add new server models to the core functionality of the program. InterAKT has already implemented a new version of PHAkt, allowing Dreamweaver MX to be used with databases other than MySQL.

The following sections go through some of the key features of Dreamweaver MX that relate to the current PHP/MySQL implementation.

The Bindings Panel

The server-side functionality of Dreamweaver MX is in the Bindings, Databases, Components, and the Server Behavior panels. Bindings are so called because they "bind" the data on your page to a server-side construct, such as a recordset or a variable. The elements that reside on the Bindings panel are called *data sources*, and vary in complexity from the simple (sessions and requests) to the complex (recordsets).

The Recordset Data Source

Recordsets are the key element to the dynamic Web page—the back-end database gives the static HTML page dynamic content. To create a new recordset, you need to first define a connection to your MySQL database (connections are described in Chapter 20). The connection is placed into an include file, and the connection information is placed into variables that are then used on the page. A line like this in your page is the link to the connection file that Dreamweaver MX creates:

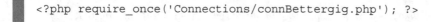

```php
<?php require_once('Connections/connBettergig.php'); ?>
```

After the connection exists, you can name your recordset and then write a SQL statement to retrieve data from the database. To define a basic SQL statement, you can use the Simple dialog box (shown in Figure 18-3) or the Advanced dialog box. With the Simple recordset dialog box, you can choose columns from one table, and choose to filter by a parameter. The Simple recordset dialog box is limited to one table, one parameter, and one sort column.

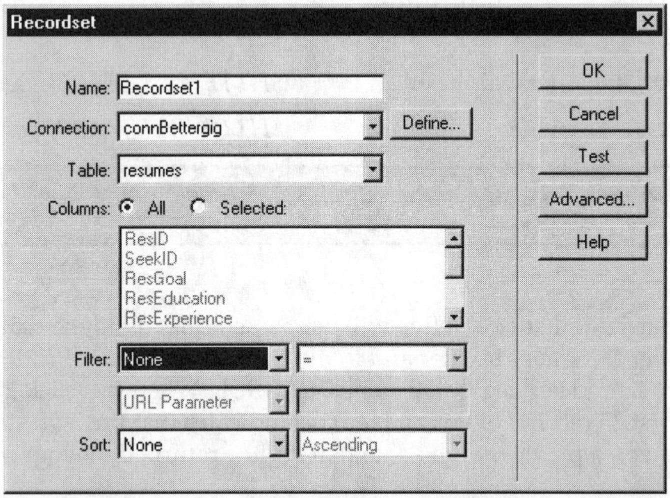

Figure 18-3. *The Simple recordset dialog box in Dreamweaver MX*

For most SQL statements, you'll probably want to stay with the Advanced dialog box, in which you can define variables and attach them to other data sources, such as request objects and session objects. You are also free to create more complex SQL statements that join multiple tables and use multiple parameters. A typical SQL statement might read like this:

```
SELECT UserID
FROM AdminUsers
WHERE Username = 'frmUsername'
AND Password = 'frmPassword'
```

The PHP implementation of Dreamweaver MX doesn't allow you to insert your parameters directly into the SQL statement, but instead gives you a box in which you can enter the variable names, default values, and run-time values that will substitute the variables in the SQL with the correct values. For example, in the preceding SQL statement, the two variables *frmUsername* and *frmPassword* have to be declared using values similar to those shown in Table 18-1. (See Table 18-2 for more.)

Note that the default value is a value that will be declared on the page as a default in the event there is no incoming value. In a testing situation, you might want to include a default value that is in your database so that you can see the data on the finished page; however, in a real-world situation, the default value should always be something that won't appear in your database, such as a special character or sequence of characters.

Name	Default Value	Run-Time Value
frmUsername	notavaliduser	*$HTTP_GET_VARS['username']*
frmPassword	none	*$HTTP_GET_VARS['password']*

Table 18-2.   *Setting variables in the Advanced recordset dialog box*

The SQL statement that you define will get passed directly to the database—both in the Dreamweaver MX query builder and in the deployed Web application. The syntax of the statement should be a legal statement for MySQL. When you click the test button, you'll see the first 25 records of your table. This indicates that the SQL statement is valid and gives you a preview of the data that will be returned by your recordset.

Other Data Source Variables

The PHP model in Dreamweaver has a few other data sources that you can easily use in your pages with the Bindings panel. Again, the advantage of declaring the variables in the Bindings panel is so that the variables will be available to other parts of Dreamweaver, such as recordsets or server behaviors. The data sources simply give you a place to store the names of the variables that you might use on your page. You simply insert a name for the variable, and it will show up on the Bindings panel. Once it's in the panel, you can drag it to the page, or use it in recordsets, form elements, property inspectors, or other constructs. Session variables that are set up in this way on one page will be available for use in the entire site.

The following data sources are available in the PHP model:

- Form variable
- URL variable
- Session variable
- Cookie variable
- Server variable
- Environment variable

The Server Behaviors Panel

Server Behaviors are the main server-side code generators of Dreamweaver MX. These Server Behaviors insert code into your documents to perform a variety of functions. Most of these functions are related to the display of the recordset on the page and the recordset paging. The use of Server Behaviors is covered in Chapters 24–27, but here's a brief introduction to some of these behaviors.

Repeat Region

The Repeat Region Server Behavior enables you to loop through a recordset with a simple point-and-click interface. The Repeat Region is inserted around your selection on the page, and uses a *do/while* loop to iterate through a recordset, like this:

```php
<?php
do {
?>
//your region
  <?php
} while ($row_Recordset1 = mysql_fetch_assoc($Recordset1));
?>
```

One of the advantages to using the Repeat Region rather than hand-coding is that it is a way to set up the Recordset Paging Server Behaviors. When you apply a Repeat Region to the page, variables interact with the behavior that allow interaction with the other Server Behaviors. Like the recordset Server Behavior, the Repeat Region has to be inserted for many of the other Server Behaviors to work with your code.

Hide/Show Region

This behavior allows you to hide or show a specific region on the page based on a specific condition that you can set up in the behavior. The available choices are to Hide/Show Selected Region:

- If Recordset is Empty
- If First Record
- If Last Record
- If Recordset Is Not Empty
- If Not First Record
- If Not Last Record

Recordset Paging

This is a group of Server Behaviors that interact with a recordset and a Repeat Region Server Behavior. They allow you to move to the First, Previous, Next, Last, and Specific records. A special server object exists that will insert the First, Previous, Next, and Last links into a table on your page as a bundled unit to save a few steps. The server objects are located on the Application tab of the Insert toolbar, and also in the Insert menu under Server Objects.

Dynamic Elements

The Bindings panel allows you to apply dynamic text items to the page, and also allows you to insert values into other objects, such as form objects. Another way to do this is to use the Dynamic Elements menu entry in the Server Behaviors panel and click one of the five items:

- **Dynamic Text** A text item, such as a recordset column or a session variable that's on the page

- **Dynamic List/Menu** A list/menu form element that gets its values from a data source

- **Dynamic Text Field** A text field form element that gets its value from a data source

- **Dynamic Check Box** A check box form element that gets its checked value based on a data source

- **Dynamic Radio Buttons** A set of radio buttons that get their values from a data source

PHP Objects

The Insert bar was covered earlier in the book, but this chapter on PHP wouldn't be complete without showing you the PHP objects that are available from the bar. Figure 18-4 shows the PHP bar.

These items will insert a generic code block in your page to give you a starting point to hand-code your own functionality.

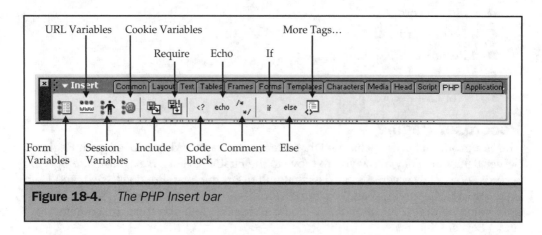

Figure 18-4.   *The PHP Insert bar*

Summary

This chapter was intended to provide a general introduction to PHP. PHP is a popular server because of its ease of use and because it's available as a free download for most of the popular server platforms. PHP is even pre-installed with Macintosh OS X, making it a perfect choice for someone who wants to build a dynamic Web application in an all-Mac environment. PHP is also probably the most popular server platform for Linux servers, and ties in well to the Apache Web server and MySQL database server on that platform.

Chapter 19

ASP.NET

Active Server Pages has been around for several years and is one of the most popular application servers there is. The large number of Windows servers means that ASP is available to the millions of people who use shared hosting. It is powerful and relatively simple to learn, and UltraDev has made it even easier to use. There is a large base of ASP programmers, all of whom should consider making a change.

Microsoft recently released its new .NET Framework. The .NET Framework is an expansive revision of the way that most of Microsoft's development tools work. In much the same way that Macromedia is streamlining and building integration into its MX product line, Microsoft is uniting its development tools within .NET. Visual Studio is now Visual Studio.NET. Visual Basic is now VB.NET. C++ is still around, but a brand new language called C# (C sharp) was created just for .NET.

There are still a large number of Windows servers, and the .NET Framework is still free to run on them. Luckily, .NET was solidified just in time for Macromedia to implement it in Dreamweaver MX, which makes it easier to use and provides a much needed design environment. But it is not as easy to learn.

.NET represents a significant shift in the way you must think about programming Web applications. Microsoft has learned well from its competitors and has implemented a wealth of new features. It is powerful, well supported, flexible and its object model is thorough and expansive. It may take some time to get your head around .NET, but it will be time well spent.

A recent trip to the bookstore reminded us just how difficult this chapter could be. There was a shelf with literally 30 brand new books, each at least 600 pages, all about .NET. The best we can hope to do is acquaint you with the concepts of .NET and teach you how to use Dreamweaver's implementation. We hope that is enough to get you started.

Moving from ASP

If you have not read Chapter 15 on ASP, we recommend you do so before reading this chapter. Some of the object models in ASP.NET are inherited from ASP, though it may work a little differently now. This chapter makes reference to these similarities, but does not try to cover them over again. A good understanding of ASP is helpful in grasping how the basics of ASP.NET work.

ASP, as it is typically used, is an inline scripting language. VBScript or Jscript is used within the HTML of your pages to insert dynamic data in the stream that becomes the browsed file. Even when used as it was originally intended, with COM doing a lot of the heavy lifting, a lot of intermingling still goes on in traditional ASP.

ASP.NET represents a paradigm shift in the way that your pages are constructed. You can still use its core languages (VB.NET and C#) in a messy inline scripting format, but the entire design of ASP.NET encourages you to do it differently. In ASP.NET, everything is an object all the way up to the page itself, which has its own properties and events. Although you may be used to the concept of events from client-side

JavaScript, you must now get used to the idea of server-side events, things that the user does on a page that trigger the firing of events back at the server.

Some things are the same, or are basically the same with a .NET twist. ASP has a global.asa file, ASP.NET has global.asax. *Response*, *Request*, *Application*, and *Session* objects are all present, and work essentially the same, though there are some stricter usage requirements. VBScript users should be able to get comfortable with VB.NET fairly quickly. In addition, DLLs are still around, but they are much easier to deploy and use, especially in a hosted environment.

But there are a bunch of new things that you need to become familiar with. Web controls, user controls, server-side events, the CLR, Web Services, and the Web.config file are just a few of the changes that await you inside ASP.NET.

First things first, though: let's get you set up to develop in and run ASP.NET by installing the .NET Framework.

The .NET Framework

The .NET Framework is the core set of services that are required for you to develop and run ASP.NET (and all other .NET) applications. It contains the Common Language Runtime (CLR) and class libraries, such as Windows Forms, ADO.NET, and ASP.NET, that allow applications from a variety of sources to run in an integrated fashion.

The .NET Framework runs on Windows NT 4 with Service Pack 6a, Windows 2000, and Windows XP, and it must be downloaded and installed from Microsoft. You can get a run-time version that will allow applications to run, but will likely need the 131MB SDK (software development kit) version if you plan to do any heavy-duty development that includes compiling DLLs.

The core of the framework is the CLR, which is the middleware that allows applications written in so many languages to work the same way. It is, in many ways, the Java Runtime Engine of the Microsoft world, except that it promises to run applications from a variety of sources on one platform instead of the other way around. For the time being, the CLR exists only for Windows-based servers, but projects are underway to replicate the CLR on Unix servers, meaning that C# and ASP.NET applications would run on those servers as well.

Note *It is an important point that the languages of .NET work so much alike. In fact, except for one small debugging flag that exists only in C#, VB.NET and C# have exactly the same functionality and produce exactly the same run-time code. This is an incredible boon for VB developers, whose functionality was always a bit behind that of C++ in the power department. You will find that VB.NET is more verbose than C#, but every bit as capable.*

Once you have downloaded the .NET Framework, you can install it on your server or development machine. It will hook right in with Internet Information Services 5 and allow the running of ASP.NET pages on your server. You can still run ASP pages the way that you always have. ASP.NET pages will have a .aspx extension, identifying them as such.

Let's get a couple of things out of the way early on. Two of the very significant parts of ASP.NET are Web Forms and Code-Behind. Web Forms are the HTML forms you can create in Visual Studio.NET, much like you would a regular Visual Basic application form. They generate HTML and a separate file of server-side code, called Code-Behind, that runs on a .NET server. Dreamweaver doesn't work this way and does not, in and of itself, take advantage of these methodologies. So, although they are important, we don't spend the little room we have talking about things that you will not see in Dreamweaver.

The installation of the .NET Framework is pretty intuitive. Once you have it installed, with a possible reboot, you should be ready to run ASP.NET pages on your computer. Next, let's look a little more closely at the differences in the ASP.NET programming model.

Differences Between ASP and ASP.NET

On the whole, a move to ASP.NET is a fundamental change in the way things work. That does not mean, however, that it is totally unrelated to the methods that you may be familiar with in traditional ASP. There are several things that we can compare that should help you get your head around the things that have changed and the reasons that they did so.

Structural Differences

There are some high-level structural differences in the way that ASP.NET operates. They are improvements to the overall structure of the platform that increase security, performance, and usability.

Interpreted vs. Compiled Code

The most obvious difference in ASP and ASP.NET pages, and the one that tells you what a particular site is using, is the page extension. ASP files use the .asp extension, and ASP.NET files use .aspx. But the difference is more substantial than the simple addition of a letter. Because both ASP and ASP.NET pages can run on the same server, this page extension signals exactly how a particular page will be processed.

ASP pages are interpreted at run-time. They contain scripting code that must be parsed out from HTML each time a page is called on the server. This is done by the asp.dll utility, which does not have much of a memory. If 10 people call a page, that DLL will parse the page independently for each of the 10 visitors like it was the first time it had seen the file. This builds an inherent lag into the delivery of your content, and although an ASP server is pretty quick about its work, there comes a time when this methodology will bog down a busy server.

ASP.NET compiles its pages into native code to improve performance. The first time a page is called, it is compiled to an intermediate language (IL), and then the compiler in the .NET Framework will compile that IL code into native code. This compiled page is then cached by the server and used each time the page is requested. The cached file remains available until you make changes to the page or the cache expires.

You don't have to do anything for this to happen; you don't even have to know that it is happening. The .NET Framework takes care of it for you and dramatically improves the performance of your site.

Namespaces

If you have ever done any traditional programming in Visual Basic or C, you are likely familiar with the concept of code libraries and references. Code libraries are organized chunks of functionality that you can use in your program when you need them. Because they are not always needed, however, it is more efficient to only include them when you need to use some of their features.

Although you can make use of DLLs that exist on a server to include additional functionality, like CDONTS or a file upload utility, ASP kind of is what it is. It does not give you access to much in the code library arena.

ASP.NET, on the other hand, contains a massive collection of objects that are arranged into namespaces. These namespaces are the way in which you include and reference functionality. For instance, HTML controls exist in the *System.Web.UI.HtmlControls* namespace, and server controls exist in the *System.Web.UI.WebControls* namespace.

You can find complete references to the classes in the .NET Framework using the .NET Framework class browser. You can access the class browser at this address: http://samples.gotdotnet.com/quickstart/aspplus/doc/classbrowser.aspx. Click the Run Example link to run the browser and explore the available classes.

 The class browser is expansive because the object model in the .NET Framework is expansive. Don't let that deter you. Most of what you will need is located in the System.Web namespaces. Get familiar with what is there and you will be a long way down the road.

Events

If you have done any HTML and JavaScript programming, you are familiar with events. Events, such as *onClick* and *onMouseOver*, are actions that can be responded to. They can be triggered by the user or by code, as in the *onError* events. They indicate that something has happened, and you can use that information to determine what direction the application should go in next.

ASP.NET extends the events that you are familiar with by creating server events. For instance, a button might have an *onClick* event, which when triggered displays an alert box or loads a URL. Now in ASP.NET, a button could have an *onServerClick* event indicating that action needs to be taken on the server. This button will exist within a form with the attribute *runat=server*. This indicates that the actions taken by the elements within the form require the form to be posted to the server so that its events can be handled. These elements that utilize the server for their functionality are called server controls.

Server Controls

Server controls have a lot in common with the HTML controls you are used to. They are ASP.NET versions of text boxes, drop-down menus, and buttons that you use to build forms on your pages. But server controls have a couple of differences.

Server controls run at the server. They do this for a couple of reasons. First, this enables them to call server-side functions rather than just browser functions. That means that you can trigger almost any kind of code through your form elements. Second, running at the server offers automatic state management, allowing the server to handle and forward form information as users progress through your application. Because of this, server controls will always have the *runat=server* attribute and will exist in a form with the same attribute.

XML

XML is an important part of the .NET Framework. Even the configuration of your .NET server is handled through an XML file called web.config. Although ASP Servers take much of their configuration from server-level settings, or page-level directives, the web.config file allows you to set your configurations specifically and separately for each application. Dreamweaver uses the web.config file to store connection settings to your databases.

Specific Differences

There are a few specific differences that we should look at. These involve the way in which pages are built and the way that you write code and interact with the HTML on your pages.

Method Calls

Method calls in ASP.NET must always be in parentheses. For instance, in ASP you could shortcut a *Response* call like this:

```
Response.Write Request("name")
```

In ASP.NET, you must include the parentheses for the *Response* object:

```
Response.Write(Request("name"))
```

Page Rendering

In ASP, you could mix your HTML and ASP code by switching in and out of ASP tags to create page rendering as follows:

```
<html>
<% If logged = 1 Then %>
Hello <%= Session("name") %>. Thanks for coming.
<%End If%>
</html>
```

In ASP.NET, you should separate code and content by using page events and web controls:

```
<%@ Page Language="VB" ContentType="text/html"
ResponseEncoding="iso-8859-1"%>script runat="server">
Sub Page_Load(Src As Object, E As EventArgs)
        test.Text = " Hello" & Session("name") & ". Thanks for coming."
End Sub
</script>
<html>
<head>
<title>Untitled Document</title>
<meta http-equiv="Content-Type" content="text/html;
charset=iso-8859-1">
</head>
<body>
<asp:label ID="test" runat="server"></asp:label>

</body>
</html>
```

Functions

In ASP, functions were defined within the <% %> tags of the page, indicating that they were server-side functions that ran on the back end of the site:

```
<%
Sub Add()
Response.Write(2 + 2)
```

```
End Sub

Add
%>
```

Because the page is an object in ASP.NET, functions are defined within script tags:

```
<script language="VB" runat=server>
Sub Add()
Response.Write( 2 + 2)
End Sub

</script>
<%
Add()
%>
```

Set

In ASP, when an object was created and set to a variable, the *Set* keyword was used:

```
Set objCDO = Server.CreateObject(CDONTS.NewMail)
```

The *Set* keyword is no longer required in ASP.NET:

```
objCDO = Server.CreateObject(CDONTS.NewMail)
```

Languages

You can no longer use more than one language on a page, like switching between VBScript and JScript. It was never a great idea in ASP anyway, but it is not allowed at all in ASP.NET.

File Extensions

ASP pages used the .asp file extension. In ASP.NET, you are liable to see one of three file extensions:

- **.aspx**   Normal ASP.NET files
- **.ascx**   ASP.NET user controls
- **.asmx**   ASP.NET Web Services

ASP.NET Concepts

In addition to those things that can be expressed as differences between ASP and ASP.NET, some concepts are brand new to the .NET Framework.

User Controls

We have talked a little about server controls. User controls are nothing more than server controls that are created by you, the user. User controls can be as simple as a bit of HTML, or as complex as the best code that you can write. They are stored with a namespace that you create and reference on your pages just like the inherent ASP.NET objects. This makes the class-based architecture of the .NET Framework quite extensible. You can create your own sets of reusable code and save them as ASCX files or compile them into DLLs.

Entire books are being written on user controls, and you certainly don't need to understand all about them to use ASP.NET with Dreamweaver MX. Locate a good reference when you are ready to move on in your .NET experience.

The BIN Directory

Each application has a BIN directory. It is literally a folder at the root of your Web site called /bin. The name refers to an abbreviation for *binary*, as a folder where the binary files were stored in CGI days, or to a bin where you throw stuff, depending on your perspective.

The BIN directory holds the supporting files that are used in your ASP.NET pages. User controls (ASCX files) and compiled DLLs are two things you will see here often. When using ASP.NET in Dreamweaver MX, a file called DreamweaverCtrls.dll contains functionality for Macromedia's .NET implementation. You must deploy this file for each .NET application that you do. We cover that later in the "Deploying Your Support Files" section.

The *PageLoad* Event

Actually, the *PageLoad* event is only one of a host of events that might be included in your application. But it does provide the opportunity to examine what happens in an ASP.NET page.

The *PageLoad* event is an event that fires any time the page loads into a browser. Within that event, you can place code and functions that perform any tasks that you want completed when a page is viewed. In contrast to an ASP page which runs from top to bottom, this event-driven model allows you to better organize your code.

In the *PageLoad* event, you might have code that creates connections, or sets up datasets, or populates arrays for use on the page. Using it and its related functions, you can precisely control when in the page-creation process certain things happen.

PostBack

PostBack is a methodology in ASP.NET that allows for its server event–driven functionality and also allows for much of the state management that is provided by .NET. PostBack is the act of posting a form back to the page on which it resides rather than posting it to a separate page. All forms with the *runat=server* attribute (forms that contain server controls) must post back to themselves.

Each time a page loads, a function called *isPostBack* evaluates to determine if this is the first time the page is loading, or if it is posting back to itself. You can utilize a conditional statement (*if isPostBack()*) to determine functionality that runs only if the form is being posted back, meaning that the server controls should now have information in them that has been evaluated. .NET handles all of this for you. It will know all by itself whether the page is loading for the first time or not. You just need to know how to respond to its answer.

Web Services

Web Services are XML-based applications that run in a distributed environment over the Internet. There are sites full of sample Web Services that do everything from adding numbers together to providing traffic and weather information. We do not have time to go into the creation of Web Services. Just know that Dreamweaver MX does provide a easy way to take advantage of available Web Services.

VB.NET or C#

Although there are several languages available to use in .NET, there are two primary ones that most developers are migrating to: VB.NET and C#. You can do basically the same things in these languages, but they do have some differences.

At a low level, the languages have some different features, for instance late-binding is built into VB.NET, although it can be achieved only through interoperability in C#. And VB.NET has not built in support for operator overloading. But those things are beyond the scope of most ASP.NET work. Let's look at the practical differences in three main areas of coding.

Conditionals

Conditionals are the places in your code where decisions must be made based on some criteria, such as the value of a variable or the status of a login. Conditionals are typically referred to as *If* statements: If a certain thing is true, do this; otherwise, do this.

VB.NET

If statement:

```
if a = b then
     'conditional code goes here
end if
```

Select statement:

```
Select case myVariable
    case 1:
          'code for case 1 goes here
    case 2:
          'code for case 2 goes here
end select
```

C#

If statement:

```
if (a == b){
     //conditional code goes here
}
```

Select statement:

```
Switch(myVariable){
    case 1:
         //case 1 code goes here
Break;
    case 2:
         //case 2 code goes here
}
```

Looping

Loops are sections of code that repeat based on some value or time period. For instance, if you wanted to send an e-mail to everyone in a dataset, you would loop through a section of code that sent an e-mail however many times it was necessary to send the e-mail to each record, advancing one record each time.

VB.NET
Do loop:

```
do while a < b
    'loop code here
loop
```

For loop:

```
for I as Integer = 0 to 10
    'loop code here
next
```

C#
Do loop:

```
do {
    //loop code here;
} while (a < b);
```

For loop:

```
for (Int32 I=0;I < 10;I++) {
    //loop code here;
}
```

Variables

Variables are the references that you use in code to hold values and objects while they are manipulated. They are created and referenced slightly differently in VB.NET and C#.

VB.NET

```
dim varName as string
```

C#

```
string varName;
```

These are just a few of the common differences in the major ASP.NET languages. These are likely the pieces that you will be using most often. The decision of which language to use is a personal one. Many people are more comfortable with the syntax and readability of VB, but C# is a more efficiently syntaxed language. You will likely find more examples done in VB, but it seems that most serious developers are moving towards C#.

Dreamweaver's .NET Implementation

We are beginning to see, with Dreamweaver MX, a divergence in the way that the included server models work. This is actually a good thing, because it allows Dreamweaver to take advantage of the strengths of newer models like ColdFusion MX and ASP.NET without being worried that each of the server models contains exactly the same functionality and works exactly the same.

This is especially true of the ASP.NET server model. ASP.NET works differently, and so does Dreamweaver's implementation of it. In fact, Dreamweaver's implementation works differently than most people would code ASP.NET. That is not necessarily a bad thing. Macromedia has taken advantage of the extensibility of the platform and created the DreamweaverCtrls.dll control we mentioned earlier to facilitate the development of ASP.NET in Dreamweaver. Here are a few things you need to know.

Deploying Your Support Files

Whenever you create an ASP.NET site in Dreamweaver, you need to deploy the DreamweaverCtrls.dll file from Macromedia so that your data binding will work correctly. Macromedia exposes the data layer through this DLL so that it will work with the Server Behaviors and objects that make up Dreamweaver.

From the Commands menu, select Deploy Support Files. A dialog box will ask you where your bin directory is. Point it to the root of your application, where a bin directory will be created. The support files will be deposited here.

You can find the DLL and its source, which you should become familiar with if you plan to do advanced development or extensions in .NET, in your configuration folder here:

X:\Program Files\Macromedia\Dreamweaver
MX\Configuration\ServerBehaviors\Shared\ASP.Net\Scripts

Interestingly, any files placed in this folder get deployed when you choose to deploy support files. This means that extension developers will be able to create .NET extensions based on user controls and have them automatically deployed by Dreamweaver. This opens up a tremendous opportunity for both the creators and users of extensions.

Data Binding

Data binding to the ASP.NET server controls can be a little tricky. For some of them, like the text box, you can simply drag a field from the DataSet in the Bindings Panel and the data will bind up. For others, like the Dropdown menu, you have to know what you are doing to get data into them, and it is a little cryptic. Let's look at the Dropdown menu.

Set up a .NET site in Dreamweaver and create a new page. Change to the ASP.NET tab of the Insert bar and select the Dropdown menu. The dialog box shown in Figure 19-1 will appear. You need to set an ID in the General category, but the category you are concerned with is Data.

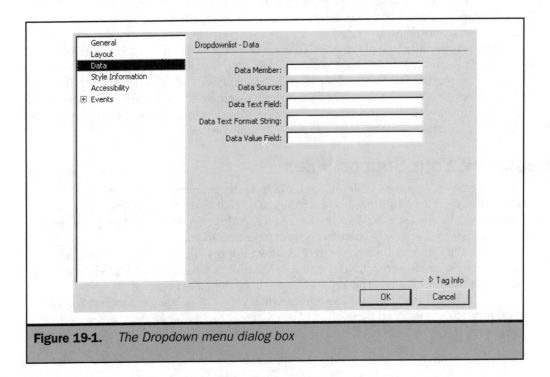

Figure 19-1. *The Dropdown menu dialog box*

Unlike other Dreamweaver objects, no help is available for filling in this information. There are no user interfaces for selecting connections or datasets or fields to populate the value and display of your drop-down box. There is not even a Help button to assist in the syntax that is expected here. By reading the source of the DreamweaverCtrls.dll, though, you can figure out what they are looking for.

Data Member is a .NET construct. It is necessary when you build complex datasets that can include multiple tables and relationships and indexes. For instance, you could have a dataset that contained a number of different tables. Data Member lets you enter the name of the table to which you are referring in these settings.

Data Source is the dataset in which your data resides. It is a dataset that you have already created in the Bindings panel. In the DataSource text box, type

```
<%# datasetname.theDS %>
```

<%# is the .NET data binding tag. *Datasetname* is the name you gave to your dataset. *TheDS* is a Macromedia property defined in the DreamweaverCtrls.dll file that binds the dataset to the object.

Data Text Field is the field in your dataset that contains the values you want displayed in the drop-down menu. It could be product names or people's names. It is the text that the user will pick from when using your application. Type the field name here.

Data Text Format String is the formatting you want applied to the display text. It is optional.

Data Value Field is the field in the recordset that holds the values that correspond to the text in the Data Text Field. For a product, it would be a product number. For a person, it might be an employee ID or some other identifying number.

Once you have completed this dialog box, your drop-down will bind to the dataset and work on your .NET server.

Summary

Perhaps more than anything else, you need to have a pretty good grasp of ASP.NET while using Dreamweaver to create an application. It can make development easier and provide great design-time tools that are not available anywhere else, but it is not as intuitive to use as the other server models. Unfortunately, it takes volumes of books to teach .NET, and we have only a limited space to allot. This information should get you started, though, as you make a transition to ASP.NET.

The
Complete
Reference

Dreamweaver
MX

Part IV

Adding Database Features to Your Site

Chapter 20

Making a Database Connection

Dreamweaver MX is designed to work with many configurations of server languages, Web servers, and databases. One of the primary reasons for choosing to use a dynamic Web authoring environment such as Dreamweaver MX is to connect your Web application to a database. There are indeed more ways to connect to a database than there are databases.

You can look at the database connection as the wire that connects your Web application to your database or database server. You have to know how to connect that wire and where to connect it. You can't just plug it in anywhere and expect it to work.

Dreamweaver MX is capable of connecting to your database in a variety of ways, depending on the configuration on your machine and on the server that you are deploying your site from.

History of Dreamweaver Connections

UltraDev 1 was the first Dreamweaver platform application that featured database connectivity. UltraDev 1 offered both design-time and run-time connections, so you could easily build a ColdFusion site, for instance, that depended on a ColdFusion connection, and not even have ColdFusion installed on your system. In the Macintosh version of UltraDev 1, all the design-time database connections were done through Java Database Connectivity (JDBC) on a remote Windows machine, connecting a JDBC:ODBC bridge to an ODBC connection. This created all sorts of problems for Mac users who couldn't find a host that would install the JDBC driver.

The connection interface changed considerably from version 1 to version 4 of UltraDev, and with Dreamweaver MX the connection methods have become even more diverse. UltraDev 4 was a breakthrough product for Mac users, who could connect to a database on the server in the same manner as a Windows user, using the HTTP interface.

Dreamweaver users have never had to worry about database connection through the program. With Dreamweaver MX, Macromedia has merged UltraDev with Dreamweaver making one big happy program. Web developers who are familiar with Dreamweaver but not UltraDev may not have dealt with database connections before.

The Database Panel

The connection is made from the Databases panel. This panel is new to Dreamweaver MX, and it offers a new way to view your databases. All connections are visible in this panel, and can be expanded to show the tables, views, and stored procedures in your database.

The database connections are defined as one of two options, depending on what server model you are using:

- Using a connection on the local machine
- Using a connection on the application server

You make a connection by clicking the plus sign (+) in the Databases panel. When you do this, a server model-specific dialog box will be invoked. This will allow you to implement a database connection using the method for that server model. In an ASP site, for example, you can choose to use a DSN or a connection string. In JSP, you have a choice of JDBC drivers. When you've chosen your method and filled in the required parameters, the database will appear in the Databases panel (see Figure 20-1). The tables, views, and stored procedures are expandable and will show the column name, data type, and special characteristics (such as primary key) for tables and views, and the parameters for stored procedures, along with the data type of the parameter and whether it's an input or output parameter.

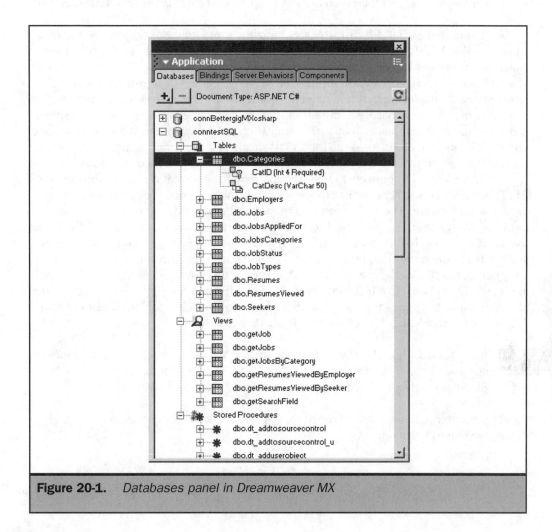

Figure 20-1.   *Databases panel in Dreamweaver MX*

The Connection

The connection information is saved in an include file that resides in the Connections folder of your site. By changing the connection information in this one file, all pages in your site that depend on the connection will reflect the changes. In the first version of UltraDev, the connection information was written to each individual page, making it more difficult to make a simple change in connection information.

Note *The new ColdFusion server model doesn't use a connection include file, but supports its use by allowing you to declare a variable to use as a data source. This is a very flexible strategy that leaves the decision to the developer as to how to implement the connection.*

As mentioned earlier, Macintosh users have the same methods for connecting to databases that Windows users can enjoy. All of the following sections apply to Macintosh machines as well as Windows machines. The only limitations for Macintosh users are that you have to connect to your application server to get the design-time database connections. Considering that you need an application server to be able to implement a data-driven site, this is hardly a limitation. This typically means setting up your site on a remote machine that has an available application server, such as a Windows machine for an ASP site or a Linux machine for a PHP site. If you are running the OSX operating system you can connect to a local PHP or JSP server running on the Macintosh.

Dreamweaver MX connects to your database on the application server through an HTTP request. This is very similar to what happens when a browser requests a page from the Web server. The server receives the request and sends the page back to the browser. In this case, the database information is sent back to Dreamweaver MX. There is a special file inside the _mmServerScripts folder inside your site that Dreamweaver MX writes to the server that takes care of the connection and communication with the program during the design phase. On an ASP server, this is an ASP file; on a JSP server, it's a JSP file; and on a ColdFusion server, it's a ColdFusion file. The file connects to the database on the server as it is called, and sends the information back to Dreamweaver MX in the form of XML. All of this is invisible to the user.

Tip *If you upgrade from UltraDev 1 to Dreamweaver MX, you can convert your recordsets and other Server Behaviors created in UltraDev 1. Simply open the recordset from the Bindings panel and then click OK. The recordset will be modified.*

This chapter reviews a few of the more popular methods for connecting Dreamweaver MX to a database.

Types of Dreamweaver MX Connections

Each server model that Dreamweaver MX supports has its own way to connect to a database. Some of the server models have different methods of connecting within that model, using different techniques. The next sections discuss the different connection methods for Dreamweaver MX, broken down by server model.

ASP

ASP was the most popular server model in UltraDev 4, but with the release of ASP.NET, that distinction may be short lived. Classic ASP, which we'll call ASP 3.0, is a scripting-based server model allowing pages to be created in VBScript or JScript. The connection methods are the same for both.

ODBC

ODBC, or Open Database Connectivity, is probably the most widely used connection method, given the number of Microsoft Windows machines out there. ODBC drivers come preinstalled with Windows and provide a standard way to connect to most databases. The vast majority of databases that run on Windows are ODBC-compliant.

ODBC was developed as an answer to the ever-present problem of compatibility between different machines, different operating systems, and different software. When you connect to an ODBC data source, you are connecting to the ODBC driver for that database, not to the actual database. The driver does the job of translating your commands into something that the database can understand—similar to speaking through an interpreter. You communicate to the driver with a SQL statement that complies with a limited generic subset of the SQL language. By translating the statements through ODBC, a small performance penalty occurs, but nothing significant in the grand scheme of things in Web time.

 Note *Dreamweaver MX needs the MDAC version 2.1 at the very minimum, so if you have version 1.5 or 2 installed, you need to upgrade. The MDAC is available from www.microsoft.com/data.*

When using ODBC, the Web page doesn't need to know where the database is located on the machine. In fact, it doesn't even have to be on the same machine, and is often located on a machine that is specifically set up as a database server and accessed through a network. You give the connection to the database a *data source name (DSN)*

ADDING DATABASE
FEATURES TO YOUR SITE

that enables you to refer to the connection by name in your program (or Web application). As long as the DSN points to the database in the ODBC Data Source Administrator interface, the Web page will be able to communicate with the database.

If you are developing ASP, JSP, or ColdFusion (version 5 and earlier) pages, you can connect to the database through ODBC. In JSP, JDBC:ODBC bridge drivers can be used to connect via JDBC to an ODBC data source, making it necessary to define your data sources in both the ODBC administrator and the JSP server administration page. In ColdFusion, all the system DSNs appear in the ColdFusion Administrator and are accessible by all ColdFusion pages. In addition, if you have direct access to the ColdFusion Administrator, it allows you to remotely create and edit DSNs.

Note *Depending on which database you are using, the drivers may or may not be preinstalled with the MDAC. If you are running Microsoft Access, FoxPro, or SQL Server, the drivers are preinstalled and ready to run. Other preinstalled drivers include dBase, Oracle, Paradox, and Visual FoxPro. Drivers for MySQL and other databases are available on the Web, or from the database manufacturer.*

The first thing you need to do is define an ODBC connection in the ODBC Data Source Administrator, shown in Figure 20-2, which is located in the Control Panel folder. Each ODBC driver interface is a little different, but the principles of each are the same. As an example, an Access database will be used. Dreamweaver MX requires a System DSN to recognize the database. A System DSN is available to all users and all services (on Windows NT), as opposed to a User DSN, which is available only to the current user, or a File DSN, which has the DSN stored in a file (independent of users).

Note *If you are using a Web-hosting company, it will set up the data source for you. You simply need to upload the database to the Web site to a folder on the server (preferably a cgi-bin or a similarly secured directory for safety) and give the Web-hosting company the information about the directory, database name, and DSN it should use. An administrator from your ISP can then set up the connection on the computer that your database resides on. Also, many Web-hosting companies allow the user to interact with the DSN administrator through a Web-based user interface.*

Click Add in the ODBC Data Source Administrator. This brings up the Create New Data Source dialog box, shown in Figure 20-3, which enables you to create a new data source.

After choosing the appropriate driver for your database, click Finish. This takes you directly to the ODBC setup for the particular driver that you are adding. Again, each driver has its own unique interface, but the result is the same. Figure 20-4 shows the ODBC Microsoft Access Setup screen.

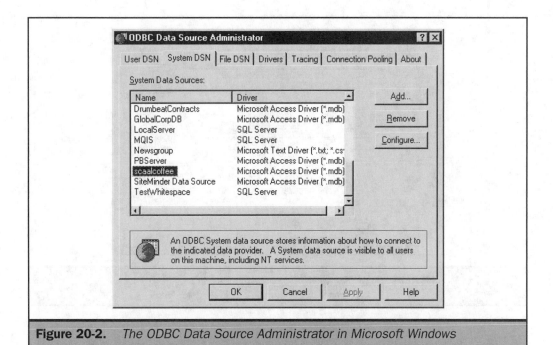

Figure 20-2. *The ODBC Data Source Administrator in Microsoft Windows*

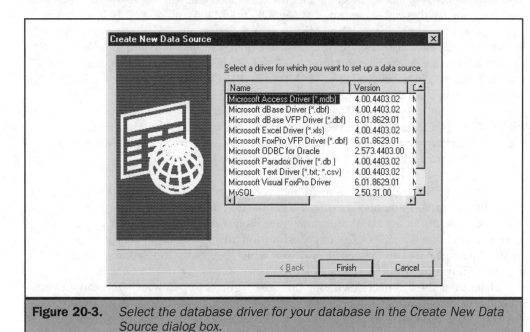

Figure 20-3. *Select the database driver for your database in the Create New Data Source dialog box.*

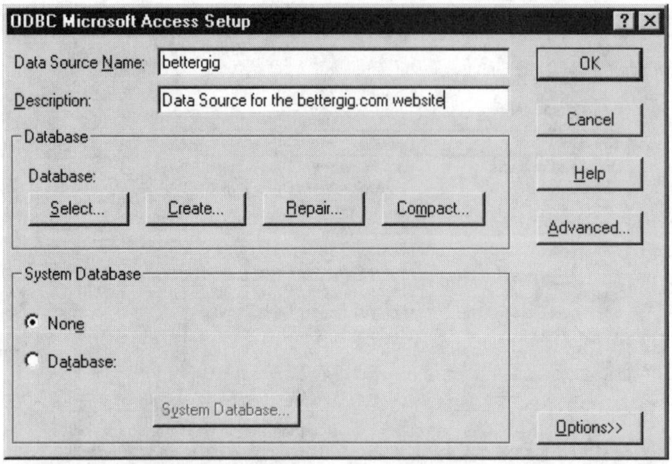

Figure 20-4. Setting up a DSN for Microsoft Access

Insert a DSN and a description (if you like, although the description is not mandatory), and then select the database. By going into the Advanced tab, you can also set a login name and password. Other databases, such as MySQL, might have all of their options on one screen, and some databases, such as Microsoft SQL Server, use the wizard metaphor. The bottom line is that you are assigning a DSN to a database, enabling you to refer to that database by name from this point forward. The DSN information is then stored in the system's Registry in the HKEY_LOCAL_MACHINE\SOFTWARE\ODBC\ODBC.INI key so that it can be used at any time by any application.

Tip *The ODBC Microsoft Access Setup screen also offers options for repairing and compacting databases. These come in handy if you don't have a copy of MS Access on that particular machine.*

Connecting through ODBC is a simple process, and connecting with Dreamweaver MX is even simpler. You need to define a connection in one of two ways. You can click the plus sign in the Databases panel (see Figure 20-1), which allows you to choose Data Source Name or Custom Connection String. The other way is to go to the Bindings panel and choose Recordset, which brings up the Recordset dialog box (see Figure 20-5), and then click Define.

That opens the Connections dialog box (see Figure 20-6), in which you can choose to edit an existing connection or create a new connection by clicking New. An option for Duplicate also exists, in case you want to copy a connection under a different name. This list of data sources is the same list that you'll find in the Databases panel.

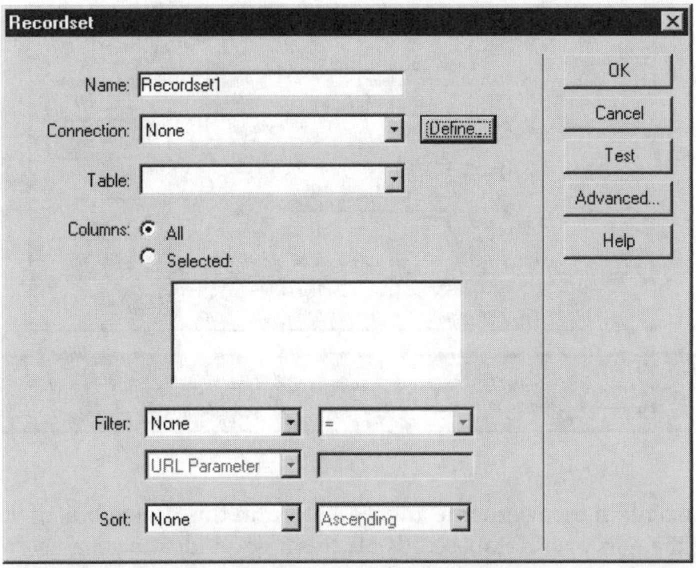

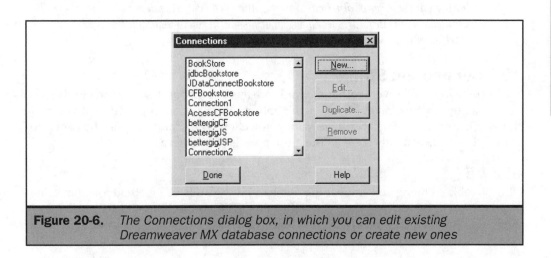

Figure 20-5.   *You can also define a connection directly from the Recordset dialog box by clicking Define.*

When you click either New or Edit, the Data Source Name dialog box opens (see Figure 20-7). This box has two radio buttons: one for a local machine and one for an application server connection (the Macintosh doesn't have this option).

Figure 20-6.   *The Connections dialog box, in which you can edit existing Dreamweaver MX database connections or create new ones*

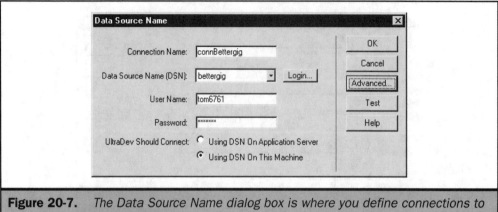

Figure 20-7. *The Data Source Name dialog box is where you define connections to the database.*

You can also fill in the username and password in this dialog box, if you've implemented them in your database. It's always a good idea to set a username and password on any database that might be accessible to others. Even if you are not worried about malicious attack, you'll want to keep the database secured—if only to prevent possible corruption of data from somebody opening the database by mistake.

If you've made a successful connection, after you click Done, you should see a drop-down list of all the tables in your database (if you are in Simple view of the Recordset dialog box) or a tree view showing all of your tables (if you are in Advanced view).

  If you are using a Web-hosting company, a security issue exists with ODBC data sources. You might find that you can access all of the data sources on the server— including data sources of other customers of the Web host. A tech note on the Macromedia Web site addresses this security issue, at www.macromedia.com/ support/ultradev/ts/documents/odbc_ini.htm.

ADO Connection String

If you are using ASP, several other methods are at your disposal with which to connect to a database. Dreamweaver MX gives the option to use a connection string, if you choose Custom Connection String as your connection type. Connection strings are also varied, so we present only some of the more popular types here.

OLE DB

OLE DB (object linking and embedding database) is the preferred method for connecting to a database in Windows. When you define an ODBC connection, you are putting a wrapper around an OLE DB connection to the database, and adding another step to the connection process. By connecting directly to OLE DB, you eliminate the middleman, so to speak, and create a connection that is a little speedier and a little more stable. OLE DB connections are not as universally compatible as ODBC connections, but their use has become fairly widespread. Also, many Web-hosting companies require a DSN-less connection or an OLE DB connection, because these require no intervention on the company's part.

Instead of using the ODBC DSN, as in the previous examples, you use the *provider*, which is specific to the database that you are working with. When you install the MDAC, several OLE DB providers are installed, including an ODBC provider, which enables you to access any ODBC-compliant database through an OLE DB connection. You have the option to access the database through the native provider or through the ODBC provider, which is not the same as accessing the database through the ODBC DSN connection. The following is a typical Microsoft Access connection string using the native provider:

```
Provider=Microsoft.Jet.OLEDB.4.0;
Data Source=C:\inetpub\wwwroot\cgi-bin\bettergig.mdb;
User ID=username;Password=password;
```

Here, note also that you are connecting directly to the database by using a path to that database. This speeds up the connection, because your system doesn't have to access the Registry to look up the DSN—it goes directly to the database. This method is not to be confused with a DSN-less connection, which is outlined next.

The way to enter the OLE DB connection string into Dreamweaver MX is to first bring up the Data Connection dialog box by clicking the plus sign (+) in the Databases panel, and then create a new connection. This time, instead of choosing Data Source Name, choose Custom Connection String, which opens the Custom Connection String dialog box, shown in Figure 20-8.

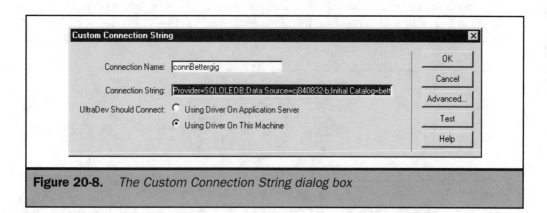

Figure 20-8.   *The Custom Connection String dialog box*

ADDING DATABASE
FEATURES TO YOUR SITE

In the empty box for Connection String, you can put the preceding Access connection string, if you are using the Access database, or use the following string for SQL Server:

```
Provider=SQLOLEDB;Data Source=myMachineName;
Initial Catalog=bettergig;User ID=username;Password=password;
```

If you enter the correct string and click Test, you should see the dialog box shown in Figure 20-9. Note that Initial Catalog refers to the actual database name in SQL Server, and Data Source refers to the actual machine name that the SQL Server resides on. Keep in mind that you must substitute your own username and password, as well as the server name, the database path for Access databases, and the Initial Catalog for SQL Server.

ODBC DSN-less Connections

Another form of connection is available to the ASP developer—a DSN-less connection. This connection is often preferable to the ODBC connection, because you don't need to have a system DSN set up to use it. The DSN-less connection is available for most of the databases that are ODBC-compliant, and uses the ODBC driver to connect to the database. The following string is in the format for an Access database:

```
Provider=MSDASQL; Driver={Microsoft Access Driver (*.mdb)};
Dbq=c:\inetpub\wwwroot\cgi-bin\bettergig.mdb;
UID=username;PWD=password
```

 The driver name inside of the curly braces { … } is the exact driver name as it appears in the ODBC Data Source Administrator. You can look at the Drivers tab of the Administrator to see which drivers are available and what the correct syntax is.

The Provider attribute is the default ODBC provider and is sometimes omitted from the string. ADO assumes that you are using the MSDASQL provider (the default ODBC provider) if you don't specify otherwise. It's a good idea to specify the provider directly.

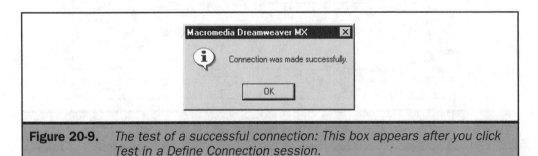

Figure 20-9. *The test of a successful connection: This box appears after you click Test in a Define Connection session.*

The DSN-less connection is identical to the ODBC connection with one difference: The connection is hard-coded into your application instead of being stored in the Registry, thereby saving a trip to the Registry.

Using the Microsoft Text Driver

One of the little-known features of ADO is the ability to define a connection to a text file. The text file can have an extension of .txt, .csv, .asc, or .tab. The text file should be set up as a comma-separated-values file with column names in the first row. You can set up an ODBC DSN for a text driver connection, or you can use a DSN-less or OLE DB connection string. Using the DSN-less connection, you must fill in the ADO connection string, as follows:

```
Driver={Microsoft Text Driver (*.txt; *.csv)};
Dbq=c:\somepath\;Extensions=asc,csv,tab,txt;
Persist Security Info=False;
```

Of course, you should place all of this on one line in the Custom Connection String dialog box. The driver works a little differently than the standard database drivers insofar as you define a *directory* instead of a path to a physical database or a physical file. The file that you are trying to access will appear as the "table" in your SQL statement.

Another way to access a text file is with an OLE DB connection string, like this:

```
"Provider=Microsoft.Jet.OLEDB.4.0;Data Source=C:\yourpath;Extended
Properties='text;FMT=Delimited'"
```

To use this OLE DB connection string you have to enter all of the quotes in the Custom Connection String dialog box as well.

After defining the connection, you should be able to click Test and make a successful connection. In defining the recordset, you'll see a list of text files in the directory specified by the connection string, instead of a list of tables. When you define your SQL statement, you'll be using the filename of the text file instead of a column name. A typical SQL statement using the text driver might look like this:

```
SELECT * FROM C:\inetpub\wwwroot\cgi-bin\addresses.txt
```

Make sure that the backslashes are all in the proper place in the file path. Some limitations may exist when using the text driver (text files can't be updated like a regular database), but being able to display data in an organized fashion directly from a text file has many benefits.

ADDING DATABASE
FEATURES TO YOUR SITE

Sample ADO Connection Strings

Note that in the Connection dialog box, the connection strings will be placed on one line in the ADO Connection String text field.

- Access ODBC DSN-less connection

```
Driver={Microsoft Access Driver (*.mdb)};
Dbq=c:\somepath\dbname.mdb;Uid=Admin;Pwd=pass;
```

- dBase ODBC DSN-less connection

```
Driver={Microsoft dBASE Driver (*.dbf)};
DriverID=277;Dbq=c:\somepath\dbname.dbf;
```

- Oracle ODBC DSN-less connection

```
Driver={Microsoft ODBC for Oracle};
Server=OracleServer.world;Uid=admin;Pwd=pass;
```

- SQL Server DSN-less connection

```
Driver={SQL Server};Server=servername;
Database=dbname;Uid=sa;Pwd=pass;
```

- Text Driver DSN-less connection

```
Driver={Microsoft Text Driver (*.txt; *.csv)};Dbq=c:\somepath\;
Extensions=asc,csv,tab,txt;Persist Security Info=False;
```

- Visual FoxPro DSN-less connection

```
Driver={Microsoft Visual FoxPro Driver};
SourceType=DBC;SourceDB=c:\somepath\dbname.dbc;Exclusive=No;
```

- Access OLE DB connection

```
Provider=Microsoft.Jet.OLEDB.4.0;
Data Source=c:\somepath\dbname.mdb;User Id=admin;Password=pass;
```

- Oracle OLE DB connection

```
Provider=OraOLEDB.Oracle;Data Source=dbname;
User Id=admin;Password=pass;
```

- SQL Server OLE DB connection

```
Provider=SQLOLEDB;Data Source=machineName;
Initial Catalog=dbname;User ID=sa;Password=pass;
```

- MySQL DSN-less connection

```
driver={mysql}; database=yourdatabase;
server=yourserver;uid=admin;pwd=pass;option=16386;
```

Using *Server.Mappath* in a Connection String

Many ASP developers prefer to use the server function *Server.Mappath* in the connection string when using a file-based database such as Microsoft Access. What this function does is to map the path to the database on the server if you supply the relative path to the database. For instance, if your database resides at e:\inetpub\wwwroot\bettergig\cgi-bin\bettergig.mdb, you could use the following connection string (all on one line):

```
"Provider=Microsoft.Jet.OLEDB.4.0;Data Source=" &
Server.Mappath("\bettergig\cgi-bin\bettergig.mdb")
```

This option allows greater flexibility when you have a Web-hosting company and you may not know the directory path to your Web site or your database. UltraDev 4 introduced the capability to use this type of path: Simply choose Using Driver On Application Server as your connection method and supply a Custom Connection String like the preceding example. This method works with both OLE DB and DSN-less connections. The path has to be the relative path of the database to the site root including a preceding backslash (\) as outlined.

Using a Password-Protected Access Database

When your Access database has a password on it, you have to change the way you compose your connection string:

```
Provider=Microsoft.Jet.OLEDB.4.0;
Data Source=c:\somepath\mydatabase.mdb;
Jet OLEDB:Database Password=pass;
```

You may have to specify the system OLE DB database file in the string as well. This one should work in a default installation of Windows 2000:

```
Provider=Microsoft.Jet.OLEDB.4.0;
Data Source=C:\somepath\mydatabase.mdb;
Persist Security Info=False;
Jet OLEDB:System database=C:\Program Files\Common Files\System\System.mdw;
Jet OLEDB:Database Password=pass;
```

And this one should work in a default installation of Windows NT 4:

```
Provider=Microsoft.Jet.OLEDB.4.0;
Data Source=C:\somepath\mydatabase.mdb;
Persist Security Info=False;
Jet OLEDB:System database=C:\winnt\system32\System.mdw;
Jet OLEDB:Database Password=pass;
```

For more information on creating Access OLE DB connection strings, check out the MS tech note at http://support.microsoft.com/support/kb/articles/Q264/6/91.ASP.

ASP.NET

ASP.NET is new to Dreamweaver MX. The method of connection to the database is similar to what it was for ASP using an OLE DB connection string. If you are comfortable with creating OLE DB connection strings, you should have no problems. If not, Dreamweaver MX actually allows you to create the connection string using Microsoft's own Data Link Properties dialog box on a Windows machine or by using one of the predefined templates.

When you create a connection for ASP.NET, the connection information is stored in an include file that is located in the Connections folder in your site. If your site is a C# site, the include file is written in C#, and if your site is a VB site, the include file is written in VB.

If you haven't read the preceding section on ASP connection strings, you should go back and read it because it contains most of the preliminary information that you'll need to understand the various connection methods of ASP.NET.

OLE DB

The first step to creating the connection is to click the plus sign (+) on the Databases tab and then click OLE DB. This will bring up the dialog box shown in Figure 20-10.

There are two buttons on the box: Build and Templates. If you click Build, you'll see the Data Link Properties dialog box (shown in Figure 20-11). This box allows you to choose between various OLE DB connection types and dynamically build the connection

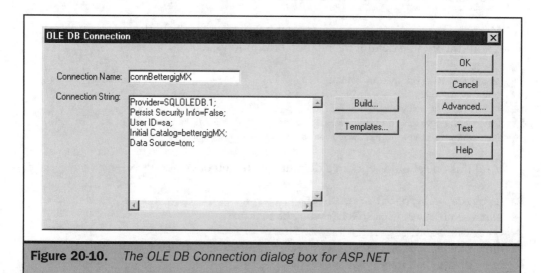

Figure 20-10. *The OLE DB Connection dialog box for ASP.NET*

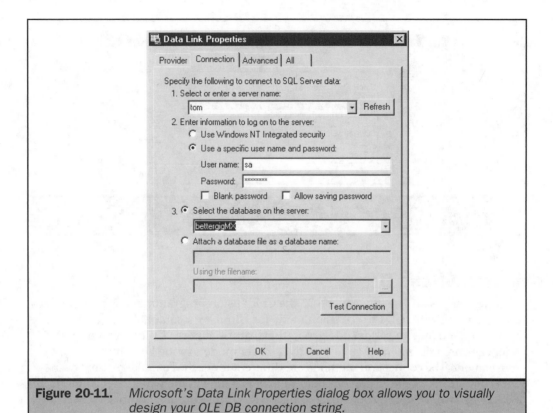

Figure 20-11.   *Microsoft's Data Link Properties dialog box allows you to visually design your OLE DB connection string.*

string by using the wizard-like interface. The values that you choose will be sent back to the Dreamweaver MX environment and will appear in the OLE DB Connection dialog box.

    Macintosh users can choose only from the Templates option.

If you choose Templates, the Connection String Template dialog box is shown (Figure 20-12). These templates are similar to what you would get if you used the Data Link Properties box, only the values shown in brackets are dummy values that you can replace with your own database values.

SQL Server Connection

This connection setting is similar to the OLE DB connection setting described in the previous section. The only difference is that the connection string template is coded into the dialog box when you open it up, allowing you to create the connection string more quickly.

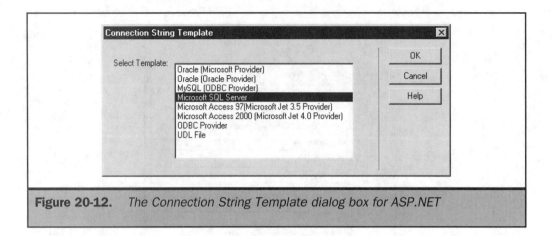

Figure 20-12. *The Connection String Template dialog box for ASP.NET*

ColdFusion 4 and 5

When working with Dreamweaver MX, the ColdFusion programmer has two different modes to work with: UD4-ColdFusion mode for UltraDev 4 compatibility, and ColdFusion mode with better code generation featuring more "ColdFusion-esque" code. They are implemented as two distinct server models in the Dreamweaver MX environment. The connection methods are different for each. To make matters even more complicated, ColdFusion has made a major change in the way that it connects to databases from ColdFusion 5 to ColdFusion MX. This section attempts to cover the various methods that are available, depending upon your own situation and what you will be working with.

UD4-ColdFusion and ODBC

ColdFusion 5.0 and earlier allows the user to connect to a database using a system DSN much like the ASP method previously outlined. In fact, if you go to the ColdFusion Administrator contained within ColdFusion Server and click ODBC in the Data Sources menu, you are taken to a screen that shows you all the ODBC DSNs available on that particular machine. Not only can you access the data sources from the Administrator, but you also can edit, add, or delete data sources right from the Web interface. Defining ODBC and OLE DB data sources remotely is one of the great features of ColdFusion.

 Defining a data source using the CF Administrator in ColdFusion 5 is just like using the Control Panel. In other words, the data source will show up as a system data source within the Control Panel.

To be able to access a database in Dreamweaver MX for a UD4-ColdFusion site, you need to have a data source set up in the ODBC administrator as a system DSN (setting up an ODBC data source was outlined earlier under the section "ODBC"). To create the connection, click the plus button (+) in the Databases tab or click Define on the recordset declaration dialog box to bring up the dialog box shown in Figure 20-13. Next, do the following:

1. Give the connection a name.

2. Click Login to log in to the ColdFusion RDS server. Use your CF Administrator password here. In most cases, the CF Administrator doesn't have a username, so you can leave the Username field blank.

3. Choose the ColdFusion Data Source Name from the drop-down box.

4. Fill in your username and password (if they are implemented).

5. Choose either Use DSN On This Machine or Use DSN On Application Server.

The code for the connection is automatically written to a connName.cfm file in the Connections folder after you create the connection, where *connName* refers to the actual name that you give the connection. All you have to worry about when you define your connection is that you are using a valid DSN, username, and password. Dreamweaver MX will do the rest.

The Data Source Name—Advanced dialog box (shown in Figure 20-14) is available to UD4-ColdFusion users to allow the use of a JDBC driver to connect to a local database. The JDBC driver is provided for Macintosh users who can't run a local copy of ColdFusion, but still works with Dreamweaver MX and connects to a local database at design time. The functionality is also available in the Windows version to allow for collaborative development in a situation where one user has a Macintosh and another user has a Windows PC. The section "JDBC Connections" explains the JDBC driver connection method for Dreamweaver MX.

ADDING DATABASE FEATURES TO YOUR SITE

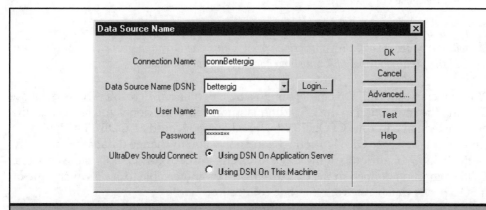

Figure 20-13.   *Assigning a ColdFusion DSN name in the Data Source Name dialog box for a database connection in UD4-ColdFusion mode*

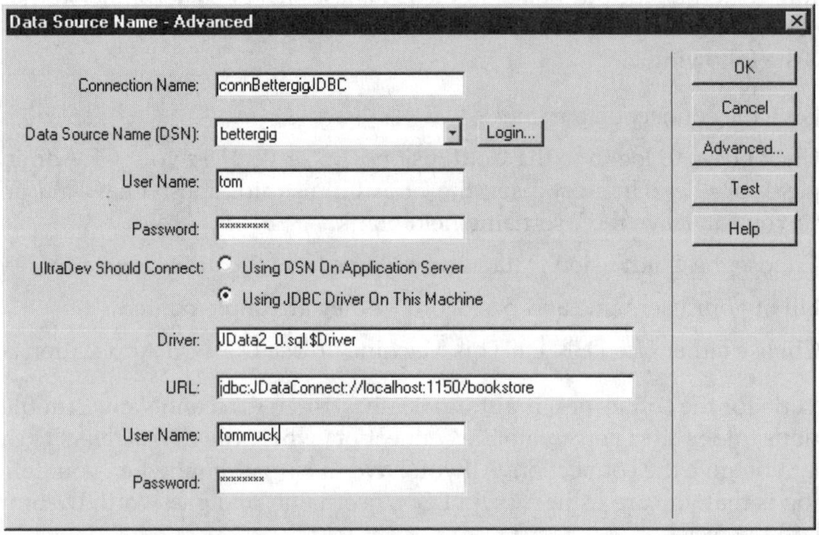

Data Source Name - Advanced   ☒

Connection Name:	connBettergigJDBC
Data Source Name (DSN):	bettergig ▾ Login...
User Name:	tom
Password:	********
UltraDev Should Connect:	○ Using DSN On Application Server
	⦿ Using JDBC Driver On This Machine
Driver:	JData2_0.sql.$Driver
URL:	jdbc:JDataConnect://localhost:1150/bookstore
User Name:	tommuck
Password:	********

OK
Cancel
Advanced...
Test
Help

Figure 20-14.   *The Data Source Name—Advanced dialog box for UD4-ColdFusion*
allows a local JDBC connection to be used.

OLE DB

If you are in UD4-ColdFusion mode, ODBC connections are the only types of connections
that are supported for use in the Dreamweaver-generated server behaviors. There are
other types of connections available to you though, such as OLE DB connections. You
can hand-code these connections.

  *If you are in UD4-ColdFusion mode and you hand-code connections on the page, you
will not be able to edit the connections from within the Dreamweaver MX environment,
and the Bindings panel will not show your recordset columns.*

You can create an OLE DB connection to a SQL Server or Microsoft Access database
by defining the connection in the CF Administrator. With that done, you can access the
datasource by name in your CFQUERY tag just like you would an ODBC DSN with
one important catch: the OLE DB connection allows you to change databases on the fly
using the DBNAME attribute of the CFQUERY tag. You can conceivably have only one
OLE DB connection defined in the CF Administrator and be able to access every one of
your SQL Server databases from that one connection.

OLE DB connections are no longer supported in ColdFusion MX. Because of that,
it is not recommended that you continue to build pages that use them.

DSN-less Connections

ColdFusion 5 introduces DSN-less connections for ODBC drivers that use the same syntax as the DSN-less connections that ASP programmers have grown accustomed to. Dreamweaver MX doesn't support these connections, but you can hand-code them in your ColdFusion page with a little knowledge of how the syntax works. One caveat is that these connections are no longer available in ColdFusion MX, but if you are running a ColdFusion 5 server, you are free to use them.

ColdFusion 5 introduced several new options to the CFQUERY tag. One of these is a DBTYPE of "dynamic". This allows the use of connection strings with the CONNECTSTRING attribute of the CFQUERY tag:

```
<cfquery name="rs"
    dbtype="dynamic"
    connectstring="Driver={Microsoft Access Driver
*.mdb)};Dbq=c:\db\mydb.mdb;Uid=Admin;Pwd=;">
SELECT SeekId, SeekUsername, SeekPassword
FROM Seekers
</cfquery>
```

If you define a CFQUERY in this manner, you can't use the Bindings palette within Dreamweaver MX for your recordset information, such as the columns and views returned from the query, but you can hand-code these.

The advantage of this method is that you don't need to define your connection to the CF Administrator—it can be done completely on the fly using path information for the database (if it's a file-based database) or the server name/database name for server-based databases such as SQL Server and MySQL. The connection string typically supplies the username and password, as well as any other values that the database needs for a successful connection.

The following connection strings are some of the more popular ODBC connection strings that you can use to declare your connection on the fly. You should place the connection string in quotes on one line entirely using the CONNECTSTRING attribute.

- MS Access ODBC DSN-less connection

```
Driver={Microsoft Access Driver
(*.mdb)};Dbq=c:\somepath\dbname.mdb;Uid=Admin;Pwd=pass;
```

- Oracle ODBC DSN-less connection

```
Driver={Microsoft ODBC for Oracle};
Server=OracleServer.world;Uid=admin;Pwd=pass;
```

- MS SQL Server DSN-less connection

```
Driver={SQL Server};Server=servername;
Database=dbname;Uid=sa;Pwd=pass;
```

- MS Text Driver DSN-less connection

```
Driver={Microsoft Text Driver (*.txt; *.csv)};
Dbq=c:\somepath\;Extensions=asc,csv,tab,txt;Persist Security Info=False;
```

- MySQL DSN-less connection

```
driver={mysql}; database=yourdatabase;server=yourserver;
uid=username;pwd=password;option=16386;
```

Note *OLE DB connection strings don't work in ColdFusion 5.*

Using *ExpandPath* in the ConnectString

ExpandPath is a built-in ColdFusion function that will retrieve the full path of a file (including the drive letter) given the relative path of the file. A relative path cannot begin with a slash or backslash:

```
#ExpandPath('..\bettergig\cgi-bin\bettergig.mdb')#
```

You can use this in your CONNECTSTRING attribute to complete the string if you are uploading a file to a remote server and don't know the physical path of your database file:

```
Driver={Microsoft Access Driver (*.mdb)};
Dbq=#ExpandPath('..\bettergig\cgi-bin\bettergig.mdb')#;
Uid=Admin;Pwd=pass;
```

The complete CFQUERY tag for this string would look like this:

```
<CFQUERY NAME="rs"
 DBTYPE="dynamic"
 CONNECTSTRING="Driver={Microsoft Access Driver *.mdb)};
Dbq=#ExpandPath('..\bettergig\cgi-bin\bettergig.mdb')#;
Uid=Admin;Pwd=pass;">
SELECT SeekId, SeekUsername, SeekPassword
FROM Seekers
</CFQUERY>
```

The connection string could be built up in a variable to make it easier to read as well:

```
<cfset rsUser="Uid=#form.username#;">
<cfset rsPass="Pwd=#form.password#;">
<cfset theDatabase="#ExpandPath('..\bettergig\cgi-bin\bettergig.mdb')#;">
<cfset theString="Driver={Microsoft Access Driver (*.mdb)};Dbq=">
```

```
<cfset theString=theString & theDatabase & rsUser & rsPass>
<cfquery name="rs"
   dbtype="dynamic"
   connectstring="#theString#">
SELECT SeekId, SeekUsername, SeekPassword
FROM Seekers
</cfquery>
```

ColdFusion MX

ColdFusion MX is Macromedia's latest generation of ColdFusion server. With this version, ColdFusion is now written entirely in Java, thereby changing the way that database connections are made. All connections are either made through JDBC drivers that are preinstalled with the ColdFusion server, or you can use your own. The switch from ODBC to JDBC drivers, however, has not changed much the way your ColdFusion page uses the connection. The major change is how ColdFusion connects to the database internally.

If you are upgrading from ColdFusion 5 to ColdFusion MX, all of the ODBC and OLE DB connections will be migrated to the new JDBC connection type. Databases such as Access, SQL Server, and DB2 have new JDBC drivers that are specifically designed for that database. There is also a JDBC bridge connection to ODBC (called the *ODBC socket*) that can be used for other databases that may not have a specific connection available.

The ColdFusion server model in Dreamweaver MX is the only server model without the plus sign (+) in the Databases tab. Instead, there is a little connection icon (see Figure 20-15). The connection icon is tied to the ColdFusion Administrator Web interface, so by clicking the icon you'll have to log into the Administrator. If you don't have rights to the Administrator, you won't be able to connect to the database during your design phase. Your best option if this is the case is to keep a local copy of your database and a local copy of ColdFusion server running as well.

The Databases tab lists a five-step procedure to set up a data source:

1. Create a site that contains the file.
2. Choose a dynamic document type.
3. Set up the site's application server.
4. Specify the RDS information.
5. Create a ColdFusion data source.

The key to making the datasource work, as in the other server models, is making sure your application server is set up properly with the URL prefix. This prefix should be the same URL that you use to browse the pages, such as http://localhost/myfolder. If you can preview the page by pressing F12, chances are your URL prefix is correct. If

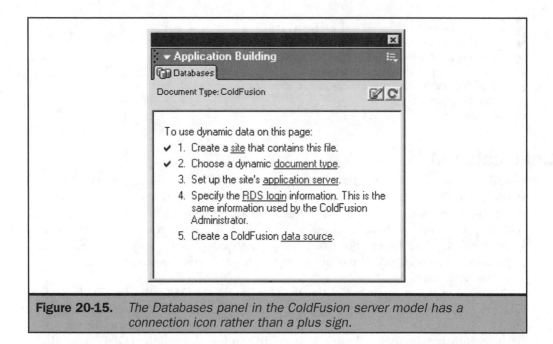

Figure 20-15. The Databases panel in the ColdFusion server model has a connection icon rather than a plus sign.

you have a Web host that doesn't allow RDS connections, you'll have to use a local server and a local RDS connection.

 RDS, as used in this chapter, is Macromedia's own Remote Development Service technology, not Microsoft's Remote Data Service. Using RDS allows the developer to connect to a remote server as if it were his own machine. The file system and data sources are available to the remote development environment.

Clicking the icon will bring up the Administrator. After logging in, you can click the Data Sources link to take you to the data sources page (shown in Figure 20-16). Here you'll find all of the available data sources on your server. Each data source has buttons available to allow you to edit the connection or delete it. If you upgraded from a ColdFusion 4 or 5 server, the ODBC and OLE DB connections that were migrated should be showing up in this list as well.

If you create a new data source, or edit an existing data source, there are many available options, including permission levels for most typical database operations (see Figure 20-17). You can, for example, set the database to accept only SQL SELECT operations from the Web application for added security. These permission levels are in addition to any permission levels you set at the database level. These are ColdFusion-specific permissions that enhance the level of security.

After you create the data source, it will appear in the Dreamweaver MX Databases panel. The panel will show all available ColdFusion MX database connections.

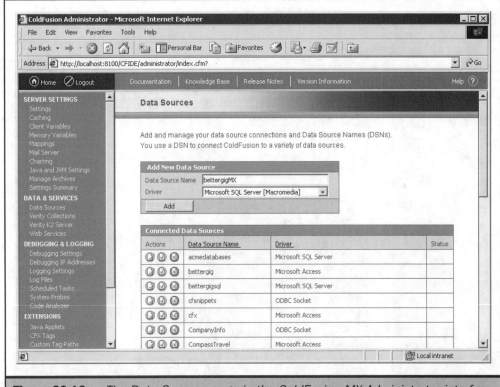

Figure 20-16.   *The Data Sources page in the ColdFusion MX Administrator interface*

The connections are also available from all of the Dreamweaver MX data sources and server behaviors that require connections, such as the Recordset, Stored Procedure, Insert, Update, and Delete server behaviors.

PHP

Chapter 18 talked a little bit about the history of PHP inside of the Dreamweaver and UltraDev platform. There was a very popular extension available for UltraDev 4 that created a complete PHP server model for UltraDev, allowing Web developers to build PHP sites in the UltraDev environment. The PHAkt extension and the commercial version, ImpAKT, were both produced by Interakt, a company in Romania that specializes in custom software development. The PHP server model extension relied on a database abstraction layer called ADODB to allow the user to connect to any database. Dreamweaver MX implements a different strategy using the native PHP/MySQL connection code.

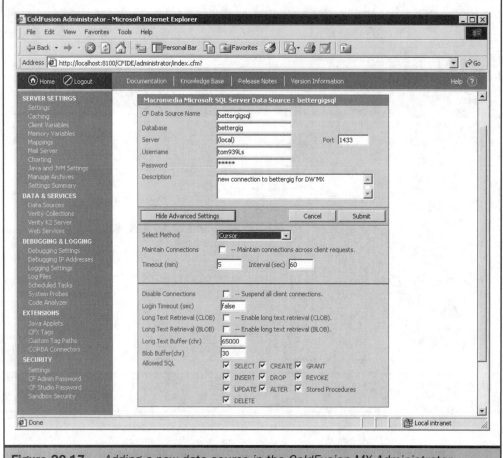

Figure 20-17. *Adding a new data source in the ColdFusion MX Administrator*

Native MySQL Connectivity

One of the strengths of PHP is the fact that it is closely tied in with the MySQL database server. The two programs are almost inseparable, and most PHP applications connect to a MySQL database.

After MySQL, the second most popular database for PHP development is PostgreSQL though Dreamweaver MX doesn't support PostgreSQL out of the box. You can use the PHAkt server model from www.interakt.ro if you want to utilize a PostgreSQL database server.

Connection is made through native PHP code. Unlike ASP or ColdFusion, which have a generic method of communicating with any database, PHP has native code that is different for each database. The MySQL code will be different from the PostgreSQL code, and vice versa. This is viewed as a strength of PHP by many PHP developers because the code has been optimized for a particular database. One of the problems with this approach is that the code that you write will work only with that particular database. In other words, if you code an application to work with a MySQL database, you can't go back later and upgrade to a DB2 database without rewriting all of your code. If you are planning to implement a PHP/MySQL site, however, this is hardly a limitation. The combination will serve you well for most small- to medium-scale sites.

To make the connection, click the plus sign (+) in the Databases panel and click MySQL Connection, or click Define in the Recordset dialog box. This will bring up the dialog box shown in Figure 20-18. There are five parameters to fill in, and a successful connection depends on your MySQL server being set up with the proper permission levels to be able to access it from the Web application.

- **Connection Name**   Give a name to your connection. A good habit is to put *conn* before the database name, as in *connDatabaseName*.

- **MySQL Server**   This is the name of your server, or the IP address.

- **User Name**   You should have a user set up in MySQL to work with the database. Never use the Root user, because you can run into security problems.

- **Password**   The user's password.

- **Database**   The database that you want to connect to. Click Select to pull up the dialog box shown in Figure 20-19. All of the available databases are shown.

After setting up a successful connection, the connection will appear in the Databases panel, along with a list of all of the tables available in MySQL. Views and stored procedures aren't supported by MySQL as of this writing, so those trees will be empty in the Databases panel. Future versions of MySQL promise to support these standard database features.

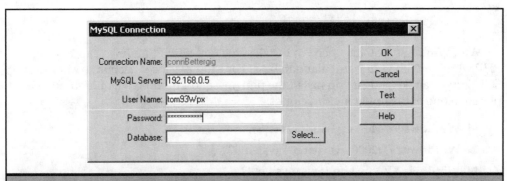

Figure 20-18.   *Adding a MySQL connection*

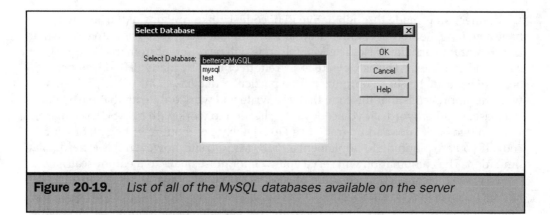

Figure 20-19. *List of all of the MySQL databases available on the server*

Using a Database Abstraction Layer

Dreamweaver MX is capable of creating any type of site, but the PHP model that is included with the program will generate only PHP/MySQL code. If you need to work with another database server, you'll have to use a third-party add-on server model, or you can create your pages by hand-coding.

A company named Interakt created a PHP server model for Dreamweaver MX named PHAkt, which utilizes a third-party database abstraction layer called ADODB. The ADODB code is included at runtime as a PHP include file. The code allows you to use a similar syntax when addressing any database. When making the connection, you have to specify the database type that you are using, and the PHAkt extension will write the appropriate code for you.

To use a database other than MySQL with PHP, you also have to make sure you have the correct modules loaded with PHP. The PHP server by default is preloaded with the MySQL module, but support for other databases has to be specified when installing the server or by reconfiguring the PHP server and adding the appropriate configuration lines, such as this line for PostgreSQL on a Linux box:

```
--with pgsql=/usr/local/pgsql
```

With Windows, you may need to install some of the PHP modules in order to get PHP working with your particular database. For example, a connection to Microsoft SQL Server can be made if you install the php_mssql.dll module. The file should be placed in one of the following directories:

- **Windows 9x/Me**   c:\windows\system
- **Windows NT/2000**   c:\winnt\system32
- **Windows XP**   c:\windows\system32

Information about installation of PHP modules can be found at www.php.net in the installation section of the PHP manual.

Other database abstraction layers are available as well, such as PEAR, Metabase, and PhpLib.

JDBC Connections for JSP

JDBC is the standard for connecting a Java application or Web page to a database, much like ODBC is the standard for ADO. The JDBC technology is central to the Java platform, and is the primary method to connect a JSP page to a database. The JDBC classes are located in the java.sql package. As with the ASP and ColdFusion connections, the Dreamweaver MX JSP connection requires the data source to be specified in a connection string. Those familiar with JSP will note that you need only to provide the driver, username, password, and URL string in the connection definition dialog box. Dreamweaver MX takes care of writing the code to actually connect to the database, manipulate the recordset, and then disconnect with a *recordset.close()* method and a *connection.close()* method.

JDBC, like ODBC, uses a generic SQL implementation rather than trying to cater to one specific database. Java was designed as a cross-platform language, and JDBC was designed as a cross-database connection to provide a Java application with the capability to talk to a database in an independent fashion.

Four basic classifications of JDBC drivers exist for JSP and Java, as outlined in Table 20-1.

Driver Type	Description
Type 1	The first JDBC drivers to come along were bridges to ODBC. Because this driver type had to "bridge the gap" to the ODBC driver, it wasn't a pure Java driver. Drivers such as the Sun JDBC:ODBC bridge are Type 1 drivers.
Type 2	Type 2 drivers were the next step. These drivers connect to native database drivers without relying on the ODBC interface. Again, this driver type isn't 100 percent Java, and requires binary code on the client machine.
Type 3	This driver type generally is a 100 percent Java implementation that still requires server middleware to connect to the database.

Table 20-1. *The Four Basic Classifications of JDBC Drivers Available for JSP Pages*

Driver Type	Description
Type 4	This driver type is a true Java implementation that connects to the database directly through a native network protocol. This is the latest and best type of driver to use for your database connection, and generally is proprietary for each individual database.

Table 20-1.   *The Four Basic Classifications of JDBC Drivers Available for JSP Pages* (continued)

Dreamweaver MX is ready to run with the Sun JDBC:ODBC Bridge, provided you are accessing a server with ODBC data source availability. To use the Bridge connection, you need to do the following:

1. Open the Connections dialog box by clicking the plus sign (+) in the Databases panel to bring up a drop-down list of available drivers.

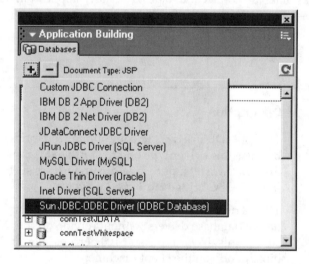

2. Choose the Sun JDBC:ODBC Driver from the drop-down list, or choose Custom JDBC Driver to type it in manually.

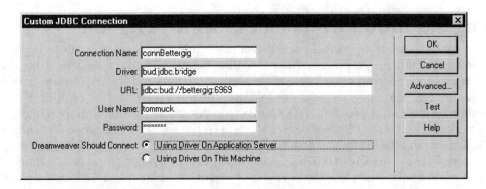

3. Give the datasource a name (such as connBettergig).

4. Choose a username and password, if you've defined them for your database.

5. Fill in the URL field, or substitute your own database information for the variable that might be in a preformatted URL field, such as [odbc dsn]. This, again, is specific to the driver that you use. In the case of the Sun driver, you fill in the following:

```
jdbc:odbc:yourdsnName (replacing the jdbc:odbc:[odbc dsn])
```

6. Choose either Use Driver On This Machine or Use Driver On Application Server.

The Sun driver, although fairly easy to use, isn't recommended for anything other than testing. It's actually very unreliable on certain JSP servers, such as the JRun 3.0 Server from Macromedia as documented on the Macromedia Web site. We recommend a Type 4 JDBC driver that's tailored specifically for the database that you plan to implement. A comprehensive list of the available JDBC drivers is available at the Sun Web site, at http://java.sun.com/products/jdbc/driverdesc.html. IBM DB2 comes with its own JDBC drivers, as does Oracle. If you are implementing an Access or MS SQL Server database, you'll have to find a third-party driver.

Note   *Macromedia's JRun now ships with JDBC drivers for many popular databases, including SQL Server.*

Generally, third-party JDBC drivers don't come cheap, but trial versions of these drivers often are available for download. In many cases, the software vendors will allow you to use the driver indefinitely as a developer, and only prohibit you from using the driver in a production environment. In any case, it is wise to test a driver fully before deciding to purchase it.

Getting the JDBC Drivers into Dreamweaver MX

The process of installing a third-party driver and having Dreamweaver MX recognize it isn't a straightforward process. After installing the driver into your machine, per the software vendor's instructions, you still must perform a few additional steps to have Dreamweaver MX recognize your driver. First, you must copy the JAR or ZIP file containing the Java classes to the JDBCDrivers folder inside the Configuration folder. By performing this step, Dreamweaver MX will recognize the driver when you choose Use Driver On This Machine. Then, when you click New in the Connections dialog box, you can choose to use Custom JDBC Connection and type in your driver information.

If you want the driver to appear in the drop-down box automatically, additional steps are involved. You have to create your own connection extension, which is a simple HTML file in this case. Open the Configuration | Connections | JSP folder and then open the Mac or Win folder, depending on which machine you're using. In that folder are the interface files (dialog boxes) for the various connections that are implemented in Dreamweaver MX. If your driver isn't here, you'll have to create your own interface for it. The following are the general steps you must follow to create the driver interface:

1. Copy one of the other driver files, such as the db2app_jdbc_conn.htm file, and open it in Notepad or your text editor of choice.

2. Change the <title> tag to reflect your new driver name. In this example, the JDataConnect driver, from NetDirect is used:

   ```
   <title>JDataConnect JDBC Driver</title>
   ```

3. Find the global variables section and replace the individual variables with your own driver information.

   ```
   //Global Variables
   var DEFAULT_DRIVER = "JData2_0.sql.$Driver";
   var DEFAULT_TEMPLATE="jdbc:JDataConnect://[hostname:port]/[odbc]";
   var MSG_DriverNotFound = "JDataConnect Driver not found!";
   var FILENAME = "JDataConnect_jdbc_conn.htm";
   ```

4. Save the file with the filename used in the *FILENAME* variable in the proper folder (Win or Mac).

5. Restart Dreamweaver MX and create a new connection by clicking the plus sign (+) in the Databases panel. Your new driver interface should appear in the list of available drivers (see Figure 20-20).

The *DEFAULT_DRIVER* variable is the driver name that will appear in the Driver text field when you create the new connection. The *DEFAULT_TEMPLATE* variable is the URL of the driver that acts as a template, with brackets surrounding information that the user can supply. The *MSG_DriverNotFound* variable is the error message that will be displayed if an error occurs. The *FILENAME* variable is the present connection file's name. The extensibility chapters (Chapters 31 and 32) cover the various methods for extending Dreamweaver MX by creating your own extensions such as this one.

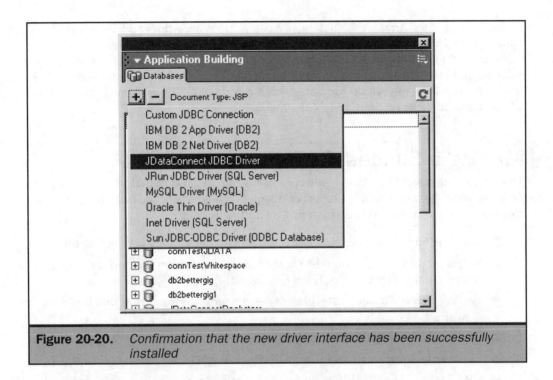

Figure 20-20. *Confirmation that the new driver interface has been successfully installed*

Macintosh Database Connections

The Apple Macintosh has long been a favorite with graphic artists and Web designers. With the advent of the iMacs and the newer G4 Macintoshes, Apple is once again a viable alternative to Windows as a tool for professional Web developers. Until now, however, Macintosh Web developers didn't have access to the same types of dynamic Web page creation tools using database connections to ADO, JSP, and ColdFusion. Dreamweaver MX bridges that gap by providing a *design-time* connection to a live database that resides on the application server. This application server can be a Windows server, a Unix/Linux server, or even a native Mac OS X server running PHP or JSP.

UltraDev 1 was the first Dreamweaver application that had database connectivity built in, and had a fairly complex setup procedure. Local connections were maintained through a Java JDBC driver named RmiJdbc, which resided on the Mac, but they also had to communicate with an RmiJdbc driver that resided on a Windows server. One of the problems that faced many Mac users was that many Web-hosting companies were reluctant to have the JDBC driver running on their servers. It had to be run from a command line, and didn't work as a service on NT machines.

Also, no method was in place for having a local Mac database used for the design of a site. This alienated users of Filemaker Pro and other Macintosh databases who wanted to work exclusively on a Mac. In addition, Linux and Unix servers were out also, because the RmiJdbc driver required by UltraDev ran only on a Windows server.

ADDING DATABASE FEATURES TO YOUR SITE

Beginning with UltraDev 4, all database connections are achieved through HTTP, allowing Macintosh and PC users to enjoy the same types of connections. To set up a connection, you must have an application server (such as PHP) running on your local machine, or you can be connected to the Internet and have access to a remote application server. A popular combination for a Macintosh running OS X is an Apache Web server, a PHP application server, and a MySQL database server.

Making a Successful Connection

The key to a successful database connection is the Site Definition dialog box. When defining your site, the Application Server dialog box has to be filled out properly to connect to your server. You need to define the following items:

- **Server Model** Choose the application server that you are connecting to.
- **Server Access** This should be set the correct connection method for your setup, usually either FTP or Local/Network.
- **Testing Server Folder** The directory on the application server that hosts the Web site.
- **Login** Your username (for the FTP setting).
- **Password** Your password (for the FTP setting).
- **URL Prefix** The IP address and path to your site; this is the key ingredient to a successful connection.

If you have defined your site correctly and are able to view your pages by previewing (using F12), then the database connections should work as well. The URL prefix will be the determining factor in getting the connection to work. If your site is located at http://192.168.0.4/mysite, that's exactly where the URL prefix should be pointing.

Caution *A common error is to put a page name in the URL prefix box. This box should contain only a path to the directory of your site, not an actual page in your site.*

Another factor in creating a successful connection is your username and password combination. Make sure your database is set up properly with correct permissions to allow you to access the database. For databases such as Access, this might not be an issue, but databases such as MySQL may require extra effort to set up the proper login permissions (typically by using a GRANT statement on the database server.) Also, username and password settings are usually case-sensitive.

Summary

This chapter has reviewed a few of the connection methods available to the Web developer in Dreamweaver MX. Not all possible connection methods are available in Dreamweaver MX, but chances are good that they will be implemented in future versions. In addition, the connection methods are extensible, as are most features in Dreamweaver MX, so that third parties can create new connection methods. Chapters 31 and 32 cover the Dreamweaver MX extensibility API.

After the connection is made, the next step is to retrieve the data from the database that you want to display on the page. The next few chapters detail designing and implementing a database for use in a Dreamweaver MX site, and accessing the data to be displayed on the page.

The Complete Reference

Dreamweaver MX

Chapter 21

Designing a Relational Database

If you are going to store something, especially a lot of something, it is a pretty good idea to have a system for storing it that lets you find it and get it back out of storage when you need it. Filing cabinets have alphabetical folders, the library has the Dewey Decimal System, and databases have the Relational Design Model.

In 1970, E. F. Codd, then a researcher at IBM, published a paper that was the first conception of what we now know as the Relational Database Design Model. Codd was concerned with the mechanics of storing and retrieving data in large database applications. His model stood in contrast to the models that were in use at the time, which were more reliant on the physical storage of the data and were significantly less flexible than Codd's vision.

Note   *Many people think that Codd's design model is called "relational" because of the way that tables are "related" to one another when querying a database. Actually, Codd's terminology was somewhat different than today's. What we call a "table," Codd called a "relation" because, by definition, that table should hold information about individual items that are in some way related to one another. What we call "columns" and "rows," Codd called "attributes" and "tuples."*

Since that time, Codd has revised and expanded the rules that govern relational database design. The last 30 years have proven the validity of the relational concept, and it is the model on which all modern databases are built. In order for you to access data from an application built with Dreamweaver MX, you are going to need to design that data store.

The design of a data store is really a separate issue from how you connect to the database or how you query data from it. Although closely related to your overall goal, database design is a discipline all to itself. In this chapter, we cover the points that you need to know to design a database that will be flexible and powerful enough to serve your application well.

What Is a Database?

Perhaps the best way to think of a database is like a big filing cabinet that you have squeezed onto the hard drive of your computer. In that filing cabinet, you have file folders. In those folders, there is paper; and on that paper is information. If you think carefully about how you set up your filing cabinet, it can be a quick-and-easy way to put your hands on the data you need.

Suppose that you need to collect information about all of the players in a golf tournament that you have started. For the most part, you need the same information about each player. You might want to collect the following information:

- Name
- Address

- Phone number
- Payment method
- Handicap (a method of tracking average score related to par, and thereby skill level)
- Team number (which team of four players this person is assigned to)
- Score (this team's score for the tournament)
- Ranking (the ranking of this team in relation to other teams in the tournament based on their score)
- Notes (any miscellaneous information you may need to store about this player)

In order to collect this information, you might whip up a quick form in your favorite word processor and print off a copy for each player you expect to register. Once you have filled out the form (which, keep in mind, is identical for every player) with each player's individual information (which is obviously different for each player), you can store those forms in a file folder for future reference. To make sure that you can always find this information, you place this folder in a drawer in your filing cabinet.

So, in the current example, five items are necessary to collect and store information about the players in your golf tournament: a filing cabinet, a filing drawer in the cabinet, a file folder, a basic form design, and an individual form for each player. These physical items relate directly to the basic parts of a modern database system. They are as follows:

- Database management system
- Individual database
- Tables
- Columns
- Rows

 Other parts of a database, such as stored procedures and triggers, are discussed later in this chapter. The elements in the preceding list represent the basics and are sufficient for this discussion.

The Database Management System

The database management system is the overall application framework within which you design, house, and manage all of the databases you create for your individual projects. Figure 21-1 shows the SQL Server Enterprise Manager. The Enterprise Manager is a centralized place where you can view, open, interact with, and maintain your databases.

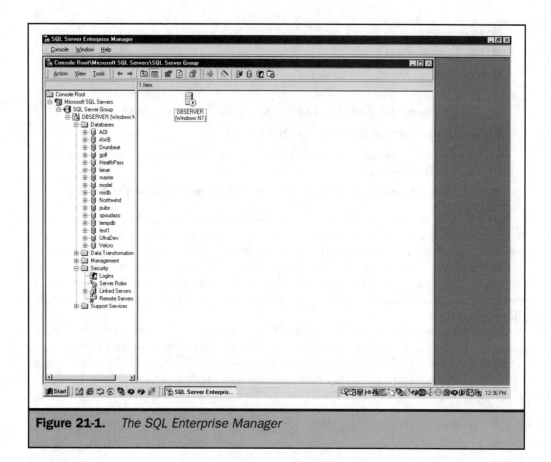

Figure 21-1.   *The SQL Enterprise Manager*

Smaller, file-based database applications, such as Access, don't provide the same level of database management as their server-based big brothers, but you can think of the basic Access program as a place where you can quickly manage the individual database files that you have created. The principal difference is that you will use Access to find and open an individual file on your computer rather than having all of the files located and displayed for you within a management system (see Figure 21-2).

In the current example, the database application or management system represents the filing cabinet in which your filing drawers are kept. You may have several drawers within the cabinet, but they are all available to you right there in the filing cabinet along with the rest of the data.

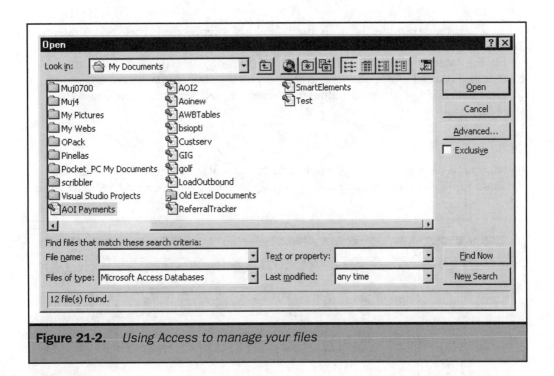

Figure 21-2.   *Using Access to manage your files*

 Note   *In a filing cabinet, you have only so many drawers, usually two or four. One of the great things about a database management system is that you can keep adding drawers (databases) as you need them to hold more data.*

The Individual Database

Within your database management system are individual databases that you have created. An individual database is a set of components and data that serve a particular purpose for a particular project. Although you can keep shoving data into one expanding database to serve multiple purposes, such a database will quickly become unorganized and useless. It is highly advisable to create separate databases for each project—and sometimes even more than one for a project if the project is of sufficient size and scope to require it.

Note   *The decision of how many databases are required to service a project is a many-faceted consideration. You need to investigate topics such as security, performance, maintenance, and data compatibility in the design stage in order to make a reasonable determination.*

In the current example, the individual database is represented by the file drawer. The file drawer is housed within the filing cabinet, just as the database is housed within the database application. Just as you might designate a drawer in your file cabinet for financial information, contracts, or golf tournament participation, you would create and populate individual databases for each type of data you need to store (see Figure 21-3).

Tables

Just as you have organized the places in which you will store data by selecting a database application and creating an individual database to segregate related data, you

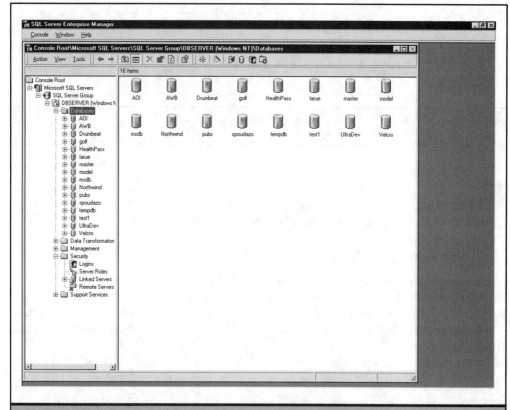

Figure 21-3. *A selection of databases within the SQL Server Enterprise Manager*

must organize the data being stored within each database. In addition to the players in your golf tournament, you may need to store information about sponsors, advertisers, judges, golf courses, and prizes. Trying to store all of this information within the same file folder would be a mistake, just as it would be a mistake to jumble it all together within your database.

Tables are the components of your database that are responsible for holding your data. Typically, you will have a table for each set of related data you need to store. In the present example, you would create a different form on which to write information about the participants, advertisers, and golf courses if you were doing this on paper. There are a couple of reasons for this.

First, different forms for each type of contact make it easier to identify the data that the form holds. Each player has at least one thing in common: each is a player in this golf tournament. Likewise, each advertiser has in common an advertisement at the tournament. It is logical to keep those groups of contacts segregated by the thing they have in common—their type of participation in the event.

Second, you are likely to need different kinds of information about different kinds of contacts. The information you might need about the players was discussed at the beginning of this section. It would be silly to put a place to store the team assignment or score of an advertiser, but you would need a place to put the type of advertisement, the rate they paid, and their billing information—information that you do not need to collect about your players. When the specific information you need to collect and store differs to this degree, it is a strong indication that it should be stored on two different forms, or in two different database tables.

Note *Looking back up the chain of data constructs you are creating, you can clearly see the relation that each has to the other. No matter how many tables you create, they all relate to your golf tournament, and hence belong in your golf tournament database. That golf tournament database, in turn, is one of your projects; therefore, it belongs in the database management system that houses your projects.*

Figure 21-4 illustrates the tables that you might create within your golf tournament database.

Columns

On the form that was created in this example to hold information about the players in the golf tournament, several pieces of information needed to be collected about each player. This information represents attributes of the individual players. These translate to your database table as the columns of the table. Although these attributes are not

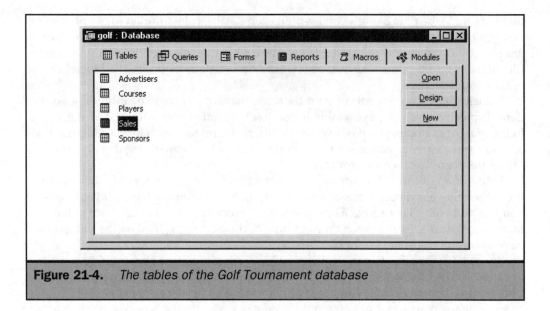

Figure 21-4. *The tables of the Golf Tournament database*

always represented as columns, the datasheet view, a common way of looking at data, looks much like a spreadsheet with the *attribute*, or *field*, names listed across the top. You can see this in Figure 21-5, which makes it clear why "columns" is the common name for this part of the table.

In essence, each column represents a question about the topic of the table. For instance, in the players table, each column relates to one of the attributes of the player. In filling out each column for each player, you are, in effect, answering a question about that player that represents information you have decided your database needs to know about the players in order to manage the tournament effectively.

Rows

Closely related to the columns of the database are the *rows* that make up the left-hand axis of the datasheet in Figure 21-5. These rows are represented in the current example by the individual copies of your form that hold the information about the individual players in your tournament. In the database table, each player is entered on his or her own row of the table. That row holds information about that player and only that player. On each row, a field is available for each column in which you can enter information about that player that answers the question represented by the column, such as what the player's name is, or which team the player is assigned to.

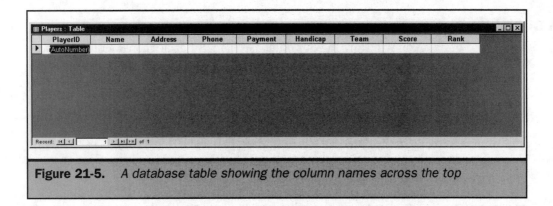

Figure 21-5. *A database table showing the column names across the top*

Designing a Relational Database

Some people's filing cabinets are nothing but collecting spots for excess paper they can't decide what to do with. The drawers barely open and close and they quickly become useless space wasters. If you are not careful and organized, your database will end up the same way: overstuffed, useless, and difficult to open and close.

Despite all that computers can do for you, sometimes setting them aside and starting with a pencil and a piece of paper is a good idea. When you first begin to sketch out the functionality of a computer project, and especially a database schema, get out a good number 2 pencil and a legal pad and try to get your thoughts organized so that the job of actually implementing the database can be done right the first time.

Note   *If you are new to programming, we cannot overemphasize the importance of doing things right the first time. True, you will almost always have bugs that need to be fixed and maintenance to perform, but you can significantly reduce these and eliminate more major problems by spending the time to design your application properly.*

You need to answer several questions before you can begin constructing your database:

- What kind of data will you be storing?
- How will the database be accessed?
- Will your users need to add and change things in the database or just look things up?
- What kind of special functionality might you need access to?
- What changes might you need to make in the future?

Your Data

What kind of data you will store in your database is an important consideration, both in selecting the database management system (or application) you will use and how its structure is defined. If, for instance, you will be storing only text information, such as names and addresses of clients and simple product information, you are pretty safe in assuming that any modern system can accommodate your needs. If, however, you need the capability to store things like BLOBS (Binary Large Objects), such as images and sounds, directly in the database tables (rather than just storing references to them), you will need to do some extra research to make sure that your database selection supports them and find out whether they require any special considerations.

An important point in this day and age is the security level of the information you will be storing. Financial, medical, and other personal information is stored in databases all over the world. If you will be handling information of this nature, you will need to pay special attention to the security scheme that you implement to ensure that the data remains secure.

Database Access

Determining how your database will be accessed is also an important consideration. For instance, will this database service only a Web site, and only one Web site? Or will it need to be accessed by multiple applications such as a sales site, an administration site, and an internal office application written in another language such as Visual Basic so that your sales staff can query information and maintain the site's data?

Think also about how the different uses of the database might affect your security needs. It is unlikely that a standalone Access database that lets users look up ZIP code information, for instance, would pose the same security risk as a large database management system operating at a financial institution. Likewise, a database that allows only office users to access it may not need the same level of security planning as one that makes data available over the Web. Because you are contemplating data access over the Internet with Dreamweaver, you will likely need to spend some time in this important area.

 Adequately covering database security is not possible here. Security is a complex matter with different implementations, depending on the software you need to use. If you are unsure as to the steps required to successfully secure your data, please seek competent help before you attempt to place sensitive information in a Web-connected database.

Use of the Database

The purpose for which your database will be used is also an important point to consider. In the preceding section, a ZIP code lookup function was mentioned. In such an application, the user would most likely be providing some simple information on which a database query would be constructed. The database would return to the user information based on the input the user had provided. For example, if the user supplied a ZIP code, the application might tell him or her for which cities that ZIP code was valid. The functionality could likely be accomplished with only a table or two of data. Such a database would be used to query data from the tables, but it is unlikely that you would ever allow a user to add or change ZIP code information. That kind of information is updated by official sources on a periodic basis, and your own maintenance procedures are all that should be allowed to alter any data within the tables.

However, the golf tournament database discussed in the previous section required several tables to store all of the data. In addition, not only will you and visitors to your site need to query data out of this database, but some of these tables will need regular updating as new players and advertisers sign on and team assignments and scores are updated. Designing a database of even moderate complexity like this can take careful consideration.

For example, it is important to keep data that needs to be updated separated from static or private data, so that users don't inadvertently change something that they shouldn't. In addition, you can save a significant amount of space and simplify maintenance of your site if you use properly normalized data, which we discuss later in this chapter in the "Database Normalization" section.

Database Functionality

If you are new to databases, it may seem strange to talk about a database doing anything besides storing data in tables. In reality, several additional functions can be performed inside the database itself that can increase or improve the performance of your overall application. Some of the most useful functions are listed here:

- Stored procedures
- Triggers
- Views
- Security
- Relationship management

Stored Procedures

Stored procedures are a method of storing the code you use to interact with your database within the database itself. Instead of passing a series of commands into the database every time you need to perform an action, you can create stored procedures that are callable from your application.

Stored procedures enable you to create database code in a modular format that you can reference each time you need to perform a particular task. They can accept input parameters, execute complex series of code, and return recordsets and values to the calling application.

In addition, stored procedures provide the following enhancements:

- **Increased execution speed** Because they are precompiled by the database, stored procedures execute more quickly than the same code passed in from your application.

- **Reduced network traffic** Calling a stored procedure already stored in the database takes fewer commands, and, therefore, less traffic is sent across the network.

- **Increased security** A user can be given permission to execute stored procedures that execute code that the user would not be authorized to run on his own. You can, therefore, better control the combinations of commands that users can execute, increasing the control you have over access to your data.

Triggers

Triggers are a special kind of stored procedure that you can set to run in reaction to changes in your database's data. When an Insert, Update, or Delete command runs, you can set a trigger to run and enforce sets of business rules that you describe.

For example, referential integrity, the assurance that related records remain in sync, is a very important consideration for your database. Maintaining referential integrity in your database requires that you set up rules so that data cannot be altered with impunity in your tables. The triggers that you set up will be responsible for checking to see that any modification of your data conforms to the rules you have described.

For example, in one table you may store information about an employer that will be posting job opportunities to the Bettergig Web site. In another table, you may store information about each of those jobs. If an employer in the first table terminated their relationship with Bettergig.com, you might choose to delete them from the database. If you stopped there, what would you be left with? The answer is a bunch of job opportunities in another table with no information about the company that is offering the jobs. These records become *orphan records* because the parent information that makes them meaningful is gone. Without the employer information, the job information is useless and needs to be deleted from the database at the same time as the employer record. You can set up a trigger on the table that runs each time an employer is deleted. When you delete an employer, you can set that trigger to check the jobs table for job opportunities that were offered by that employer, and the trigger will delete them at the same time.

Likewise, you can set triggers to run when records are added or updated in your database. You can run combinations of triggers in response to single events to allow for complex data manipulation when data is modified in your tables.

Views

A view is a virtual table. That means that its contents are defined by a query, not by an actual physical table that contains data. When a view is created, it is really defined as a query that is run when the view is called from an application or another query. Each time it is called, the query is re-executed so that the data you receive remains current.

In one way, a view is like a stored procedure in that it is a predefined query that can be called when needed. But a view is intended to return data just as a call to a table would; it doesn't perform complicated manipulations and return values as a stored procedure does.

An interesting use of views is the combination of similarly structured data that exists across servers, perhaps in different departments or different divisions of a company. With a view, you can combine, for instance, sales numbers from a variety of departments that all store their data on separate database servers.

In addition, data can be updated through the use of views as long as the view follows these rules:

■ There is at least one table in the From clause, meaning that the view is not based entirely on tableless calculations.

■ There are no aggregate functions in the view. (See Chapter 14 for a discussion of aggregate functions.)

■ Each field in the view must be based on a simple column expression, meaning that no functions or mathematics have been applied.

Security

As mentioned earlier, security is a major concern for any database that you will be placing on the Web. Most database management systems provide a means of defining users and setting security options for individual users or groups of users. Make sure that you understand how your database authenticates users and their appropriate roles before you put data of a sensitive or personal nature anywhere near a Web site.

Relationship Management

When you are setting up your tables in a new database, you need to identify relationships among the data that is stored in the tables. Once again, this relates to database normalization, and relationships will no doubt make more sense after the normalization discussion coming up in this chapter. But a quick example here should help you get started.

When you set up the data for the Bettergig.com Web site, you will see that this database stores information about employers and the jobs they are offering on the site. In one table of the database, information about the participating employers is stored. Information about the jobs they are offering is stored in a different table. How do you know what jobs belong to what employers? Good question.

You could store the name and other information about the employer that is offering a particular job in the table alongside the job details. But this is impractical and unnecessary when you are working within the relational database model. Instead, information about the employer can be stored once in a different table. In that table, each employer is assigned a unique identifying piece of information, usually an integer or small piece of text that you can use to reference that specific employer wherever you need its information. In the jobs table, all you need to do is supply a field in which you can store the identifier of the employer that is offering the job. Then, whenever you reference that job, you can look in this field of the table and identify the employer.

But that little identifier will quickly become useless to you by itself, because you cannot possibly remember all of the employers and their identifiers as the database gets larger. By defining a relationship between the jobs table that holds the identifier and the employers table that tells you which employer that identifier belongs to, you can be sure you always have access to all of the information you need about a job offering.

A database of any size will likely have a number of relationships defined. Figure 21-6 shows a database diagram with several table relationships defined.

In addition to helping you identify your data, relationships can help you make sure that your data remains meaningful. For instance, in this example, suppose that someone tried to assign an identifier to a job for which there was no employer defined in the employers table. The database would throw an error warning you that you were about to corrupt the integrity of your data by assigning a nonexistent employer to a job. In this way, the database can help you enforce the fact that it is proper to set up an employer before entering jobs that they have to offer.

Several different kinds of relationships exist between database tables. These are discussed in the upcoming section "Table Relationships."

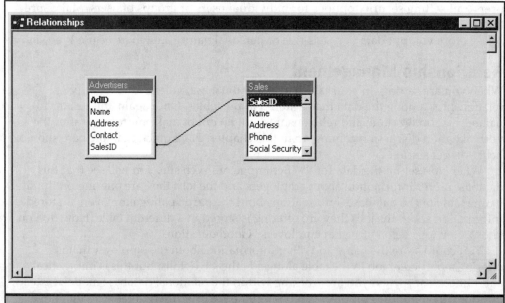

Figure 21-6. *Table relationships are displayed when you view your database diagram.*

Database Maintenance

The last item on the list of considerations when designing a database is the methods you will use to perform maintenance. Ideally, you will need to do as little maintenance as possible, but the real-world facts are that you will end up performing some maintenance on your database as you go. Careful planning will help minimize the number of alterations you need to make, but the sheer complexity of some sites means that you are bound to either miss something or experience an honest to goodness change in how you need the database to work.

One of the primary concerns about altering databases once they are in use is what happens when you find yourself needing to add or change fields (or columns) in a table. In either case, you will likely have existing data that will be affected by the change, and you will need to carefully consider how your changes will impact that data. Give special notice to how existing data will react if you need to change a data type—meaning changing a field from a text data type to an integer, for instance. Think also about existing records if you must add a field to a table. What will it mean that all of the existing records have had no data inserted into that new field, and how can you best address collecting and inserting the appropriate values for each existing record?

Uniqueness and Keys

Suppose that you had several bills of U.S. currency of different denominations in front of you, from a $1 bill up to a $100 bill. If someone asked you to hand him a particular bill that had a U.S. president's picture on it, how would you know which one he meant? Not all U.S. currency has a president on it (Benjamin Franklin was never president), but certainly more than one denomination has a president on it.

Luckily, the bills contain unique information. Each has a different denomination that can identify the bill when compared to others. But even that would not be sufficient in, say, a stack of $10 bills. In that case, you would need to look at the serial number on each bill to be sure that you could identify each bill uniquely.

The records in your database are much the same. Many of them may have information in common. Just as many U.S. bills have presidents on them, many of the players in your golf tournament may live in Georgia. You can go a level deeper and look only for the players from Atlanta. That may work, just as you may have had only a single $10 bill, but it is just as likely that you could have multiple players from Atlanta. In order to be sure that you can identify a single player without question, you need to have information that is unique to that player. Although we are not collecting this information, you might think of something like a social security number, which is guaranteed by an outside source to be unique to each person. Although it may be inappropriate to demand players' social security numbers just so they can play golf, you can approximate the role of the social security number by telling your database to assign a unique identifier to each entry in the database.

Think about why table uniqueness is so important. First, from a common-sense standpoint, how much sense does it make to store multiple copies of identical data in your table? If nothing is different about a second or third record, why waste space storing them?

Second and more important, when you attempt to update or delete a database record, the database must be able to identify exactly which record you are trying to operate on. If it can't do so, the database will likely throw an error rather than risk corrupting your data by altering the incorrect record. Records can be identified by the use of three kinds of keys:

- Candidate keys
- Primary keys
- Foreign keys

Candidate Keys

A candidate key is a set of one or more columns in your database that are unique across all occurrences. For instance, consider the following table of data:

ZIP Code	City
32811	Orlando
32835	Orlando
34749	Ocoee
32789	Winter Park
32790	Winter Park

In this sample, two possible candidate keys exist based on their uniqueness. The first is the ZIP Code column. Because no value repeats, it can be considered a candidate key. In addition, although the city names in the City column do repeat on occasion, the combination of the ZIP Code and City columns together never repeat, providing another possible candidate key. Because the City column does repeat, it has no value by itself for identifying unique records.

Note *Just because the values in these columns do not repeat in the sample data does not necessarily mean that they never will. The designation of a candidate key is based upon your knowledge of the data that will be placed in your tables and your knowledge that certain combinations of columns will remain unique. Once designated, this decision will be enforced in your database to call attention to attempts to duplicate data that you have identified as a candidate key.*

Another consideration when identifying a candidate key is where it is possible for a particular record to be null for a key column. Because null values cannot be guaranteed to be unique, no candidate key can contain nulls.

Primary Keys

A primary key differs from a candidate key only in that it has been arbitrarily designated as the primary key from the selection of candidate keys already defined. Although primary keys, in the current thinking, are not strictly necessary in your tables, they are quite useful—especially because of their minimalist nature.

> **Note** *There is another kind of relational key called an alternate key. An alternate key is any candidate key that has not been designated as the primary key for a table.*

Whereas a given candidate key may be up to several columns in complexity, a primary key is often designated as a single column that uniquely defines a row in the database. Sometimes this single column has no real relationship to the actual data that is being stored, other than the fact that you have designated it as an arbitrary identifier. Developers will often use an autonumber or Identity function to have the database itself create a random or incremental integer or whole number that is used as the primary key. In many cases, you can construct the database so that the number becomes meaningful for the data in question, such as making the generated number a group or account number, but this is not strictly necessary. Primary keys are of the greatest use when used to refer to table data being referenced from a foreign key.

Foreign Keys

Foreign keys are not strictly keys at all, in that they do not typically have any impact on the uniqueness of a particular record. The job of a foreign key is to refer to the primary key (or candidate key, to be proper) of a table that holds more detailed information about some topic that is related to the current record.

For example, let's return to the golf tournament database. In that database, a table was created to hold information about advertisers at the golf tournament. Suppose that this year, the tournament is becoming quite an event, and you must hire some sales people to handle the transactions with your advertisers. You have promised those sales people a commission, so you must, of course, track the sales they have made. To do this, you will need to add a table to hold data about your sales staff. Consider Table 21-1.

Note that the SalesID column is designated as a primary key (PK) for the table. The SalesID is a unique value that is automatically assigned by the database when a new sales rep is entered. As mentioned earlier, this autonumber field has been given significance by making it the sales representative's identification number.

PK	SalesID	Integer
	Name	Text
	Address	Text
	Phone	Text
	Social Security	Text
	Commission Rate	Integer

Table 21-1. *The Sales Table*

Now look at the structure of the advertisers in Table 21-2.

The advertisers table also has a primary key assigned. In addition, the SalesID field has been designated as a foreign key (FK). When you enter a new advertiser into the table, the ID of the sales rep who sold the transaction is entered in the SalesID column. By relating the SalesID foreign-key column from the advertisers table to the SalesID primary-key column in the sales table, you gain a couple of distinct advantages. First, information about your sales staff has to be stored only once and then can be referenced by a simple integer from wherever else in your database you need this information. This saves space in the database, as well as data entry time. Second, you can very easily assign multiple accounts in the advertisers table to the same sales rep, creating a one-to-many relationship between the tables. Table relationships are discussed next.

PK	AdID	Integer
	Name	Text
	Address	Text
	Contact	Text
FK	SalesID	Integer

Table 21-2. *The Advertisers Table*

Table Relationships

There are three types of relationships between database tables:

- One-to-one
- One-to-many
- Many-to-many

One-to-One Relationships

A one-to-one relationship between two tables means that for each record in the first table, there can be one and only one related record in the second table. This type of relationship is rarely used, but when it is, it is usually because of some limitation of the database application that requires a piece of information unique to one record to be stored separately, perhaps because of its size.

One-to-Many Relationships

One-to-many relationships are by far the most common in relational databases. A one-to-many relationship means that one record in the first table may have multiple related records in the second table, usually identified by a foreign key. The golf tournament database is a good example of this. In it, there is one record for each sales representative. The sales representative's ID, however, might show up in multiple records in the advertisers table if one sales rep sold advertisements to many different companies. The one-to-many relationship is the most useful type of relationship, and is a core component of the relational database model.

Many-to-Many Relationships

A many-to-many relationship exists when many records in one table are related to many records in a second table. In reality, this relationship cannot be properly illustrated using the relational database model. To do so would require the use of several overlapping one-to-many relationships. Thus, it is unlikely that this relationship would be used in a well-designed database.

Database Normalization

An in-depth discussion of database normalization could take many chapters; indeed, it has in some books. For the purposes of this book, you need to understand that normalization is the process of organizing data to reduce duplication. This is most often accomplished by separating data into two or more related tables. When done properly, advantages are more storage space, better performance, ease of use, and easier maintenance.

At least five normal forms can define how data is laid out in a database. The most common form through which databases are normalized is the third normal form.

 The third normal form represents a good compromise between performance and design considerations, as well as the total eradication of data duplication. When you get beyond the third form, the recommendations for how data can be organized get rather absurd and unworkable in the modern environment.

The First Normal Form

The first normal form holds that each field in a database table must contain different data. For instance, in the golf tournament players table, you could have only one field in which the score was entered.

The Second Normal Form

The second normal form says that no field of data may be derived from another field. For example, if in the players table you were storing the date of birth of the players, it would be improper to have a second field that stored the year of birth alone because that data would be redundant.

The Third Normal Form

The third normal form says that duplicate information is not allowed in the database. The third normal form is what was achieved in the golf tournament foreign-key example. Instead of storing information about the sales rep for an account directly in the advertisers table each time the sales rep sold a new account, a sales table was created to hold that information, which was then referenced by a foreign key in the advertisers table.

Summary

When you are getting ready to design a database for use on the Web, you need to take several aspects into account, including performance, security, data layout, and functionality. Fortunately, you can take advantage of years of research and save yourself the trouble of determining an efficient means by which to implement your data needs by applying the principles set forth in the relational database model, such as relationships, keys, and normalization. Volumes have been written on database design, and you are encouraged to learn as much as you can—it is an important topic that is often overlooked. If this is the job that you have chosen to do, you are well served to learn as much as you can about the mechanics of constructing a well-designed database.

The Complete Reference

Dreamweaver MX

Chapter 22

Setting Up Your Data

The two preceding chapters have reviewed some of the preliminaries of database connections and database design. Now it's time to put together the actual database that will drive your Bettergig.com Web site. Several sample Bettergig databases have been included in the download at www.osborne.com, including a Microsoft Access 97 version, in addition to several scripts to generate databases for Microsoft SQL Server 7 (or 2000), IBM DB2 7.x, PostgreSQL 7.x, and MySQL 3.x. With the Bettergig sample database in place, you'll be able to follow the examples in the next few chapters.

Before getting to that, however, you need to design the database. Designing the database for the site is arguably the single most important aspect of a dynamic Web site. Without a proper database design, all other aspects of the site become less efficient and more difficult to implement than they need to be. With a proper database design, the SQL statements will be easier to create, and data will be easier to display. Not only that, but the larger the database becomes, the slower it becomes. With a proper design, speed doesn't become as much of an issue.

OLTP and OLAP Databases

The database you'll be designing will be an *online transaction processing (OLTP)* database. Most databases these days are of this variety. OLTP databases are designed with transaction processing in mind. This does not refer to a monetary transaction; rather, by our definition, a *transaction* simply means that the database will be capable of *interaction* with a user through the Web interface you design, and it will allow data to be inserted, updated, and deleted. A typical transaction might be a user changing his or her contact information, such as his or her e-mail address. OLTP databases try to eliminate redundancy for both performance and data integrity.

The other type of database is an *online analytical processing (OLAP)* database. These databases typically are used to report information and rarely have updates to them. In these kinds of databases, redundancy isn't really an issue, and can even help the performance. A typical OLAP database might be a U.S. ZIP code database, in which the data doesn't change very often and needs to be searched quickly.

The Data

The purpose of this database is to hold the data that drives the Bettergig.com Web site. Because the site is a job-search tool, the database has to hold data about available jobs. It also has to hold personal data about the people who are looking for jobs, as well as their resume information. Finally, it must hold data about the employing companies.

A database holds raw data, but the Web application needs to deliver information to the end user. With a proper database design, you can organize the data in a logical fashion so that it can be retrieved in a way that makes it useful to the end user.

List the Items

Proper advance planning is key to a successful database design. Start with a list of the data that you need and organize it into logical tables. Each table should hold data that belongs to one unit/object/entity. Each field in a table should hold one item that pertains to the table. After you organize the data in a logical fashion, you'll go through the *normalization* procedure to eliminate redundant data and to avoid problems with inserting, updating, and deleting data, which you may run into later.

Start by listing the things that you need in your database. The following list should include everything, and also make it clear when multiple items will be needed:

- Job Category 1
- Job Category 2 (and so on)
- Job Type
- Job Location
- Job Status
- Job Salary
- Job Education
- Job Description
- Job StartDate
- Job Term
- Job Citizenship
- Employer Name
- Employer Address
- Employer Contact
- Employer Phone
- Employer Fax
- Employer E-Mail
- Employer Username

- Employer Password
- Employer AccessGroup
- Résumé Goal
- Résumé Education
- Résumé Experience
- Résumé Citizenship
- Résumé Available
- Résumé Status
- Résumé Salary
- Résumé Contact
- Job Seeker Name
- Job Seeker Address
- Job Seeker Phone
- Job Seeker Fax
- Job Seeker E-Mail
- Job Seeker Username
- Job Seeker Password
- Job Seeker Access Group

Normalizing the Data

After you've made the list, you can begin the database normalization process. The first thing you'll want to do is to break the data into separate entities. Looking over the list, you can see four fairly distinct entities: jobs, job seekers, employers, and résumés. These four main entities will make up the four main tables in the database:

- **Seekers**   Holds personal data about the people who are looking for jobs
- **Employers**   Holds data about the employing companies that have jobs available
- **Jobs**   Holds a list of current jobs available
- **Résumés**   Holds current résumés of the job seekers

These tables will simply hold your raw data. The data doesn't have to be in any particular order, and it is generally ordered "as entered." When a new row is added, the data typically gets added to the end of the table, but it could also be inserted somewhere else. The tables are simply storage facilities for the data. The data in the database is organized by indexes and keys, and the physical order of the data means nothing.

Caution	*When naming your tables and database objects, avoid the use of terms that might be reserved words for the database server. Because all databases have different reserved words, it's beyond the scope of this book to give a complete list. However, words such as date, data, time, name, table, field, user, password, or any other generic word that might be used inside of the functionality of the database or SQL should be avoided. For a list of reserved words for your particular database, consult the documentation that came with it.*

Each table holds all the data for one *specific* entity. In the case of the Seekers table, that entity is the personal information of the job seekers. One thing you want to avoid is combining different entities in one table. For instance, at first glance, the Seekers and Résumés could have been contained together in one table. Each job seeker will have a corresponding résumé. Upon closer inspection, though, the job seekers and the résumés are two distinct entities, so it's logical to split them into two tables. By clearly separating distinct entities, you are able to keep your logic easy to understand.

Most tables will have a *plural* name, because they are *collections* of individual rows of data. The fields generally have a *singular* name, because a field should hold only one item of data. This section looks at the fields for the four main tables and how the tables relate to each other. Note that you aren't actually working with the database at this point. You'll map out your tables and columns on paper and then figure out the relationships before moving on to the normalization phase.

Some of the fields declare multiple items. Job Seeker Name, for example, can be broken down into first name and last name. You could even go as far as middle initial and salutation if you so desire. No column should hold more than one item, so before you go any further, you should redefine some of the items in the list to accommodate correct database protocol:

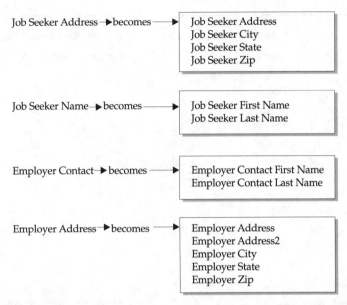

The preliminary field lists for the database tables are given in Tables 22-1 through 22-4. The data types are listed for a Microsoft Access database. The data type comparison chart, shown in Table 22-5, shows the data type conversions for five popular databases (Access, MS SQL Server, PostgreSQL, MySQL, and DB2). The primary key columns are auto-incrementing integer types, and could be MS Access autonumber types or equivalent.

Name	Type	Size	Special Characteristics
SeekID	Number (Long)	4	Primary key (autonumber column)
SeekFirstName	Text	50	
SeekLastName	Text	50	
SeekAddress	Text	60	
SeekCity	Text	50	
SeekState	Text	2	
SeekZip	Text	10	
SeekPhone	Text	20	
SeekFax	Text	20	
SeekEmail	Text	50	
SeekUsername	Text	12	
SeekPassword	Text	12	
SeekAccessGroup	Text	20	Default value "Seekers"

Table 22-1. *Seekers Table, for Job Seeker Personal Information*

Name	Type	Size	Special Characteristics
EmpID	Number (Long)	4	Primary key (autonumber column)
EmpName	Text	50	
EmpAddress	Text	60	
EmpAddress2	Text	60	
EmpCity	Text	50	
EmpState	Text	2	
EmpZip	Text	10	
EmpContactFirst	Text	50	
EmpContactLast	Text	50	
EmpPhone	Text	20	
EmpFax	Text	20	
EmpEmail	Text	50	
EmpUsername	Text	12	
EmpPassword	Text	12	
EmpAccessGroup	Text	20	Default value "Employer"

Table 22-2. *Employers Table, to Hold Company Information*

Name	Type	Size	Special Characteristics
JobID	Number (Long)	4	Primary key (autonumber column)
EmpID	Number (Long)	4	Foreign key to Employers
JobCategory	Text	50	
JobCategory2	Text	50	
JobType	Text	50	
JobLocation	Text	50	
JobStatus	Text	50	
JobSalary	Text	50	
JobEducation	Text	50	
JobDescription	Text	255	
JobStartDate	Text	50	
JobTerm	Text	50	
JobCitizenship	Text	50	

Table 22-3. *Jobs Table, to Hold Job Information*

Name	Type	Size	Special Characteristics
ResID	Number (Long)	4	Primary key (autonumber column)
SeekID	Number (Long)	4	Foreign key to Seekers table
ResGoal	Text	255	
ResEducation	Text	255	
ResExperience	Text	255	
ResCitizenship	Text	50	
ResAvailable	Text	50	
ResStatus	Text	50	
ResSalary	Text	50	
ResContact	Text	50	

Table 22-4.   *Résumés Table, to Hold Data about Individual Résumés*

Access	SQL Server/MSDE	PostgreSQL	DB2	MySQL
AutoNumber (Long)	int (w/IDENTITY property)	serial	integer	int (AUTO_ INCREMENT)
Byte	smallint	smallint	smallint	tinyint
Currency	money	decimal	-	decimal
Date/Time	datetime	date or time	date or time	datetime
Hyperlink	-	-	-	-
Memo	ntext	text	clob	text, mediumtext, longtext
Number (Decimal)	decimal	decimal	decimal	decimal
Number (Double)	float	double precision (float8)	double	double
Number (Integer)	smallint	integer	integer	int
Number (Long)	int	bigint (int8)	bigint	bigint
Number (ReplicationID)	uniqueidentifier	-	-	-
Number (Single)	real	real (float4)	real	float
OLE Object	image	bytea	blob	blob
Text	varchar	varchar or text	varchar	varchar or text
Yes/No	bit	bit	-	-

Table 22-5.   *Data Types Comparison Chart for Several Leading Databases*

An identifying prefix is prepended to each field in the table so that the field can be identified as a member of that table. For instance, SeekFirstName is used in the Seekers table (refer to Table 22-1) for the first name of a job seeker. This keeps things more organized when you start writing your SQL statements with joins in them, and it also helps you keep track of foreign keys in other tables. For instance, the SeekID field is the primary key of the Seekers table, but it is also a foreign key in the Résumés table, identifying the individual job seeker by his or her unique identifier. We've done this as our naming convention, but you can use any method that you feel comfortable with. The important thing is to have a naming convention and use it consistently.

Tip   *Several methods exist for making your field names unique. Spaces are not permissible in naming conventions, nor are special characters. You can use a prefix in small letters, such as seekFirstName, or simply capitalize the first name of every word, as we do in this book. Another typical naming convention uses underscores, as in Seek_First_Name.*

Starting with the Seekers table, note that it contains all the personal information about the job seeker, such as name and address, a username and password, and an AccessGroup level. The SeekID field will be the primary key of the table. You can use this field now as a foreign key in another table to reference a particular job hunter. Most of the fields will correspond directly to the form fields that the job seeker will fill out in the Web application.

Note   *Primary keys, foreign keys, and other database terms were introduced in Chapter 21.*

The AccessGroup field is set up as a special field that automatically inserts a value of "Seeker" into the field every time a new row is added to the table. This is accomplished by defining a default value for the column. Not all database servers allow a default value, but you should use it if you can. This is an easy way to make sure that everyone inserted into this table has an AccessGroup level of "Seeker." This way, you don't have to complicate your Web application with any of the details of logic—simply inserting the row with the Seeker information will automatically insert the AccessGroup level.

The Employers table is similar to the Seekers table in design, but it will hold the data about each particular employer who may use the site. The employers will be the group responsible for posting the jobs and the job information. Also, they will be the group that is able to search the résumés for likely candidates for the jobs. The EmpID field is the primary key for the table; it will be used to reference a particular employer in other tables as a foreign key. As in the Seekers table, an AccessGroup field exists for the access level of the employer. This field also has a default value—"Employer." Employers will have access only to those areas of the site that have an access level of "Employer."

The Jobs table is the job listing provided by the employer. The primary key is the JobID field, which is used as a unique identifier to be able to refer to any particular job.

The EmpID field is a foreign key from the Employers table. Each job will be supplied by one particular employer, and this field will reference that employer. This provides a one-to-many relationship between the Employers table and the Jobs table. Although each job has a specific employer that it references, each employer could have many jobs being offered.

The Jobs table also contains fields for job categories, job location, salary, description, and education requirements, among other things. In short—all the data about a particular job will be held in this table. The fields will correspond directly to the form fields that the employer will use to insert the job into the database from the Web application.

The Résumés table will hold individual résumés of the job seekers. We've elected to pull the résumé information from form fields entered into a Web form, so the fields in this table will represent the results of those Web forms. The other option was to have the user upload an actual résumé to the server, but that presents other problems and complicates the issue at hand. For one thing, you would need an upload component if you were to have an ASP or JSP site. Also, the information wouldn't be readily available to the database for searches. The file would have to be broken down into a text-only file, and the keywords would have to be extracted from it. We'll leave that for the next version of the Web site.

The fields in the Résumés table contain all the information that a person would generally enter on a résumé, such as work experience, education experience, and so forth. The ResID field is the primary key for the table. The SeekID field is a foreign key from the Seekers table, because the résumés will be submitted by the job seekers.

The four tables comprise all the information that you need to complete your application, but there are some scenarios that you need to think about before you commit to this design. If you remember the first rule in database normalization, each field should contain different data. The Jobs table clearly has a few instances where duplicate or redundant data is being stored.

The JobCategory and JobCategory2 fields in the Jobs table, for instance, both apply to the same thing. Because you may need to have two different job categories, this may be a contender for a separate table. The data could come from a predefined list of categories, which prevents redundant information from being entered and also prevents cases of users entering two similar values, such as S/W Design and Software Design.

The JobsCategories table is a simple listing of all Jobs and their related categories, which form a *many-to-many* type of relationship. A job can have zero or more categories using this structure with no redundant data. The information is no longer stored in the Jobs table. Likewise, a category could have zero or more jobs associated with it. A table with a many-to-many relationship will usually be named after the two tables that it joins—in this case Jobs and Categories.

The nice thing about having a many-to-many relationship here is that you can find related data easily by joining tables in the SQL statements. Whereas in the previous design a Job could have only two related categories, a job can now have an infinite number of categories with no associated overhead. When a new job is entered, a row is created in the JobsCategories table for each category that applies to the job. For example, if an Employer on Bettergig.com lists a job that requires skills in databases, VBScript, SQL Server, and Web design, there will be four corresponding rows in the JobsCategories table. You can query the table for a particular job to retrieve all of the associated categories, or you can query the table to retrieve all of the associated jobs.

The JobsCategories field doesn't require a primary key, because the JobID and CatID form a *composite key*. A composite key is simply a primary key that is composed of two or more fields. In this case, the JobID is the primary key of the Jobs table, and the CatID field is the primary key of the Categories table. They are both foreign keys to their respective tables, but together they form a composite key.

The JobTypes field in the Jobs table, on the other hand, will have only one value, but it is the type of value that would be best served by a list. This way, duplicate data will not be stored in the Jobs table, and data search and retrieval will be quicker. For example, if 100 jobs had "Web Development" as their job type, that would be a lot of redundant data in the table. By simply listing Web Development once in a central table, you can reference it with a foreign key in the Jobs table, which typically will take up only four bytes of storage and will be much faster to search. Searches in integer fields are typically much faster than searches in text fields.

The JobStatus field, like the JobTypes field, can contain a one-word description of the status of the job, such as "Temporary" or "Permanent." The status should be kept in a separate table, so that redundant information won't be stored in the Jobs table, and searches for a particular job status will be quicker.

The four new database tables are shown in Tables 22-6 through 22-9.

> **Tip**
>
> *Tables such as the Categories and JobTypes tables that simply list some unchanging data are frequently used to feed list menus on Web pages. If the user has to update or insert some information into a table, it's best that the choices also come from the database, rather than being hard-coded in the page.*

The normalization process is almost complete. Now that you've created these data tables, you have to go back to the Jobs table and change the plan for the JobCategory, JobCategory2, and JobTypes fields. Eliminate the JobCategory and JobCategory2 fields completely. For the JobTypes field, change the data types from Text to Number (Long) types, and use the field as a foreign key to the primary key just created in the JobTypes table. For the JobStatus field, change the data type from Text to Number (Long) type, and use the field as a foreign key to the primary key just created in the JobStatus table. Again, you shouldn't be working with the database at this point yet, only plotting your strategy on paper. The new Jobs table is listed in Table 22-10.

The tables could be normalized even more by creating a States table listing all U.S. states and referencing the primary key in the Jobs, Seekers, and Employers tables. Getting too deeply into database design, however, is beyond the scope of this book. For now, the database is normalized to the point where the main rules of normalization are being followed and the tables are still easily understood.

Name	Type	Size	Special Characteristics
CatID	Number (Long)	4	Primary key (autonumber column)
CatDesc	Text	50	

Table 22-6.   *The Newly Created Categories Table Is a Reference for Categories for the Jobs Table*

Name	Type	Size	Special Characteristics
CatID	Number (Long)	4	Foreign key to Categories
JobID	Number (Long)	4	Foreign key to Jobs

Table 22-7.   *The Newly Created JobsCategories Table Is a Reference for All Job/Category Joins*

Name	Type	Size	Special Characteristics
JobTypeID	Number (Long)	4	Primary key (autonumber column)
JobTypeDesc	Text	50	

Table 22-8.   *The Newly Created JobTypes Table Is a Reference for Job Types in the Jobs Table*

Name	Type	Size	Special Characteristics
JobStatusID	Number (Long)	4	Primary key (autonumber column)
JobStatusDesc	Text	50	

Table 22-9.   *The Newly Created JobStatus Table Is a Reference for Job Status in the Jobs Table*

Name	Type	Size	Special Characteristics
JobID	Number (Long)	4	Primary key (autonumber column)
EmpID	Number (Long)	4	Foreign key to Employers
~~JobCategory~~	~~Text~~	~~50~~	
~~JobCategory2~~	~~Text~~	~~50~~	
JobType	~~Text~~ Number(Long)	~~50~~ 4	
JobLocation	Text	50	
JobStatus	~~Text~~ Number(Long)	~~50~~ 4	
JobSalary	Text	50	
JobEducation	Text	50	
JobDescription	Text	255	
JobStartDate	Text	50	
JobTerm	Text	50	
JobCitizenship	Text	50	

Table 22-11.   *The Newly Modified Jobs Table*

Typical Uses for the Data

You also have to consider other information that you might need to store in the database. People generally think of a database in terms of *information*, but a database, in fact, holds only raw *data*. After that data is processed by an application, it becomes information. All the basic data that you need is already in the database, but now you must think in terms of the end user, and what sorts of information the user will want from the database.

A typical user of the Bettergig.com Web site will be a job seeker who will come to the site, enter personal information, and compose his or her résumé. The following are some other things a job seeker might want to do:

- Search the job database
- View a list of employers
- View the job database by category
- Check the status of his or her résumé to see whether anyone has looked at it

- Update personal information
- Update his or her résumé
- Delete his or her account
- Apply for jobs

As you address the functionality, you'll see that several of these tasks can already be performed using the data previously entered. Searching the job database or viewing by category will entail setting up a search form and searching the Jobs table. Viewing a list of employers is also easy, by displaying information from the Employers table. What about checking who has viewed each résumé? Right now, no way exists to keep track of this information, although the data is already in place. You need to use the ResID field from the Résumé table to keep track of which résumé is being looked at, and the EmpID field from the Employers table to see who has viewed it. A new table called ResumesViewed is created to hold these two pieces of data, as shown in Table 22-11; this table contains a new field to hold a unique ID number for the row.

The resumesViewedID field is the primary key; it is an Access Autonumber field (or an equivalent field in the database of your choice). The ResID field is the primary key of the Résumés table, and it acts as a foreign key here. A one-to-many relationship exists between the Résumés table and the resumesViewed table, because one résumé may be viewed any number of times. The EmpID field is the primary key of the Employers table and acts as a foreign key in this table. A one-to-many relationship exists here as well, because one employer can view many résumés.

In your Web application, you'll have to add the functionality to achieve these results, but now you have a table to hold the data. With this information, you can offer the job seeker a count of how many times his or her résumé has been viewed, or even give information about the various employers that may have viewed the résumé. By the same token, this table will give employers information about the number of résumés they've viewed.

Next, you need to include the capability for job seekers to update their personal information and résumés. This is a straightforward process, as well, and doesn't require any additional database functionality.

Name	Type	Size	Special Characteristics
ResumesViewedID	Number (Long)	4	Primary key (autonumber column)
ResID	Number (Long)	4	
EmpID	Number (Long)	4	

Table 22-11.   *The ResumesViewed Table, Containing Two Foreign Keys Referencing the Résumés Table and the Employers Table*

Deleting the data is another gray area. When a job seeker deletes his or her résumé or personal information, do you purge it from the database or simply mark his or her data as "inactive" with a Boolean value (yes/no or bit data type)? In this case, you'll allow a purge of the record. This is always an option when you design your own database. By allowing the user to delete an entry, rather than simply marking the user as "inactive," you eliminate all traces that the user ever existed. That's fine for this demonstration, but in your own real-world database, you might want to keep track of the deleted entries as well. One way to do this is by use of a *trigger* that would allow you to perform operations on any insert, update, or delete to any given table. Using a trigger, you would be able to track any changes to your database.

To ensure referential integrity (described in Chapter 21), you need to make sure that if a job seeker decides to delete his personal data, any entries in the Résumés table will be deleted as well. This can be done at the application level or at the database level. In Access, when you are building your relationships, you can specify to "ensure referential integrity." SQL Server has this functionality built into the visual tools as well, as shown in Figure 22-1. By specifying the relationships in the diagram, the

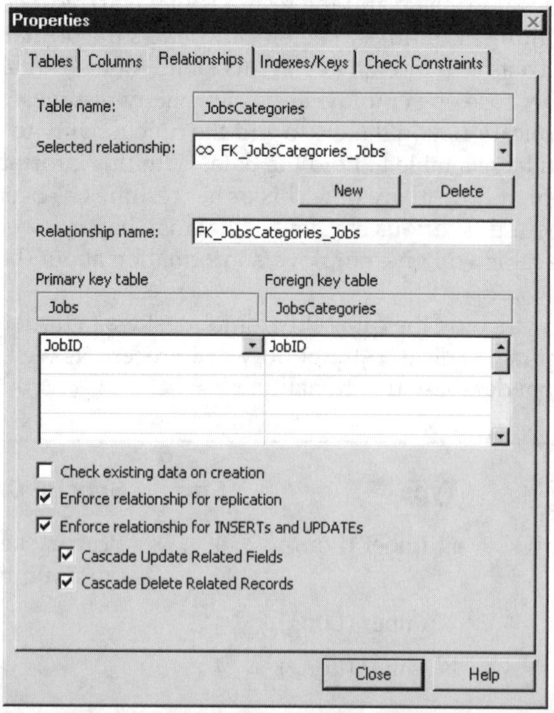

Figure 22-1. *Adding constraints to a table in SQL Server using the diagram*

database server automatically creates the relationships internally and enforces referential integrity.

| Caution | *Although SQL Server 2000 supports cascading delete, SQL Server 7 doesn't. Also, MySQL 3.x has no support for constraints or referential integrity.* |

If your database server doesn't have visual tools, or if you prefer to use SQL scripting, these constraints can be scripted as well, as in the following example:

```
ALTER TABLE Resumes ADD
   CONSTRAINT FK_Resumes_Seekers FOREIGN KEY
   (SeekID) REFERENCES Seekers(SeekID)
      ON DELETE CASCADE
      ON UPDATE CASCADE
```

As you can see, each constraint has a unique name so that the database can keep track of the object.

The last item on the list for the job seeker is the ability to apply for jobs. Currently, no way exists to keep track of jobs that are applied for in the database. Thus, Table 22-12 is created (called JobsAppliedFor) to hold the SeekID field for the job seeker and the JobID field for the job, as well as a new field to hold a unique identifier for the row.

This table provides a new relationship: jobs to seekers. The JobsAppliedID field is the primary key, and it is an Access Autonumber field (or an equivalent field in the database of your choice). The Jobs table has a one-to-many relationship to the JobsAppliedFor table, because one job could have many applicants. The Seekers table also has a one-to-many relationship to the JobsAppliedFor table, because the job seeker could have applied to many jobs. The table contains a column that tracks the date/time that the job was applied for. This should be set up as a default value generated by the database server. In SQL Server, the function *getdate()* gives you a current date/time value. In Access, you can use *Date()*.

Name	Type	Size	Special Characteristics
JobsAppliedID	Number (Long)	4	Primary key (autonumber column)
SeekID	Number (Long)	4	Foreign key to Seekers table
JobID	Number (Long)	4	Foreign key to Jobs table
JobsAppliedDate	Datetime	8	Default value of current date

Table 22-12.   *The JobsAppliedFor Table Tracks the Jobs for Which a User Has Applied*

If you look at a diagram of the relationships, shown in Figure 22-2, you can see the entire database as it stands now. The little "keys" signify the primary key of a certain table, linked to an "infinity" sign, showing the one-to-many relationship. The built-in diagram editor of Microsoft SQL Server 2000 was used to generate this diagram. A diagram like this should be drawn by hand before starting on the actual implementation. Spending the time in the design phase of the database before committing it to your server is important. It's the same principle as building a house. You wouldn't give the carpenters a pile of wood and tell them to start building without first committing the design of the house to a set of blueprints. This database diagram is the blueprint for the database, and it exists on paper before the first table is created in your database.

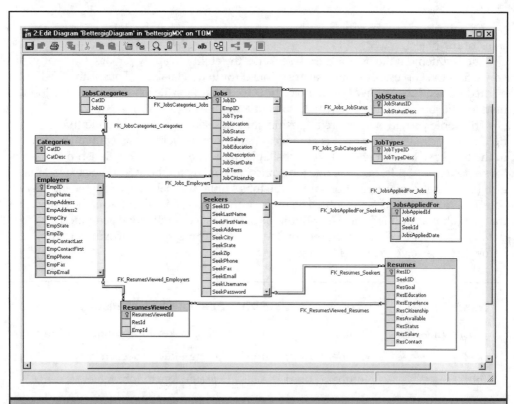

Figure 22-2.   A diagram of the physical structure of the Bettergig database

Indexes

One last thing that you'll need to concern yourself with in any database is where to place the indexes. What is an index? Indexes in a database table are similar to indexes in a book—rather than page through the entire book to find a specific topic, you can look in the index to find the exact page. For example, if you were to look for the word *indexes* in this book, it might take you hours to find it if you started on page one and scanned each page until you found it. By looking in the index, you can see that the word is found on several pages, and you can then go directly to those pages to find the instance of the word. A search using the index of a book might take you minutes instead of hours.

Indexes in the database act the same way. If you are searching for a particular e-mail address, and your table has 100,000 rows, if the e-mail address field is indexed, the search will require only a few accesses to the data. If the field isn't indexed, the database may have to look through 99,999 rows (worst case) before it comes to the one row containing the e-mail address you need. Similarly, if you are retrieving records from the Seekers table and sorting by last name, if the SeekLastName field is indexed, the sort will take much less time, and the data will be returned to the application much more quickly.

Indexes come at a cost, however. You can overuse indexes. In general, you should index only two or three columns in a table at the most. Indexes can create bottlenecks in database performance when it comes time to update or insert data. A well-managed database has a careful balance of cost versus value when it comes to indexes.

The general rules for indexing a column in a table are if

- It is frequently used in a table join.
- You are frequently searching for an exact match in that field. A good indication is if your SQL statement has a WHERE clause that points to one specific field.
- It is frequently used in an ORDER BY clause.
- It is used in GROUP BY queries.
- It is used in range queries (such as SELECT * from mytable WHERE access_date BETWEEN '01/01/02' AND '01/31/02').
- It is used in aggregate functions.

Again, all of these may apply multiple times to any one table, but it is up to the database designer to implement the best strategy to take into account the different situations for which the data will be used.

Tables also have "built-in" indexing—any time you have a primary key or unique key constraint on a table, the primary key is used as an index.

When should a field not be indexed? There are several rules here, but in general you don't want to index something if a table scan is more cost-effective, taking into account the extra work the database has to do to manage the index. Using the book index analogy, if a page in a book only has a few words on it and you are looking for one particular word, it would be quicker to scan the page than to go to the index of the book and retrieve the page number. Even though the JobTypes table will be searched frequently, there are only a few items in the table, making an index not as desirable. Also, it goes without saying that if a database column is not going to be used in queries that it would not be a good candidate for an index.

The Jobs.JobDescription field may be searched frequently, but it is a long field and will seldom be searched based on the sort order—the searches of this field will be within the text of the field itself, making an index almost useless. As an example, look at the following job description:

> "This job calls for an ASP programmer with 5 years of experience in Visual Basic, SQL Server, and other related technologies. Knowledge of Visual Interdev would be a plus."

If a job seeker were to search for "Visual Interdev," the index on this field would have absolutely no value because it is based on the first word in the field: "this."

Tip	*SQL Server has full-text indexing as an added feature, but use it only when needed.*

The Bettergig database has a few places where an index will be useful. For example, both the Employers table and the Seekers table have a username field—this field will be accessed for one value every time a user logs in to the site. Also, every time the user modifies something in the database, the user's account information is retrieved by using the username. For that reason, putting indexes on the SeekUsername and EmpUsername fields might make sense.

The Jobs table has a column that will be accessed frequently in job searches: JobTypes. This makes a good candidate for an index. The JobsCategories table has only two fields, but the CatID field will be accessed in a lot of searches because it points to the jobs that contain matches that a job seeker might want to find. For that reason, we'll index CatID in that table.

Implementing the Database

Now that the design is complete, you can implement the database. You should never use a production database server while building and testing your application, so it is wise to have a design-time connection to a local database server. The connection methods were outlined in Chapter 20. The run-time connection is the connection to the database that resides on your Web server. The server could be a computer at your shop or an unknown computer located at a remote location at an Internet service provider (ISP) somewhere.

You may decide to make the design-time and run-time connections to the remote Web server and not even implement a local database. Although it's certainly an option, you'll find that having a local copy of the database makes your Web site creation much less painful. A process that is popular is to use a local copy of Microsoft Access and upsize the database to a remote copy of Microsoft SQL Server for your run-time connection. To change the connection, you simply have to redefine it in the Dreamweaver MX environment so that the connection file that resides in the Connections folder is different for the remote Web server.

Caution   *Although you may be tempted to use the same database and connection for your design-time and run-time connections, it's not a good idea to work with critical live data while you are in the design phase. At the very least, you should be working from a "copy" of the original database, and not the actual database.*

If you are working on a local copy of Access, SQL Server, or any other database, creating the database and tables will be easy. In Access, you simply choose File | New and give the database a name. After creating a "new" database, you can create the tables simply by typing the information into the table design interface (see Figure 22-3).

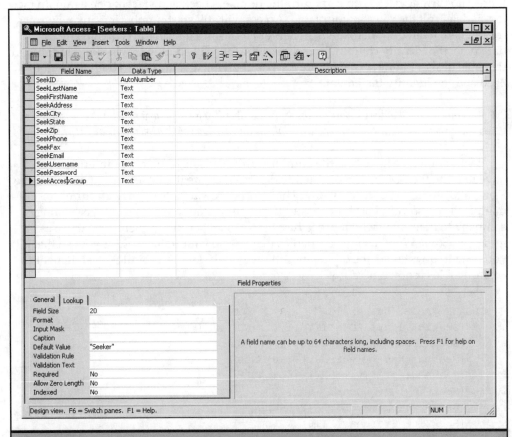

Figure 22-3.   *The table design interface in Microsoft Access*

Most RDBMS software has a user interface of some kind that makes creating databases and tables easy. Some, such as MySQL, don't come with visual interfaces, but third-party products have been built to allow visual editing of the database.

You'll be assigning the field names and data types, as well as the maximum length for the individual fields. This is often a gray area. You don't want to use too much space for your fields, but you also don't want to take the chance that the data won't fit into the field. Use your own discretion when deciding on your field lengths. In SQL Server, there are varchar and nvarchar fields that allow variable length data. It's still a requirement to declare a field size, but the actual data will take up only as much space as it needs. Varchar is a one-byte character, and nvarchar is a two-byte character (Unicode). With that in mind, a 50-character varchar field can take 50 bytes for storage, whereas a 50-character nvarchar field can take 100 bytes for storage.

Access has a special Autonumber field that typically is used for the primary key. Access will automatically increment the previous number for any new row that is being inserted. Keep in mind, however, that after Access starts to autonumber a field, there's no turning back. You can't turn the numbers back and start at one again. In fact, if you delete all the rows in your table, Access will still start numbering any new rows from where it left off. Microsoft SQL Server has a similar structure when using the int data type: the Identity column. You choose the Identity column by checking Identity in the table design interface (see Figure 22-4) and giving a value of 1 to both the Identity Seed and the Identity Increment.

Caution   *You can use identity or autonumber fields liberally for primary keys, but you should not use them as identifiers for secure applications because of their sequential nature.*

If you don't have access to the administrative console or database interface, you'll have to write the SQL code to create the database, create the tables, and then create the views and stored procedures, if any. This procedure varies from manufacturer to manufacturer, so you'll have to consult the documentation from your Web-hosting company to determine which procedure to use to create and implement databases on its server. Some Web-hosting companies may create your databases for you, so that all you need to do is create the tables and fill them with data. A typical SQL statement to create a table is shown here:

```
CREATE TABLE [Seekers] (
    [SeekID] [int] IDENTITY (1, 1) NOT NULL ,
    [SeekFirstName] [varchar] (50) NULL ,
    [SeekLastName] [varchar] (50) NULL ,
    [SeekAddress] [varchar] (60) NULL ,
    [SeekCity] [varchar] (50),
    [SeekState] [varchar] (2) NULL ,
    [SeekZip] [varchar] (10) NULL ,
    [SeekPhone] (20)NULL ,
```

```
    [SeekFax] [varchar] (20) NULL ,
    [SeekEmail] [varchar] (50)NULL ,
    [SeekUsername] [varchar] (50) NULL ,
    [SeekPassword] [varchar] (50) NULL ,
    [SeekAccessGroup] [varchar] (50)NULL
)
```

This statement creates the Seekers table. You'll need to become completely familiar with the implementation of SQL for your particular database if this is the route you intend to take. Databases such as MySQL and PostgreSQL aren't implemented with a GUI, and table creation can be something of a nightmare—especially from a remote location. These database servers also allow the use of a SQL script file that can be loaded in and executed. Script files for these databases are included in the download at www.osborne.com, along with instructions on how to load and run them.

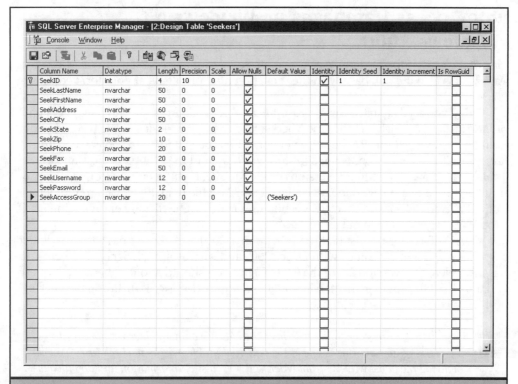

Figure 22-4.   *The table design interface in Microsoft SQL Server 7*

Deploying Your Database

Deploying a database on the Web server is going to vary depending upon which database you're using. An Access database, for instance, is a file-based database, so it's simply a matter of including the Access MDB file in the root of your Web site and uploading it with Dreamweaver MX's built-in FTP tools. Choose the file from the Site Manager and then either use the *put* command or drag and drop the database into the appropriate Web folder on the server. If you have security concerns about leaving the database at the root of the site, you can use a third-party FTP program to upload the database to the proper location. If the database is at the root of the site, you can keep it inside a secure folder with permissions set up by the Web server administrator.

You'll find that as you deploy databases on the server, a Web-hosting company with good customer service is essential. There are permission issues, DSN issues, and a host of possible problems that will need personal attention from a representative from your Web-hosting company. If you find that you can't reach them by phone or e-mail, and you can't get your service set up with a database connection, it's probably time to switch Web-hosting companies.

Remote Access Databases on Windows NT and Windows 2000

One of the most popular databases for small- to medium-sized Web sites is Microsoft Access. It is also the database with the most potential problems, if you don't configure it correctly.

The server needs to have the Microsoft Data Access Components (MDAC) version 2.1 or later installed, which includes the Microsoft Jet Database Engine 4. We recommend nothing less than MDAC 2.5, because version 2.1 has been known to become corrupt and cause the database connections to stop working until the MDAC is reinstalled. Table 22-13 shows the different versions of the MDAC. If you aren't sure of your version number, find either the Msdadc.dll or the Oledb32.dll file (usually in a shared folder under Program Files), and check its version number by right-clicking and viewing its Properties page, as shown in Figure 22-5.

MDAC 2.5 comes preinstalled with Windows 2000 and doesn't have to be installed separately. Version 2.1 comes with Office 2000 and Microsoft SQL Server 7. Microsoft has also released a version 2.6 of the MDAC, but you should avoid it, because it doesn't contain OLE DB providers for the Jet database engine (MS Access), although you can add these components separately.

 Some installer programs will write over the MDAC with an older version. If things stop working for you, this is one of the potential problem areas to check first. You can download the latest MDAC from Microsoft's Web site. Information and downloads are at www.microsoft.com/data.

Name	New Name	Ship Vehicle	Release Date
MDAC 2.7 RTM	MDAC 2.7 RTM (2.70.7713.4)	Microsoft Windows XP	October 2001
MDAC 2.6 SP1	MDAC 2.6 SP1 (2.61.7326.6)	Microsoft SQL Server 2000 SP1	June 2001
MDAC 2.6 RTM	MDAC 2.6 RTM (2.60.6526.3)	Microsoft SQL Server 2000	September 2000
MDAC 2.5 SP2	MDAC 2.5 SP2 (2.52.6019.2)	Microsoft Windows 2000 SP2	
MDAC 2.5 SP1	MDAC 2.5 SP1 (2.51.5303.5)	Microsoft Windows 2000 SP1	August 2000
MDAC 2.5 RTM	MDAC 2.5 RTM (2.50.4403.12)	Microsoft Windows 2000	February 2000
MDAC 2.1 SP2	MDAC 2.1.2.4202.3 (GA)	Microsoft Universal Data Access Web site	July 1999
MDAC 2.1 SP1a	MDAC 2.1.1.3711.11 (GA)	Microsoft Universal Data Access Web site	April 1999
MDAC 2.1 Internet Explorer 5 SP1	(a subset of MDAC 2.1.1.3711.11(GA))	Microsoft Internet Explorer 5.0	March 1999
MDAC 2.1 SDK updater	MDAC 2.1 SDK updater	Microsoft Universal Data Access Web site	January 1999
MDAC 2.1 RTM	MDAC 2.10.3513.2 (SQL7)	Microsoft SQL Server 7.0	November 1999

Table 22-6. *MDAC Version Numbers*

In the best possible scenario, the database should reside in a folder that's apart from the root of your site. For instance, if the site is located at e:\inetpub\wwwroot\mysite, your database could be at e:\databases. If you have a Web-hosting company, that might not be an option for you. It is important, however, for your database to reside in a folder that is not available to Internet Information Server (IIS) to read from. Typically, there is a cgi-bin directory on the server located in the root of the site. That folder is protected from within IIS from prying eyes by having its read permission turned off.

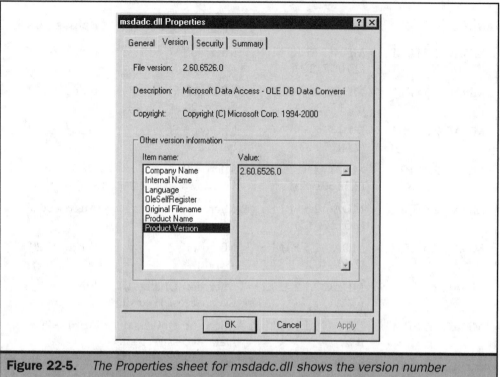

Figure 22-5. *The Properties sheet for msdadc.dll shows the version number*

This is not the Windows NT read permission, but rather the IIS read permission, which is accessible through the IIS Administrator interface, shown in Figure 22-6.

 You can check whether the read permission is set correctly by trying to browse to the database from your local machine. When you put a known path to the database in the Web browser, such as www.mysite.com/cgi-bin/mydatabase.mdb, you should see an error page. If the File Download dialog box pops up, you know that the permissions are set incorrectly!

Also, the actual folder needs to have full IUSR_MACHINENAME permissions set up on it under Windows NT. When IIS is installed, a user account is created in Windows NT, which you can view by going to Start | Programs | Administrative Tools (common) | User Manager For Domains. Again, if your database is on a remote server owned by the Web-hosting company, they will have to make sure the proper permissions are set.

In addition to the folder having full access to the IUSR account, the database must have it as well. Frequently, the database is uploaded to the folder or copied from another

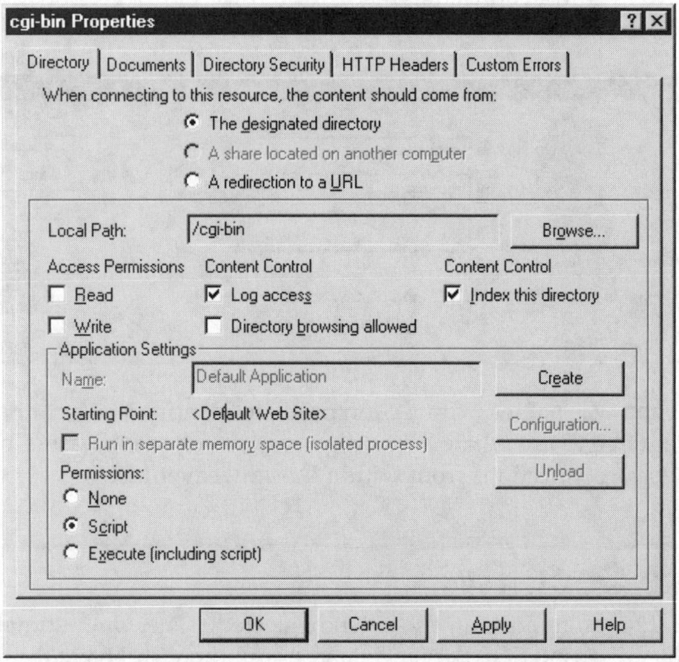

Figure 22-6.   *Access permissions to folders can be set in IIS*

location and doesn't inherit the permissions from the folder. You should explicitly check the permissions of the database. One of the most common errors for Access database users in ASP is the following:

```
Microsoft OLE DB Provider for ODBC Drivers error '80004005'
[Microsoft][ODBC Microsoft Access 97 Driver] Operation must use
an updateable query.
```

This error message actually usually has nothing to do with the query. The error will occur if the database isn't in a folder with IUSR permissions, or if the database itself doesn't have these permissions. This is another example of a cryptic Microsoft error message. Luckily, Microsoft has a very good Knowledge Base from which errors like this can be tracked down easily. In many cases, if you copy and paste the entire error message into a Microsoft Knowledge Base search query, you will find white papers dealing with the errors in question.

The Dreamweaver MX connection made for our Access 97 version of the database in an ASP site is shown here:

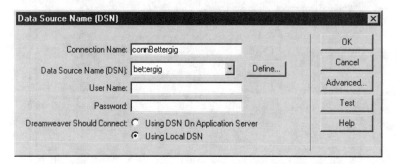

The connection was named with a conn prefix to identify it as a connection, although you are free to use whatever naming convention you please. Chapter 20 details the database connections from within Dreamweaver MX.

Database Security

Database security is an important, and often neglected, issue. One estimate says that 25 percent of the Microsoft SQL Server databases out there still have the default "sa" system administrator account set up with no password. This is asking for trouble. Your database should always be set up with a username and strong password to access it. If your database has some critical data on it that you don't want to be made available to hackers, you might consider some sort of encryption/decryption software. Although the server-based databases are the most secure, your data is secure only if you have complete trust in your Web-hosting company. No one is 100 percent safe from hackers.

Tip *A strong password is a password that can't be easily broken by "brute force." Hackers can use programs that determine passwords by simply trying every combination of letters available. If you use combinations of upper- and lowercase letters and special characters, the password is much more difficult to break.*

In addition, if you have a database server such as MS SQL Server, IBM DB2, PostgreSQL, or MySQL, you should isolate database privileges for the Web application to the bare minimum. For example, for a site that just displays table data, there is no reason to allow the Web application to have insert, update, or delete privileges on the tables that display the data.

Tip *Most databases have views that allow you to define queries that represent "virtual tables" in your database. This allows you to isolate privileges to specific columns in a table. Rather than allowing access to the entire table, you can create a view that accesses only certain columns. By allowing the Web application to use the view and not the table, you are effectively limiting the access to certain columns in the table.*

If you have an administration section of your database allowing an administrator to update, insert, or delete data, you should isolate those pages to that specific user and have another user set up for the display pages. You can set up user privileges in the visual interface of your database server, or you can set them up by using a GRANT statement:

```
GRANT select
ON Seekers
TO webuser
```

or for a site administrator:

```
GRANT select, insert, update, delete
ON Seekers
TO TomTheAdmin
```

Caution   *Never use the system administrator account (sa in MS SQL Server, or root in MySQL) when you set up the Web pages for your Web application. This allows a hacker to have full privileges to your entire database server if he or she can find a way in.*

Summary

By now, you should have some idea of how to create your database, and how to deploy one. Whichever database you decide to use, you need to become familiar with its intricacies. Creating tables remotely, or even creating the whole database remotely, is sometimes a necessity. Knowing only the basics is going to get you into trouble.

These days, becoming a Web developer means you have to wear many hats. Dreamweaver MX makes the hats fit a little better by giving you some powerful tools to ease the whole process and hide some of the complexities of the underlying code. The next chapter covers the SQL language used in communicating with the database.

Chapter 23

An Overview of the Structured Query Language

Once you have a database set up for your site, you will need to turn your attention to getting data in and out of it. The kind of site you are planning to build will, in some ways, dictate how familiar you will need to be with the language of data access. If you just need to provide your users with access to existing data and to allow them to search and view what is already there, you may be able to get by with just a small portion of the capabilities of your database system. If, however, you will be collecting and deploying information in a true dynamic environment, you will want to become very familiar with the subject of this chapter.

In this chapter, we cover the language of the modern database. Structured Query Language (SQL, pronounced "sequel") began life in the IBM labs of the late '70s. As the relational model of database design took hold, a need evolved for a structured way to interact with the individual tables that make them up. Utilizing fewer than 30 keywords, SQL is a simple yet powerful means of performing a variety of operations on your chosen database.

Note	*At least two SQL standards are proffered by ISO and ANSI, plus the variants that are implemented by the manufacturers of the different database programs. This chapter attempts to adhere to the ANSI standard. When you select the database application you will use for your site, you will do well to obtain a SQL reference specific to the brand and version you have chosen.*

The individual commands that you construct using the SQL language are known as *statements*. SQL statements range from very simple, with as few as four words, to very complex, with intricate joins and subqueries. Entire books have been written on the topic, and this chapter cannot hope to adequately cover everything you might want to know about it, but an overview will be very helpful as you get started with Dreamweaver MX. This chapter serves as an excellent jumping-off point for further study as your needs develop.

Basic SQL

A vault full of money is no good if you don't have the combination. A book full of knowledge is no good if you can't read. And a database full of information is no good if you don't have a way to get it out. SQL provides a means of getting information out of your database through the use of *queries*. Although they are not written like questions, the purpose of the SQL query is to ask for information from your tables.

Note	*The name Structured Query Language can be misleading. SQL can actually do much more than just ask for information from your database. It can create tables and modify their structures. It can insert, update, and delete data. The term "query" is simplistic compared to the actual power of the language.*

The questions you can ask are limited only by the data that you have chosen to store in your tables. For instance, your database may have a table that holds information about architects. You can write a SQL query to ask that table for a listing of all of the left-handed, commercial architects that live in Orlando. As long as you store the city where each architect lives, their specialty, and whether they are right-handed or left-handed, your database will respond with a list of architects that meet the criteria you have specified. If, on the other hand, you have never established dexterity as a field of data to be collected, your database will not know how to handle a query that uses it as criteria.

So, it is very important that you consider the kinds of questions you will need to ask your tables when you are setting them up. You don't want to collect a bunch of data, only to find out that you missed an important component that makes it useless for your intended purpose. Because the tables in the Bettergig database are a little too big to illustrate easily, let's create a new table that tracks the receipt of payments.

Consider the things that you need to know about a payment you have received in order to store it in a meaningful way. You need to know what account to credit the payment to, the date it was received, the check number, and the amount. You might also want to set up a field to serve as a unique identifier for a particular transaction. This field would be a numeric field that automatically increments each time a new record is added to the table.

Note   *A concept of a unique identifier for each record is an important one to grasp. Most databases offer some means of automatically creating an incremented counter for each record as it is added to the table. In Access, it is called an autonumber data type; in SQL Server, it is an Identity field.*

The database structure for the Payments table is shown next.

Field Name	Data Type	Width
Transaction	Autonumber	4
Account	Text	5
CheckNumber	Text	10
Amount	Money	8
DateReceived	Date	8

Next, the table needs some data that you can work with.

Transaction	Account	CheckNumber	Amount	DateReceived
1	12345	301	200.53	10/25/00
2	47638	1245	100.00	10/26/00
3	75892	746	503.42	10/30/00
4	12345	321	150.04	11/03/00

Transaction	Account	CheckNumber	Amount	DateReceived
5	75892	803	400.00	11/05/00
6	12345	340	623.00	11/10/00

The *Select* Statement

The foundation on which the SQL language is built is the *Select* statement. Just as its name implies, the *Select* statement is used to select a row or rows of data from a table or tables that meet the set of criteria that you provide. Although a *Select* statement can be very complex, the simplest form provides two pieces of information for the database to act upon: what you want to see and where it comes from. For instance, the following *Select* statement retrieves all of the fields from all of the records in the Payments table:

```
Select * From Payments
```

The asterisk is shorthand for "show me all of the fields," so the preceding statement produces identical results to the following statement:

```
Select Transaction, Account, CheckNumber, Amount, DateReceived From Payments
```

This simple query is actually providing a number of pieces of information to the database:

- *Select*   The *Select* keyword is used to identify the statement that follows as a query to the database for information. You might use other keywords such as *Update*, *Insert*, or *Delete* in this position to implement other actions (which we cover later).
- *** or field names**   The asterisk or a comma-separated list of field names tells the database which fields you want to see and in what order.
- *From*   The *From* keyword is required for all *Select* statements and identifies in which table or tables the requested data is found.
- **Table names**   The listed table or tables are used to fulfill the request.

There is also another piece of information provided because this SQL statement ends where it does. The lack of any additional information beyond the Table Name indicates that you want to see all of the records in the specified table. You can, of course, filter your results by any number of criteria, which we cover shortly.

Returning to the original query, it becomes clear what data will be returned.

```
Select * From Payments
```

or

```
Select Transaction, Account, CheckNumber, Amount, DateReceived From Payments
```

returns the following resultset:

Transaction	Account	CheckNumber	Amount	DateReceived
1	12345	301	200.53	10/25/00
2	47638	1245	100.00	10/26/00
3	75892	746	503.42	10/30/00
4	12345	321	150.04	11/03/00
5	75892	803	400.00	11/05/00
6	12345	340	623.00	11/10/00

Selecting Specific Fields

You can select only specific fields from the table by identifying them in your query as in the following:

```
Select Account, Amount From Payments
```

which returns the following:

Account	Amount
12345	200.53
47638	100.00
75892	503.42
12345	150.04
75892	400.00
12345	623.00

Changing the Order of the Returned Fields

You can also change the order in which fields are returned by specifying in your statement the order you want:

```
Select Transaction, Account, DateReceived, Amount, CheckNumber From Payments
```

which returns:

Transaction	Account	DateReceived	Amount	CheckNumber
1	12345	10/25/00	200.53	301
2	47638	10/26/00	100.00	1245
3	75892	10/30/00	503.42	746
4	12345	11/03/00	150.04	321
5	75892	11/05/00	400.00	803
6	12345	11/10/00	623.00	340

Selecting Only Unique Records

Suppose that you need to find out which accounts are represented in your Payments table. You might execute a SQL query like this:

```
Select Account From Payments
```

which would, of course, return:

Account

12345

47638

75892

12345

75892

12345

This result does show you all of the accounts that are represented on your Payments table, but it gives every instance of each Account number, which can be unwieldy in a larger table. SQL provides a means of identifying and displaying only unique values in your table. You still get a resultset that contains all of the individual Account values that are represented in your database, but you get each value only once. This is accomplished with the *Distinct* keyword as follows:

```
Select Distinct Account From Payments
```

which returns:

Account

12345

47638

75892

Expressions and Conditions

As stated earlier, a SQL statement can do much more than just ask for a listing of all of the records in a database table. This section covers manipulating data with expressions and filtering data with conditions.

Expressions

You may be familiar with expressions from other programming that you have done. An expression is anything that returns a value, such as 2 + 2 or variable1 + variable2. You can also use expressions within SQL statements to perform operations on the values in your tables and return a result in your query. To help illustrate this, add a new Accounts table that will go along with the Payments table from the earlier example. The structure of the table is shown next:

Field Name	Data Type	Width
Account	Text	5
FirstName	Text	20
LastName	Text	20
City	Text	25
State	Text	2
ZipCode	Text	5

This table simply holds information about the accounts that will be sending payments. There is a first name, a last name, a city, a state, and a ZIP code for each account. These tables will help illustrate many of the powerful capabilities of expressions in SQL statements.

Note *You will likely want to capture much more information about an account holder than just their name, city, state, and ZIP code, but this amount of information will serve to demonstrate the point without introducing extraneous detail that would only be confusing.*

Because three accounts are making payments (as seen in the previous example), you need to make sure that those three accounts are represented in the Accounts table. Here is some sample data:

Account	FirstName	LastName	City	State	ZipCode
12345	Jim	Randolph	Orlando	FL	32886
47638	Susan	Tudor	New York	NY	10011
75892	Trevor	Patrick	El Paso	TX	79925

You can certainly get information out of this table using the same kinds of queries we used earlier:

```
Select * From Accounts
```

This would return the following:

Account	FirstName	LastName	City	State	ZipCode
12345	Jim	Randolph	Orlando	FL	32886
47638	Susan	Tudor	New York	NY	10011
75892	Trevor	Patrick	El Paso	TX	79925

But what if you needed the account holder's full name to display on a screen or on a letter or a bill? If you have had any experience with databases before, you know that it is impossible to get two separate fields such as FirstName and LastName to line up together for every record. You need a way to put the FirstName and LastName fields together so that they display properly. You can use an expression for that.

The expression that we use will join two strings (pieces of text) together. This is known as *concatenation*. Depending on what brand of database you are using, this may be done in a slightly different way. Following are the two most common methods of concatenation.

The idea behind concatenating two strings in a SQL query is to combine the field values together, possibly with some literal text that makes it display properly. To combine the field values, you will use either the & operator or the + operator, depending on your database brand and version.

 Note *The + operator is often used to concatenate strings, but you can get unpredictable results if you are not sure of your data types. When a + operator is used on two numbers, they will be added together. When it is used on two strings or one string and one number, the two values will be concatenated.*

Consider the following SQL query:

```
Select Account, FirstName, LastName from Accounts
```

This statement returns the following:

Account	FirstName	LastName
12345	Jim	Randolph
47638	Susan	Tudor
75892	Trevor	Patrick

But you need the first name and last name together, so you might try this:

```
Select Account, FirstName & LastName As Name From Accounts
```

Notice that the & operator was used. Your statement may need to read like this:

```
Select Account, FirstName + LastName As Name From Accounts
```

Also notice the *As* keyword. This keyword is used when an expression is entered to provide a name by which the results will be referenced. It creates a kind of virtual field name that can be referenced just like a real table field once the result set is generated. This query will return a field called Name, which is not really a field at all, just a title that you have given to the results of your expression.

You might think that you are in good shape with this query, but look at the results:

Account	Name
12345	JimRandolph
47638	SusanTudor
75892	TrevorPatrick

The database has taken your instructions quite literally and has concatenated the string values right next to each other. As mentioned earlier, you must often combine field values with some literal string values to get the proper display values from the query. Try this:

```
Select Account, FirstName & ' ' & LastName As Name From Accounts
```

which returns:

Account	Name
12345	Jim Randolph
47638	Susan Tudor
75892	Trevor Patrick

The previous statement concatenates not only the two database fields but also a literal space to result in the logical display of the first name and last name. The following query takes this concept one step further:

```
Select Account, FirstName & ' ' & LastName As Name, City & ', ' & State & ' ' ¬
& ZipCode As Address From Accounts
```

which returns this:

Account	Name	Address
12345	Jim Randolph	Orlando, FL 32886
47638	Susan Tudor	New York, NY 10011
75892	Trevor Patrick	El Paso, TX 79925

This statement concatenates the City, State, and ZipCode fields together with a comma and a space between the City and State and a space between the State and ZipCode fields to result in the expected display format for the address of the account holder.

You can use expressions to do any number of additional manipulations on your data. You can multiply a unit price times a number of units to get a subtotal, or you can multiply a subtotal times a sales tax figure to get the sales tax. Expressions are a powerful way to manipulate your data against itself or against external values that you introduce.

Conditions

So far, you have had practice retrieving data from your database in blocks that include everything that is available in the tables. Chances are, however, that you will need to filter the results of your data so that only certain records are retrieved. You can filter data by the use of conditional clauses such as the *Where* clause. The *Where* clause enables you to specify criteria against which the data in your tables will be compared.

Only those records that meet your criteria will be returned in the resultset. Consider the following SQL statement:

```
Select * From Payments Where Account = '12345'
```

Depending on your brand of database, this query may need to read:

```
Select * From Payments Where Account Like '12345'
```

Note   *In this example, the account number is enclosed in quotes because the field was defined as a text field. Had this field been identified as a numeric field, the quotes would not be necessary.*

The previous statement returns these records:

Transaction	Account	DateReceived	Amount	CheckNumber
1	12345	10/25/00	200.53	301
4	12345	11/03/00	150.04	321
6	12345	11/10/00	623.00	340

Notice that only records with the account number 12345 were returned, because that is the criteria you specified in the query. You can also use the *Where* clause in the Accounts query used earlier:

```
Select Account, FirstName & ' ' & LastName As Name, City & ', ' & State & ' ' ¬
& ZipCode As Address From Accounts Where LastName = 'Randolph'
```

This returns:

Account	Name	Address
12345	Jim Randolph	Orlando, FL 32886

Additional Operators

In addition to the equal (=) operator, several other operators are available for you to use as part of expressions and conditions. Table 23-1 lists many of the operators and their intended use.

Operator	Use
*	The multiplication operator; multiplies field values by one another or by literal values that you provide.
/	The division operator; divides field values by one another or by literal values that you provide.
–	The minus operator; subtracts field values from one another or performs subtraction with field values and literal values that you provide.
>	The greater-than operator; used in conditional *Where* clauses such as *Select * From Payments Where Amount > 300.00.*
<	The less-than operator; used in conditional *Where* clauses, such as *Select * From Payments Where Amount < 300.00.*
>=	The greater-than or equal-to operator; used in conditional *Where* clauses.
<=	The less-than or equal-to operator; used in conditional *Where* clauses.
<>, !=	Not-equal-to operators; used in conditional *Where* clauses.
AND	The logical AND operator; used in conditional *Where* clauses, such as *Select * From Payments Where Account = 100.00 AND Amount > 400.00.*
OR	The logical OR operator; used in conditional *Where* clauses, such as *Select * From Payments Where Amount < 100.00 OR Amount > 400.00.*
LIKE	The LIKE operator; used in conditional *Where* clauses when a wildcard is necessary. For example, *Select * From Accounts Where LastName Like 'Ran%'* would return any record in which the LastName starts with "Ran".
NOT	The NOT operator; used in conditional *Where* clauses such as *Select * From Accounts Where LastName Not Like 'Ran%'.*
_	The single character wildcard operator; used when you don't know a single character. For example, *Select * From Accounts Where State Like 'C_'* would return any record where the State field contained "CA", "CO", "CT", or "C" plus any other one character.
%	The multiple character wildcard operator; used like the _ operator except that it allows for multiple characters.

Table 23-1.   *Common SQL Operators and Their Uses*

Functions

While you can choose to implement certain operators within expressions that you construct to manipulate your data, there is also a selection of *functions*. Functions are, in essence, prewritten snippets of code that perform an operation and return a value. The code snippets are available to you by simply calling the function and providing the value or values on which it will operate. This section covers common SQL functions and their uses.

Note   *Again, you will need to reference the language guide for your brand of database to see the full range of available functions. Some of the functions discussed here may not be available; others may be specific to your implementation.*

Date and Time Functions

Data and Time functions enable you to perform manipulations on dates and times that you have stored in your database. Much like expressions, these functions are called within the *Select* statement. You can use the *As* clause to give the resulting value a unique name with which to refer to the results.

Because there is a Date field in the Payments table, try the following examples using that data.

```
Select * From Payments Where DateReceived Like '10/25/00'
```

This would return:

Transaction	Account	DateReceived	Amount	CheckNumber
1	12345	10/25/00	200.53	301

But suppose you want to find all of the accounts for which you have received a payment in the last 30 days. Try this:

```
Select * From Payments Where DateReceived > DateAdd(m,-1,Date())
```

The results that this query returns depend on the date that you run it. If the date is 12/1/2000 when you run the query, it will return:

Transaction	Account	DateReceived	Amount	CheckNumber
4	12345	11/03/00	150.04	321
5	75892	11/05/00	400.00	803
6	12345	11/10/00	623.00	340

This query makes use of two functions (both of which are Microsoft database functions, but there will be equivalents for the product you are using). The *Date()* functions get today's date. The *DateAdd* function adds a variety of date parts to a supplied date to get a result. This query uses *DateAdd* and passes in three values:

- The unit of time that will be added to the supplied date (in this case, *m* for month; it can also be *d* for day, *w* for week, or other available values)

- The number of units to add (in this case, –1, so one month will be subtracted)

- The supplied date (in this case, the result of the *Date()* function, or 12/01/2000 if that is the current date)

So the result of the *DateAdd* function (if the date is 12/01/2000) is 11/01/2000. To the database, this query looks like this:

```
Select * from Payments Where DateReceived > '11/01/2000'
```

This returns the records in which the DateReceived field is greater than November 1.

The Date() *function gets the system date on the machine where the code is being run. If the database resides on your local machine, its system date will be used. If the database is on a Web server or its own database server machine, that computer's system date and time will be used for these functions. To get the most consistent results, make sure that your remote computers are synchronized with your development machine. This can be difficult if your ISP's server is in a different time zone or a different country. You may have to make systematic adjustments for the time difference between your local site and your ISP's location.*

Other Date and Time functions are available for your use, depending on the database you choose to use. If you can define in prose the end result you need to obtain, there is most likely a function or combination of functions that will allow you to manipulate your dates and times to return the proper set of records.

Aggregate Functions

Aggregate functions allow you to retrieve results that are based on the combined data of records in your table. For instance, you might need to determine the amount of the largest payment you have ever received or the average of the payments made during a particular period of time. Aggregate functions allow you to do this.

The following five Aggregate functions are covered in this section:

- *Count*
- *Sum*

- *Avg*
- *Min*
- *Max*

You may have others available.

The *Count* Function

You can use the *Count* function, obviously, when you need to count something, such as the number of account holders who live in Wyoming or the number of payments received during a specific period of time. Suppose you need to determine the number of payments received during the month of November 2000. There may be a couple of ways to do this, but here is one way using the *Count* function:

```
Select Count(Transaction) As Payments From Payments Where DateReceived >=
'11/01/00' and DateReceived <= '11/30/00'
```

This query returns:

Payments

3

In the query, a unique identifier (the transaction number) was selected as the field value to count. The database then selected all of the records in which the payment was received in November, counted the number of unique transaction numbers, and returned 3. You can use the *Count* function to count any unique set of values in your tables.

The *Sum* Function

The *Sum* function returns a sum of a collection of fields. Suppose, in addition to the number of payments received in November, you also need to know the sum of those payments. The *Sum* function will select the records that match the criteria in your *Where* clause, add them up, and return the value to you:

```
Select Sum(Amount) As Total From Payments Where DateReceived >= '11/01/00' and
DateReceived <= '11/30/00'
```

This returns:

Total

1033.01

The *Avg* Function

The *Avg* function returns the average of the values in the field that you select for the records that meet your criteria. If you need to know the average payment received in the month of November, you can just run the two queries previous and then divide the *Sum* result by the *Count* result. Or, you can do this:

```
Select Avg(Amount) As Average From Payments Where DateReceived >= '11/01/00' and
DateReceived <= '11/30/00'
```

which returns:

Average

344.34666

The *Min and Max* Functions

Keeping with the November payments theme, you may also need to know the amount of the smallest and largest payments received during November. To get the smallest, use the following:

```
Select Min(Amount) As Minimum From Payments Where DateReceived >= '11/01/00' and
DateReceived <= '11/30/00'
```

This returns:

Minimum

150.04

To get the largest payments, use this:

```
Select Max(Amount) As Maximum From Payments Where DateReceived >= '11/01/00' and
DateReceived <= '11/30/00'
```

which returns:

Maximum

623.00

Arithmetic Functions

A number of Arithmetic functions are available. Their uses are similar to the other functions. Table 23-2 lists some common arithmetic functions and their uses.

Arithmetic Function	Use
ABS	Returns the absolute value of the value operated on
CEIL	Returns the smallest integer greater than or equal to the value operated on
FLOOR	Returns the largest integer less than or equal to the value operated on
COS	Returns the cosine of the value where the value is the radians (not degrees)
COSH	Returns the hyperbolic cosine of the value where the value is the radians
SIN	Returns the sine of the value where the value is the radians (not degrees)
SINH	Returns the hyperbolic sine of the value where the value is the radians
TAN	Returns the tangent of the value where the value is the radians (not degrees)
TANH	Returns the hyperbolic tangent of the value where the value is the radians
EXP	Raises the mathematical constant e by the provided value
MOD	Returns the modulus (remainder) of two provided values
SIGN	Returns a –1 if the value provided is less than 0, a 1 if it is greater than 0, or a 0 if the value is 0
SQRT	Returns the square root of the value provided
POWER	Raises one value to the power of a second value
LN	Returns the natural logarithm of the value
LOG	Returns the logarithm of one value in the base of a second value

Table 23-2.   *Common SQL Arithmetic Functions and Their Uses*

String Functions

String functions operate on text values. They work in a similar fashion to other functions, with a value or values (either literals or field references) being provided. Table 23-3 lists common String functions and their uses.

Your database application will likely have additional string functions available.

String Function	Use
CHR	Converts an ASCII value to its string equivalent
CONCAT	Concatenates (splices together) two values
INITCAP	Capitalizes the first character of each word and makes all of the remaining characters lowercase
UPPER	Capitalizes all of the characters in the string
LOWER	Makes all of the characters in the string lowercase
LPAD	Pads the left of a provided string with a provided character with as many spaces as you indicate
RPAD	Pads the right of a provided string with a provided character with as many spaces as you indicate
LTRIM	Trims all spaces from the left of a string value
RTRIM	Trims all spaces from the right of a string value
REPLACE	Takes three values: the string to be searched for, the string within the searched string, and what to replace each occurrence of the string with. If the third value is omitted, the found characters are deleted and replaced with NULL
SUBSTR	Returns a piece of a string value starting at the character position you provide and continuing for as many characters as you specify
LENGTH	Returns the length of a provided string value

Table 23-3. *String Functions and Their Uses*

Clauses

Clauses are optional parts of a SQL statement that specify additional criteria for the query or additional work that needs to be done before the results are returned. The *Where* clause was covered earlier in this chapter. You need to be aware of two other clauses:

- The *Order By* clause
- The *Group By* clause

The *Order By* Clause

The *Order By* clause provides a means by which you can sort your data in either ascending or descending order. Depending on the type of application you are developing and the specific use of the query you are working on, you may want to sort account holders by their last names or payments by the date they were received. The Order By clause lets you specify which field or fields are used to sort your data.

Note
One of the premises of the relational database is that physical storage is of little importance. Depending on how data is entered and what indexes operate on it, you may well find that the most recently entered records in a particular table do not appear at or near the end of the table. If it is at all possible that the sorting will matter when the data is used or displayed, you should specify how you want data ordered.

An unordered query on the Accounts table like this:

```
Select * From Accounts
```

returns this:

Account	FirstName	LastName	City	State	ZipCode
12345	Jim	Randolph	Orlando	FL	32886
47638	Susan	Tudor	New York	NY	10011
75892	Trevor	Patrick	El Paso	TX	79925

But you may want to have the data sorted by the account holders' last names. If so, you can add an *Order By* clause as in the following:

```
Select * From Account Order By LastName
```

which would return:

Account	FirstName	LastName	City	State	ZipCode
75892	Trevor	Patrick	El Paso	TX	79925
12345	Jim	Randolph	Orlando	FL	32886
47638	Susan	Tudor	New York	NY	10011

You can also add the *ASC* designation for ascending, making the records sort from A to Z. This is the default option, though, so it is not necessary. If you want them in Z to A order, however, you need to specify the descending option, as in the following:

```
Select * From Account Order By LastName DESC
```

which would return:

Account	FirstName	LastName	City	State	ZipCode
47638	Susan	Tudor	New York	NY	10011
12345	Jim	Randolph	Orlando	FL	32886
75892	Trevor	Patrick	El Paso	TX	79925

Ordering by More Than One Column

You can also order by more than one column at a time. Say, for instance, that you want to order by the account number in the Payments table and then by the amount, so that you will get a result ordered by the account number in which the payment amounts are ordered from smallest to largest.

```
Select * From Payments Order By Account, Amount
```

This would return:

Transaction	Account	DateReceived	Amount	CheckNumber
4	12345	11/03/00	150.04	321
1	12345	10/25/00	200.53	301
6	12345	11/10/00	623.00	340
2	47638	10/26/00	100.00	1245

Transaction	Account	DateReceived	Amount	CheckNumber
5	75892	11/05/00	400.00	803
3	75892	10/30/00	503.42	746

The *Group By* Clause

The *Group By* clause enables you to perform aggregate functions on groups of records and display them by group rather than operating on the entire table. For instance, if you want to find out how many payments were received into the Payments table, you can run the following query:

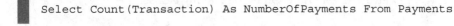

```
Select Count(Transaction) As NumberOfPayments From Payments
```

which would return:

NumberOfPayments

6

But you may need to see how many payments each account has made and group the payments by account number, so that you get a list of each account and the number of payments made to that account. The *Group By* clause lets you do this:

```
Select Account, Count(Transaction) As NumberOfPayments From Payments Group By
Account
```

This returns:

Account	NumberOfPayments
12345	3
75892	2
47638	1

The *Having* Clause

Closely related to the *Group By* clause and other aggregate functions is the *Having* clause. If you are using the *Group By* clause and need to set criteria to be applied to the data, you cannot use a *Where* clause because of the order in which the various parts of the statement are processed. In this case, you need to use the *Having* clause, as in the following:

```
Select Account, Count(Transaction) As NumberOfPayments From Payments Group By
Account Having Account Like '12345'
```

which would return:

Account	NumberOfPayments
12345	3

You can also apply an aggregate function in the Having clause.

```
Select Account, Avg(Amount) AS AveragePayment From Payments Having Avg(Amount) >
400.00
```

This would return:

Account	AveragePayment
75892	451.71

Joins

So far, all of these examples have pulled data from only one table at a time. It is very likely, however, that you will spend a great deal of your time mixing the data from more than one table into your results. To do so, you will need to use *joins* to identify the ways in which tables relate to one another. There are several kinds of joins; we cover two basic types:

■ Inner joins
■ Outer joins (left and right)

There is also a type of outer join known as a full join, or Cartesian Product, in which all records from both tables are returned regardless of whether they relate to records in the other table. Although there is some limited use for these, we do not cover them here.

Inner Joins

Inner joins are the most common type of join. You use these when you want to see all of the records in two tables that have a direct relation to each other. For instance, review the records in the Accounts and Payments tables used in the prior examples. You will notice that each record in the Accounts table (identified by the Account Number) has related records in the Payments table. In other words, every account in the Accounts table has made at least one payment.

Each time a query was run in the previous sections, it was run on only one table. But suppose you want to return information that spans both tables? Maybe you need to see not only the account numbers and payment amounts, but also the names of the account holders that made those payments. When you want to see only the records that are related in the two tables, you can use an inner join, as in the following:

```
Select Acccounts.Account, Accounts.FirstName, Accounts.LastName, Payments.Amount
From Accounts Inner Join Payments on Accounts.Account = Payments.Account
```

This returns:

Account	FirstName	LastName	Amount
12345	Jim	Randolph	150.04
12345	Jim	Randolph	200.53
12345	Jim	Randolph	623.00
47638	Susan	Tudor	100.00
47638	Susan	Tudor	400.00
75892	Trevor	Patrick	503.42

Outer Joins

There will likely be times when you need to query data from tables in which you know or suspect that unrelated records exist. For instance, it is entirely possible that you have an account holder set up in the Accounts table that has not made any payments yet. To help illustrate, add a fourth account holder to the Accounts table.

Account	FirstName	LastName	City	State	ZipCode
12345	Jim	Randolph	Orlando	FL	32886
47638	Susan	Tudor	New York	NY	10011
75892	Trevor	Patrick	El Paso	TX	79925
98734	Victor	Patitucci	Atlanta	GA	30305

If you were to run the inner join query that you just ran on the two tables now, you might be surprised to see the exact same results as you did before you added your new account holder. Because there are no related records in the Payments table, the new account is ignored by an inner join query. To see the new account in the results, you must use an outer join.

There are three types of outer joins: left, right, and full. The types relate to which tables are given the special attention that an outer join provides. If you think about the tables that you join being next to one another on a board or a data environment display, the first one referenced in the join expression is on the left and the second is on the right. As mentioned earlier, the full outer join (or Cartesian Product) is of dubious use and is not covered here.

So, using the previous example, say that you want to make sure that all of your account holders are listed, whether or not they have made a payment. The Accounts table will be on the left, so you will get a listing of all accounts and their related payments in addition to a listing of the accounts that have no payments:

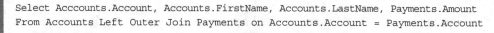

```
Select Acccounts.Account, Accounts.FirstName, Accounts.LastName, Payments.Amount
From Accounts Left Outer Join Payments on Accounts.Account = Payments.Account
```

This returns:

Account	FirstName	LastName	Amount
12345	Jim	Randolph	150.04
12345	Jim	Randolph	200.53
12345	Jim	Randolph	623.00
47638	Susan	Tudor	100.00
47638	Susan	Tudor	400.00
75892	Trevor	Patrick	503.42
98734	Victor	Patitucci	

The right outer join is used when you suspect that there are records in the right-hand (payments) table that have no account holder. The need for right outer joins can indicate a data integrity problem in your tables. Although it is perfectly acceptable to have an account holder who has made no payments (to your database, if not to your accounting department), it is problematic to have payments that have no account holder. Nonetheless, you can use right outer joins to display records in your related table that have no corresponding records in the main table.

> **Note**
>
> *Notice the dot notation in the preceding query. When you are using tables that have the same field name in each of them, you must identify from which table you intend the data to come. Use the format table_name.field_name to clearly identify your intentions to the database. There is also a method in which each table is given an alias within the query, making it simpler to reference.*

Subqueries

Subqueries are queries within another query. Sometimes it is not possible to construct a resultset directly from the data in your raw tables. You may need to do some "preprocessing" in order to develop a subset of data that you wish to query. If you are familiar with Access queries, you may have queried a query before and will have a good idea of the concept. In some other languages, such as FoxPro, you can actually select data into a cursor and then query that cursor directly. SQL itself does not have a way to do that, but you can include queries within your queries to simulate the same thing.

> **Note**
>
> *Some databases, like MySQL, do not support subqueries, but there are often ways to get around using them by using complex Where clauses instead. Subqueries can be handy, however, if you have access to them.*

Two types of subqueries are covered in this section:

- The *In* statement
- The embedded *Select* statement

The *In* Statement

The *In* statement is used with the *Where* clause of a SQL query to identify a list of values to be used as criteria for the primary query. For a simple example, suppose you want to select all of your account holders who live in New York or Florida. Using the *In* statement, you can create the following query:

```
Select * From Accounts Where state In ("NY", "FL")
```

The *In* statement allows you to specify a list of criteria against which the primary query will be tested. Any record in which the state is NY or FL will be pulled in the preceding query. You can also use an embedded *Select* statement within the *In* statement.

The *Embedded Select* Statement

An embedded SQL statement is a complete query, including any legal portion of a *Select* statement that is contained within the *Where* clause of the primary query used, along with the *In* statement. Suppose you want to see a list of account holders who have made payments on their accounts. Consider this statement:

```
Select * From Accounts Where Account In (Select Distinct Account From Payments)
```

Notice how the various elements of the SQL statement begin to come together as the queries get more complex. In this statement, a distinct (or unique) list of account numbers that appear in the Payments table is created. Then the primary query pulls the records from the Accounts table that have account numbers that appear in the subquery list.

If you want to see the opposite, those account holders who have not made payments, you can insert the NOT operator as follows:

```
Select * From Accounts Where Account NOT In (Select Distinct Account From Payments)
```

  Note   *You may find it interesting to know that you can also use an* embedded Select *statement within the From clause of the primary query. Queries this complex are beyond the scope of this chapter; but as you become more proficient with the SQL language, you will likely find a use for the capabilities that this structure provides.*

 # Action Queries

In addition to *Select* queries, there are queries that perform some action on your database. This section covers three types of Action queries:

- *Insert* queries
- *Update* queries
- *Delete* queries

Insert Queries

If you are planning to collect information from your users, the time will quickly come when you need to insert information into a table. The *Insert* statement lets you do just that. There are two ways to use the *Insert* statement.

The first way is the direct insertion of values into the fields of the database. Used this way, the *Insert* statement enables you to identify the fields that you wish to populate and the values you wish to place in those fields. Suppose that you need to add an account holder to the Accounts table:

```
Insert Into Accounts (Account, FirstName, LastName, City, State, ZipCode) Values
('73647', 'Theresa', 'Andrews', 'Chicago', 'IL', '60606')
```

Running this statement causes a new record to be added with the specified values. You can also use a *Select* statement to provide the insertion values for your *Insert* statement. Suppose that you have a backup Accounts table with the same structure as the Accounts table, and you want to copy the Accounts table data into it.

```
Insert Into BackupAccounts (Account, FirstName, LastName, City,
State, ZipCode) Select * From Accounts.
```

The *Select* statement used in place of the *Values* clause provides the insertion values. This statement can be any legal SQL statement that provides the correct number of fields in the correct order with the correct data types to insert data into the indicated table.

Update Queries

If data never changed, you would not need the *Update* statement, which enables you to change data in your tables. However, it does change. For instance, suppose that one of your account holders got married and changed her last name:

```
Update Accounts Set LastName = "Thomas" Where Account = '73647'
```

This query locates the record for account number 73547 and changes the LastName field to Thomas.

Delete Queries

Delete queries delete records from your tables when provided criteria are met. If you want to delete all records (much like selecting all records), no criteria are supplied:

```
Delete From Accounts
```

This statement deletes all records from the Accounts table, ruining your data and, probably, your job. To be selective in what is deleted, provide criteria that uniquely identifies the record or records you want to delete:

```
Delete From Accounts Where Account = '73647'
```

This statement deletes only the record for Theresa Andrews that was created and altered in earlier sections.

You can also delete multiple records at once. Suppose you needed to purge all payments received before a certain date from the Payments table:

```
Delete From Payments Where DateReceived < '01/01/1990'
```

This statement deletes all records that contain payments received before 1990.

Variables

Within your use of Dreamweaver, you will likely need to use variables in your SQL statements to dynamically filter data. Although the specifics of this operation are covered in a later chapter, it is important that you understand the concept here.

Each of the queries performed in this chapter so far have been based on hard-coded criteria, where, for example, you specified a date or series of dates to search for or specified the last name of the account holder you wanted to find. In most real-life cases, however, you will not know this information until your user begins to interact with your application and tell you the things they need to find. Within your ASP, JSP, PHP, ASP.NET, or CF code, you will allow for the capture of this data into variables that you can insert into your SQL statements, thus dynamically creating a query that is customized to the visitor's needs.

Remember that a SQL statement is really just a line of text. It does not get parsed out and take on meaning until it arrives at the database as a query. Until the statement is sent to the database, you can perform a number of common programming techniques on it to construct it as you see fit. One of the most common procedures is to use variables in the *Where* or *Having* clause.

Suppose that you know that a certain portion of your application will need to pull payments from a particular account number. Maybe account holders can sign in and view the payments posted to their accounts. But you won't know which account holder's information to pull until an account holder logs in and requests his or her payment history. By capturing account numbers at log in, you can be prepared to show account holders their payments by setting up your SQL statement as follows.

You can begin by writing your SQL statement as if you knew the account number you wanted to view, like the following:

```
Select * From Payments Where Account Like '12345'
```

Then go back and take the hard-coded value out and prepare the statement to accept a variable. In this case, the variable name will be *acct*:

```
Select * From Payments Where Account Like & acct
```

 Note   *Depending on your database implementation, you may need to use the + operator instead of the & operator.*

This code will actually be processed by the code in your page, and Dreamweaver helps you set this up without having to code it by hand. By the time the query gets to the database, it is fully formed and in a format that the database expects to see. If the visitor logged in with a username that indicated an account number of 12345, the SQL statement with the variable in the preceding code would look exactly like the one before it to the database. This method allows you to put off the designation of the account number until run time when it can be determined by the user's information.

Summary

Structured Query Language (SQL) and its various permutations is a powerful programming language. Part of its power lies in its capability to use a relatively simple set of commands and keywords in a variety of combinations that build on one another and provide a means of manipulating data in almost any way you can imagine. Using SQL in a programming environment increases the kinds of manipulations you can perform on your data so that you can query, display, and use it in any way your application might require.

This chapter introduced you to the language, functions, and uses of SQL in a general fashion. It is intended to help you get started with Dreamweaver's data access capabilities and provide you with an idea of SQL's structure, so that you will be able to determine your needs and know in what direction you are likely to find help for the problems you face. Because Dreamweaver is so helpful in constructing, implementing, and manipulating your SQL statements, this information should allow you to successfully build a number of different kinds of sites.

However, there is not room enough to cover other significant topics—such as referential integrity, stored procedures, and triggers—all of which are very important to a development effort of any size. If this chapter enables you to get started and prepares you to expand into these topics, it has served its purpose.

The Complete Reference

Chapter 24

Adding Database Features to Your Site

The primary reason to use an application server such as ASP, JSP, PHP, ASP.NET, or ColdFusion is to be able to serve live content from a database. Although there are other reasons, databases are the key to a successful dynamic site. In this chapter, we'll add many of the standard types of database functionality that you might use with your own site. We'll build upon the basic structure that was set up for the Bettergig.com Web site, and use the database that was built in Chapter 22 to demonstrate the server-side functionality of Dreamweaver MX.

| Note | *Not all of the server models in Dreamweaver MX support all of the available Application Objects or Server Behaviors, but we'll note the differences.* |

Defining the Database Connection

Database connections were covered in Chapter 20. If you haven't read the chapter and don't know how to create a connection, now would be a good time to go back and read it. Each server model has its own specific way to connect to a database, so it's important to have a live connection working before adding live content to the pages.

If you are going to try the examples, make sure the database is created and in the proper location. The database is needed for all of the examples. On the Osborne Web site (www.osborne.com), you will find SQL scripts for creating an IBM DB2, MySQL, PostgreSQL, or Microsoft SQL Server database. Instructions for running the scripts are included in the ReadMe files that accompany the databases in the Zip file. Also included is an Access 97 version of the database. If you are using the Access version, you should place the file in a secure folder on the server. If you are on a Windows NT or 2000 Server and using IIS, the folder has to have IUSR permissions for the local machine. To secure the folder, you must do one of two things:

■ Place the folder in which the database resides outside of the site root. For example, if your site is in the folder e:\inetpub\wwwroot\bettergig, you can put the database in a folder such as e:\databases.

■ If the folder has to reside in the site root (such as in a shared environment with a Web host), make sure that the Web server Read permissions are turned off for that folder. Typically, a Web host will provide a secure folder (such as a cgi-bin folder) for your databases or scripts.

Create a new connection for the site (if you haven't done so already). You should name the connection connBettergig and test it to make sure that it works before proceeding. Once you have a working connection to the Bettergig database, you can proceed with the examples.

If you have a successful connection, your database will show up in the Databases panel. This feature is new to Dreamweaver MX. The Databases panel gives you access to your database tables, views, and stored procedures.

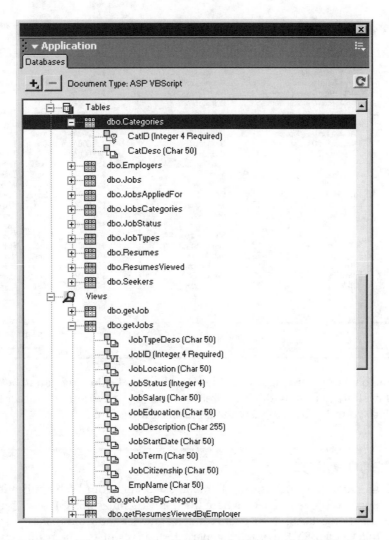

If you right-click on the connection name inside the panel, you have the option to edit, duplicate, delete, or test the connection.

The panel is handy for viewing your data directly from the design environment. By right-clicking on a table or view from within the panel, you can have access to all the data returned by that table or view.

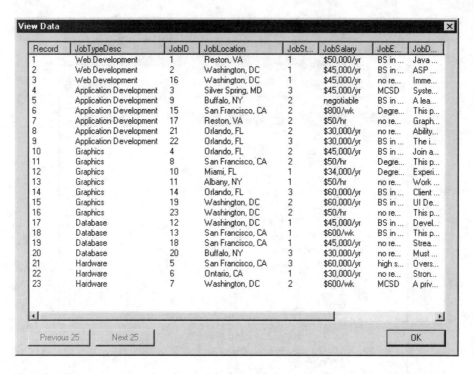

Also, the data types are plainly visible from the panel, allowing you to better plan your display strategy from within the Dreamweaver MX environment rather than going back to your database to view the table or view design.

The Recordset

The data is stored in the database, but to make use of it in your Web application you need to be able to retrieve it. That's where the *resultset* comes in. ASP users will know this as a *recordset* object: ASP.NET users call it a Data Set and ColdFusion users can access it with a CFQUERY tag, but the generic term is resultset. The resultset is not a physical thing that you can point to on your database server. Nor is it a table, a column, a row, or a query. It is, in effect, the response to an inquiry that you send to the database—the question is in the form of a SQL statement. You say to the database "give me all names of all employers, along with their city and state" in the form of a SELECT statement, like this:

```
SELECT EmpName, EmpCity, EmpState FROM Employers
```

The resultset is a direct response from the database, giving you only the information that you requested and nothing more. The results are passed to your page, after which the page can do whatever it needs with it, whether it is displaying the data, sending it to a file, or merely comparing it to some other data. We'll refer to the resultset as *recordset* for consistency with Dreamweaver MX.

To recap, you need to do several things to retrieve the data:

- Connect to the database.
- Create a SQL statement that retrieves the data that you need.
- Send the SQL statement to the database.
- Retrieve the results.

Creating the Query

You can find the recordset data source as an Application object on the Insert bar, the Insert | Application Objects menu, or the Bindings panel. The easiest method to employ if you have your Insert bar open is to use the Recordset button on the Application bar. After clicking this, the Recordset dialog box will pop up.

You can create the query in Dreamweaver MX by using the Simple interface, which is point and click: Choose your tables, columns, and filters, and click OK. Figure 24-1

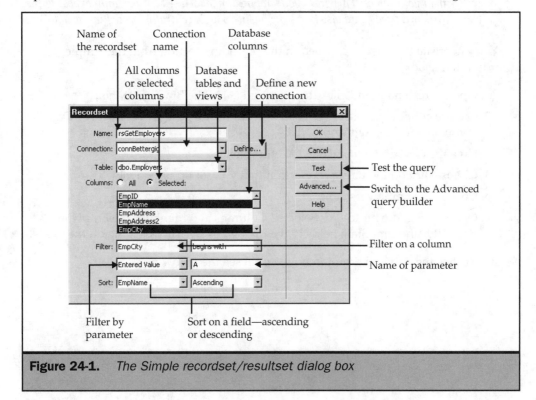

Figure 24-1.   *The Simple recordset/resultset dialog box*

shows the Simple recordset dialog box, which is similar across all server models. You can SHIFT-select multiple columns in the column list.

 The Simple recordset dialog box should be used only for very simple queries that require access to only one table or view, one parameter, and one sort field.

You can click Advanced to go into Advanced view, or the SQL builder view. In this dialog box, you can have access to your SQL statement that is being served to the database. If your SQL statement is simple enough, you can continue to switch back and forth between the two views. If you are unfamiliar with SQL, this is a good way to learn the basic SELECT statement of the SQL language.

Dreamweaver doesn't have any of the sophisticated SQL building tools like some of the relational database systems have, such as Microsoft SQL Server, Access, or IBM's DB2, but the Advanced dialog box allows you to write your own. Also, the dialog box includes a tree view of all tables, views, and stored procedures in your database that you can add to your SQL statement by clicking the SELECT, WHERE, or ORDER BY buttons.

 You should avoid the tendency to create complex SQL in your Web application. Instead, put your SQL statements into a query, view, or stored procedure in your database and use your Web application to retrieve results from that query, view, or stored procedure rather than your tables. This gives your application added security by only exposing the elements that it needs, and also keeps the business logic centrally located in the database.

You can create the query described in the preceding section from the Simple recordset dialog box:

1. Open a fresh page and click the plus sign (+) in the Bindings panel.

2. Choose either Recordset (Query) if you are in ASP, CF, JSP, or PHP, or Data Set if you are working with ASP.NET.

3. Give the recordset a name like rsGetEmployers.

4. Choose the connBettergig connection that you set up previously.

5. Choose the Employers table.

6. Choose the radio button for Selected Columns and highlight the EmpName, EmpCity, and EmpState fields in the dialog box by SHIFT-clicking on the fields.

If you click the Advanced button now, you'll see the following:

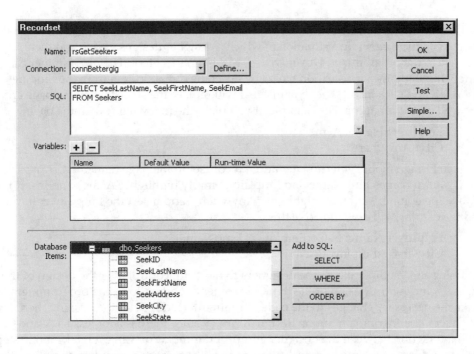

If you click OK now, the query will be saved to the page in the form of a recordset, resultset, cfquery, or data set, depending upon which server model you are working with. From here on, we use the term *recordset* to keep the explanations simple, because that is the term that Dreamweaver MX uses in most of its dialog boxes.

Displaying the Results

Displaying data is generally the easy part of putting together the dynamic site. It involves writing a SQL statement to extract the data from the database that you want to display and then inserting the data into the page. If you are in Design view, you'll see a placeholder representing the data. This placeholder can be moved, dragged, cut, copied, or pasted; it can also have styles applied to it as if it were static text. If you are in Live Data view, you'll see the actual data from the database on the page. Again, this dynamic text can be treated as if it were static text and manipulated the same way.

You can insert the data into your page in several ways:

- Dragging the database column from the Bindings panel to a spot on the page where you want it displayed and dropping it there.

- Putting your cursor on the page where you want the data to be displayed, selecting a column in the Bindings Inspector, and clicking the Insert button. The dynamic text will be inserted at the position of the cursor.

- Hand-coding your pages, including items that are coming from a data source. You might, for example, want to include a recordset column in a hand-coded server-side script.

One technique that may help you design your pages is to set up placeholders for all of the dynamic content. In a situation in which a designer designs a page and then passes the page to the programmer, Dreamweaver MX is a perfect tool. The programmer can simply highlight the static text on the page, select the dynamic item from the Bindings Inspector, and click Insert. The dynamic text will replace the static text on the page and retain all of its formatting. For example, if you place the following text on the page

Employer Name: Acme
City: Anywhere

while in Design mode, you can later add a recordset to the page named *rsGetEmployers* with column names EmpName and EmpCity. Simply highlight "Acme" and insert the EmpName column, and then highlight "Anywhere" and insert the EmpCity column, and the display will now look like this:

Employer Name: {rsGetEmployers.EmpName}
City: {rsGetEmployers.City}

Using this method allows the designers to have full control over the design of the pages, including the design of the dynamic content. It also allows the programmers to make the necessary changes to the code without interfering with the design. There is a far greater chance of maintaining design accuracy since there is a lot less back-and-forth interaction between the designer and programmer. You can even take it one step further and have the designers lock all regions of the page in a template and allow the insertion of only the dynamic data.

Using the page you just created with the *rsGetSeekers* recordset on it, you can place fields from the recordset on the page by using any of the methods shown in the preceding section. After doing this, you should be able to press the F12 key to preview the page. You should be seeing data from the database on the page now.

Using the Dynamic Table Application Object

The Dynamic Table is a new feature of Dreamweaver MX. It allows you to display the results of a query in the form of a table, complete with column headings that match the names of your recordset fields. This can be a quick method of getting your data on the page, after which you can go back and adjust the style and format of the table later.

The Dynamic Table adds a simple table to the page with two rows and as many cells (columns) as it needs to display all of the database columns returned in the recordset. You can insert the Dynamic Table from the Insert | Application Objects menu. A button is also available. The button to insert a Dynamic Table is located in the Application tab of the Insert bar, as shown here:

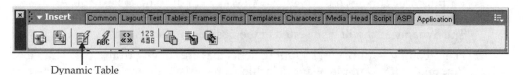

Dynamic Table

When you insert a Dynamic Table, the dialog box looks like this:

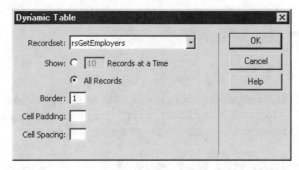

You can choose the recordset that you want to use to populate the table, how many records per page (or all records), and table attributes border, cellspacing, and cellpadding. To see this in action, use the page that you just created and follow these steps:

1. Click Dynamic Table from the Application tab of the Insert bar.

2. Choose the *rsGetEmployers* recordset.

3. Click the radio button to Show *x* Records At A Time, and enter **5**.

4. Leave the rest set to the default (border of 1, no cellspacing, no cellpadding).

5. Click OK.

After inserting the table, your page will contain the table complete with headers, dynamic data, and a repeat region. The repeat region is explained in detail later in the chapter.

   ASP.NET users don't have a Dynamic Table object, but instead have a DataGrid *object, which is similar in concept.*

You can save this page in the site as view_employers.asp (or .cfm, .jsp, .php, or .aspx) under the get_a_gig folder.

Sorting the Results

The table displays the data exactly as it comes from the database. Therefore, if you want to sort the table by employer name, for example, you have to tell the database to give you the results in that order. You can do that with an ORDER BY clause, as explained in Chapter 23, in one of two ways in Dreamweaver MX: You can use the Simple recordset box and choose the Sort field, or you can write the SQL by hand from the Advanced recordset box.

To see this in action, open the Bindings panel for the view_employers page and double-click the *rsGetEmployers* recordset. This will show the recordset box again, allowing you to edit the SQL code. If the box is in Advanced view, click Simple. At the bottom of the dialog box you'll see a field for Sort. Choose the EmpName column and choose Ascending for the sort type. If you click the Advanced view now, you'll see this SQL statement:

```
SELECT EmpName, EmpCity, EmpState
FROM Employers
ORDER BY EmpName ASC
```

As you can see, the Sort parameter in the Simple recordset dialog box simply added an ORDER BY clause to the SQL statement. If you save this page again and press F12, you can preview the page and see the results in a sorted order now.

Navigating Through the Recordset

The Dynamic Table object includes code that makes it easy to add navigation to your recordset. Recall that when you added the object to the table, you could specify the number of records to display on the page. If you were to choose the number 5, only 5 records would be displayed on each page. In order for this to be of any use, there has to be a way to get to the second page.

That's where the Recordset Navigation Bar object comes in. It is located in the Insert | Application Objects menu, and also on the Insert bar in the Application tab. To add one of these bars to the view_employers page, simply follow these steps:

1. Position your cursor where you want the navigation bar to appear, usually directly above or directly below the table.

2. Click Recordset Navigation Bar on the Application Objects insert bar.

3. Choose the *rsGetEmployers* recordset from the drop-down list.

4. Choose text or images for your navigation scheme. If you choose images, the images will be copied to the folder that your page is in.

5. Click OK.

After applying the object, you should be able to browse the page by pressing F12, and you'll be able to navigate through your pages.

If you look at your Server Behaviors panel after applying the Recordset Navigation Bar, there are actually eight new Server Behaviors showing. These are the individual Server Behaviors for Show Region and Recordset Paging. They can be applied individually as well. For example, you could have an image that takes you to the first record, and simply apply a Move To First Record Server Behavior to that image.

 One of the most flexible aspects of Dreamweaver MX is the way that Server Behaviors, Application Objects, and Data Sources can interact with each other and can be edited at any time individually.

Displaying the Record Numbers

The links that you applied with the Recordset Navigation Bar show as First, Previous, Next, and Last. This doesn't help you determine which page you are on or which records are showing. For that, there is another Application object: Recordset Navigation Status. This object displays a text string like this:

> Records 1 to 5 of 20

To apply this object, follow these steps on the view_employers page:

1. Position your cursor where you want the navigation status bar to appear, usually directly above or directly below the table.

2. Click Recordset Navigation Status on the Application Objects insert bar.

3. Choose the *rsGetEmployers* recordset from the drop-down list.

4. Click OK.

After applying the object to the page, you should be able to preview the page by pressing F12, and your recordset status display will be showing. Figure 24-2 shows the completed view_employers page with the recordset, Dynamic Table object, Recordset Navigation Bar object, and Recordset Navigation Status object in place and functioning.

Master-Detail Page Set

The View All Gigs and View A Gig pages will bring into play an Application object called Master-Detail Page Set. This object automates the process of creating a Master page containing a list of records that each link to specific Details pages. This is a typical recordset navigation technique that is used on most sites that have dynamic content. For example, when you search for a book on Amazon.com, a list of books that match your search criteria will be displayed, with links to the details of each book upon clicking its title.

Note *The ASP.NET and PHP server models do not contain the Master-Detail Page Set.*

Creating the Recordset

For the Master Detail object to work, you must first specify a recordset. The recordset will contain all of the items that you want displayed on the Details page. For the Jobs page to work, you'll need to have a fairly complex statement. If you recall, the JobTypes fields is drawn from a separate table. This dramatically decreases the size of the database, but it also dramatically increases the complexity of the SQL. However, SQL is a powerful language that is designed specifically for retrieving items from a database. Once again, until you become comfortable with the language, it's a good idea to create SQL statements with a graphical interface, such as the View builder interface that is included in Microsoft SQL Server (shown in Figure 24-3). Most modern databases have a similar

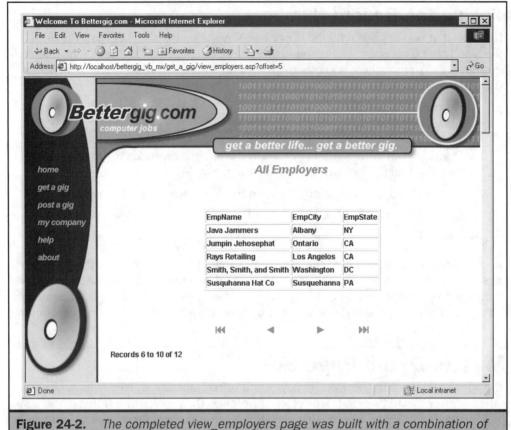

Figure 24-2. *The completed view_employers page was built with a combination of four different Application objects.*

interface that will allow you to choose the columns that you want to be displayed, as well as the columns that are needed for the joins.

The SQL statement needed here is as follows:

```
SELECT JobTypes.JobTypeDesc
, Jobs.JobID
, Jobs.JobLocation
, Jobs.JobStatus
, Jobs.JobSalary
, Jobs.JobEducation
, Jobs.JobDescription
, Jobs.JobStartDate
, Jobs.JobTerm
, Jobs.JobCitizenship
, Employers.EmpName
```

```
FROM Jobs
   INNER JOIN JobTypes
      ON Jobs.JobType = JobTypes.JobTypeID
   INNER JOIN dbo.Employers
      ON Jobs.EmpID = Employers.EmpID
```

The SQL statement should be created as a view in your database. If your database doesn't support views (such as MySQL), you can use this statement on your page. This is the getJobs view in the Bettergig database.

You can save debugging time when writing queries by putting the commas that exist between fields at the beginning of each line. This way, when you are debugging your SQL statements, you can comment out the line easily with two dashes (--).

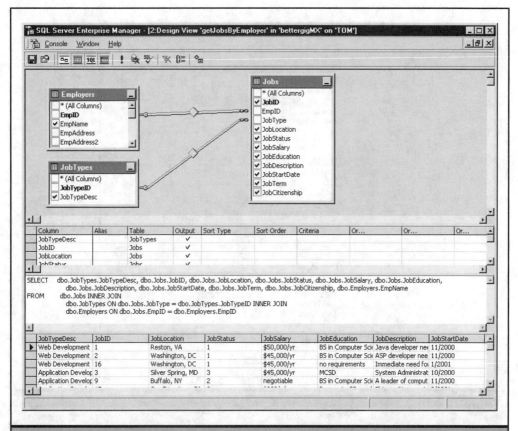

Figure 24-3. *The New View builder in Microsoft SQL Server allows you to graphically create your SQL statements.*

ADDING DATABASE
FEATURES TO YOUR SITE

On your page you will need to define a recordset named *rsGetJobs*. The SQL needed will be very simple because you are retrieving only the information that you need inside of the view:

```
SELECT * FROM getJobs
```

As a matter of practice, you should not use SELECT * unless you specifically need to retrieve all columns. In this case, the view is prewritten to return only the columns that are needed.

Adding the Insert Master Detail Application Object

This Application object, like the others, is accessed either from the Insert bar in the Application panel, or by clicking Insert | Application Objects | Insert Master-Detail Page Set. This will bring up the dialog box shown in Figure 24-4.

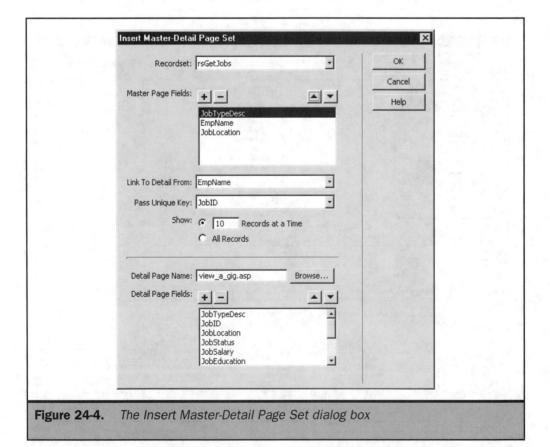

Figure 24-4. *The Insert Master-Detail Page Set dialog box*

When you use this object, there are two pages that are affected—the current page will be the Master page, and the Detail page can be specified from this dialog box. Follow these steps for the view_all_jobs and view_a_job pages:

1. Choose the newly created recordset *rsGetJobs*.

2. Choose your Master Page Fields. These will be displayed in a table and are only meant to be a summary of the jobs available. Pick the JobTypeDesc, EmpName, and JobLocation from the list of fields and remove the rest.

3. Set the Link To Detail From attribute to the JobTypeDesc field.

4. Set the Pass Unique Key to the JobID field.

5. Click the Show *x* Records At A Time radio button and leave it set to the default (10).

6. Type in **view_a_gig.asp** (or whichever server model you are working with) for the Detail Page Name.

7. At Detail Page Fields, click the up and down arrows to reorder the fields in a logical order for display on the page.

8. Click OK, and the object will be inserted into this page. In addition, the Detail page will be updated if it exists (or created if it doesn't exist) with a table containing all of the fields that were specified.

Note *If your Preferences are set to have one window open at a time, Dreamweaver MX will prompt you to save the page after applying this object. You should click Yes, because the page must be closed in order for Dreamweaver MX to open up the Detail page and insert the recordset and table into that page.*

If you look at Figure 24-5, you'll see that Dreamweaver MX has inserted about 16 different Server Behaviors just on the Master page. First, a table is inserted containing column headings and the database columns that were specified. Next, a Repeat Region Server Behavior is applied to the table row containing the dynamic data. Then, another Application Object is inserted—the Recordset Navigation Bar. This object holds eight different Server Behaviors by itself, showing First, Previous, Next, and Last links to allow the user to browse through the records. Last, another Application Object is inserted as part of the package—the Recordset Navigation Status display, which shows the typical First to Last of Total Records display.

Note *When you use an Application Object, you aren't merely inserting a bunch of code. The object is actually inserting specific Server Behaviors that can later be edited, changed, or removed from the page. In the case of the Master page, there are 16 separate Server Behaviors that can later be manipulated.*

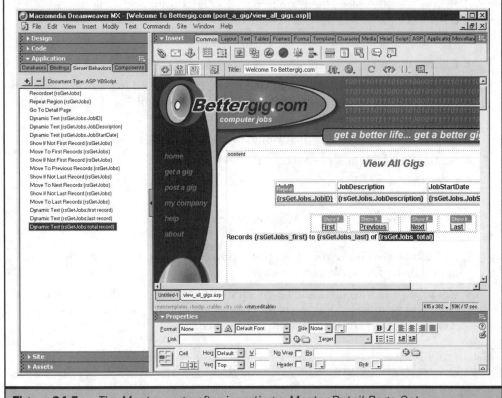

Figure 24-5. *The Master page after inserting a Master-Detail Page Set*

One final thing to do is add a back link to the view_a_gig page. Put the text **<<<back** on the page and set a link equal to the following JavaScript, which you can type directly into the property inspector Link field (as shown in Figure 24-6) for the text that you just inserted:

```
JavaScript:history.go(-1)
```

The tag selector is a good place to add CSS to a specific tag. Figure 24-6 shows the tag selector in use to add a class to a <p> tag.

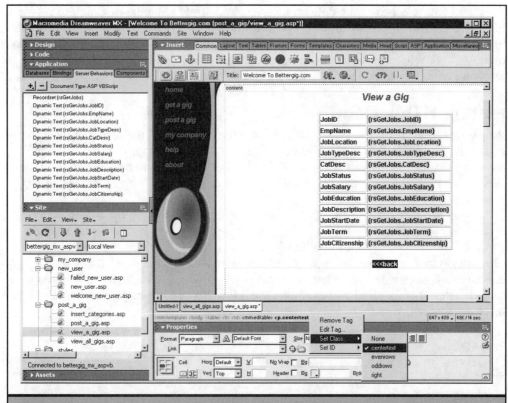

Figure 24-6.   *Using the property inspector to create an A tag by entering the link information, and using the tag selector to enter the class of a tag*

The Repeat Region Server Behavior

You've been dealing with some of the great features of Dreamweaver MX that allow the use of Application Objects, which automate the process of creating data-driven pages. Users of UltraDev become accustomed to using the Repeat Region Server Behavior. This Server Behavior was inserted into the Master page using the Insert Master-Detail Page Set object in the previous example. In many situations, it's important to be able to use the Repeat Region by itself, so we'll go over some of its uses next.

The Repeat Region is located in the Server Behaviors panel. There is also a button on the Insert bar in the Application tab. It is the second button on the left, right next to the Recordset button. You can apply the Server Behavior only to a selection you've made in Dreamweaver MX, such as a table row, list item, or other area in the Dreamweaver MX environment.

When you select dynamic data on the page and apply a Repeat Region, the Server Behavior inserts server-side looping code around your selection. In addition, there are built-in variables that keep track of your loop so that you can show your data in blocks of 5, 10, 20, or whatever value you choose. The key to using this Server Behavior is knowing what is going on beneath the surface.

Repeating HTML Code

When the server reads the page, it will execute the code within the server tags. In the case of ASP and JSP, these are the <% open tags and %> close tags. For ColdFusion, anything that begins with <CF is a valid ColdFusion tag that will be translated by the server. For PHP, the code will be typically enclosed inside of <?php open tags and ?> close tags.

A loop can take many forms, but in most cases, it is a *for/next* loop, a *do/while* loop, or a *while/wend* loop. Although each language has its own syntax, the functionality is similar. ColdFusion has looping built into several of its tags, which makes writing a ColdFusion loop much easier than a similar loop in ASP, PHP, or JSP. If the server encounters a loop, whatever is between the loop is processed for as many times as the loop dictates or is required. For example, the following pseudo-code will display a table with three rows:

```
<table>
<% For I = 1 to 3 %>
   <tr>
       <td>Loop number <% = I %></td>
   </tr>
<% Next %>
</table>
```

When the server code executes, the following table will be output to the browser:

```
<table>
   <tr>
       <td>Loop number 1</td>
   </tr>
   <tr>
       <td>Loop number 2</td>
   </tr>
   <tr>
       <td>Loop number 3</td>
   </tr>
</table>
```

Not only is the code within the loop repeated, but the variable that contains the loop index is also output to the browser. This opens up many possibilities, and the Repeat Region Server Behavior simplifies many of these operations.

Repeat Region on a Table

The most often used Repeat Region is a dynamic table. You saw a table like this in action earlier with the Dynamic Table object, but now you'll learn the parts that make up the object. We'll create an Administrator page in the admin folder named all_seekers and apply the Repeat Region Server Behavior to the page. The steps to apply the Server Behavior to a table are as follows:

1. Create a recordset that returns more than one row of data. For this example, create a recordset named *rsSeekers* using the following SQL:

   ```
   SELECT SeekFirstName, SeekLastName, SeekEmail FROM Seekers
   ```

2. Insert a table on your page. The table can have one row and as many columns as you have dynamic data to display. Alternately, you can insert a two-row table and make the first row the column headings. In this example, we apply a two-row, three-column table to the page.

3. Drag and drop or insert the dynamic text, text fields, images, check boxes, or whatever other item you might want repeated into the table cells. For this example, insert the columns SeekFirstName, SeekLastName, and SeekEmail into the second row of the table.

4. Select the table row containing the dynamic data and apply the Repeat Region Server Behavior to the row. Select the table row by dragging the cursor across the cells in the row, or by clicking the <tr> icon in the tag selector on the bottom bar of the document window.

5. The Server Behavior will allow you to specify the number of rows you want repeated or All Records. Choose All Records for this example.

6. The first row will contain the column headings, so you can type in the text for First, Last, and Email in the table cells.

7. You can turn the e-mail address into a hyperlink by applying a link to the rsSeekers.email placeholder. Simply right-click (CTRL-click on the Macintosh) and choose Make Link. Set Select Filename From to Datasources by clicking the appropriate radio button. Choose the SeekEmail field from the menu. Lastly, type the text **mailto:** in front of the dynamic data and click OK.

The page in the design environment should look like Figure 24-7. If you browse the page at this point, you'll have a list of all job seekers in the Seekers table.

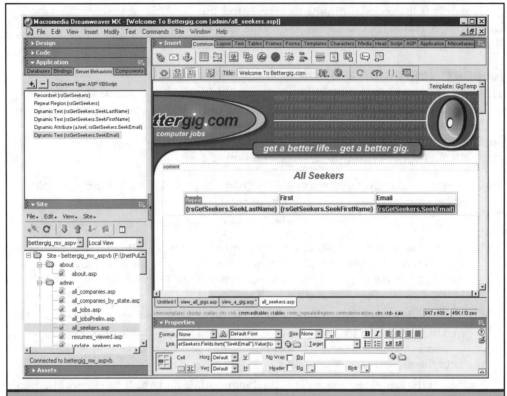

Figure 24-7.   The all_seekers page in the Dreamweaver MX design environment after applying a Repeat Region to the table row

   Avoid putting a repeat region on a row with one table cell. Because of a bug in Dreamweaver MX, the table cell will become selected (the <td> tag) rather than the table row, and the results will repeat horizontally instead of vertically.

Repeat Region in a Dynamic List

Repeat Regions can be applied to more than just tables. For example, you can place some dynamic text on the page, insert a <br> tag next to it in source view, and apply the Repeat Region Server Behavior to the dynamic text. The text will show up as multiple lines seperated by <br> tags when you browse it. In other words, the <br> tag is repeated along with the dynamic text.

This technique can also be used with a dynamic list. Lists can be bullets (unordered lists) or numbers (ordered lists), or they can have a graphic as a bullet. Whichever one you choose, you can do it dynamically with a Repeat Region. We create another

Administrator page in the admin folder named all_companies and apply a Repeat Region to a list. The steps are as follows:

1. Create a recordset named *rsEmployers* from the Employers table and use the following SQL statement:

```
SELECT EmpName, EmpPhone FROM Employers
```

2. Place some dummy text on the page (to be replaced later).

3. Apply a list to the text by right-clicking (CTRL-clicking on the Macintosh) on the selected text and choosing List | Unordered List.

4. Drag the EmpName column onto the selected text. It will replace the text.

5. Add a space and then insert the EmpPhone dynamic text right next to it.

6. SHIFT-select both placeholders of the dynamic text to show the <li> tag in the tag selector, and select the <li> tag.

7. Apply a Repeat Region Server Behavior to the page, choosing All Records.

Figure 24-8 shows the page with Live Data turned on. You can see that the bullets appear in front of each row from the database. If you look at the underlying code, you'll see that the code is broken down like this (pseudo-code):

```
<ul>
<% loop code %>
<li><% recordset columns %></li>
<% end loop code %>
</ul>
```

Just like the dynamic table, the Repeat Region wraps a loop around the line items of the unordered list, allowing you to create a dynamic list. If you had chosen Ordered List from the menu, the bullets would have been replaced by numbers from one to however many items are returned from the database.

Repeating a Show/Hide Layer Using Repeat Region

One of the great ways to use a looping construct in a page that's executed on the server is to give unique names to HTML elements. This is done by using the index number of the loop or, in the case of ColdFusion, the internal *CurrentRow* variable and appending the counter to the end of the HTML element name, like this:

```
<input type="text" name="txtTitle<%=Repeat1__index%>">(ASP or JSP)
<input type="text" name="txtTitle#Recordset.CurrentRow#">(CF)
```

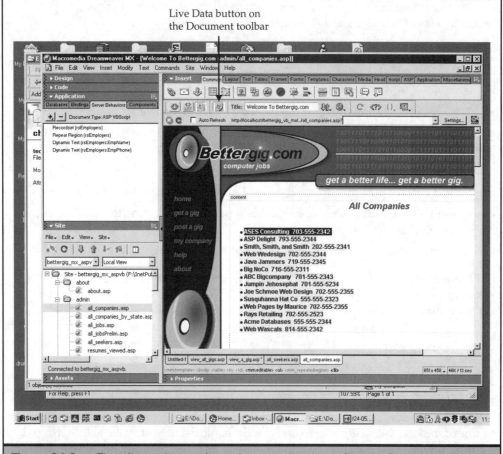

Figure 24-8. *The all_employers dynamic page showing a Repeat Region applied to a bulleted list*

ASP.NET and PHP don't have a counter variable like this, but you can create your own and increment it within the loop, as in this PHP version:

```
<?php $Repeat1__index = 1; 'declare the variable outside of the loop ?>
<!-- loop code -->
<input type="text" name="txtTitle<?php echo $Repeat1__index++;?>">
```

Note *The ASP.Net variation of the dynamic Show/Hide tutorial is not possible to achieve in Dreamweaver using the standard behaviors and Server Behaviors.*

If this code were within a Repeat Region loop, the code that is output would look like this:

```
<input type="text" name="txtTitle1">
<input type="text" name="txtTitle2">
<input type="text" name="txtTitle3">
etc.
```

Obviously, this technique has many uses. One advanced use of it is to name a layer on the page with a dynamic name such as this, and then use the Show/Hide Layers standard Dreamweaver MX behavior to allow the generation of a custom layer for each element in the loop. This can be done by hand-coding, but it can also be accomplished with a little ingenuity using the graphical design elements of Dreamweaver MX.

Open up the all_jobs file in the admin folder and create a recordset named *rsJobs*. The SQL statement for the recordset will look like this:

```
SELECT Employers.EmpName, Jobs.JobDescription, Jobs.JobEducation,
    Jobs.JobLocation, Jobs.JobSalary, Jobs.JobStartDate, Jobs.JobID
    FROM Employers
INNER JOIN (JobTypes
    INNER JOIN Jobs
      ON JobTypes.JobTypeID = Jobs.JobType)
      ON Employers.EmpID = Jobs.EmpID
```

This SQL statement will return a list of all jobs with a few selected fields from the table, as well as the Employer name from the Employers table. We'll use the image details.gif for the mouseover to show/hide the layer on the page. The page will display a list of all jobs in "short" form (as in a Master page), and the layer that is being shown/hidden will contain the information for the individual jobs (as in a Details page). Additionally, a Go To Details Page Server Behavior will be added.

Note   *The method shown involves the nesting of layers, which may not work in some versions of Netscape.*

The technique used to get the dynamic show/hide layers to work properly requires careful attention to the correct order of steps:

1. Go to Modify | Convert | Tables to Layers. This will change all tables on the page to layers using <div> tags. This is necessary because you shouldn't have a layer defined inside a table. (The page will have to be detached from the template first.)

2. Insert a new layer on the page by clicking Insert | Layer, and then drag the new layer to a place on the page in the content region. The layer should be sized so that it takes up the left half of the area, shown here:

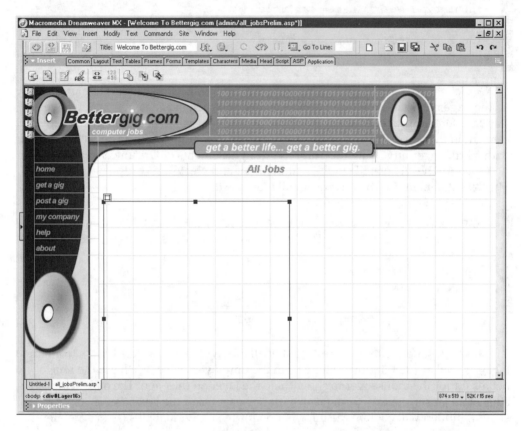

3. Insert a table that's one row and three columns into the layer at a width of 300 pixels with no border. Inside this table you can type in the text for the column heads—**Company Name** and **Location**. Leave the third column blank—it's there for alignment purposes only.

4. Below that table, but inside the same layer, insert another table that is one row and three columns and set to 300-pixels wide with no border.

5. Inside this table, in cell 1 insert the EmpName column, and in cell 2 insert the JobLocation column. In cell 3 insert the image details.gif.

6. Click anywhere inside the layer and insert another layer. Drag the new layer to the right of the first layer so that the two layers are approximately the same size (the page up until this point is shown next). If you look at the code, the <div> tag has been created as a child tag of the first layer that you inserted.

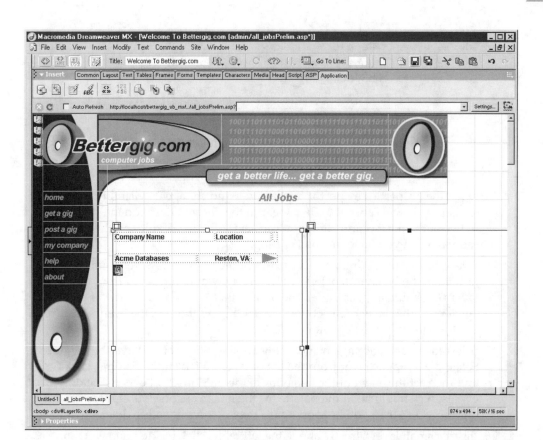

7. SHIFT-select the entire second table (the table with the dynamic data in it) and the new layer tag together. The layer tag should be directly next to or below the table.

8. Apply a Repeat Region to the selected area showing 10 records.

9. Click inside the second layer that's on the right half of the page and insert a table that is two columns and six rows with no border, at 300 pixels wide.

10. Drag the EmpName, JobLocation, JobSalary, JobEducation, JobStartDate, and JobDescription fields to the table cells of column 2 of the table inside the second layer, and place appropriate descriptive labels in column 1 that correspond to the fields.

11. Select the layer once again, and right-click (CTRL-click on the Macintosh) and choose Edit Tag | <div>. Here is where you are going to give the layer a dynamic name.

12. As you open it, the layer ID should be highlighted. Change the ID attribute to match the code that follows (inside the quotation marks with no spaces) so that it appears like this (see the following illustration):

```
id="LayerDyn<%=Repeat1__index%>" (ASP and JSP)
id="LayerDyn#rsJobs.CurrentRow#" (ColdFusion)
id="LayerDyn<?php echo Repeat1__index++;?>"(PHP)
```

```
Edit Tag: <div id="LayerDyn<%=Repeat1__index%>"
          style="position:absolute; left:351px;
          top:0px; width:370px; height:413px;
          z-index:17; visibility: visible;">
```

13. Open the Properties Inspector for the layer and change its visibility (vis) to hidden. This will cause it to disappear in the design environment. If you need to tweak the positioning later, you can set it back to default and then set it to hidden when you have finished editing.

14. Select the Details.gif image and apply a Show-Hide Layers behavior to it, located in the Behaviors palette. Select the new dynamic layer from the list of layers (it should appear under one of the other layers because it was created "inside" of that layer). Click Show, click OK, and then set the event to onMouseOver in the Behaviors palette.

15. Select the image once again and apply another Show-Hide Layer behavior to it. Select the dynamic layer from the list of layers, click Hide this time, click OK, and then set the event of the behavior to the onMouseOut event. The only two events that should be in the palette for the image are onMouseOver and onMouseOut. If any others pop up (as they do occasionally), delete them.

16. Insert a small layer directly above the left table, click inside that layer, and apply the Recordset Navigation Bar Application Object. This object will insert First, Previous, Next, and Last links to the page, allowing you to browse the recordset.

17. Apply a Go To Details Page Server Behavior to the image (details.gif). For the Details page attribute, browse to the view_a_gig page and use the JobID column as the URL parameter.

You can also set the background color of the layer, making for a truly dynamic page. By clicking the bgcolor icon in the Property Inspector of the layer, you can use the Color Picker eyedropper to pick a color on your page to apply to the layer. Note for ColdFusion users: Whenever you insert a color into a dynamic area of the page, you have to manually edit the code to insert an extra # sign (such as ##009999).

If you've followed all of these steps, the page should look something like Figure 24-9. You should now be able to browse the page and mouse over the images in the table to show the details of the jobs. This technique is based on a technique from the award-winning Massimo Foti, whose Dreamweaver extensions have opened up new possibilities for Web designers.

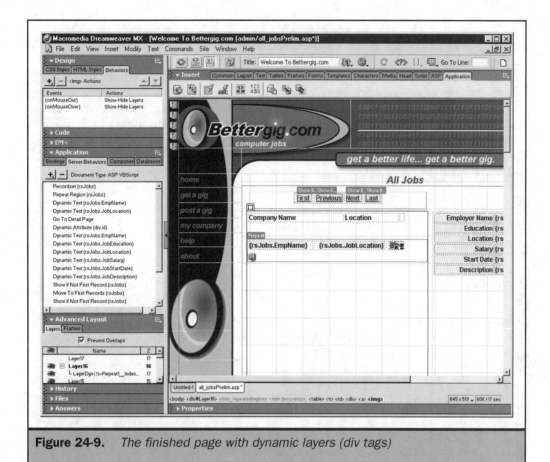

Figure 24-9.   *The finished page with dynamic layers (div tags)*

ADDING DATABASE
FEATURES TO YOUR SITE

Alternating Colors in a Repeat Region

One of the most frequently used techniques for a dynamic table is to alternate the colors of the table rows. There's nothing built into Dreamweaver MX to take care of this for you but by doing a little bit of hand-coding, you can accomplish this fairly easily.

As you saw in the Show/Hide example, you can manipulate the index variable to achieve dynamic effects. In that example, you appended the number to a layer name to give each layer a different name. To get the effect of an alternate-colored table, you have two colors that you want to alternate. The effect is easy to implement with the Modulus math function, which gives the remainder of an integer division—either 1 or 0. For example, 3 MOD 2 = 1, because the remainder of 3, divided by 2, is 1. In fact, the modulus of any integer divided by 2 is going to be either 1 or 0, so you can set up a simple *if* statement to test for the value and set the colors accordingly.

The first step is to make sure that you have two different CSS classes previously defined. You can define new styles by right-clicking (CTRL-clicking on the Macintosh) on the page and choosing CSS Styles | New Style. This technique will also work with the BGCOLOR attribute of the <tr> tag if you prefer, but the *Class* attribute will allow you to use CSS, which is much more versatile.

After your Repeat Region is applied to the page, you can open up the Code view and navigate to the <tr> tag of the repeating row. Or, you can edit the tag by right-clicking (or CTRL-clicking on the Macintosh) the correct <tr> tag in the tag selector in the lower left of the design page; then you can edit the tag directly. The code is as follows, for different languages:

```
VBScript
<tr class = "<%If (Repeat1__index MOD 2) Then
    Response.Write("yourclass1")
Else
    Response.Write("yourclass2")
End If%>">


JavaScript or Java
<tr class = "<%if(Repeat1__index % 2 == 1) {
    out.println("yourclass1");
}else{
    out.println("yourclass2");
}%>">


ColdFusion
<tr class = "¬
    #IIF(CurrentRow MOD 2, DE('yourclass1'),DE('yourclass2'))#">


PHP
<!-- in PHP make sure you initialize a counter first
<tr class = "<?php if($Repeat1__index++ % 2 == 1) {
    echo "yourclass1";
}else{
    echo "yourclass2";
}?>">
```

Notice that the ending tag half for the <tr> tag is after the server markup tags in the ASP and JSP implementations. Two closing >"> tags with a quotation character might look wrong, but the server tags will be stripped out by the server, including all server-side code, leaving just the class name and the closing tag. After the page is browsed, the code will look something like this:

```
<tr class = "yourclass1">
   <td>stuff</td>
</tr>
<tr class = "yourclass2">
   <td>more stuff</td>
</tr>
<tr class = "yourclass1">
   <td>stuff</td>
</tr>
etc.
```

If you apply this code to the table and Repeat Region on the view_all_gigs page, the result will look like Figure 24-10. You can apply this technique in all sorts of different ways. If you desire a checkerboard effect, for example, you can apply a similar technique to a <td> tag instead, using your own counter-variable.

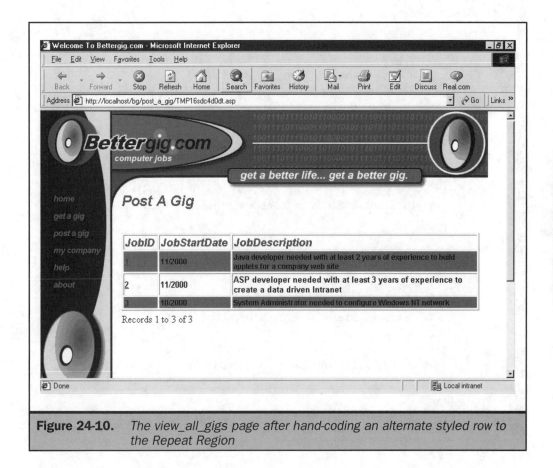

Figure 24-10.   *The view_all_gigs page after hand-coding an alternate styled row to the Repeat Region*

Code fragments such as the previous alternating row example make good candidates for Snippets. The Snippets panel can contain all of your most-often-used code fragments to make it easier to add functionality to your pages.

Alternating Colors in an ASP.NET Page

The ASP.NET Repeat Region makes use of the Repeater Web Server Control. This control allows you to create a template of how you want your HTML to look, and the control will fill in the dynamic data where specified. This is a tag-based control and includes <ItemTemplate> tags for your main rows, but also has a <AlternateItemTemplate> tag to specify an alternate row. This is exactly where you can put in an alternate style for your alternating colors:

```
<table width="75%" border="1">
    <td>JobID</td>
    <td>JobStartDate</td>
    <td>JobDescription</td>
  </tr>
  <ASP:Repeater runat="server" DataSource='<%# DataSet2.DefaultView %>'>
    <ItemTemplate>
      <tr class="oddrows">
        <td>
          <%# DataSet2.FieldValue("JobID", Container) %>
        </td>
        <td>
          <%# DataSet2.FieldValue("JobStartDate", Container) %>
        </td>
        <td>
          <%# DataSet2.FieldValue("JobDescription", Container) %>
        </td>
      </tr>
    </ItemTemplate>
    <AlternatingItemTemplate>
      <tr class="evenrows">
        <td
          <%# DataSet2.FieldValue("JobID", Container) %>
        </td>
        <td>
          <%# DataSet2.FieldValue("JobStartDate", Container) %>
        </td>
        <td>
          <%# DataSet2.FieldValue("JobDescription", Container) %>
        </td>
```

```
      </tr>
    </AlternatingItemTemplate>
  </ASP:Repeater>
</table>
```

The *DataSource* property controls how the ItemTemplate and AlternatingItemTemplate rows will look. There are other tags for the *Repeater* control as well: the <HeaderTemplate>; <FooterTemplate>; and <SeparatorTemplate> tags. They can't be bound to data, but they will appear even if no data is returned. The opening <table> tag in the previous example could have been placed in a <HeaderTemplate>, and the closing </table> tag could have been placed in the <FooterTemplate>.

Using Stored Procedures

Stored procedures are available to many of the databases that you can work with in Dreamweaver MX. They are precompiled SQL scripts that reside in your database and can be called by your program. Why use a stored procedure over a query? There are many reasons and here are a few:

- Stored procedures are faster than regular queries because they are compiled and their execution plans are recorded.

- Stored procedures place the important business logic into your database server.

- Stored procedures offer much greater security than direct queries to your tables. If you query a table, you are also opening up security holes for hackers to access your database. A knowledgeable hacker can attach a second query to a URL to delete your tables if you aren't careful. Stored procedures can't be hacked in this way.

- Stored procedures can contain complex logic, looping, and other programming structures that are typically found in programming languages. One stored procedure can contain one query or a hundred queries.

- Stored procedures can call other stored procedures, offering much more flexibility in code creation.

We'll show you a simple stored procedure and how to use the built-in Stored Procedure Server Behavior that is built into Dreamweaver MX.

Because MySQL doesn't support stored procedures at the time of this writing, the PHP server model can't be used with stored procedures.

Simple Stored Procedure

The simplest of stored procedures is a SELECT * FROM mytable. We go one step beyond that by creating a stored procedure that accepts a parameter. One of the powerful features of stored procedures is that you can pass parameters to the stored procedure. Here is a stored procedure that takes one integer parameter: *@jobid*. This parameter can then be matched to the appropriate rows in the database so that only matching records are returned.

```
CREATE PROCEDURE spGetCategories
  @jobid int
AS
SELECT Categories.CatDesc
FROM Categories
INNER JOIN JobsCategories
ON JobsCategories.CatID = Categories.CatID
WHERE  JobsCategories.JobID = @jobid
```

To your Web page, this stored procedure will do the exact same thing as a query that would have been defined on the page, but now the logic is in the database as a compiled statement. Your own syntax may vary depending on the database that you are working with, but this example works with Microsoft SQL Server and PostgreSQL. Open the view_a_gig page that was created previously for the Master-Detail Page Set tutorial. This stored procedure will add job categories to the page.

To use the stored procedure from Dreamweaver MX, open the Bindings panel and click Command (Stored Procedure). That will bring up the dialog box shown in Figure 24-11. The actual menu item will vary depending on what server model you are using. Follow these steps to add the stored procedure to the page:

1. Type in a name for the stored procedure in the Name field. Use the name **cmdCategories**.

2. Choose the connection that was set up for the Bettergig site.

3. The Type drop-down box should be set to Stored Procedure.

4. The Return Recordset box should be checked, and the recordset name should be filled in as **rsCategories**.

5. Move down to the Database Items box and expand the Stored Procedures tree. Choose the spGetCategories stored procedure. This will populate the rest of the dialog box.

6. Fill in a size of **4** and a default value of **0** for the @jobid parameter. The other information should have been populated automatically.

7. Click OK.

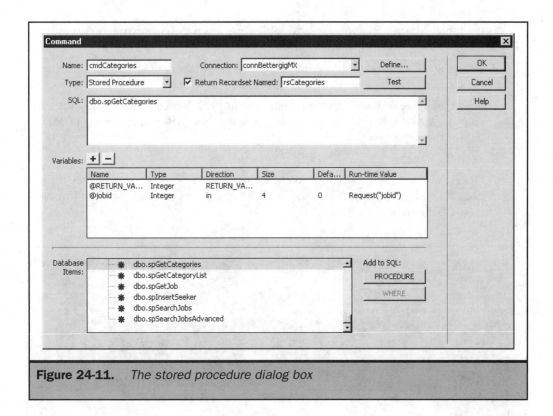

Figure 24-11. *The stored procedure dialog box*

This adds the stored procedure to the page, but also adds a recordset named *rsCategories* that is returned by the stored procedure. The available fields are listed in the Bindings panel in the tree under the command name. You can insert these into your page exactly the same way as the standard recordset fields.

Modifying the Display Page

This page has been previously set up to display the data from the *rsGetJobs* recordset. You can make modifications to the page to allow for the new data to be displayed.

1. Select the display table. You can select it by clicking on the border, or by using the tag selector on the bottom bar of the document window and clicking the <table> tag.

2. If the Property Inspector isn't open, open it by clicking Window | Properties.

3. Add one row to the table inside of the Inspector by typing in the new number. For example, if it reads 11, type in **12**. This will add a new row to the bottom of

the table. Alternately, you can add table rows from the contextual menu for the table: Table | Insert Rows or Columns.

4. Drag the rsCategories.catdesc field from the Bindings panel to the new empty table cell.

5. Select the table row with the new field and apply a Repeat Region showing all records. Make sure you choose the rsCategories recordset from the drop-down list for the Repeat Region.

6. Save the page.

7. Open the view_all_gigs page and click on any of the jobs. The new view_a_gig page should display the jobs along with all categories for each job. The finished page is shown in Figure 24-12.

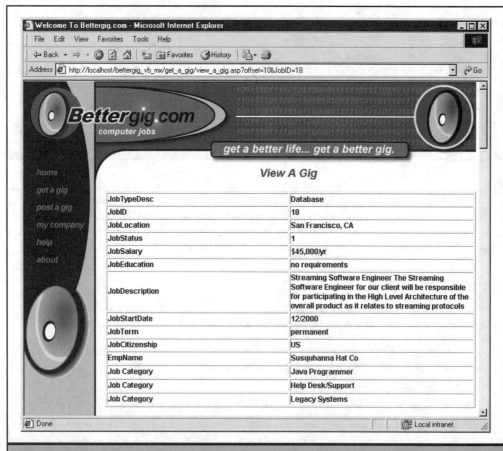

Figure 24-12.   *The newly modified view_a_gig page has one repeating row for job categories.*

The Record Insertion Form Application Object

Now that we've explained the concepts of displaying the data, it's time to add some data to the database. The SQL statement structure that is used to insert data to the database looks like this:

```
INSERT INTO [table] ([fields]) values ([values])
```

Dreamweaver MX writes the SQL for you automatically, and even puts the form and all the form elements on the page for you, while mapping the form elements to specific database columns. This is done through the use of the Record Insertion Form.

To demonstrate this functionality, we use the new_user page. This page will allow a user to insert his or her personal information into the database. The Record Insertion Form object actually does all the work, so you can start with a completely blank page. To use the object, choose it from the Insert | Application Objects menu or click the Record Insertion Form button on the Application Objects insert bar. That will show the following interface:

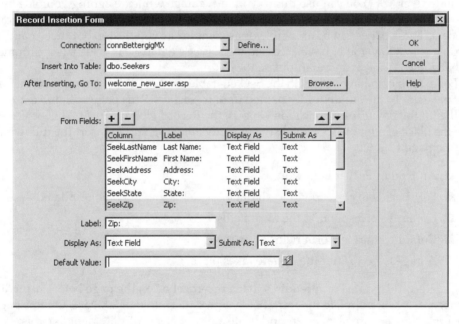

Fill in the form as follows:

- **Connection**   Choose the connection that you've set up for Bettergig.
- **Insert Into Table**   Choose the Seekers table.
- **After Inserting, Go To**   Browse to the welcome_new_user page.

■ **Form Fields**   Remove the SeekID and SeekAccessGroup fields using the minus sign.

■ **Label**   Change the label for each field so that it is a user-friendly label.

■ **Display As**   Leave this set to the default Text. This can be any valid form element, such as a drop-down list or check box.

■ **Default Value**   Leave this field blank for all fields.

With all of the boxes filled in, click OK, and the form will be inserted into the page. If you browse the page, you can now insert a new user into the database. Chapter 25 builds upon this page using the User Authentication Server Behaviors to validate that the username is unique.

Adding Administrator Pages

As we've pointed out previously, the new Application Objects that automate the process of developing certain types of dynamic pages is one of the nicest features of Dreamweaver MX. You can use this to your advantage while designing your site by creating temporary or Administrator pages for viewing, inserting, and updating your test data. These pages can be as simple or as complex as you desire, but their main purpose is to allow you to have access to the server's database in a visual environment so that you can look at and manipulate the data.

For example, to have access to the Seekers table on the server, you can open up a new page under the admin folder named update_seekers. This page will make use of another of the powerful Application Objects: the Record Update Form. This object will take the place of a lot of labor-intensive work by allowing you to insert the following into the page:

■ An Update Server Behavior

■ Form fields to correspond to all database fields that are being updated

■ Labels to correspond to the form fields

■ Default values for form fields

■ A page to go to after the update takes place

The Record Update Form requires that a recordset be on the page before using it. The recordset will populate the form fields with data from the database. On this page, create a recordset named *rsSeekers* and write a basic Select All statement like this:

```
SELECT * FROM Seekers
```

This statement is the simplest of SQL statements and will return all of the columns in the database. After creating the recordset, position your cursor in the middle of the content area where you want the Update table to be inserted, and click Insert | Application Objects | Record Update Form.

The Record Update Form looks a lot like the Record Insertion Form. Fill in the form as follows:

- **Connection**   Choose the connection that you've set up for Bettergig.
- **Table to Update**   Choose the Seekers table.
- **Select Record From**   Choose the *rsSeekers* recordset.
- **Unique Key Column**   Choose the SeekID field with a numeric value.
- **After Updating, Go To**   Browse to the welcome_new_user page.
- **Form Fields**   Remove the SeekID and SeekAccessGroup fields using the minus sign.
- **Label**   Leave these set to the default.
- **Display As**   Leave this set to the default Text. This can be any valid form element, such as a drop-down list or check box.
- **Submit As**   Leave this set to the default as well.
- **Text**   This field should be left set to the default, which is the value coming from the recordset.

The only modification you have to make to the listed form elements is to remove the SeekID field from the form. This is to prevent database errors because the SeekID is the Autonumber field that gets written automatically by the database. When you are inserting a record to the database, the autonumber field is generated by the database so your form does not need to insert it. When you update the record, the autonumber is not going to change so it doesn't need to be included in the update. Make sure this field is chosen as the key column in the form so that the proper record is updated.

Because the primary purpose of a page like this is to be able to view your database and make updates to it, you can leave all of the default labels in place—these are the actual column names that will make it easier to keep track of things.

After applying the object, you have to apply two more objects: Record Navigation Status and Record Navigation Bar. The Record Navigation Status object will insert the recordset information listing the first record displayed, the last record displayed, and the total records in the recordset. The display will show something like this:

Records 1 to 5 of 50

In the case of an update form, there is only one current record showing at any one time, so the first and last records in the status display will be the same, like this:

Records 1 to 1 of 50

Luckily, this text is editable, as are most objects in Dreamweaver MX, so you can change the text to look like this:

Record 1 of 50

The Recordset Navigation Bar can insert either text or images. The text that it will insert, as we've seen when it was automatically inserted along with the Master-Detail Application Object, is this:

First Previous Next Last

If you choose to use images, they will be little arrow icons and will automatically be copied by Dreamweaver MX into the folder that the page resides in. These are also completely editable and can be changed for images of your choice.

The finished page, which took about five minutes to put together, looks like Figure 24-13. You can create a page like this for each one of your database tables, if you like. When you are accessing data on a remote server, it is frequently difficult to get a birds-eye view of the data, but this technique is easily applied and gives you total

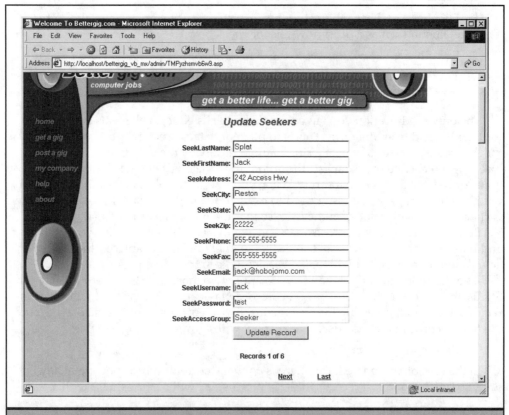

Figure 24-13. The finished update_seekers page that was built using several Dreamweaver MX Application objects

control over your test data. Later, the pages can be turned into Admin pages with special access levels to allow the system administrator to tweak the data easily.

Other Uses of the Bindings Panel

The Bindings panel is not only a place where recordsets and stored procedures live, it is a place where other data sources can be found. A data source, if you remember, is dynamic data that can be displayed. When a data source is defined in the Bindings panel, it can be dragged from the panel and dropped on the page, or it can be selected in the panel and inserted into the data source at the cursor's position with the click of the Insert button.

The different server models in Dreamweaver MX contain different items in the Bindings panel. For example, ASP has menu items for Session, Application, and Request variables. When you choose one of these data sources from the panel, you can define a name for the variable (shown next). In doing this for session and application variables, nothing is actually inserted on the page—instead, an entry is made in the _notes_ folder for your site, and the data source then appears in the panel for every page in the site. This makes it very easy to insert data sources into the page.

More importantly, when a data source is defined in this way, it is available to all server behaviors, behaviors, objects, and other extensions that have the lightning bolt icon (shown in Figure 24-14).

Furthermore, you may now add server formats to the data source to format the display of the data. Server formats can be accessed directly from the dialog box when clicking the lightning bolt. They are also available when you have a data source on the page—the data source becomes "active" in the Bindings panel if it is on the page. When you click on it in the Bindings panel, you see a drop-down list of available server formats that can be applied to the data source on the page.

Once you choose a server format in the Bindings panel, the format is actually applied to the code on the page, but the data source is still available for the current page and other pages. If you have more than one instance of the data source on the page, you can select each instance on the page and the listing in the Bindings panel will reflect that instance. The Bindings panel listing will show any server formats that have been applied to that particular instance of the data source.

Data sources can also be found as extensions, so that more data sources can be added to Dreamweaver MX. Chapter 31 shows how to build a simple data source extension.

ADDING DATABASE FEATURES TO YOUR SITE

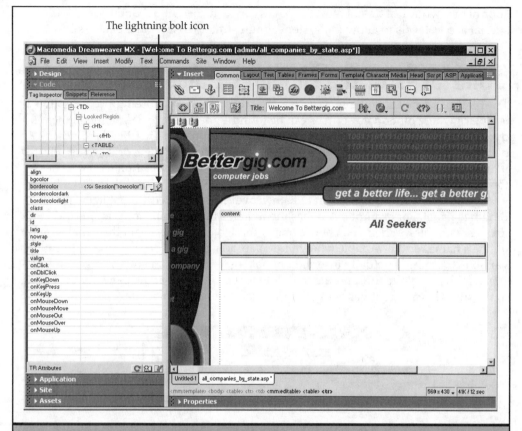

Figure 24-14.   *The lightning bolt icon allows you to invoke a list of data sources.*

Summary

Dreamweaver MX offers a rich assortment of dynamic features that make creating data-driven Web applications easy. Application Objects speed up the process of development considerably. Also, the standard Server Behaviors, such as Repeat Region, offer versatile functionality that goes beyond the surface. You're limited only by your imagination, as we showed with the dynamic Show-Hide Layer functionality. In the next chapter, we get into some more complex database and server features to add more functionality to the Bettergig site.

The
Complete
Reference

Dreamweaver
MX

Chapter 25

User Authentication

I n a Web application, a page typically exists where users can register a username and a password they will use each time they log in to the site. There is also typically an access level set for the user. This allows the user to see only those pages that have the same access level attached to them. We go through a few examples here using some of the standard Dreamweaver MX Server Behaviors for data access, as well as some of the Application Objects that add complex functionality to your pages.

Note   *The ASP.NET and PHP server models in Dreamweaver MX don't contain User Authentication Server Behaviors. PHP users can work with the PHAkt extension from www.interakt.ro, which does have User Authentication Server Behaviors included. You can also hand-code the functionality.*

Session Variables

Session variables were explained in Chapters 15 through 19 for each language, but they play an important part of authentication, so we include a quick refresher here. Session variables are available in the server models that Dreamweaver MX supports and have similar implementations in each. A *session* is created when a user requests a page with server-side code in it, such as an ASP page. The application server creates a session with a session ID number and keeps track of these numbers internally by storing the information in memory and on the user's machine in a cookie. Every time the user asks for another page, the server looks at the cookie on the user's machine and then checks its memory to see if the user has a current session.

Note   *Cookies are needed for session management, but the cookie contains only a session ID to identify the user to the server. The username and password information are stored securely in the server's memory.*

Session variables can store pertinent information about a user or about the current session. Because the Web is a stateless environment, session variables play a key part in keeping information "alive" as the user accesses various pages in the site. Although there are other methods of maintaining state, session variables are the easiest and most widely used method. Typically, a user is given an ID number or username that is stored in a database and used when he logs in to the site.

The Dreamweaver MX User Authentication Server Behaviors take care of the details of assigning the session variables. All you have to worry about is where to store the user information. Your database should have a table containing user information. Among the columns of information stored about each user should be a username column and a password column. Optionally, you can have an access level column as well, to define the role the user will play in the site. Just be sure to give yourself full administration privileges so you can see the pages you build.

If you are using ColdFusion, you'll have to create an Application.cfm page to use session variables and the User Authentication behaviors. See the box titled "The Application.cfm File." A tech note on the subject is available at www.macromedia.com/support/ultradev/ ts/documents/cfsessionerror.htm.

When the user logs in, the username and password are compared to values in the database. If they match any row in the database table, a session is created for the user. If the login fails, no session is created and the user is either given the boot or given the option to try again.

If a user has cookies turned off on his machine, sessions will not work unless you have made provisions beforehand. You would have to hand-code some additional functionality into your site for such users, or simply display a message that states that cookies must be enabled to access certain features of the site. One method for authenticating users if they have cookies turned off is to pass a unique ID in the URL variable so that each page that has an access level set up on it can authenticate users using the URL variable instead of session variable. Some application servers, such as ColdFusion, provide easy access to the session information so that you can add it easily to the URL.

Before the user can be validated, however, he has to exist in the database.

The Application.cfm File

ColdFusion users will need to have an Application.cfm page in place before any work can be done with this site. In general, the Application.cfm page will allow you to "turn on" session variables in the site. A typical Application.cfm page will look like this:

```
<cfapplication name="Bettergig"
 clientstorage="Registry"
 clientmanagement="yes"
 sessionmanagement="yes"
 applicationtimeout="#CreateTimeSpan(0,2,0,0)#"
 sessiontimeout="#CreateTimeSpan(0,0,20,0)#">
```

The CFAPPLICATION tag is the only requirement for the file. The session-management attribute is the requirement for the Bettergig site: it needs to be set to "Yes" for session variables to be used. Also, any pages using ColdFusion and Dreamweaver's user authentication Server Behaviors will need the Application.cfm file defined in this manner. Consult the ColdFusion documentation that came with the ColdFusion server or at the Macromedia Web site for more information about the Application.cfm page.

There are a couple of standard techniques that you will always see on a page like this:

■ Three input fields for Username, Password, and Confirm Password. The Password and Confirm Password fields have to match in order to proceed.

■ A search of the database for the Username so that you don't have two identical usernames in the database.

In the last chapter, a new page was created named new_user.asp (or new_user.jsp, new_user.aspx, new_user.php, or new_user.cfm) in the new_user directory. You'll add functionality to that page to validate the fields as well as test the database for duplicate usernames.

Adding a Validate Form Behavior

The fields are all going to be required fields, so you'll have to add a FormValidation behavior to the Submit button. To add this behavior, perform the following steps:

1. Select the form by clicking it in the tag selector or right-clicking the red form outline in the design environment.

2. If the Behaviors panel isn't showing, select it from the Window menu.

3. Click the plus sign (+) in the Behaviors panel.

4. Choose Validate Form from the drop-down list.

5. The Validate Form behavior has a check box for Required. Check this box for each element in turn (see Figure 25-1). For the e-mail field, you can click the Accept Email Address radio button.

6. Click OK.

If you have applied it properly to the form tag, it should show up in the Behaviors panel in the *onSubmit* event of the form. Dreamweaver MX provides some basic form validations, but you can find others on the Macromedia Exchange that provide more functionality, such as checking for length and illegal characters.

 Validating your form elements before submitting them to the database can prevent many errors down the line. Some forms will even validate that an address is valid before allowing any database insert. Other types of validation are for valid numbers, e-mail addresses, ZIP codes, states, or credit card numbers.

Inserting a Custom JavaScript Function

One feature that hasn't been included in the form yet is a confirm password box. This feature is usually put in place to make sure that the user doesn't type in the password incorrectly. With a bad password, the user would never be able get back into the site. The new_user page in its current form doesn't have this feature, but you can add it easily.

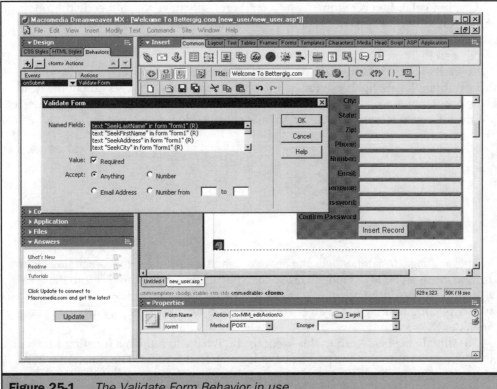

Figure 25-1.   *The Validate Form Behavior in use*

The first step is to add another form field to the page inside of the table. To do that, follow these steps:

1. Select the table. You can do this by clicking the outside border of the table or by selecting the <table> tag in the tag selector.

2. Change the Rows attribute of the table in the Property inspector and increment it by one, or right-click the table and choose Add Row. With a little practice, you can add a row anywhere in the table.

3. Copy the password text field and paste a copy into the new, blank table cell below the password field.

4. Add the appropriate text, like **Confirm Password**.

5. For added protection, change the Type attribute of each of these text fields to Password.

One last validation is required, and you'll probably have to hand-code this one unless you can find a behavior that does this on the Exchange or on a third-party site: You must validate that the Password and Confirm Password fields match. To do this, you'll need to insert a little custom JavaScript.

To insert JavaScript into your page, you need to be in Code view. Because you've already added JavaScript behaviors to the page, there is already a section in the head of the document with JavaScript functions. If this weren't the case, you would have to add the following language declaration inside the head tags:

```
<script language="JavaScript" type="text/JavaScript">
<!--
//insert functions here
//-->
</script>
```

The language declaration tells the browser that the next lines will contain JavaScript. The next line is an HTML comment tag so that the functions will be invisible to the HTML rendering engine of the browser (for old browsers). After including the functions, a JavaScript comment tag hides an HTML close comment tag. The closing script tag concludes the section.

To validate the password in this section, you'll have to type in a function that will allow you to confirm that the password fields match each other. The function will be called from the *onSubmit()* event of the form object. The function looks like this:

```
function form1_onSubmit() {
    if(document.form1.SeekPassword.value !=
        document.form1.SeekPassword2.value) {
        alert("The passwords didn't match");
        return false;
        }
    return true;
}
```

The function was named *form1_onSubmit* as a way of describing the functionality of the JavaScript function. As you build your own libraries of functions, you can also make the functions more flexible so they work with any form or form element, and when doing so, give them more generally descriptive names like *confirmPassword()* or *doFieldsMatch()*. The function simply checks to make sure that the values of the two text fields match each other. If they don't, the function returns false to the caller, and if they do, the function returns true.

To call the function, you'll have to edit the form tag to insert an *onSubmit()* event. You can do this in several ways:

- Go into Code view and hand-code the event.
- Right-click (CTRL-click on the Macintosh) the red form outline in the design window and choose Edit Tag <form>.
- Choose the form tag from the tag selector in the lower-left corner of the design window, right-click (CTRL-click on the Macintosh), and choose Edit Tag (shown in Figure 25-2).

With the tag editor open, find the piece of code that looks like this:

```
return document.MM_returnValue;
```

That code is the key to the validation. The return value has to be true in order for the form submit to take place. The form validation Behavior that you put on the page returns a true or false value in the document.MM_returnValue variable. You simply have to make sure that your true or false value from the custom JavaScript function gets taken into account before the form gets submitted. Change the code to look like this:

```
return document.MM_returnValue && form1_onSubmit()
```

Notice that the function is not called directly, and instead we "return" the function to the *onSubmit* event along with the *document.MM_returnValue* using Boolean logic (*&&* is the operator for the *AND* keyword). In Boolean logic, true *AND* true is true;

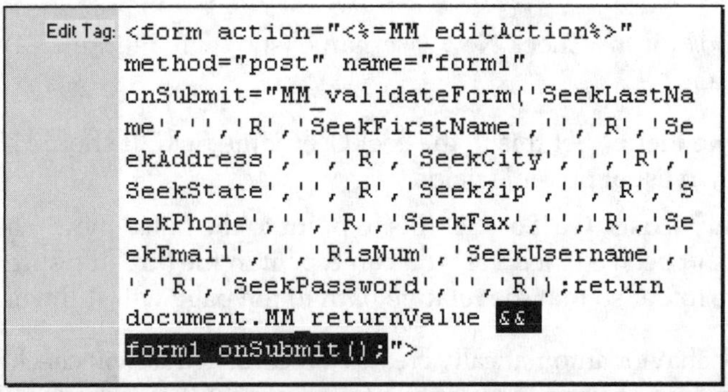

ADDING DATABASE
FEATURES TO YOUR SITE

Figure 25-2. *After clicking the <form> tag in the tag selector, the tag editor is available from the contextual menu.*

false *AND* true is false; and, false *AND* false is false. So in other words, both values have to be true in order for the form to be submitted. You can use this technique in your own custom JavaScript functions to validate form fields or test for other conditions.

If you test the page now, the page should not submit anything to the database unless all fields are filled in and the two password fields match (shown in Figure 25-3).

 There are extensions available that will compare two fields, such as Jaro von Flocken's Check Form and Massimo Foti's Compare Fields. Extensions will be covered in Chapter 30.

Testing for a Duplicate Username

On a standard database insert, you can use the Insert Record Server Behavior from the Server Behaviors panel by itself or use the Record Insertion Form Application object. The insert action on this page will be a little different, however, because you have to first search the database for the username. If it exists, you'll send the user back to the new_user page to try again. This is accomplished by using the User Authentication set of Server Behaviors. There is one called Check New Username, which is exactly what is needed.

In order to use this behavior, the form and Insert Server Behaviors need to be applied to the page first. This Server Behavior will check to see that the Insert behavior is in place. If it isn't, you'll see an error message telling you to put an Insert Record behavior on the page first:

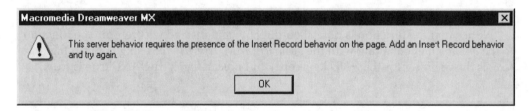

The dialog box for the Check New Username (shown in Figure 25-4) prompts you for two parameters:

- **Username Field**   Set this to the SeekUsername field. It should show up in the drop-down list of possible fields.
- **If Already Exists, Go To**   Set this to point to the failed_new_user page. If the page hasn't been created yet, you can type it in the box—be sure to create it in the same folder so that the relative path to the page will still work.

This Server Behavior automatically creates a recordset that will check your database for the username and redirect the user to a failed page if the username already exists. The recordset doesn't show up as a recordset in the Bindings panel; it is specific to this behavior. If you remove the Server Behavior from the page, the recordset will be removed as well.

Figure 25-3.   *The form fields are now required before the form can be submitted.*

Creating the failed_new_user and login_user Pages

The failed_new_user page will do nothing but display a message to the user if he has entered a username that already exists. The page should be based on the same template as the other pages to maintain consistency. Place a message on the page: "Username exists. Please go back and choose another." Then put a link on the page using the text "<<<back" to link back to the new_user page. Do this with a bit of JavaScript. Highlight the text that you entered (that is, "<<<back") and open up the Properties inspector. In the Link text field, insert the following script:

```
JavaScript:history.go(-1)
```

This JavaScript command will allow you to return to the previous page using the browser's history. With this method, you can use the page as an all-purpose error page for duplicate usernames (for the job seekers and employers).

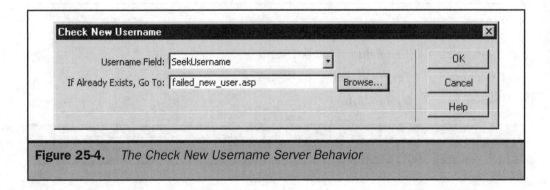

Figure 25-4.   *The Check New Username Server Behavior*

The login_user Page

The login_user page will allow the newly inserted user to officially log in and begin to use the site. A login page will typically serve several purposes:

- It will check the database for the username/password combination.

- It will retrieve a unique identifier such as a user ID number for the person who has just logged in and store it in a session variable so that it is available to all pages that the user might go to. In the case of the built-in Dreamweaver MX Server Behaviors, the username is the unique identifier.

- It will retrieve an access group level for users so that they will only be allowed on the pages that their access level is set for. The access level is typically stored in a session variable as well.

Start the page by making sure that it is based on the template that you've been using. Next, insert a three-row, two-column table into the Content editable region on the page. The table will be set up like Table 25-1.

With the form on the page, all you have to do now is apply another of the Dreamweaver MX Server Behaviors: Log in User. This behavior will retrieve a recordset based on the username and password that is entered on the page, and it will insert the username and access level of the user into session variables. Once this is complete, the user will be redirected to the page they came from.

Any page can have protection on it so that a user has to be logged in to use the page. If users try to access the page without logging in, they'll be directed to the login page. Upon a successful login, users will be redirected to the page that they tried to access the first time. This saves a lot of complex logic to determine where to send a user after logging in.

To apply the Server Behavior, simply click the plus sign (+) on the Server Behavior panel and choose User Authentication | Log in User. That will bring up the dialog box shown in Figure 25-5.

Text	Form Element
Username	Text field named txtUsername
Password	Text field named txtPassword
(blank)	Submit button

Table 25-1.   *Format for the User Login Table on the login_user Page*

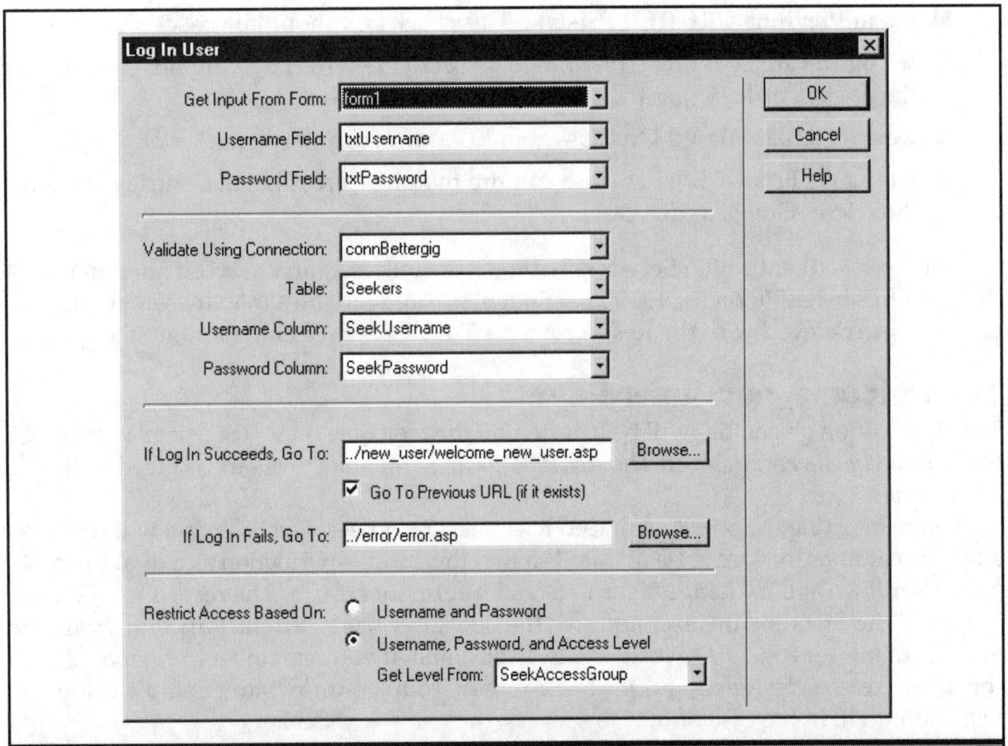

Figure 25-5.   *The Log In User Server Behavior allows the automatic generation of the server-side script to log in a user.*

The parameters for the Server Behavior should be filled in as follows:

■ **Get Input from Form**   Drop-down list of all forms on the page (*form1*, in this case).

■ **Username Field**   *txtUsername*.

■ **Password Field**   *txtPassword*.

■ **Validate Using Connection**   The database connection used in the validation (*connBettergig*, in this case).

■ **Table**   The database table in which the user information is stored (*Seekers*, in this case).

■ **Username Column**   *SeekUsername*.

■ **Password Column**   *SeekPassword*.

■ **If Log in Succeeds, Go To**   welcome_new_user page. Click Browse to find the page so that you get the correct relative path.

■ **Go to Previous URL (If It Exists)**   This check box should be checked.

■ **If Log in Fails, Go To**   This should be set to the error page. Again, browse to the page in order to get the correct relative path.

■ **Restrict Access Based On**   Username, Password, and Access Level.

■ **Get Level From**   The database column that the Access Level is retrieved from (*SeekAccessGroup*, in this case).

The User Authentication Server Behaviors were all designed to work hand in hand. By using this behavior on the login_user page, session variables that are set on this page can be retrieved with the Restrict Access To Page Server Behavior on other pages.

The welcome_new_user Page

The Application object that will be inserted on the welcome_new_user page will be the *Record Update Form* object. The *Record Update Form* object was introduced in the last chapter.

Before inserting the object, you need to create a recordset. The recordset will retrieve all of the columns that are to be updated so that this form can function as a dual-purpose New User form and a Change Your Personal Information form. The record for the user is created the first time the user accesses the new_user page, but the only entries are the SeekUsername and SeekPassword fields. In addition, if you remember in Chapter 22, the database was designed and the SeekAccessGroup column had a default value inserted into it. In the case of the job seekers, the value was Seekers.

Session variables that Dreamweaver MX creates for the User Authentication Server Behaviors can be used for other things. The session variables created by Dreamweaver MX are named *MM_Username* and *MM_UserAuthorization*. These variables can be placed into the Bindings panel for easy drag-and-drop functionality, or you can hand-code your script on the page using these variable names. The *MM_UserAuthorization* variable is useful for showing or hiding various sections of a page depending on access level. You might have one page that works for all users, but show certain parts to authorized users only. An example might be a button to edit a record that would be shown only to administrators, while everyone else would just see the data. The *MM_Username* variable can be used to greet the user by username, or it can be used when it is necessary to insert the username into the database for a transaction of some sort. In this case, you'll use it to filter a recordset. This is a secure way to filter a recordset so that the user sees only the data that relates to his own account.

Create a new recordset by clicking the plus sign (+) in the Bindings panel and choosing Recordset. Name the recordset *rsGetSeeker*. This recordset will be filtered by a session variable. Actually, the word *filtered* is not entirely accurate, although it is used in this context all the time, and is indeed part of the language of the Simple recordset dialog box. In actuality, the database will return only the values that meet the criteria of the *WHERE* clause in the SQL statement. It's not so much a filter as it is a pick-and-choose query.

You'll be writing the SQL statement in Advanced mode. The SQL statement will look like this:

```
SELECT SeekUsername, SeekAddress, SeekCity, SeekEmail, SeekFax,
  SeekFirstName, SeekLastName, SeekPhone, SeekState, SeekZip, SeekID
FROM Seekers
WHERE SeekUsername = 'svUsername'
```

The parameter *svUsername* in the SQL statement has to be defined in the Variables box in the Recordset dialog box. The variable should be set up as shown in Table 25-2. Users of the new ColdFusion server model should consult the box titled "Recordsets in the New ColdFusion Server Model."

To insert the Update object, position your cursor at the spot on the page where you want the object to be inserted. Then go to the Insert menu and click Application Objects | Record Update Form, or click the Record Update Form button on the Application tab of the Insert bar (see Figure 25-6). This will display the Record Update Form dialog box shown in Figure 25-7. There are quite a few options in this box, and the time savings is enormous. The parameters that you need to include are as follows:

- ■ **Connection**   Choose your Bettergig connection for this field. If it's not defined, click the Define button. Connections are covered in Chapter 20.

- ■ **Table to Update**   The database table that the form will update.

- ■ **Select Record From**   The recordset that is used to get the correct record.

- ■ **Unique Key Column**   Usually the Primary Key of the database table. Use the SeekID field.

- ■ **After Updating, Go To**   You should use the Browse button to fill in this field with the page that the user will be redirected to. In this case, it's going to be the post_resume page.

- ■ **Form Fields**   This is where the fun begins. Column (database column), Labels (descriptive text), Display As (form field), and Submit As (data type) are listed for each form element. These should correspond with each column in the recordset; however, several columns will not be needed. Remove *SeekUsername*, SeekPassword, SeekAccessGroup, and SeekID by clicking the minus (–) sign after highlighting the field. Also, you can adjust the labels to something that is more user friendly (such as First Name instead of *SeekFirstName*). All of the fields can be submitted as text.

Server Model	Name	Default Value	Run-time Value
ASP	*svUsername*	%	*Session("MM_Username")*
JSP	*svUsername*	%	*session.getValue("MM_Username")*
UD4-ColdFusion	*svUsername*	%	*#session.MM_Username#*

Table 25-2.   *Variable Declaration for* rsGetSeeker

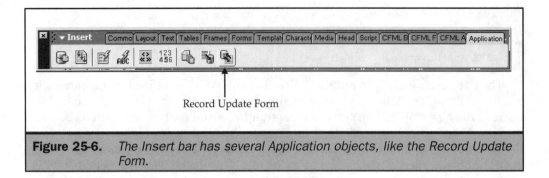

Record Update Form

Figure 25-6. *The Insert bar has several Application objects, like the Record Update Form.*

After changing each form field, setting the labels to something user friendly, and making sure all of the Submit As columns are filled in with Text, click OK. This Application object will insert an Update Server Behavior on the page, as well as a table with the form fields and descriptive labels. At the bottom of the table is a Submit button. In addition, each form field is set as a Dynamic Text Field retrieving the data from the

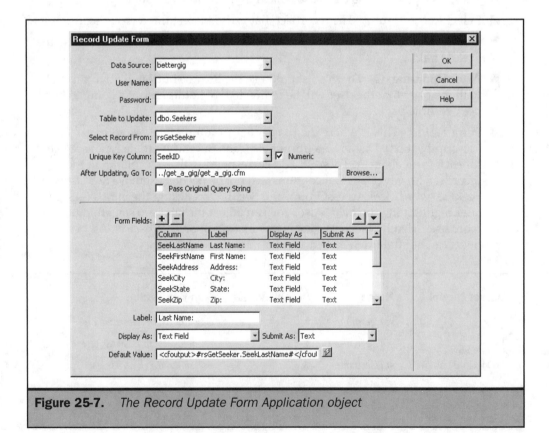

Figure 25-7. *The Record Update Form Application object*

Recordsets in the New ColdFusion Server Model

Dreamweaver MX comes with two server models for ColdFusion, named ColdFusion and CF-UD4, the latter giving backward compatibility for UltraDev 4. When using the CF-UD4 server model, the settings for creating variables in Recordset, Insert, and Update dialog boxes are similar to the way it is done for ASP, JSP, PHP, and ASP.NET. When using the new ColdFusion server model, however, it is a little different.

For the welcome_new_user example, the *rsGetSeeker* query would look like this:

```
SELECT SeekID, SeekUsername, SeekAddress, SeekCity, SeekEmail, SeekFax,
  SeekFirstName, SeekLastName, SeekPhone, SeekState, SeekZip
FROM Seekers
WHERE SeekUsername = '#variables.svUsername#'
```

Notice that a variable is placed directly in the SQL statement. This could have been a form variable, URL variable, or any other type of valid variable. When using Session variables, it is a good practice to lock them whenever using them. For that reason, in the previous example, it is a good idea to assign the session variable value to a temporary page-level variable, such as the *variables.svUsername*.

When you use the variable in the Recordset dialog box, Dreamweaver MX will prompt you for Page Parameter. This is simply a name of a variable and an optional default value. The ColdFusion server model is more versatile than the other server models in this regard because the other server models require a default value, even if you don't want to use one.

The code that is inserted for a parameter looks like this:

```
<cfparam name="variables.svUsername" default="session.MM_username">
```

Because this is a session variable, you should lock the entire statement, in this way:

```
<cflock timeout="20" type="readonly" scope="session">
  <cfparam name="variables.svUsername" default="session.MM_username">
</cflock>
```

You can find more information about locking at the Macromedia Web site at www.macromedia.com/v1/handlers/index.cfm?id=17318.

ADDING DATABASE
FEATURES TO YOUR SITE

database to be displayed in the form field as the default value. Two hidden fields are added as well: *MM_recordid* (or the actual name of your key field) and *MM_update*. These are fields that the Update Server Behavior needs in order to work properly. The *MM_recordid* hidden field contains the value of the *SeekID* field of the current record, so that the update will occur on the correct record.

If the table didn't insert into the proper place, you can select it and drop it into the place on the page where you want it to reside. If you move it around, however, you'll need to make sure that the table, including the hidden fields, is within the form tags.

Server-Side Validation

In the previous section, client-side validation with JavaScript was used. Client-side validation uses JavaScript in the end user's browser. This is usually effective in about 90 to 95 percent of the cases, but it isn't foolproof. Malicious users can disable JavaScript or post from their own form to your database, and cause database errors to occur. The best way to take care of this problem is to supply both client-side and server-side validation code to your pages. This is a little extra work, but your site will be much more bulletproof if you utilize both technologies. The client-side validation will take care of most of the incoming form field data, and the server-side validation is there as a backup method for the remaining cases where the client-side validation failed. Client-side validation is more user-friendly because it doesn't have to make a round trip to the server, which also increases the server load. The best scenario involves client-side validation handling most of the validation of data with server-side validation as an additional safety measure.

Server-side validation can take many forms. None of it is available from Dreamweaver MX out of the box, but by hand-coding the functionality, you can take advantage of whichever method your particular server model favors.

Regular expressions play a valuable role in validating data. Regular expressions were covered briefly in Chapter 8, and are addressed again more thoroughly in Chapter 32 in the section about building Server Behaviors. Regular expressions are similar in all technologies, but it is a good idea to become familiar with the implementation in the server model of your choice.

ASP/VBScript

The easiest way to do server-side validation in ASP VBScript is to use one of the built-in VBScript functions to validate a specific data type, which all return true or false. The built-in VBScript functions are:

- *IsNumeric* Is the value numeric?
- *IsDate* Is the value a valid date?
- *IsEmpty* Does the variable contain anything?
- *IsNull* Is the variable null (not defined)?

Here is an example of how you would do this:

```
<%
If IsNull(Request.Form("myFormElement")) Then
  Response.Redirect("error.asp")
End If
%>
```

Another example assumes that all form fields are required:

```
<%
Dim checkIncoming
checkIncoming = True
For i = 1 to  Request.Form.Count
    checkIncoming = checkIncoming AND Request.Form.Item(i) <> ""
Next
If checkIncoming = False Then
    Response.Redirect("error.asp?all+form+fields+required")
End If
%>
```

Regular expressions are also very useful for building validation functions. Here is an example that checks for a valid e-mail address:

```
Function RegExpCheck(theExpression,theString)
    dim theMatch
    Set myRegExp = New RegExp
    myRegExp.Global = True
    myRegExp.IgnoreCase = True
    myRegExp.Pattern = theExpression
    set theMatch = myRegExp.Execute(theString)
    RegExpCheck = theMatch.count
End Function
Dim txtEmail
txtEmail = Request.Form("SeekEmail")
If Not RegExpCheck("^[\w\.=-]+@[\w\.-]+\.[a-z]{2,4}$", txtEmail) Then
    Response.Redirect("error.asp?error=must+be+a+valid+email+address")
End If
```

ASP/JScript

If you are building a server-side validation function in ASP/JScript, you won't have some of the same built-in functions that are available to VBScript users, but you are also at a distinct advantage because of the built-in functionality of the JavaScript language. Regular expressions are much easier to use in JScript, and as such, you can create sophisticated server-side validation functions using regular expressions. The following example tests the SeekEmail field for a valid e-mail address and the SeekFirstName field for a valid alphabetical character:

```
var txtEmail = String(Request.Form("SeekEmail"));
var txtFirstName = String(Request.Form("SeekFirstName"));
var theExp = /^[\w\.=-]+@[\w\.-]+\.[a-z]{2,4}$/
if (!theExp.test(txtEmail)) Response.Redirect("error.asp");
theExp = /^[a-zA-Z]+$/;
if(!theExp.test(txtFirstName)) Response.Redirect("error.asp");
```

The regular expression is held in the variable named *theExp*. It is tested with built-in JScript regular expression functionality, and the user is redirected to the error page if the form field does not match the criteria of the regular expression.

ColdFusion

ColdFusion users have many different types of validation available to them since ColdFusion has built-in server-side validation using hidden form fields, as can be seen in this example:

```
<input type="hidden" name="SeekEmail_required "
 value="Email address is a required field">
```

The ColdFusion server sees the *_required* and knows that the form field named SeekEmail needs to be validated as a required field. The other types of validation are *date, eurodate, float, integer, range,* and *time.* Because this method depends on the client-side hidden field in order to work, this can't be considered a 100 percent server-side solution and may have some of the same security issues as client-side JavaScript.

ColdFusion also has a built-in function for determining a valid date—*IsDate(string).*

One of the best methods to validate the incoming form field data in a ColdFusion page is to use the CFPARAM tag and the *type* attribute. The type attribute is not put into the CFPARAM tags by default in Dreamweaver MX, but you can add it in manually or double-click a CFParam entry in the Bindings panel.

Here are some of the different validation types for use in the CFPARAM tag that are useful in form validation:

- **date**   A date-time value
- **numeric**   A numeric value
- **string**   A string value or single character
- **variableName**   A variable name

To use this type of validation, your CFPARAM tags could be enclosed in a CFTRY block to capture the error:

```
<cftry>
    <cfparam name="form.ResID" type="numeric">
    <cfparam name="form.Address" type="string">
    <cfparam name="form.SeekFirstName" type="string">
    <cfparam name="form.SeekLastName" type="string">
    <cfcatch type="expression">
        There was an error: <cfoutput>#cfcatch.Message#<cfoutput>
        <cfabort>
    </cfcatch>
</cftry>
```

ColdFusion users also have the regular expression option available, with one of the built-in regular expression functions, such as this regular expression to validate an e-mail address:

```
<cfif Not
 REFindNoCase("[a-zA-Z0-9_\.=-]+@[a-zA-Z0-9_\.-]+\.[[:alpha:]]{2,4}",
 #Form.SeekEmail#)>
    <cflocation url="error.cfm?error=must+be+a+valid+email+address">
</cfif>
```

PHP

PHP has a rich set of over 7,500 functions available. Many of these functions are useful for form validation, such as these:

- *is_float*
- *is_int*
- *is_null*
- *is_numeric*
- *is_string*

Also, PHP has excellent regular expression support. The *eregi* function will do a case-insensitive regular expression match, as in this example for validating an e-mail address:

```
if(!eregi("^[a-zA-Z0-9_]+@[a-zA-Z0-9\-]+\.[a-zA-Z0-9\-\.]+$",
    $SeekEmail)) {
    header("Location: error.php?error=must+be+a+valid+email+address ");
}
```

ASP.NET

ASP.NET is perhaps the easiest of all server models for doing simple server-side validation. ASP.NET provides several server controls that are built specifically for validating data. Also, ASP.NET uses the principle of the "post-back form," in which the form is posted back to itself. Dreamweaver also makes use of this principle in most of its built-in Server Behaviors as well.

ASP.NET validation controls are available in the tag library (right-click and choose Insert Tag). That brings up this dialog box, giving you options to insert the different ASP.NET validation controls:

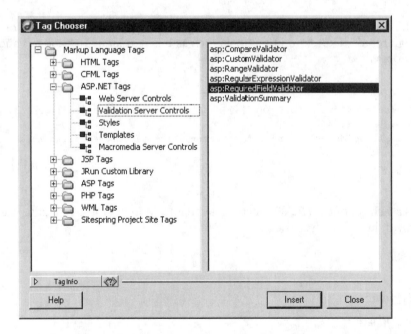

If you insert one of these, a custom interface is available to allow you to add the attributes to the tag quickly and easily:

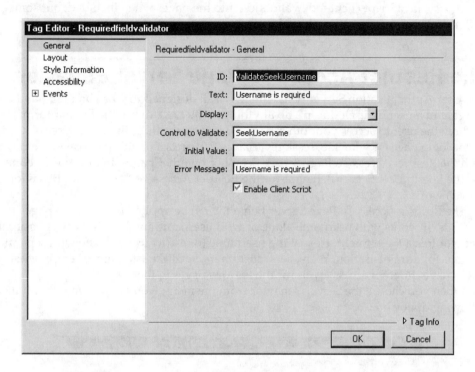

JSP

You can validate a form several ways in JSP, depending upon what type of programming you are doing. You can create a scriptlet on the page to take care of the validation. These would be compiled with the page. An example of this type of validation would look like this for an integer validation:

```
boolean isInt = true;
int temp;
try {
    temp = Integer.parseInt((String)request.getParameter("ResID"));
} catch (NumberFormatException e) {
    isInt = false;
}
if(isInt){response.sendRedirect("error.jsp?error=there+was+an+error")};
```

Also, many tag libraries are available that make it much easier for the Java programmer to include validation with his form fields. Many of the tag libraries that are available insert basic JavaScript client-side validation into the pages when included, but some will include server-side validation as well.

The Restrict Access to Page Server Behavior

The User Authentication Server behaviors were all designed to work hand in hand. Logging in a user by itself doesn't do anything—you have to use the login information to allow the user to access your other pages. By using the built-in Log In User behavior on the login page for your site, session variables that are set on this page can be retrieved with the Restrict Access To Page Server Behavior on other pages. In fact, you need to use the Log In User Server Behavior for the Restrict Access To Page Server Behavior to even work.

The Restrict Access To Page Server Behavior can be applied to any or all pages in your site. It works with username alone or with username and access level. A basic site that requires a login might use just the username to restrict users. A site with separate sections for administration, Web users, customers, special customers, or employees, might have different access levels for the various pages in the site.

When you choose the Server Behavior from the menu, you are presented with the following dialog box:

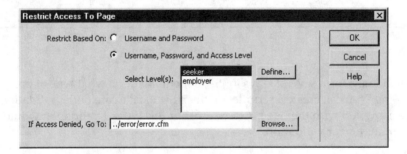

The two radio buttons on the interface allow you to choose to verify the user with username and password, or username, password, and access level. If you choose the second option, the Select Levels box is made active so that you can choose one or more access groups that are allowed on the page. The Define button allows you to define access groups for the site. These site-wide settings will be available to each page that you want to apply this behavior to. There is also a box labeled If Access Denied, Go To. This is the page to redirect any users that aren't authenticated.

Clicking Define brings up the Define Access Levels dialog box:

This box has the familiar plus and minus buttons on the interface to allow you to add or subtract access levels. These access levels are stored for your entire site so that you need to define them just once and you'll have access to them on any page.

This behavior can be applied to all pages in the site, one at a time. If you have any pages that don't need to be restricted, you don't need to use this behavior on them.

 If you have any HTML pages in your site, be sure not to attempt to use any Server Behaviors on those pages, or to change your file extension from a dynamic page to an HTML page—the code won't work unless the page has a recognized server. Many users attempt to apply the Restrict Access To Page Server Behavior to all of their pages, never realizing that the code will not execute on an HTML page.

Live Data Mode

Live Data mode has been around since UltraDev 1, but it is more accessible to the designer/programmer now with the Live Data Mode button on the toolbar. Live Data gives you the ability to view your page *in the design environment* as if it were a Web page being served by the application server. This gives you the ability to edit and design pages in an environment that is as close to the way the end user will see the page as is possible.

Live Data Settings

Frequently, on a dynamic page you will need to supply parameters to the page in order to view the page properly. In our particular case, the page will assume that a user is already logged in and that the username is stored in the session variable *MM_Username*. This can be easily simulated with the Live Data settings of Dreamweaver MX. What these settings do is allow you to insert some server-side script into the Dreamweaver MX environment that will get executed before the page is served to the Live Data server.

ADDING DATABASE
FEATURES TO YOUR SITE

In the past, you would have to actually insert the code on the page itself temporarily in order to test the page; but with the Live Data settings, you can let Dreamweaver MX handle the details. You can use the Live Data Settings dialog box to define any script blocks that you want executed before the page loads, and also to pass any request variables to the page that might be needed for the page to execute properly.

Go to View | Live Data Settings to see the dialog box shown next. In this dialog box, you are allowed to specify URL variables with a name/value pair, and you can write your own custom initialization script. The settings that you specify here can be saved so that whenever you want to work on the page, the Live Data settings will automatically revert to whatever you previously saved.

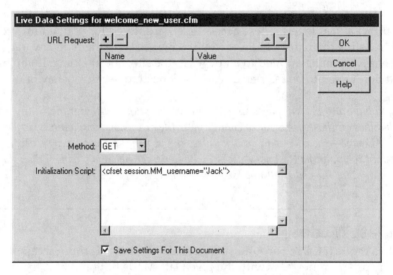

This is the place where you can write script that is required to make your page work independently of other pages. A user login/authentication script, such as the Restrict Access To Page Server Behavior, requires that session variables be set up to allow access to the page. By placing the variable declaration in the Live Data Settings dialog box, Dreamweaver will set the session variables before the page is previewed.

The Initialization Script should be valid syntax for whichever application server you are working with. For example, to work in Live Data for the view_resume page that you are about to design, you could insert one of the following initialization scripts, depending upon which server model you are using:

```
<%Session("MM_Username") = "jack" %> (ASP)

<% session.putValue("MM_Username", "jack") %> (JSP)

<CFSET session.MM_Username="jack"> (ColdFusion)
```

Log Out User

What goes up must come down. When a user logs in, you should also allow the user to log out. You can use the Log Out User Server Behavior to give the user the option to log out. What this Server Behavior actually does is kill the current session for the user. If the user has any desire to continue browsing in the site, he or she will have to log in again. The Log Out User Server Behavior looks like this:

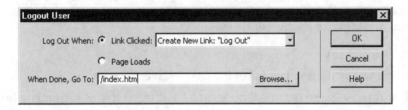

There are two options for the Server Behavior:

- Log the user out upon page load
- Log the user out by clicking a link

The first option is the most basic—it will simply kill the session as the page loads. The second option allows you to set a link on the page that says "Log Out" or something similar. This is handy for intranets and situations where the user might leave the machine so that another person can use the machine and log in under a different username.

After logging out, you can set an optional page to redirect the user to. If you are using the link option of the Log Out User Server Behavior, this is probably a good idea.

ADDING DATABASE
FEATURES TO YOUR SITE

What to Do If You Don't Have User Authentication Server Behaviors

As of the writing of this book, Macromedia has not provided User Authentication Server Behaviors for ASP.NET and PHP. All is not lost, however, as the User Authentication Server Behaviors do some basic things that can be achieved by hand-coding. Here is a run-down of what the User Authentication Server Behaviors do and what you can do to mimic their behavior:

Check New Username

You can duplicate this Server Behavior with SQL and a little ingenuity. You want to allow the user to enter a username and password, and then check the database for an existing record with that username. You can write a SQL statement that will do this:

```
SELECT SeekUsername FROM Seekers
WHERE SeekUsername = 'rqUsername'
```

You should set up the variable of *rqUsername* as your incoming username form element. The logic for the Server Behavior is this:

- Detect if any rows were returned from the database.
- If a row is returned, redirect the user to an error page.
- If no rows were returned, perform a basic *Insert* to the database to insert the new username and password.

Log In User

The Log In User Server Behavior does these things in this order:

- It checks the database to see if the user exists.
- If the username/password combination exists, the username and access level fields are placed into session variables named *MM_username* and *MM_ UserAuthorization*. After the successful login, the user is then directed to another page.
- If the username/password combination doesn't exist, the user is directed to an error page.

Restrict Access to Page

This Server Behavior will do two things—both can be replicated by hand coding. If you want to restrict users by username only, you can simply check for the existence of the *MM_username* variable. If it exists, that means the user was successfully logged in. If not, you can redirect the user.

The same thing applies to access levels. After the user passes the username test, you can check for the correct access level.

Log Out User

This Server Behavior kills a session. To duplicate its functionality, put some code on your page to kill the session.

Inserting to the Database Using a Recordset Field

The next page to create for the new job seeker is the post_resume page in the get_a_gig folder. On this page, the user will be able to insert the data necessary to complete an online resume. Rather than allowing the user to upload a resume as a file, the Bettergig site allows the user to create a resume using predefined form fields. This will allow for easy searching of the database.

Similar to the *Update Record Application* object is the *Record Insertion Form Application* object, both of which were introduced in the previous chapter. The *Record Insertion Form Application* object doesn't generally require a predefined recordset because it is only inserting and not updating data, but in this case, we need to retrieve the *SeekID* for the job seeker in order to be able to insert a resume to the correct user. In the next chapter, we illustrate several methods of hand-coding to allow you to keep values such as these in session variables.

Create a new recordset named *rsGetSeekID* using the *connBettergig* connection. As always, you should use the Advanced dialog box for the recordset. The SQL statement will look like this:

```
SELECT SeekID
FROM Seekers
WHERE SeekUsername = 'svUsername'
```

After writing your SQL statement, you'll need to define the variable that is used (see Table 25-3). The PHP and ASP.NET are added for completeness, but it is assumed that you've hand-coded the user login functionality that is missing from Dreamweaver MX.

Server Model	Name	Default Value	Run-time Value
ASP	*svUsername*	0	*Session("MM_Username")*
JSP	*svUsername*	0	*session.getValue("MM_Username")*
ColdFusion	*svUsername*	0	*#session.MM_Username#*
*PHP	*svUsername*	0	*$_SESSION["MM_Username"]**
*C#	*svUsername*	0	*(Session["MM_Username"] != null) ? Session["MM_Username"] : "0"*

* The PHP and ASP.NET server models don't contain User Authentication Server Behaviors to set up these session variables, but you can hand-code the functionality.

** This PHP code works in PHP 4.1.0 and higher. Earlier versions of the server have other methods to access session variables.

Table 25-3. *Variable Definition for the* rsGetSeekID *Recordset*

To insert the Record Insertion form, choose Insert | Application Objects | Record Insertion Form or double-click the icon in the Application tab on the Insert bar. This will bring up the Insert Record Insertion Form dialog box. You can place your cursor where you want the object to appear, otherwise, it will be inserted at the bottom of the page and you can drag it into position.

The parameters that you need to define for this Application object are as follows:

- **Connection**   Set this to *connBettergig*.
- **Insert into Table**   Set this to the Resumes table.
- **After Inserting, Go To**   Set this to the view_resume page (click Browse to ensure that your relative path will be accurate).
- **Form Fields**   These fields will be created automatically by the *Record Insertion Form* object. Set them up as shown in Table 25-4.

The *ResStatus* menu needs to be filled in with a couple of entries: Currently Employed and Currently Available. You can do this by clicking the Menu Properties button. This will bring up the dialog box shown in Figure 25-8, in which you can set the Label and Value options as shown.

Using the Menu option allows you to set a predefined list of options for the user. These can also come from a recordset, which makes it an easy way to set up a dynamic menu.

Column	Label	Display As	Submit As
ResAvailable	Available	Text Field	Text
ResCitizenship	Citizenship	Text Field	Text
ResContact	Contact	Text Field	Text
ResEducation	Education	Text Area	Text
ResExperience	Experience	Text Area	Text
ResGoal	Goals	Text Area	Text
ResSalary	Salary Requirement	Text Field	Text
ResStatus	Status	Menu	Text
SeekID		Hidden Field	Numeric

Table 25-4.   *Form Field Definition for the Record Insertion Form*

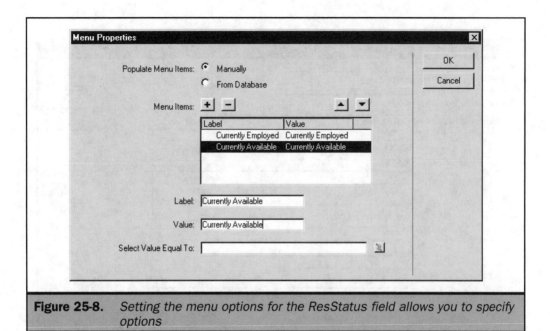

Figure 25-8. *Setting the menu options for the ResStatus field allows you to specify options*

The SeekID column needs to have a default value added to it by clicking the lightning bolt icon (shown in Figure 25-9) and browsing the SeekID column of the *rsGetSeekID* recordset. This will ensure that the resume will be added to the database with a reference to the correct user.

Writing the SQL Statement

When you want to display the data from the database, the SQL (Structured Query Language) statement is the key. With the SQL statement, you are able to pick and choose the data that you want to retrieve. Writing good SQL is an art in itself, and it is necessary to learn for a successful dynamic Web site. Many popular database programs, such as Microsoft Access, Microsoft SQL Server, or IBM DB2, can generate SQL. In these programs, there are query or view builders that take the hassle out of writing SQL by hand. Use these tools in conjunction with Dreamweaver to help design your queries. Dreamweaver is great at building Web pages, but needs assistance in building SQL statements.

Simple SQL that retrieves data from one table is relatively easy to write. As you've seen in previous examples in this chapter, and the chapters on database design and SQL, you must use a *SELECT* statement to retrieve the values that you want to display. When you're dealing with only one table, it's just a matter of picking the columns from the Dreamweaver MX query builder.

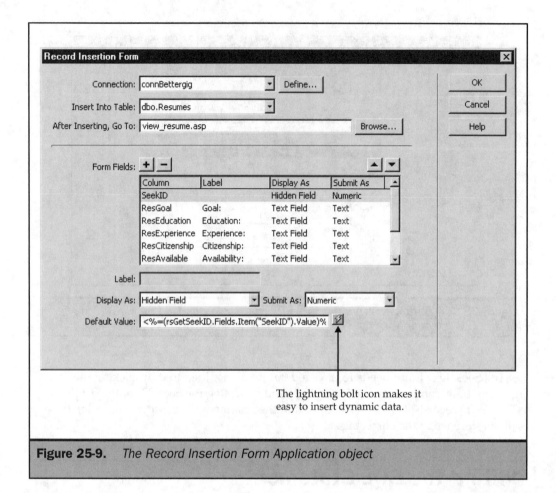

The lightning bolt icon makes it easy to insert dynamic data.

Figure 25-9. *The Record Insertion Form Application object*

However, when you have complex joins between tables, you need to know the language inside and out. The SQL statement for the view_resume page will get its data from two tables that are related by the *SeekID* number of the end user (the job seeker). The SQL will be filtered by the session variable that is set up for the user when he logs in, and will use an inner join to relate the tables to each other. The SQL is as follows:

```
SELECT Resumes.ResGoal, Resumes.ResEducation,
       Resumes.ResExperience, Resumes.ResCitizenship,
       Resumes.ResAvailable, Resumes.ResStatus,
       Resumes.ResSalary, Resumes.ResContact, Resumes.ResID,
       Seekers.SeekFirstName, Seekers.SeekLastName,
```

```
        Seekers.SeekAddress, Seekers.SeekCity,
        Seekers.SeekState, Seekers.SeekZip,
        Seekers.SeekEmail, Seekers.SeekFax, Seekers.SeekPhone
FROM Resumes
INNER JOIN Seekers
ON Resumes.SeekID = Seekers.SeekID
WHERE (Seekers.SeekUsername = 'svUsername')
```

The variables needed for this statement are the same as in Table 25-3.

As you can see, the SQL is drawing its data from two tables: Seekers and Resumes, which are joined on the SeekID column. To further complicate matters, the SeekID is retrieved from the Seekers table by using the session variable that was set up in the previous pages: *MM_Username*. The session variable needs to be assigned to a special variable inside the Dreamweaver MX environment. This variable is named *svUsername* and is inserted into the SQL statement to take the place of the session variable. This is one of the idiosyncrasies of Dreamweaver MX that needs to be adhered to if you want to be able to access the recordset through the Bindings panel.

You can see from the SQL statement that we've added the table name as a prefix to each column. This isn't always necessary, but it's a good practice to get into when you start getting into more complex SQL statements. Using this technique allows you to ensure there's no confusion in the columns. In this case, there is a SeekID field in both tables, so this column would have to be referred to with a table name prefix.

In any event, now that you have the SQL, you can create the recordset named *rsDisplayResume* based on the *connBettergig* connection. After testing it to make sure it is error free and works, click OK, and the recordset will appear in the Bindings panel. All of the columns that are going to be displayed are shown in the Bindings panel and can now be inserted easily into the page.

To begin inserting the data, you can add a table to the page, or simply begin typing in the content region and use <p> tags to separate your content. Whichever method you prefer, the technique for getting the data to the page is the same: Put your cursor where you want to insert the dynamic text, select the column in the Bindings panel, and click the Insert button. The other method is to simply drag the column from the Bindings panel and drop it on the page where you want it.

If you are viewing the page in Live Data mode, the data from the database will be displayed on the page (see Figure 25-10). If you're not in Live Data mode, you'll see placeholders for the dynamic data. In either case, the dynamic text can be manipulated in the design environment to allow for text styles and placement.

Preserving the Whitespace with HTML
 Tags

After you've added each database column to the page in turn, you will have a completed page displaying the resume of the logged-in user. Remember, the browser doesn't

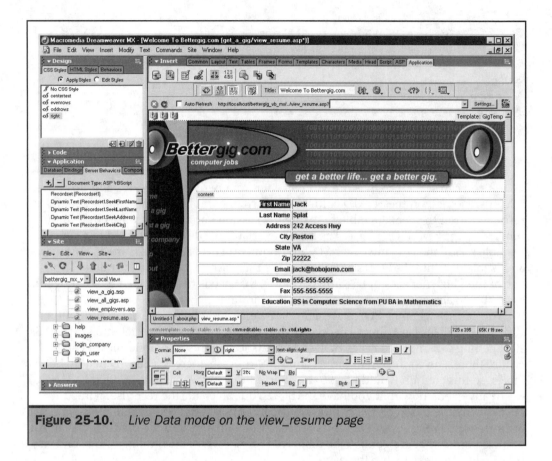

Figure 25-10. *Live Data mode on the view_resume page*

recognize line breaks, so you must insert <br> tags wherever there is a line break in the text. These must be hand-coded and will be different for each server model. The code to do this is as follows (replace *[column]* with your own dynamic data representation):

```
Replace([column],chr(10),"<br>" & chr(10)) [VBScript]
[column].replace(/\n/g,"<br>\n") [JavaScript]
[column].replace("\n","<br>\n") [Java]
ParagraphFormat([column]) [ColdFusion]
nl2br([column]); [PHP]
```

Adding the Company Pages

The Bettergig site has two basic types of users: the job seeker and the company representative. The companies will post jobs that are available, and the job seekers will post their resumes to be viewed. So far, the job seeker has been able to insert himself in the database, log in, insert a resume, and view the resume. The next step is to include the functionality for the company representative to post job information for the job seeker to be able to search.

The my_company Pages

Company representatives using the Bettergig.com Web site will have to log in also. Rather than complicate the site with scripting, we've separated the sections for job seekers and company representatives. They are also separated in the database with the company data being stored in the Employers table. What you'll have to do is to create pages similar to the new_user pages already created. You can create the following pages using the same steps that you used for the seeker pages:

- welcome_company_user
- new_company_user

Although it might seem wasteful to have almost exact copies of certain pages on the server, remember that we are dealing with server-side code, not HTML pages. If you have to insert server script into a page to differentiate between different users or different situations, the server has to execute more code, creating greater overall strain on the server. It's preferable to have extra pages doing simple things rather than extra code doing more complex things.

Inserting Company Records

The company representatives that come to the Bettergig site will have two primary reasons for coming to the site: to post new jobs and to search for a job seeker who might fit into a position with their company. We'll start with the post_a_gig page.

The functionality of this page will be similar to the post_a_resume page with a few small changes. The JobType field in the Jobs table is a foreign key to the JobType table. What this means is that the lists of job types is actually stored in another table to allow for a more dynamic and expandable database. If more job types are added, they only need to be added to the JobTypes table.

What this means to our post_a_gig page is that we only want the user to be able to choose from the list of job types from the database. This is typically accomplished with a drop-down list menu. The difference here is that the lists will be generated dynamically. By doing it in this way, if new job types are added to the database, the Web pages will not need to be updated—all of the information will be coming from the database, and, therefore, it will always be up to date. In a large site that contains numerous references to job types, this can be a tremendous organizational time saver.

Adding the Recordsets to the Page

This page will need two recordsets.

- *rsGetJobTypes* will pull all information from the JobTypes table. Use a Select statement like this:

```
SELECT * from JobTypes
```

- *rsGetEmpID* will get the employer's UserID (the EmpID primary key field) for insertion in the Jobs table. Use a *Select* statement like this:

```
SELECT EmpID
FROM Employers
WHERE EmpUsername = 'svUsername'
```

Once again, the variable needs to be set up for the Dreamweaver MX environment. The variables needed for this statement are the same as in Table 25-3.

Adding the *Record Insertion Form Application* Object

The next thing you'll have to do is insert another Application object: the Record Insertion Form. This time you'll set up the drop-down menu boxes with the information coming from the *rsGetJobTypes* recordset. Start by positioning the cursor at the Content editable region, and then choose the Record Insertion Form from the Insert menu, or double-click the object from the Application tab of the Insert panel. There is a lot of information associated with this one step, so make sure you follow along closely.

- **Connection**   This will once again be the *connBettergig* connection.
- **Insert into Table**   This will be the Jobs table.
- **After Inserting, Go To**   Set this up by clicking Browse and navigating to the view_all_gigs page.
- **Form Fields**   These will be a little tricky this time. We address them separately in the following section.

Setting Up the Form Fields for the Insert

The EmpID column will have no label because it will be a hidden form field. The Submit As field should be set to Numeric, and the Default Value will require a special step. Click the lightning bolt icon to bring up the Dynamic Data dialog box (see Figure 25-11), and then click the EmpID field in the *rsGetEmpID* recordset. This will set the value of the form field to the value in the EmpID field based on the record you retrieve when querying the database with the Username contained in the session variable.

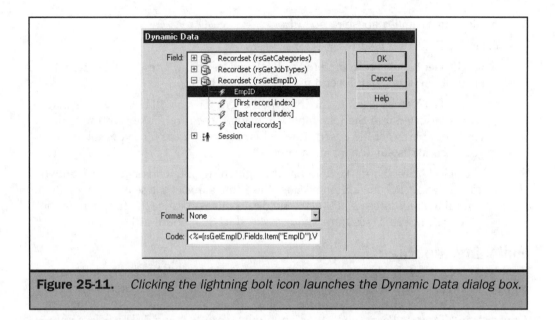

Figure 25-11.   *Clicking the lightning bolt icon launches the Dynamic Data dialog box.*

Setting Up Dynamic Menu Fields

The JobType column will have a recordset attached to it. To properly set up this field, follow these steps:

1. Set the Label field to a user-friendly label, such as Job Type.

2. Set the Display As field to Menu.

3. Set the Submit As field to Numeric.

4. Click the Menu Properties button; the dialog box shown here will pop up.

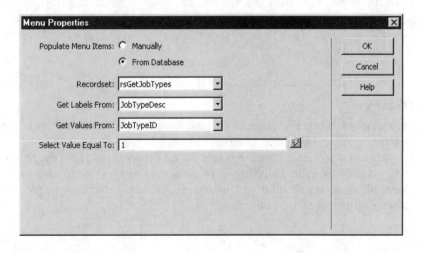

5. Click the From Database radio button.

6. Set the Recordset field to rsGetJobTypes.

7. Set the Get Labels From field to the JobTypeDesc field. These will be the actual drop-down items that the end user will choose from.

8. Set the Get Values From to the JobTypeID field. These will be the values that will be inserted into the Jobs table. By using these foreign keys in the table, you'll be able to get the description fields easily from the JobTypes table when you need to display the Job data later.

9. The Select Value Equal To field has the lightening bolt icon once again, but you don't have to click the button because this is the value of the selected menu item. Just fill in the number **1** in the text field and this will cause the first item in the table to be selected (assuming your tables start their count at 1).

Finishing the Page

That will take care of the dynamic menus in the form, but you'll have one static menu as well: JobStatus. This menu should be set to populate manually. Fill in three menu items by clicking the plus sign (+) in the dialog box and set the labels to Permanent, Contract, and Temp to Perm. The values should be set to 1, 2, and 3. The Select Value Equal To box should once again be set to 1 to select the first item.

The other form fields can all be set to Text Fields, with the exception of the JobID form field—make sure you remove this item, because the database will create this number automatically if it is set up as an Autonumber or Identity column in the database.

One of the mistakes many people make is to try to do an Insert or Update statement with the Primary Key included in the statement. This will usually cause a database error, because the database itself takes care of incrementing this value. When inserting your Insert or Update statement, make sure no Autonumber or Identity columns are chosen.

After setting up all of the form elements in the Insert form and double-checking all items, click OK. The form should be inserted exactly at the point where the cursor was positioned. If it is located elsewhere, you can select the table and drag it where you would like it to be inserted.

Summary

In this chapter, we've shown you some of the basic user authentication methods available within the Dreamweaver MX environment. Macromedia has not provided the same user authentication methods across the board for all server models, so the techniques necessary to achieve this functionality in other server models were also outlined. In addition, several pages were built in the Bettergig site that depend on the *MM_Username* session variable being set by an authorized user.

The
Complete
Reference

Dreamweaver
MX

Part V

Advanced Data Integration

The Complete Reference

Dreamweaver MX

Chapter 26

Advanced Database Features

A database exists for the purpose of storing data in some defined manner so that it can be accessed and presented in a meaningful or useful way. The key to a successful database is the organization of the tables within that database, and the key to a successful data-driven Web site is being able to retrieve the information that you need from a well-organized database. Furthermore, the key to programming a data-driven site is being able to write the SQL statements needed to retrieve the desired information. SQL is the language that you'll need to use and become proficient in if you want to build a more advanced site, no matter which server platform you are working with.

In Chapter 24, we examined some of the ways to include dynamic content in a Web site using Dreamweaver's built-in Application Objects and Server Behaviors. In this chapter, we continue to build upon the Bettergig.com site by adding some of the more advanced features of a data-driven site, beginning with a search page.

Search Pages

The ability to search a database for specific information is one of the most popular features of a data-driven site. Search engines such as Yahoo, Google, or Hotbot all use databases that are searchable by using highly optimized search algorithms and indexed tables. Although your Web site probably won't require the industrial-strength engines of these search sites, a search page will likely be a desirable addition to your site.

A Basic Search Page

Searching the database can be simple or complex. The simplest search to perform on a database is to find a match for a piece of data in one field of the database. To perform a search like this, the SQL statement needs to retrieve only those rows in which the field contains the search criteria.

The Job Search

A job seeker will either be posting a resume to the site or looking for a job that's been posted. To search for a job, the job seeker will have to search the job description for a keyword and be able to view the jobs that match that keyword. Later, we'll add the ability to search more than one field or more than one keyword.

Open the get_a_gig page in the site. Start the page by inserting a form with a form field and a Submit button within that form. This page will accept a word and then display the results of the search, also allowing for another search by having the form field on the page available for a new search. The text field should be named **searchfield**, and the action of the form should be set to this page (get_a_gig).

Next, you'll need to create the recordset that retrieves the form field and queries the database for a match. Create a new recordset, name it *rsGetAGig*, and write the SQL using the JobDescription field of the Jobs table:

```
SELECT JobDescription, JobID from Jobs WHERE JobDescription LIKE
'%txtSearchfield%'
```

> **Tip**   *The* Select *statement used in a typical search operation uses the* Like *keyword with wildcard characters. This allows for keyword searches within a database field. The standard wildcard character for "anything" is %. If you put this character before and after your keyword variable, the text contained in the variable can be matched anywhere in the field.*

You'll have to set up a variable in the recordset dialog box, as shown in Table 26-1.

After defining the variable, the SQL statement should be ready to test. With the "dummy" data in the Default Value column, the SQL statement won't return any rows. This is because there is no match in the database within the JobDescription field. The Default Value is one of the safeguards that Dreamweaver adds to the code: It exists to help prevent database errors from occurring if the expected incoming variables are null.

Adding the Data and Repeat Region

After defining your SQL statement, the next step is to put the database fields on the page. This time, the process will be manually using a table and a Repeat Region. Insert a two-row, two-column table on the page and label the cells in the first row **Job ID** and **Description**. In the second row, you are going to insert the corresponding database columns, which are rsGetAGig.JobID and rsGetAGig.JobDescription.

Next, select the table row by using the tag selector in the lower-left corner of the design window or by CTRL-clicking (CMD-clicking on the Macintosh) the two table cells. Next, apply a Repeat Region to the area showing all records. Finally, select the entire table and apply a Show Region If Recordset Is Not Empty Server Behavior to the area. This will allow the table to be shown *only* if there are search results.

If you save the page and try it out, it should show only the search field and button. If you enter a word that is contained in the description of one of the jobs, the table will be displayed with the ID number and the description for each matching record. But if no matches are found, only the search field will be displayed again. It's also a good idea to include alternate text in the event of an empty search.

Server Model	Name	Default Value	Run-Time Value
ASP	*txtSearchField*	xyz	*Request("searchfield")*
JSP	*txtSearchField*	xyz	*request.getParameter("searchfield")*
ColdFusion	*txtSearchField*	xyz	*#searchfield#*
PHP	*txtSearchField*	xyz	*$searchfield*
ASP.Net	*txtSearchField*	xyz	*Request.Form("searchfield")*

Table 26-1.   *Variable Values in the Recordset Dialog Box*

Inserting Alternate Text

Although there are several ways of doing this—most of which would involve some hand-coding—you can once again include alternate text with Dreamweaver's built-in Server Behaviors. The opposite of the Show Region If Recordset Is Not Empty is the Show Region If Recordset Is Empty Server Behavior. The steps are as follows:

1. Type the text **No Matching Records** next to or beneath the table you inserted.

2. Select the text.

3. Apply the Show Region If Recordset Is Empty Server Behavior.

The page should now look like the page in Figure 26-1. Now, when you browse the page, your text will be visible if there are no records; and if there are records, your table with the results of the search will be visible.

Figure 26-1. *The basic search page includes alternate text for an empty search.*

Adding a Link to the Detail Page

The search page as it stands will show the summary of all matches of your search, but the page shows only the job description. To view all information for an item returned from the search, you'll have to link to a Detail page. If you recall from Chapter 24, a Master-Detail page set was built automatically with the Insert Master-Detail Page Set Application Object. You can reuse the view_a_gig page by simply linking to it with the appropriate variable, which in this case is the JobID.

A built-in Dreamweaver Server Behavior (once again) simplifies the whole process. Simply select the JobID field in the design environment and choose the Go To Detail Page Server Behavior (shown in Figure 26-2).

The required parameters for the behavior are as follows:

- **Link**   This should be filled out automatically to reflect the selected recordset column on the page.

- **Detail Page**   Browse to the view_a_gig page in the post_a_gig folder by clicking Browse. This will ensure that the proper relative path to the page is used.

- **Pass URL Parameter**   This should be set to the JobID field of the recordset.

- **Recordset**   This will be the *rsGetAGig* recordset.

- **Column**   Once again, this should be set to the JobID field.

- **Pass Existing Parameters**   These can be left blank for now.

After clicking OK and saving the file, you can browse the page to search for a job, click the link, and be taken to a Detail page listing all the information about that job.

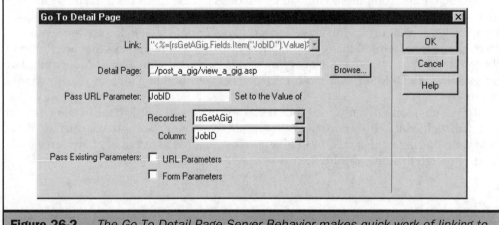

Figure 26-2.   *The Go To Detail Page Server Behavior makes quick work of linking to a Detail page.*

ADVANCED DATA
INTEGRATION

Adding Advanced Search Features

Now that the basic search page is working, it's time to add some more advanced search features to the page. A job seeker may want to enter keywords that might be within one of several fields in the database. Rather than have a different form field for each database field, it's possible to include them all in one search.

Combining Fields

Although there are certainly many ways to combine your database fields for a search, one of the easiest involves concatenating the fields at the database level. This technique will work in all databases, so those without the benefit of stored procedures will be able to use this technique.

Create a view in your database named *getSearchField*. If you are using Microsoft Access, *queries* is the term that is used for Access views, but the functionality is similar. The view can be accessed from the recordset dialog box in Dreamweaver just as a table can. Use the following SQL in the view:

```
SELECT JobTypes.JobTypeDesc +
 Employers.EmpName +
 Jobs.JobLocation +
 Jobs.JobDescription AS SearchField,
 Jobs.JobID, Employers.EmpName
FROM JobTypes INNER JOIN
    Employers INNER JOIN
    Jobs
ON Employers.EmpID = Jobs.EmpID
ON JobTypes.JobTypeID = Jobs.JobType
```

The SQL looks complicated, but all it will do is get the fields from the Jobs table that you'll want to search—JobLocation, JobDescription—as well as the related fields from related tables such as JobTypeDesc and EmpName. These fields are retrieved through the Inner joins to the related tables based on the foreign keys that are stored in the Jobs table. You can write the query by hand or create it with a visual query builder interface in your DBMS. The Microsoft SQL Server view building interface is shown in Figure 26-3.

The visual tools will only take you so far, however, and a little hand-coding of your SQL will yield you a little more flexibility. In this case, you'll want to concatenate the fields into one big field named SearchField. You can also insert a space between each field, although this isn't absolutely necessary with this type of search.

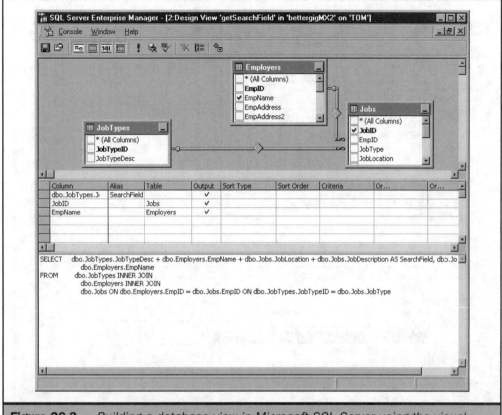

Figure 26-3. *Building a database view in Microsoft SQL Server using the visual tools of SQL Server*

The fields are concatenated with the plus (+) sign, but your own database may have a different method. The result is that all relevant fields are tacked together, and a few other necessary fields are also retrieved: Jobs.JobID, Employers.EmpName, and JobTypes. JobTypeDesc. We'll use these in the HTML table that shows the search results.

Modifying the Original Search Page

After creating and saving the view, move back to the get_a_gig page and open up the recordset *rsGetAGig*. You'll need to change the SQL statement to retrieve data from the new view instead of from the Jobs table. You should be in the Advanced Recordset dialog box and choose the *getSearchField* view from the Views Database Item at the bottom of the box (see Figure 26-4). The variable declaration will remain the same, but the SQL statement needs to be changed.

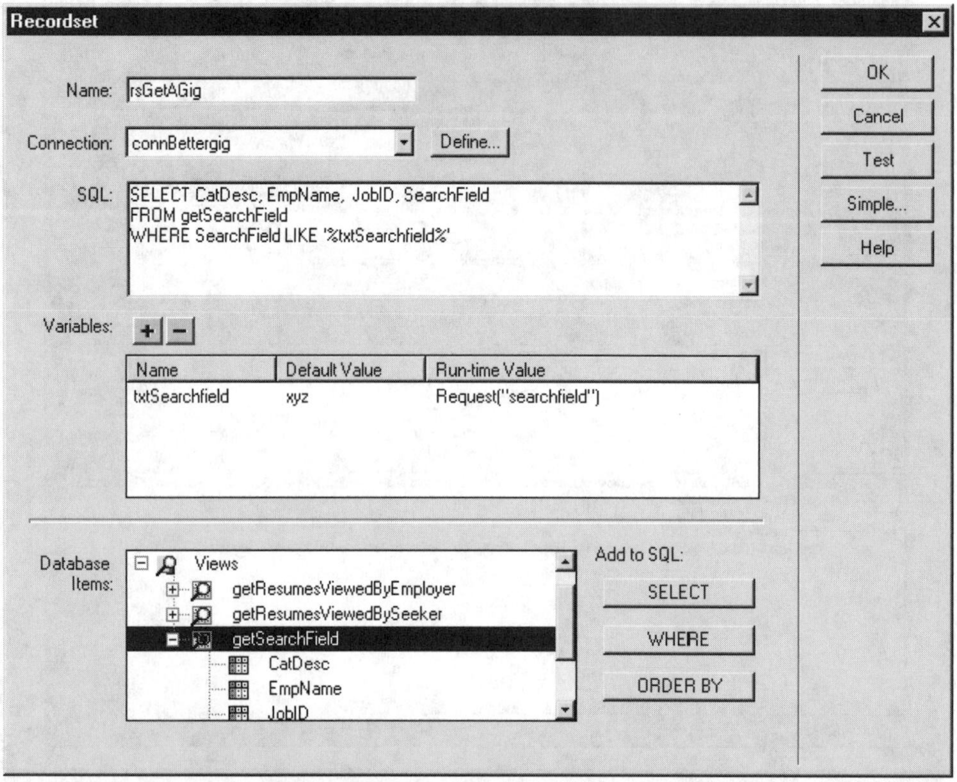

Figure 26-4. The Recordset dialog box after changing the SQL statement to reflect the new view

Write the SQL as follows:

```
SELECT CatDesc, EmpName, JobID, SearchField
FROM getSearchField
WHERE SearchField LIKE '%txtSearchField%'
```

As you can see, only the table name and the column names changed. The *Where* clause remains the same.

Note
Modifying recordsets is often a much easier process than creating one from scratch, particularly if the SQL statement is complex. Also, remember that you can copy recordsets from one page to another by right-clicking (CTRL-clicking on the Macintosh) the recordset in the Bindings panel, choosing Copy, opening up another page, and choosing Paste.

Notice that you now have four fields in the recordset and that the JobDescription field no longer exists. You'll have to modify the page slightly to accommodate the new fields, but there is a simple method of doing this that will help speed up the process. The steps are as follows:

1. Select the table that the Repeat Region has been applied to.

2. Open the Property inspector for that table.

3. Change the Cols field from 2 to 3. This will add a blank column to the table. Notice that this new column is also within the Repeat Region.

4. Add a heading to the newly created third column, **Employer Name**.

5. Drop the EmpName column into the empty cell beneath the heading.

6. Select the rsGetAGig.JobDescription in the second column and delete it.

7. Move to the Bindings panel and click the CatDesc field.

8. Click Insert on the Bindings panel to insert this field into the newly vacated empty cell in the second column of the table.

By making these few simple modifications to the page, you now have a more sophisticated search page that actually searches five separate fields for the keyword and returns the JobID, employer name, and category description from the database for the matched records. Also, the Go to Detail Behavior still works, because you are using the same JobID field.

As you can see, modifications to existing pages are easily accomplished with Dreamweaver and can be huge timesavers after you get the hang of it. It's not always necessary to start from scratch when you want to create a new page.

Adding Multiple Search Words

Sophisticated search engines allow you to enter many different combinations of search criteria. Although it's beyond the scope of this book to go into detail about the different methods, you should be aware of what you might need and possible approaches to the problem.

Obviously, the most basic requirement is to allow for multiple words in the search. Predicting how the user will enter the data, however, is impossible. You can specify the requirements on the page, such as "Enter your search words separated by commas—phrases can be enclosed in quotes." As you can imagine, these two simple requirements can drastically increase the complexity of the code contained in the page.

There are basically two ways to approach the problem:

■ Add server-side code to the page to handle the different situations.

■ Build a stored procedure within the database to handle the tasks.

Using Server-Side Code

Hand-coding requires a knowledge of the server language that you are working with. The task of creating a dynamic SQL query is fairly straightforward, but it requires string manipulation and knowledge of SQL as well. Also, Dreamweaver has strict rules governing its recordsets; and if you change the way that the SQL is created by adding server-side conditional logic into the SQL, the recordset will cease to work in the Bindings panel. As long as you already have your recordset columns on the page where you want them, this isn't a problem.

What you'll have to do is remove the *Where* clause from the SQL statement while you are in Code view on the page, not from the recordset dialog box. The remaining SQL statement will then look like this:

```
SELECT CatDesc, EmpName, JobID, SearchField
FROM getSearchField
```

The next thing to do is to add a block of code to the page to parse the text field into three possible situations:

- One word or a group of words is entered.
- A group of words is entered inside of quotes.
- A group of words is entered separated by commas.

The first option will use the standard *Where* clause that was previously created. The second option will require the quotes to be stripped off before using the standard *Where* clause that was previously created. The third option requires that the words be separated. For instance, if the job seeker enters the words **web,asp,vbscript**, the words need to be added to the *Where* clause like this:

```
WHERE SearchField LIKE '%asp%' AND SearchField LIKE '%web%' AND
SearchField LIKE '%vbscript%'
```

The difficulty lies in the fact that there is no way of knowing how many words will be entered. You can write a short script to take care of the three situations. This pseudo-code illustrates the functionality that the script will accomplish:

```
Define SQLstr to hold the 'where' clause of the SQL statement
myField holds the incoming form field data
IF myField has quotes
    remove the quotes
    Build SQLstr as the Where clause using the
      phrase that had quotes around it
```

```
ELSE IF myField has commas
     separate the parts of myField
     construct a Where clause to allow for all of the substrings
        in myField
ELSE
     use myField as it stands and construct the Where clause
END OF IF STATEMENTS
Execute the SQL adding the Where clause to it
```

Following is the code for all the server languages that you should insert right before the recordset is created.

VBScript Version

```
Dim SQLstr
Dim myField
myField = rsGetAGig__txtSearchField
If instr(myField,chr(34)) Then
   myField= Replace(myField,chr(34),"")
SQLstr = " WHERE SearchField LIKE '%"
SQLstr = SQLstr + replace(myField, "'", "''") + "%'"
ElseIf instr(myField,",") Then
     Dim splitField
     SQLstr = " WHERE"
     splitField = split(myField,",")
     for i = 0 to ubound(splitField)
         SQLstr = SQLstr & " SearchField LIKE '%"
         SQLstr = SQLstr & replace(splitField(i), "'", "''") & "%'"
         if i < ubound(splitField) Then SQLstr = SQLstr & " AND "
         Next
Else
     SQLstr = " WHERE SearchField LIKE '%"
     SQLstr = SQLstr & Replace(myField, "'", "''") & "%'"
End if
%>
```

JavaScript Version

```
var SQLstr;
var myField = rsGetAGig__txtSearchField;
if (myField.indexOf('"')!= -1) {
```

```
    myField= myField.replace(/"/g,'');
    SQLstr = " WHERE SearchField LIKE '%"
    SQLstr = SQLstr + myField.replace(/'/g, "''") + "%'"
}else if (myField.indexOf(',')!= -1) {
    var splitField = myField.split(",");
    SQLstr = " WHERE";
    for (var i = 0; i < splitField.length;i++){
        SQLstr = SQLstr + " SearchField LIKE '%";
        SQLstr = SQLstr + splitField[i].replace(/'/g, "''") + "%'";
     if (i < splitField.length-1) SQLstr = SQLstr + " AND ";
    }
}else{
    SQLstr = " WHERE SearchField LIKE '%"
    SQLstr = SQLstr + myField.replace(/'/g, "''") + "%'"
}
%>
```

ColdFusion Version

```
<cfset myField = rsGetAGig_ _txtSearchField>
<cfif (find('"',myField))>
  <cfset myField= Replace(myField,'"','',"all")>
  <cfset SQLstr = " WHERE SearchField LIKE '%#myField#%'">
<cfelseif (find(',',myField))>
  <cfset SQLstr = " WHERE">
  <cfloop INDEX="splitField" LIST="#myField#">
    <cfset SQLstr = SQLstr & " SearchField LIKE '%">
    <cfset SQLstr = SQLstr & splitField & "%'">
    <cfif splitField NEQ ListLast(myField)>
      <cfset SQLstr = SQLstr & " AND ">
    </cfif>
  </CFLOOP>
<cfelse>
  <cfset SQLstr = " WHERE SearchField LIKE '%#myfield#%'">
</cfif>
```

Java Version

```
String SQLstr;
String myField = rsGetAGig_ _txtSearchField;
if(myField.indexOf('"')!= -1) {
```

```
    myField = myField.replace('"',' ').trim();//space inserted
    //and then removed because the replace method doesn't work
    //with null values
    SQLstr = " WHERE SearchField LIKE '%";
    SQLstr = SQLstr + myField + "%'";
}else if (myField.indexOf(',') != -1){
    SQLstr = " WHERE ";
    java.util.StringTokenizer tokens = new
        java.util.StringTokenizer(myField,",");//one line!
    String[] splitField = new String[tokens.countTokens()];
    for (int i=0; tokens.hasMoreTokens(); i++) {
        splitField[i] = tokens.nextToken();
        SQLstr = SQLstr + " SearchField LIKE '%";
        SQLstr = SQLstr + splitField[i] + "%'";
        if(tokens.hasMoreTokens()) SQLstr = SQLstr + " AND ";
        }
}else{
    SQLstr = " WHERE SearchField LIKE '%";
    SQLstr = SQLstr + myField + "%'";
}
%>
```

PHP Version

```php
<?PHP
$myField = rsGetAGig__txtSearchField;
if (strstr($myField, '"')) {
    $myField= str_replace('"', '', $myfield);
    $SQLstr = " WHERE SearchField LIKE '%" ;
    $SQLstr .= str_replace("'", "''",$myField);
    $SQLstr .= "%'" ;
}else if (strstr($myField,',')){
    $splitField = explode(",", $myField);
    $SQLstr = " WHERE";
    for ($i = 0; $i < count($splitField); $i++){
        $SQLstr .= " SearchField LIKE '%";
    str_replace("'", "''", $splitField[$i]);
        $SQLstr .= $splitField[$i];
        $SQLstr .= "%'";
        if ($i < count($splitField) -1) $SQLstr .= " AND ";
    }
}else{
```

```
$SQLstr = " WHERE SearchField LIKE '%" ;
$SQLstr .= str_replace("'", "''", $myField);
$SQLstr.= "%'" ;
}
?>
```

ASP.Net (C#) Version

```
<%
string SQLstr;
string myField = rsGetAGig__txtSearchField;
if (myField.IndexOf("\"") != -1) {
   myField= myField.Replace("\"","");
   SQLstr = " WHERE SearchField LIKE '%";
   SQLstr += myField.Replace("'", "''") + "%'";
}else if (myField.IndexOf(",") != -1) {
    string[] splitField = myField.Split(Convert.ToChar(","));
    SQLstr = " WHERE";
    for (Int32 i = 0; i < splitField.Length;i++){
       SQLstr += " SearchField LIKE '%";
       SQLstr += splitField[i].Replace("'", "''") + "%'";
      if (i < splitField.Length-1) SQLstr += " AND ";
    }
}else{
    SQLstr = " WHERE SearchField LIKE '%";
    SQLstr += myField.Replace("'", "''") + "%'";
}
%>
```

After inserting the script, you also have to change the Dreamweaver-generated SQL statement to reflect the change. What you are going to be doing is removing the *Where* clause from the Dreamweaver SQL and inserting the SQLstr to take its place. Your new SQL should look like this for ASP and JSP:

```
"SELECT SearchField, JobID, EmpName, CatDesc FROM getSearchField"¬
+ SQLstr
```

ColdFusion users can insert the variable directly into the SQL, like this:

```
"SELECT SearchField, JobID, EmpName, CatDesc FROM ¬
getSearchField #PreserveSingleQuotes(SQLstr)#"
```

ADVANCED DATA
INTEGRATION

Tip   *When hand-coding, it's a good idea to get all of your Server Behavior and Data Bindings work out of the way first. Also, if you need the Data Bindings functionality again, you can do this simply by removing the SQLstr variable from the end of the SQL statement. All of the Dreamweaver functionality will return when the SQL is recognizable to the program once again.*

You'll notice that after you add the variable to the SQL statement, the recordset no longer shows up inside the Data Bindings Inspector, and you'll see red checkmarks next to several items in the Server Behaviors panel. This is normal and merely indicates that Dreamweaver no longer recognizes the items as the items that it generated. When you begin hand-coding, you can close the Bindings panel and Server Behaviors panel—they are useless at this point.

Note   *If you attempt to edit a Server Behavior with a red check mark in it, you should make sure that the red check mark isn't there because you changed the code manually. By re-editing the Server Behavior, the red check mark will disappear, but so will your hand-coded script!*

Hand-coding your page is always an option when you want to add more functionality to the page, but it also forces you to put your programming logic in the page. In many cases, placing your logic in the database is preferable. That's where stored procedures come in.

Using a Stored Procedure

Stored procedures allow for more complex database transactions and are available for most of the top database systems, including Oracle, IBM's DB2, and Microsoft SQL Server. A stored procedure allows you to create sets of commands inside your database that execute faster and are capable of much more complex combinations of commands that would be impossible to accomplish with a standard SQL statement from within a Web page. Also, the ability to make batches of commands and transactions allows for more secure transactions to the database. For example, in an online transaction, a stored procedure could execute multiple-order updates, account debiting, and accounting all within one stored procedure.

Additionally, the stored procedures are compiled, allowing for quicker execution times within the RDBMS. They also allow for the complex business logic of the site to be confined to the database, where the highly optimized database engine can handle the task. Many programmers would argue that all business logic should be confined to the database by defining the parameters in your Web application and sending them to the stored procedure to process. The stored procedure would process the parameters, execute whatever commands might be contained within, and then send back to the application any return values that are defined.

A stored procedure to conduct a basic search of the jobs table could be written as follows. Note that this is a Microsoft SQL Server stored procedure, and your own RDBMS might have a slightly different syntax:

```
CREATE PROCEDURE spSearchJobs
@SQLstr varchar (255) = "xyz"
AS
SELECT SearchField, JobID, EmpName, CatDesc
FROM getSearchField
WHERE SearchField LIKE '%' + @SQLstr + '%'
```

You can save this stored procedure with the name *spSearchJobs* (we add the *sp* prefix to all of our stored procedures). Notice also that it is calling the *getSearchField* view that was created earlier. Later, you can incorporate the view directly into the stored procedure for more speed and efficiency, or turn it into a separate stored procedure that you can call from this stored procedure.

Note   *Another advantage of stored procedures is that you can call one stored procedure from within another.*

To allow the Web page to execute the stored procedure, you'll have to create a new search page similar to the basic search page created earlier. The page should have the text field named searchfield and a Submit button, with the action of the <form> tag pointing to the page itself. There also should be a two-row, three-column table inserted to receive the values that will be returned by the stored procedure.

Next, you'll have to add a Command object to the page from the Bindings panel. This is applied much like the recordset and accepts these parameters:

- **Name**   *cmdGetAGig*
- **Connection**   *connBettergig*
- **Type**   Stored Procedure
- **Return Recordset Named**   *rsGetAGig*
- **SQL**   *dbo.spSearchJobs*
- **Variables**   Should be set up as in Table 26-2

Name	Type	Direction	Size	Default Value
@@SQLstr	VarChar	in	255	xyz

Table 26-2.   *Variables Defined for the spGetAGig Command*

Additionally, the run-time values need to be set up to reflect the server model that you are working with. Refer to Table 26-1 for the run-time values for this attribute. The Command dialog box is shown in Figure 26-5. After clicking OK, the Command will show up in the Bindings panel just like a recordset (shown in Figure 26-6), and the fields can be inserted into the page in exactly the same manner. Repeat Regions can be applied as well.

You should now be able to apply a table to the page, insert the stored-procedure return columns, and apply a Repeat Region to the page to complete the simple search page.

Note   *Using stored procedures also allows for greater security within the database. Although users of Microsoft Access might enjoy the power of being able to access the actual production tables of the database, giving your end user access to these tables is generally not good practice. Using a stored procedure allows you to give the user permission to access the table only through the carefully constructed stored procedure rather than the table itself.*

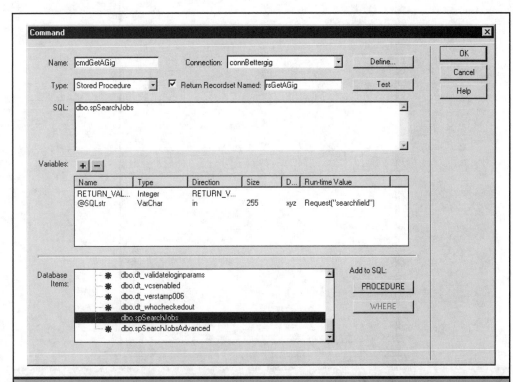

Figure 26-5.   *The Command Server Behavior allows stored procedures (as well as* Insert, Update, *and* Delete *commands) to be inserted into a Web page.*

ADVANCED DATA
INTEGRATION

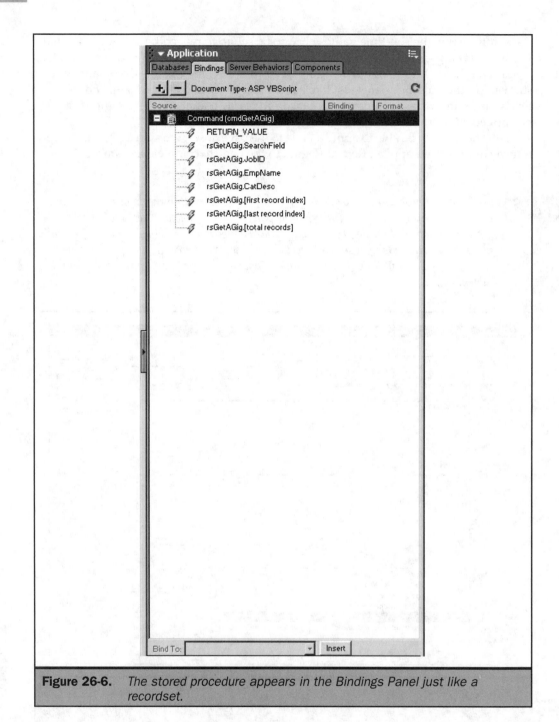

Figure 26-6. *The stored procedure appears in the Bindings Panel just like a recordset.*

To add the complex search functionality to the stored procedure, you need to have more than just a basic knowledge of SQL. SQL is capable of complex programming logic. There are looping and conditional statements associated with it as in any other programming language. To implement a more complex stored procedure for searching the database, you could modify the stored procedure that was already written, or write a new stored procedure such as the following:

```
CREATE PROCEDURE spSearchJobsAdvanced
     --set the incoming parameter
@SQLStr varchar(255) = "xyz"
 AS
   --then declare some variables.
Declare @temp varchar(255)
Declare @searchstring varchar(255)
   --We are going to allow 4 search variables.
Declare @searchstring1 varchar(255)
Declare @searchstring2 varchar(255)
Declare @searchstring3 varchar(255)
Declare @searchstring4 varchar(255)
   --set the default values of the search variables
Select @searchstring1 = '%'
Select @searchstring2 = '%'
Select @searchstring3 = '%'
Select @searchstring4 = '%'
   --declare a counter for the number of criterion
Declare @counter int
Select @counter = 0
   --@index will hold the current comma position
Declare @index int
   --set the initial value of the @temp variable to the
   -- entire incoming @SQLstr parameter
Select @temp = @SQLstr
   --strip off any quotes and replace with spaces, then trim
   -- the spaces.  SQL doesn't allow empty strings.
Select @temp = rtrim(ltrim(Replace(@temp,char(34)," ")))
--check for a null string
if @temp is null RETURN
--begin a loop. The @temp variable will have search strings
-- removed one at a time
WHILE @temp is not null
BEGIN
```

```
--look for comma
Select @index = CHARINDEX(',', @temp)
if @index = 0
--if no comma, then the whole string is used.
BEGIN
    SELECT @searchstring = ltrim(rtrim(@temp))
    SELECT @temp = null
END
else
--if there's a comma, separate the first part from the second part
BEGIN
    SELECT @searchstring = ltrim(rtrim(LEFT(@temp, @index-1)))
     --the new searchstring
    SELECT @temp = RIGHT(@temp,LEN(@temp) - @index)
     -- the rest
END
    SELECT @counter = @counter + 1
--set the variables depending on what position they were in.  For
-- example, a string like 'asp,web,vbscript' has 3 substrings
-- so the @searchstring4 would always contain the default '%'
if @counter = 1 Select @searchstring1 = '%' + @searchstring + '%'
if @counter = 2 Select @searchstring2 = '%' + @searchstring + '%'
if @counter = 3 Select @searchstring3 = '%' + @searchstring + '%'
if @counter = 4 Select @searchstring4 = '%' + @searchstring + '%'
END
--the parsing of the search parameters is finished.  Get the data
-- from the getSearchField view that was created earlier
Select SearchField, JobID, EmpName, CatDesc
FROM getSearchField
WHERE SearchField LIKE  @searchstring1
AND SearchField LIKE @searchstring2
AND SearchField LIKE @searchstring3
AND SearchField LIKE @searchstring4
```

This stored procedure can be applied in the same manner as the simple stored procedure that was built previously, because it accepts only one parameter and returns the same fields. In fact, if you are modifying the existing stored procedure, it isn't necessary to change the page at all. However, now the new stored procedure is much more flexible, and the functionality remains similar to the multiple-search criteria server-side script approach.

Note

As shown, the stored procedure was modified to make the Web application more flexible, but the Web application had no changes to it. This is one of the advantages of stored procedures—they allow you to move the logic into the database and out of the Web application. It also illustrates the "black box" approach—hiding the details of the functionality from the application.

Adding the my_company and find_a_seeker Pages

The my_company and find_a_seeker pages will allow the company user to have access to the various resumes that are available. The my_company page will be a set of simple links to the various pages that are available to the employer, including the find_a_seeker page, which will be a list of resumes available. You should set up the my_company page with links to all of the pages that are available to the employer. You could also create a search page similar to the get_a_gig page that was created earlier that searches resumes instead of jobs. The my_company page should have a Restrict Access To Page Server Behavior on it that allows only employers to access the page. This behavior was described in the last chapter.

The find_a_seeker page—also containing the Restrict Access To Page Server Behavior—will be a simple list of all resumes. Clicking a link will take you to the view_resume page that has already been created. To create this list, follow these steps:

1. Apply a recordset named *rsGetResumes* to the page. The SQL should read as follows:

   ```
   SELECT ResID, ResGoal FROM Resumes
   ```

2. Insert a two-row, two-column table on the page.

3. Add column headings and insert the two database columns into the table.

4. Add a Repeat Region to the second row showing ten records.

5. Add a Recordset Navigation Bar Application Object to the page.

6. Add a Go To Detail Page Server Behavior to the view_resume page using the ResID column as the URL parameter.

Note

If in doubt as to how to apply any of these steps, see Chapter 25, in which the various Server Behaviors were explained in detail.

Adding a Resumes Viewed Page

Every time a potential employer views a resume, the employer's ID number (EmpID), as well as the resume ID number (ResID), will be stored in another table that was created just for this purpose. The table name is ResumesViewed and is a *linking* table because it contains foreign keys from the Employers table and the Resumes table that effectively link the two tables together when the fields have something in common. In the case of the ResumesViewed table, the fact that the employer has viewed the resume is the common thread between the two tables. Each time the resume is viewed, it will cause a line to be added to this table storing the ResID, EmpID, and ResumesViewedID fields.

You can add functionality like this by placing an *Insert* command on the view_ resume page. This is not the Insert Server Behavior that was used when form fields were involved. Rather, the Insert command is accessed through the Command Server Behavior by using the drop-down menu (see Figure 26-7). This method of applying an insert gives you a little more flexibility with your *Insert* statement. With the Insert Server Behavior, you are limited to form fields.

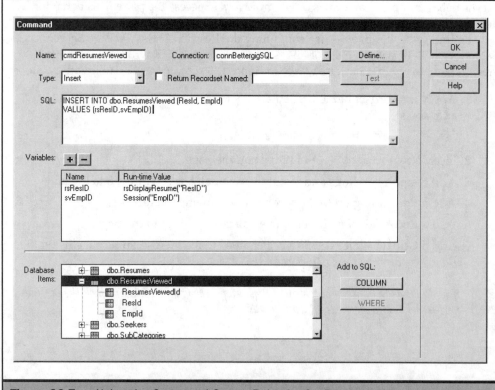

Figure 26-7.   *Using the Command Server Behavior for Database Insert*

Set up the insert by using the following parameters:

- **Name** *cmdResumesViewed*
- **Connection** *connBettergig*
- **Type** *Insert*
- **SQL** INSERT INTO ResumesViewed (ResID,EmpID) VALUES (rqResID,svEmpID)
- **Variables** As shown in Table 26-3

The session variable for *EmpID* hasn't been set up yet, but it can be hand-coded on the welcome_company_user page that the company users will see when they log in.

 ColdFusion users should use the standard recordset dialog box to write the SQL to handle the insert to the database.

Hand-Coding a Session Variable

Adding a session or application variable declaration is an easy process, but it requires basic knowledge of server-side scripting. Depending upon the data your variable is going to hold, you have to put the declaration in the proper place in the application. For the purposes of the *EmpID* session variable, the *EmpID* from the database has to be

Server Model	Name	Run-Time Value
ASP	*rqResID*	*Request("ResID")*
JSP	*rqResID*	*request.getParameter("ResID")*
ColdFusion	*rqResID*	*#ResID#*
PHP	*rqResID*	*$ResID*
ASP.Net	*rqResID*	*Request.Form("ResID")*
ASP	*svEmpID*	*Session("svEmpID")*
JSP	*svEmpID*	*session.getValue("svEmpID")*
ColdFusion	*svEmpID*	*#Session.svEmpID#*
PHP	*svEmpID*	*$svEmpID*
ASP.Net	*svEmpID*	*Session("svEmpID")*

Table 26-3. *Setting up Variables for the* Insert *Command*

there. There is a place in the application where that occurs, and that is on the welcome_ company_user page immediately after the recordset *rsGetEmployer* has been called.

When hand-coding inside the Dreamweaver environment, it's usually a good idea to separate your code from the Dreamweaver-generated code. That way you ensure that your hand-coding won't get written over by Dreamweaver. The reasoning behind this is simple: Dreamweaver has specific patterns of code that it searches for when editing a Server Behavior that it has inserted on the page. In most cases, the pattern begins at the start of a given script block and ends at the end of the block. For example, in a script block for a Server Behavior, you have an opening tag, the script, and then the closing tag. If you insert some extra script inside the tags, you run the risk that Dreamweaver will not be able to recognize its own Server Behavior anymore or, if it does, that it might strip off the code you inserted. This is not true in every case; but, in general, you should separate your code by enclosing it in its own script tags.

After the *rsGetEmployer* recordset is declared, insert the following line:

```
<%session("EmpID") = rsGetEmployer("EmpID")%> (ASP, ASP.NET)
<%session.putValue("svEmpID",rsGetEmployer.getInt("EmpID"))%> (JSP)
<CFSET Session.svEmpId = rsGetEmployer.EmpID> (ColdFusion)
<?PHPsession_register("EmpID") = $rsGetEmployer("EmpID")?> (PHP)
```

Adding Conditional Logic

The view_resume page will be accessible by the job seeker and by the employer. The ResumesViewed table will be updated only when the employer views the page. This is accomplished by adding conditional logic to the page. You saw it earlier with the Show Region Server Behavior. This behavior works very well for showing and hiding things that are going to be seen on the Web page. In this particular case, however, the item that you need to hide is a section of server-side code on the page before the <body> tags that performs the database insert. This functionality will have to be hand-coded.

Once again, the server-side script can be enclosed in its own script tags to ensure that the Dreamweaver-generated script isn't tampered with. You can do this by first finding the code for the *Insert* command and then applying your conditional code around it. In general, when you have a condition, there is a Begin condition tag and an End condition tag. Next you'll find the sample conditional code that you can use around the *Insert* command:

VBScript Version

```
<%If (session("svEmpID")<> "") Then %>
<%
''
''insert code
''
```

```
%>
<%End If%>
```

JavaScript Version

```
<%if(String(Session("svEmpID"))!="undefined") {%>
<%
//
//insert code
//
%>
<%}%>
```

ColdFusion Version

```
<CFIF IsDefined(Session.svEmpID")>
<!---
---insert code
--->
</CFIF>
```

Java Version

```
<%if(session.getValue("svEmpID")!=null) {%>
<%
//
//insert code
//
%>
<%}%>
```

PHP Version

```
<?php
if($EmpID){
//
//insert code
//
}
?>
```

ASP.Net Version

```
<%
if(Session("EmpID") != null){
//
//insert code
//
}
%>
```

In ASP, there will be slight performance degradation by having the server-side tags opening and closing, but the loss will be minimal, and probably not even discernable. The important thing to remember about using this method is that it will allow the Server Behaviors to remain separate and functional within Dreamweaver. When your page is finished, you can remove the extraneous tags if you feel that it is necessary. JSP pages are compiled into servlets (as explained in Chapter 9), so the extra tags don't affect the page performance at all. ColdFusion, of course, is entirely made up of tags, so there is no performance penalty here.

Adding a resumes_viewed Page to the Admin Section

There are several ways to use the data in the ResumesViewed table. For example, job seekers can check how many times their resumes are viewed. Also, the employer could get a feel for how many times other employers have looked at a particular resume. For the site administrator, the table can supply general summary data for the site. You'll add this functionality to the resume_viewed page in the Admin subfolder.

Using Count(*)

SQL has aggregate functions that allow you to examine data in your database as groups of data rather than individual pieces of data. A *Sum* function, for example, will return the sum of all items in a column. A *Min* or *Max* function will return the lowest and highest values in the table.

The *Count* function allows you to get counts of your data, depending upon conditions that you set in the SQL statement. If you wanted to get a count of how many times the employers actually viewed the resumes, you could write a SQL statement like this:

```
SELECT COUNT(ResumesViewed.ResId) AS ResumeByEmployer,
    Employers.EmpName
```

```
FROM ResumesViewed INNER JOIN
    Employers ON
    ResumesViewed.EmpId = Employers.EmpID
GROUP BY Employers.EmpName
```

This SQL statement counts the number of times each employer viewed resumes. This statement doesn't separate the resumes by individual seeker, but rather gives the total count of how many times a specific employer viewed *any* resume. The Count is given the alias *ResumeByEmployer* so that you can reference the number on your Web page. The ResumesViewed table contained only the EmpID number, but by using an Inner join in the statement you can get the employer's name as well; this gives the data more meaning to the end user. When the statement is run, the result might be something like Table 26-4.

The SQL statement could be copied and pasted as is into the Dreamweaver query builder, or you can create a view named *getResumesViewedByEmployer* out of the statement and then access it with a SQL statement inside of the Dreamweaver environment like this:

```
Select ResumesByEmployer, EmpName FROM getResumesViewedByEmployer
```

The latter method is preferable; but whichever you choose, the result is that you should create a recordset on the page named *rsGetResumesViewedByEmployer*. After creating this recordset, you can insert a table on the page, add the column headings and column information as you've done before, and apply a Repeat Region to the row containing the data. When browsing the page, the results of the SQL statement will be shown.

Another count that you'll want on this page is the resumes viewed by job seeker. This count will show how many times each individual resume was viewed. It could also be used on a page specific to job seekers to allow them to see how many times the resume was viewed. For now, however, you can insert it on this Admin page.

ResumesByEmployer	EmpName
8	Acme Databases
21	Smith, Smith, and Smith Enterprises
7	Susquehanna Hat Co.

Table 26-4.   *Sample Count of How Many Times an Employer Viewed a Resume*

ADVANCED DATA INTEGRATION

The SQL statement should read as follows:

```
SELECT COUNT(ResumesViewed.ResId) AS ResumesCount,
    Seekers.SeekFirstName + ' ' + Seekers.SeekLastName as FullName
FROM Resumes INNER JOIN
    ResumesViewed ON
    Resumes.ResID = ResumesViewed.ResId INNER JOIN
    Seekers ON Resumes.SeekID = Seekers.SeekID
GROUP BY ResumesViewed.ResID, Seekers.SeekLastName,
    Seekers.SeekFirstName
```

The statement is similar to the *getResumesViewedByEmployer* statement; however, this one retrieves information about the job seeker. To do this, you need an Inner join to the Resumes table, which, in turn, needs to be joined to the Seekers table. Also, the *SeekFirstName* and *SeekLastName* are combined—with a space inserted between them—to form the *FullName* alias. Upon running this query, you might have results like that found in Table 26-5.

Once again, you can create a view named *getResumesViewedBySeeker* and access it with a simple SQL statement from within Dreamweaver, like this:

```
SELECT FullName, ResumesCount FROM getResumesViewedBySeeker
```

Create a recordset named *rsGetResumesViewedBySeeker* using this statement and again, apply the table, column headings, columns, and Repeat Region to the page. Now the page should have two tables on it that give accurate counts containing data pertaining to both the job seeker and the employer.

FullName	ResumesCount
Jack Splat	8
Thomas Testdata	10
Jack Springer	5

Table 26-5.   *Counting the Resumes Viewed for Each Job Seeker*

Adding the Error Page

An error page can be as simple or as complex as you want to make it, but its primary purpose is to alert the user to an error condition. In this site, the error page is a one-stop place where a user is redirected if an error occurs on a page.

One error condition you'll want to catch is the attempt to access a page without the proper authorization. You'll want the user to have the chance to log in properly and be taken back to the page he or she attempted to access. This is accomplished fairly easily with the built-in User Authentication Server Behaviors—simply redirect the user to the login page from the Restrict Access To Page Server Behavior. If you recall, we set this parameter in all cases to this Error page instead.

When a user encounters an error condition, you may want to log the error so it can later be examined. Also, several pages in the site will be accessible by different types of users—administrators, job seekers, and employers. Because these different groups all have their own login pages, you'll want them to log in on the appropriate page.

The Restrict Access to Page Server Behavior will append a querystring variable of *accessdenied* to the end of the URL when it redirects the user to the error page. This *accessdenied* variable contains the relative location of the page that the error occurred on. By picking up this variable, you can append it to the proper link to redirect the user to the appropriate page. For example, the view_a_gig page can be accessed by all three groups, and there is no way of knowing which group the person belongs to if he hasn't logged in yet. You can simply set up a link for each login page and put the appropriate text on the page:

Are you a Job Seeker? Sign in or Register now.
Are you an Employer? Sign in or Register now.

The job seeker will be redirected to the login_user page in the login_user directory, and the employer will be redirected to the login_company_user page in the login_company_user directory. Make the link by highlighting the words "Sign in" and then right-clicking (CTRL-clicking on the Macintosh) and choosing Make Link. Browse to the page that you are setting the link to.

You'll have to manually code the querystring at the end of the link by placing your cursor at the end of the link in the URL field of the Make Link dialog box and placing the following server-side code:

```
?<%=Request("query_string")%> (ASP, ASP.NET)
?<%=request.getParameter("query_string")%> (JSP)
?<CFOUTPUT>#cgi.query_string#</CFOUTPUT> (ColdFusion)
?<%PHP echo $query_string %> (PHP)
```

ADVANCED DATA INTEGRATION

Next, highlight the word "Register" in each line and set the link to the appropriate registration page. In the case of the job seeker, it will be the new_user page in the new_user directory, and in the case of the employer it will be the new_company_user in the my_company directory.

After doing this, whenever users encounters an error that is the result of not being logged in, they will be redirected to this error page, at which time they can choose to log in properly or register if they are a new user. After a successful login, they will be redirected back to the page on which the error originally occurred.

By appending a querystring variable for other types of error conditions, you can catch those variables on this error page and write the code to apply the appropriate actions depending on what type of error it is.

Summary

In Chapter 24, the Server Behaviors and Bindings panels were introduced. In this chapter, we've taken the functionality a little further with more advanced concepts, including stored procedures, commands, hand-coding, and aggregate queries using the *Count* keyword. We could certainly cover a lot more that would add more functionality to the site, but this chapter was meant only as a starting point.

As the languages and technologies used on the Web get more complex, it is increasingly important that you take the time to learn as much as you can about the platform that you choose to use for your applications. Hopefully, this chapter has shown you how you can expand on Dreamweaver's built-in functionality to take advantage of all of the power that these platforms provide.

Chapter 27

Advanced
Scripting Topics

This chapter covers some scripting topics that are more advanced than regular page design but don't really belong in the database section either. These items represent things that many Dreamweaver users ask about. Some are specific to a particular platform, and others can be executed in any language if you know the syntax.

E-Mail

Sending e-mail is an important part of many data-driven Web sites. The ability to respond to users by e-mail can be used to confirm orders, provide usernames and passwords, or notify users that a site's content has changed.

There are several basic parts of an e-mail message, listed here:

- **From** The name or e-mail address the message is sent from
- **To** The e-mail address that the mail is intended for
- **Subject** The subject of the e-mail
- **Body** The text of the e-mail message
- **CC** An address to which you want to send a carbon copy of the e-mail
- **BCC** An address to which you want to send a blind carbon copy (a copy that the primary recipient has no knowledge of)
- **Attachment** A file that is attached to the e-mail
- **Priority** The priority setting of the e-mail

No matter which method you choose to create and send your e-mail, you will be setting some or all of these properties in your code and then calling a method that sends the e-mail.

CDO Mail

CDO mail is a Windows/ASP method of creating and sending e-mail. It relies on the cdonts.dll file that is a subset of Windows Collaborative Data Objects. Setting up the cdonts.dll component was covered in Chapter 2.

Once your server is configured to use CDO, constructing and sending an e-mail is as easy as typing a few lines of code.

```
<%
Dim CDOMail
Set CDOMail = Server.CreateObject("CDONTS.NewMail")

CDOMail.From = "ray@workablesolutions.com"
CDOMail.To = Request("customeremail")
CDOMail.Subject = txtSubject
```

```
CDOMail.Body = "Thank you for writing. Attached is a file that explains our
order process. Please let us know if you have any questions"
CDOMail.CC = "ray@workablesolutions.com"
CDOMail.AttachFile = ("d:\files\orders.txt")
CDOMail.Send

Set CDOMail = nothing
%>
```

An explanation of the above code follows.

```
Dim CDOMail
```

Here, a variable is created. In ASP, all variables are variants, meaning that they can hold any kind of data. The variable will be used to hold an object, assigned in the next step.

```
Set CDOMail = Server.CreateObject("CDONTS.NewMail")
```

This line assigns an object to the variable *CDOMail* based on the *NewMail* class of the CDONTS object. If you have set up CDO mail as covered in Chapter 2, this step should complete itself without incident.

```
CDOMail.From = "ray@workablesolutions.com"
CDOMail.To = Request.Form("customeremail")
CDOMail.Subject = txtSubject
CDOMail.Body = "Thank you for writing. Attached is a file that explains our
order process. Please let us know if you have any questions"
CDOMail.CC = "ray@workablesolutions.com"
```

This code illustrates several ways to assign values to the properties of the *CDOMail* object. The From line assigns a static string value that is hard-coded. The To line uses an ASP request object to get a value from a form field named *customername* and assign it to the *To* property of the object. The Subject line uses a variable (that must have been defined and assigned a value earlier in the code) called *txtSubject* to assign a subject value. You can see that you can use any of a number of common programming methods to collect data and assign it to the properties of the *CDOMail* object.

```
CDOMail.AttachFile = ("d:\files\orders.txt")
```

The *AttachFile* property is used to attach a file to the e-mail, much as you might attach a file to an e-mail you send from Outlook or Eudora. Keep in mind that the path described here is to a physical file on the Web server from which this e-mail is being sent.

```
CDOMail.Send
```

The *Send* method is used to complete the assignment of properties and send the e-mail.

```
Set CDOMail = nothing
```

As with any ASP object, you need to set the variable reference to nothing in order to free unneeded server resources.

JMail

JMail is an alternative to CDO mail available from dimac.net. Its syntax is a little different, but it works basically the same as CDO. Following is an example of a JMail e-mail:

```
<%
Set JMail = Server.CreateObject("JMail.SMTPMail")
JMail.ServerAddress = "exchange.emailserver.com"
JMail.Sender = "ray@workablesolutions.com"
JMail.Subject = "txtSubject"

JMail.AddRecipient Request.Form("customeremail")
JMail.Body = "Thank you for writing. Attached is a file that explains our
order process. Please let us know if you have any questions"
JMail.Priority = 1

JMail.AppendBodyFromFile "d:\email\email_footer.txt"

JMail.AddAttachment " d:\files\orders.txt "

JMail.Execute

Set Jmail = nothing

%>
```

Other ASP E-mail Programs

Several other e-mail components are available for little or no cost. You may find one that you like better, or you may be forced by your ISP to use a particular version. Just keep in mind that most operate in the same fashion as the preceding examples, and follow these steps:

- Dimension (Dim in VBScript) a variable to hold an object.
- Set the object as an instance of the component class.
- Set static text, ASP objects, or variables to each of the component's properties that you want to make use of.
- Call a method of the component to send or execute the e-mail.
- Set the object equal to nothing to free server resources.

No matter what program you choose to use, there will be some documentation or examples that explain the properties and methods of the component. Referencing these, you should be able to make quick work of the implementation of any component.

ColdFusion Mail

ColdFusion mail was discussed briefly in Chapter 10. Sending an e-mail in ColdFusion is simply a matter of including a CFMAIL tag on your page:

```
<CFMAIL TO="#myToVariable#"
FROM="#myFromVariable#"
SUBJECT="Your order was received">
Thank you for submitting your order!
</CFMAIL>
```

Although that is all you need to send a simple e-mail, other attributes of the tag allow you to add other options to the e-mail:

- **CC="copy_to"**   Specify a CC address.
- **BCC="blind_copy_to"**   Specify your BCC address.
- **TYPE="msg_type"**   You can set this to "html" for an HTML e-mail.
- **MAXROWS="max_msgs"**   If your e-mail is coming from a query, you can specify the maximum number to send.
- **MIMEATTACH="path"**   Specify an attachment. You can specify other attachments with a CFMAILPARAM tag.
- **QUERY="query_name"**   Used if you want to send an e-mail to every name in a database, or if you want to send a series of e-mails to one person based on the results of the query. One e-mail is sent for every row returned by the CFQUERY tag.
- **GROUP="query_column"**   Use this feature if you want to group the output within one e-mail, such as an Order Details result within an e-mail to a customer.

- **GROUPCASESENSITIVE="yes/no"** The default is "yes" and case is considered while grouping records. Set it to "no" if you want to ignore case and keep the recordset intact.

- **STARTROW="query_row"** Start the e-mails at this row of the recordset.

- **SERVER="servername"** This will override the default mail server setting in the CF Administrator or specify a server if there isn't one previously defined in the Administrator.

- **PORT="port_ID"** Overrides the default port of 25.

- **MAILERID="headerid"** You can specify a mailer ID to be passed in the X-Mailer SMTP header. This header identifies the mailer application, which is set to Allaire ColdFusion Application Server by default.

- **TIMEOUT="seconds"** Specify a timeout in seconds to stop waiting for the e-mail server.

To demonstrate a slightly more advanced use of the CFMAIL tag, assume that you have an e-mail statement that is personalized for customers in your database as they order something online. A generic e-mail is stored as an HTML page in your Web folder (GenericOrderPage.htm), and the customer's account information is stored in the database along with the other customer information, such as name, address, and the orders placed. For the sake of this example, assume that all information is coming from the *getOrderDetails* view that is stored in the database. The view retrieves related information from the Customers, Orders, OrderDetails, and Products tables, but that's not important for the understanding of this example and is covered later.

This is what the page would look like:

```
<CFQUERY Name="rsOrders" DSN="#mydsn#">
Select * from getOrderDetails where OrderID = #OrderID#
</CFQUERY>
<CFMAIL TO="#rsOrders.emailaddress#"
    FROM="sales@acmedatabases.com"
    SUBJECT="Your order number #Order ID# is on its way!"
    TYPE="HTML">
<CFINCLUDE TEMPLATE="GenericOrderPage.htm">
<table><CFLOOP QUERY="rsOrders">
    <tr>
        <td>#rsOrders.ProductID#</td>
        <td>#rsOrders.ProductName#</td>
        <td>#rsOrders.Price#</td>
        <td>#rsOrders.Quantity#</td>
<CFSET TotalLineItem = rsOrders.Price * rsOrders.Quantity>
        <td><b>TOTAL:</b> #TotalLineItem#</td>
```

```
    </tr>
</CFLOOP>
</table>
Total Order cost = #rsOrders.TotalPrice#
<CFINCLUDE TEMPLATE="ThankYou.htm">
</CFMAIL>
```

The small amount of code in this example performs the following tasks:

- Retrieves the order information from the database, including the customer's information.

- Includes a generic HTML e-mail text that is stored on the server (GenericOrderPage.htm) for the first part of the e-mail.

- Loops through all the orders, adding up the line items as it goes and formatting the order details into a table.

- Includes another include file that has the closing thank you information.

You can see that by using a combination of include files, looping constructs, and HTML tags, you can create truly dynamic e-mails with ColdFusion. You can even include variables in the included HTML page. You can embed them into the HTML include file like this:

```
Hello #rsQuery.FirstName#.  Thank you for your order of #rsQuery.TotalPrice#.
```

The ColdFusion server reads through and evaluates everything sequentially up to the closing CFMAIL tag.

The CFQUERY tag in this example doesn't affect the number of e-mails sent, because you didn't specify a *Query* attribute in the CFMAIL tag. The example in Chapter 10 demonstrated the use of bulk e-mails using a *Query* attribute.

Please make sure to check the documentation for whichever e-mail method you choose so that you'll know all the properties and methods that are available to you.

PHP Mail

Sending e-mail in PHP is made simple by the inclusion of the *mail()* wrapper function. This function's responsibility is to gather up information about the mail you want to send and ship it off to an available SMTP server for processing. If the delivery is successful (the function found the specified SMTP server) the function returns TRUE.

The first thing that you need to check is that there is a valid SMTP server set up in the php.ini file on your server. If you are running a Windows server, you can likely use the localhost SMTP server that comes with Windows. On Unix, the sendmail program is almost always present.

In the INI file, there will be a category called mail function with a parameter or two, depending on the platform you are using. In Windows it looks like this:

```
[mail function]
SMTP = localhost
sendmail_from = youraddress@domain.com
```

On a Unix server, you simply need the path to the sendmail server.

```
[mail function]
sendmail_path = path
```

The default is the local sendmail program.

The mail function accepts three required arguments: an e-mail address, a subject, and a body. These can be hard-coded into the function call, or loaded into variables.

```
<?php
$email_to = "somebody@somewhere.com";
$email_subject = "Make sure to sign up for TODCON";
$email_body = "It is going to be great!\n";
$email_body .= "Don't miss it!\n";

if(mail(@email_to, $email_subject, @email_body))
        echo "Mail sent.";
else echo "Mail failed.";
?>
```

This will attempt to deliver an e-mail to the specified SMTP server for delivery to somebody@somewhere.com. If the *mail()* function finds the SMTP server, the message Mail sent will be displayed, otherwise, Mail failed will appear.

The *mail()* function will also accept a fourth argument that allowed for the sending of additional headers such as CC and BCC. Again, these can be hard-coded, passed as variables, or even collapsed into a single headers variable. Look at the previous example with a couple of additional headers:

```
<?php
$email_to = "somebody@somewhere.com";
$email_subject = "Make sure to sign up for TODCON";
$email_body = "It is going to be great!\n";
$email_body .= "Don't miss it!\n";

if(mail(@email_to, $email_subject, @email_body,
```

```
"From:me@mydomain.com\r\nCc:him@hisdomain.com\r\nBcc:hidden@nodomain.com"))
     echo "Mail sent.";
else echo "Mail failed.";
?>
```

Notice that these additional headers are comprised of one string separated by new lines. Do not input them as multiple arguments with commas in between.

You can use these additional headers to perform any regular e-mail functions like attaching files and setting priorities. The actual procedure for performing more advanced tasks is beyond this book, and we would refer you to a good PHP reference, but this should get you started responding to your users with basic information.

.NET Mail

Although you can use CDO mail on a .NET server, .NET's architecture provides for built-in functionality that was not available in traditional ASP. .NET has a built in SMTP control that makes sending e-mail much simpler.

The key to using built-in controls in .NET is to remember to import the namespace that contains them. You can learn more about this in Chapter 19. In the following code, you import the *System.Web.Mail* namespace that contains the *SmtpMail* control. From there, it is as simple as passing in the details of the mail as variables or strings:

```
<% @Page Language="C#" %>
<% @Import Namespace="System.Web.Mail" %>
<%
string strTo = "somebody@somewhere.com";
string strFrom = "me@mydomain.com";
string strSubject = "Make sure to sign up for TODCON";
SmtpMail.Send(strFrom, strTo, strSubject,
  "It is going to be great!");
Response.Write("Mail sent.");

%>
```

Again, make sure that your server has a valid SMTP server set up in its IIS configuration.

Controlling Where Script Is Run

Traditionally, scripts have been run in the normal course of page execution, meaning that a script that appears at the top of the page is going to run when the form loads. The pages that come before it are responsible for gathering information that the script needs so that when the scripted page loads, the code is ready to go. This is still a very valid and useful way to do many things, but there is a different method of placing scripts and their predicate requirements on the same page. This can also be a very efficient means of handling traffic through your application. The idea is that you can place code on a page that expects data that is also collected in a form on that page. The invocation of the script code is then made dependent on the value of the button that posts the form.

> **Note** *The .NET platform has really capitalized on this method of page handling with its post-back functionality. Understanding the way that this concept works will help you to grasp the power of encapsulating code onto pages that perform specific tasks.*

If you have done much work with forms, you may know that the Submit button also has a value that can be gleaned from the post. When the Submit button has been clicked, that value is available on the page that the form posts to in the request object. Thus, when a page loads, you can determine whether it is a result of the click of a certain button by checking for that button's value in the post. If it has no value (it equals "") or it is null, the page loaded because of a call from a different page and no information is available for the script. If, however, the value of the button is set, you know that the page loaded as the result of the form being submitted to it, and values are available for the script to execute.

> **Note** *For this method to work, you must set the form on the page to post back to the same page. For instance, if the page you are working on is called CDOTest.asp, the form on that page should post to CDOTest.asp.*

Very often when the page reloads from the form post, the display part of the page is never reached the second time through. The purpose of this method is to process the form data into the necessary code and then send the user off to the proper place with a redirect statement. The following code illustrates using a CDO e-mail component this way.

```
<%@LANGUAGE="VBSCRIPT"%><% if (cStr(Request("Submit")) <> "") Then
Dim objCDO
Set objCDO = Server.CreateObject("CDONTS.NewMail")
objCDO.From = "ray@workablesolutions.com"
objCDO.To = Request("to")
objCDO.CC = ""
objCDO.Subject = "Test"
objCDO.Body = "test"
```

```
objCDO.Send()
Set objCDO = Nothing
Response.Redirect("mailsent.asp")
End If
%>
```

If the Submit button in this example has been clicked, the *If* statement is invoked, the e-mail is constructed and sent, and the user is redirected to the mailsent.asp page. If the button has not been clicked, this code is skipped and the HTML beneath it displays an HTML form to collect the information to send the e-mail.

This method can be very efficient because it eliminates the need for processor ASP pages that handle code and direct the user but serve no display purpose. Many of the functions and behaviors in Dreamweaver use this method. The code that you see generated by Dreamweaver will be easier to understand once you have a handle on this way of doing things.

The *FileSystemObject* Object

The *FileSystemObject* (FSO) object provides a means for your ASP pages to access the file and drive systems of the server on which they are running. There are four objects in the FSO collection, listed in Table 27-1.

Using the FSO object, you can do pretty much anything you need to regarding the file system of the computer your pages are running on. You can create files and write to them, delete files, move files around, and even create databases and search files.

The FSO model is available in a Microsoft-provided dynamic link library called scrrun.dll. You can access the functionality of this DLL from any application that

FSO Object	Description
Drive object	Enables access to physical and network drives.
FileSystemObject object	Enables access to the computer's file system.
Folder object	Enables access to folders and their properties.
TextStream object	Enables access to a file's contents.

Table 27-1. *The Objects of the File System Object Collection*

provides access to objects, such as Visual Basic or Access. To access it from ASP, you must create an object, much as we did with the *CDOMail* object earlier.

```
<%
Dim fso
Set fso = Server.CreateObject("Scripting.FileSystemObject")
%>
```

The *FileSystemObject* object has several methods available to it by which you can perform your tasks. The most commonly used are listed in Table 27-2.

Once you have created a *FileSystemObject* object in your code, you can call these methods to perform operations on your file system. For instance, suppose that you have collected information about a person from a form and you want to write that information to a text file for later use (say as a guest book). You can use the information you have collected to write to a file.

```
<%
Dim fso, file
Dim name, zipcode, email
name = Request("name")
zipcode = Request"(zip")
email = Request("email")

path = "c:\guestbook\book.txt"

set fso = Server.CreateObject(Scripting.FileSystemObject")

set file = fso.opentextfile(path, 3, TRUE)

file.write(name) & vbcrlf

file.write(zipcode) & vbcrlf

file.write(email) & vbcrlf

file.close

set file = nothing
set fso = nothing
%>
```

FSO Method	Description
CopyFile	Copies files from one place to another.
CreateTextFile	Creates a text file and returns a TextStream object so that you can write to the file.
DeleteFile	Deletes a file.
OpenTextFile	Opens a file and creates a TextStream object that you can use to read from the file or append to the file. This method can also create the file if it does not exist, if you have set its parameter to allow it to do so.

Table 27-2. *The File System Object Methods*

The preceding code gathers information from a preceding form into a collection of variables. It then sets a path to the file that will be written. The path is a file on the server computer and must be an actual file path. It does not affect the file system of the client computer that is viewing these pages.

Once the FSO is created, the *opentextfile* method is called to open a file. This method takes three parameters: the path to the file (provided here by a variable), an indication of the purpose for which you will use the file (represented by a 1 here; see Table 27-3), and a true or false setting that tells the method whether or not to create the file referenced in the path if it does not already exist.

After the file is opened, you can use the methods of the *TextStream* object that is created by the *OpenTextFile* method to write to the open file. In the preceding code, the values of the variables were written to the file using the *write* method. The *vbcrlf* command was used to place a carriage return after each line.

File Use Integer	Description
1	The file is opened for reading.
2	The file is opened for writing.
3	The file is opened for appending.

Table 27-3. *Options for How a File Is Opened*

VBCRLF is a VBScript command that stands for Visual Basic Carriage Return Line Feed. It is used to place a carriage return (return to the far left of the line) and a line feed (go to the next line on the page) in the output of your code.

Once this is complete, the file is closed and the File object and the FSO object are set to nothing to free server resources.

The *TextStream* object also has methods, such as *Readline* and *Skipline*, that allow you to navigate through the contents of a file. See Microsoft's documentation or the MCDN Web site for a more complete description of the *FileSystemObject* object and the tasks you can accomplish with it.

PHP File Handling

You can handle files in PHP in much the same way with its built-in functions.

```php
<?php
$path = "c:\guestbook\book.txt";
$guestfile = fopen($path, a);

fwrite($guestfile,"Jim Robinson\r\n");

fclose(%guestfile);

?>
```

In this example, you open a file for appending. The file is identified by the $path variable. When the *fopen()* function is called, the *$guestfile* variable is set as a reference to the file you will be appending. Notice the second argument "a" in that statement. This argument tells PHP to open the file for appending. Other possible arguments are listed in Table 27-4.

Value	Description
R	Open file for reading. The file position indicator is placed at the beginning of the file.
R+	Open the file for reading and writing.

Table 27-4. *Parameters of the* fopen() *Function in PHP*

Value	Description
W	Open the file for writing only. Existing data will be lost. If the file does not exist, PHP will attempt to create it.
W+	Open the file for reading and writing. Any existing data will be lost. If the file does not exist, PHP will attempt to create it.
A	Open the file for appending only. Data will be written to the end of the file.
A+	Open the file for reading and appending. Data will be written to the end of the file.
B	Open the file as a binary.

Table 27-4. *Parameters of the* fopen() *Function in PHP* (continued)

A great many more functions exists in PHP, which assist you in the creation and manipulation of files, directories, and their contents. You can control information by files or by a character at a time.

ASP.NET File Handling

Although some of the older technologies have functionality that can be explained quickly in a chapter like this, the newer languages have more available in them than can reasonably be covered in a book about Dreamweaver. Following is a quick ASP.NET example that you can build on as you learn more about the language:

```
using System;
using System.IO;

public class FileDemo
{
public static void Main()
{
    string path=" c:\guestbook\book.txt";
    StreamWriter filewrite=File.CreateText(path);
    filewrite.WriteLine("Jim Robinson");
    filewrite.Close();
}
}
```

After referencing the *System* and *System.IO* namespaces (which you can learn more about in Chapter 19), you have access to the *Streamwriter* control, which is used here to create a file called book.txt in the guestbook directory. You then simply use the *WriteLine* method to add a name and then close the file.

Basic functions get simpler as languages evolve. ASP.NET actually has a lot of the component information that you referenced in the FSO example earlier all bundled in an easy-to-use control. But as the new languages get more powerful, there is also more you can do with them, which means, again, you need a good reference to the tools of your choice.

Debugging and Troubleshooting Common Errors

No matter how careful you are, some problems are likely to pop up that you will need to resolve to get your pages working. If you are working with Internet Information Server and ASP, the errors that you will receive can be rather confusing and not at all indicative of the true nature of the problem. Here are some of the more common errors that occur and their possible remedies.

Microsoft OLE DB Provider for ODBC Drivers error '80004005' [Microsoft][ODBC Microsoft Access Driver] Operation must use an updateable query

This is usually because of the write permissions on the NT directories. You can read from databases anywhere on the drive, but to write to them they have to be in a directory to which the IUSR_ user has write permissions. The IUSR_ user is the default user that your visitors access your site under. Speak to your ISP or network administrator about the proper permission to allow users to write to the database on your server; this will usually fix the error.

If this doesn't help, check to make sure you are not using joins in your query. Queries with joins are not updateable.

Error 0156: 80004005 The HTTP headers have already been written to the browser. Changes in HTTP headers should occur before page is written

Your ASP page is most likely trying to redirect to another location after data has already been written into the HTML response stream. This can occur if programmatic decisions in the body of your page try to send the user to another page after elements of the current page are already on the way to the browser. To prevent this problem, put the following code at the top of your ASP page:

```
Response.Buffer = true
```

The *Response* object, including the *Buffer* property, is covered in Chapter 8.

Microsoft OLE DB Provider for ODBC Drivers error '80004005' Data source name not found and no default driver specified

This error indicates that a Data Source Name (DSN) has not been set up on the server. It is most commonly encountered the first time you upload a site to your remote server. You may have been developing and testing on a computer that has the DSN set up correctly, but you must also set one up on the server machine that maps the correct path to the database (or have your ISP do it for you).

Keep in mind that if you are using an Access database, the database file (.mdb file) must also be uploaded to a directory on the server. This directory might end up being different from the one on your development machine, and the server's DSN will need to be mapped appropriately. The directory needs to have read and write permissions set for the IUSR_<machine_name> user, or you will end up getting the 80004005 error.

The IUSR_<machine_name> user is a special user that IIS sets up to accommodate visitors to your Web site. It represents the default user account that anonymous users will access to be allowed privileges on your server. The actual name of this user depends on the name you have given your computer. For instance, if the computer's name were WWW, this account would be IUSR_WWW.

Microsoft OLE DB Provider for ODBC Drivers error '80040e14' [Microsoft][ODBC Microsoft Access 97 Driver] Syntax error in INSERT INTO statement

This error is often caused by a reserved word used as a column name. Make sure that you do not have a column named "date" or some other reserved word.

Microsoft OLE DB Provider for ODBC Drivers error '80040e10' [Microsoft][ODBC Microsoft Access 97 Driver] Too few parameters. Expected 1

This error usually occurs when a column name in your query does not exist. Make sure that you are using the actual column names rather than alias names and that you have spelled all of your column names properly.

My Script Is Showing Up in the Browser Window Instead of Being Run By the Server

There are a couple of possible causes for this problem, which are illustrated in Figure 27-1.

First, you may have created an ASP page but given it an .html or .htm extension. This can be a common problem in Dreamweaver if you set .html as you default page

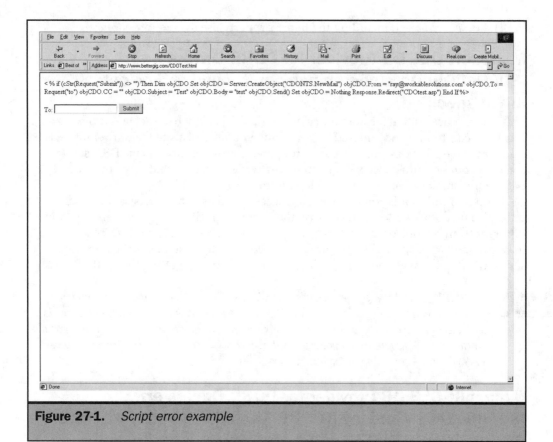

Figure 27-1.   *Script error example*

extension and then save pages without specifying the .asp extension. This can be a stealthy problem because it may cause your page to display correctly in the browser, but your ASP code is viewable in the source view of the page, exposing what should be secure information. Check the page you are trying to access to see that it has the proper extension.

Note   *It is sometimes wise to set the default extension to .html in your site definition. Many times, a site has only a few pages that contain code that needs to be processed by the ASP, JSP, or CF engine. Those pages, if given an .asp, .jsp, or .cfm extension, will access the engine and slow performance even though there is no code on them to run. Setting your default to .html in Dreamweaver can help you save regular Web pages as HTML files. This processes more quickly, but you will have to remember to save your coded pages with the appropriate extension.*

Second, you may have hand-written code that is not properly delineated with script tags (<% %>, etc.). If you have missed tags, or mistyped them, portions of your code will be treated as text rather than being sent through the processing engine, and the code will display as text in the user's browser.

Third, it is possible that the mapping in your Web server that tells the server where to run script code has been corrupted. For example, when running ASP on Internet Information Server, the server knows from the .asp file extension that the file needs special handling. It gets instructions on how to process the file from the Applications Settings dialog box in the Web site's properties in IIS. In Figure 27-2, you will see that IIS holds a list of file extensions and the processing libraries that are needed to interpret them. If this list becomes corrupted, or the dynamic link library (DLL) that is referenced is missing or corrupted, the server may either display the ASP file or try to download it to the user's computer. Either one is bad.

To repair this problem, you usually need to reload IIS or PWS on the problem computer. The ASP DLLs will be replaced with the reload, and the files should interpret properly.

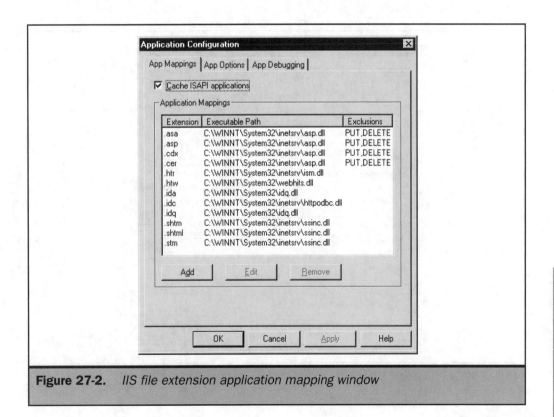

Figure 27-2.   *IIS file extension application mapping window*

Debugging Server-Side ASP

Internet Information Server provides a means for debugging server-side VBScript or JScript. To do this, you must enable debugging for the Web site in the Microsoft Management Console. In the properties for the site, choose Configuration on the Home Directory tab (see Figure 27-3) and enable ASP server-side debugging on the App Debugging tab (see Figure 27-4).

In your ASP script, include the debugging keyword appropriate to your server-side language choice immediately before the line where you want the debugger to pause. For VBScript, the keyword is *Stop*.

```
<%
    Response.Write "The debugger will start right after this line"
    Stop
    Response.Write "The debugger has paused the page"
%>
```

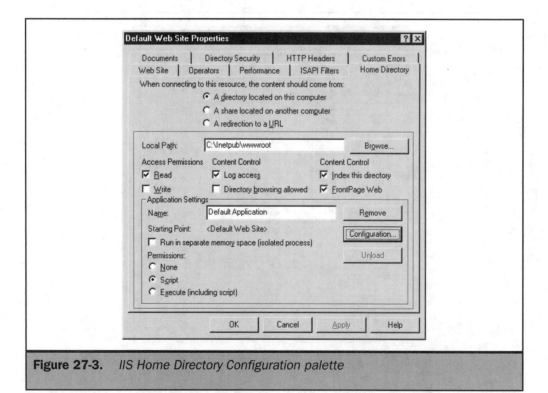

Figure 27-3. *IIS Home Directory Configuration palette*

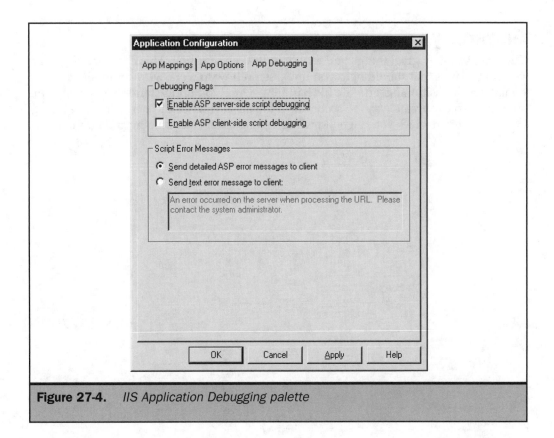

Figure 27-4. *IIS Application Debugging palette*

For JScript, use the *debugger* keyword.

```
<%
    Response.Write "The debugger will start right after this line"
    debugger
    Response.Write "The debugger has paused the page"
%>
```

When viewed in a browser, the page will pause and allow you to inspect assigned variables before they are passed on.

Those are just a few tips for troubleshooting and debugging script problems. Even if you are not using ASP, these issues should give you some idea of where to look to find what your problem might be. Remember to check permissions for your database, your file extensions, your database connection strings or DSN, and your tags and syntax, and you will eliminate most of the common errors that people encounter.

Summary

There are so many great things you can do with Web scripting. This chapter has given you some basics that should help you understand how to work with components, e-mail, script positioning, and the file handling. Once you understand these basics, you should be able to create ways to accomplish the tasks you need to perform—or at least have a base upon which you can build when seeking out further training and information.

The
Complete
Reference

Dreamweaver
MX

Chapter 28

Server-Side
Flash Integration

C hapter 11 covered some of the basic topics dealing with Flash within the Dreamweaver environment, but now we dive into some of the more advanced (and interesting) areas of integration. Flash MX (shown in Figure 28-1) is Macromedia's newest platform for building dynamic user interfaces. Flash MX even looks like Dreamweaver MX to give the Web developer a common look and feel across the entire MX suite. Flash MX is closely tied to ColdFusion MX, JRun 4, XML, Web Services, and Dreamweaver MX to enable Web applications to reach beyond the limitations of HTML and Web browsers. Dreamweaver MX is now more than just a simple Web page builder: It is the glue that enables you to deliver dynamic Web applications by tying all of these technologies together.

The Flash experience that most people are familiar with is an SWF file embedded in an HTML page, which livens it up with animation, colors, sounds, and movement. Flash MX reaches far beyond that, however. Using Flash MX you can build true client/server applications that don't have to be bound by the rules and limitations that you've learned building Web pages in the past. The Flash player can communicate easily with the server in such a way that the experience for the end user is seamless. No more

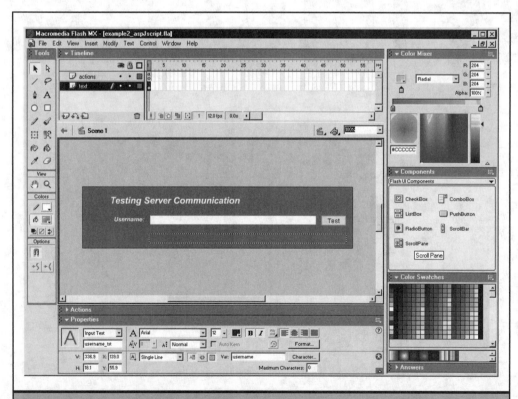

Figure 28-1. The Flash MX interface

round-trips to the server waiting for pages to load in or refresh. The Flash player puts a friendly face on the browser and hides the communication with the server from the user. In addition, Flash can maintain session state within the Flash player.

Flash MX interfaces are not limited to simple HTML form elements. Flash MX ships with some standard controls (new in Flash MX) that can be extended to provide all sorts of new functionality. A second set of controls is available from the Macromedia Web site, and third parties are developing more advanced controls.

The Flash experience that we discuss in this chapter is the client/server architecture without all the flashy graphics and animations. This communication is best done with Macromedia's own technologies, ColdFusion MX and JRun 4, but we also cover the methods available to other server-side technologies as well.

 Some knowledge of Macromedia Flash MX and ActionScript is assumed in this chapter. The intention is to provide information on using the Macromedia technologies together, but we are assuming you are somewhat familiar with Flash MX.

Tools

HTML is easy to use for simple client/server applications. The HTML language contains quite a few user interface elements that everyone has grown accustomed to using: text fields, list boxes, check boxes, and radio buttons to name a few. One of the problems with HTML is that the set of controls is fairly limited. You can spice them up with CSS styles, or you can "fake" the functionality of more complex objects by using DHTML (such as tree controls), but HTML at its core is a limited markup language intended for simple two-step communication. With HTML, the user fills in the form fields and then clicks a Submit button. The data is sent to the server, and a new page loads in.

Flash has a completely different approach. When you submit a form from a Flash movie, the page typically does not have to be refreshed and new pages don't have to be loaded in. The communication takes place seamlessly behind the scenes.

The object-based approach of Flash MX brings the ease-of-use of HTML to the Flash environment by adding UI Components to the Flash developer's arsenal.

UI Components

UI Components are the Flash equivalents of the standard HTML elements that everybody is familiar with. The standard set (shown in Figure 28-2) consists of the following elements:

- CheckBox
- ListBox
- RadioButton

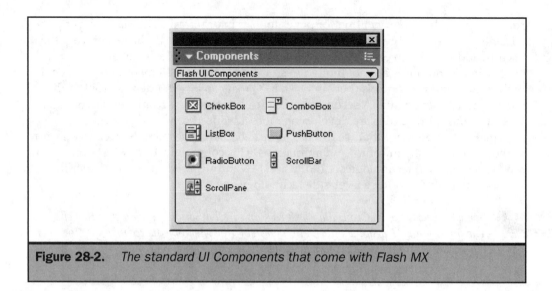

Figure 28-2. *The standard UI Components that come with Flash MX*

- ScrollPane
- ComboBox
- PushButton
- ScrollBar

In addition, you can create a simple text field by using Flash text and setting the Text Type property to Input Text.

Because Flash MX has an object-based approach, you can easily customize these elements. This is something that you can't do easily with HTML. For example, you could customize the ListBox to add color, text styling, or other special effects to the selected elements. When you add functionality to a control, it becomes a completely new control that you can save and reuse.

You can find information on modifying and creating custom UI components at www.macromedia.com/support/flash/applications/creating_comps/.

The UI components also have properties and methods that are similar to the corresponding HTML controls, but allow for many variations. For example, the CheckBox has the following features:

- **onChange** Allows you to define a callback function for *onChange*.
- **Label** Text that appears next to the CheckBox.
- **LabelPlacement** Text can appear on the left or right.

- **getEnabled**   Is the CheckBox enabled?
- **getLabel**   Get the value of the label.
- **getValue**   Get the value of the CheckBox.
- **registerSkinElement**   Allows you to change the look of the element.
- **setChangeHandler**   Set the callback function for the CheckBox.
- **setEnabled**   Set the enabled property of the CheckBox.
- **setLabel**   Set the label of the CheckBox.
- **setLabelPlacement**   Set the placement of the label.
- **setSize**   Set the size of the CheckBox.
- **setStyleProperty**   Set the style of the CheckBox.
- **setValue**   Set the value of the CheckBox.

If you are unfamiliar with Flash and ActionScript, using the UI Components within Flash is a lot like using HTML and JavaScript. ActionScript is based on the ECMAScript specification, which is the same specification that JavaScript is based on.

UI Components Set 2

Corresponding with the release of Flash MX, Macromedia released a second set of UI Components, which is available from the Macromedia Exchange (www.macromedia. com/exchange). The components are fully documented—go to Window | Component Help—UI Set 2.

The second set of components (shown in Figure 28-3) gives the Web developer a core set of advanced controls that allow for a more refined user experience. These controls are essential to using Flash for sophisticated client/server interaction. The controls are as follows:

- Calendar
- IconButton
- ProgressBar
- ScrollBar
- SplitView
- Tree
- DraggablePane
- MessageBox
- PushButton
- ScrollPane
- Ticker

ADVANCED DATA
INTEGRATION

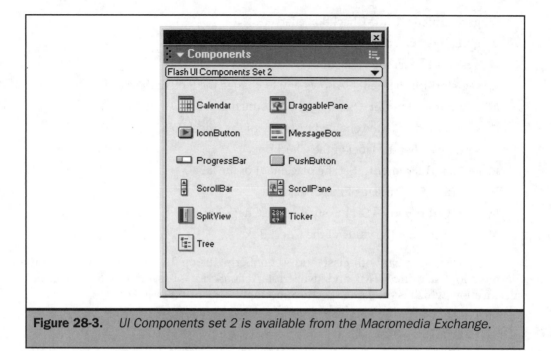

Figure 28-3.   *UI Components set 2 is available from the Macromedia Exchange.*

These controls are also very easy to use, and you can extend them to create new controls as well.

Charting Components

Creating a chart or a graph in HTML is possible, but it's not easy. The best option for presenting a chart to the end user is to use Flash. Macromedia has released a set of components that make it easy to create custom charts and graphs that can be dynamically generated by server-side code that you create. You can download the components from the Macromedia Exchange (www.macromedia.com/exchange), and you should consider them essential to your Web tools arsenal. The chart types that are available are the following:

- Line charts
- Bar charts
- Pie charts

These types of charts have been available to ColdFusion users as part of the ColdFusion language beginning with ColdFusion 5, but now you can use these custom Flash components with any server platform by utilizing some of the client/server techniques available in Flash MX.

Using Dreamweaver for ActionScript Programming

When you are building Flash MX interfaces, the Dreamweaver environment is the logical place to do your ActionScript coding. Dreamweaver offers color-coding of ActionScript keywords, code insight, and code completion. In addition, you can download ActionScript reference books developed by third parties that extend the Dreamweaver Reference panel. The ActionScript reference book was developed by Waldo Smeets and is available from www.udzone.com. The Dreamweaver environment is more suited to scripting than the Flash environment. By coding your ActionScript in Dreamweaver, you can take advantage of all of the great Dreamweaver tools and functionality, such as the multiple document interface, toolbars, and Snippets.

You can include an external ActionScript file into your movie with a line like this:

```
#include "scripts/myFunctions.as"
```

The *include* directive will insert the code into your Flash movie upon publishing. The path in the *#include* directive should be a relative path from the .fla file to your ActionScript file.

In addition, you can export and import your ActionScript code from a Flash movie from the Actions panel pop-up menu (shown in Figure 28-4). The menu is located on the far right edge of the Actions bar.

Using Get and Post

Flash MX is a groundbreaking application. Before Flash MX, a Flash programmer had to work with many limitations. The Flash application interface didn't provide standard user-interface elements for use in your Flash movies, and the client to server communication was done with simple name/value pairs of variables or with XML that had to be transformed on the client and on the server, literally eating up processing time as it did so.

 Working with name/value pairs and XML are still the best methods to use if you aren't working with ColdFusion MX, ASP.NET, Websphere, or JRun 4. Flash MX is optimized for these methods much better than Flash 5 was, however.

Where Flash MX really shines is in the native communication with ColdFusion MX and JRun 4 servers. The Macromedia Flash Player 6 can play movies created in Flash MX that take advantage of new functionality. The Flash Remoting components allow direct communication between the Flash 6 movie and the server. In addition, the Flash Remoting components are being released for ASP.NET and Websphere as well. Flash Remoting will be discussed later in the chapter, in the section "Flash Remoting."

ADVANCED DATA
INTEGRATION

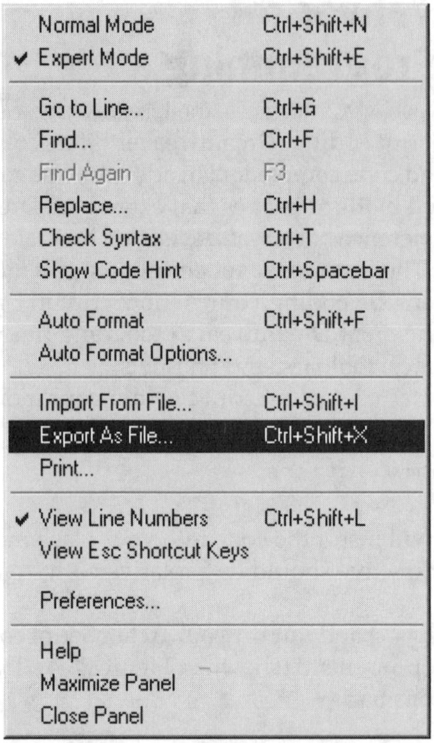

Normal Mode	Ctrl+Shift+N
✔ Expert Mode	Ctrl+Shift+E
Go to Line...	Ctrl+G
Find...	Ctrl+F
Find Again	F3
Replace...	Ctrl+H
Check Syntax	Ctrl+T
Show Code Hint	Ctrl+Spacebar
Auto Format	Ctrl+Shift+F
Auto Format Options...	
Import From File...	Ctrl+Shift+I
Export As File...	Ctrl+Shift+X
Print...	
✔ View Line Numbers	Ctrl+Shift+L
View Esc Shortcut Keys	
Preferences...	
Help	
Maximize Panel	
Close Panel	

Figure 28-4. *The Popup menu in Flash MX allows you to export your script to an external file.*

There are methods available that work with older Flash players and other server technologies. The most basic form of Flash/server interaction is done via HTTP using *Get* and *Post*.

Get

The Flash ActionScript programmer has a few methods at his or her disposal of dealing with incoming data from a server. A simple line like this in a Flash movie can retrieve variables from the server:

```
loadVariables("http://www.bettergig.com/login.php", _root.isLogged, GET);
```

That works in Flash 5 as well as Flash MX. The domain that you are retrieving variables from has to be the same domain that your page is served from. This could be considered a limitation, but it was actually put in place for security reasons. Also, the path specified has to be a full path to the page.

In Flash MX, a new object-based approach is recommended that will work with all server models, and is much easier to use. The *LoadVars()* object takes the functionality of *loadVariables* and abstracts it into an easy-to-use object with methods that give you easy access to the variables. You can utilize *LoadVars* like this example (the Example 1 files that you can find at www.osborne.com), which loads two variables named *username* and *serverTime*:

```
function onSubmit() {
  //instantiate the LoadVars object
  var myMessage = new LoadVars();
  //initialize two properties (our variables)
  myMessage.username = "";
  myMessage.serverTime = "";
  //define an onLoad handler function, named handleReply
  myMessage.onLoad = handleReply;
  //load the server-side script (substitute your own domain and path)
  myMessage.load("http://www.bettergig.com/flash/example1.cfm","",GET);
}
//handle the reply from the server with this function
function handleReply(success) {
  if (success) { //communication with the server was successful
    //the success parameter is the result of the communication
    greeting_txt.text = "Hello, ";
    greeting_txt.text += this.username;
    greeting_txt.text += ". The server time is ";
    greeting_txt.text += this.serverTime;
  } else { //communication with the server failed
    greeting_txt.text = "There was a problem communicating with the server";
  }
}
```

Note   *For a brief explanation of object-oriented programming, see the box in Chapter 31 titled "Object-Oriented Programming in Dreamweaver MX."*

The *onSubmit* function is fired when the user clicks the Submit button. The function creates the *LoadVars* object (named *myMessage*) and sets two variables: *username* and *serverTime*. The variables are initialized to empty values. You can see that the *LoadVars* object is easy to use because you can address the variables within the object with simple dot notation. Next, the *onLoad* callback function is declared. That involves simply using dot notation once again to name the function:

```
myMessage.onLoad = handleReply;
```

Finally, the *load* method of the *LoadVars* object is invoked, and the variables are loaded in from the server. When using the *LoadVars* object, the default HTTP method that is used is *Post* unless you specify *Get*.

The *handleReply* function handles the response from the server. If the communication with the server was successful, the *success* variable will be set to true. Then we simply use the variables that were retrieved to write the text to the Flash movie. If the communication failed, an error message is written to the movie.

The *Get* method of sending and retrieving data from the server is utilized by using the *text/html* standard MIME header. You can accomplish this in your server-side script by setting the MIME header before sending the data back to the client browser, or by simply leaving off the header, because text/html is the default. It is good practice to specify the header in your scripts when you are communicating with Flash to differentiate the *Get* method from the *Post* method.

It is up to the server-side code to supply the correct values that the Flash player is expecting. The following code will supply two variables named *username* and *serverTime* to the Flash movie (note that we are hard-coding the username variable, but it could have just as easily come from a session variable or from the database). Notice that the content type is set to text/html and the *serverTime* variable is set equal to the actual time on the server:

ColdFusion

```
<cfsetting enablecfoutputonly="YES">
<cfcontent type = "text/html">
<cfset username = URLEncodedFormat("Tom")>
<cfset serverTime = URLEncodedFormat(TimeFormat(now(),"hh:mm:ss"))>
<cfset sendToFlash = "&username=#username#&serverTime=#serverTime#">
<cfoutput>#sendToFlash#</cfoutput>
```

PHP

```
<?php
header("Content-Type: text/html");
$username = urlencode("Tom");
$serverTime = urlencode(strftime("%I:%M:%S"));
$sendToFlash = "&username=$username&serverTime=$serverTime";
echo $sendToFlash;
?>
```

ASP VBScript

```
<%
Response.AddHeader "Content-Type","text/html"
```

```
username = Server.URLEncode("Tom")
serverTime = Server.URLEncode(Time)
sendToFlash = "&username=" & username & "&serverTime=" & serverTime
Response.Write(sendToFlash)
%>
```

ASP JScript

```
<%@LANGUAGE="JAVASCRIPT"%>
<%
var d = new Date();
var seconds = d.getSeconds()< 10? "0" + d.getSeconds():d.getSeconds();
var minutes = d.getMinutes()< 10? "0" + d.getMinutes():d.getMinutes();
var hours = d.getHours()< 10? "0" + d.getHours():d.getHours();
var theTime = hours + ":" + minutes + ":" + seconds;
Response.AddHeader("Content-Type","text/html");
username = Server.URLEncode("Tom");
serverTime = Server.URLEncode(theTime);
sendToFlash = "&username=" + username + "&serverTime=" + serverTime;
Response.Write(sendToFlash);
%>
```

ASP.NET VB

```
<%@ Page Language="VB" ContentType="text/html" %>
<%
Dim username, serverTime, sendToFlash
username = Server.URLEncode("Tom")
serverTime = Server.URLEncode(TimeValue(Now))
sendToFlash = "&username=" & username & "&serverTime=" & serverTime
Response.Write(sendToFlash)
%>
```

ASP.NET CSharp

```
<%@ Page Language="C#" ContentType="text/html" %>
<%
string username = Server.UrlEncode("Tom");
string serverTime = Server.UrlEncode(DateTime.Now.ToLongTimeString());
string sendToFlash = "&username=" + username + "&serverTime=" + serverTime;
Response.Write(sendToFlash);
%>
```

JSP

```
<%@ page contentType="text/html"
language="java" import="java.util.*, java.text.*" %>
<%
SimpleDateFormat formatter = new SimpleDateFormat("hh:mm:ss a");
Date d = new Date();
String theTime = formatter.format(d);
String username = response.encodeURL("Tom");
String serverTime = response.encodeURL(theTime);
String sendToFlash = "&username=" + username + "&serverTime=" + serverTime;
out.println(sendToFlash);
%>
```

The *Get* method in Flash communication suffers from the same limitations as the *Get* method in a standard HTML page. The size limitation varies among different browsers, but is usually between 1,000 and 2,000 characters. Also, the *Get* method is limited to ASCII characters. For most Flash communication you'll want to use the *Post* method.

Post

The *Post* method is the default method of communication when using the *LoadVars* object, or the *loadVariables* function of ActionScript. *Post* is more secure than *Get*, doesn't have the size limitation, and can also be used to transmit more complex objects. The *Post* method uses a MIME type of *application/x-www-form-urlencoded* or *application/x-www-urlencoded*. You should specify these in your server script.

To demonstrate the *Post* method, we'll modify the previous example to show two-way communication between the Flash player and the server. We'll remove the server time functionality and add a new element to it: a text field to allow the user to enter a username. We'll also add simple server-side validation that will allow only alphabetic characters. Here is the ActionScript for the simple Flash movie:

```
function onSubmit() {
  var send_data = new LoadVars(); //outgoing form data
  var myMessage = new LoadVars(); //incoming POST data
  myMessage.username = "";
  myMessage.validated = 0;
  myMessage.onLoad = handleReply;
  send_data.username = username_txt.htmlText
  send_data.sendAndLoad("http://127.0.0.1/flash/example2.asp",
    myMessage, POST);
}
function handleReply(success) {
```

```
   if (success) {
     if(this.validated) {
       greeting_txt.text = "Hello, ";
       greeting_txt.text += this.username;
       greeting_txt.text += ".";
     } else {
       greeting_txt.text = "Please Enter a valid username";
       username_txt.htmlText = "";
     }
   } else {
     greeting_txt.text = "There was a problem communicating with the server";
   }
 }
```

The ActionScript code is similar to what was used in the previous example for the *Get* method. This time, however, we use two *LoadVars* objects. The first (*send_data*) is set up for the post to the server page. It will contain the value of one form element in the Flash movie. The second *LoadVars* object is *myMessage*, which is set up the same way as it was in the previous example. This time, however, we will use the *sendAndLoad* method of the *LoadVars* object:

```
send_data.sendAndLoad("http://127.0.0.1/flash/example2.asp",
   myMessage,POST);
```

This method will send the values in the *send_data* object that we set up, but will also load any incoming values into the *myMessage* object (the second parameter).

The *handleReply* function is similar to the version used in the previous example with one exception: We are now testing an incoming variable named *validated*. If the value is 0, the function displays a message to the user ("Please Enter a valid username"). If the value is 1, the form submission was successful and the values are displayed to the page.

Now we'll look at the server-side code that will interact with the Flash movie. The following code samples for Example 2 in each server model perform the following steps:

- Content type is set to *application/x-www-form-urlencoded*.

- Variable named *username* is initialized to the incoming Flash form variable.

- Variable named *validated* is set to 1 initially.

- The variable named *username* is checked for all alphabetic characters (this process differs in each server model, but the result is the same).

- If any bad characters are found, the *validated* variable is set to 0.

- The return string is built up and returned to Flash.

ColdFusion

```
<cfsetting enablecfoutputonly="YES">
<cfcontent type = "application/x-www-form-urlencoded">
<cfset username = URLEncodedFormat(form.username)>
<cfset validated = 1>
<cfif REFind("^([a-zA-Z])+$",username) EQ 0>
  <cfset validated = 0>
</cfif>
<cfset sendToFlash = "&username=#username#&validated=#validated#">
<cfoutput>#sendToFlash#</cfoutput>
```

PHP

```
<?php
header("Content-Type: application/x-www-form-urlencoded");
$username = urlencode($_POST["username"]);
$validated = "1";
if (!preg_match("/^([a-zA-Z])+$/",$username)) $validated = 0;
$sendToFlash = "&username=$username&validated=$validated";
echo $sendToFlash;
?>
```

ASP VBScript

```
<%
Response.AddHeader "Content-Type","application/x-www-form-urlencoded"
username = Server.URLEncode(Request.Form("username"))
validated = 1
For i = 1 to Len(username)
  theChar = Asc(UCase(Mid(username,i)))
  If  theChar < 64 OR theChar > 90 Then
    validated = 0
  End If
Next
sendToFlash = "&username=" & username & "&validated=" & validated
Response.Write(sendToFlash)
%>
```

ASP JScript

```
<%@LANGUAGE="JAVASCRIPT"%>
<%
Response.AddHeader("Content-Type","application/x-www-form-urlencoded");
var username = Server.URLEncode(Request.Form("username"));
var validated = 1;
if (!username.match(/^([a-zA-Z])+$/)) validated = 0;
sendToFlash = "&username=" + username + "&validated=" + validated;
Response.Write(sendToFlash);
%>
```

ASP.NET VB

```
<%@ Page Language="VB" ContentType="application/x-www-form-urlencoded" %>
<%
Dim username, validated, sendToFlash
username = Server.URLEncode(Request.Form("username"))
validated = "1"
Dim r As Regex
Dim m As Match
r = new Regex("^([a-zA-Z])+$", RegexOptions.Compiled)
m = r.Match(username)
if Not m.Success Then validated = "0"
sendToFlash = "&username=" & username & "&validated=" & validated
Response.Write(sendToFlash)
%>
```

ASP.NET CSharp

```
<%@ Page Language="C#" ContentType="application/x-www-form-urlencoded"%>
<%
string username = Server.UrlEncode(Request.Form["username"]);
string validated = "1";
Regex r;
Match m;
r = new Regex("^([a-zA-Z])+$", RegexOptions.Compiled);
m = r.Match(username);
if (!m.Success) validated = "0";
string sendToFlash = "&username=" + username + "&validated=" + validated;
Response.Write(sendToFlash);
%>
```

JSP

```
<%@ page contentType="application/x-www-form-urlencoded" %>
<%
String username = response.encodeURL(request.getParameter("username"));
String validated = "1";
if(username.length() < 1) validated = "0";
for (int i=0; i<username.length(); i++) {
  if(!Character.isLetter(username.charAt(i))) validated = "0";
}
String sendToFlash = "&username=" + username + "&validated=" + validated;
out.println(sendToFlash);
%>
```

The user enters a username and clicks the Submit button. The field is sent to the server, which performs validation on the form field. If the validation was successful, the field is sent back to the Flash player (see Figure 28-5). If not, an error message is sent back.

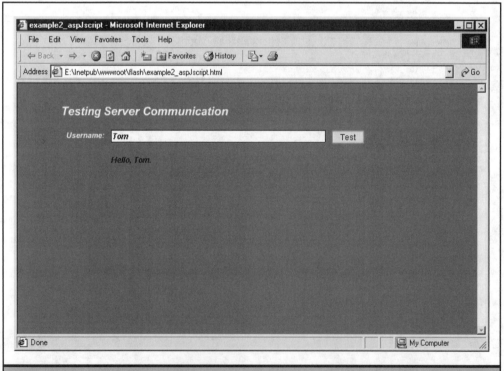

Figure 28-5. *The Flash player communicates seamlessly with your server-side code.*

This was a very simple example, but the idea is to show how form variables can be sent from Flash to the application server and back again, without refreshing the page or redirecting to another page. Also, you can utilize whatever server functionality you need, such as validating fields, searching databases, sending e-mails, or managing the file system.

Using XML

You can get a lot of mileage out of using *Get* and *Post* with simple variables, but sometimes you need to have more complex client/server interaction in your Web pages. Flash has built-in support for XML that was made even more powerful in Flash MX.

XML is a multipurpose language that allows you to describe your data as you are sending it. It is a tag-based language, like HTML, but it is much more versatile because you create your own tags based on what they contain. For instance, an HTML page will have <html>, <body>, and <head> tags. An XML document might have <firstName>, <lastName>, <address> tags that describe the data that they contain. A typical XML document might look like this:

```
<?xml version="1.0" encoding="iso-8859-1"?>
<myValidation>
     <username>flash</username>
     <password>xml</password>
</myValidation>
```

XML is supported by most server platforms. ASP, for example, has several methods for dealing with XML depending on how you are utilizing it. The MSXML object can be used to create, access, send, or store an XML document. This can be particularly handy for building XML structures on the fly and sending them to the Flash player on the client. The ADO *Recordset* object has methods that allow you to transform data from a database into XML. Other technologies have similar methods for dealing with XML.

The Flash MX XML object is structured similarly to the *LoadVars* object that was used in the previous examples—it has some of the same properties and methods that were used in those examples. There are also many properties and methods of the object that you can use to parse, create, load, or send XML documents.

The *sendAndLoad* method is similar to the *sendAndLoad* method that was used for the *LoadVars* object in the second example. After you create an XML document structure in your Flash movie, the *sendAndLoad* method allows you to send the document to a server-side script (which can be used by any server technology), which in turn processes the XML document and returns another XML document. You should set up your Flash movie to parse and act on the XML that it receives.

The following is a very simple ActionScript code listing (Example 3 from www.osborne.com) that will take a username and password entered by a user, build an XML document using the values, send it to the server, and display a message signaling a successful or failed login attempt. The XML document was built as a string to keep things simple for the example, but it could have been built dynamically by the Flash movie as well:

```
// ActionScript Document
function onSubmit () {
  // set up a new XML object
  var returnXML = new XML();
  // remove white space from the xml
  returnXML.ignoreWhite = true;
  // set the callback function for the response from the server
  returnXML.onLoad = handleReply;
  // create an XML string
  // form fields are replaced in the string
  var my_xml = '<?xml version="1.0" encoding="iso-8859-1"?>';
  my_xml += '<myValidation>';
  my_xml += '<username>' + username + '</username>';
  my_xml += '<password>' + password + '</password>';
  my_xml += '</myValidation>';
  var flash_xml_object = new XML(my_xml)
  // create an XML object to send to the server
  // send it to the server and then load it into the myXML object
  flash_xml_object.sendAndLoad("http://127.0.0.1/flash/example3.cfm",
  returnXML);
}

function handleReply(success) {
  if(success) { //the server communication was successful
    if(this.firstChild.attributes.logged == "1"){ //login was successful
      greeting = "Hello " + this.firstChild.attributes.username;
      greeting += ". Login was successful";
    } else {
      greeting = "Login failed";
    }
  } else {
    greeting = "There was a communication failure.";
  }
}
```

The Flash movie (shown in Figure 28-6) has username and password fields that you can fill out. The script to supply the successful login XML is shown here for ColdFusion:

```
<cfset my_xml = XMLParse(URLDecode(GetHttpRequestData().content))>
<cfset username = my_xml.myValidation.username.xmltext>
<cfset password = my_xml.myValidation.password.xmltext>
```

```
<cfset logged = "1">
<cfif username NEQ "flash" or password NEQ "xml">
  <cfset logged = "0">
</cfif>
<cfset returnXML = "<return username=""" & username>
<cfset returnXML = returnXML & """ logged=""" & logged & """ />">
<cfoutput>#returnXML#</cfoutput>
```

There is a lot more to XML communication than we were able to cover here, but hopefully the preceding example is enough to show you the basic principle.

Flash communication using XML is available to any server technology that can parse XML. The ColdFusion example is shown here for simplicity, but other methods can be utilized for ASP, JSP, PHP, or ASP.NET.

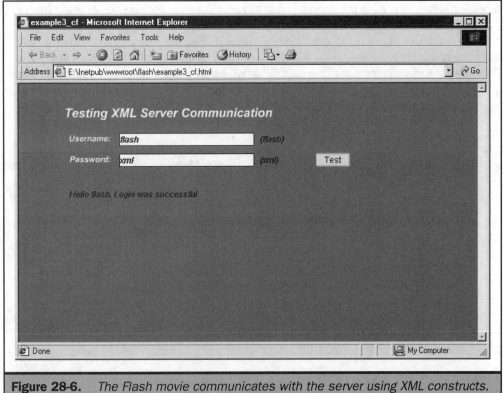

Figure 28-6.   *The Flash movie communicates with the server using XML constructs.*

Flash Remoting

The most exciting new functionality in Flash MX, ColdFusion MX, and Dreamweaver MX is the Flash Remoting service. Flash Remoting is preinstalled on a ColdFusion MX server or a JRun 4 server. In addition, you can use an ASP.NET component to utilize Flash Remoting from an ASP.NET application, or a Java class is available to allow you to use Flash Remoting from a J2EE server. You can download the component from the Macromedia site and install it on your server. Once installed, Flash MX movies can communicate with the server natively.

> **Note** *You can download Flash Remoting components at www.macromedia.com/software/ flash/flashremoting/. As of this writing, the ASP.NET and Java Flash Remoting services were in beta and not available yet. JRun 4 and ColdFusion MX have Flash Remoting pre-installed.*

Flash Remoting offers many advantages over the other methods, such as using XML and *LoadVars* objects. Because the server component can communicate directly with the Flash movie, more complex objects can be transferred, such as structures and recordsets. Also, because the server contains functionality that can be accessed directly, the Flash code can be more concise. Recordsets can be loaded into Flash movies using a new *Recordset* object of Flash, making it easy to sort and page through results directly from the client browser. Also, *DataGlue* is a new set of functions that allows you to bind Flash user interface elements to the data. Flash Remoting also offers debugging of client- and server-side code using the NetConnect debugger. With all of these new features, Web programming has finally come of age.

To utilize Flash Remoting services, you have to follow these general steps in your Flash movie:

- Include the Flash Remoting classes located in NetServices.as in your movie. If you are going to utilize *DataGlue*, include the DataGlue.as classes as well.
- Define any event handlers you might need.
- Connect to the URL where your Flash Remoting service lives.
- Create the connection.
- Create the service object.
- Call any service functions that you are utilizing.

We'll go through a simple example in ColdFusion MX. First, we'll use Dreamweaver MX to build a ColdFusion Component (CFC) to search the Bettergig database. Then, we'll write a simple ActionScript in Flash MX to utilize the CFC and display the result to the user.

Creating the ColdFusion Component

ColdFusion Components are at the heart of the new Flash Remoting capabilities for ColdFusion MX. Dreamweaver MX allows you to build a ColdFusion component visually from the Components panel.

1. Open the Create Component dialog box by clicking the plus sign on the Components panel, which will bring up this dialog box:

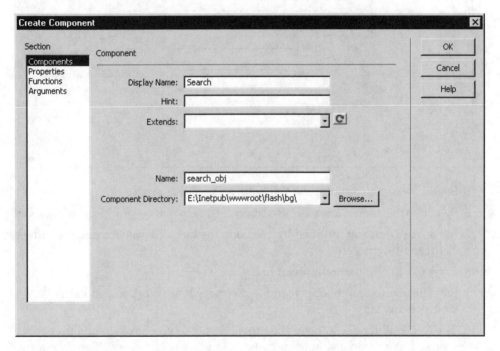

2. Name the component **search_obj**.
3. Navigate to a directory on your server for the Component Directory.

4. Skip the Properties page and move to the Functions page. Add one function and name it **getSearchResult**.

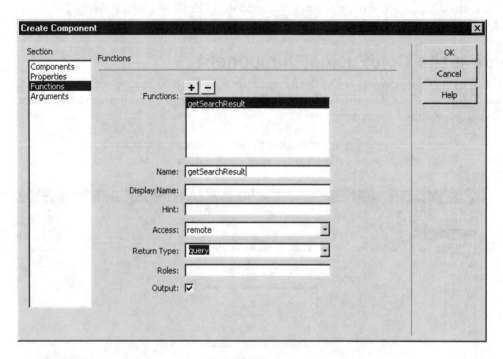

5. Set the Access to remote, and the Return Type to query.

6. Switch to the Arguments tab and add an argument named *searchField* of type *string*.

7. Make the argument required by checking the box and give it a default value of % (percent sign).

8. Click OK to add the component to the page.

9. Save the file as **search_obj.cfc** in the directory that you specified in the Components tab.

10. The CFC builder doesn't add the function body—you have to code that yourself. We'll add a simple query here, in place of the *<!--- getSearchResult body --->* placeholder:

```
<cfquery name="rsGetJobs"
 datasource="bettergig">
SELECT JobDescription, EmpName
FROM Jobs INNER JOIN Employers
ON Employers.EmpID = Jobs.EmpID
WHERE JobDescription LIKE '%#searchField#%'
</cfquery>
```

11. Make the return value a query value, by modifying the <cfreturn> tag like this:

```
<cfreturn rsGetJobs>
```

12. Save the page again. The return value will be the entire query, which will be able to be displayed by the client that calls the function, which in this case will be the Flash player. The component is finished, and it's time to move to Flash MX.

Adding the Flash ActionScript

In Flash MX, we've created a simple interface with a text field named *search_txt* to supply the argument to the searchField parameter of the CFC and a submit button. Also, there is a dynamic text element on the page that will display the result from the search. We'll simply display the number of records returned.

The ActionScript will be simple as well:

```
//required include file for Flash Remoting
#include "NetServices.as"
if (connected == null) {
//init just one time to set the connection to the service
//variable named connected will be a global variable
  connected = true;
//the gateway url needs to be established
  NetServices.setDefaultGatewayUrl
  ("http://127.0.0.1:8100/flashservices/gateway");
//the connection needs to be set up
//my_conn uses the _conn naming convention to enable code hints
  var my_conn = NetServices.createGatewayConnection();
//myService is the actual CFC that we created in Dreamweaver MX
  var myService = my_conn.getService("search_obj",this);
}
submit_btn.onRelease = function() {
    myService.getSearchResults(search_txt.text);
}
function getSearchResults_Result(result) {
//set a variable to the results of the call to the component
  var theRecordset_rs = result;
//display the result
  results = "There were " + theRecordset_rs.getLength;
  results += " records returned."
}
```

| Note | *The NetServices.setDefaultGatewayUrl method requires the path to your server. In the above example, the local 127.0.0.1 IP address was used.* |

The results of any call from a Flash movie to a method on the server will be available from the *[method name]_Result* function. In this case, the getSearchResult_ Result function. Another function is available as well for checking the status of the transaction between the Flash movie and the server—*[method name]_Status*. That wasn't utilized here to keep things simple, but can be utilized to check for successful or failed communication.

Displaying the Results

The previous example was a very simple example, but we can use the same ColdFusion Component and create a more complex Flash movie that will actually display the results of the search and allow the user to page through the resultset with first, previous, next, and last buttons. To create the movie, we've simply added a few more dynamic text elements that will display the results to the user, and a few more lines of ActionScript. Here is the ActionScript:

```
// ActionScript Document
#include "NetServices.as"
if (connected == null) {
  connected = true;
  NetServices.setDefaultGatewayUrl("http://127.0.0.1/flashservices/gateway");
  //my_conn uses the _conn naming convention to enable Flash coding hints
  var my_conn = NetServices.createGatewayConnection();
  var myService = my_conn.getService("search_obj", this);
  var theRecordset_rs = null;
  var recNum = 0;
  var recLength = 0;
}
submit_btn.onRelease = function() {
  //send the text of the search field to the service
  myService.getSearchResult_(search_txt.text);
}
function getSearchResult_Result(result_rs) {
  theRecordset_rs = result_rs;
  recLength = theRecordset_rs.getLength();
  results_txt.text = "There were " + recLength + " records returned.";
  firstRecord();
}
function getRecord() {
  if (recLength == 0) {
    description_txt.text = "";
    empname_txt.text = "";
    recordnumber_txt.text = "No records";
  } else {
    description_txt.text = theRecordset_rs.items[recNum].JobDescription;
```

```
    empname_txt.text = theRecordset_rs.items[recNum].EmpName;
    recordnumber_txt.text = "Rec. No. "+(recNum+1)+" of "+recLength;
  }
}
function nextRecord() {
  recNum++;
  if (recNum >= recLength) {
    recNum = recLength-1;
  }
  getRecord();
}
function previousRecord() {
  recNum--;
  if (recNum<0) {
    recNum = 0;
  }
  getRecord();
}
function firstRecord() {
  recNum = 0;
  getRecord();
}
function lastRecord() {
  recNum = recLength-1;
  getRecord();
}
```

The connection function is virtually identical to the previous example, except that we are initializing a couple of global variables to hold the current record number and the length of the recordset. The *getSearchResults_Result* function once again packs the resultset into a variable, but this time the resultset is displayed. *getRecord()* is a general-purpose function to show the current record. The four functions correspond to the OnClick events of the first, previous, next, and last buttons are *firstRecord*, *previousRecord*, *nextRecord*, and *lastRecord*. The Flash movie will load a new recordset each time the user hits the submit button—the client/server interaction is completely transparent to the user. The completed movie is shown in Figure 28-7.

ASP.NET Flash Remoting

Flash Remoting for ASP.NET can be utilized with Web Services built using ASP.NET or you can access ASP.NET pages directly. The main difference in the ActionScript that was utilized for ColdFusion is the connection method. For ColdFusion, the connection was like this:

```
NetServices.setDefaultGatewayUrl("http://127.0.0.1:8100/flashservices/
gateway");
```

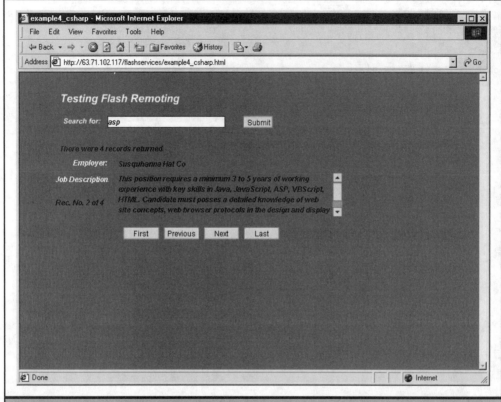

Figure 28-7.   *The Flash movie acts as a search/results interface to the database.*

For ASP.NET, you can create the connection like this:

```
NetServices.setDefaultGatewayUrl("http://127.0.0.1/flashservices/
gateway.aspx");
```

The difference is the .aspx at the end of the URL. The ASP.NET implementation is in the form of a dll named flashgateway.dll that resides on the server. The Flash Remoting installation places this dll in the [Web root]\flashservices\bin folder. You should copy this dll to the bin folder in your ASP.NET application. The following lines will need to go into your web.config file as well:

```
<httpModules>
  <add name="GatewayController"
```

```
type="FlashGateway.Controller.GatewayController,flashgateway" />
</httpModules>
```

After the server is set up in this way, you can utilize the Flash Remoting service by placing custom tags into your ASP.NET page. The tag and namespace need to be registered first:

```
<%@ Register TagPrefix="MyTag" Namespace="FlashGateway"
 Assembly="flashgateway" %>
```

After doing that, you can use the tag in your page to establish the connection from the server-side page to Flash:

```
<MyTag:Flash ID="Flash" Runat="server" />
```

The Flash movie from the previous example can be utilized in an ASP.NET script. The ColdFusion version utilized a CFC named search_obj. For the ASP.NET version, you can create a folder named search_obj and place a file in it called getSearchResults.aspx. The getSearchResults.aspx page will have a simple query on the page set up as a DataSet. To create the aspx page, follow these steps in Dreamweaver:

1. Create a new C# page.
2. Create a DataSet named getJobs using this SQL:

   ```
   SELECT JobDescription, EmpName
   FROM dbo.Jobs INNER JOIN  dbo.Employers  ON Employers.empid = Jobs.empid
   WHERE JobDescription LIKE ?
   ```

3. Add a parameter to the SQL: QueryString variable named JobDescription.
4. Click OK and apply it to the page.
5. Modify the parameter in Code View by modifying the code. Change the Parameter tag to read like this:

   ```
   <Parameter  Name="@JobDescription"  Value='<%# "%" +
   Flash.Params[0].ToString() + "%" %>'  Type="VarChar"   />
   ```

6. Add the registration for the Flash tag at the top of the page:

   ```
   <%@ Register TagPrefix="MyTag" Namespace="FlashGateway"
    Assembly="flashgateway" %>
   ```

7. Add the Flash tag after the DataSet:

   ```
   <MyTag:Flash ID="Flash" DataSource="<%# getJobs.DefaultView %>"
    Runat="Server" />
   ```

8. Save the page as getSearchResults.aspx.

ADVANCED DATA
INTEGRATION

Now if you publish the Flash movie and browse the page, you should be able to search the database using the Flash movie, and also page through any results using the First, Previous, Next, and Last buttons.

Most Flash Remoting in ASP.NET would be built using Code Behind, but this is just a simple example. It also shows that a Flash movie that was built for interaction with a ColdFusion script can be used virtually untouched in an ASP.NET implementation. You could also easily create a JRun or Websphere application that would utilize this same process.

For more information on Flash Remoting, consult the developer's section of the Macromedia Web site at www.macromedia.com/desdev.

Using Server-Side ActionScript

Server-side ActionScript allows the Flash programmer to store scripts on the server and communicate directly with the ColdFusion MX server, for Flash programmers who might not want to learn a new technology. The server-side ActionScript file will become a service to the client-side Flash movie.

There are two new additions to the ActionScript language for server-side coding:

- **CF.query**   Access the ColdFusion query object just as you would in ColdFusion using the <cfquery> tag

- **CF.http**   Access HTTP methods (*post* and *get*) just as you would with the <cfhttp> tag.

You can create server-side ActionScript files in Dreamweaver MX (or any text editor) and save them with an .asr file extension (ActionScript Remote). The ASR file resides on the server in a directory that will become part of the service name. For example, if the filename is *getAllJobs* in the *bettergig* directory, you would reference it as *bettergig.getAllJobs* in your client-side ActionScript. The client-side ActionScript for this service might look this:

```
#include "NetServices.as"
NetServices.setDefaultGatewayUrl("http://127.0.0.1:8100/flashservices/gateway");
my_conn = NetServices.createGatewayConnection();
myService = my_conn.getService("bettergig.getAllJobs",this);
```

After doing that, you will be able to access any of the functions in that server-side .asr file directly from the client by using the myService object with dot notation. A function named *getMyResults* might be called like this:

var theResults = myService.getMyResults('searchfield');

For more information on ASR files, consult the developer's section of the Macromedia Web site (www.macromedia.com/desdev).

Summary

Flash MX and Dreamweaver MX can be looked at as competing products if you are talking about HTML interfaces versus Flash interfaces, but in the grand scheme of the Web, you should use the best tool for the job. In many ways, Flash MX opens up new opportunities for Web developers to augment their toolsets. Flash MX and Dreamweaver MX can be complementary tools, and you can use them both to communicate with your server-side code on whichever platform you decide to work with. Admittedly, Flash MX is ideally suited for ColdFusion development with extra functionality built into the ColdFusion server and the Flash MX development environment, but there are also numerous ways for Flash MX to communicate with any server technology out there.

The Complete Reference

Dreamweaver MX

Chapter 29

E-Commerce with Dreamweaver MX

The buzzword on everybody's lips these days is "e-commerce." You can't turn on the radio or television without hearing about a company's e-commerce or transaction capabilities on their Web site. Everybody's doing it, but what exactly is it? What is an e-store?

Simply put, when you buy something from a Web site, you are conducting an electronic-commerce, or *e-commerce*, transaction. It could be as simple as buying a book from Amazon.com or as complex as procuring fighter jets in an auction at Exostar.com. These Web sites are considered *e-stores* because they provide a *virtual* storefront where you enable the exchange of goods or services. The only difference is that you can sit in the comfort of your own home while you shop.

The e-store has to operate under the same principles as a regular store. It must be able to provide merchandise, keep inventories, conduct transactions, and ship merchandise to the customers. Of course, many of these functions are often outsourced to other companies. For instance, a third party could take care of your credit card transactions, and the actual inventory could come from somewhere else—even from your own hard drive, if you are selling software.

Typically, an e-store is based on a shopping cart model. A shopping cart is usually nothing more than a cookie, variable structure, or database that stores the items a user has selected. When UltraDev was first released, there was a lot of clamor for a shopping cart. The product that UltraDev was replacing, Drumbeat 2000, had e-commerce capability built into the program. Many people looked at UltraDev as a downgrade rather than an upgrade, because of its lack of basic e-commerce functionality. The UltraDev Shopping Cart was released shortly thereafter. Our first edition focused on that shopping cart.

Since that time, however, several shopping carts have been introduced which are much more advanced than the original cart. This chapter outlines the basic functionalities of a shopping cart–based e-store using the general concepts that are inherent to most of the shopping carts on the market.

The Shopping Cart

A *shopping cart* is simply a place where data can be stored while a transaction is in progress. Just like a real shopping cart in a store, it holds the items for you until you check out. The typical shopping scenario involves a person going to a Web site, choosing items to buy from the site, adding items to a shopping cart, and then checking out. The typical shopping cart extension for Dreamweaver MX automates the process of getting the product information from the database and storing it in the temporary cart on the user's machine in preparation for the transaction.

The cart contents are maintained for a predefined length of time, so that if the user decides to leave and then come back, his or her cart will still contain the same merchandise. This is generally done through the use of cookies stored on the user's machine. The server can read the cookie whenever the user comes back to the site, and the cart will be repopulated with the items that were originally in it by retrieving the values from the cookie and then reconstructing the contents of the cart. A typical e-store will allow the user to maintain the contents of the cart anywhere from 30 days to an indefinite period of time. Because the user's machine is the storage facility for the cart, running out of storage space is never a concern.

One of the downsides of a cookie-based cart system is that the user could have cookies turned off. For that reason, many cart systems also store the cart info in server memory while the user is at the site. Only upon leaving the site will the contents of the cart be cleared.

ASP sessions will not be usable if the user has cookies turned off, and for that reason, it is wise to implement a temporary cart system in your database as well, to mimic the session systems of PHP or ColdFusion.

The following sections describe some of the third-party shopping cart solutions that are available for Dreamweaver MX and UltraDev.

The UltraDev Shopping Cart

Rick Crawford, formerly of Elemental Software and creator of the Drumbeat shopping cart, created and built through his company, PowerClimb, the original UltraDev Shopping Cart. This cart is available for free from the Macromedia Web site and also from the PowerClimb Web site at www.powerclimb.com.

The UltraDev Shopping Cart was developed to be a limited shopping cart model. It was never intended to be a complete e-store solution—just a shopping cart that can be built upon. Whereas Drumbeat 2000 boasted a complete e-store with credit card transactions through CyberCash, the UltraDev Shopping Cart is a more basic foundation on which to develop an e-store.

The UltraDev Shopping Cart is not entirely compatible with Dreamweaver MX, but can be used with UltraDev 1 and UltraDev 4. It is available as a 1.1 version for ASP, and as a 1.2 beta version for JSP and ColdFusion from the PowerClimb site. There is also an Authorize.Net back-end settlement behavior available from the PowerClimb site, which simplifies sending credit card data.

The UltraDev Shopping Cart menu is shown in Figure 29-1.

UltraCart II

Soon to follow, the UltraCart II was developed by Joe Scavito as an upgrade to the original UltraDev Shopping Cart. Joe developed some of the patches to the original UltraDev Shopping Cart that allowed the extension to be used with UltraDev 4, and then later expanded on it and created a brand new cart system for ASP. The UltraCart II goes far beyond the original cart implementation. Figure 29-2 shows the Server Behaviors available with the UltraCart II. The UltraCart II is an ASP-only solution available for JScript and VBScript. It is a cookie-based cart system similar to the original UltraDev Shopping Cart.

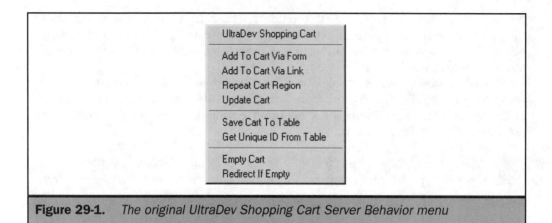

Figure 29-1.   *The original UltraDev Shopping Cart Server Behavior menu*

UltraCart II comes with plenty of examples and documentation, making it very easy to learn and implement. An e-store can be a complex thing, but after you've built your first e-store with the UltraCart II, you'll find that you can utilize the same techniques for other e-store sites as well.

The UltraCart II is available from www.thechocolatestore.com/ultradev.

Intellicart

Intellicart is a product of Tim Green, and is a PHP-only solution that was developed for UltraDev 4 using the PHAkt or ImpAKT server models from www.interakt.ro. Tim is updating the cart to work with Dreamweaver MX as well. Figure 29-3 shows the Intellicart Server Behavior menu.

The Intellicart is one of the most flexible and easy-to-use carts on the market. If you are building a PHP e-store, this package will be all you need to implement your site functionality. It contains back-end payment processing Server Behaviors to make it easy to connect to PayPal, Payflow Pro, or Energy Flow.

The Intellicart also contains several server objects that make it even easier to apply than most carts. The server objects create the entire cart display tables, with choices of different themes that are built into the extension (shown in Figure 29-4).

The Intellicart is available at www.rawveg.org.

Charon Cart

The Charon Cart is developed by Julian Roberts, and is an ASP-based solution. It was developed for UltraDev 4 as well, and has been updated for Dreamweaver MX. The cart only works in ASP VBScript as of this writing. This is a great cart for people on a budget because it's free. As a free extension the support is not as robust as with some of the commercial carts, but Julian is one of the top ASP developers in the Dreamweaver and UltraDev communities, and the cart works well.

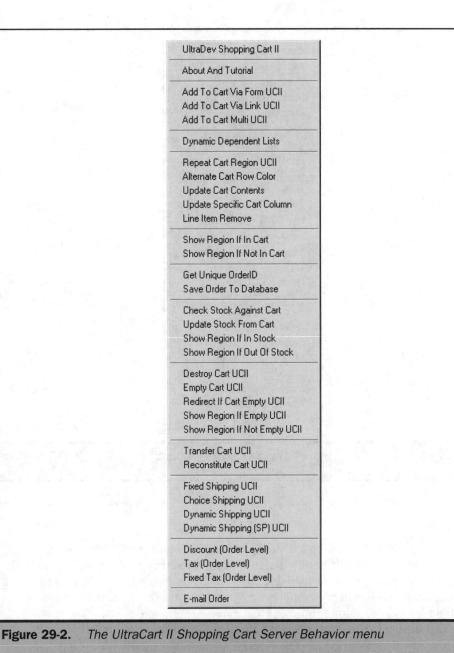

UltraDev Shopping Cart II
About And Tutorial
Add To Cart Via Form UCII Add To Cart Via Link UCII Add To Cart Multi UCII
Dynamic Dependent Lists
Repeat Cart Region UCII Alternate Cart Row Color Update Cart Contents Update Specific Cart Column Line Item Remove
Show Region If In Cart Show Region If Not In Cart
Get Unique OrderID Save Order To Database
Check Stock Against Cart Update Stock From Cart Show Region If In Stock Show Region If Out Of Stock
Destroy Cart UCII Empty Cart UCII Redirect If Cart Empty UCII Show Region If Empty UCII Show Region If Not Empty UCII
Transfer Cart UCII Reconstitute Cart UCII
Fixed Shipping UCII Choice Shipping UCII Dynamic Shipping UCII Dynamic Shipping (SP) UCII
Discount (Order Level) Tax (Order Level) Fixed Tax (Order Level)
E-mail Order

Figure 29-2.   *The UltraCart II Shopping Cart Server Behavior menu*

The Charon Cart menu is shown in Figure 29-5 and is available from www.charon.co.uk.

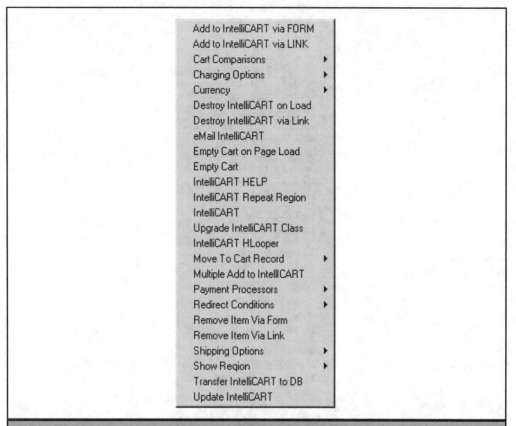

Add to IntelliCART via FORM
Add to IntelliCART via LINK
Cart Comparisons ▸
Charging Options ▸
Currency ▸
Destroy IntelliCART on Load
Destroy IntelliCART via Link
eMail IntelliCART
Empty Cart on Page Load
Empty Cart
IntelliCART HELP
IntelliCART Repeat Region
IntelliCART
Upgrade IntelliCART Class
IntelliCART HLooper
Move To Cart Record ▸
Multiple Add to IntelliCART
Payment Processors ▸
Redirect Conditions ▸
Remove Item Via Form
Remove Item Via Link
Shipping Options ▸
Show Region ▸
Transfer IntelliCART to DB
Update IntelliCART

Figure 29-3. *The Intellicart shopping cart Server Behavior menu*

Cartweaver

Cartweaver is a ColdFusion-based shopping cart solution from Lawrence Cramer. It is implemented a little differently than the other carts. It is implemented as a set of ColdFusion custom tags and is available from the Dreamweaver or UltraDev interface as snippets. Because it is implemented as custom tags and snippets, the cart is also compatible with ColdFusion Studio or Homesite.

The cart is easy to use. It comes as a complete sample store, with full documentation. Because it is ColdFusion-based, it is easily modified.

Cartweaver is available from www.cartweaver.com.

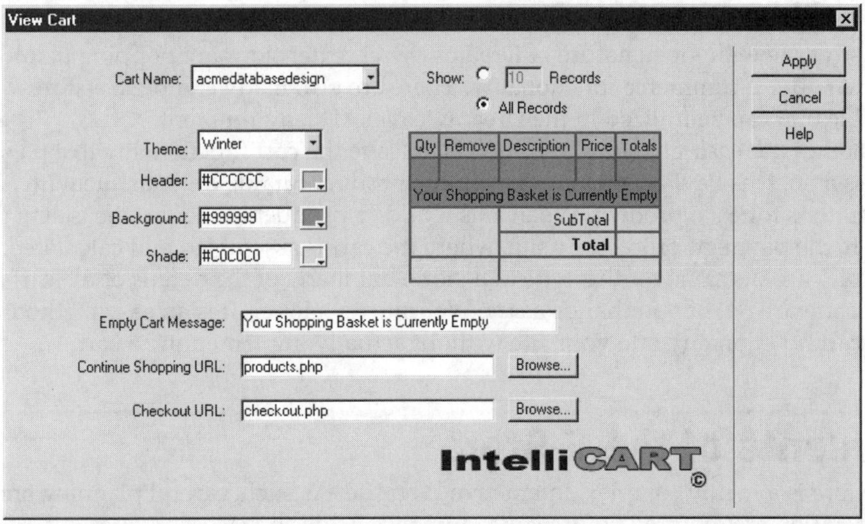

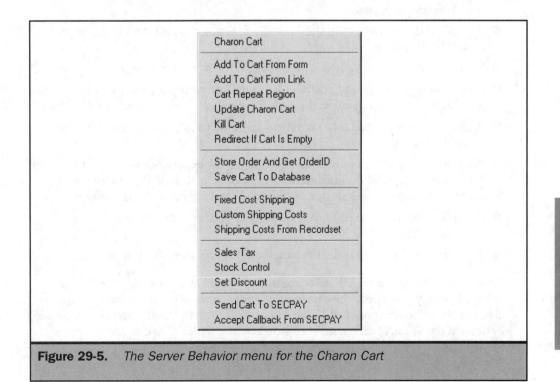

Figure 29-4. *The View Cart server object makes it easy to build cart display pages automatically.*

Figure 29-5. *The Server Behavior menu for the Charon Cart*

Other E-Store Extensions

Because of the wide-open nature of Dreamweaver, extensions are popping up all the time that offer e-commerce functionality. There are also many complete e-stores available that can be utilized in the Dreamweaver MX environment.

Another increasingly popular option is to leave the cart functionality to a payment processor such as PayPal. You implement the product catalog on your site with Add to Cart buttons for each product. When a user adds a product to the cart, he is actually taken to the payment processor's site, where the cart is assembled and calculated. The principles are the same for this type of e-store, but many of the details of the cart and transaction are out of your hands as the Web site developer. It is an easy method to build cart functionality into your site without actually implementing a cart.

Elements of the E-Store

An e-store is a highly complex, interactive Web site. As such, careful planning and consideration are required before you commence its design. Most e-stores will follow a similar structure, though. Typically, you'll have the following pages in your e-commerce site:

- A products overview (or master) page (or series of pages) that lists all products with brief descriptions

- A product detail page, built dynamically for each product, that lists complete details of the product

- A search page that usually ties in to the products overview page

- A cart page, which you typically link to on all of your pages with a View Cart graphic or link, displaying to the user the items that are currently in the cart

- A checkout page or series of pages in which the user is asked to pay for the items purchased

- A signup page, so that a user can personalize his experience by adding relevant purchase or registration information, and oftentimes a login page for visits thereafter, so the user is recognized immediately along with his preferences.

- An order confirmation page, where the user confirms the order before committing to it

- A "thank you" page that displays the details of a successful transaction

Most of the Dreamweaver MX carts are implemented as data sources or Server Behaviors. The way you apply the cart to your site is to choose it from the Bindings panel or Server Behaviors panel and give it the attributes you need—cart name, cookie expiration (in days), cart fields, and computed fields, which you can use to apply computations to a specific field. After you define a cart on one page, the other pages in your site that use the cart will have to have the *identical cart on each page*. For this reason, most of the cart implementations make use of an include file to act as the actual cart. This is to ensure that the structure is identical for the cart throughout the site. If you had a cart on one page that stored a price column, and the cart on the next page didn't have the price column defined, that price column would be lost from all other pages as well. In addition, depending on which cart you are using, not having identical carts can have serious consequences leading to page errors or other more serious problems.

The Cart Server Behaviors

In addition to the data source that is the *actual* cart, you can apply to a page Server Behaviors that will do several different things. Here is a basic rundown of cart Server Behaviors that are fairly consistent among the various cart implementations:

- **Add to Cart Via Form** Adds an item (or items) to the cart by using a form and a Submit button. You can use this Server Behavior if you need to populate a list, for example, and have the user choose an item on the list; or you can use it when the user is allowed to manually insert text into a form field.

- **Add to Cart Via Link** Does the same thing as the Add To Cart Via Form Server Behavior, but will send only the unique product ID number to the next page in a URL variable. Typically, you would use this method if you already have all of the information that is needed (no color or size decisions to make) or if you are implementing a Detail page with a list of items.

- **Repeat Cart Region** Similar to the standard Repeated Region (which won't work with the cart) that you can apply to data from a database, except that it only works with the cart. Typically, you would use this on your View Cart page to display everything that has been put into the cart.

- **Update Cart** For use on a page where you might be changing quantities or changing items. You need to have a form and a text field (or other form field) on the page to use this.

- **Save Cart to Table** Used to save the contents of the cart to a database table. Frequently, you'll want to also submit the data to a credit card company or online commerce server, so keep that in mind when you are ready to save the cart data.

- **Get Unique ID from Table** Gets a specified column from the database and increments the number by 1 to use as a unique ID number. Typically, this is used with an "autonumber" style of column, as in Microsoft Access.

- **Empty Cart** Empties the cart of its contents. Actually, it destroys the cart cookie and re-creates it as a new cart.

ADVANCED DATA
INTEGRATION

- **Redirect If Empty**   Used on a Cart Display page to redirect the user to another page if there isn't anything in the cart. Again, this is an optional behavior, and can be used to provide a more elegant method of displaying an empty cart by having a specific EmptyCart page to go to.

- **Kill Cart**   This is used to completely destroy the cart and its contents.

- **Add Shipping**   Shipping can be done in a variety of different ways, such as fixed amount, per item, or by weight.

- **E-Mail Cart Contents**   Use this one if you want your customer to be able to send a copy of the cart contents to himself.

This was just a short introduction to the cart concept and some of the available carts for Dreamweaver MX. Next, we go through some of the key concepts in building your own e-store.

The Cart Site

This section describes a typical implementation of a small e-commerce site. Aside from the shopping cart, you'll need an e-store database that contains product information, customer information, and order information. You'll also need to implement a login system and a customer insert/update form for keeping track of customers. The site will be for a typical online software company, called Acme Databases, that offers downloadable software as well as product software on CD-ROM. In addition, it offers hardcopy documentation such as books and/or manuals.

The tutorial is kept as generic as possible, so that no matter which database or server model (ASP, JSP, ColdFusion, PHP, or ASP.NET) you're using, you'll be able to follow along. Because Dreamweaver MX supports so many different languages and implementations, only the general concepts are covered.

The Database Structure and Other General Database Issues

A database structure for an e-store is not something that you should gloss over quickly. The more effort you spend in creating the database, the fewer issues you will have to deal with later. You should always plan the database with expansion in mind, as well. Here are a few other general specifications and details about the database implementation.

Use of Text Data Types

In the tables listed later in the chapter, RDBMS-specific syntax isn't given, but instead we have focused on the general data types and lengths. For instance, the PhoneNumber column is listed as text/30, but could just as easily be stored as a number. Generally, it is logical to store fields that need to be calculated in some way as a number, and other numeric fields that don't have to have any calculations performed on them as text, varchars, or strings. For instance, a phone number will never be added, subtracted, multiplied, or divided in any way, so there's no need to store it as a number. Also, text fields tend to reduce database errors, for instance in the case when a person enters a letter instead of a number. Formatting of the phone numbers, or other fields of this type, can be done at the application level upon entering the field data (with client-side JavaScript or server-side validation of fields) or at the display level upon retrieval of the field from the database.

A price, on the other hand, should be stored as a special *money* field. Computers often have errors in rounding when it comes to floating-point (non-integer) values, and database manufacturers have taken this into account when implementing special *money* data types. The currency symbol should *never* be stored in the database along with the amounts. For example, your database field will never contain "$230.90". It would, instead, contain a numeric value of "230.9" and your Web application could supply the logic to display it properly as a currency field on your page.

> **Tip** *Formatted numbers, prices, phone numbers, ZIP codes, and other numeric/textual data should never be in your database fields. You can format these data at the Web application level by using custom scripting or Dreamweaver MX Server Formats, or you can preformat them inside of your database views or stored procedures upon retrieval.*

Autonumber Fields

Autonumber or identity columns are used in this example for all of the primary keys, but this was merely a choice of convenience. In the real world, special algorithms to determine a unique identifier would be better suited for an e-store. Autonumber fields are great for noncritical information, or as a way to reference the database fields from within your RDBMS, but they shouldn't be exposed to the end user via a form element or URL variable, which can lead to security problems. Instead of sequential integer numbers, you could choose to use a combination of the person's name with a 16-digit random number, timestamp, or an RDBMS-specific globally unique identifier.

A typical way to implement this is to have both types of fields in your database. When your stored procedures are doing the work inside of the RDBMS, they can be using the autonumber fields to take advantage of the speed of an integer column. When your Web application is accessing the data, it should use a more secure method, however. Say for example, you have a customer ID field. In your URL, you would never want to expose a customer ID in the following manner:

```
customer_details.cfm?customerid=232
```

All a user would have to do to get the details of another customer is change the ID number in the URL. This is not very secure, and you should avoid it at all costs. On the other hand, a products page that references a product details page is a good use for an autonumber field.

Referential Integrity

After building the tables, make sure you identify the foreign key constraints for the tables to maintain referential integrity. This is done differently depending on your database. Make sure you know your RDBMS inside and out to be able to implement primary and foreign key constraints. In Access and SQL Server, it's simply a matter of building a diagram of the database and connecting the primary and foreign keys together.

Implement the Connection

After the database is in place, tested, and ready to run, you'll want to deploy the database to the proper Web folder (if it's a file-based database) or create it on the server (if it's a server-based database), and create your connection to the database. This might be an ODBC data source, which means that you'll have to have the server administrator set up the DSN on the remote server. If you're using a DSN-less or OLE DB connection, you'll need to find the correct path to the database. For a JDBC connection, make sure you have all the details you'll need, such as the driver type and URL, and that the class path for these drivers is accessible to both Dreamweaver MX and to the JSP application server. Connections were covered in depth in Chapter 20.

The Database for the Acme Databases Site

The first thing to do when building a site is to determine and develop a database plan. The database design may be the single most important aspect of the e-store. With a carefully constructed database, all other aspects of the e-store will fall into place easily. The plan for this particular site is to sell online software, CD-ROMs, and documentation in the form of books. You are going to need several tables for this database, which are listed in Table 29-1. These tables are typical for a small-scale e-store.

Microsoft SQL Server and Microsoft Access come with a sample e-store database called Northwind that has a similar e-store structure.

Customers Table

The title of the Customers table is a bit of a misnomer, because the entries in the table are not actual customers until they buy something. People can be assigned a customer ID when they sign up to shop at the online store. Certain information can be "required" at the time of signup, but not all information. When the customer places an actual order, he or she will have to fill in the missing blanks of information. For example, a customer's address won't be considered to be required while he or she shops, but after the order is placed, the information is needed for shipping or contacting the customer. You'll implement this by having a "signup" form with minimal requirements, and then by implementing an "orders" form that requires more complete information.

The Customers table contains two ID values. The first is a special, auto-incrementing data type to allow quick access to your data from your database views and stored

Table Name	Description
Customers	Names, addresses, and personal information about the customers
Products	List of all available products with detailed information
Orders	List of order information to keep track of individual orders
OrderDetails	Line items of individual orders
ShippingMethods	Types of shipping and cost for each
PaymentMethods	Types of payments accepted
Payments	List of all payments made
MyCompanyInfo	Information about the company

Table 29-1. *A Typical E-Store Database Structure*

procedures. These data types are not secure for an e-store, so another ID is added that the customer will be exposed to. This can be generated by the database server or it can be a special identifier of your own design.

The column information for the Customers table is shown in Table 29-2. The Size column is generally a gauge of the length of the field, but this is not a hard-and-fast rule.

As in the database that was covered in Chapter 22, the fields listed are generic and will apply to Microsoft Access. You should adapt the field data types to your own RDBMS system—for further information consult Chapter 22.

Name	Type	Size	Special Characteristics
CustomerID	Autonumber or identity	4	Primary key
CustomerSecureID	Unique Identifier	8	Special RDBMS-specific identifier (see text)
CompanyName	Text	50	

Table 29-2. *Customers Table for the Acme Databases Web Site*

Name	Type	Size	Special Characteristics
ContactFirstName	Text	30	
ContactLastName	Text	50	
BillingAddress	Text	255	
City	Text	50	
StateOrProvince	Text	20	
PostalCode	Text	20	
Country	Text	50	
ContactTitle	Text	50	
PhoneNumber	Text	30	
FaxNumber	Text	30	
Username	Text	20	
Password	Text	20	
AccessGroup	Text	20	

Table 29-2. *Customers Table for the Acme Databases Web Site* (continued)

Products Table

The Products table will contain information about the individual products that the store will be selling. A products table can be simple or robust, depending on the complexity of the products you are selling. In this case, only a few fields are needed, but in your own implementation of an e-store, you can make this table as robust as you need it. It can even tie into other tables, such as a Supplier table. Other possible columns for a Products table are

- Units in stock
- Color
- Units on order
- Date of order
- Discontinued product
- Units level before reorder
- Supplier ID
- And so on

Our Products table, however, will be somewhat simple. In addition to product name and description, the table will have a column named Download that is a simple *bit* column—that is, it can hold either a 1 or a 0. This acts as a flag to determine whether the product is a download or not. If it is, another column will apply to the product: DownloadLink. The DownloadLink column will contain a physical location in the Web site so that the product can be downloaded. There is also a column for Weight, which will obviously be 0 for a download, but will contain a weight for an actual physical item. ProductID will be the primary key for the table, and will contain an autonumber or identity column to make that part of the data entry automatic—every item that gets added to the database will have an ID number assigned to it.

The column information for the Products table is shown in Table 29-3.

Orders Table

The Orders table will contain one entry for each order placed. The table is not the place for specific order details, such as which items are on the order; you'll implement an Order Details table specifically for that. The table will, however, hold shipping information (because it frequently differs from the billing information), freight charges, and tax rate. The primary key is the OrderID column and will be an autonumber or identity column. Again, because an order requires security, a special OrderSecureID column is introduced as well. The CustomerID is a foreign key to the Customers table, and the ShippingMethodID is a foreign key to the ShippingMethods table.

The payment information isn't stored in this table because you're going to consider the Payment as a complete entity that is independent of the physical Order that is placed. They conceivably could have been grouped into the same table, but the rules of database design dictate that you should separate entities whenever possible.

Name	Type	Size	Special Characteristics
ProductID	Autonumber or identity	4	Primary key
ProductName	Text	50	
UnitPrice	Money	8	
Description	Text	255	
Download	Bit or Boolean	1	
Weight	Number (int)	4	
DownloadLink	Text	50	

Table 29-3. *Products Table for the Acme Database Design E-Store*

The chart in Figure 29-6 shows that the Orders table sits in the center of the chart. The whole concept of an e-store revolves around a customer placing an order. In your case, and in the case of any e-store, the order is the key component of the transaction. It holds links to the customer who made the order, the products on the order (via the Order Details table), the method of shipping that order, and the payment made on the order. By accessing one row in the Orders table, you can—through SQL statements— find all the information that relates to that order to create an invoice.

The column information for the Orders table is shown in Table 29-4.

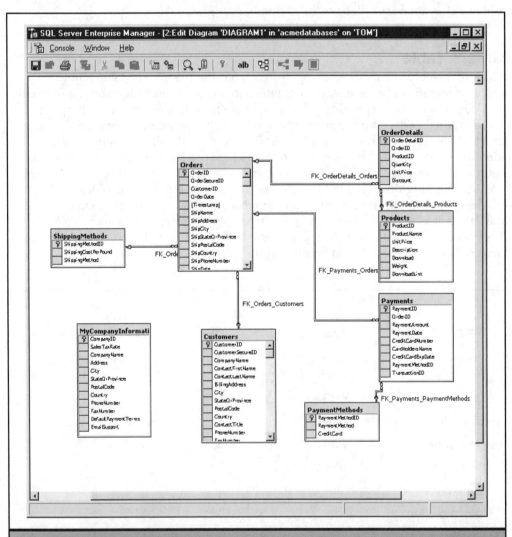

Figure 29-6. *The SQL Server diagram for the Acme Databases e-store database showing the relationships between tables*

Name	Type	Size	Special Characteristics
OrderID	Autonumber or identity	4	Primary key
OrderSecureID	Unique Identifier	8	Special RDBMS-specific identifier (see text)
CustomerID	Number (int)	4	Foreign key to Customers
OrderDate	Text	30	Could be date/time, but text is used for complete compatibility
PurchaseOrderNumber	Text	30	
ShipName	Text	50	
ShipAddress	Text	255	
ShipCity	Text	50	
ShipStateOrProvince	Text	50	
ShipPostalCode	Text	20	
ShipCountry	Text	50	
ShipPhoneNumber	Text	30	
ShipDate	Text	30	
ShippingMethodID	Number (int)	4	
FreightCharge	Money	8	
SalesTaxRate	Number (float)	8	

Table 29-4. *Orders Table for the Acme Databases Web Site*

OrderDetails Table

The OrderDetails table will contain line-item information for the orders that are placed. The OrderDetailID will be the primary key for the table and will contain a unique identifier for that particular transaction. For instance, a typical order might contain three items. Each item would be contained in one row in this table, and each would reference the OrderID through the foreign key contained in the table.

Other columns in the table will be UnitPrice, Quantity, and Discount. The UnitPrice will come from the Products table, but is kept separately in this table so that it can be modified on an individual order basis. For instance, a customer could call up and ask to receive a special price on an item because he or she can find it somewhere else for a cheaper price. You don't want to change the unit price of the item itself, but you can change it on this one particular order by noting it in the Discount column. The ProductID field references the product, and is a foreign key to the Products table. The Quantity column indicates the number of orders for a particular item and is used to calculate the line item price and the shipping weight. These calculated fields aren't stored in the database, but are implemented in your application.

The column information for the OrderDetails table is shown in Table 29-5.

ShippingMethods Table

Because there can be many different shipping options, you should implement a table that contains shipping method information. It will hold the information about the different shipping methods that are available. Even if you are using only one type of shipping, this table will allow for future expansion. The primary key will be the ShippingMethodID and will be an autonumber or identity column. There are also columns for ShippingMethod, which is a descriptive name of the method, and ShippingCostPerPound, which can be used for shipping calculations for your Orders table. This table can also hold other information about the shipping methods involved, such as a support site for the shipper, to name just one aspect to consider.

The column information for the ShippingMethods table is shown in Table 29-6.

Name	Type	Size	Special Characteristics
OrderDetailID	Number (int)	4	Primary key
OrderID	Number (int)	4	Foreign key to Orders
ProductID	Number (int)	4	Foreign key to Products
Quantity	Number (int)	4	
UnitPrice	Money	8	
Discount	Number (float)	8	

Table 29-5.   *OrderDetails Table for the Acme Databases Web Site*

Name	Type	Size	Special Characteristics
ShippingMethodID	Autonumber or identity	4	Primary key
ShippingMethod	Text	20	
ShippingCostPerPound	Number (int)	4	

Table 29-6.   *ShippingMethods Table for the Acme Databases Web Site*

PaymentMethods Table

This table will contain information about the various payment methods that are available. The PaymentMethodID will be an autonumber or identity column that will act as the primary key for the table. The name of the payment method will be kept in the PaymentMethod column and is just a simple, descriptive name for the method. The CreditCard column is a bit datatype and contains either a 1 or a 0 as a flag for whether or not the payment method is a credit card. The bit datatypes are handy for quick-and-dirty, "yes/no" types of problems. Typically, a payment method page will have different form fields for a credit card payment, so a yes/no test for credit card can tell you whether to display the form fields or not. Among other methods, a payment method could be a check, money order, COD, or a company account.

The column information for the PaymentMethods table is shown in Table 29-7.

Payments Table

This table will contain information about all the payments that are made. If a person orders something online and makes the purchase with a credit card, details of the transaction will be contained in one row of this table. You could consider it a "monetary transactions" table, because the table will detail each and every transaction that is made, with one row for each transaction.

Name	Type	Size	Special Characteristics
PaymentMethodID	Autonumber or identity	4	Primary key
PaymentMethod	Text	50	
CreditCard	Bit	1	

Table 29-7.   *PaymentMethods Table for the Acme Databases Web Site*

ADVANCED DATA INTEGRATION

The PaymentsID column will be an autonumber or identity column, and it will be the primary key for the table. OrderID is a foreign key to the Orders table, and will reference a specific order number from that table. The PaymentAmount column will contain the amount of payment, which would be equal to the computed values of the unit price for each item purchased, multiplied by the quantity of that item, with sales tax, shipping, and any discounts also figured into the mix. PaymentDate will contain the actual date that the payment was made, which should also correspond to the date of the purchase, unless you are implementing some sort of installment schedule or other method of payment. If a person were to pay by check, for instance, the PaymentDate would be different from the OrderDate contained in the Orders table.

Other columns in the table deal with the credit card number, cardholder's name, and expiration date, along with the PaymentMethodID—which will be a foreign key to the PaymentMethod table. The reason behind keeping the methods in a separate table is to prevent faulty information from being entered. Typically, the payment method will be a radio button or select list on a form so that only one method can be chosen, and it will correspond to a list of choices on the Web page.

Storing credit card numbers in a database is something you should consider only if you are implementing a secure system using a robust database server such as SQL Server or Oracle, and have a security system in place. Depending on who is processing your payments, most online processing can be done by the online processing provider, thereby eliminating your need to store any critical information such as credit card numbers. Some of these providers will provide you with a transaction ID upon a successful transaction, which is also implemented in the table design.

The column information for the Payments table is shown in Table 29-8.

MyCompanyInfo Table

The MyCompanyInfo table will be the only unrelated table in the database. It is there simply to keep the Acme Databases company information in one place. This can be used for invoices, e-mail messages, Web pages, or places where you might need to insert your company data. The information stored in here is simply the name, address, phone and fax numbers, and so forth.

One column in this table needs a little explanation. The column DefaultPaymentTerms is a 255-character column that contains the payment terms for the company. This can be a short descriptive paragraph detailing payment terms that resides only in this column and therefore needs to be updated only in this one place for use anywhere in the site, invoices, e-mail messages, and so forth. You may also add things to this table that might be pertinent to your own company, such as a standard disclaimer whose wording might change, or the information for various contacts, such as technical support, customer service, or the sales department.

The column information for the MyCompanyInfo table is shown in Table 29-9.

The Site Tree for Acme Databases

The home page of the Acme Databases site can be called simply home.asp, home.cfm, home.php, or home.jsp, depending on the server model you're working with. Some

Name	Type	Size	Special Characteristics
PaymentID	Autonumber or identity	4	Primary key
OrderID	Number (int)	4	Foreign key to the Orders table
PaymentAmount	Money	8	
PaymentDate	Text	30	
CreditCardNumber	Text	30	
CardHoldersName	Text	50	
CreditCardExpDate	Date/time	4	
PaymentMethodID	Number (int)	4	
TransactionID	Text	50	

Table 29-8.   *Payments Table for the Acme Databases Web Site*

Name	Type	Size	Special Characteristics
CompanyID	Autonumber or identity	4	Primary key
SalesTaxRate	Number (money)	8	
CompanyName	Text	50	
Address	Text	255	
City	Text	50	
StateOrProvince	Text	20	
PostalCode	Text	20	
Country	Text	50	
PhoneNumber	Text	30	

Table 29-9.   *MyCompanyInformation Table for the Acme Databases Web Site*

Name	Type	Size	Special Characteristics
FaxNumber	Text	30	
EmailSupport	Text	60	
DefaultPaymentTerms	Text	255	

Table 29-9. *MyCompanyInformation Table for the Acme Databases Web Site (continued)*

people prefer to use index.htm, but hackers have specifically targeted the name "index" in recent years. For that reason, it is better to use something nonstandard.

It's a good idea to create blank pages for all pages in the site before doing anything on the site, so Table 29-10 shows a list of the page names and their purpose. The items with asterisks (*) are the pages that contain an actual Cart on the page. You can create a blank page by right-clicking in the Site Files window and choosing New File. You can

Page	Description
Home	Your home page, with a Login form for registered users.
SignUp	The page that records the new username and password.
Cart*	Lets the user view the cart and its contents.
AboutUs	Details the Acme Databases company information.
Products*	The complete list of products available, with links to the Details page for each product.
Details*	Lists individual products with more detailed information for each.
CustomerInfo*	The page on which users confirm personal information for the purchase.
CheckOut*	Presents the confirmation of the user's order and totals for shipping and sales tax.
ShippingConfirmation	Presents a form for the user to enter any shipping information.
Payment	Processes the payment.
ThankYou	A "thank you" page to signify a successful order.

Table 29-10. *The Pages Needed for Acme Database Design*

Page	Description
Download	Any files that have been paid for can be downloaded from this page—links to DownloadCount.
EmptyCart	If a user chooses to View Cart and the cart is empty, the user is redirected to this page.
Error	An all-purpose Error page for failed logins, access levels, and unfulfilled orders.

Table 29-10.   *The Pages Needed for Acme Database Design* (continued)

name them in the Site Files window immediately after creating them, which is usually the easiest way to create new pages. Also, it is easy to drag/drop files from folder to folder within the site tree directly from the site panel.

The flow of logic between pages is shown here:

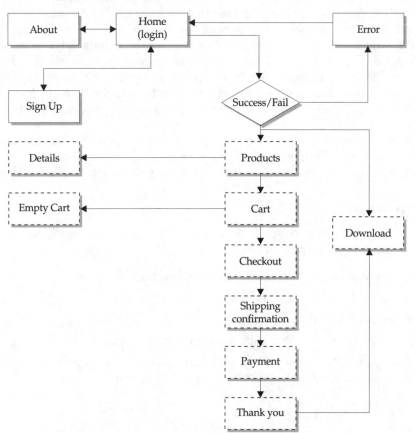

The home page acts as a login page. From the home page, the user can also sign up to become a new customer, or view the "About Us" page. If the user has a successful login, he can begin to shop. The pages with the dotted outlines are all "secured" pages. That is, they have Restrict Access To Page Server Behaviors applied to them.

The products page is a general listing of products, which also links to the detail pages of individual products. The customer can add items to the cart from either page, and also choose to view the cart. If the customer is finished shopping, he can move to the checkout page and proceed through the purchase process, which also includes the payment and shipping confirmation pages. When the customer is finished, he is presented with a "Thank you" page after which time he can proceed to the download section, or await shipping of any tangible goods. The error page is used by all pages in the site as a general error display page, but is shown in the diagram as a pass-through page for unsuccessful logins. An unsuccessful login is just one of the many types of errors you'll need to manage.

The About Us Page

The About Us page (shown in Figure 29-7) is a typical page that you might find in an e-store—it simply contains information about the company. For your Acme Databases site, you'll be drawing the information from the database using the MyCompanyInformation table. You could just as easily hand-code the information in the Web page itself, but you want the information to be maintainable by someone other than the Web designer. By putting the information in the database, if any information changes, someone from the company can update the information directly in the database or from a Web form instead of going back to the Web designer. This is especially helpful if the information is going to be on several pages in the site.

 When designing a site for a client, it's a good idea to leave as much of the site maintenance as possible in the hands of the client. This prevents service calls to update the Web site and allows the client to perform trivial tasks such as updating a contact name or address.

The Home Page

The Home page in the site serves as a welcome to the site and a user login page. The main items that you need on the page are as follows:

- A form that has its Action attribute set to the Success page
- A text field named username
- A text field named password
- A Submit button that has its action set to Submit form
- A Register Now link pointing to the SignUp page, with appropriate text, such as "If you haven't registered yet, you need to sign up"

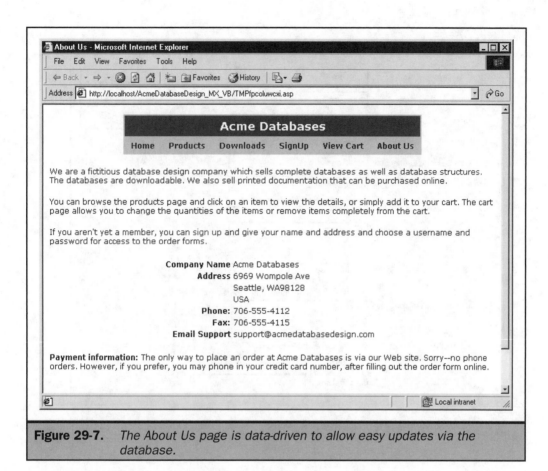

Figure 29-7. *The About Us page is data-driven to allow easy updates via the database.*

With these HTML elements in place, you will also need to apply a Log In User Server Behavior to the page. This will allow the user to login and begin shopping. The Log In User Server Behavior is shown in Figure 29-8. It allows you to set an error page and a success page, as well as the HTML field and database field mappings. Upon a successful login, the customer will be directed to the products page.

The SignUp Page

You need to implement a basic SignUp page that asks the user to choose a username and password, and then allows them to shop securely on the site. Because the user will be registering for the first time, there won't be a unique CustomerID yet and as a result, this page won't need the Restrict Access to Page Server Behavior on it.

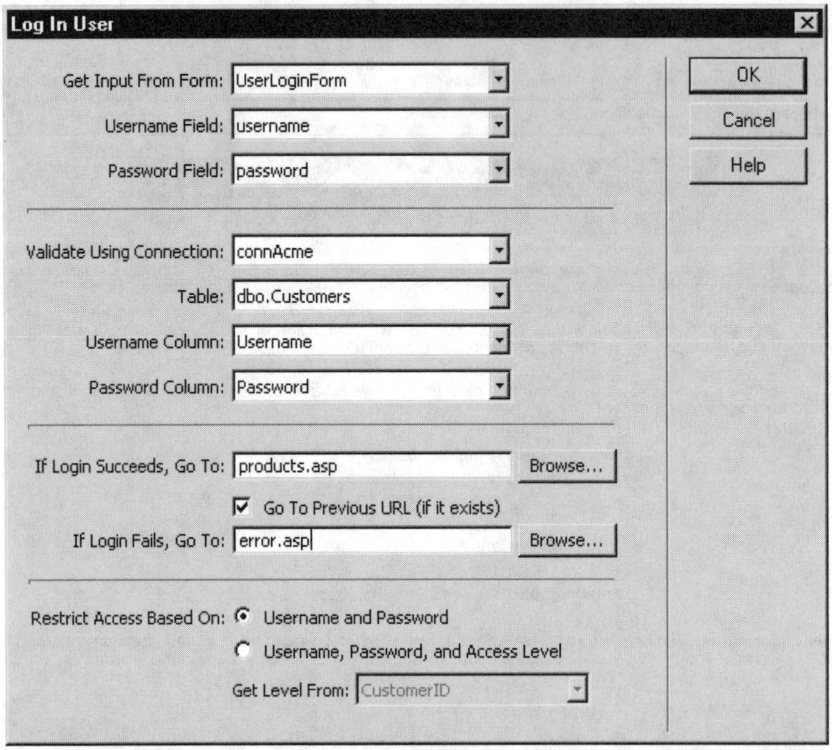

Figure 29-8. *The Log In User Server Behavior facilitates easy point-and-click user authentication.*

Several things need to happen when the user signs in for the first time:

1. The user enters a username, which must be unique—it must not exist in the database.

2. The user enters a password, which should be entered twice for confirmation that the first typed password is the intended password.

3. The username and password are inserted into the database and a CustomerID is issued to the user.

Implementing the Products Page and Detail Page

The Products page will contain an instance of the cart. As stated earlier, the cart is an object that has to reside on any page that will need to access it. In the case of a products or product details page, the cart has to be in place so that a user can add an item to the cart.

This page will contain a complete list of products available to the customer, as well as a search field to allow a user to narrow down the search, if there are a lot of products. Here, the user will be able to select a product to add to the cart, or select a link to view the product in greater detail. The Detail page will have the cart added to it as well. The user will be able to add items to the cart from both pages, and will be redirected to the Cart page upon adding an item to the cart.

> **Note** *When working with a shopping cart, it is important to realize that the cart is stored as a cookie on the client machine. If you decide at some point to change the functionality of the cart during the testing phase—adding or deleting columns, for instance—you need to locate the cookie on your test machine and delete it manually. You can locate the cookie by searching the folder where your temporary Internet files are located for your particular machine. Or, you could write a custom page specifically to kill the cart when needed.*

The Products Page

You can set up the products and products detail pages by using a Master-Detail server object from the Insert bar. This object was described in Chapter 24. You can also create the pages manually. On the products page, you'll need to add the following elements:

- Search field
- Recordset
- Table with column headings
- Recordset fields in row two
- Repeat Region on row two
- Recordset Navigation Bar
- Search field
- Link to detail page on the product name

Putting the search field directly on the page makes it more convenient for customers to browse, so that they don't have to click a bunch of links or use the Back button to get the information they want. The finished products page is shown in Figure 29-9.

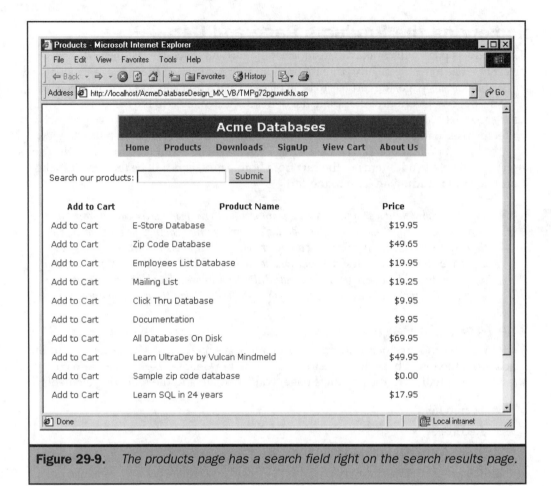

Figure 29-9. *The products page has a search field right on the search results page.*

These pages should also have Restrict Access To Page Server Behavior applied to them (shown in Figure 29-10).

Keep in mind when browsing to the pages in this site that you are dealing with a Web application, and the entry point for that application is the Home page. Attempting to access another page in the application without first logging in from the home page will cause an error. You can prevent this by either logging in each time or setting up Live Data scripts in the Live Data Settings dialog box. Live Data Settings were explained in Chapter 25.

The products page will have an Add To Cart text link, button, or image applied to each table row. This is accomplished by adding the text link, button, or image to a table

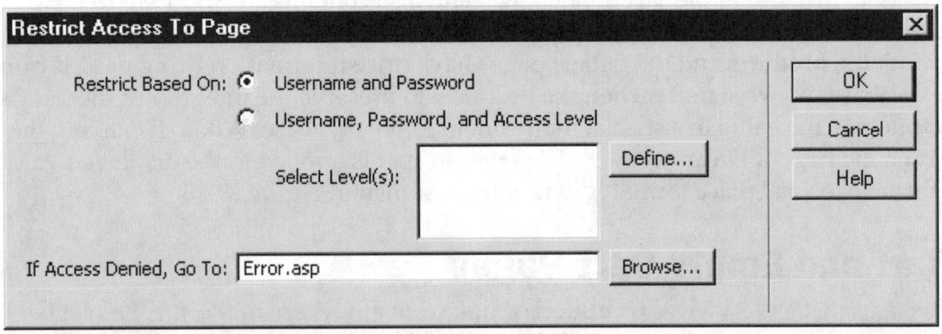

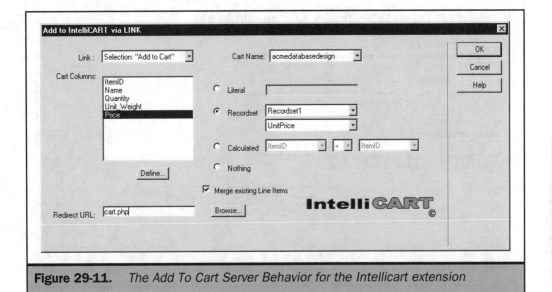

Figure 29-10. *The Restrict Access To Page Server Behavior using only username and password to validate a user*

cell within the repeat region. Then, you can apply an Add To Cart Server Behavior to the item. Most cart implementations have a Server Behavior that will do this. Figure 29-11 shows the Intellicart implementation of the Add To Cart Server Behavior.

The Product Details Page

One half of the Master-Detail page-set is the details page. This page takes a record number or unique identifier from the URL, and filters a recordset based on this parameter. The page can then display the details of one specific product. This page

Figure 29-11. *The Add To Cart Server Behavior for the Intellicart extension*

also has an instance of the cart on the page, and also contains an Add Item to Cart Server Behavior as well. The details page is shown in Figure 29-12.

Both the products and the details pages have price information being passed from the database. As we stated earlier, the best way to preserve the integrity of the data is to store only the value in a special money field in the database. When displaying the field on the page, a Dreamweaver MX server format is applied to the displayed value so that a 2 decimal place format is maintained, shown in Figure 29-13.

The Cart and Empty Cart Pages

When a user clicks a View Cart button or link from anywhere in the site, he will be shown the Cart page. This page contains several key elements:

- The shopping cart
- A table that holds the shopping cart fields

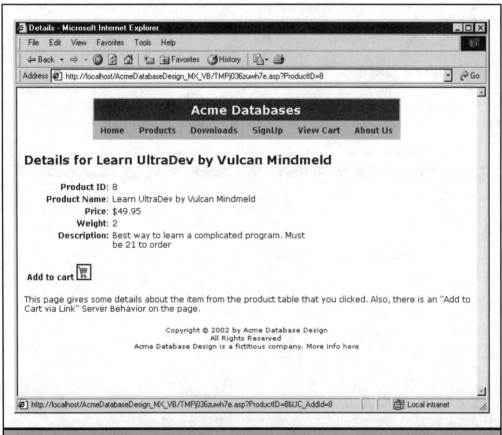

Figure 29-12. *The finished details page is part of the "drill-down" mechanism of the Master-Detail page-set.*

- A special Repeat Region made especially for the cart
- Subtotals and totals
- A Server Behavior to empty the cart contents
- Link to the CheckOut page
- A Server Behavior to redirect the user to the empty cart page upon emptying the cart

One final touch is required to format the cells that contain monetary values. You must apply a currency format to the individual price cells by selecting the individual script blocks and applying Server Format | Currency | Default to the highlighted item. You should do this for each of the monetary values on the page. The finished cart page is shown in Figure 29-14.

One nice feature of an e-store is to have a small pop-up window listing the contents of the cart. You can do this by creating a duplicate of your cart page, formatting it especially as a small pop-up window. Then, on your other pages that have a link to

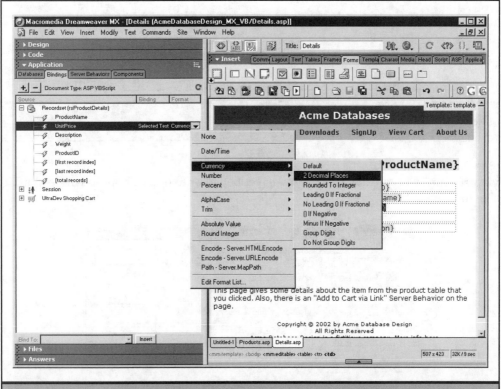

Figure 29-13.   *Using server formats to dress up the displays of monetary values from the database*

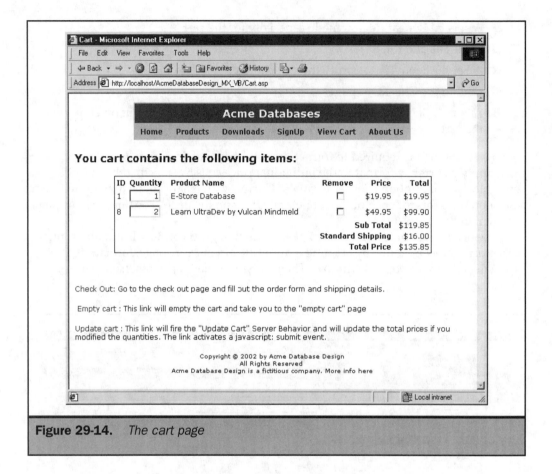

Figure 29-14. The cart page

view the cart, you can attach a Dreamweaver behavior to open a pop-up window, as shown here:

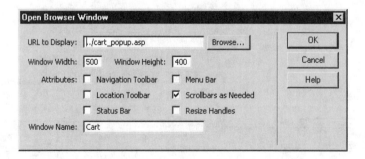

The EmptyCart Page

On the EmptyCart page, you'll simply put a statement that says, "Your Cart is empty. Back to Products."

The Check Out Pages

The scenario at this point is this: The user has chosen some items to buy, and has clicked the link to Proceed to Checkout. At this point, you need to gather the user information, the order information, the shipping information, and the type of transaction—whether it's a credit card transaction or a "bill me" transaction. You can implement the functionality in a fashion similar to the "wizard" metaphor that you've seen in programs before.

The user will need to have personal data stored in the database. The first thing to do is to get the user's personal data from the database, if it already exists, and place it into various predetermined form fields on the page. Then, the user can either choose to accept what is there (if he or she is a past customer), or enter new information if the information in the database is inaccurate or incomplete. You can implement this with an Update server object from the Insert bar.

Shipping Confirmation

After users have viewed or updated their personal information, they may want to update the shipping address information. One way to implement this is to prepopulate the text fields for the shipping address with the customer's own personal address information. If any changes need to be made, the customer can make them from the form. In most cases, they will probably choose to ship to their current address.

The easiest way to populate form elements from a database is to create a recordset and then drag the fields from the Bindings panel and drop them onto your form elements one at a time. This makes the shopping experience easier for the customer if they don't have to type the same address information in again.

Saving the Cart to the Database

At some point in the purchase process the cart contents need to be stored to the database. The database has two tables set up for purchases: Orders and OrderDetails. The Orders table contains one line for each order. This is linked to the OrderDetails table by using an order number from the Orders table. Each line item in the cart will occupy one line in the OrderDetails table. The shopping cart Server Behaviors will typically take care of the details of saving the cart to the appropriate tables. Simply apply a Save Cart To Table Server Behavior.

Note that the Weight, Name, TotalWeight, and Total columns are typically not saved to the database. The items are in the cart so that a Cart Display page can show the contents of the cart with the details of the products, without another trip to the database. The weights and names are stored in the Products table of the database and do not need to be stored in the OrderDetails table. That would add redundant data to the database. Furthermore, the totals shouldn't be stored, because they are calculated fields. One rule of database design, you may remember, is that calculated fields shouldn't be stored in the database because they depend on another column for their result. If someone were to change the Unit Price of an item, the total price would then be inaccurate.

Paying for the Order

There are many methods for accepting credit cards on your e-commerce site. Most small Web sites will have the e-commerce functionality implemented by a third party. Generally, you need to provide a form that posts the following transaction information to the service:

- Amount of transaction
- Invoice number
- Credit card type
- Credit card number
- Expiration date
- Name on card
- Account name
- Account number

These details can be submitted to the payment processor through a hidden form field. Most of the payment processors have detailed instructions available from their Web site that show you exactly how to implement a transaction.

Some payment processors actually create the shopping cart functionality for you, so that all you need to do is simply send the details about the products to them. This is becoming increasingly common, and is a quick way to build e-commerce functionality into your site.

The Thank You Page

A thank you page is the last step in the transaction. If you've created the payment functionality yourself, this is the last page in the procedure. If you've submitted the payment details to a third-party payment processor, the URL for the thank you page will also have to be sent along with the payment details so that the payment processor can redirect the user back to your site when the transaction is complete.

The Download Page

Recall that you are offering file downloads on the Acme Databases site as part of the products list. After users purchase software, you must have a way for them to retrieve their downloads. You can do this by going directly to the OrderDetails table in the database and pulling out the information about purchases. When a user reaches the Download page, the user's CustomerID is stored in a session variable. That's all you need to make the connection between the Customer, the Orders table, the OrderDetails table, and the Products table. Another method would be to create a lookup table in your database that includes the customer's ID number and the product information. Lookup tables break some of the rules of database design because they duplicate data, but in a real-world scenario they offer quick access to important information whenever speed or availability is an issue.

The Error Page

You can implement an error page that will serve as a universal error page to which all errors will be redirected. Put some generic text on the page, such as "There was an error." As your site gets more complex, you can customize your error pages to specific problems that the user might encounter. One method is to redirect a user to an error page and include a query string variable (or URL variable for the ColdFusion users). You could pass an error variable named *error* with a value that consists of a predetermined error number, as in *error.asp?error=3*. In pseudocode, the error page would look like this:

```
Switch (error)
    Case 1
        Display "You need to log in"
    Case 2
        Display "You need a valid password"
    Case 3
        Display "There was a database error"
```

Another method is to pass the actual error text to the error page, as in the following statement:

```
Response.Redirect("Error.asp?error=Failed%20login")
```

On the error page, you could then display the incoming *QueryString* variable on the page, as in

```
There was an error: <%=Request("error")%>
```

If you implement the error page in this fashion, you will also need to create a link back to the page that the user requested originally. You can do this in any number of different ways. One technique is to pass the referring page in the URL along with the error number or error message.

E-Mailing the Customer

One feature that you may want to include in your site is a way to e-mail customers after they've made a purchase. In many cases, the payment processor will take care of this for you. If not, however, you'll need to create the e-mail yourself.

Some of the Dreamweaver MX extensions that are available can take care of the dirty work of creating the e-mail. If one is not available, here are a few pointers to help you create an e-mail using dynamic fields from the cart or the database.

An e-mail is simply a string of text. Most e-mail components work in a similar fashion. You must build the string of text that will become the body of the e-mail before adding it to the e-mail component. You can accomplish this in many different ways, but the easiest way is to hand-code the string concatenation into your code before calling the e-mail component. You also have to include line breaks in the e-mail where you need them, or format the text as HTML. A typical string concatenation method for ASP VBScript would look like this:

```
<%Dim theBody
theBody = "Your order was processed on " & Date() & vbcrlf
theBody = theBody & "in the amount of "
theBody = theBody & session("totalWithShipping") & vbcrlf
While Not (rsOrder.eof)
    theBody = theBody & rsOrder("product") & vbcrlf
    theBody = theBody & "Quantity: " & rsOrder("quantity") & vbcrlf
    theBody = theBody & "Total: " & rsOrder("unitprice") & vbcrlf
    theBody = theBody & "-----------------------------" & vbcrlf
Wend
theBody = theBody & "Thank you for your order!"
%>
```

Some of the Dreamweaver MX shopping carts will actually format the e-mail for you. Custom Server Behaviors are available on the Web that can do this for you as well.

A Few Notes About Scaling the Site

The site as it stands is a good starting point for a small-scale e-store. Keep in mind, however, that certain techniques were used to keep the site small and simple. When scaling to a larger or more secure site, you need to consider several things:

- Databases such as Microsoft SQL Server, IBM's DB2, and Oracle9i have stored procedures that allow the use of transactions. You should use stored procedures to allow the use of multiple queries, multiple inserts, and return values.

- Move business functionality to components on the server. In ASP, these could be COM components; in JSP, you can use Enterprise JavaBeans (EJBs); and in ColdFusion, you can use custom tags. Another option would be to move more functionality into the database as stored procedures.

- You need to secure download links of purchases in such a way as to prevent unauthorized use. Also, store the files in a directory that doesn't have Read access. The files could be downloaded by sending a binary stream to the browser instead of being linked to. A link to a file will usually pass the path information to the end user, which jeopardizes the security of the files.

- Don't store anything in a database that is subject to privacy issues, such as credit card numbers; but, if you do, you should encrypt them. Don't leave user IDs, usernames, passwords, and other private pieces of data unsecured for hackers to access.

- The current cart is configured only as a cookie. If the user leaves the site and then comes back to the site from another machine, the cart contents won't be there. You could implement another database table to accommodate "active" carts, which would permit shoppers to view their carts from anywhere.

Summary

E-commerce is a complicated subject with many facets. Most e-commerce sites follow a standard structure with minor variations. Because of this, you can purchase e-commerce extensions for Dreamweaver that make it easy to put together a complex site. Another alternative is to purchase a complete e-store solution, although these methods are never as flexible as the hand-built sites utilizing shopping cart extensions. Whichever method you decide to use, Dreamweaver MX can make implementing an active e-store much easier.

ADVANCED DATA
INTEGRATION

The Complete Reference

Dreamweaver MX

Part VI

Getting the Most Out of Dreamweaver MX

Chapter 30

Extensions and the Extension Manager

D reamweaver MX comes with a lot of features out of the box. When you first start up Dreamweaver MX, you may be a little overwhelmed by the amount of things that you need to learn. Once you become familiar with the program, however, you'll find that you frequently want it to do more. You might wish that you had your own menu of favorite help files accessible from the program. Or maybe you would like to be able to count how many words are in the document. Maybe you want to hide a section on your page if a person hasn't logged in, or hide a section of the page if he or she *has* logged in. These are examples of Dreamweaver MX extensions that you can download and install into the program to make the Web development environment more productive.

What Is an Extension?

What is meant when we talk about extending Dreamweaver, or the extensibility of any product or platform in general? Typically, something is extensible if you can add to it, if you can make it do things that it wasn't originally able to do by learning enough about it that you can change its features in some way. Now, that doesn't mean that when you lose your hammer and have to use the handle of a screwdriver to hang a picture that the screwdriver is extensible. Extensibility is something that is built into a product by providing a methodology that encourages people to find ways to make it grow. And a feature or function that you add to a product is called an extension because it extends the core product in some way.

Allowing the user to add new features to programs has been a long-standing tradition in the computer world. Many people build macros in Microsoft Word or Corel WordPerfect that allow them to enhance their work environments. The concept of the macro is taken a step further in Dreamweaver MX. A majority of the features that you have come to know in the program are completely within the grasp of the user. For example, when you click Insert | Table, the Table dialog box pops up.

Insert Table		☒
Rows: `3` Cell Padding: `    `		OK
Columns: `3` Cell Spacing: `    `		Cancel
Width: `75` `Percent ▾`		Help
Border: `1`		

You've probably seen this dialog box 100 or 1,000 times by now. What you may not know is that the dialog box is nothing but an HTML file that is in your Configuration folder. In fact, all of the objects on the Insert bar are located in a folder named Objects. The Behaviors in the Behaviors panel are located in a folder called Behaviors. If you know what you're doing, you can go into these folders and modify the files that are in there or create your own. The table.htm file looks like this in the Dreamweaver MX environment:

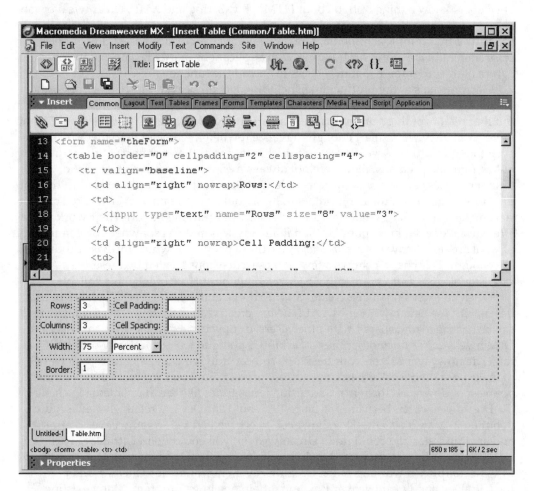

As you can see, there is no mystery about the interface. It is simple HTML. Chapter 31 explores these files in detail and shows you how to create your own extensions. The text fields in the dialog box are nothing more than standard HTML text fields. There is also a corresponding JavaScript file that does the dirty work of inserting the table code into your document.

This is possible because the designers of Dreamweaver MX have enabled the entire program with an *application programming interface* (API) that allows the user to build extensions to the program in HTML and JavaScript. Also, many of the menus and other features of the programs are stored as simple XML documents. Because most Web developers know a thing or two about HTML, JavaScript, and XML, Dreamweaver can be extended using the languages they already know. This was a stroke of genius that has truly paid off for Macromedia. Dreamweaver MX is currently the number one environment in the world for building Web applications, partly because of the open nature of the program that allows users to extend the functionality.

Macromedia's entire product line, including Dreamweaver, Flash, Fireworks, and others, is exceptionally capable of performing the tasks for which they were designed. But the creators of these programs were smart enough to realize that users would want more. Well, they were smart enough to realize it when it was shown to them. You see, even though the things we discuss in this chapter are at the very heart of the structure of Macromedia products, they were not always meant for end-user consumption. It took the tireless efforts of some very talented people digging around within the directory structure on their computers to figure out how Dreamweaver worked and to start making it do things that it wasn't originally programmed to do. Their work made Dreamweaver even more popular than it already was and has spawned the community of what are now known as *extensionologists*: those people for which the base product is not enough. This chapter shows a few of these extensions created by these extensionologists, but we are only just scratching the surface of what is available.

When an extensionologist creates an HTML file and enables it with JavaScript that ties in with the Dreamweaver MX API, he has created an extension. These extensions can be packaged and shared with other users, or they can exist solely for that user. Dreamweaver MX on another user's desktop is going to look completely different than Dreamweaver MX on your desktop. You can add whichever features you want to make your own work environment more productive. You can create these features yourself, or download them from extension repositories like the Macromedia Exchange.

Dreamweaver has been around since 1997, but UltraDev is a relatively new product, debuting in May 2000. UltraDev, however, was based on the Dreamweaver platform, and anything that you could do in Dreamweaver, you could do in UltraDev. This includes using Dreamweaver extensions within the UltraDev program. Dreamweaver MX is a complete reworking of the Dreamweaver environment to include all of the UltraDev and Dreamweaver functionality in one huge program. Many existing UltraDev extensions written for UltraDev 1 or UltraDev 4 will work in the Dreamweaver MX environment.

| Caution | *Even though some UltraDev 4 extensions and most Dreamweaver 4 extensions will work in Dreamweaver MX, it is advisable to install them one at a time and note any incompatibilities that you may encounter before installing more extensions. The API of Dreamweaver MX is considerably different than the API of previous versions of the program.* |

Dreamweaver MX extensions include (but aren't limited to) the following types:

- **Objects**   Objects are "things" that you can insert into your document, such as tables, form elements, Flash movies, or characters.

- **Behaviors**   If objects are the nouns, behaviors are the verbs. They perform an action on the page or to an object.

- **Commands**   Commands are versatile extensions that can do just about anything, and usually perform some sort of code manipulation on the page, such as Clean Up HTML.

- **Floaters**   When you add a floating panel extension to the program, you are adding a completely new floating window that can do whatever you program it to do.

- **Inspectors**   These are the contextual Property Inspectors that appear when something is selected or the cursor is within a section of code on the page.

- **Toolbars**   These are bars that reside above the document windows that can be extended to include new buttons that add custom functionality, or new buttons to add existing functionality in a new way.

- **Server Behaviors**   These are to server-side code what behaviors are to client-side code. They typically enable an action that the page can execute on the server.

- **Data sources**   These are the *sources of dynamic data*, like recordsets, session variables, or JavaBeans that can display some information coming from the server onto the page.

- **Server formats**   These extensions allow you to format the dynamic data in a meaningful way, such as adding a dollar sign and decimal point with two decimal places to a number for money formatting.

- **Connections**   These are the files that allow you to connect to a database. They contain the functionality needed by Dreamweaver MX to build a connection to the database.

Extension Packages and the Extension Manager

We've talked about extensions and how they can be built to add functionality to the program, but how do you get them into the program and how do you keep track of them? Dreamweaver MX itself doesn't have any functionality to enable the packaging or installation of new extensions, but Macromedia has created a program that works with UltraDev, Dreamweaver, Dreamweaver MX, Fireworks, and Flash. It's called the Extension Manager, and it is installed by default with all of those programs—you can download it for free from the Macromedia Web site.

The Extension Manager

If you open your Macromedia folder on your hard drive, you'll see the Extension Manager folder alongside the Dreamweaver MX folder. If you have other Macromedia programs installed, such as Flash MX or UltraDev 4, they will all share this one Extension Manager. The Extension Manager has several uses:

- It allows you to install extensions that you may have downloaded or found on a CD-ROM.
- It keeps track of all extensions that are installed, by placing them in a list.
- It has a built-in extension packager to allow you to package new extensions.
- It allows you to import your extensions from a previous version, a networked remote computer, or another program.

You can open the Extension Manager from several places. On a Windows machine, it is located in the Start menu under Macromedia Extension Manager. It will also open automatically if you double-click on an extension package (MXP) file or an extension installation (MXI) file. It is also accessible from the Commands menu by clicking Commands | Manage Extensions.

 Version 1.5 of the Extension Manager no longer supports older programs such as Dreamweaver 3 or UltraDev 1.

When you open it, you will see a list of all extensions installed on your machine.

Turn extensions on and off   Version number of extensions   Author of extension

Remove extension completely   Go to Macromedia Exchange

List of installed extensions   Type of extension

Get help information

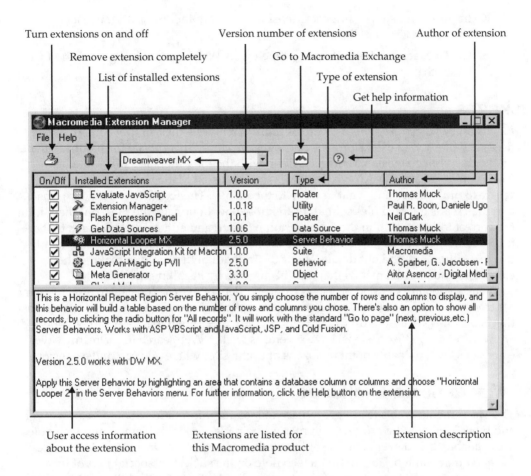

User access information   Extensions are listed for   Extension description
about the extension   this Macromedia product

The Extension Manager also has these features on the File menu:

- **Install Extension**   Browse to an extension package on your computer.
- **Package Extension**   Package an extension you have written.
- **Submit Extension**   Submit your extension to the Macromedia Exchange.
- **Remove Extension**   Permanently remove an extension.

- **Import Extensions**   Import extensions from another program, such as Dreamweaver 4 or UltraDev 4.
- **Go To Macromedia Exchange**   Open your Web browser and go directly to the Exchange.

Packages

Extension packages are similar to Zip or StuffIt archives—they simply contain all the necessary files for an extension. The packages are stored in a special format that can be read only by the Extension Manager. Along with the files, there is a Macromedia Extension Installation (MXI) file that gives the Extension Manager instructions on where to put the files and what to write to the menus. The Extension Manager unpacks and then reads the MXI files so that it can know how to unpack the files, put them into the correct locations within the Configuration folder, and add any menu items that are included in the package. If you know a little about XML, you can open these MXI files in a text editor and find out details about the individual files used in making the extension, and also the menus that may be affected by installing the extension.

You can obtain extension packages from a variety of places. You can go directly to the Macromedia Exchange (www.macromedia.com/exchange/) and search for extensions there, but that's only the tip of the iceberg. Our sites (www.basic-ultradev.com and www.dwteam.com/extensions) have several as well. A Web search for "Dreamweaver extensions" will probably point to dozens of useful sites where you can find extensions.

The Macromedia Exchange

The Macromedia Web site is a great place to look for information about Dreamweaver and other Macromedia products. Numerous help files, updates, demos, and tech notes are available. If you ever have a problem with some aspect of Dreamweaver, chances are good that you'll be able to find a tech note on the subject. A special part of the Macromedia site has been set up for extension developers to upload their extensions so that anyone can download and install them into their own computer. It's called the Exchange and it's online at www.macromedia.com/exchange.

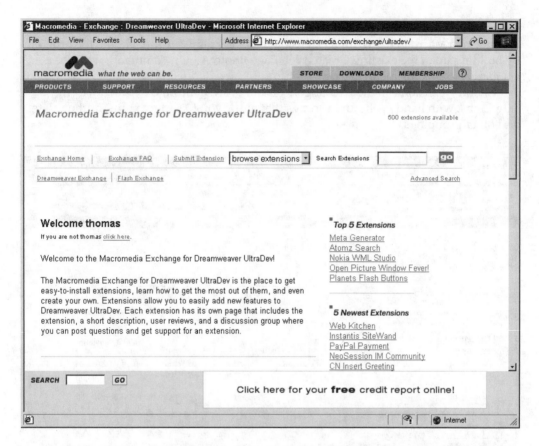

To use the Exchange, you have to sign up first, but it's just a formality. Most of the extensions available on the Exchange are free. As of this writing, more than 500 extensions were available for Dreamweaver users. Many of these are UltraDev extensions that are fully operational in Dreamweaver MX. Several Dreamweaver MX Server Behaviors are available as well.

Third-party developers wrote most of the extensions on the Exchange, but there are also a number written by Macromedia as add-ons to the program. The Dreamweaver command Create Web Page Photo Album 2.0, available on the Exchange, is a good example of a Macromedia-written extension that adds more functionality to the program by building upon the existing Create Web Page Photo Album command, which is a standard Commands menu item.

To find extensions on the Exchange, you can browse through a list of all of the extensions, with handy column headings that allow you to sort by name, author, date, and other groupings.

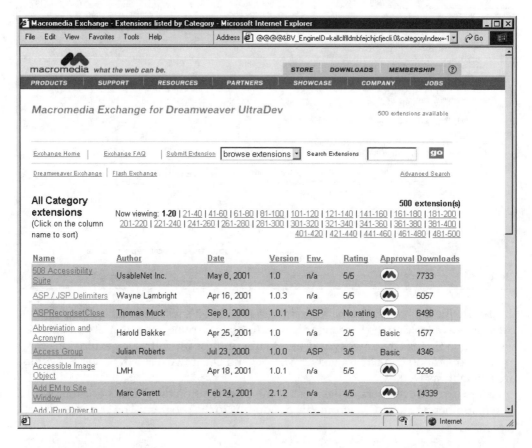

The list is quite long, but on your first visit it is a good idea to see everything that is available. After you get an idea of what's there, you can go back from time to time and search for extensions that you might need for any given task. An advanced search page allows you to search the extensions by almost anything.

Each extension has its own page with the extension description and download links for PC and Macintosh. There is a discussion group for the extensions where you can post questions about extensions. There is also a place where you can rate the extension from 1 to 5, or post comments about the extension. You'll notice that some of the extensions have the Macromedia logo next to them—they are Macromedia-approved extensions. This simply means they've undergone more stringent testing and conform to certain Macromedia interface standards.

Tip
Macromedia has tested all extensions on the Exchange before being posted, so it is usually a safe bet to install an extension if you find it on the Exchange.

Other Extension Sites

There are many popular sites for downloading extensions. Many of these sites offer free downloads of extensions, and some may charge a small fee for an extension.

Extensions have become a business for some people because the use of extensions has become fairly widespread. Many of the extension developers are well-known members of the Dreamweaver MX community, and can usually be trusted to deliver top-quality software at a low price. If you are unsure of a particular Web site or extension, you can usually find information in the Macromedia forums by simply asking the advice of people in the newsgroups.

Using Extensions

To use an extension, you have to install the MXP file into your Dreamweaver MX. What this will do is unpack the files in the package and place them in the appropriate folders inside the Configuration folder in Dreamweaver MX. This is a simple process:

1. Download the extension you wish to install.

2. Save the file on your computer in a central location so that you'll be able to find it. There is a folder named Downloaded Extensions in the root Dreamweaver MX folder that is a perfect place to store and keep track of third-party extensions.

3. Navigate to the folder where you downloaded the extension.

4. Double-click the extension file package. This should bring up the Extension Manager. If it doesn't, you may need to reinstall Dreamweaver MX or the Extension Manager.

5. The first screen you'll see is the Macromedia Extensions Disclaimer licensing agreement. You should read this before proceeding. It tells you, among other things, that the extensions are the property of the person who wrote the extension and that there is no warranty of any kind. In other words, install at your own risk and don't redistribute the extensions.

6. Click Accept to install the extension.

7. If you get any dialog boxes that tell you there is a file installed that is older than the one you are about to install, you can usually click Yes and safely overwrite this file.

8. If you get any dialog boxes that tell you there is a file installed that is newer than the one you are about to install, you should probably click No so as not to overwrite the newer file. It is up to the extension developer to make sure that these shared files don't conflict with each other. The Extension Manager doesn't keep track of different versions of files—only different versions of extensions.

9. You should now see a dialog box that tells you the extension has been installed successfully.

10. One thing you will want to do is to read the information available in the Extension Manager after installing the extension. After clicking OK in step 9, you'll see the information page of the Extension Manager, which lists descriptions

of all extensions you've installed. One reason to read this is because the extension may be hard to find in Dreamweaver MX. There are many places where an extension can show up. In the case of a server format, you may expect it to be in the Server Behaviors panel, but it isn't: It will show up on a particular data source in the Bindings panel as a drop-down list. Armed with that information, you can start Dreamweaver MX and try to apply the extension.

11. If Dreamweaver MX is running, you'll have to shut it down and restart it to be able to use a new extension. This is because Dreamweaver MX loads references to all current extensions into memory when you start it up. When you install a new extension, Dreamweaver MX doesn't know about it until you restart it.

12. Open the appropriate menu for the extension you just installed. It should appear.

Tips for Using Extensions

If you think of extensions as pretested bits of code that can be parameterized, then you begin to appreciate the power of them, but also the limitation. Most extensions are fairly flexible in their implementation. You can add your own code to the page and Dreamweaver MX will still recognize the extension. For example, if you add a Show-Hide Layers Behavior to your page, you can add hand-coded bits of JavaScript to your <head> section of the page and the Show-Hide Layers behavior will still show up in the Behaviors panel. One thing that you can't do is to make changes to the key areas that allow the extension to be recognized by Dreamweaver MX.

| Tip | *The most important tip of all was also step 10 from the previous section: After installing an extension, read the description in the Extension Manager, but also read any documentation that may have come with the extension. Extensions can be found in many places and on many different menus inside of the Dreamweaver environment, and can be used in many different ways.* |

In the case of Behaviors, the function name has to be intact in the code on your page in order for the extension to be recognized by Dreamweaver MX. For example, you can't change the name of the *MM_validateForm* function to *myFormValidation* and expect Dreamweaver MX to still be able to recognize the function. Similarly, you can't edit the actual functions and then attempt to reapply the Behavior—Dreamweaver MX might overwrite your changes.

You are always free to use your own hand coding within Dreamweaver MX. That is one of the program's strongest points. But don't expect the automated parts of the program to remain automated after you've modified them. Dreamweaver MX is a very flexible environment that allows you to create your own code or use the automated code-generating functionality of Behaviors, Objects, Server Behaviors, and other built-in extensions. Dreamweaver MX also won't overwrite your own code. However, when a piece of code belongs to Dreamweaver MX, like a Behavior, Dreamweaver MX will take ownership of the code and attempt to correct it if it has been modified.

Server Behaviors are no different. In many cases, when you modify the code generated by a Server Behavior, many times you will see a red check mark in the Server Behaviors panel. This is not necessarily a bad thing. When you see this, it can mean one of two things:

- You have modified the Server Behavior code in some way intentionally.
- The Server Behavior code has been corrupted in some way and should be corrected.

If you have modified your code and the Server Behavior shows up with a red check mark in the Server Behaviors panel, don't attempt to open up the Server Behavior from the panel any more—any changes you've made will be "corrected" when you click OK in the Server Behavior dialog box. This is very handy to correct a corrupted section of code, but it is frustrating if you have made extensive changes to the code. The best approach is to use the Server Behaviors to get your code onto the page, but don't use them any more if you are making changes to the code.

Using the Bindings panel for many people means adding a recordset to the page and nothing more. The true power of the Bindings panel, however, is that you can define many different types of page-level and site-wide variables in the panel. After doing this, the variables are available to any extension or dialog box that has a text field with a lightening bolt icon next to it. For example, if you define your session variables for the site in the Bindings panel, they will be available for use inside of tag attributes in the Tag Inspector (found in the Code panel group). This can be handy for creating a color preference for a user of your Web site by placing the user's color preference in a session variable, or by defining a dynamic ID attribute for a dynamic <div> layer on your page.

Some Popular Extensions

Dreamweaver and UltraDev have been around for a while, and there are literally hundreds—if not thousands—of available extensions that will work in Dreamweaver MX. Many of these are available from the Exchange and other places. Many extensions that were written for earlier versions of Dreamweaver will not work in Dreamweaver MX, but many will. Following is a description of some of the more popular extensions.

Horizontal Looper Repeat Region

The Dreamweaver MX Repeat Region Server Behavior creates a loop that repeats all data vertically, with no option for horizontal repeats. The Horizontal Looper is so-called because it repeats your data from your database horizontally as well as vertically. It acts in a similar fashion to the standard Repeat Region that is supplied with Dreamweaver MX, but instead of "number of records," you are prompted for Rows and Columns. This can give you greater flexibility for the types of data display pages you can create. For example, if you have a page of image thumbnails, you can display them in a 4×4 grid easily with the Horizontal Looper. This extension is available from www.dwteam.com.

When you want to use the Horizontal Looper, you have to consider that it will build a table for you automatically. Whereas the Repeat Region will loop over your data and create the server-side code for the loop, the Horizontal Looper actually has to put your data into an HTML table so that it can be neatly formatted in rows and columns.

The steps to use this Server Behavior are as follows:

1. The first thing you need to do is to put a data connection and a recordset on your page. You can do this in the standard way. For this example, use the Bettergig database and the Employers table. Use a SQL statement like this:

```
SELECT EmpName, EmpCity, EmpState, EmpPhone
FROM Employers
```

2. Insert a one-column, four-row table on the page with no border, and 100 percent width.

3. Drag or insert each database field from the Bindings panel into the table cells. There should be one field per cell.

4. Select the entire table. This is most easily accomplished by using the tag selector on the bottom of the document window.

5. Apply the Horizontal Looper to the table. The input parameters should be two columns and three rows. At this point, you can browse the page and you will see the display being repeated horizontally and vertically. It is only the first six records, though, and you'll want to page through the results just as you do with a Repeat Region.

6. Add a Recordset Navigation Bar object to the page. You can find this in the Application tab of the Insert bar, or in the Insert | Application Objects menu.

Now you should be able to browse the page *and* page through the results. You can dress up the display any way you want now, such as changing the CSS style for the *EmpName* field to make the display more readable (as shown in Figure 30-1).

CF XHTML Editor

The CF XHTML Editor was developed by Massimo Foti. Massimo is one of the most prolific and talented extension developers around. This particular extension was the winner of Macromedia's extension contest that helped kick off the preview release of Dreamweaver MX.

Figure 30-1. *The Horizontal Looper builds a display that repeats the data horizontally and vertically.*

The extension is for ColdFusion only and offers the Web developer the capability to insert an area on a Web page that is like a mini-word processor. It can be used in content management systems or other types of data entry applications where you want to allow the user to enter clean XHTML code or styled text. The extension is implemented as an Object, a Behavior, and a custom ColdFusion tag. This extension is available from www.massimocorner.com.

You can use this object on a ColdFusion site, so we'll make an addition to the post_a_gig.cfm page to allow the employer to insert XHTML formatting on the job description field. To apply the object, follow these steps:

1. Remove the JobDescription text field. The XHTML Editor will be the new JobDescription field. Leave your cursor in the table cell that was once occupied by the JobDescription textfield.

2. Choose the XHTML Editor from the ColdFusion Advanced tab of the Insert bar.

3. Make the fieldname JobDescription, and give the XHTML Editor a width of 500 and a height of 350.

4. Click OK.

If you browse the page, you should be able to fill in the database fields with text, and the Job Description field will allow you to add styling to your text, such as lists, <em> and <strong> tags, and different block-level tags (shown in Figure 30-2).

The extension works only on Windows using Internet Explorer 5.5 or higher, but the code it produces can be used in any browser.

Check Form

Dreamweaver MX comes with a Behavior for validating form fields, but it is very limited. Jaro von Flocken is one of the top extension developers, and his Check Form (shown in Figure 30-3) is one of those extensions that every Dreamweaver developer has in his arsenal. This extension is available from www.yaromat.com.

Check Form can be applied to the *onSubmit* event of the <form> tag. That is usually the best place to apply a client-side JavaScript validation. To apply the behavior, there needs to be form elements on the page also. The extension will be grayed out in the Behaviors menu if there are no form elements on the page.

To apply the behavior, follow these steps:

1. Select the form tag in the tag selector on the bottom bar of the document window. The Behaviors panel should have the <form> Actions heading in the title bar of the panel.

2. Open the Behaviors panel and choose Yaromat | Check Form.

3. Cycle through your form elements one at a time to apply the appropriate validation to each form element. Also, make sure you add your own custom error messages to each form element as well.

4. Click OK and the Behavior will be applied to the page.

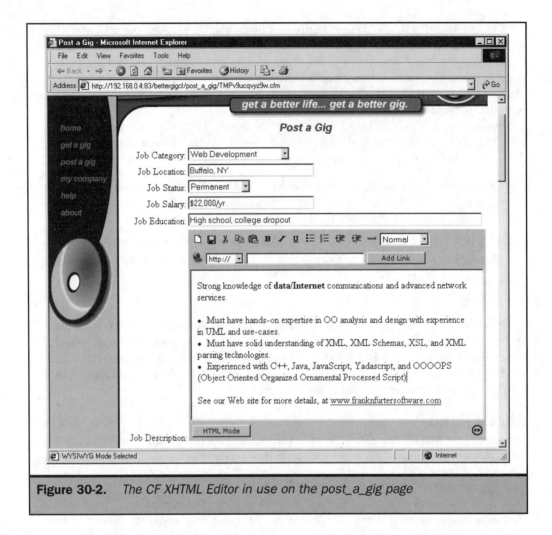

Figure 30-2.   *The CF XHTML Editor in use on the post_a_gig page*

If you browse your page at this point, you should not be able to submit the form unless the validation rules that you applied to the form are being met.

JavaScript form validation is a great first-line defense against bad data.

DWMX Tidy

This extension was written by Daniele Ugoletti and Paul R. Boon of www.dwfile.com. It is based on HTML Tidy, only tailored for the Dreamweaver MX interface. The extension is extremely configurable, allowing you to choose from a predefined list of

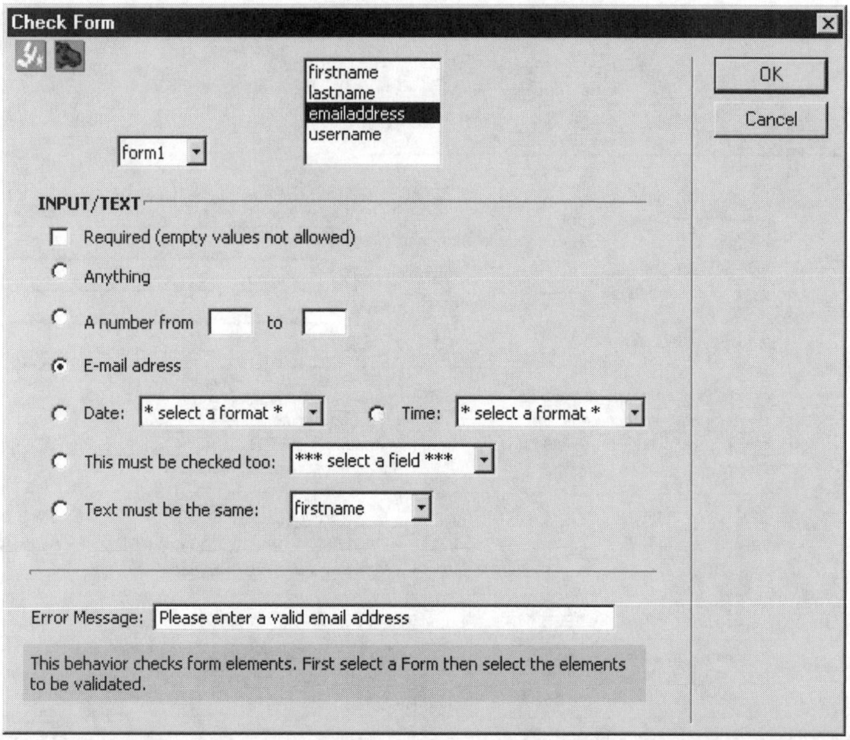

Figure 30-3. *The Check Form extension has many options for validating form elements.*

available "tidy" settings for your page or your site, and the ability to define your own custom settings. This extension is available from www.dwfile.com.

To use the extension, choose Team DWFile.com I DMX Tidy from the Commands menu and then choose the options you want from the interface (shown in Figure 30-4). The extension is Windows only.

Expression Builder

The Expression Builder is an extension that was written to bring some of the ColdFusion Studio functionality into Dreamweaver MX. It is a Flash MX–based floating panel that allows you to add functions to your code from a predefined dictionary that is loaded into the extension. The extension is also extensible, allowing you to add your own dictionaries to the extension. The extension was written by Neil Clark and is available at www.fluidik.com/products/extensions/.

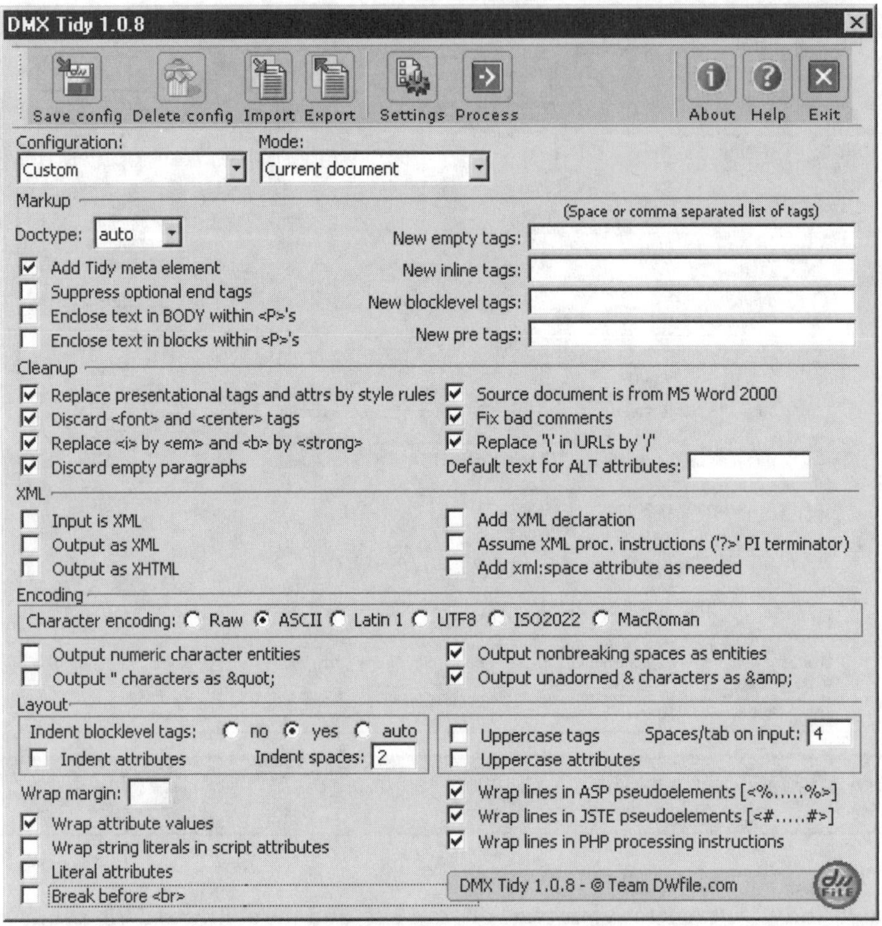

Figure 30-4. *The DMX Tidy extension, from www.dwfile.com*

To use the extension, choose Window | Others | Expression. You can then choose any expression from the list to insert into your document.

JavaScript Integration Kit for Flash 5

The JavaScript Integration Kit for Flash 5 is a Macromedia-authored extension that adds several things to Dreamweaver MX, but at the forefront is the Advanced Form Validation Behaviors. These Behaviors include several form field validations like credit card, email, entry-length, US Phone, US Zip code, and many others. The extension also includes several Flash control Behaviors, for adding VCR-like controls to a Flash movie. This extension is described more fully in Chapter 11.

Calculate Form

This is another great Yaromat extension from Jaro von Flocken. This extension allows you to add calculations to form elements. You can create some pretty sophisticated calculations using the extension, because it allows you to treat the form elements as if they were numbers in a calculator (shown in Figure 30-5). The extension creates all the JavaScript for your page automatically.

To use the extension, you need to have form elements on your page that are to be calculated. There also should be a form element in which to put the result of your calculation. The calculations can be done between form elements or with a hard-coded constant. Parentheses are included in the extension that you can use to aid in the calculation.

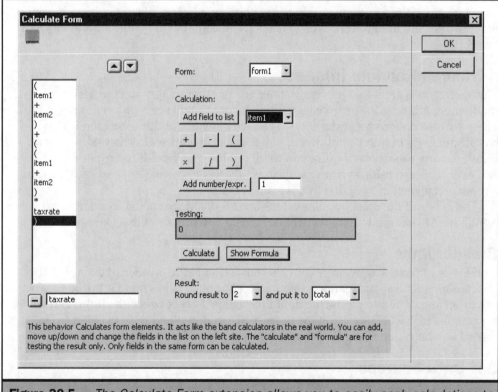

Figure 30-5.   *The Calculate Form extension allows you to easily apply calculations to form elements.*

Layer AniMagic

The Layer AniMagic extension from Project Seven makes it easy to add animation effects to layers on your page. You can choose from several preset movements or you can create your own, setting the speed and position of the layers. This extension is available from www.projectseven.com.

The extension can be used in place of Timelines. The code that is generated by the Timelines features is very robust, but it also consumes a lot of space and resources. Many times you don't need all the capabilities of Timelines, and in those cases the Layer AniMagic extension is more efficient.

Auto Layers

This extension by Project Seven is like an automated way of applying the Show-Hide Layers Behavior that ships with Dreamweaver. It is a Behavior with a memory. When you select a layer to show, it remembers the layer so that next time you apply it, that layer will be hidden, as well as all other layers that have been shown with the behavior.

The extension is a good candidate for building your own dynamic menus using layers. Many of the solutions out there are very code-heavy, like the dynamic menus of Fireworks, but the Project Seven extensions all contain very compact and efficient JavaScript.

Advanced Random Images

This extension is great for showing banner ads or other images to your visitors randomly. Each time the user visits the site, he or she will see a different image. There are also options for slideshows. The nice thing about this extension is that it has productivity in mind by allowing you to select an entire directory of images at once. So many extensions require you to fill out too many fields, or apply them over and over. This extension is from Paul Davis of www.kaosweaver.com. Paul also has a commercial version available that is even better.

This is one of the most popular extensions on the Macromedia Exchange and rightly so. At last count, there were over 140,000 downloads of this extension.

Breadcrumbs

Paul Davis of www.kaosweaver.com also has a client-side JavaScript extension that inserts a breadcrumb navigation system into your page (shown in Figure 30-6). The extension allows you to define the delimiter that is used between the links, and also has options to use CSS styles on the links. You can download the extension from www.kaosweaver.com and find it in the Commands | Kaosweaver menu.

Get Data Sources

The Bindings panel is a great way to keep track of your session and application variables for a site, but there is no easy way to add them other than typing them in

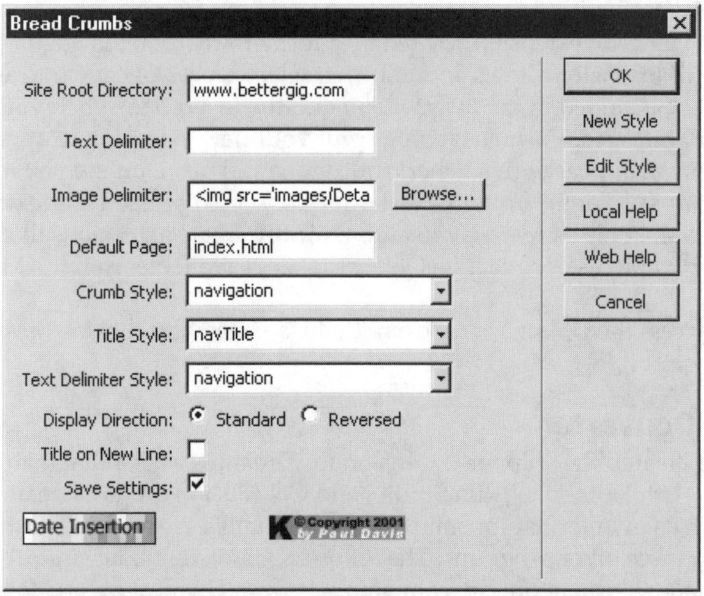

Figure 30-6.   *The Breadcrumbs navigation extension from Kaosweaver*

one by one. This extension, written by Tom Muck, searches your site for all instances of session or application variables and displays them in the Bindings panel. This extension is available from www.dwteam.com, and works with JSP, ASP, CF, and PHP.

Links List

This extension, which won the Macromedia award in 2000 for best UltraDev extension, allows you to add recordset navigation on your page that is a list of links, like 1-10 | 11-20 | 21-30 | 31-40. It works with the standard Dreamweaver MX recordsets and Repeat Regions in ASP, JSP, ColdFusion, and PHP. You can find the extension at www.dwteam.com.

Open Picture Window Fever!

This is the original open picture window extension for Dreamweaver, written by Drew McLellan. This extension allows you to open a new browser window around a picture. The picture dimensions can be retrieved automatically by the extension, making it very easy to apply the Behavior without having to know the actual image dimensions. The latest version of this extension also gives you the option to open a new window with a Flash movie. The extension is available from dreamweaverfever.com/grow.

Object Maker

The Object Maker is an extension written by a former Macromedia engineer named Joe Marini. This extension allows you to turn a selected area of code into an Object that will then be included in the Insert menu and the Insert bar. When you apply the extension, you can specify which tab you want your new extension to appear in. The extension will appear with a generic question mark icon, unless you manually create your own icon for the object. Object extensions are discussed in the next chapter, but the Object Maker is a great way to automatically create extensions that simply insert predefined pieces of code. The Object Maker is available from the Macromedia Exchange.

You can access the Object Maker from the Insert menu by clicking Save Selection As Object.

Snippets Converter

Massimo Foti created the Snippets extension for Dreamweaver 4 that maintained compatibility with Homesite, JRun Studio, and ColdFusion Studio. Dreamweaver MX came out with its own format for snippets that is totally incompatible with older snippets from these other programs. The Snippets Converter extension, also written by Massimo, allows you to import your snippets from Dreamweaver, Homesite, JRun Studio, or ColdFusion Studio. The newly imported snippets will be accessible from the Snippets panel in Dreamweaver MX.

The Snippets Converter is available from www.massimocorner.com.

Built-In Command Maker

One of the most powerful features of Dreamweaver is the capability to take a group of actions that were performed on the page and replay them using the History palette. Even better, you can take this same group of actions and make a command out of it by selecting the history steps that you want to replay and then clicking the Save button (the floppy disk image) or choosing Save As Command from the contextual menu of the History palette. This can save you a lot of time.

When you save a set of history steps as a command, the command automatically appears on the Commands menu, and it also appears as an HTML file in the Commands folder. For example, if you were to insert a table with two rows and three columns, with width set to 100 percent, cellspacing set to 0, and cellpadding set to 0, you could save the action as a command and then you would be able to run this from the commands menu. If you have a site where certain table sizes are being used frequently, you could even have a whole group of these in a submenu.

History commands have many uses, and once you start using them, you will find all sorts of shortcuts that will help you in your Web page creation. Did you know that you can save a history command to the clipboard and re-apply it to the page? For example, let's say you wanted to change a paragraph to an <h3> tag, apply a CSS style, and add a link to section of text. You could perform those actions on to the text, then go to the History palette and select the three history steps. By using the contextual menu (right-click on a PC and CTRL-click on a Mac), you can save the commands to the clipboard so that you can apply the same steps to other sections of text. After saving the steps, you can simply select another section of text and click Paste, and your steps will be replayed on the current selection. This can be very handy when you have multiple instances of something on the page that you need to apply the same steps to.

Summary

In this chapter, you learned about extensions. Extensions are the Dreamweaver MX equivalent to macros, only much more powerful. You were also given a tour of the Macromedia Exchange, a central repository for extensions, and shown several of the more popular extensions available. In the next chapter, you'll learn how to build your own extensions to Dreamweaver MX.

The
Complete
Reference

Dreamweaver
MX

Chapter 31

Dreamweaver MX
Extensibility Model

One of the most exciting features of Dreamweaver MX is the capability to add your own features to it, or *extend* it. Dreamweaver MX is built around a document object model (DOM), much like a fourth-generation browser. Dreamweaver MX is, in fact, built upon a combination of a subset of the Netscape Navigator 4 DOM and a subset of the World Wide Web Consortium (W3C) DOM inside of the HTML interfaces of extensions and dialog boxes. The rendering engine of Dreamweaver MX is based on the Netscape DOM, so the extensions conform more closely to the syntax and specifications of that DOM. New to Dreamweaver MX is the built-in JavaScript 1.5 interpreter, which supercedes the 1.2 interpreter that was in Dreamweaver 4 and UltraDev 4.

 With the added power of the JavaScript 1.5 interpreter comes a few problems, however. JavaScript 1.5 syntax is not nearly as forgiving as JavaScript 1.2 syntax. Many extensions that were written for Dreamweaver 4 may have problems because of this.

The principles behind the DOM have their basis in object-oriented programming (OOP). In short, everything in your document is an object, from an image or form item, to comments and tags. The document itself is an object and is the root level of the DOM. Everything in the document can be accessed through the document object.

The extensions are written in HTML and JavaScript, with the ability also to write more complex extensions in C or C++. For example, when you click the Table object in Dreamweaver MX, the pop-up interface that appears is an HTML form, with a JavaScript include file that does the dirty work of putting the code together and inserting it into the document where you want it. The idea that you can extend an HTML tool with HTML itself is ingenious—it allows Web developers with HTML and JavaScript experience to add features to the tool to make it more productive in their own environment. The Dreamweaver MX on your desktop will be very different from the Dreamweaver MX on another's desktop, because you will likely have added the features that make working with Dreamweaver MX easier for you.

Understanding Extensions

To access the extensibility features of Dreamweaver MX, you need to be fairly proficient in JavaScript. Several good JavaScript books are available and having a good one handy at all times is wise. Also, many of the extensibility features rely on regular expressions, a part of JavaScript that is not well documented. You can find information on regular expressions, also known as *regexes*, or *RegExps*, in Perl resources as well, because the syntax is very similar. After you are comfortable with regexes, you will be able to write complex Server Behaviors and other extensions where text manipulation is important.

All the extensions to Dreamweaver MX reside in the Configuration folder at the root of the Dreamweaver MX folder. If you look inside the folder, you'll see folders for

Commands, Objects, Floaters, Inspectors, Menus, Server Behaviors, Toolbars, and Translators, among others. The files in these folders correspond directly to the different areas of Dreamweaver MX that are extensible. For example, every item on the Commands menu of Dreamweaver MX has a corresponding HTML file in the Configuration | Commands folder. Every object on the Insert bar has corresponding files in the Configuration | Objects folder. By modifying these files or creating your own, you can effectively change the functionality of Dreamweaver MX.

Note | *Dreamweaver MX uses a new (to this version) multiuser Configuration folder in operating systems that support it (like Windows 2000 and Mac OSX), so when an extension is installed, it will be installed to a Configuration folder inside the current user's multiuser folder.*

Adding features to Dreamweaver MX is valuable, but the best part of it is that your HTML and server-side script is "live" in the code window while you work on your page. Repeat Region is a perfect example of this. This Server Behavior consists of some very sophisticated JavaScript to get the Behavior to work with the page, but the results are astounding. When you apply the Behavior and switch to "Live Data" (SHIFT-CTRL-R), the page is rendered in "real time," giving you not only a chance to "preview" the page, but also the ability to edit the page in a form that exists only in concept.

To explain further, when a user requests your page, the server fetches the page—if it has the proper file extension (.jsp, .asp, .aspx, .php, or .cfm)—and executes the code, sending only HTML and client-side scripts to the browser. Dreamweaver MX, however, is retrieving your server code on the fly from the server, showing you the results of your server code as if it were the result of an HTTP request. The page you are editing inside of the Dreamweaver MX environment in Live Data view is a rendition of how your page will look in a browser, but it doesn't actually exist in that form. Dreamweaver MX goes one step further than other Web-development tools by letting you edit this "ghost" page in a visual environment as if it were your final product.

Dreamweaver was designed with extensibility in mind. As mentioned earlier, Dreamweaver MX has a DOM similar to a browser. The DOM is described in detail in the "Extending Dreamweaver MX" document included in the Dreamweaver MX help menu, and also on the Dreamweaver MX CD-ROM as a printable PDF document. You can also get a bound version from Macromedia for a small fee. The Dreamweaver MX application programming interface (API) has about 700 JavaScript functions that are not accessible by the DOM of a standard browser because Dreamweaver MX relies on *selection,* which is not a necessity in a browser. The capability to *select* areas of HTML, objects, and script, and apply commands or Behaviors to the selection, is what makes Dreamweaver MX a powerful HTML-authoring environment.

Extensions are essentially *code that is inserted into the page,* but they can also be a lot more than that. Unlike a text editor or a text-based HTML editor, such as Homesite or BBEdit, the HTML tags are *rendered* into actual objects that you can see and manipulate by moving, dragging, assigning attributes, or changing the code. When you drop an image on the page, for instance, you can go back and select the image to be presented with a Property Inspector that shows you the attributes that go along with the image. If you happen to change some of the code in HTML source view, those changes are reflected on the screen visually, as well as in the attributes of the Inspector. These are all things that you have to consider when you are writing your own extensions to Dreamweaver MX. An object extension, such as a table, has an associated Property Inspector. In addition, when you are writing Server Behaviors, you must consider the different server-side languages that are part of Dreamweaver MX. When you write a Server Behavior extension, it is usable only by someone working within the same server environment as you. In other words, if you create a ColdFusion Server Behavior, someone using the ASP VBScript server model would not be able to use it.

The Extension Interface

Most extensions have an *interface* for receiving attributes from the user. This interface can be designed inside of the Dreamweaver MX environment, because it is just an HTML form. Most of the standard rules of HTML apply, and you can use standard HTML form elements to accept input from the user. There are also some special form elements that were built for the MX environment only, such as the editable select list. You can also use some of the special JavaScript objects that form "controls" within the Dreamweaver MX environment. These controls form the basis of the Server Behavior Builder, but the code can be used in other extensions as well.

You can go about designing the interface in several ways. Generally, you should start with a basic table and add your attributes to it, as shown in Figure 31-1.

One thing to think about when you are designing your interface is that your text fields and other form fields should have meaningful names. When you are writing your code to manipulate the data that you retrieve from the interface, a text field named firstRowColor is certainly more readable than textfield2. Other considerations also exist. You might think that your extension looks great in purple, but Macromedia has strict guidelines that you should follow to remain 100-percent compatible with Dreamweaver MX:

- Don't use font or background colors. Use the standard Dreamweaver MX colors that are picked by default.

- Don't use font styles.

- Your company or personal logo can be in the interface, but it should be on the bottom. Alternatively, you can put an About button on the interface and link it to an HTML page or another tab in your interface.

- You can include a brief help text on the bottom of the interface itself, with the color set to #D3D3D3.

- Extensions should have a Help button. This can be implemented in many cases by simply including a *displayHelp()* function in your extension.

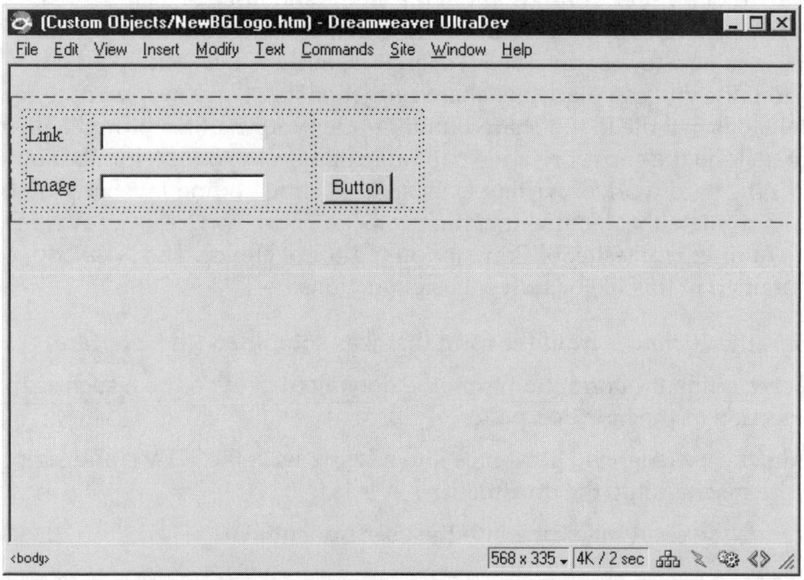

Figure 31-1.   *Typical basic extension interface*

These are just a few of the guidelines. You can find a full list in the file ui_guidelines.html under \Macromedia\Extension Manager\Help\.

To get the visual look of your interface, you can design it in the Dreamweaver MX environment. Set up a site with the root folder as the Configuration folder and you'll be able to edit extension files as if they were part of a site. You can also edit your files in Homesite, Ultraedit, BBEdit, or your text editor of choice to clean up the code. Make sure to remove all styles, colors, and fonts that may have been added to the page during the design process.

In addition to the HTML elements, your interface can include all the JavaScript functions that are used in the execution of the extension, or it can have a line at the top, such as the following, to import the JavaScript functions as an include file:

```
<script src="myextension.js"></script>
```

This file should have the same name as your HTML file, except with a .js extension. This JavaScript file should contain only the localized functions that are necessary for your particular extension. When you have your interface file ready, save it into the appropriate folder under Configuration. It is not mandatory to include your JavaScript functions in a separate file, but it can be helpful in creating localized versions of your extensions, and also to separate the JavaScript from the GUI.

Additionally, you can place any shared functions that you may want to reuse in other extensions in a file in the Shared folder under your name or your company name. Be sure to include the correct relative path information in your script declaration.

Most of the hard work of writing extensions is hand-coding JavaScript into the JS file to manipulate the document, which you can do in the Dreamweaver MX environment or in Homesite, BBEdit, or your editor of choice. The JavaScript code that is contained in this file has a few basic functions:

- Gets the attributes from the form that was submitted (the interface)
- Gets pertinent information from the document being edited, such as the current selection or the insertion point
- Puts the user-defined attributes into a string with the HTML and script that is to be inserted into the document
- Inserts the resulting string into the user's document

 One of the advantages of working with another program such as Homesite to create and edit extensions is that you will want to test them out using a real Web page in Dreamweaver MX. This is especially true of server-side extensions such as server behaviors. You'll want to have full preview and live data functionality within Dreamweaver MX while you are working on the extension.

Selections and Offsets

Sometimes extension writing is a fairly simple procedure, but other times it may require some very complex document and string manipulation to accomplish, as in the case of Server Behaviors. The same principles apply to all extensions, though, from the basic Objects and Behaviors to the complex Server Behaviors and Data Sources. Depending on what your extension is doing, it could work with either a *selection* or an *insertion point*. A *selection* is a highlighted area on the page. An *insertion point*, which is a specified point in your document, is either where the cursor is located or any point within the document. Here is an example that retrieves the highlighted code or object from a page using the *getSelection()* method of Dreamweaver, which is a function from the Dreamweaver MX API for getting a selection:

```
var theSelection = dw.getSelection();
```

This function will return an array of two values that represent the beginning of the selection and the end of the selection as *offsets* from the beginning of the document. The offset values are integer values that refer to the character positions within a document.

For example, in the following snippet, if you were to select the words "hello there," the selected code would have offsets of 12 and 23:

```
<html><body>hello there</body></html>
```

To check whether an actual selection is made, or whether you are simply dealing with an insertion point, you make a test to see whether the two values match— meaning nothing is selected. You make a test with a block like this:

```
if (theSelection[0] == theSelection[1]) {
    //we have an insertion point, not a selection
}else{
    //we have a selection
};
```

You can use this function both ways—and you can use it to display an error message if the extension requires a selection and the user hasn't selected anything. You can then manipulate the document yourself by using the powerful function *getDocumentDOM()*, which returns the contents of the document in object form:

```
var theDom = dw.getDocumentDOM('document');
```

You can use the object that is returned, *theDom*, to get the actual selection in text format by first getting the *documentElement* property of the document node (*theDom*). After you have that, you use the *outerHTML* property of the *documentElement* to get the actual text of the entire document:

```
var theDom = dw.getDocumentDOM('document');
var theSelection = theDom.getSelection();
var theEntireDocument = theDom.documentElement.outerHTML;
var theSelectedText = theEntireDocument.substring(theSelection[0], ¬
theSelection[1]);
```

Now, the variable *theSelectedText* contains the actual text that is highlighted in the document window. If this happens to be an object such as an image, the variable will contain the entire object, including tags and attributes. You can start to see that this becomes a very powerful tool for inserting things into your document, or for editing things that are already in your document. Highlighting an image, for example, will put the contents of the entire HTML code block to render that image into the variable, which you can then manipulate, alter, or give Behaviors.

Another way to highlight a block of HTML on the page is to click the tag name in the Tag Selector in the lower-left corner of the document window. This highlights the corresponding code in the HTML source window and the corresponding object in the design window.

You can also get the text before the selection or the text after the selection by manipulating the selection with string functions using the offsets to the selection. Added to the previous code, the following lines of code will return the two blocks of text around the selection:

```
var beforeTheSelectedText = theEntireDocument.substring(0, ¬
theSelection[0]);
var afterTheSelectedText = theEntireDocument.substring(theSelection[1]);
```

The first variable (*beforeTheSelectedText*) starts at the zero position on the page and gets all text up to the beginning of the selection. The second line gets all text starting at the point where the selection ends. This gives you three parts now— *beforeTheSelectedText* contains all code before *TheSelectedText*, *theSelection* contains the selection, and *afterTheSelectedText* contains all code after the selection. You could easily take these three parts of the page and put them back together or manipulate the text in one or more of the parts. Suppose you want to make the selection a link. You could do that with a simple <a href> tag around the selection, like this:

```
var newSelection = ' <a href="http://www.myhomepage.com">' + ¬
theSelectedText + '</a>';
```

Notice that the preceding code just concatenated the string with the opening tag, the selection, and the closing tag. Now, the *newSelection* variable holds the original selection wrapped in a link. To write it back to the page, you have to concatenate the strings like this:

```
var theDom = dw.getDocumentDOM('document');
theDom.outerHTML = beforeTheSelectedText + newSelection + ¬
afterTheSelectedText;
```

Now your updated page contains a link around the text that you had selected.

Nodes

Nodes are essential to the understanding of the DOM, both in browsers and in Dreamweaver MX extensions, and are required for some of the complex HTML manipulation within Dreamweaver MX. Every tag in the document can be considered a node. Nodes have many properties that can be used by the developer to build extensions. The properties are accessed through standard *dot* notation, as in *myNode.property*. The terminology that will be used may be more familiar to those comfortable with the Netscape 4 DOM, which is quite different from the DOM that Internet Explorer programmers are used to. When building extensions, you'll be accessing objects and their properties as you would when working with the Netscape 4 browser. There are several exceptions as well—Dreamweaver MX allows the use of innerHTML and outerHTML, for example, which are part of the Internet Explorer DOM. The Dreamweaver MX DOM is a complex mix of these browser DOMs, with much more added as well.

A knowledge of nodes and the DOM is essential to building Dreamweaver MX extensions and is becoming more and more essential to basic Web programming. Dynamic HTML, XML, and XHTML all use the DOM as a way to access a document.

The following are the four basic types of nodes, which you can check with the *nodeType* property:

- **DOCUMENT_NODE**   The document-level node that enables you to have access to all parts of the document

- **ELEMENT_NODE**   A node for an HTML tag, such as <table>

- **COMMENT_NODE**   An HTML comment surrounded by <!- ->

- **TEXT_NODE**   A block of text that is on the page

To better understand nodes, examine the following:

```
<table>
    <tr>
        <td>First</td>
        <td>Last</td>
        <!--this is a comment node-->
    </tr>
</table>
```

The <table> tag is the outermost node in the example. It is an ELEMENT_NODE type node, and it contains nodes within, called *child nodes*, accessible through the *childNodes* property of the table node. The one item in the *childNodes* array is the <tr> node. That node has a *childNodes* array as well, with three items in it—two <td> tag pairs and a COMMENT_NODE type node. Nodes also have parents, accessible through the *parentNode* property. The *parentNode* of <tr> is the <table> node. Not seen here is the <body> node, which is parent of the <table>, the <body> node. Parent to the <body> node is the <html> node, which is the DOCUMENT_NODE *nodeType*.

You've already seen the *outerHTML* property of the document node—this was the entire document, including the tags that made up the node. Another property is the *innerHTML* property, which retrieves what is *between* the tags. This property is useful for getting text and properties that are contained within a tag. Another handy property of a node is the *tagName* property. The *tagName* property of the <table> tag is table, which you could use in a situation in which you are looking for a particular node, like this:

```
for (var i=0; i<someNodes.length; i++) {
    if(someNodes[i].tagName.toLowerCase() == "table") {
        //found a table tag--do some stuff to it
    };
};
```

You can use this method to your advantage if you are trying to insert some code into a specific tag, such as adding a JavaScript rollover Behavior to an <image> tag, or putting some server-side code into a repeat-region table tag to alternate colored rows. Another way to find a tag is to use the function *findTag(tagName)*, located in the DOM.js file.

Dot Notation

Accessing properties of the DOM or objects in the DOM is done with standard *dot* notation. The root of the "tree" is the document, and all objects can be accessed through it. The objects that you will be accessing in your extension interface will be predominantly form items, such as text fields (or edit boxes), check boxes, radio buttons, and drop-down select boxes. Getting to these is easy through the document root. Start with *document.formname* to get the form, and then access your form element by its name, like this:

```
document.formname.elementname
```

Depending on what kind of element it is, different properties will be associated with it. A check box will have a "checked" property; a text field will have a "value" property. The code looks like this:

```
var isCheckboxChecked = document.myForm.myCheckbox.checked;
//true or false value for myCheckbox: is it checked?
var myText = document.myForm.myTextfield.value;
//actual text value of the textfield named myTextField
```

Dot notation can be pretty complicated, but after you are able to follow the logic of it, getting the properties of any object will be easy. The following example is a little more complex. Suppose you have a select box in an HTML form that will access a list of recordsets available to the page. After the user has made a selection, you now will be able to retrieve it. You start with a select box on the form named *selectRecordset*. You can use dot notation to retrieve the text. To illustrate the complexity, the following shows the entire statement on one line, using dot notation:

```
var myRecordset =
    document.forms[0].selectRecordset.options[document.forms[0]. ¬
selectRecordset.selectedIndex].text;
```

You start with "document" and get to the "forms" array next. Because you have only one form on the page, you access the first element in the array, which has a zero index—*forms[0]*. If you knew the name of the form, you could have used that in its place, but *forms[0]* is a good general-purpose way of getting the form object on a page. Next, you access the name of the element in the form, *selectRecordset*. The options of the select box are numbered from 0 to however many recordsets are on the page, so you want to pick the option that is selected. No "selected option" property exists, but there is a *selectedIndex* property. Because you need the actual text and not the index, you will access the DOM again with *document.forms[0].selectRecordset.selectedIndex* to get your *[index]* number. Now, you have the selected option value from the box, and all that remains is to get the text of that option. You do that with the "text" property. This complexity is required because of the Netscape 4 DOM inside of the extension interface and the fact that the *value* attribute is not supported.

You could organize this into more easily readable lines by accessing the individual objects and properties in a hierarchical fashion, as follows (note that the following code retrieves the same text property):

```
var theForm = document.forms[0];
var theSelectBox = theForm.selectRecordset;
var theIndex = theSelectBox.selectedIndex;
var theOption = theSelectBox.options[theIndex];
var theText = theOption.text;
```

In any event, you can see how the hierarchical approach is implemented in the DOM. You can access the properties, methods, and events of any particular object by using dot notation.

The Dreamweaver MX API Methods

The DOM also has methods. Methods can be considered built-in functions of the DOM. To access the methods of the DOM, you use dot notation as well:

```
theNode.theMethod();
```

getElementsByTagName(tagName)

Given the name of the tag, the method simply retrieves the tag that you are searching for. You can call this method with a node, or with the entire DOM. If you are searching for all images on the page, you would call it like this:

```
var myImageNodeList = ¬
dreamweaver.getDocumentDOM().getElementsByTagName("img");
```

or

```
var theDom = dreamweaver.getDocumentDOM();
var myImageNodeList = theDom.getElementsByTagName("img");
```

hasChildNodes()

This method returns true or false. Use it to determine whether any child nodes are within the node that you are calling it from, as in the following:

```
if (myNode.hasChildNodes()) {
    //do this
};
```

getAttribute(attrName)

Use this method if you need to find any given attribute of a node. If your node (*myNode*) contains the following text, you can get the image source path with *myNode.getAttribute("src")*:

```
<img src="myImage" height=30 width=40>
```

setAttribute(attrName, attrValue)

This method does the opposite of *setAttribute* and returns no value. You supply the attribute name and the value you want the attribute to have, and *setAttribute* will write the HTML to your page for you. For example, if you have a table node named *myTable*, and you want to set the width to 50 percent, put the following line in a command:

```
myTable.setAttribute("width","50%");
```

removeAttribute(attrName)

This method removes a given attribute as well as its value from a node.

As mentioned earlier, Dreamweaver MX has over 700 built-in functions that you can use. You'll be exploring more of these as you build extensions in this chapter and the next chapter.

Shared Folder Functions

You don't need to reinvent the wheel when writing your extensions, so it's always a good idea to reuse whatever you can. In addition to the standard methods of the DOM, hundreds of functions are available in the Shared folder under Configuration—some are well documented and some aren't. After you learn your way around the Shared folder, you'll be writing extensions much more quickly. You can streamline certain repetitive tasks by using the appropriate function. The following sections take a look at a few of them.

> **Tip**
>
> *Many of the shared functions that you'll be using when developing extensions are in the dwscripts.js file, which is a new file for Dreamweaver MX. The dwscripts.js file is found in Configuration | Shared | Common | Scripts. Many of the common functions from previous versions of Dreamweaver are now found in this file, which is loaded in memory at startup. Simply include the dwscripts.js file in your extension to use the functions within.*

findObject(objName, parentObj)

This function (located in .. \Shared\MM\Scripts\CMN\UI.js) will be one of your most-used functions. It replaces a lot of repetitious DOM accesses. What it does is allow you to avoid using standard dot notation in certain situations where you know the name of the element that you are addressing—you can simply call that element by name using *findObject*.

When the OK button is clicked in your extension, your JavaScript needs to fetch the values from the form that was just submitted. Suppose that you have a text field in your interface named *recordset* and a drop-down box named *myOptionsBox*. You could use standard dot notation like this:

```
var recordsetName = document.forms[0].recordset.selectedIndex;
var myOptions = document.forms[0].myOptionsBox.options[document.forms[0]. ¬
myOptionsBox.selectedIndex].text;
```

or use the *findObject* function like this:

```
var recordsetName = findObject("recordset").value;
var myOptions = ¬
findObject("myOptionsBox").options[findObject("myOptionsBox"). ¬
selectedIndex].text;
```

The first method uses the standard DOM methods of retrieving the object's properties, whereas the second method uses the *findObject* function and is a little easier to read. The *findObject* function returns the actual object that you are looking for, with all of the properties intact. We generally prefer using the *findObject* function, but we illustrate both methods in the extensions we build in the following chapters.

*You may notice that Dreamweaver MX actually inserts a function similar to findObject() in your HTML pages called **MM_findObj()** as a function of some of the built-in Behaviors. This function performs similar actions within the confines of the browser. When creating Dreamweaver MX behaviors or custom JavaScript code for a Web page, **MM_findObj** can make it easy to access elements of your page.*

The *findObject()* function can also be replaced with the new Dreamweaver MX functionality contained in the *dwscripts.findDOMObject()* function.

getAllObjectTags(tagName)

This function (located in .. \Shared\MM\Scripts\CMN\docInfo.js) returns an array of all tags of the same type as the *tagName* attribute that you send to the function. For example, if you are looking for all tables on a page, you would call this function and assign the resulting array to a variable, such as the following:

```
var myTableTagArray = getAllObjectTags("table");
```

getSelectedObject()

This is a simple function (located in .. \Shared\MM\Scripts\CMN\docInfo.js) that returns the object that is currently selected in the document, like this:

```
var theObject = getSelectedObject();
```

If you take a look at the actual function, it is pretty basic, and it illustrates another method of accessing an object. The entire function consists of two lines:

```
var currSel = dreamweaver.getSelection();
return dreamweaver.offsetsToNode(currSel[0],currSel[1]);
```

The first line gets the selection in the document made by the user, and the second line uses a built-in DOM method, *offsetsToNode*. This method converts the two offsets from the beginning of the document into the *node* that the selected code is contained within. In the following example

```
<table>
    <tr>
        <td>Hello</td>
    </tr>
</table>
```

if you highlight "Hello" in the document and pass the *offsets* (the number of characters into the document to the first character of the selection, and the number of characters into the document to the first character after the selection) to the *offsetsToNode* built-in function, you are returned the object that contains the <td> tag set. You can test this using the following:

```
var test = getSelectedObject();
alert(test.outerHTML);
```

If you run this little script in an extension, an alert box pops up with <td>Hello</td> in it, as shown in Figure 31-2. So, while "Hello" is the selection, the selected object is the <td> node. This also illustrates your best method of debugging your extensions—alert boxes. Dreamweaver MX has no built-in debugger, and no JavaScript debugger will work with extensions within the Dreamweaver MX environment, so you are left with using alerts to check your work.

createUniqueName(tagName,tagString,arrToSearch)

You use this function (located in ..\Shared\MM\Scripts\CMN\docInfo.js) if you are adding a tag for an object on the page and want the object to have a default name that is unique. Suppose your object inserts a check box on the page, but you want it to have a name such as *checkbox2* if a *checkbox1* already exists on the page. This function will do that for you.

The *tagName* variable is your tag that is being searched for. The *tagString* variable is the name that you want to use, such as "checkbox" to return *checkbox1* as your name. This name can be anything, and it doesn't have to match the default name for the tag in question. The *arrToSearch* variable is an optional array of elements that the search will occur in. If no array is given, the whole document is searched by default.

This function can be replaced in most cases with new Dreamweaver MX functionality *dwscripts.getUniqueNameForTag(tagType, baseName)*.

selectionInsideTag(tagName)

This function (located in ..\Shared\MM\Scripts\CMN\docInfo.js) returns true or false, depending on whether the currently selected text is within a particular tag.

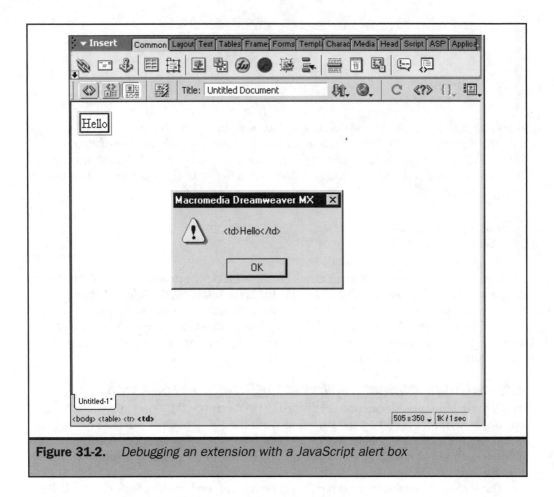

Figure 31-2. *Debugging an extension with a JavaScript alert box*

Suppose your extension depends on the selection being within a table cell. You could access this function as follows:

```
if (selectionInsideTag("td")) {
    //it is!  do something with it
} else {
    //it's not.  Error condition
};
```

findTag(tagName)

This function (located in . . \Shared\MM\Scripts\CMN\DOM.js) returns a node containing the object of a specific tag for which you are looking. You can also pass it a *startNode* variable as the second element in the *tagName* array. This is an optional variable, and if it isn't given, the function will search the entire document.

> **Note**
>
> *The* findTag *function is a recursive function and is a good example of the recursion technique. Recursion enables you to traverse through a tree and its nodes without leaving the function. Basically, you start with your root node and examine it; if you don't find what you are looking for in the root node, you move through the child nodes successively by calling the function again within the function itself for each child node. This causes the function to continue looping until all nodes are searched, or until it finds a match.*

For example, if you want to remove all bold tags from the document, you can do so like this:

```
function stripBolds(){
    var boldTag = findTag("b");  //get the tag
    var insideBold = boldTag.innerHTML;  //get what's inside the tag
    boldTag.outerHTML = insideBold;  //set the outside equal to the inside
    //effectively stripping off the tag
    if(findTag("b")) {
        stripBolds();//more recursion -- if there's another bold
        //do the function again
    }
}
```

nodeList(startNode)

This function (located in . . \Shared\MM\Scripts\CMN\DOM.js) returns an array of all nodes that are within a node passed to the function. If, for example, you pass it the node consisting of the following text

```
<table><tr><td>hello</td></tr></table>
```

the result returned will be a three-element array with the <table> node, the <tr> node, and the <td> node.

dwscripts.isInsideTag(node, tagTypes)

This function is passed two parameters: the tag name you are searching for, and the list of tags in which to search for it. The *tagNames* variable is a comma-separated list of tags that you want to check for the existence of a specific tag name. For instance, if you want to see whether there is a <b> tag within any heading tags, you can call the function like this:

```
if (dwscripts.isInsideTag("b","h1,h2,h3,h4,h5,h6")) {
    //it is--do something
} else {
    //it isn't--do something else
};
```

dwscripts.browseFile(fieldToStoreURL, stripParameters)

With this function, you pass a textfield name into the *fieldToStoreURL* variable. Typically, you invoke this function with a button or an image of a small folder next to the text field that you want to store the filename in and call it in the *onClick* event of that button or image field. It brings up the Select File dialog box (see Figure 31-3) and inserts the result into the text field. The second parameter can be set to true if you want the parameters stripped from the URL that is returned.

```
myFile = dwscripts.browseFile("myTextField");
//bring up the file dialog and
//save the filename in the "myFile" variable
```

> **Tip** *You can create your own function that is more versatile than* browseFile *by using the built-in API call to* dreamweaver.browseForFileURL(). *Using this built-in function, you can add your own title to the dialog box, as well as create an open, select, or save dialog box.*

checkForFormTag(formItemStr)

This function (located in . . \Shared\MM\Scripts\CMN\form.js) is handy if you happen to be inserting a form element, such as a special-purpose text field or check box that you've designed. Simply pass the string containing the HTML that you are putting on the page, and the function will check to see whether the text is contained within a form tag after it gets inserted. It does this by checking the currently selected text and checking up the tree until it finds a form tag. If there is no form tag, the function will put a form tag around your text and make sure it has a unique name. If your selection is contained within a layer, the function will search only within the layer, because a form element will not span across layers.

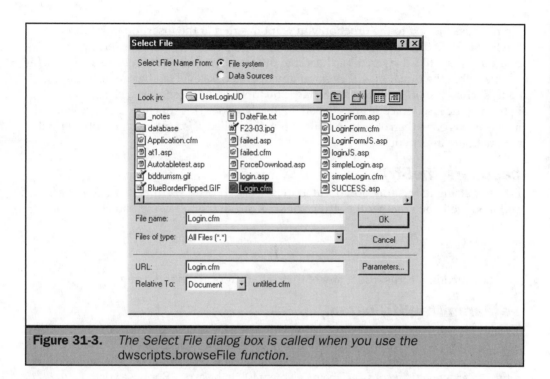

Figure 31-3. *The Select File dialog box is called when you use the dwscripts.browseFile function.*

Note *When referring to layers in the Dreamweaver MX environment, the term generally refers to absolutely positioned <div> and <span> tags. A <div> tag is a block-level element, while a <span> tag is mostly used as an inline element.*

For example, if you are inserting a custom *textfield* object that you designed, and you want to make sure it is inside of a form tag, you can do so like this:

```
var textfieldToInsert = myTextfield.outerHTML; //get the HTML from the
//code you are inserting
checkForFormTag(textfieldTextToInsert); //wrap it with a form tag if it's
//not inside of a form
```

When passed an object (node), this function (located in . . \Shared\MM\Scripts\ CMN\form.js) indicates whether the given object is a layer by checking for all possible layer tags—<layer>, <ilayer>, <div>, and <span>.

insertIntoDocument(textStr, bBlockTag)

This function (located in . . \Shared\MM\Scripts\CMN\form.js) inserts a string of text into a document, plain and simple. The text can be anything—HTML, text, or JavaScript.

Simply pass the text to the function you want inserted at the insertion point through the *textStr* variable, and set the *bBlockTag* to true if the text you are inserting is a block-level tag, like a layer, table, heading, or form. The reason for setting the *bBlockTag* to true is that the function will close off any open block-level tag before inserting the code, such as if there is an open <p> tag. The function will generate a closing </p> tag in front of the inserted code and reopen it after the code. This function is generally used in extensions other than objects. A built-in function called *objectTag()*, used in objects, will automatically insert your text.

badChars(theStr)

Pass any string to this function (located in . . \Shared\MM\Scripts\CMN\string.js), and it will tell you whether the string contains one of the following bad characters:

```
~!@#$%^&*()_+|`-=\{}[]:";'<>,./?
```

The function returns true if any of these characters are in the string.

getParam(tagStr, param)

This function (located in . . \Shared\MM\Scripts\CMN\string.js) returns the value of any named parameter from a string passed to it. In the example *<cfquery name="recordset1">*, *tagStr* is equal to *<cfquery name="recordset1">* and *name* is the parameter. The function will return an array with "recordset1" being element [0] in the array. Suppose you pass the following string

```
<td><img src="trans.gif" align="left" width="1" height="1"></td>
<td><img src="trans.gif" align="left" width="89" height="1"> </td>
```

using this expression

```
var myWidthArray =  getParam(theString, "width");
```

the function would return "1" as *myWidthArray[0]* and "89" as *myWidthArray[1]*.

quote(textStr, quoteType)

This function (located in . . \Shared\MM\Scripts\CMN\string.js) simply wraps the *textStr* variable that is passed to the function in single or double quotes, depending on the value of *quoteType*. Use "1" for single quotes and "2" for double quotes. The file dwscripts.js also contains useful functions for working with quotes:

- *dwscripts.isQuoted(str)* tells you if a string has quotes around it.

- *dwscripts.trimQuotes(str)* trims quotes from a string.

- *dwscripts.escQuotes(str)* adds a backslash character before quotes in a string.

stripSpaces(theStr)

This function (located in . . \Shared\MM\Scripts\CMN\string.js) strips the leading and trailing spaces from a string that is passed to it.

These are just some of the functions available. As you develop extensions and rework existing extensions, you will find yourself doing some tasks over and over. The functions contained within the Shared folder will greatly enhance your workflow. Also, as you write functions that you might need to reuse, you can package them with your extensions and place your own folder in the Shared folder.

In addition to extending the environment by giving yourself more commands, Behaviors, objects, and so forth, you can change the menus within the Dreamweaver MX environment. This takes a little knowledge of XML, but it's not much different from the standard HTML that you are accustomed to using. At the most basic level, Dreamweaver MX automatically places certain things in the menus as you put files into the Configuration folder. If you put the file My Server Behavior.htm into the ServerBehaviors folder, the next time you open up Dreamweaver MX, you will have a new Behavior in the menu.

> **Tip**   *All the menu files are written in XML. In addition, the MXI files that are required to package an extension are written in XML. It is not truly valid XML and can't be displayed in a dedicated XML editor, but rather is a limited version of XML that Dreamweaver MX uses and understands. The Dreamweaver MX derivation allows special characters ('<>"&) that have to be substituted in real XML.*

As a matter of practice, you won't always want to rely on Dreamweaver MX to put the extensions in the menus. You're usually better off specifying where you want your item to appear. You can also add commands to your contextual menus, and you can add submenus where needed. Suppose you have a set of extensions for adding text formatting to your pages. Your extensions might consist of formats or phrases that your company uses on a day-to-day basis. You might decide that the best place to put these is in a submenu on the contextual menu for the document. That way, your much-needed commands are only a right-click away. By manipulating the menus.xml file, you can customize the Dreamweaver MX interface itself by changing the menus and menu items.

Configuration Folders

If you open up the Dreamweaver MX program directory, the Configuration folder contained within holds all of the menu items—Commands, Behaviors, Server Behaviors, Toolbars, and other extensions to the Dreamweaver MX environment. The files are contained within individual folders whose names correspond to their menu items. Also, several folders don't have a corresponding visible menu in the Dreamweaver MX environment but contain files that are necessary internally for the operation of the program. The following is a description of some of those folders:

- **Behaviors**   Contains actions that your objects can take, which usually are JavaScript functions that respond to different events on an HTML page. The files in this folder correspond to the menu items in the Behaviors floater.

- **BrowserProfiles**   Contains the information needed by Dreamweaver MX to verify that a given browser can handle the various tags, properties, methods, and events on the page. If you choose File | Check Target Browsers, the command will use data from these files to determine whether your page meets the requirements of a given browser. Any page with server-side code will be parsed and executed before it is checked against the target browser.

- **Commands**   Includes the actions that you can apply to your page when you choose an item from the Commands menu on the standard Dreamweaver MX menu bar. Typically, a command also has a corresponding menu item in contextual menus for ease of use. Additionally, many commands can be called by other extensions and can perform a wide variety of tasks that make them perhaps the most flexible extension available.

- **Connections**   These are the database connection methods of Dreamweaver MX. This folder contains one subfolder for each server model defined in Dreamweaver MX.

- **DataSources**   Contains the files that appear in your Bindings panel. The file DataSources.xml contains the information for the Bindings menu. You could, for example, decide on a different approach for how your page connects to your database and write a new extension called *NewRecordset* to handle it.

- **Dictionaries**   Contains the spelling-check features of Dreamweaver MX, accessible through the Text menu. You can download new dictionaries from the Macromedia site, or make your own. The Personal.dat file includes any personal words that you may have added to the dictionary. You can examine this file in Wordpad, BBEdit, or any text editor of choice. If you move to another machine and use the spelling-check feature a lot, you may want to copy this file to your new machine. In Dreamweaver MX, this folder was moved inside of the Content folder.

- **Encodings**   Contains the information for various document character encodings, as shown in the Document Encoding drop-down box in the Page Properties dialog box under the Modify menu. Several character encodings are available by default. These are listed in the EncodingMenu.xml file. If you want to add your own encoding format, you should also change this file to reflect your new encoding file.

- **Extensions**   By its very name, you would think that this is where Dreamweaver MX extensions reside. It is, in fact, the repository for the MXI files (files with an .mxi file extension) that accompany any extensions that you have installed. These

MXI files are actually XML files that contain instructions to the Extension Manager for installing an extension into Dreamweaver MX.

- **Floaters**   Stores your custom floaters, if you decide to implement them. Since Dreamweaver MX came out, these are known as *panels*, but they continue to reside in the Floaters folder.

- **Inspectors**   Contains the Inspectors, or Property Inspectors, which are the little attribute sheets that pop up at the bottom of the screen when you make a selection in the document. The Inspector's job is to find all the attributes of the selected object or Behavior and display them so that the user can edit them. Typically, when writing an extension, you can also write an Inspector to go with it.

- **JDBCDrivers**   If you're a JSP programmer and use custom classes for your JDBC database drivers, this is where you can put them to have Dreamweaver MX recognize them. Copy your JAR or ZIP files to this folder, and Dreamweaver MX will recognize them.

- **JSExtensions**   By its name, you might think that this is where your JavaScript extensions go—it's not. This is where the various DLLs (shared libraries) from C-level extensions reside. The name JSExtensions relates to the fact that these shared libraries give you more JavaScript functionality in your extension writing. You can create extensions in C that interact with JavaScript extensions and the Dreamweaver MX API.

- **Menus**   Contains the main Dreamweaver MX menu, menus.xml, as well as a backup copy. Although you can manually edit the menus.xml file, writing your changes to the file as an extension in an MXI file is a better practice so that the changes can be easily uninstalled. In a multiuser system, you may have to manually edit the multiuser menus.xml file to get your changes to appear to Dreamweaver.

- **Objects**   Includes the objects that reside in your Insert panel (or Objects floater if you are working with Classic Dreamweaver 4 workspace). The folder is organized into subfolders, each of which has a corresponding tab in the Insert panel.

- **Plugins**   The UnsupportedPlugins.txt file contains a list of plug-ins that are not supported by Dreamweaver MX. You can place plug-ins that you use into this folder.

- **Queries**   Stores your Find/Replace patterns when saved. You may have noticed a little disk icon in the Find/Replace dialog box. When you click this icon, your search pattern is saved into this folder for reuse.

- **ServerBehaviors**   Contains the complex server-side scripts that turn Dreamweaver MX into a database-aware development environment. Server Behaviors are typically the hardest of the extensions to write. The main folder has subfolders for each of the server languages. These are discussed in the next chapter.

- **ServerFormats**   Contains the various formats for displaying different types of data in Dreamweaver MX, depending on which server format you happen to be using. These formats are accessible through Dynamic Data | Format. You can edit the ServerFormats.xml file to add more menu items to the menu, and edit the Formats.xml file to add new formats to the mix.

■ **ServerModels**   Includes the files that define some of the functions common to the specific server model that you happen to be working on. If you want to add a new server model, such as PHP, you have to define the various standard Dreamweaver MX functions in this folder, such as *findAllRepeatedRegionNames()* and *findAllRecordsetNames()*.

■ **Shared**   Contains a wealth of functions and general information in the form of fully commented JavaScript for use by extension developers to add to the functionality of Dreamweaver MX.

■ **SiteCache**   Stores information about links in your site. The folder is empty until you define your sites. You are prompted "Would you like to create a cache file for this site?" when you create a site. The results of the cache reside in this folder.

■ **Startup**   Scripts that need to run as Dreamweaver MX starts up are placed in this folder.

■ **Templates**   Contains the empty template files for your use as a Web developer. You can place skeleton HTML, ASP, JSP, CF, or whatever files you use frequently into this folder, which will save you time in development. The file default.htm is the standard start file for all new pages. You can modify this particular file for your own use, as well.

■ **ThirdPartyTags**   Stores tags other than the standard HTML tags. You'll find files for ASP, CF, JSP, and other third-party tags in here. You can edit these or add new files. If Dreamweaver MX comes across a tag that it doesn't understand, it looks in this folder for a match.

■ **Translators**   Contains translators that will translate content on a page. For example, a recordset field is translated into readable text in the design environment. Note also that the Live Data translator files reside in this folder.

■ **Builtin***   This folder contains such built-in documents as templates, CSS files, framesets, and *TemplatesAccessible*. These are all options when you choose File | New.

■ **CodeColoring***   These XML files enable the code coloring when you are in code view. You can also create your own code coloring for different document types.

■ **Components***   Contains subfolders for each of the server models. The available component extensions for the individual server models are located in here. For example, the ColdFusion folder contains a CFCs folder for ColdFusion Components functionality. ASP.NET contains a WebServices folder for the functionality of this component within Dreamweaver MX.

* New to Dreamweaver MX

- **Content*** Contains some of the content that is available to Dreamweaver MX, including the Reference panel and the built-in spell check functionality available from the Dictionaries folder.

- **DocumentTypes*** These are the document types available when you choose File | New. You can add new document types in this folder and add the appropriate menu entry to the MMDocumentTypes.xml file, and they will appear when you choose File | New.

- **Flash Player*** The Flash MX player resides here.

- **Reference*** Contains useful reference materials, such as the HTML, JavaScript, and CFML references that are part of Dreamweaver MX. You can also create your own reference materials and place them in this folder. This folder is located inside of the Content folder, but deserves a separate mention because of its usefulness.

- **ServerDebugOutput*** Dreamweaver MX supports server-side debugging directly through the design window. The results of debugging are displayed in the Results panel below the document window. Currently this feature is enabled only for ColdFusion, but you can add your own debugging functionality by adding a server model-specific folder inside of this folder.

- **Snippets*** Snippets have been around for years in Homesite, CF Studio, and JRun Studio, but they are now part of Dreamweaver MX as well. The Snippet extension type is an XML file that stores the information about your Snippet. You can package these Snippets as extensions as well.

- **Strings*** Contains XML files filled with strings that are used in the Dreamweaver environment. You can conceivably create your own string files and use them to create locale-specific extensions.

- **TagLibIntrospection*** The extensions in this folder allow Dreamweaver MX to introspect tag libraries. ASP.NET and JSP 1.2 tag library functionality is included out of the box.

- **TagLibraries*** Tag Libraries are an important new feature in Dreamweaver MX; you can import your own tag libraries and create your own interfaces to these tags and store them in this folder. The concept comes from Homesite/CF Studio, and the VTM file format is from that program as well. The difference is in the implementation: Dreamweaver MX stores the interfaces in HTML to accommodate better with its extensibility model.

- **Toolbars*** One of the most striking new features of Dreamweaver MX is the Toolbars extensibility, allowing users to create custom toolbars that access built-in or custom extensions. The toolbars folder contains the XML files that contain the toolbar functionality.

- **WebServices*** Contains functionality for introspecting Web Services.

* New to Dreamweaver MX

As you can see, all parts of Dreamweaver MX are open for customization. The API is laid out in such a way as to simplify the process of writing your own objects, commands, Behaviors, and whatever else you may require. The 700+ page "Extending Dreamweaver MX" document, available in the Help menu and also as a PDF file on the Dreamweaver MX CD-ROM, contains technical information on the techniques and methods of extension writing. Also, the help files in the Extension Manager folder give the ground rules for writing "official" extensions that you can package and submit to Macromedia for approval, or post on the Macromedia Exchange.

The best way to start writing extensions, though, is to dive right in and write one. At some point, the Library items won't give you all the functionality you need, and you'll want to create a custom extension to insert some code on the page. Extensions give you the power to add user-defined attributes to a block of code easily, and go back and edit those attributes if necessary. The easiest extension to start with is the object.

Objects

Objects are simply snippets of HTML and script that are written to the Web page as a predetermined string of code. They usually represent "visual" elements of HTML, such as images, form fields, tables, and other "physical" things a user can see on the page. Objects are also the most basic of extensions that you can write yourself.

Objects reside in the Objects folder under Configuration, and are available from the Insert bar or the Insert menu. If you look inside this folder, you'll see other subfolders— Characters, Common, Forms, Frames, Head, and Invisibles. These folders appear in the corresponding tabs of the Insert panel in Dreamweaver MX. In addition, Dreamweaver MX adds many new objects to the mix, depending upon which server model you are working with. If you add your own folder inside of the Objects folder, you can effectively add a new tab to the Insert bar. All you need to do is to create an entry in the insertbar.xml file inside of that folder to correspond to your new folder. If you plan to write Object extensions, it's a good idea to separate them from the standard extensions by putting your own folder in here.

Note   *Previous versions of Dreamweaver and UltraDev would automatically recognize any folders placed inside the Objects folder. Dreamweaver MX doesn't allow this, but adds a file called insertbar.xml inside the folder where you can specify your new Objects.*

Objects can have three corresponding files:

- **HTML File**   Contains the user interface and the form to get any attributes from the user.

- **JS File**   Contains the functions that do the work to create your object. The JS file is optional, because you can include your JavaScript in the HTML file. In general, if the JavaScript occupies more than a few lines, you can include it as a separate file.

■ **GIF File** An 18×18 pixel GIF image that will be the icon in the Insert panel. If the GIF file is missing, Dreamweaver MX gives your object a generic icon.

Note *Standard icons (files with the .ico extension) are 16×16, so converting them into a GIF file using a dedicated icon editor such as Microangelo (www.impactsoft.com) is a snap. Dreamweaver MX Object GIF files will even work fine at 16×16. You can create one in any good image-editing program as well.*

These files all have the same name—the name of the object—each with its own respective file extension. For example, a Table object will have Table.htm, Table.js, and Table.gif files associated with it.

Modifying an Object

You'll start by modifying a simple object, before you dive in and create a new one. Begin by copying the Table.htm, Table.js, and Table.gif files from the Common folder to a new folder under Objects, named Custom Objects. You'll also need to add the following items to the insertbar.xml file. Make sure you save a copy of the original insertbar.xml file somewhere safe before modifying the existing file:

```
<category id="DWMXTCR_Insertbar_Custom_Objects" folder="Custom Objects">
    <button id="DWMXTCR_Table_W_Layer"
    image="Custom Objects\table.gif"
    enabled=""
    showIf=""
    file="Custom Objects\table.htm" />
</category>
```

Save the file and then start up Dreamweaver MX. You should find your new Custom Objects tab in the menu. Click it, and the Table object should now be on the menu.

Start with a very basic change—you'll wrap the table with a layer automatically so that it can be dragged around on the screen in true WYSIWYG fashion. To do this, you need to add one function to the JS file—*objectInsertLayer()*.

Open the Table.js file in HomeSite, BBEdit, Notepad, or any text editor of choice; add the following function to the file; and then save it:

```
function objectInsertLayer() {
    return "TRUE";
};
```

After you save the file, it is ready for use, but if you have Dreamweaver MX open, it won't change until you "reload" your extensions by restarting the program.

Click the Table object in the panel and "draw" a table onto your page by clicking anywhere on the page, and holding the button down as you move the mouse downward and to the right. When you release the mouse button, your table should be there, wrapped in a layer. If you desire to change the sizes of the layer or the table, you can click the handles of the layer or table and resize it so that they match, or differ, as your need dictates. Now, you can move the table around on the page by clicking and holding on the little drag handle in the upper-left corner of the layer box. This trick works with most objects, and it approximates the WYSIWYG approach of desktop publishing programs that is lacking from most Web design software. Some Dreamweaver MX users have made entire panels of these objects.

Dreamweaver MX recognizes the table and the layer as two separate objects. They can easily become separated, because they are not actually combined as one unit. But, with this example, you can see how easy it is to make a significant change in the functionality of an object.

Now that you've had exposure to the power of extensibility, you're ready to delve into the world of objects.

Object Files

An object file is built as a basic HTML page. The most basic form of object is raw HTML that you may insert into your file. If you have some code that you want to put into your page, and it's something that you use frequently, you can put the code into its own HTML page, package and save it as an object, and then it will be available for use any time you need it. These kinds of objects are known as *simple objects,* because they require no user interaction or user-defined attributes of any kind. They are simply inserted as is into the open document at the insertion point. You could also save these as Library items, but they are more easily transferable as objects from site to site and from computer to computer. In addition, you can go beyond the basic functionality of a Library item when you include user-defined attributes.

Always avoid using <head>, <body>, <meta>, or other similar tags that are considered standard in a well-formed HTML file within an object file that uses the "simple" object form (no objectTag() function). Also, you should always put the string of code you want to insert inside a single pair of <html> tags. If not, Dreamweaver MX may add redundant <meta> and <style> tags to the document where the object is inserted.

Suppose you have a company logo and tagline that are included in various places within your pages. Use the Bettergig.com site logo from the Osborne Web site as an example. You could insert an image, navigate to the correct file on your hard drive, and then insert your tagline—a procedure that you can repeat as many times as is required. However, if the procedure is something that you may need to do frequently, making it into an object would be to your advantage. This will certainly speed up the process of design.

You are now going to create this simple extension, using the BGigLogo.gif file that can be downloaded from www.osborne.com. Create a new site called TestExtensions in a folder named TestExtensions under your root, and then place the BGigLogo.gif file into that folder. Open your text editor of choice, and enter the following HTML code onto a blank page:

```
<html>
<a href="http://www.bettergig.com">
<img src="BGigLogo.GIF" align="center" hspace=5
alt="Get a better life. . .get a better gig!"></a>
<b> Get a better life. . .get a better gig!</b><br>
This site and its contents &copy;2002 by Bettergig.com
</html>
```

Now, save the file under the Custom Objects folder, inside the Objects folder, as BGLogo.htm. You'll also have to add a new button to the insertbar.xml file, just as you did with the table object that you modified earlier. Add these lines within the new <category> tag that you already created:

```
<button id="DWMXTCR_BGLogo"
 image="Custom Objects\BGLogo.gif"
 enabled=""
 showIf=""
 file="Custom Objects\BGLogo.htm" />
```

To include an icon with the object, copy the BGLogo.gif file from the download package available from www.osborne.com to the Custom Objects folder. Restart the program and the new extension should be ready for use. Go ahead and click the icon. The logo with the tagline should appear on your page (see Figure 31-4). This technique will work with any HTML that you need to insert into a page. It will always insert the object at the cursor insertion point. Now, the generic icon should be replaced with a custom icon to match your extension.

The *objectTag()* Function

So far, the object is little more than a piece of HTML that could have been built as a Snippet or Library item. Suppose you want to make more complex objects. This is where the *objectTag()* function comes into play. You can expand your simple objects to create more complex entities with user-defined attributes. The way that most of the objects in Dreamweaver MX work is that the HTML file contains form elements that

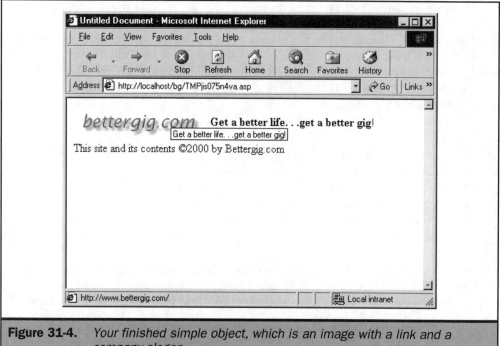

Figure 31-4.   *Your finished simple object, which is an image with a link and a company slogan*

the user is able to fill out with the various attributes that the object requires. For instance, in the Table object, you are prompted for rows, columns, cell padding, cell spacing, width, border, and percent/pixels. These text fields are all form elements in the HTML file, Table.htm. The JS file then takes these user-defined attributes and formats them in such a way as to create a string of HTML code that represents an HTML table. After the formatting is complete, the *objectTag()* function returns the string to Dreamweaver MX that contains the complete table, which is then inserted into the source and rendered by Dreamweaver MX to the page visually.

Note   *In Dreamweaver MX, a fine line sometimes exists between Library items, Snippets, and Objects. Generally speaking, items such as those in the example you just completed are fine as Snippets or Library items. They become Object material only when you need to reuse them frequently throughout your Web site development and add the ability to apply any user-defined attributes to them.*

The *objectTag()* function is built into the Dreamweaver MX DOM and is called when an object is selected, if it exists. If the function doesn't exist, the entire HTML file is inserted into the document, as it was earlier with the simple object. Take advantage of the simple object whenever you don't have any user-defined attributes to be concerned with. If you do have user-defined attributes, create a JS file and include the *objectTag()* function, along with whichever other functions are necessary to format your attributes properly for the final page. The way to include the JS file in the object is to place an include line into the HTML file, like this:

```
<script src="Table.js"></script>
```

You may also include any other files that you may need. Many useful functions are available in the Shared directory in the Configuration folder. This Shared directory is also where you should put your own often-used functions within your own folder that you have named. By Macromedia's standards, an extension stored in the root folders under Configuration should have only one of each of the three file types mentioned—JS, HTM, and GIF. For example, the BGLogo extension could consist of BGLogo.htm, BGLogo.js, and BGLogo.gif. Place anything else in the Shared directory. This is where things such as JavaScript files of shared functions, images, or temporary directories should go. Then, you can reference your file like this:

```
<script language = "javascript"¬
src="../../Shared/Bettergig/BGFiles/Functions.js">
```

Using the *objectTag()* Function in the Company Logo Example

To demonstrate a few of the principles previously discussed, you now are going to build another object. You'll build the company logo-generating object, but this time you'll use the *objectTag()* function to put it on the page. When you previously built the simple object, the actual HTML from the object file was written to the page. That's fine when a predefined piece of code is being inserted on the page. But, in the case where you are receiving input or attributes from the Web developer, you need to do a little string manipulation to put the user-defined attributes together with the HTML.

Create a new HTML file named NewBGLogo.htm. Begin by inserting a script declaration in the head section referencing your JS file:

```
<html>
<head>
<script language = "javascript" src="NewBGLogo.js"></script>
</head>
<body>
</body>
</html>
```

This enables you to use functions in a NewBGLogo.js file in your object. Save the file in the Custom Objects folder, along with NewBGLogo.gif from the Osborne Web site, and create a new entry in the insertbar.xml file to correspond to the new Object:

```
<button id="DWMXTCR_NewBGLogo"
 image="Custom Objects\NewBGLogo.gif"
 enabled=""
 showIf=""
 file="Custom Objects\NewBGLogo.htm" />
```

Now, you need to create the NewBGLogo.js file. You can do this in any text editor, such as BBEdit on the Mac or HomeSite on the PC. Start with a blank page and insert the following function:

```
function objectTag() {
    var tag = '';
    tag ='<a href="http://www.bettergig.com">';
    tag += '<img src="BGigLogo.GIF" align="center" hspace=5 ';
    tag += 'alt=" Get a better life. . .get a better gig!" ></a>\n';
    tag += '<b> Get a better life. . .get a better gig!</b><br>\n';
    tag += 'This site and its contents &copy;2002 by Bettergig.com';
    return tag;
}
```

Save the file as NewBGLogo.js in the Custom Objects folder, and then restart Dreamweaver MX.

> **Tip** *When building strings that contain quotes, take advantage of JavaScript's capability to utilize both types of quotes characters (single and double). By using single quotes around the entire string, you can liberally use double quotes inside of the string where needed.*

This object does exactly the same thing that your original simple object does—insert the code at the cursor insertion point. What is different, however, is that the code that you want to put on the page is actually now built as a string, and then returned by the *objectTag()* function to Dreamweaver MX. If you apply the object to the page, you'll see the same object as before. Also notice that when you use this approach, you have to make sure your spaces are in all the right places. Insert a space after the alternate text declaration (to allow for other image attributes to be inserted), and also insert a space after the *hspace* declaration, because you are adding the next line *immediately* after this line. Also place newline characters (\n) into the text to break up your source code. These will not affect how end users see the page when they browse, but using them will make your source code easier to read.

This approach is very powerful, because you now can get parameters from the user and add them to the string to make the object more functional. In the Dreamweaver MX environment, open the file NewBGLogo.htm that you just created. To do this, you should first define a new site as Custom Objects with the Custom Objects folder as the root of the site. You can leave the Server Model and Server Access pages blank. Now, open the file. Your page will be blank. Add a table with two rows and three columns (see Figure 31-5) with the following attributes applied to the objects:

- Text field named *txtLink*
- Text field named *txtImage*
- Button named Browse

This provides a way for the developer to put his or her own image into the object without hard-coding the name of the image into the object. The link will be user-defined, as well.

Now save the file. If you restart Dreamweaver and click your NewBGLogo file, the dialog box will be invoked. It doesn't do anything yet, because you haven't added any functionality to it, but you can see that Dreamweaver MX has added the OK and

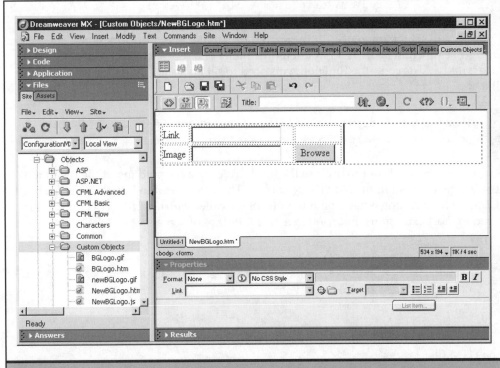

Figure 31-5.   *Creating an interface for the* NewBGLogo *object*

Cancel buttons to the form. These will be on every object. You can add a third button, Help, simply by adding a *displayHelp()* function. Dreamweaver MX will automatically add a Help button if it sees this function.

Now examine how to get the parameters from a form. You'll be accessing the form elements with the *findObject()* function, as described earlier in this chapter. The *txtLink* field will be a standard text field HTML object, getting text from the user. The *txtImage* field will get its value from a filename that you designate by browsing files with the Browse button. You want to invoke a function of the *onClick* method of the button to bring up a dialog box that will fetch the filename of an image on your hard drive. There's a built-in function that does this—*browseFile(fieldToStoreURL)*—and it will take a text field object as the parameter. This function resides in the File.js file in the \Shared\MM\Scripts\Cmn directory. To get the text field object, you'll use the *findObject(objName)* function. This resides in the UI.js file. You'll have to set up these shared files as include files to be able to access the functions. At this time, add the following lines after the other script-declaration line in the NewBGLogo.htm file:

```
<script language = "javascript"¬
src="..\..\Shared\MM\Scripts\Cmn\UI.js"></script>
<script language = "javascript"¬
src="..\..\Shared\MM\Scripts\Cmn\file.js"></script>
```

This will set the references to the shared files that contain the functions. The *browseFile* function takes as a parameter the name of a form field in your form. You'll use *txtImage*. To access the function, you need to set an *onclick* event for your button, like this:

```
<input type="button" name="browse" value="Browse"
onclick="browseFile(findObject('txtImage'))">
```

This enables the user to browse the hard drive for a file, and insert the result into the Image text field in the *NewBGLogo* object. Then, you need to initialize the user interface by inserting a function into your JS file called *initializeUI()*. This function is used in most extensions that contain a user interface of some sort.

```
function initializeUI() {
  findObject("txtLink").focus(); //sets the focus
  findObject("txtLink").select(); //sets insertion point
}
```

You then invoke the function by referencing it in the <body> tag's *onload* event in the HTM file:

```
<body onload="initializeUI()">
```

> **Note** *Putting a function in the* onload *event of the <body> tag of an extension is directing the extension to call this function first as the object is being applied to the page.*

Go ahead and save the object and then try to use it. At this point, when you click the Browse button, the Select File dialog box should pop up and ask you to select a file. If the file you choose doesn't reside in your Web folder, the function will ask you whether you want to copy it there. After you indicate that you would like to copy the selected filename, it will be copied in your text field, ready to be inserted into your object.

All that you need to do now is take the information that the user has entered in the two form fields and insert it into the tag string. You'll use the *findObject()* function to get the values in this way, inserted at the beginning of the *objectTag()* function:

```
var theImage = findObject("txtImage").value;
var theLink = findObject("txtLink").value;
```

As noted earlier, you could have used dot notation to access the document node also, as in the following:

```
var theImage = document.forms[0].txtImage.value;
var theLink = document.forms[0].txtLink.value;
```

Both ways are valid, but you should get into the habit of doing one or the other to maintain consistency in your extensions. We prefer to use the *findObject()* function to keep things consistent and readable. Once you have the values of the text fields assigned to variables, manipulating your string of HTML will be very easy. Simply remove the hard-coded values for the link and image source and replace them with your variable names. We use plus signs (+) to put our string together. Your final *objectTag()* function looks like this:

```
function objectTag() {
    var tag = '';
    tag='<a href="' + theLink + '">';
    tag+='<img src="' + theImage + '" align="center" hspace=5 ';
    tag+='alt=" Get a better life. . .get a better gig!" ></a>\n';
    tag+='<b> Get a better life. . .get a better gig!</b><br>\n';
    tag+='This site and its contents &copy;2002 by Bettergig.com';
    return tag;
}
```

This example also demonstrates that you can include quotes in your strings by using single quotes around the string. If you need to include actual single quotes in the string, you surround your string, including the single quotes, with double quotes.

JavaScript is flexible in that it allows both single and double quotes to surround a string. The other possibility is to use an escape code—a backslash (\)—to include double quotes in the string, as in this line:

```
tag = "\"Hello,\" said John"
```

Display Help

Building a help file is something you might want to consider if your extension is complex or requires any special instructions. The help file can be a basic HTML page with instructions, or a complex series of pages with images and hyperlinks. However you decide to do it, the basic method for displaying a help file is with the *displayHelp()* function. This is a function that Dreamweaver MX will look for when a user accesses your extension. If the function exists in your extension file in any form, the extension interface will have a Help button below the Cancel and OK buttons.

 Note *Some extensions, such as Property Inspectors and Floating panels, will have a little question mark icon displayed instead of a Help button.*

At its most basic level, the *displayHelp()* function can just flash an alert box like this:

```
function displayHelp() {
    var alertText = "Choose two styles from the drop-down lists\n"
    alertText += "or click the 'New' button to create new styles."
    alert(alertText);
}
```

At a more advanced level, you can use the built-in *browseDocument(path)* function of Dreamweaver MX, which causes your default browser to pop up the Web page that is passed to the function. You can call the function like this:

```
dw.browseDocument(myHelpPage);
```

 Keep in mind that you have to pass the entire path to the function; otherwise, Dreamweaver MX won't know where to find it.

Another built-in function, *getConfigurationPath()*, enables you to find the path of the Dreamweaver MX program on the hard drive. This works on both the Mac and in Windows. The *getConfigurationPath()* function will return the full path to the Configuration folder. You call it like this:

```
var pathToConfig = dw.getConfigurationPath();
```

You can store your help files in the ExtensionsHelp folder under Configuration. This is the standard location for third-party extension developers to store help files. After you have that information, you can append the location of your help file to it, like this:

```
var fullPath = pathToConfig + ¬
 "/ExtensionsHelp/MyFolder/Helpdocs/CustomTable.htm";
```

The full *displayHelp()* function for the *CustomTable* object would look like this:

```
function displayHelp() {
    var pathToConfig = dw.getConfigurationPath();
    var fullPath = pathToConfig + ¬
"/Shared/MyFolder/Helpdocs/CustomTable.htm"
    dreamweaver.browseDocument(fullPath);
}
```

Instead of putting a help file into the Shared folder, you could have it on the Web somewhere, and just point to your Web site using the full path of the file, like this:

```
dreamweaver.browseDocument("http://www.mysite.com/help/CustomTable.htm");
```

Creating a Server Object

In this section, you will build an object that will display the last access date of the page to the user. You'll need to use the File System object of ASP to do it, and you'll write a VBScript and a JavaScript version of the object.

Generally speaking, if your code fits into one code block and resides inside the <body> tag, you can easily create an object out of the code.

The following is the VBScript code that you are going to use:

```
<%
DateFile = Server.MapPath("\DateFile.txt")
On Error Resume Next
Set TM_fs = Server.CreateObject("Scripting.FileSystemObject")
Set a = TM_fs.OpenTextFile(DateFile, 1, 0, 0)
LastDate = a.ReadLine
InStream.Close
```

```
Application("lastAccessDate")= LastDate
LastDate = Month(Now) & "/" & Day(Now) & "/" & Year(Now)
LastDate = LastDate & " " & Time
set b = TM_fs.CreateTextFile (DateFile, 1, 0)
b.WriteLine LastDate
b.Close
%>
This page was last viewed on
<% Response.Write(Application("lastAccessDate"))%>
```

As you've just read, now you simply need to build the code into a string that will
be returned to the Dreamweaver MX environment and then be inserted into the page.
Server-side code has a few additional caveats. For one, you need to make sure that the
language declaration is at the top of the page. Also, because Dreamweaver MX handles
several server models, you need to make sure that you are currently in the correct
language for the object. You accomplish this in much the same way that you did in the
CustomTable object. However, in this case, you'll flash an alert box if the user is in a JSP,
PHP, ASP.NET, or ColdFusion site, or doesn't have a server model declared. Your code
skeleton, before you add the return object to it, is as follows:

```
<html>
<head>
<title>Insert Last Access Date</title>
<meta http-equiv="Content-Type" content="text/html;¬
charset=iso-8859-1">
<script language = "javascript"¬
src="../Shared/MM/Scripts/CMN/docInfo.js"></SCRIPT>
<script language = "javascript"¬
src="../Shared/MM/Scripts/CMN/DOM.js"></SCRIPT>
<script language="javascript">
//--------------      API FUNCTIONS    ---------------
function insertLanguageDeclaration() {
  var theDom = dw.getDocumentDOM();
  var serverLanguage = theDom.serverModel.getServerLanguage();
  if (serverLanguage == "VBScript" || serverLanguage == "JavaScript") {
    var htmlNode = theDom.getElementsByTagName("html")[0];
    var preHeadCode=htmlNode.outerHTML;
    var pattern = new RegExp('<%@LANGUAGE=[^%]*%>');
    var theNode = pattern.exec(preHeadCode);
    if(theNode == null) {
        theNode = "<%@LANGUAGE=" + serverLanguage.toUpperCase() +¬
              "%>\n";
        EndSection = preHeadCode;
    }else{
        EndSection = RegExp.rightContext;
```

```
      };
      htmlNode.outerHTML =  theNode + EndSection;
    }
    return serverLanguage;
}

function objectTag() {
    var serverLanguage = insertLanguageDeclaration();
    var tag = "";
    var myScriptObject = "";
    if(serverLanguage=="VBScript") {
       myScriptObject = new VBScriptObject();
    }else if(serverLanguage=="JavaScript") {
       myScriptObject = new JavaScriptObject();
    }else{
       alert("Object not compatible with Server Model");
       return"";
    }
    tag = myScriptObject.text;
    tag = '<p>' + tag + '</p>';
    return tag;
}
</script>
</head>
<body>
</body>
</html>
```

Tip   *A good rule when designing Web pages is to test your code in all the various browsers that you are targeting. The same rule should carry over to testing the code that your extensions will produce.*

Note that two shared folders are included that contain some functions you'll be using. After the script declaration and function assignments, the *objectTag()* function begins by assigning your server language to a variable by calling the *insertLanguageDeclaration()* function. This function gets the HTML node (the entire document) and puts the *outerHTML* into the variable *preHeadNode*. After you have the entire document in a string, you can do a search for the language declaration line. You do this by using regular expressions, or *RegExps*. Regular expressions will be addressed in greater detail in Chapter 32. The following two lines do the search and then assign the result to a variable:

```
var pattern = new RegExp('<%@LANGUAGE=[^%]*%>','gi');
var theNode = pattern.exec(preHeadCode);
```

The *pattern* variable is your regular expression. You create the expression with the *RegExp* constructor. The variable consists of the code that you are searching for, and both a special negated-character class, *[^%]*, which represents any character up to but not including the percent sign, and a special repetition character, *, which represents zero or more of the previous character. The combination of the two, *[^%]**, means "zero or more of any character up to but not including %." You end the string with a %>, which is the closing ASP bracket. Your resulting expression is looking for <%@LANGUAGE= and any characters up to and including %>. The *gi* parameters allow you to do a global document search and a case-insensitive search.

The next line executes the pattern against the *preHeadCode* string with the *exec* method of *RegExp*, which in effect searches the entire document for the occurrence of your language declaration.

When you execute *RegExp*, you can access various attributes of the string that were searched for a match. The variable, *theNode*, now contains the matched string, if there was a match, or nothing at all, if there was no match. The *rightContext* contains everything to the right of the match, and the *leftContext* contains everything to the left of the match. At this point, check whether the string is null. If it is null, you'll assign the language declaration to the string with the following line:

```
theNode = "<%@LANGUAGE=" + serverLanguage.toUpperCase() + "%>\n";
```

Next, you'll assign the *preHeadCode* contents to the variable *EndSection*. This variable contains the entire document, which is now going to be the "end section" of code when you concatenate the string. If it isn't null and there *is* a match, you'll assign *RegExp.rightContext* to the *EndSection* variable. Then, you just put the two sections together and put it back into the DOM with the following line:

```
htmlNode.outerHTML =  theNode + EndSection;
```

The document at this point includes the language declaration.

Using Objects in Your Object

Note that you have two functions yet to create—*VBScriptObject()* and *JavaScriptObject()*. These two functions are going to build up the string of code for your *objectTag()* function. By doing it in this way, you have the flexibility to easily add other server models by simply adding another block of code to the object. You will be calling the variables a little differently, though. You'll *instantiate* each variable as an object, and assign the new instance of the object to the *myScriptObject* variable that you already created. By using JavaScript's built-in object-oriented functionality, you have greater flexibility with your code. Although it is not a "true" OOP language, because it doesn't have a well-defined "class" notion, the functionality can be easily simulated. The special box titled "Object-Oriented Programming in Dreamweaver MX" gives a brief introduction to one way of implementing OOP using JavaScript.

Object-Oriented Programming in Dreamweaver MX

OOP is, at its root, a concept in programming that you can apply to virtually any program that you may want to build. You have to think of an object in terms of a physical thing. You can think of it as a black box. In a black box, you know what the box does, and you know how to interface with it, but you don't have to know the details of how it works. Consider a VCR, for example. All VCRs have a place to insert the tape. They have a Play button; Record button; and buttons for Rewind, Fast Forward, On, and Off. All VCRs aren't the same, but they are all derived from the same basic principles, which is called the *class* in programming terms. This class describes the various properties, methods, and events of the object.

To implement the VCR class in JavaScript, you would put it in a function, like this:

```
function VCR(theName) {
     this.name = theName;
     this.buttons = new Array();
     this.speeds = new Array();
     this.manufacturer = "";
     this.color = "";
     this.state = false; //on or off
     }
```

The function describes the *properties* that the object has. Then, when you want to create the object *instance* in a program, you call it with the new keyword, like this:

```
var myVCR = new VCR("Panasonic");
```

After defining the object, you can give it any properties that it may need. You can now define the properties by referring to the object by the name of this instance—myVCR:

```
myVCR.buttons[0] = "Stop"
myVCR.buttons[1] = "Play"
myVCR.buttons[2] = "Rewind"
myVCR.buttons[3] = "On/off"
```

Your VCR only has four buttons. You can access the length of the Buttons property of the object like this:

```
var howManyButtons = myVCR.buttons.length
```

And, you can access the names of these buttons by looping through the array, like this:

```
for(i=0;i<howManyButtons;i++) {
    alert (myVCR.buttons[i]);
    }
```

You can give your objects methods by attaching them to the *prototype* of the object, like this:

```
VCR.prototype.play = VCR_Play
function VCR_Play(Tape_Is_Inserted) {
    if (Tape_Is_Inserted) {
        alert("Now playing the tape")
    }else{
        return false;
    }
    return true;
}
```

Now, the *play()* method can be called by referencing the object, like this:

```
myVCR.play(true);
```

This code passes a "true" to the object, indicating that a tape is inside the machine. The *play()* method will then flash the alert box saying that the tape is playing. The *play()* method only takes one *parameter*—a true or false value indicating whether or not the tape is in the machine.

This is a working JavaScript object. What use is this? Well, actually, you probably don't have use for a VCR in a program, but this just shows the versatility of the approach. By defining an object, giving it properties and methods, and making those attributes known to other programmers, the object can be implemented in programs for whatever functionality the program demands. The *play()* method works in all objects of the VCR class. As a programmer, you don't have to know how it does it—you just know that it is passed a true or false value, and that it will play the tape if it is sent a true value. The function is *encapsulated* in the black box.

You could implement another VCR object with 20 buttons, and it would be a completely different object, but it would be based on the same class and have the same methods as the previous myVCR object instance. They are both members of the VCR class, but they have different properties that distinguish them. The methods remain consistent—they both have a *play()* method that can be accessed. If the VCR program is rewritten, other programs that rely on the VCR class will still work if the rules are kept intact, and the *play()* method still has the same attributes.

A method you can use to instantiate a class in JavaScript is to define a function and reference it within the function as "this." The function is called the *constructor* and doesn't return any value. To call it, you will use the keyword *new*, which creates an *instance* of the object. After that point, you can access the public properties of the object. You're giving it only one property—text. However, you could have a name property, a type property, a language property, or even a favoriteFood prope…rty. As you build more complex extensions, you may create more complex classes with their own properties and methods. The classes you build are limited only by what you store in the object. Chapter 32 looks at the Server Behavior classes that you can use to create Server Behaviors.

The *VBScriptObject()* Class

The following is the *VBScriptObject()* class, which you can insert above the *objectTag()* function:

```
function VBScriptObject() {
tag = '\n<%';
tag += '\nDateFile = Server.MapPath("\DateFile.txt")';
tag += '\nOn Error Resume Next';
tag += '\nSet TM_fs = Server.CreateObject("Scripting.FileSystemObject")';
tag += '\nSet a = TM_fs.OpenTextFile(DateFile, 1, 0, 0)';
tag += '\nLastDate = a.ReadLine';
tag += '\nInStream.Close';
tag += '\nApplication("lastAccessDate")= LastDate';
tag += '\nLastDate = Month(Now) & "/" & Day(Now) & "/" & Year(Now)';
tag += '\nLastDate = LastDate & " " & Time';
tag += '\nset b = TM_fs.CreateTextFile(DateFile, 1, 0)';
tag += '\nb.WriteLine LastDate';
tag += '\nb.Close';
tag += '\n%>';
tag += '\nThis page was last viewed on';
tag += '\n<%';
tag += '\nResponse.Write(Application("lastAccessDate"))';
tag += '\n%>';
this.text = tag;
}
```

This function's sole purpose is to build the string of code that you want to insert. You assign the tag variable to the text property of the object. Notice that you stop and start the ASP tags around the phrase "This page last viewed on," because the ASP code is hidden on the page. This one line will be inserted into the document as if the user had typed it into the design window. By doing it like this, instead of by using a *Response.Write* statement, the user is allowed to view the phrase in design mode.

Note   *You are calling your objects* VBScriptObject *and* JavaScriptObject *in this example, but these are just names—you could have called them anything. If you give your objects and methods names that are descriptive, the code will be easier to maintain.*

The *JavaScriptObject()* Class

Next, you'll create a JavaScript class for use with an ASP JavaScript site:

```javascript
function JavaScriptObject() {
tag += '\nsPath = Server.mapPath("DateFile.txt");';
tag += '\nApplication.Lock();';
tag += '\nvar TM_fs = Server.CreateObject("Scripting.FileSystemObject");';
tag += '\nif (!TM_fs.FileExists(sPath))  {';
tag += '\n  TM_fs.CreateTextFile(sPath);';
tag += '\n  DateFile = TM_fs.OpenTextFile(sPath,2);';
tag += '\n  DateFile.Writeline(0);';
tag += '\n  DateFile.Close()';
tag += '\n  }';
tag += '\nvar DateTime = TM_fs.OpenTextFile(sPath,1);';
tag += '\nLastDate = (String(DateTime.ReadLine()));';
tag += '\nDateTime.Close();';
tag += '\nApplication("lastAccessDate") = LastDate;';
tag += '\nLastDate = todayStr() + " " + nowStr();';
tag += '\nDateFile = TM_fs.OpenTextFile(sPath,2);';
tag += '\nDateFile.Writeline(LastDate);';
tag += '\nDateFile.Close();';
tag += '\nApplication.Unlock();';
tag += '\nTM_fs = null;';
tag += '\nDateFile = null';
tag += '\nfunction nowStr() {';
tag += '\n  //returns the current system time as a string.';
tag += '\n  var now = new Date()';
tag += '\n  newHours = hours = now.getHours()';
tag += '\n  if (hours==0) newHours = 12';
tag += '\n  minutes = now.getMinutes()';
tag += '\n  seconds = now.getSeconds()';
tag += '\n  timeStr = "" + ((hours > 12) ? hours - 12 : hours)';
tag += '\n  timeStr += ((minutes < 10) ? ":0" : ":") + minutes';
tag += '\n  timeStr += ((seconds < 10) ? ":0" : ":") + seconds';
tag += '\n  timeStr += (newHours >= 12) ? " PM" : " AM"';
tag += '\nreturn timeStr';
tag += '\n}';
tag += '\nfunction todayStr() {';
tag += '\n//returns the current system date as a string.';
tag += '\nvar anydate = new Date()';
tag += '\nvar year = anydate.getYear()';
tag += '\nyear = year + 1900 * (year<2000)';
tag += '\n    return anydate.getMonth()+1+"/"+anydate.getDate()+"/"+ year';
```

```
tag += '\n}';
tag += '\n%>';
tag += '\n This page was last accessed on ';
tag += '\n <% Response.Write(Application("lastAccessDate"))';
tag += '\n%>';
this.text = tag;
}
```

Your final JavaScript routine, shown in the preceding code, is a little more complex only because JavaScript doesn't have the built-in date and time manipulation that VBScript has. Regardless, the final functionality will be the same.

One final option is included in case the server language is not JavaScript or VBScript. This code is inserted intentionally at the end of the function as a fail-safe. If there is no language match, the program will drop down to this block of code, which will alert the user that the object doesn't work with the current server configuration.

> **Note** *The "trickling down method" is one way to approach this type of coding. You check your code as it makes its way through a series of If/Then/Else statements, and if it doesn't find a match, it ends up on a default condition.*

All that remains after you've instantiated your *VBScriptObject()* is to assign it to a variable so that the *objectTag()* function will return the result to Dreamweaver MX. The text property of the *scriptObject* contains the complete script to be inserted. You can add more HTML to the tag, such as the <p> tag that was added here. At this point, the language is inconsequential.

You'll also have to add another entry in the insertbar.xml file, under the same Custom Objects category:

```
<button id="DWMXTCR_LastAccessDate"
 image="Custom Objects\LastAccessDate.gif"
 enabled=""
 showIf=""
 file="Custom Objects\LastAccessDate.htm" />
```

If you save the object now in your Custom Objects folder and restart Dreamweaver MX, you can apply the object to the page (see Figure 31-6). You'll see the text "This page last viewed on" surrounded by two ASP tags. You can apply text styles to the object, if you wish, by selecting the <p> tag in the tag selector and applying one of your page styles to the tag.

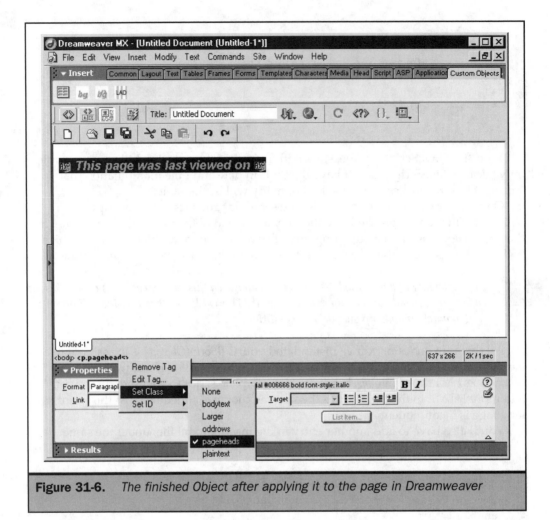

Figure 31-6. *The finished Object after applying it to the page in Dreamweaver*

If you preview the page in a browser, the date won't be filled in the first time you view it, because this is the first access of the page. Close the browser, reopen it, and view it a second time. The date and time appear on the page:

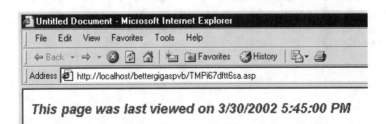

Adding a ColdFusion Version

Now that you have a nice framework already set up, you are ready to add the ColdFusion version of the code. At this point, two steps are required:

1. Create a *ColdFusionObject()* class constructor.

2. Insert the two lines necessary to instantiate the constructor.

To create the constructor, use the following code:

```
function ColdFusionObject() {
var tag='<CFSET LastAccessDate="">';
tag += '\n<CFSET FILENAME=#getdirectoryfrompath(gettemplatepath())#¬
    & "DateFile.txt">';
tag += '\n<CFIF #FileExists(filename)is "Yes">';
tag += '\n<CFFILE ACTION="read" FILE="#filename#"';
tag += 'VARIABLE="LastAccessDate">';
tag += '\n</CFIF>';
tag += '\nThis page was last viewed on ';
tag += '<CFOUTPUT>#LastAccessDate#</CFOUTPUT>';
tag += '\n<CFFILE ACTION="write" FILE="filename"';
tag += 'OUTPUT="#DateFormat(Now(),"mm/dd/yy")# #TimeFormat(Now(),¬
    "hh:mm:ss tt")#">';
this.text = tag;
}
```

ColdFusion is a tag-based language that has a lot of functionality already built into the server. File manipulation is straightforward in ColdFusion, so you can create an object with similar functionality to the ASP object with only a few lines of code. The one thing that you are doing differently is finding the path to the current page, because the CFFILE tag needs a path for the file to be read/written. You do that by using the two built-in ColdFusion functions *GetDirectoryFromPath()* and *GetTemplatePath()*. Now, you'll instantiate the object in your *objectTag()* function body, right after the test for the JavaScript object:

```
}else if(serverLanguage=="Cfml") {
    myScriptObject = new ColdFusionObject();
```

That's all there is to it. Now the object works for ColdFusion as well. This extension uses some of the principles and object-oriented approach that Macromedia engineers applied when building Dreamweaver MX, although on a much smaller scale. After you have your basic extension finished, making the extension usable in another server language isn't difficult. You could just as easily add JSP, ASP.NET, or PHP code to the object. That was just one of the side benefits of using the object-oriented approach.

Tip
Another way to discover the language of the current document is to use the function dw.getDocumentDOM().documentType. *When using this function, however, you will return values such as "ASP-VB" and "ASP-JS", rather than "VBScript" and "JavaScript".*

Commands

Commands are perhaps the most powerful of the extensions, because they can perform powerful document and site manipulation, and can be called from any other extension. Some of them appear on the Commands menu of Dreamweaver MX and include such things as Clean Up HTML and Add/Remove Netscape Resize Fix. A command can add code to a page or manipulate code that's already on the page. Sometimes, a fine line separates commands, objects, behaviors, and Server Behaviors; but no matter what you decide to do with your code, knowing all the available possibilities is a good idea.

A Command file is similar to the HTML files that you created for objects and Server Behaviors, but differs in a few respects. For one, not every command has a corresponding menu item. If you look inside the Commands folder, you'll see quite a few commands that don't appear on the Commands menu. To keep the command from appearing on the menu, simply put the following as the first line in your command file:

```
<!-- MENU-LOCATION=NONE -->
```

There are a few ways you can use commands to enhance your other extensions. You can invoke a command with a *dw.runCommand()* function call or with the *dw.popupCommand()* function call.

This is done for many reasons. Commands are more versatile than some of the other extensions. A Property Inspector, for example, must reside in a small interface to conform to the predefined size of an Inspector. Frequently, you will have to invoke a command to display a larger interface for editing some code or attributes. If you look at the Asp.js file in the Inspectors folder, for instance, you'll notice the *launchASPEditDialog()* function, which gets the selected object and then calls the *dw.popupCommand("EditContent")* to invoke a code editor for the ASP code block that was selected by the user. You can do this in your own Property Inspectors, as well.

Tip
As always, looking at existing code is a great way to learn how to apply the techniques to your own programming. The existing Command files offer a wealth of information.

The following syntax presents a very basic command to show you how to manipulate the document. This command simply wraps any selected text or object with comment tags, so that you can freely comment your HTML without leaving the design environment. You can also choose to "comment out" some text or an object while designing your site, which is useful for debugging.

```
<html>
<head>
```

```html
<title>MakeComment</title>
<script language="javascript">
<!--
function makeComment() {
  var openTag = '<!--\n'
  var closeTag = '\n-->';
  // Get Selected text and wrap with comment tags
  var dom = dw.getDocumentDOM(); //get the DOM
  var sel = dom.getSelection(); //get the selected text or object
  var wrapthis = dom.documentElement.outerHTML.substring(sel[0], sel[1]);
  wrapthis = openTag + wrapthis + closeTag; //wrap the selected text
  dw.getDocumentDOM().insertHTML(wrapthis); //insert into the document
  window.close();
}
//-->
</script>
</head>
<body onLoad="makeComment()">
</body>
</html>
```

The code is fairly simple. First, it declares two variables for your opening and closing comment tags. Then, it declares the *makeComment()* function, which is called from the body *onLoad* event of the extension. The *makeComment()* function simply gets the document DOM, and then it acquires the selected text by using the offsets that were returned by the *getSelection* method of the DOM and getting the *outerHTML* property. Then, all that is left to do is to wrap the opening and closing comment tags around the selection, and insert the entire string back into the document.

At this point, if you save the extension in the Commands folder with the name Make Comment.htm and restart Dreamweaver MX, you can apply it by making a selection on the page and then choosing Make Comment from the Commands menu. When you do this, any selected text or object will be collapsed into a comment tag. How are you going to "uncomment" the item now? You'll write another command, Strip Comment Tags, to accomplish this. Here is the code for that command:

```html
<html>
<head>
<title>Strip Comment Tags</title>
<script language="javascript">
<!--
function stripComment() {
  // Get Selected comment and strip comment tags
  var doc = dw.getDocumentDOM(); //get the DOM
  var sel = doc.getSelection(); //get the selection
  var theNode = dw.offsetsToNode(sel[0],sel[1]);
```

```
if(theNode.nodeType==Node.COMMENT_NODE) {
   sel=theNode.data;
   dw.getDocumentDOM().insertHTML(sel);
  }
  window.close();
}
//-->
</script>
</head>
<body onLoad="stripComment()">
</body>
</html>
```

This command works in a similar fashion to the Make Comment command. However, after getting the selection, the command first checks to see whether the selected node is a comment node. If it is a comment, it gets the *data* property of the node. The data property contains the area that's inside the tags in *comment* nodes and *text* nodes. It's similar to the *innerHTML* property of the *element* nodes. After getting the data property, you then write the HTML to the document without the comment tags.

You can use these techniques to add server-side code, as well. You could easily modify the Make Comment command to insert any of the server markup listed in Table 31-1, or to insert code before and after the selected text simply by changing the *openTag* and *closeTag* variables.

OpenTag	CloseTag
<% =	*%>*
<%Response.Write("	*")%>*
<cfoutput>	*</cfoutput>*
<%try{	*}catch(java.lang.Exception e){;}%>*
<%If Session("Username")<>"" Then %>	*<%End If%>*
<cfif IsDefined("Session.Username")>	*</cfif>*
<%if(MM_offset != 0)%>	*<%}%>*
<?php echo	*; ?>*
<cftry>	*<cfcatch>Error code</cfcatch></cftry>*

Table 31-1.   *Possible Open and Close Tags for a Modified Command File*

Another feature worth mentioning about Command files is the capability to define the buttons for the interface on the fly—making them contextual depending upon conditions that you can set up programmatically. One good example of this technique is the Add/Remove Netscape Resize Fix command. In that command, the button shown in the interface depends upon whether or not the user has already applied the command to the page. If the command has been applied, the user is shown the Remove button; whereas if the command hasn't been applied yet, the user is shown the Add button. You could easily adapt the Make Comment and Strip Comment commands to share one single interface by using this technique. There is a file available from www.osborne.com demonstrating this approach.

Toolbars

Toolbars are new to Dreamweaver MX, and are easily implemented. How often have you wished that you could call your favorite command from a button? Now you can do it, and all that is required is to put a small XML file in the Toolbars folder that conforms to the Toolbar extensibility API. In addition, you'll have to include GIF images that will act as the toolbar buttons for your toolbar.

Toolbars have been a much-requested feature throughout the life of Dreamweaver. Other programs, such as MS Word, Homesite, and CF Studio have toolbars, but Dreamweaver users have been without this feature until now. Some of the most popular commands have already been included in Dreamweaver MX in the Standard toolbar, such as File | New, File | Open, and File | Save.

Toolbars consist of a *toolbarset* tag, within which is one or more toolbar tags. Within the toolbar tags is any number of toolbar controls, which can be any of the following types:

- **Button**   Standard push button to invoke a command. The new file button is a Button type.
- **Checkbutton**   Like a check box, the check button has a checked and unchecked state. The live data button is a check button type.
- **Radiobutton**   This control acts similarly to a radio button on a Web page—when one button is pressed, the other buttons are unpressed. Radio buttons are grouped, as the Code/Split/Design view buttons.
- **Menubutton**   This control will pop up a menu when clicked, like the Preview in Browser button.
- **Dropdown**   This control acts just like a standard drop-down box on a Web page.
- **Combobox**   This control is an editable drop-down box.
- **Editcontrol**   Like a text field in a Web page, this control allows you to type into it, but it will fire an event when the focus is shifted off it. The Title box in the Document toolbar is of this type.
- **Colorpicker**   This control will pop up a color picker to allow a color to be selected. It is typically used with an editcontrol.

The toolbar control can work with a Command file, menu command file, or with an inline JavaScript command within the toolbar file itself.

You create a toolbar with the following XML code skeleton:

```
<?xml version="1.0"?>
<!DOCTYPE toolbarset SYSTEM "-//Macromedia//DWExtension toolbar 5.0">
<toolbarset>
   <toolbar id="DWMXTCR_Toolbar_Custom" label="TCR">
<!-- toolbar controls go here -->
   </toolbar>
</toolbarset>
```

You could add two new buttons to this toolbar to add the comment commands that were created in the previous section to the toolbar. You'll also have to copy the DWMXTCR folder from the Chapter 31 zip file that is available on the Osborne Web site to the Toolbars folder. This folder contains the images used for these buttons. Add the following controls to the preceding skeleton, and save it into the Toolbars folder as Custom_toolbar.xml:

```
<button id="DWMXTCR_stripcomment"
   image="Toolbars/DWMXTCR/stripcomment.gif"
   tooltip="Strip Comment"
   domRequired="TRUE"
   file="Commands/Strip Comment.htm" />
<button id="DWMXTCR_makecomment"
   image="Toolbars/DWMXTCR/makecomment.gif"
   tooltip="Make Comment"
   domRequired="TRUE"
   file="Commands/Make Comment.htm" />
```

You can also include the functionality right inside of the toolbar button control, if the code is short enough. The following toolbar button will prompt a user for how many new documents to open up. Dreamweaver MX will then open up that number of new documents:

```
<button id="DWMXTCR_multiple"
   image="Toolbars/DWMXTCR/multiple.gif"
   tooltip="Multiple new documents"
   domRequired="TRUE"
   command="var howmany = prompt('How Many?','10');
    for(var i=0;i<howmany;i++)
    dw.newDocument();" />
```

Floaters

A custom floater, or panel, is another form of extension that gives Dreamweaver MX a unique way to interact with the user. You can use a floater to incorporate special functionality of your own design into the Dreamweaver MX environment. A floater could be described as a "Property Inspector on steroids." The restrictions of Inspectors don't apply to floaters, so you can add as much functionality as you need in the floater interface. One typical use is to add a pop-up window and attach it to a button in a Property Inspector to "spread out" the Inspector and give it more functionality. This is typically done with a Command file, but there is one problem with Commands: The windows are modal, meaning that they have to be closed before you can go back to your document. By turning it into a floating panel, you aren't restricted to having to close the window, as you would be with a Command file.

Floaters don't pop up automatically when dropped into a folder, as do the other extensions. They have to be invoked by a function call either through a menu item or a button on another extension. You can invoke a floater by calling *dw.setFloaterVisibility(floatername,true)* or *dw.toggleFloater(floatername)*. The easiest way to do this is by adding a line to the menus.xml file, like this:

```
<menuitem name="MyFloater" enabled="true"
 command="dw.toggleFloater('MyFloater')"
 id="DWContext_Text_MyFloater" />
```

You can place a menu item like this anywhere, but a good place for a floater is in the Window menu on the main menu bar for Dreamweaver MX. You can also put floaters in the contextual menu; if it's something that deserves its own floater, it's probably something that you want just a right-click away. The menu item in the preceding code has an ID name that hints that it might be under the DWContext_Text menu, which is the main document contextual menu.

Now you are going to build a simple floater that will allow the evaluation of JavaScript. Begin by creating a new HTML file. Call it EvaluateJavaScript.htm and save it in the Floaters folder. Place this code in the document as the interface:

```
<html>
<head>
<title>Evaluate JavaScript</title>
<script language="JavaScript">
    //your code goes here
</script>
</head>
<body>
<form name="theForm">
  <table cellspacing="0" cellpadding="0">
```

```
<tr>
  <td nowrap>
    <input type="button" name="Submit" value="Evaluate"
     onClick="evaluateTheScript()">
    <input type="button" name="clear" value="Clear"
     onclick="clearWindow()">
  </td>
</tr>
<tr>
  <td>
    <textarea name="theCode" style="width:350px; height:200px">
    </textarea>
  </td>
</tr>
<tr>
  <td>
    <textarea name="jsEvaluate"  style="width:350px;
     height:100px"></textarea>
  </td>
</tr>
</table>
</form>
</body>
</html>
```

Now, you need to edit the menus.xml file in the DWMenu_Window section. Open the menus.xml file in your text editor and use the *find* command to search for the following text, which will display all the menu items that are currently in the Window menu in Dreamweaver MX: *<menu name="_Window" id="DWMenu_Window">*. Place the following line at the bottom of the menu before the closing </menu> for that particular menu:

```
<menuitem name="Evaluate JavaScript" enabled="true" ¬
 command="dw.toggleFloater('EvaluateJavaScript')" ¬
 checked="dw.getFloaterVisibility('EvaluateJavaScript')" ¬
 id=" DWMenu_Window_EvaluateJavaScript " />
```

Caution *If you have installed extensions on your copy of Dreamweaver MX, there may be a duplicate menus.xml file installed to your multiuser directory. If the file is located there, any changes to your menus.xml will have to be made directly to that file or the extension won't work. These problems can be circumvented by always building an extension package for your extension. The Extension Manager takes care of creating the menu entries to the correct file.*

The *checked* attribute shows your floater on the menu with a check mark next to the name if it is active in the design environment. After editing the menu in this way, you can close Dreamweaver MX and restart it, and the Evaluate JavaScript menu item appears. If you click it, the floater pops up. At this point, the functionality isn't built in yet, but it's now a working floater that can be used by itself or docked with the other floaters.

You've already put the empty script block in the document, so now you can fill in the functions that are going to be needed by the floater:

```
function clearWindow() {
   document.theForm.theCode.value= "";
}
```

The *clearWindow()* function is called by the *onclick* event of the Clear button, built previously in the HTML form. This function simply clears all text or code out of the textfield named *theCode*.

The next four functions are built-in floater API methods:

```
function isAvailableInCodeView(){
   return true;
}
function isDockable() {
   return true;
}
function getDockingSide() {
   return "left right";
}
function isATarget() {
   return true;
}
```

The first, *isAvailableInCodeView()*, simply tells Dreamweaver MX that the floater should be able to be seen in code view. If this function were not included, the floater would be disabled in code view. The *isDockable()* function tells Dreamweaver MX that the floater can be docked with other panels. If this function isn't included, the floater acts as a standalone window that can't be docked. Two other required functions for docking are *getDockingSide()*, which returns the dockable sides of the panel, and *isATarget()*, which allows a panel to accept other panels for docking as well.

The last function, *evaluateTheScript()*, actually performs all of the actions required of this particular floater:

```
function evaluateTheScript() {
   var theEval;
   var theScript= document.theForm.theCode.value;
   try {
     theEval = eval(theScript);
     // try to execute the script entered by the user
```

```
      if(theEval != null) {
        document.theForm.jsEvaluate.value = theEval;
        // if there is something to display, display it
      }
    }
  catch(e) {
      alert(e);//display an error message
      // if there is an error in the script
    }
  }
```

Upon the click of the Evaluate button, this function evaluates a piece of JavaScript that is entered into the floater. As you can see from the function, it is using the new functionality of the JavaScript 1.5 engine of Dreamweaver MX with the *try/catch* block. This prevents any JavaScript errors entered by a user to cause an error in the floater. This would have been impossible to do in previous versions of Dreamweaver. Figure 31-7 shows the new floater docked and in use.

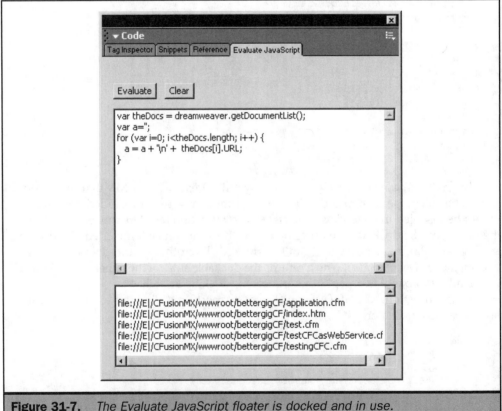

Figure 31-7. *The Evaluate JavaScript floater is docked and in use.*

As you can see, a floater is a fairly easy extension to build, and can also be a very useful item, allowing you to keep functionality open at all times in the Dreamweaver environment.

Data Sources

Data sources are the variables, recordsets, and database commands that return data to a Web page to be displayed. A session or application variable would be considered a data source, as well as a column in a recordset. Data sources are found in the Bindings panel (formerly Data Bindings in UltraDev), between the Server Behaviors panel and the Databases panel in a default installation of Dreamweaver MX.

The panel has a plus (+) and a minus (-) button just like the Server Behaviors panel, but the menu entries in this panel don't "do" anything to the page. A data source can be put on the page to display data, as you did when you dropped database columns into the design environment, but it doesn't perform any action. They are called Bindings because they "bind" data to page elements, such as text or form elements.

Data sources are extensible, too, like most features of Dreamweaver MX. You are free to modify and add to the Bindings panel by designing your own data sources or modifying existing data sources.

Data sources are also accessible by choosing Server Behaviors | Dynamic Elements | Dynamic Text. Indeed, this is the only way to edit a data source, because you can't double-click a data source from the Bindings panel to edit it. If you choose the menu from the Server Behaviors panel, it actually gives you the underlying code to the data source, which you can modify or give a *format*. The data source format is chosen from a predefined list of possible formats that include such things as date and time formatting, money formatting, and other forms of number formatting.

You'll now build an example of a data source using a type of variable that isn't available from the stock Bindings panel in most of the server models—a Local variable. A data source can get pretty complex, interacting with Server Behaviors and Translators. This discussion will just go over the basics of an actual data source implementation without the accompanying Server Behavior and Translator. This is the ASP version of the data source.

> **Tip**   *By writing a corresponding Server Behavior for a data source, you can give it extra functionality, such as the capability to apply data formats from the Server Behavior panel.*

To begin, the Data Source requires an HTML file that will reside in one of the subfolders in the DataSources folder, depending upon which server model you are working with. This one will be an ASP Data Source, so you'll need to create a LocalVariable.htm file in the ASP_Vbs or ASP_Js directory. The file will start with this code:

```
<html>
<head>
  <script src="helper.js"></script>
```

```
<script src ="../../Shared/MM/Scripts/CMN/string.js"></script>
<script src ="../../Shared/UltraDev/Scripts/ssDocManager.js">
</script>
<script language="javascript">
//The rest of the functions will go here
</script>
<title>Local Variable</title>
</head>
</html>
```

When a user first clicks the plus sign to add a data source, the *addDynamicSource()* function is called. Your implementation of that function is as follows, beginning with two global variables of your images for the Bindings panel (these are in the Chapter 31 folder of the zip file available from the Osborne Web site):

```
var local_filename = "LOC_D.gif"
var datasourceleaf_filename = "DSL_D.gif"
function addDynamicSource(){
  MM.retVal = "";
  MM.localContents = "";
  dw.popupCommand("Local Variable");
  var dom = dw.getDocumentDOM();
  var fileURL = dom.URL;
  if (!fileURL.length){
    fileURL = getTempFileURL();
  }
  if (MM.retVal == "OK") {
    var theResponse = MM.localContents;
    if (theResponse.length) {
      addValueToNote(fileURL,"localCount","local",theResponse);
    }else{
      alert("Please enter a name");
    }
  }
}
```

The function basically pops up a command (which you'll create next) that grabs the name of the local variable that the user defines and stores it in a special array in the design notes for that file, after it has checked for the existence of the notes. It stores the information about the data source in the notes so that other pages can retrieve it. The command that you are calling is just a basic HTML interface that retrieves the user's input of a variable name and returns it to this function. This is the code for the Command file, which you can name LocalVariables.htm and store in the Commands folder:

```html
<!-- MENU-LOCATION=NONE -->
<html>
<head>
  <title>Local Variable</title>
  <script src="../Shared/MM/Scripts/CMN/localText.js"></script>
  <script language="javascript">
  function commandButtons(){
    return new Array("OK","okClicked()",
      "Cancel","window.close()");
  }
  function okClicked(){
    var nameObj = document.forms[0].theName;
    if (nameObj.value) {
      MM.localContents = nameObj.value;
      MM.retVal = "OK";
      window.close();
    } else {
      alert("Please fill in a name or cancel");
    }
  }
  </script>
</head>
<body>
<form>
  <table border="0">
    <tr>
      <td align="right" valign="baseline">Name:</td>
      <td valign="baseline">
        <input name="theName" type="text" style="width:150px">
      </td>
    </tr>
  </table>
</form>
</body>
</html>
```

After getting the data source, Dreamweaver MX empties the Bindings panel and calls the *findDynamicSources()* function in each file in the DataSources folder. If the function finds a data source, Dreamweaver MX then calls the *generateDynamicSourceBindings()*

function in that file to rebuild the panel from scratch. Those two functions for your Local variable data source, which should be placed into the LocalVariables.htm Data Source file that you created, are as follows:

```
function findDynamicSources() {
  var DSL = new Array();
  var dom = dw.getDocumentDOM();
  if (dom) {
    var fileURL = dom.URL;
    if (fileURL.length) {
      copyFromTempURL();
    } else {
      fileURL = getTempFileURL();
    }
    if (fileURL.length){
      var LBindingsArray = new Array();
      getValuesFromNote(fileURL,LBindingsArray,"local","localCount");
      if (LBindingsArray.length > 0) {
        DSL.push(new ObjectInfo("Local Variables", ¬
        local_filename, false))
      }
    }
  }
  return DSL;
}

function generateDynamicSourceBindings(elementName) {
  var BindingsArray = new Array();
  var outArray;
  var dom = dw.getDocumentDOM();
  if (dom) {
    var fileURL = dom.URL;
    if (!fileURL.length)
      fileURL = getTempFileURL();
    if (fileURL.length){
      if (elementName != "local")
        elementName = "local"
      if (fileURL.length){
        getValuesFromNote(fileURL,BindingsArray,elementName, ¬
        "localCount");
        outArray = GenerateObjectInfoForSourceBindings(BindingsArray,¬
        datasourceleaf_filename);
      }
```

```
      }
    }
    return outArray;
}
```

The first function finds the values of the data sources from the file notes and adds them to the array that it returns to Dreamweaver MX. The function then creates a new *objectInfo* object for this particular data source, to which it adds the title of the data source, the image filename that gets displayed in the panel, and an "allow delete" flag. Then, the bindings are added to the panel by the call to the *generateDynamicSourceBindings* function.

> **Caution** *Data sources are perhaps the most complex extension type, and require complex interactions among commands, Server Behaviors, Translators, data formats, and the data source itself. Building one shouldn't be taken lightly!*

Next is the *generateDynamicDataRef* function, which actually builds the string that gets inserted into the document. In this case, you are simply placing <%= and %> around the variable name. This is the ASP equivalent of *Response.Write*, which is used quite often as shorthand in the body of a Web page. If this were a ColdFusion data source, you would add *<cfoutput>#(variable name)#</cfoutput>* around the variable name.

```
function generateDynamicDataRef(elementName,bindingName) {
   retStr = "<%=" + bindingName + "%>";
   return retStr;
}
```

Next is the *inspectDynamicDataRef* function, which simply returns the source (which is "Local" in this case) and binding (the variable name):

```
function inspectDynamicDataRef(expression){
  var retArray = new Array();
  // Quickly reject if the expression doesn't contain "<%="
  var exprIndex = expression.indexOf("<%=");
  if (exprIndex != -1){
    if(expression.indexOf(".")==-1||expression.indexOf('"')==-1){
      //if no dot or no quotes, must be local
      var found = expression.search(/<%=\s*(\w+)\s*%>/i)
      if (found != -1){
          retArray[0] = "Local";
          retArray[1] = RegExp.$1;
```

```
        }
      }
    }
    return retArray;
}
```

Finally, the *deleteDynamicSource()* function is defined, which is called when a user clicks the minus (–) button on the Data Sources floater:

```
function deleteDynamicSource(sourceName,bindingName){
  var dom = dw.getDocumentDOM();
  if (dom) {
    var fileURL = dom.URL;
    if (!fileURL.length)
       fileURL = getTempFileURL();
    if (fileURL.length){
       deleteValueFromNote(fileURL,"localCount","Local",bindingName);
    }
  }
}
```

The preceding code gives you a working data source for a Local variable type. Any additional functionality, such as using server formats to have the data source show up in the Server Behaviors panel as a Dynamic Text item, has to be coded separately into a Server Behavior. In addition, to get the data source to show up on the page as a viewable entity, you will have to write a Translator. Translators are covered in the next chapter.

Server Formats

Server formats are special extensions that you can apply to dynamic text elements, such as the Session and Application variables, and recordset columns. You can apply a server format by double-clicking a data source in the Server Behaviors panel. Typical formats include currency formatting, date and time formatting, upper- and lowercase formatting, and other standard text formatting. When you apply the server format to the element on the page, the extension takes care of stripping off the server tags, adding the special formatting, and then putting the tags back on. In addition, if any special functions are required for the formatting, the extension inserts the appropriate code into the head of the document.

Server formats are easy to write and often offer the best method for doing some "last minute" text formatting for database fields, variables, and other data sources.

As with other areas of Dreamweaver MX, you can extend or write your own server formats. These extensions are built a little differently than some of the other extensions. You must insert a *RegExp* pattern right into the menu file. Like the regular expressions that are used in Server Behaviors, this expression is used by Dreamweaver MX to match the format in the code on your page.

There are folders within the Server Formats folder that correspond with the server models that work with Dreamweaver MX. Each of these folders has a corresponding Formats.xml menu file as well, which is the menu where your changes will go.

The extensions are fairly consistent. You can easily take an existing server format and change it to reflect the new format that you want to implement. You'll find that most of the server formats contain three basic functions: *formatDynamicDataRef*, *applyFormat()*, and *deleteFormat()*. In addition, some of the formats will write a function to the head of the user's document. In those cases, a fourth function will build a string that contains the text of the function.

You now are going to build an ASP version of a Preserve Whitespace server format. ColdFusion, PHP, ASP.NET, or JSP versions can be built using identical techniques. This is a format that you can apply to a database field that may contain new lines and tabs that don't translate to HTML. The format will take care of replacing these instances with <br> tags and strings of nonbreaking spaces in place of the tab character.

The HTML File for Preserve Whitespace

The first thing to do, of course, is to create an HTML file named PreserveWhitespace.htm and save it in the ASP_Vbs folder or ASP_Js folder under Server Formats. The file should contain the following text:

```
<!-- MENU-LOCATION=NONE -->
<html>
<head>
<title>PreserveWhitespace</title>
<script language="javascript" ¬
src="../../Shared/UltraDev/scripts/ssCmnElements.js">
</script>
<script language="javascript" ¬
src="../../Shared/UltraDev/scripts/ssClasses.js">
</script>
<script language="javascript" ¬
src="../../Shared/MM/Scripts/CMN/dom.js"></script>
<script language="javascript" ¬
src="../../Shared/UltraDev/scripts/ssDocManager.js">
</script>
<script language="javascript" src="FormatsSupport.js"></script>
<script language="javascript" src="PreserveWhitespace.js"></script>
```

```
</head>
<body>
</body>
</html>
```

Some of the standard include files are listed here, as well as FormatsSupport.js, a new file that contains some necessary support functions for the server format that you are creating. A PreserveWhitespace.js file that will contain all the functions for this particular server format is referenced as well.

Creating the New Format

All of the main functions are going to be housed in the JS file, so go ahead and create that now. The code that you include will remove all line-feed characters and replace them with a line feed and a <br> tag. You could do a simple "replace" of the line feed with a <br> tag, but the line-feed character creates better HTML formatting when you view the source of the output page. In addition to the line feed, you're replacing the tab character (chr(9)) with a series of five nonbreaking spaces. Here's the VBScript code for the function:

```
<SCRIPT RUNAT=SERVER LANGUAGE=VBSCRIPT>
function PreserveWhitespace(str)
   tabStr = chr(160)&chr(160)&chr(160)&chr(160)&chr(160)
   str = Replace(str,chr(10),chr(10)&"<br>")
   str = Replace(str,chr(9),tabStr)
   PreserveWhitespace = str
End Function
</SCRIPT>
```

Because the function is enclosed with its own language declaration, the function will run on a site that is defined for JScript as well. The preceding code has to be built into a string and inserted into the head of the document. Because the code exists as a generic function that can be used by a data source in the body of the document, you don't have to worry about the *weights* of a Server Behavior—it can fall anywhere within the head and still function properly. The following function builds the string and returns the complete string to the caller:

```
function getWholeJSFormatFunc() {
   strRet  = '<SCRIPT RUNAT=SERVER LANGUAGE=VBSCRIPT>\n';
   strRet += 'function PreserveWhitespace(str)\n';
   strRet += 'tabStr =chr(160)&chr(160)&chr(160)&chr(160)&chr(160)\n';
   strRet += 'str = Replace(str,chr(10),chr(10)&"<br>")\n';
   strRet += 'str = Replace(str,chr(9),tabStr)\n';
```

```
  strRet += 'PreserveWhitespace = str\n';
  strRet += 'End Function\n';
  strRet += '</SCRIPT>\n';
  return strRet;
}
```

The *formatDynamicDataRef* Function Implementation

Next, you'll define a global variable that is used to name the Server Format within the extension:

```
var formatFunc = "PreserveWhitespace";
```

The following function will be called by Dreamweaver MX if the user chooses the Preserve Whitespace format from the Bindings panel or the Dynamic Text Server Behavior:

```
function formatDynamicDataRef(str, format){
  var ret = str;
  var iStart = getIndexOfEqualsForResponseWrite(str);
  if (iStart > -1){
    var iEnd = str.indexOf("%>", iStart+1);
    if (iEnd > -1){
      ret = str.substring(0, iStart+1) + " " + formatFunc + "(";
      ret += str.substring(iStart+1, iEnd)
      ret += ") " + str.substr(iEnd);
    }else{
        alert("No ASP end tag");
    }
  }else{
      alert("No equals sign");
  }
return ret;
}
```

The dynamic text, or data source, that the format is being applied to is passed to the function in the *str* variable. The second argument, format, is the JavaScript object that describes the format that's being applied.

The function marks the open and close tags for the dynamic data passed into the *str* variable and remembers the index location, and then inserts the function name along with opening and closing parentheses. The function is also doing some preliminary error checking by making sure that there is an equals sign and a closing ASP tag.

The *applyFormat()* Function

Next, you'll implement the function that does the work of inserting the function into the head of the document. You'll find that this function is almost identical in all server formats that require a function in the head. You simply use the DOM to insert the code directly before the <html> tag:

```
function applyFormat(){
  if (getFunctionVersion(formatFunc, null) == -1){
    var currSel = dw.getSelection();
    var htmlNode = dw.getDocumentDOM().documentElement;
    var oldHtmlOffsets = dw.nodeToOffsets(htmlNode);
    var wholeFunc = getWholeJSFormatFunc();
    insertBeforeHTMLTag(wholeFunc);
    htmlNode = dreamweaver.getDocumentDOM().documentElement;
    var newHtmlOffsets = dw.nodeToOffsets(htmlNode);
    var delta = newHtmlOffsets[1] - oldHtmlOffsets[1];
    dw.setSelection(currSel[0]+delta, currSel[1]+delta);
  }
}
```

The *deleteFormat()* Function

The *deleteFormat()* function does the exact opposite of the *applyFormat()* function. It goes into the DOM and removes the function that was added. The first thing that it does, however, is check to make sure that no other data sources are on the page that might need the function to remain—if so, it merely exits, leaving the function intact:

```
function deleteFormat(){
  if ((numFormatFunctionInvokations(formatFunc, 1) < 1) && ¬
     (getFunctionVersion(formatFunc, null) > -1)){
    var currSel = dw.getSelection();
    var htmlNode = dw.getDocumentDOM().documentElement;
    var oldHtmlOffsets = dw.nodeToOffsets(htmlNode);
    deleteWholeScriptContainingFunction(formatFunc);
    htmlNode = dreamweaver.getDocumentDOM().documentElement;
    var newHtmlOffsets = dw.nodeToOffsets(htmlNode);
    var delta = newHtmlOffsets[1] - oldHtmlOffsets[1];
    dw.setSelection(currSel[0]+delta, currSel[1]+delta);
  }
}
```

The only thing unusual about this function is the call to a shared function from the FormatsSupport.js file—*deleteWholeScriptContainingFunction*. The name says it all: It does the job of deleting the function in question.

Editing the Formats.xml File

The last thing that needs to be done to create a working server format is to add a menu entry to the Formats.xml file that is in the same folder as the extension. Each subfolder under Server Formats (ASP_Js, ASP_Vbs, JSP, UD4-ColdFusion, ASP.Net_Vb, ASP.Net_Csharp, PHP_MySQL, and ColdFusion) has its own Formats.xml file. The following lines need to be added after the last </menu> tag but before the closing </format> tag:

```
<menu name = "New Formats" ¬
id="DWMenu_ServerFormatDef_ASP_2_NewFormats">
<format file="PreserveWhitespace" title="Preserve Whitespace"¬
expression="<%\s*=\s*PreserveWhitespace\([^%]*%>" ¬
id="DWMenu_ServerFormatDef_ASP_2_PRES_WHITE" />
</menu>
```

Caution *Never edit a menu file without first making a backup of the file. Also, if you have installed extensions that write to this file, you may have to modify the Formats.xml file in the appropriate multiuser configuration folder instead of in this one. For that reason, it is easier to create an extension package so that your menu files can be modified automatically.*

Notice the use of the <format> tag. The <format> tag is actually a JavaScript object that will contain information about the server format needed by Dreamweaver MX to apply the format. The tag includes the following standard attributes:

- A file attribute, which is the title of the file used in the format (your PreserveWhitespace.htm file)
- A title attribute for how it is displayed in the menu
- An expression attribute, which is the *RegExp* that actually takes care of locating the format in the document after it has been applied
- An ID attribute, which must be a unique ID name

These are the required attributes, but you can also include other information about the server format here as well, and then access it through dot notation in the *formatDynamicDataRef* function. For instance, if you have a server format that displays a certain number of characters in a data source, you could have a *numChars* attribute and access it by using *format.numChars* in the function.

Packaging Extensions

As previously mentioned, menus generally should not be edited directly; but if they are edited, they must be edited very carefully. How do you make changes to a menu without physically changing one? By using an extension *package.* Dreamweaver MX comes with the Extension Manager, which also includes a built-in packager for extensions.

In addition to packaging and changing menus automatically, when you create a package with the Extension Manager, you know that the appropriate files are going to be modified correctly in the multiuser Configuration folder. Dreamweaver MX added a sophisticated framework to the program that allows extensions to be installed into the folder of the current user, located in c:\Documents and Settings*username*\Application Data\Macromedia\Dreamweaver MX\Configuration on a Windows 2000 machine.

The process of creating a package is started by writing a Macromedia eXtension Information (MXI) file with all the information about your extension. The MXI file is in a limited XML format. It's not *true* eXtensible Markup Language, and as such shouldn't be edited in a dedicated XML editor; instead, it's a variation of XML that is recognized by the Extension Manager API. To write your MXI file, you can use the template that's included in the Dreamweaver MX package, or you can modify an existing MXI file.

When you install a third-party extension, the MXI files are unpacked to the Extensions folder under Configuration. These files don't have an editor associated with them, but they can be opened in Notepad or BBEdit, or any text editor. Make sure to save as plain text after you make your changes to the file.

The next section goes through the process of creating the MXI file and packaging an extension by using the Evaluate JavaScript floating panel that you created earlier in the chapter.

Main Tag

The main tag of the MXI file is the <macromedia-extension> tag. This tag specifies the name, version, type, and the optional attribute of requires-restart. In addition, if you submit the extension to the Macromedia Exchange, Macromedia will insert an ID number into this tag, which should not be edited.

```
<macromedia-extension
   name="Evaluate JavaScript Floater"
   version="1.0.0"
   type="Floater"
   requires-restart="true" >
```

The name should be a unique name, and is usually the same as the title that you give to the extension in the HTML file of that extension. The version number consists of three digits representing the main version number, the revision number, and the minor revision number. For example, if you begin with 1.0.0 and submit the extension to Macromedia, and you are asked to make small changes in the extension, you should number the next version 1.0.1, and so on.

The type attribute should be one of the extension types recognized by Dreamweaver MX. A list of available types is shown in Table 31-2. The *requires-restart* attribute is optional and should be used if your extension requires the program to be restarted after the extension is installed.

Products and Authors Tags

The next tag is the <products> tag, which consists of the names of the programs that the extension will work with. Some commands, objects, behaviors, and other extensions might work with Dreamweaver, UltraDev, or both, but the Server Behaviors and other server-related extensions should be defined as UltraDev-only or Dreamweaver 6 by specifying them in this tag. If you specify Dreamweaver 3, the extension will install to Dreamweaver 3 and above or UltraDev 1 and 4. Dreamweaver MX is known as Dreamweaver 6 to the Extension Manager.

```
<products>
    <product name="Dreamweaver" version="6" primary="true"/>
</products>
```

Next is the <author name> tag, which you can use to identify the extension as written by you, or you can put a company name in here:

```
<author  name="Thomas Muck"> </author>
```

object	command	behavior (or action)	translator	dictionary
browserProfile	encoding	floater	propertyInspector	jsExtension
query	template	thirdPartyTags	plugin	report
suite	dataSource	serverFormat	serverBehavior	serverModel
codesnippet	toolbar	samplecontent	site	taglibrary

Table 31-2.   *List of Available Extension Types for Dreamweaver MX in the Extension Manager*

Description of the Extension

The next required tag is the <description> tag, which provides a description of the extension. Inside this tag is a CDATA attribute that sets off the start of your description data. The description should indicate the basic functionality and usage of the extension. The text of the <description> tag can contain some HTML limited to <br> tags and * * characters:

```
<description>
<![CDATA[
Floater that allows JavaScript evaluation on the fly.
]]>
</description>
```

 If your extension description is complex, make liberal use of <br> and   in your description—spaces, tabs, and newlines are ignored when the description is displayed in the Package Manager.

After the description of the extension is the <UI-Access> tag, in which you describe how the extension is accessed and applied to the Web page. The <UI-Access> tag also has the CDATA directive, and has the same HTML restrictions as the <description> tag:

```
<UI-Access>
<![CDATA[
To access this extension, choose Evaluate JavaScript from
the Windows menu.
]]>
</UI-Access>
```

Putting Your Files into the Extension Package

Before you package your extension, you should copy all the files to a staging area, which can be a central folder for all of your extension packages, or a folder that mimics the directory structure of the Dreamweaver Configuration folder. Macromedia advises against packaging the extensions directly from within the Dreamweaver environment. You can try to keep a folder that has all of your extension packages in separate subfolders within a main extension package staging area. The child tag of the <files> tag is the <file name> tag, in which you actually give the name of each file that is to be included in the extension package.

If you keep the MXI file within this same staging area folder as your files, you can keep your packaging paths simple for the <file name> tag. This path is always a relative path to the actual file that you are packaging:

```
<files>
  <file source="EvaluateJavaScript.htm"
   destination="$dreamweaver/configuration/Floaters" />
</files>
```

The filename in the source attribute of the <file> tag always has to be a relative path to the file from the MXI file. By using a staging area, you can eliminate the complex use of paths in your filenames.

The filename is given, and must be listed as a relative path to the MXI file. The destination is also given as a path, with the path referencing the Dreamweaver root folder by using a *$dreamweaver* directive. This is a built-in variable that refers to the program that is receiving the installation, and can be used for both Dreamweaver and UltraDev. Other options at the present time are *$fireworks* for a Fireworks extension, *$ultradev* for an UltraDev extension, and *$flash* for a Flash extension.

Changing the Dreamweaver Menus

Next are the configuration changes. These are the additions to the various menus within Dreamweaver. In fact, you can build an extension that is nothing but menu changes. Suppose you want a Close All Files command to be accessible from the contextual menu to conform to your work habits. You could edit the menus.xml file by hand, or you could create an MXI file with the menu change spelled out in a <configuration-changes> tag. This way, you can undo the changes by simply removing the extension from Dreamweaver. This is just a better way to handle your menus so that you can document and undo the changes you make to the menu if needed.

The <configuration-changes> tag for this particular extension is as follows:

```
<configuration-changes>
  <menu-insert appendTo="DWMenu_Window">
    <menuitem name="Evaluate JavaScript" enabled="true"
     command="dw.toggleFloater('EvaluateJavaScript')"
     checked="dw.getFloaterVisibility('EvaluateJavaScript')"
     id="TCR_DWMenu_Window_EvalJS" />
  </menu-insert>
</configuration-changes>
```

Notice the ID attribute that is added to the menu items. The ID should be something unique to your extension. Macromedia recommends adding a unique prefix to the beginning of the menu item. For instance, the preceding code adds a menu item to the DWMenu_Window menu. The new ID is given a name

DWMXTCR_DWMenu_Window_EvalJS with a unique prefix (DWMXTCR) and a unique suffix (EvalJS). The final ID is DWMXTCR_DWMenu_Window_EvalJS, and will be unique to this extension. This is necessary to avoid conflicts with other extensions written by yourself or other people.

Other Dreamweaver MX menus can be modified as well. For example, the server format that was created in the previous section can be packaged and the changes to the Formats.xml file can be added to an MXI file so that they don't need to be applied manually. The following tag can be placed inside of a <configuration-changes> tag to apply edits to the Formats.xml file:

```
<server-format-definition-changes server="ASP_Vbs">
  <menu-insert appendTo="DWMenu_ServerFormatDef_ASP_2">
    <menu name="String Formatting" id="tfm ServerFormatDef ASP 2¬
    StringFormat">
    </menu>
  </menu-insert>
  <menu-insert appendTo="tfm_ServerFormatDef_ASP_2_StringFormat">
    <format title="Preserve Whitespace"
     file="Preserve Whitespace"
     expression="<%\s*=\s*PerserveWhitespace\([^%]*%>"
     id="tfm_ServerFormatDef_ASP_2_PreserveWhitespace" />
  </menu-insert>
</server-format-definition-changes>
```

Wrapping Up the Package

After completing all of the required tags, you must close out the main tag:

```
</macromedia-extension>
```

Now that you have an MXI file for the extension, you can open it in the Macromedia Extension Manager. On a PC, right-click the MXI file and click Open With Macromedia Extension Manager; on a Mac, open the Extension Manager and click File | Open. Newer versions of the Extension Manager will open if you double-click the MXI file. Next, you are prompted for Extension to Package and the filename to Save Package As. After you complete this process, you can install the extension in any machine by using the MXP file that is the result of the packaging operation. The MXP file contains all the files of your extension, as well as the MXI file to tell Dreamweaver MX where to put the files and what changes to make to the Dreamweaver MX menus. When the extension is installed, the MXI file is installed to the Extensions folder under Configuration, so that the Extension Manager can keep track of which extensions are installed.

> **Caution**   *The Extension Manager has gone through many changes since it was created. Some versions had serious bugs in them. You should read the help files that came with the version on your computer, and check the Macromedia Web site for the newest version of the Extension Manager.*

You can submit packaged extensions to the Macromedia Exchange and share them with other users. The submission process is outlined on the Macromedia Exchange Web site, at www.macromedia.com/exchange. In addition to the submission, there is also an option for a Macromedia seal of approval, which verifies that the extension has been tested for bugs and compatibility issues by the Macromedia Quality Assurance engineers, and is a good indication that the extension is safe to install. Whether you choose to submit your extension to the Exchange or not, you should package your extensions. Packaging the extensions offers these advantages:

- It allows you to keep track of installed extensions more easily.

- Uninstalling an extension is much easier, because all extension files are removed at once.

- Changes to the menu files are reversible when the extension is uninstalled.

- Transporting the extension is easier, because all of the individual files contained in the extension are in one package.

- Extensions can be "turned off" by unchecking the package in the Extension Manager interface—they still show up in the Extension Manager, but are inactive in Dreamweaver MX.

Summary

Macromedia has added to the success of Dreamweaver by allowing third parties to easily delve into the inner workings of the program. This chapter has gone over many of the extension types available to Dreamweaver MX. You've built objects, commands, toolbars, floaters, and a few other extension types as well. This chapter has only scratched the surface. Many other extension types are available, including the capability to create extensions in C. Once you've mastered extensibility, a whole world of new options opens up for you as a Web developer.

If you can add the tools that you need to Dreamweaver MX, you can be more productive in your day-to-day Web development. Also, if you are aware of the inner workings of Dreamweaver MX, and know its limitations, you also begin to learn how to push the program to accomplish things that you might not have been able to do otherwise.

The next chapter examines the main server-side code generation extensions of Dreamweaver MX—the Server Behavior.

Chapter 32

Building Server Behavior Extensions

Dreamweaver has always had Behaviors that allowed the user to insert JavaScript functionality into their Web pages easily with a point-and-click interface. Then UltraDev came along and with it the capability to insert server-side code with point-and- click ease. Dreamweaver MX takes over for UltraDev by offering even more server-side functionality with an expanded Server Behavior Builder and a new system for managing Server Behaviors more efficiently.

Server Behaviors differ from regular Behaviors in their implementation. Typically, the server markup will go above the <html> tag, although many of the Server Behaviors can insert code directly into the body of the document, or around an area of selected code, or as the value of an attribute of an HTML tag. The idea of putting server-side code into your document is to eventually deliver an HTML page to the end user. The server-side code can therefore take many shapes, and it is the job of the Dreamweaver MX Server Behavior to automate the process of getting this server-side code into the document.

The Server Behaviors are JavaScript API objects of Dreamweaver MX that have built-in properties to enable scripts that are inserted to be positioned relative to other Server Behaviors on the page, and to allow them to be edited by double-clicking them in the Server Behavior panel. This is no small feat, because they also remember the various user-defined attributes they contain, such as recordset information, variable values, and page references. In addition, they have the capability to be removed as a unit, which is remarkable considering that some Server Behaviors contain several blocks of code, or are interspersed with HTML and text.

These are the steps that Dreamweaver MX follows when a Server Behavior is applied to a page:

1. The user selects the Server Behavior from the menu.

2. The Server Behavior first checks to see whether it can be applied. (For instance, does it need a recordset?) If not, it aborts.

3. If the page meets the requirements of the Server Behavior, the Server Behavior API functions build a list of all Server Behaviors of that type and, if necessary, generate unique names for variables and attributes (for instance, Repeat1, Repeat2, and so on). If not, it aborts.

4. It takes all the user-defined attributes and inserts them into a mask string. The mask is nothing more than the final code that will be inserted into the page, with masks holding the place of the actual attributes (for instance, ##rsname## or @@rsname@@ could hold the place of the actual recordset name that will be used).

5. After the replacements are made in the string, the code is inserted according to weight. You can find a description of weights in Table 32-1.

6. After it's inserted, Dreamweaver MX will do another search through the document for Server Behaviors to repopulate the list in the Server Behavior floater.

7. The new Server Behavior should appear in the list.

Weight Description	Inserted Where?
0–99 (numbered weights)	Above the <html> tag, relative to any other Server Behavior that has a numbered weight attached to it. A recordset has a weight of 50, so a behavior that executes after a recordset will be between 51 and 99.
aboveHTML+*nn*	Identical to the preceding, where *nn* is the weight number. This was implemented in UltraDev 4 as a replacement for numbered weights.
belowHTML+*nn*	Inserts weighted code below the closing </html> tag, where *nn* is a relative weight between 0 and 99. This was also added in UltraDev 4.
beforeNode	Before the selected node.
afterNode	After the selected node.
replaceNode	Replaces the node with the Server Behavior.
beforeSelection	If there's a selection on the page, inserted before; otherwise, inserted at the insertion point.
afterSelection	If there's a selection on the page, inserted after; otherwise, inserted at the insertion point.
replaceSelection	Replaces the current selection or inserted at the insertion point.
afterDocument	Inserted after the closing </html> tag. This weight was used in UltraDev 1 and is converted to belowHTML for backward compatibility.
nodeAttribute+attribname	Sets the attribute for attribname for the node given.
nodeAttribute	Inserts a chunk of code into the tag after the tag name.

Table 32-1   *Weights Used by Server Behavior Objects*

There are several ways to build a Server Behavior extension. This chapter covers some of those methods, beginning with a hand-coded Server Behavior, and moving on to the Server Behavior Builder that was introduced in UltraDev 4. The EDML file format is also covered. Once you know the foundation, creating complex Server Behaviors either by hand or with the Server Behavior Builder will be much easier.

If you've used the Server Behavior Builder, you might wonder why you would want to create a Server Behavior by hand. There are several reasons for this:

■ The Server Behavior Builder uses a combination of HTML/JavaScript/XML, and is a shortcut to creating Server Behaviors, but nothing more. It still follows the same principles as the hand-coded behaviors.

■ You can't create Server Behaviors with the Builder that include partial or incomplete sections of script, which is often necessary in more complex extensions.

■ The Builder doesn't organize the Server Behaviors—they exist on one big list, which soon becomes cumbersome.

■ The HTML interfaces that are created with the Builder are limited. If you know HTML, you can significantly improve the look and usability of the Server Behavior interfaces, allowing you to include your own logos, field validation, and help files.

■ It is difficult to create Server Behaviors that work with more than one server model with the Server Behavior Builder.

■ Server Behaviors are often used in conjunction with more complex data sources, commands, and server formats. Knowing what is going on behind the scenes will allow you to implement these more complex extensions.

■ Knowing what each of the functions actually does allows you to insert your own custom code into the Server Behaviors created by the Builder.

■ Code patterns created by the Server Behavior Builder can be modified to be more flexible to allow for hand-coding within the code block.

We start with building a simple Server Behavior by hand-coding the functions and EDML files that are necessary for the extension. If you are interested in using only the Server Behavior Builder, you can skip ahead to Part 2 of this chapter ("Part 2: Using the Server Behavior Builder"), because hand-coding a Server Behavior is not a project to be taken lightly.

The *ServerBehavior* Class

When we spoke of classes and objects earlier in Chapter 31, we were only scratching the surface in preparation for the *ServerBehavior*. The *ServerBehavior* is a full-fledged class with public and private properties, methods, and events. We'll use the analogy of a box. If you think of the *ServerBehavior* class as a blueprint describing how the box is built, the *ServerBehavior instance* is the actual box that you build. Inside the box is all of the information about your Server Behavior. This box can be passed from function to function and retain all of the properties that it contains.

Just as you can build more than one box from the blueprints, you can also have more than one instance of a *ServerBehavior* on any given page. Each instance will contain all properties of that particular instance and keep it separate from other Server Behavior instances—even behaviors of the same type. The four required properties of the *ServerBehavior* are:

- **title**   Title used in your behavior. This is what actually shows up in your Server Behavior floater.

- **selectedNode**   Pointer to the node of the Server Behavior. This causes the behavior to be highlighted in Code view and on the page if you select it from the Server Behaviors floater.

- **incomplete**   A Boolean flag that you can set to check whether something is missing from your behavior. If it's set, a little red exclamation point shows up next to your title in the floater.

- **participants**   An array of pointers to all of the nodes that are members of your Server Behavior. In many cases, this will only be one.

You can access the properties by using methods of the *ServerBehavior* object. For a full explanation of the *ServerBehavior* object, check the comments in the ServerBehavior.js file located in Configuration | Shared | Common | Scripts.

To declare a new instance of a *ServerBehavior*, you can use the *new* keyword, as in the following:

```
var myServerBehavior = new ServerBehavior("My Server
Behavior","",null);.
```

After creating the object, you attach the properties that belong to it by using the public methods of the *ServerBehavior* class. The *ServerBehavior* class is used by the *findServerBehaviors* function, and as such there will not usually be a need to access it directly.

Note   *In UltraDev 1 and UltraDev 4, there was a class named* SSRecord *that is still available in Dreamweaver MX, although it is deprecated. The* ServerBehavior *class takes the place of the* SSRecord. *If you have a copy of the first edition of this book, the* SSRecord *is covered. Also, in Dreamweaver MX you can still use and edit old Server Behaviors that use the* SSRecord *class.*

Steps for Building a Server Behavior Extension

Unlike objects, which we covered in the previous chapter, Server Behaviors have several functions that must be included in writing the extension. These functions take care of the housekeeping involved in the creation of an instance of a Server Behavior on your page. Following is the basic framework required to write the Server Behavior extension:

1. You need the final code that you want to use. This should be fully tested code. While you're debugging the Server Behavior, you don't want to worry about whether the final code works. After you have a working block of code, you are ready to start building the Server Behavior.

2. Create the actual HTML file that will act as the user interface for the behavior. This is pretty straightforward and consistent for all extensions. User interfaces were covered in Chapter 31.

3. Add your include file references to the document. Server Behaviors use a standard set of JavaScript files from the Shared directory. Make sure to include *all* files that contain references to functions you will be using.

4. Set some other global variables that are needed for the behavior, including the code *weight* for each code block. Weights are shown in Table 32-1.

5. Include the *initializeUI()* function. This is not a required function, but is often useful to set up the user interface if it requires any information, such as a drop-down list of recordsets. You can also implement JavaScript control objects instead of plain HTML elements in your Server Behavior and initialize them in this function. Controls are covered later in the chapter.

6. Add a search string at the top of the file. This will be a simple unique string that is found in your code. It acts as a "scout" for the behavior. When you apply any edits to your document, Dreamweaver MX will look for the search string in your document. If it doesn't find it, it won't even bother to check for an instance of the Server Behavior.

7. Create Group and Participant EDML files for your Server Behavior. These are simple XML files with a .edml file extension.

8. Write the pattern and mask variables for your code (which we'll refer to as the PATT and MASK variables). The PATT variable is a regular expression pattern used to find the code in the document, and the MASK variable is your actual code to be inserted, with "masks" in place of your user-defined attributes. These will go into the EDML participant file.

9. Write function skeletons for the five required Server Behavior functions in the HTML file, and any other functions you may need:

   - *canApplyServerBehavior()*   Checks to make sure that the page has the necessary ingredients for the Server Behavior. If the user is editing an existing instance of a Server Behavior, the function takes a ServerBehavior object as an argument.

- *findServerBehaviors()*   Returns an array of ServerBehavior object instances on the page.

- *applyServerBehavior()*   Does the work of inserting the behavior onto the page. If the user is editing an existing instance of a Server Behavior, the function takes a ServerBehavior object as an argument.

- *inspectServerBehavior()*   Takes a ServerBehavior object as an argument and updates the Server Behavior's user interface to reflect the parameters of the existing Server Behavior that the user is editing.

- *deleteServerBehavior()*   Takes a ServerBehavior object as an argument and deletes the SB from the page.

10. Implement each of the required functions in turn and any supporting functions. As you're writing the functions, you should test them along the way, making sure each part does what it's supposed to do up to that point.

11. Implement the *analyzeServerBehavior* function, if needed. This function performs a couple of tasks: making sure the code is, in fact, an instance of your behavior, and setting certain properties in the Server Behavior object (including the *incomplete* property, the *selectedNode* property, the *title* property, and the *participants* property).

12. Implement, if needed, *copyServerBehavior* and *pasteServerBehavior*. These are necessary only if you want your user to be able to copy and paste the Server Behaviors into the same document or another document.

Note   *These are intended as basic guidelines; and, as is the case with even good rules, there are times when you will break them and implement a Server Behavior a little differently.*

As you can see, it's quite a bit more complex than putting an object into your document. We go through a complete Server Behavior example step by step to illustrate how you can implement a simple Server Behavior.

Your Final Code: The First Step

You'll begin at the end—with the code that you want the Server Behavior to insert in the page. Our exercise will involve a relatively simple Server Behavior—setting a session variable equal to a timestamp. This has several uses, most notably to use when attempting to retrieve an identity column from a database after a database insert.

We show you the code for all server models (ASP, JSP, PHP, ASP.NET, and ColdFusion) and all languages (ASP VBScript, ASP JavaScript, ColdFusion, PHP, VB, C#, and Java), but you have to implement only one of these. The Server Behavior functions will remain the same.

The variable name *tfm_timestamp* was chosen because it will be unique to this Server Behavior. This technique is important in Dreamweaver MX extensions and even more important for Server Behaviors. Server Behaviors are located in the document by Dreamweaver MX through the use of *patterns*; so if you make parts of the Server Behavior unique, there is less chance of another Server Behavior finding yours by mistake.

Giving your variables unique names is one way to make sure that your code doesn't get interpreted by another Server Behavior as one of its participants. You'll notice that Macromedia uses specific naming conventions in the naming of the built-in variables, such as Repeat1__numRows *and* MM_offset.

This is your final code that you'll base your Server Behavior on in all supported languages.

ASP VBScript Code Listing

```
<%
tfm_timestamp = Timer * 1000
Session("@@Variable Name@@") = tfm_timestamp
%>
```

ASP JavaScript (JScript) Code Listing

```
<%
var tfm_timestamp = new Date().getTime();
Session("@@Variable Name@@") = tfm_timestamp
%>
```

ColdFusion Code Listing

```
<cflock name="tfm_timestamp" timeout="20" type="exclusive"
scope="session">
    <cfset session.@@Variable Name@@ = abs(gettickcount())>
</cflock>
```

JSP Code Listing

```
<%
String tfm_timestamp = String.valueOf(new
java.util.Date().getTime());
session.putValue("@@Variable Name@@", tfm_timestamp.toString());
%>
```

PHP Code Listing

```php
<?php
$tfm_timestamp = explode(" ",microtime());
$_SESSION["@@Variable Name@@"] = ¬
 ($tfm_timestamp[0] + $tfm_timestamp[1]) * 10000;
?>
```

C# Code Listing

```
<%
long tfm_timestamp = DateTime.Now.Ticks;
Session["@@Variable Name@@"] = tfm_timestamp;
%>
```

ASP.NET VB Code Listing

```
<%
Dim tfm_timestamp
tfm_timestamp = DateTime.Now.Ticks
Session("@@Variable Name@@") = tfm_timestamp
%>
```

The code listings will work with any of the server languages without any change
to the Server Behavior. Use the PATT and MASK variables that reference your server
language. In other words, if you are developing a VBScript extension, use only the
PATT and MASK variables for VBScript. The code implementation is similar for each
of the server languages, with the appropriate syntax changes for each language.

Now that the design of the final functionality is in place and the code is implemented,
you can write the Server Behavior.

Creating the HTML File: The Interface

To create your interface, you have to decide which attributes are going to be user-defined
and build an HTML form to get these attributes from the user. The code will look
like this:

```html
<!DOCTYPE HTML SYSTEM "-//Macromedia//DWExtension ¬
 layout-engine 5.0//dialog">
<html>
<head>
<title>Timestamp Session Variable</title>
```

```
<body onLoad="initializeUI()">
<form name="theForm">
  <table border=0>
    <tr>
      <td align="right" valign="baseline" nowrap>
        Variable Name:
      </td>
      <td valign="baseline" nowrap>
        <input type="text" name="Variable__Name"
style="width:150px">
      </td>
    </tr>
  </table>
</form>
</body>
</html>
```

Adding Your Include Files

The next step is to attach a list of all of the common functions that make up a Server Behavior. These functions are for string manipulation, user interface controls, file manipulation, and the Server Behavior API. The files are all fully commented, so you may go through them to better understand the files and all the functions contained within. In fact, we consider all the files in the Shared folder to be required reading for the extension developer.

```
<script language="javascript" ¬
src="../../Shared/Common/Scripts/dwscripts.js"></script>
<script language="javascript"
src="../../Shared/Common/Scripts/dwscriptsExtData.js"></script>
<script language="javascript"
src="../../Shared/Common/Scripts/dwscriptsServer.js"></script>
```

Note *Keep a list of these and other shared files handy in a separate file or in custom Snippets so that you can copy and paste the necessary code into your extensions. As you write Server Behaviors, you'll find that you will use files from this list in every Server Behavior.*

Defining Global Variables and Implementing the initializeUI() Function

Any variables that you may want available throughout your Server Behavior should be defined in a global variables section at the start of your page directly below your include file declarations. Global variables will be accessible by the entire Server Behavior, even inside of functions. First you need to define a script block in the HTML file:

```
<script language="JavaScript">
<!--
//Start global variable section here
var VARIABLE_NAME = dwscripts.findDOMObject("Variable_Name");
```

Now you can begin adding your functions with your first function: *initializeUI()*. The *initializeUI()* function will take care of setting up your interface for any user-defined attributes you may need. This is where you will put your functionality to populate select boxes with lists of recordsets or columns from recordsets that are on the page. You can also initialize JavaScript controls for your Server Behavior from within this function. The function, in this case, will simply put the cursor in the field.

```
//Start  functions
function initializeUI() {
    document.forms[0].elements[0].focus();
}
//^^^^insert the rest of your functions above this line^^^^
//-->
</script>
```

You can now save the file into one of your Server Behaviors folders (ASP_Vbs, ASP_Js, ASP.NET_Csharp, ASP.NET_Vb, JSP, PHP_MySQL, UD4-ColdFusion, or ColdFusion). After closing down the program and restarting it, the Server Behavior should appear on the Server Behavior menu. The extension still doesn't do anything, but you'll find that if you test your extensions piece by piece, you'll have far fewer debugging headaches. If you've reached this stage and the interface works, you can go on to the next step.

The Search String: Finding the Behavior in Your Document

The next thing you want to add is a search string to the very top of the file. It should be the first line in the file. Dreamweaver MX will take the search string and look for it in your document each time you make an edit. Dreamweaver MX actually goes through the list of *all* search strings in all Server Behavior files to determine whether the Server Behaviors are on the page or not. The search string can be something short, but preferably something that's unique to your behavior to make the search more efficient. If the search string is found in the document, the *findServerBehaviors* function is called to determine if the behavior is *actually* on the page.

Be careful when you create the search string. Frequently, when you are coding your behavior, you will change the code used in the behavior and the search string will no longer match. If the search string doesn't appear somewhere in your code, the Server Behavior won't be found by the findServerBehaviors *function.*

The search string works like a quick glance, skimming through the document to see if the document warrants the attention of the more powerful *findServerBehaviors* function. You may want to use a variable in your extensions that will be unique to that extension only and use this in the search string:

```
<!--Search:"tfm_timestamp"-->
```

Now whenever the string *tfm_timestamp* is found in a document, the *findServerBehaviors* function in this extension will be called. This is one of the reasons for using the variable prefix *tfm_*. You should have your own variable prefix for your own extensions.

The search string shouldn't be too complicated; it's only intended to do a quick search. It also shouldn't be something too common that will be found in many pages, because the frequent unnecessary calls to the *findServerBehaviors* function will slow down the program. Later, when we build a Server Behavior with the Server Behavior Builder, the search string will be created automatically and stored in the XML participant file.

 Don't use HTML comments in your search string if you are defining it in the HTML Server Behavior file. The Dreamweaver MX interpreter will pick up your comment as a literal comment in your Server Behavior, and the search string will never execute.

Creating Group and Participant XML Files

In UltraDev 1, PATT and MASK variables and all other properties of the Server Behaviors were created entirely in HTML and JavaScript. These types of Server Behaviors continued to work in UltraDev 4, but a new procedure for building Server Behaviors was introduced. Beginning with UltraDev 4, MASK and PATT variables are stored in XML participant files for easy access to the Server Behavior. Beginning with Dreamweaver MX, the old-style of building Server Behaviors using just HTML and JavaScript is not supported in the new server models. For that reason, it is advisable to use XML group and participant files to store your Server Behavior properties.

Also new to Dreamweaver MX is the file location of these XML files. In UltraDev 4, there was a special folder called ExtensionData where all of these XML files were stored. That folder still exists in Dreamweaver MX, but the XML files have been replaced in most of the new Server Behaviors by the new EDML files located in the Configuration | ServerBehaviors | [*server model*] folder. EDML stands for Extension Data Markup Language, and is a special file format unique to Dreamweaver that is based in XML but has several required tags and properties. For information on the XML file format used in UltraDev 4, you can consult the Extending UltraDev help documents in UltraDev 4, or see Chapter 22 of the previous edition of this book.

The Group file in Dreamweaver MX is an EDML file that contains these tags:

- **<group>** Main tag that tells Dreamweaver MX which Server Behavior the group is for, among other things.

- **<title>** This is where the title that appears in the Server Behavior panel can be defined.

- **<groupParticipants>** Main tag under which you can list the participants of this Server Behavior.

- **<groupParticipant>** Individual participants of this group. Participants are stored in separate EDML files.

The EDML Group file for the Timestamp Session Variable Server Behavior is as follows:

```
<group name="Timestamp Session Variable" version="6.0"
 serverBehavior="Timestamp Session Variable.htm">
  <title>Timestamp Session Variable (@@Variable__Name@@)</title>
  <groupParticipants selectParticipant="TimestampSession_main">
    <groupParticipant name="TimestampSession_main"
    partType="identifier" />
  </groupParticipants>
</group>
```

You can save this file with the name Timestamp Session Variable.edml in the Configuration | ServerBehaviors | [*server model*] folder for the server model that you are working with.

The Participant files are stored here as well. For this particular Server Behavior, you have only one participant. You can name the participant TimestampSession_main.edml, as it was referred to in the Group file. The participant files have these main tags that you will use in this Server Behavior:

- **<participant>** This is the main tag that surrounds the data for this participant.

- **<insertText>** This tag holds your MASK variable. This is the code that will be inserted into the document.

- **<searchPatterns>** This tag holds the PATT variable that will be used to find your Server Behavior in the document.

- **<quickSearch>** You can include a short search string here instead of in the HTML file to allow a quick scan of your document. This was explained in the previous section.

For this particular Server Behavior, the participant file will look like this:

```
<participant version="6.0">
  <insertText location="aboveHTML+49"><![CDATA[
MASK STRING GOES HERE
]]></insertText>
  <searchPatterns whereToSearch="directive">
    <searchPattern paramNames="Variable__Name" isOptional="false"
    limitSearch="all">
    <![CDATA[/PATT STRING GOES HERE/i]]>
    </searchPattern>
  </searchPatterns>
  <quickSearch>tfm_timestamp</quickSearch>
</participant>
```

You assign the code *weight*, which is a relational order that the Server Behavior uses to insert the code into the document. The recordset has a weight of 50, so you'll give this one 49 to be applied before the recordset. Next, the text field named *Variable__Name* is set up as a *paramName* reference for this Server Behavior. The *isOptional* attribute can be used if your participant is optional. In this case, however, the participant is required. The *limitSearch* attribute specifies where inside of the *whereToSearch* area the search will occur. In this case, the entire tag is searched with the attribute of *all*.

Building Your PATT and MASK Variables

This subject could warrant an entire chapter or even a book by itself. The MASK variables are the easier to implement of the two. A *mask* is simply the final code that you want on the page, with the user-defined attributes "masked" out with unique characters surrounding them, such as @@ or ##. The MASK can be pulled out and replaced with the attributes. The PATT variables, on the other hand, use complex regular expressions to enable the detection of the block of code in the document, and the parsing of the user-defined attributes.

Many Server Behaviors created for UltraDev 1 or UltraDev 4 used ## in MASK variables. Dreamweaver MX Server Behaviors use @@ as a mask, like @@Variable__name@@ in our example.

The PATT and MASK Strings in Your Server Behavior

For this particular extension, your user-defined attribute is the session variable name. The MASKs are substituted for the user-defined attributes when the extension is applied to the page. Dreamweaver MX will do these replacements automatically. The mask characters that are used are typically ## or @@, which are inserted around an identifying name for the variable. The Server Behavior Builder uses @@, so we use that here for consistency as well.

Regular Expressions Explained

Regular expressions (also known as a *regex* or *RegExp*) are a part of many popular languages, such as Perl, JavaScript, PHP, and ColdFusion, to name but a few. A regular expression is an object that contains patterns of characters that are to be matched in a string or a document. JavaScript has a built-in *RegExp* object that has several well-defined properties, methods, and events. A *RegExp* can be defined either as a string or as a set of characters within the slash (/) characters, as in the following line:

```
var thePattern = /this\s*is\s*a\s*pattern/;
```

If the pattern is defined like a string—wrapped in quotes—you must use double backslashes for the escape sequence, like this:

```
var thePattern = "this\\s*is\\s*a\\s*pattern";
```

The patterns themselves represent the text you are searching for. If you wanted to find your name, for instance, you could simply use the name literally, like this:

```
var thePattern = /Tom/;
```

But if you wanted to find any instance of Tom, Tommy, or Thomas, you could use a *RegExp* like this:

```
var thePattern = /Tom|Tommy|Thomas/;
```

The pipe (|) character acts as an "or" in the expression, as in "Tom or Tommy or Thomas." You might also want to find any name that begins with the letter *T*, like this:

```
var thePattern = /T\w+/;
```

This expression uses the *character class* \w, which stands for a letter, underscore, or number character, and the + directive, which means "one or more of the previous character." In this case, \w+ means "one or more letter/number characters up to a nonletter/number character." This expression will continue to match a word beginning with T until a nonletter/number character is found. There are several character classes in the *RegExp* object, notably:

- **[....]**   Any characters contained within brackets (for example, [abc] will match any a, b, or c character)
- **[^...]**   Any characters *not* in the brackets (for example, [^123] will match any character that's not 1, 2, or 3)
- **.**   Any character that's not a newline (\n) character
- **\d**   Any digit character
- **\D**   Any nondigit character
- **\s**   Any whitespace character (space, tab, newline)
- **\S**   Any nonwhitespace character
- **\W**   Any nonletter, nonunderscore, or nonnumeral character

In addition, the * directive means "zero or more of the previous character." A useful combination is \s*, which means "zero or more of any whitespace character." This allows for the fact that a user might insert spaces or carriage returns in the code, which would make the match for your code fail if you used only a space or carriage return character in your pattern, because it's not an exact match.

Additionally, there are certain characters that require an escape character:

```
/ \ . * + ? | ( ) [ ] { }
```

These are used within the *RegExp* object as classes and directives; therefore, to use the literal characters, you have to "escape" the character, like this (the plus sign and the question mark are escaped):

```
var thePattern = /What\s*is\s*2\s*\+\s*2\?/gi
```

This string is searching for "What is 2 + 2?" It will also find "What is 2+2?," or even
"What
is
2+2?"
We've also introduced the global identifier (g) and the case-insensitive identifier (i). The global simply means that *all* occurrences of a match will be returned, and the case-insensitive identifier will match regardless of case.

Another concept is *grouping*. When you put parts of your expression within parentheses, the *RegExp* remembers the string that is matched within the parentheses. Look at the following expression:

```
var thePattern =
'(.*)\\.ActiveConnection\\s*\\=\\s*\\"(.*)\\";';
```

The *(.*)* in the first part of the expression matches "zero or more characters up to the next character in the expression." What you're searching for in this example is the recordset name (the first set of parentheses) and the connection string (the second set of parentheses). You would have a match with the following:

```
Recordset1.ActiveConnection = "dsn=Bookstore";
```

When a match is completed, an array is returned. The zero element (*thePattern[0]*) contains the entire matched string. The first element (*thePattern[1]*) will contain what is in the first set of parentheses (*Recordset1*), and the second element (*thePattern[2]*) will contain the match from the second set of parentheses (*dsn=Bookstore*). This is information that is useful as you match your patterns to the document.

Note *The .* pattern is used frequently in regular expressions, but doesn't always return the desired match. It's known as a "greedy" expression because it sometimes matches more than you expect. It's always better to use a less greedy negated class. A negated class for the pattern defined in the preceding example would be [^.]*, which means "any and all characters up to but not including the first . (period character)." Also, beginning with Dreamweaver MX you can make an expression nongreedy by adding a ? behind it, like this: .*?*

The following shows the MASK code for each of the server languages implemented. As stated earlier, you can implement the one that you are going to use in your own code without changing the format of the Server Behavior.

ASP VBScript MASK String

```
<%
tfm_timestamp = Timer * 1000
Session("@@Variable__Name@@") = tfm_timestamp
%>
```

Notice how the code is formatted to correspond roughly with the finished code. That makes it easier to debug a faulty MASK or PATT variable. You'll find that you'll often have to go through your PATT variables one character at a time to ensure accuracy.

ASP VBScript PATT Strings

```
tfm_timestamp\s*=\s*Timer\s*\*\s*1000\s*
Session\("([^"]*)"\)\s*=\s*tfm_timestamp
```

ASP JavaScript MASK String

```
<%
var tfm_timestamp = new Date().getTime();
Session("@@Variable__Name@@") = tfm_timestamp
%>
```

ASP JavaScript PATT Strings

```
var\s*tfm_timestamp\s*=\s*new\s*Date\(\)\.getTime\(\);\s*
Session\("([^"]*)"\)\s*=\s*tfm_timestamp\s*
```

ColdFusion MASK String

```
<cflock name="tfm_timestamp" timeout="20"
 type="exclusive" scope="session">
    <cfset session.@@Variable__Name@@ = abs(gettickcount())>
</cflock>
```

ColdFusion PATT Strings

```
<cflock\s*name="tfm_timestamp"\s*timeout="20"\s*
type="exclusive"\s*scope="session">\s*
<cfset\s*session\.(.*[^\s])\s*=\s*abs\(gettickcount\(\)\)>\s*
<\/cflock>
```

JSP MASK String

```
<%
String tfm_timestamp = String.valueOf(new
java.util.Date().getTime());
session.putValue("@@Variable__Name@@", tfm_timestamp.toString());
%>
```

JSP PATT Strings

```
String\s*tfm_timestamp\s*=\s*String\.valueOf
\(new\s*java\.util\.Date\(\)\.getTime\(\)\);\s*
session\.putValue\(")(.*)(",\s*tfm_timestamp\.toString\(\)\);\s*
```

PHP MASK String

```
<?php
$tfm_timestamp = explode(" ",microtime());
$_SESSION["@@Variable__Name@@"] =
($tfm_timestamp[0] + $tfm_timestamp[1]) * 10000;
?>
```

PHP PATT Strings

```
\$tfm_timestamp\s*=\s*explode\("\s*",microtime\(\)\);\s*
\$_SESSION\["([^"]*)"\]\s*=\s*\(\$tfm_timestamp\[0\]\s*\+
\s*\$tfm_timestamp\[1\]\)\s*\*\s*10000;\s*
```

ASP.NET C# MASK String

```
<%
long tfm_timestamp = DateTime.Now.Ticks;
Session["@@Variable__Name@@"] = tfm_timestamp;
%>
```

ASP.NET C# PATT Strings

```
long\s*tfm_timestamp\s*=\s*DateTime\.Now\.Ticks;\s*
Session\["([^"]*)"\]\s*=\s*tfm_timestamp;\s*
```

ASP.NET VB MASK String

```
<%
Dim tfm_timestamp
tfm_timestamp = DateTime.Now.Ticks
Session("@@Variable__Name@@") = tfm_timestamp
%>
```

ASP.NET VB PATT Strings

```
Dim\s*tfm_timestamp\s*
tfm_timestamp\s*=\s*DateTime\.Now\.Ticks\s*
Session\("([^"]*)"\)\s*=\s*tfm_timestamp\s*
%>
```

You can insert the PATT and MASK variables into your Server Behavior at this point. They will go into the XML participant file like this example for C#:

```
<insertText location="aboveHTML+49">
<![CDATA[<%
long tfm_timestamp = DateTime.Now.Ticks;
Session["@@Variable__Name@@"] = tfm_timestamp;
%>]]></insertText>
<searchPatterns whereToSearch="directive">
  <searchPattern paramNames="Variable__Name" isOptional="false"
    limitSearch="all">
<![CDATA[/long\s*tfm_timestamp\s*=\s*DateTime\.Now\.Ticks;\s* ¬
Session\["([^"]*)"\]\s*=\s*tfm_timestamp;\s*/i]]></searchPattern>
</searchPatterns>
```

The PATT and MASK strings are placed inside <![CDATA[tag blocks. These special XML tags allow you to place literal code inside of an XML tag without translating any special characters. This is absolutely necessary for MASK and PATT strings. Also, when you have bigger, more complex patterns, you can break them into more than one <searchPattern> tag. This can give your Server Behavior greater flexibility when dealing with larger code blocks.

Explanation of Pattern Matching

Your MASK variable looks pretty basic compared to the pattern variables, which are fairly complex regular expressions. You utilized *RegExps* briefly in Chapter 31, but here is where their utility and functionality are maximized. The patterns contain all of the code that has to be matched on the page. Dreamweaver MX will perform all of this for you behind the scenes, but it is helpful to know how to do it for your own extensions. The methods you can use when utilizing a *RegExp* in JavaScript are *match()*, *exec()*, *test()*, *search()*, *split()*, and *replace()*.

What a *RegExp* will enable you to do is compare the *RegExp* to the page code, with the results of the search returned in various forms:

- A complete matched string
- Groupings of attributes that you need to retrieve, in an array and also with individual variable names (*$1, $2, $3 . . .*)
- A *leftContext* and *rightContext*, for finding the areas before and after the match
- An array of all matches if using the *exec()* or *match()* method

When building the patterns, you have to decide what is going to be a literal string in your code that will be matched, what will be variable, and what will be grouped for retrieval. You should do this line by line for the final code that you use. Take a look at this sample line of code as an example:

```
<%
If Recordset1.EOF Then Response.Redirect("failed.asp")
%>
```

In this line, the recordset name and the failed.asp page will be variables that can change and be inserted by the user. We start with those variables by substituting a pattern and grouping them like this:

```
<%
If ([^.]+).EOF Then Response.Redirect("([^"]+)")
%>
```

The next thing you need to do is to escape any special characters, which are characters that have a special meaning to the *RegExp* object. In this line of code, the following characters need to be escaped by a double backslash: parenthesis, period, space, newline, and quote. Now the line looks like this:

```
<%\s*
If\s*([^.]+)\.EOF\s*Then\s*Response\.Redirect\(\"([^"]+)\"\)
\s*%>
```

It's undeniable that the code is starting to look a little confusing. The literal parentheses are escaped by the backslash, whereas the grouping parentheses aren't. Also, the newline characters and the space characters are grouped together with \s*, which will pick up zero or more of any whitespace character. This grouping is handy if a user decides to add blank lines or remove spaces from a behavior after it's applied to the page. The next thing you want to do is to group the items together that *aren't* variable. That way, you can take the strings apart after they are matched, and put them back together with the new attributes. Your code now looks like this after going through and grouping all of the ungrouped code:

```
(<%\s*
If\s*)([^.]+)(\.EOF\s*Then
\s*Response\.Redirect\(\)"([^"]+)(\"\)
\s*%>)
```

Now all you have to do is double the backslashes so that the pattern can be used in a JavaScript string variable, assign it to a variable, and make the string more readable by separating the lines and putting single quotes around each line:

```
var myPattern = '(<%\\s*'+
'If\\s*)(.+)(\\.EOF\\s*Then'+
'\\s*Response\\.Redirect\\(\\)"(.+)(\\"\\)'+
'\\s*%>)';
```

At this point, if you perform a match on a string of code (*theDocument*, in the following example), you'll have a grouping of all elements that you need to examine. We create the *RegExp* object from the pattern and then perform an *exec* on the object using the string, *theDocument*:

```
var theRegex = new RegExp(myPattern,"i");//make a RegExp object
var newChunk = theRegex.exec(theDocument);
```

After doing this, you can examine the different elements of the match. The variable, *theRegex*, is an array consisting of every member of your grouping. The following table shows the content of each element.

Element	What the Element Contains	Variable Name
theRegex[0]	Entire matched string from *theDocument*	*$0*
theRegex[1]	<%\nIf	*$1*
theRegex[2]	Recordset1	*$2*
theRegex[3]	.eof Then *Response.Redirect("*	*$3*
theRegex[4]	failed.asp	*$4*
theRegex[5]	")\n%>	*$5*
RegExp.rightContext	Everything in *theDocument* after the match	n/a
RegExp.leftContext	Everything in *theDocument* before the match	n/a

Now you can appreciate how powerful regular expressions are. You can use this information to take the document apart, replace the user-defined attributes such as recordset name, and then put the document back together again. The better your pattern is, the more versatile your behavior becomes. Why do we do it this way?

Let's say, for example, that there is a <table> tag in the Server Behavior. You could match it with a *RegExp* like this:

```
var thePattern = /<table>/gi;
```

What happens when the user edits the table, though? Let's say a user makes the table wider and puts a style on it. Now the match doesn't work anymore, and the Server Behavior won't show up in the Server Behavior inspector because the table tag looks like this:

```
<table class="mystyle" width="50%">
```

When you build your pattern variables, make the patterns as flexible as possible so that if the document is edited, the Dreamweaver MX environment will still be able to pick out the Server Behaviors. So, if the pattern were written like this instead,

```
var thePattern = /<table[^>]*>/gi;
```

the match would still occur, because you are matching "<table and everything up to and including the > character." This could be advantageous when you want to edit a Server Behavior—you can pull apart the match from the user-defined attributes and put it back together with the new attributes without sacrificing any changes the user may have made in the document along the way. This way, changes made by a user through hand-coding aren't at risk of being overwritten by reapplying an extension. Obviously, this depends on how well the patterns are written.

Patterns in the EDML participant files can be built as one large pattern (such as the patterns that are generated by the Server Behavior Builder), or they can be broken into smaller chunks for more precise matching.

Caution *One misplaced character in a regular expression can prompt the whole match to fail and cause the Server Behavior to be unrecognizable to Dreamweaver MX.*

Writing the Function Skeletons

Put the following function skeletons into your Server Behavior:

```
function canApplyServerBehavior(sbObj) {
    return true;
}

function findServerBehaviors() {
    return Array();
}

function applyServerBehavior(sbObj) {
    return "";
}

function inspectServerBehavior(sbObj) {
}
```

```
function deleteServerBehavior(sbObj) {
}

function analyzeServerBehavior(sbObj) {
}

function displayHelp() {
    alert("Enter a session variable name to hold a timestamp");
}
```

These are all the functions you'll need to complete the Server Behavior. In addition to the five required functions, the *displayHelp* function adds a Help button to your interface to allow you to attach a help file or use the alert box that is shown here. Also, the *analyzeServerBehavior* function is added, which you'll use to make sure all your parameters are still in the code.

Implementing the *canApplyServerBehavior()* Function

This function checks to see whether the document has the necessary elements to allow the inclusion of the Server Behavior. You can use this function to make sure there is only one instance of itself on the page, if that is a requirement, or you could use it to check for an instance of a recordset on the page, if that is a requirement. In this case, we check for another instance of the Server Behavior on the page, because we don't want this Server Behavior to appear twice on one page. The function is passed a *Server Behavior* object if you're editing an existing Server Behavior, and nothing if it's a new instance. It returns false if the Server Behavior can't be applied to the page for one reason or another. A typical implementation of this function is as follows:

```
function canApplyServerBehavior(sbObj) {
  var errMsg = "";
  if((findServerBehaviors().length==1) && (sbObj == null)) {
    //if there is already an instance on the page
    errMsg = "Only one SB of this type can appear on a page\n";
    }
  if (errMsg) alert(errMsg); //pop-up error message
  return (errMsg == "");  //return false if error message exists
}
```

Here, you are calling the *findServerBehaviors* function from this Server Behavior itself, and checking to see whether there is already an instance on the page. If there is, you also check to see whether the function was passed an existing *Server Behavior* object—the *sbObj* variable—which means that you're editing an existing behavior. The error message becomes active if you have an instance on the page *and* you are working with a new instance of the behavior. If the error message is assigned, you display an alert box. The last statement evaluates to true if there is no error message and false if there is. If the function returns false, all further operations within the Server Behavior cease.

Implementing the *findServerBehaviors()* Function

This function is called whenever a user edits the document in some way and the search string at the top of the document is found in the document. This function will locate all instances of the behavior in the current document and return an array of Server Behavior objects that contain these instances. Your Timestamp Session Variable Server Behavior can have only one instance, but now you'll use a standard function that you can reuse for other Server Behaviors with one or more instances allowed. The function is as follows:

```
function findServerBehaviors() {
  var sbArray = dwscripts.findSBs();
  return sbArray;
}
```

The *dwscripts.findSBs()* function does all the work for you. It will load the PATT variable from your participant file, try to match it in the document, and if it matches, return an array of instances of your Server Behavior on the page. If not, the function returns an empty array. We move on to the *applyServerBehavior* function next.

Implementing the *applyServerBehavior()* Function

The *applyServerBehavior()* function is responsible for doing the actual insertion of your code in the page. It does this intelligently by *weight*, as mentioned earlier. The function does several things:

- It gathers user-defined attributes—in this case, a session variable name from the user interface.
- It checks to make sure the attributes entered by the user are acceptable.
- It takes the MASK string that you defined earlier and inserts the attributes into the string (behind the scenes).
- It inserts the code into the document.
- It differentiates between a Server Behavior that is being edited and a new one.
- It returns an error message if something went wrong.

The first thing the function will do is to grab the attributes from the form that was submitted and put the results into variables. It also has to check to make sure that the data is good. If the user is supposed to enter an integer, for example, and he or she uses a word instead, you have to throw an error and give control back to the interface to abort the process. Because your Server Behavior takes a session variable name as a user-defined attribute, you have to make sure that it has been provided. You should also make sure that it is a valid variable name. There is a utility function available in dwscripts.js (*dwscripts.isValidVarName*) that works quite nicely for this, so we've implemented that here. Here is your completed *applyServerBehaviors* function:

```
function applyServerBehaviors(sbObj) {
  var paramObj = new Object();
  var errStr = "";
  var theVariableName = VARIABLE_NAME.value;
  if(!dwscripts.isValidVarName(theVariableName)) {
    errStr = "Must be a valid variable name ";
  }
  if (!errStr) {
    paramObj.Variable_Name = theVariableName;
    dwscripts.fixUpSelection(dw.getDocumentDOM(), true, true);
    dwscripts.applySB(paramObj, sbObj);
  }
  return errStr;
}
```

The first thing that the function does is create a new object called *paramObj*. This is an object of parameter names and values that are used by your Server Behavior. Then a variable named *theVariableName* is set to the value from the form field. The value is then checked out in the *dwscripts.isValidVarName* function, as described earlier. If it doesn't pass this test, an error message is created in the *errMsg* variable. Finally, if there is no error message, the Server Behavior is inserted into the document with the *dwscripts.applySB* function.

Implementing the *inspectServerBehavior* Function

This function is called when a user double-clicks the Server Behavior instance in the Server Behavior panel. A *ServerBehavior* object containing the information about that Server Behavior is passed to the function. The function then pulls out any values that it needs to populate the dialog box. The dialog box of that behavior is then brought up and contains all values that the user had entered when the behavior was first applied to the page. The user can then edit the attributes of the behavior, after which the *applyServerBehavior* function is called again—this time with a *priorRecord* variable containing the *ServerBehavior* object of the behavior *before* the edits were made. It's up to the *dwscripts* class to determine which attributes are new and which are original.

This function's sole purpose is to populate the user interface with values from the Server Behavior, so the following would be the implementation for this Server Behavior:

```
function inspectServerBehavior(sbObj) {
  VARIABLE_NAME.value = sbObj.Variable__Name;
}
```

Cleaning Up: the *analyzeServerBehavior* Function

The Server Behavior is basically complete at this point. You can add the *analyzeServerBehavior* function to it if you care to do some last-minute checks. The function can check to make sure the parameter exists; if it doesn't, it will set the incomplete flag of the *ServerBehavior* object:

```
function analyzeServerBehavior(sbObj) {
  if(!sbObj.getParameter("Variable__Name"))
    sbObj.setIsIncomplete(true);
}
```

This function is checking to see whether the *Variable__Name* parameter is in place. If it isn't, the incomplete flag of the *ServerBehavior* object is set to true using the *setIsIncomplete* method of the *ServerBehavior* object. You can try out the functionality by applying the behavior to the page and then going back to the page in HTML source view and deleting the Variable Name. If you look at the Server Behavior panel, there should be a red check mark next to the item name at this point. If you were to bring up the user interface again by double-clicking the Server Behavior in the Server Behavior panel, the Variable Name field would be blank. But if you enter the attribute into the box and then click OK, the behavior will be complete again.

Implementing the *deleteServerBehavior* Function

In many cases, the *deleteServerBehavior* function is the easiest to write. This function is called when a user clicks the minus (–) button on the Server Behavior floater. Generally, in the simpler Server Behaviors, it's merely a matter of calling the *dwscripts.deleteSB* method. Here's how the *deleteServerBehavior* function is implemented for the Timestamp Session Variable Server Behavior:

```
function deleteServerBehavior(sbObj){
  dwscripts.deleteSB(sbObj);
}
```

In certain cases in which your Server Behavior might be very complex, the *dwscripts.deleteSB* method can't be used. In these cases, you may use whatever method is at your disposal to remove the Server Behavior code from the page. Using regular expressions, pattern matching, and string manipulation would be one way.

Other Functions

There are a couple of other functions that weren't used in this behavior, but are available to the writer of Server Behaviors. They are the *copyServerBehavior* and *pasteServerBehavior* functions. Their names alone should indicate the functionality they provide. If Dreamweaver MX sees these two functions in the extension, the Copy and Paste contextual menu items in the Server Behaviors panel will become activated, and you'll be able to copy and paste the extension from page to page.

Here's the *copyServerBehavior* function for your Timestamp Session Variable Server Behavior:

```
function copyServerBehavior(sbObj) {
  sbObj.preprocessForSerialize();
  return true;
}
```

As you can see, the *ServerBehavior* object is passed to the function. This happens internally through the Server Behavior API. If a user right-clicks the Server Behavior instance in the panel, and then clicks Copy, Dreamweaver MX will pass the *ServerBehavior* object to this function for manipulation. The function serializes the actual text of the object using the *preprocessForSerialize()* method of the object. The return value of true tells Dreamweaver MX that the serialization was successful—that is, the Server Behavior could be converted to a string for the clipboard. If this function returns true, the Paste menu item in the Server Behavior floater becomes active. For this simple case, we just assume that the serialization was successful and return *true*.

Another function is necessary for the *copyServerBehavior* and *pasteServerBehavior* functions to work: *createServerBehaviorObj()*. This function will create a new *ServerBehavior* object of the same type for the paste functionality:

```
function createServerBehaviorObj(){
  return new ServerBehavior("Timestamp Session Variable");
}
```

And now, here's the *pasteServerBehavior* function:

```
function pasteServerBehavior(ssRec) {
  if(findServerBehaviors().length !=0){
    alert("No more than one Timestamp Session Variable a page")
  }else{
```

```
    sbObj.postprocessForDeserialize();
    sbObj.queueDocEdits(true);
    dwscripts.applyDocEdits();
  }
}
```

Similar to the copy function, the *ServerBehavior* object is passed to the *pasteServerBehavior* function. That function now contains the serialized Server Behavior. Next, call the *findServerBehaviors* function to see if there are any existing Server Behaviors of this type already on the page. If an instance already exists on the page, an alert is flashed to the user and the function ends without pasting the behavior into the document. If not, the *ServerBehavior* object is deserialized (converted from a string back into an object), and the edits are queued up and applied using some of the new Dreamweaver MX API functionality.

| Tip | *The Server Behavior Builder in Dreamweaver MX doesn't include the copy and paste functions in the Server Behaviors it builds, but you can insert them manually by hand-coding the functionality as described in the preceding section.* |

Where Do You Go from Here?

Now that you've completed your first Server Behavior, you can see the required API methods that are used by most Server Behaviors. You've also seen some optional functions that you can use to enhance the Server Behavior (copy and paste). You can use similar techniques to build Server Behaviors for any application. Some of the functions are completely transportable to other Server Behaviors, whereas others will require extensive modification to be reusable. You can also use the PATT and MASK strings in Property inspectors or Translators to allow those extensions to find instances of your Server Behavior.

In any case, the basic framework is in place. You should now be able to use the Server Behavior API to build a Server Behavior that will insert any sort of server markup into your documents. Also, if the standard Server Behaviors that ship with Dreamweaver MX don't match your needs, you can add to them, copy them, or rewrite them to suit your own applications. The next section covers the automated method of building Server Behaviors.

Part 2: Using the Server Behavior Builder

Dreamweaver UltraDev 4 introduced a Server Behavior Builder that takes the hard work out of building simple Server Behaviors. The Server Behavior that you just created could have been created with the Server Behavior Builder. When you create a

Server Behavior using the Builder, the HTML file, the group EDML file, and the participant EDML files for the Server Behavior are created automatically.

Of course, the best way to learn how to use the Server Behavior Builder is by actually creating a Server Behavior.

Creating a Server Behavior with the Builder

Frequently, when you are accessing dynamic text, such as a database column, you may need to replace instances of the text with another character, word, or HTML tag. For example, when retrieving text from a database that has a line-feed character, the text will be displayed on the HTML page as one long string; however, HTML text must be formatted with <br> tags. Or assume that you need to replace a certain word or token in the text with the user's name, current time, current date, or some other dynamic data. You are now able to build an extremely simple Server Behavior that can address all of these situations.

Creating the Code for the Server Behavior

As with the hand-coded Server Behaviors, the most important thing to remember is that the code you use to create the Server Behavior should work properly before even beginning the creation process. Also, there are limitations with the Server Behavior Builder that you should be aware of before starting:

- The code blocks have to be completely enclosed by tags. For example, you can't insert text or code after a closing tag.

- You can't have an unclosed tag as part of a participant. For example, you can't have a <table> open tag in one participant and a </table> close tag in another.

- You can wrap a selection with a balanced tag pair, but you can't enclose a selection within a set of server-side tags.

- You can't edit the user selection in any way within the confines of the Builder. For example, if you want to enclose a dynamic database column with a server-side function, you can't do it with the Builder.

Experimentation with the Builder will enable you to develop solutions for some of the functionality you may want to achieve, but there are also some things that just can't be done.

 Trial and error is the best method for trying out the functionality of the Server Behavior Builder. The functionality is limited; but with a little ingenuity, you can create workarounds for the inherent limitations of the Builder.

The code you will be dealing with for this particular extension will, of course, vary from server model to server model. The Java code is a little more complex but accomplishes the same thing and will be inserted in the Server Behavior Builder in exactly the same way as the others. The code is as follows:

VBScript

```
<%=Replace((@@RecordsetName@@.Fields.Item("@@Column@@").Value), ¬
@@String To Replace@@, @@Replace With@@)%>
```

JavaScript

```
<%
var columnname = @@RecordsetName@@.Fields.Item("@@Column@@").Value;
var ToReplace = @@String To Replace@@;
var ReplaceWith = @@Replace With@@;
var i = columnname.indexOf(ToReplace);
while (i != -1)    {
    columnname = columnname.substr(0,i) + ReplaceWith + ¬
columnname.substr(i + ToReplace.length,columnname.length);
    i = columnname.indexOf(ToReplace,i);
}
Response.Write(columnname);
%>
```

JSP

```
<%
String columnname;   //if using this SB more than once on a page
String ToReplace;    //you should declare the variables in a
String ReplaceWith;  //separate script block
int TM_i;            //
columnname = @@RecordsetName@@.getString("@@Column@@");
ToReplace = "@@String To Replace@@";
ReplaceWith = "@@Replace With@@";
TM_i = columnname.indexOf(ToReplace);
while (TM_i != -1)     {
    columnname = columnname.substring(0, TM_i ) + ReplaceWith + ¬
columnname.substring(TM_i + ToReplace.length(), columnname.length());
    TM_i=columnname.indexOf(ToReplace, TM_i );
}
out.println(columnname);
%>
```

ColdFusion

```
<cfoutput>
#Replace(@@RecordsetName@@.@@Column@@, @@String To Replace@@, ¬
@@Replace With@@,"All")#</cfoutput>
```

PHP

```
<?php echo str_replace(@@String To Replace@@, @@Replace With@@, ¬
$row_@@RecordsetName@@['@@Column@@']); ?>
```

ASP.NET C#

```
<%# @@RecordsetNam@@.FieldValue("@@Column@@", ¬
Container).Replace(@@String To Replace@@,@@Replace With@@) %>
```

ASP.NET VB

```
<%# @@RecordsetNam@@.FieldValue("@@Column@@", ¬
Container).Replace(@@String To Replace@@,@@Replace With@@) %>
```

Giving the Server Behavior a Name

The Server Behavior Builder is accessed from the Server Behavior panel by clicking the plus sign (+) on the Server Behavior panel and then clicking New Server Behavior. This will show the New Server Behavior dialog box, shown in Figure 32-1. In this dialog box, you are given options for:

- **Server Model**   This can be any installed server model in Dreamweaver MX.
- **Name**   This is the name of the Server Behavior, which can include spaces.
- **Option: Copy Existing Server Behavior**   Select this check box to start creating your extension from an already existing Server Behavior.
- **Behavior to Copy**   This drop-down list displays all available Server Behaviors that you can copy from.

You'll name this new Server Behavior as *Dynamic Text with Replace* and then choose your server model. You can leave the Copy Existing Server Behavior option unselected. After you complete the naming process, click OK.

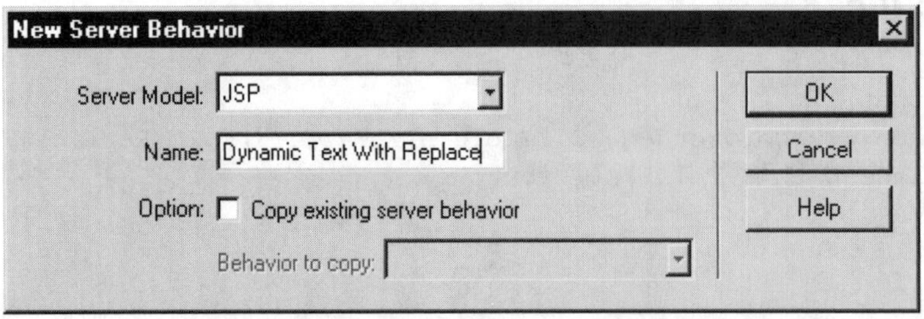

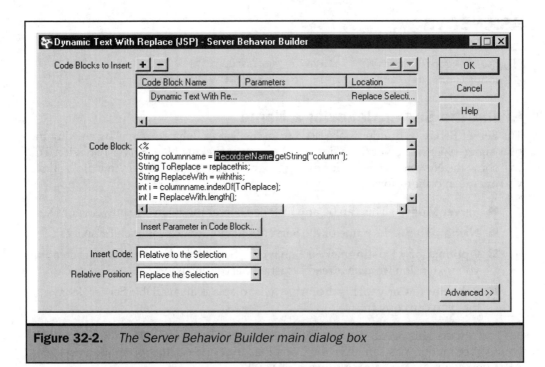

Figure 32-1.   The New Server Behavior dialog box allows you to copy from existing Server Behaviors or create a new one.

Adding the Code Block to the Builder

After clicking OK in the Server Behavior Builder, you will see the dialog box shown in Figure 32-2. You need to follow the steps shown next.

Figure 32-2.   The Server Behavior Builder main dialog box

1. Click the plus sign (+) to insert a new code block. The code block name will default to the Server Behavior name appended with _block1. This is fine for now, but later, when you develop more complex extensions, you can choose more meaningful names.

2. You should copy and paste your code block into the Code Block box.

3. Starting with the first parameter in the code block, highlight the parameter (in this case, *RecordsetName*).

4. Click the Insert Parameter In Code Block button to see the dialog box shown in Figure 32-3. Choose a name to identify the parameter, such as Recordset Name. This is the name that will appear in the Server Behavior interface when you apply the behavior to the page. If the parameter appears more than once in the code block, you will be prompted to replace all occurrences. You should always say yes to this. The parameter name is inserted into the code block surrounded by @@ to identify it as a parameter. This is how the Server Behavior Builder transforms your code block into a MASK variable.

5. Follow Steps 3 and 4 for each of the other three parameters that are in this behavior: *Column*, *String To Replace*, and *Replace With*.

6. The Insert Code drop-down box has several options. For this Server Behavior, choose Relative To The Selection.

7. The Relative Position drop-down box also has several options that vary according to which position you choose for the Insert Code box. For this Server Behavior, choose Replace The Selection.

8. Click Advanced. This will extend the dialog box with some advanced features (as shown in Figure 32-4).

9. The Server Behavior Title box shows you the title that will actually appear in the Server Behavior inspector. The parameters that you inserted into the behavior are listed to the right of the Server Behavior name in parentheses. You can leave these here, or if there is a long list of them, put only the parameters in here that will give your Server Behavior title some meaning when you see the

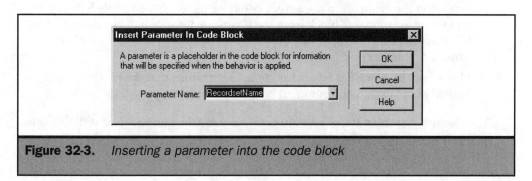

Figure 32-3.   *Inserting a parameter into the code block*

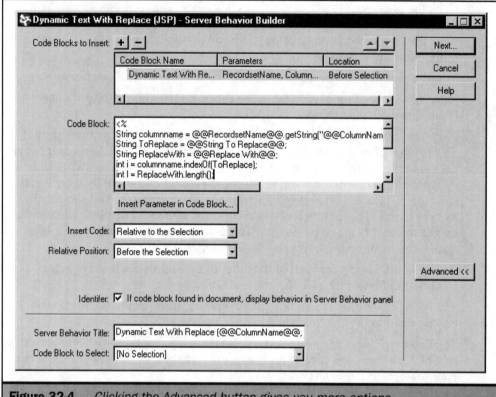

Figure 32-4.   *Clicking the Advanced button gives you more options.*

title in the Server Behavior inspector. For this particular behavior, leave this set to the default.

10. The Code Block To Select box is set to the default (No Selection). This box gives you the option to have your code highlighted in the design environment when you select the behavior in the Server Behavior panel. To accomplish this, you must choose your code block from the drop-down list of blocks available. For this extension, there is only one block—Dynamic Text With Re_block1 (or similar depending on the name you gave it).

11. Make sure the Identifier box is selected. This ensures that the block is highlighted in the design environment based on the choice you made in Step 10.

After completing these steps, you can click Next to take you to the next dialog box.

Creating the HTML Interface for Your Server Behavior

Upon clicking Next in the Server Behavior Builder, you are taken to the Generate Behavior Dialog Box screen, shown in Figure 32-5. This dialog box allows you to choose from the following types of HTML interface controls for the Server Behavior:

- **Recordset Menu**   This allows you to choose from a list of recordsets on the page.
- **Recordset Field Menu**   This gives you a list of columns in your recordsets.
- **Editable Recordset Menu**   This allows you to choose from a list of recordsets on the page or type in a value*.
- **Editable Recordset Field Menu**   This gives you a list of columns in your recordsets, or you can type in a value.
- **CF Data Source Menu**   Choose from a list of ColdFusion data sources.
- **Connection Menu**   Choose from a list of your available connections.
- **Connection Table Menu**   If you have a Connection Menu in the Server Behavior, you can use this to display a list of the tables available for a particular connection.
- **Connection Column Menu**   This will show a list of columns in a table if you have a Connection Menu and a Connection Table Menu in the Server Behavior.
- **Text Field**   This is a plain text field.
- **Dynamic Text Field**   This will place a lightning bolt button next to your text field so that a dynamic text item can be chosen.
- **URL Text Field**   This option places a Browse button next to the text field so you can choose a path to a file.
- **Numeric Text Field**   This is a plain text field that will validate for a numeric value only.
- **Recordset Fields Ordered List**   This control will generate a list box with recordset fields, a plus and minus button, and up and down buttons (shown in Figure 32-6). A Recordset Menu is required for this to work.
- **Text Field Comma Separated List**   This control returns a list of text fields on your page.
- **List Menu**   This is a list menu control that adds a standard HTML select element to your Server Behavior.
- **Checkbox**   Adds a check box to your Server Behavior.
- **Radio Group**   Allows you to add a group of radio buttons to your Server Behavior.

* New to Dreamweaver MX is the capability to define an editable <select> tag in your extensions. You can do this by adding an editable="true" attribute to a <select> tag.

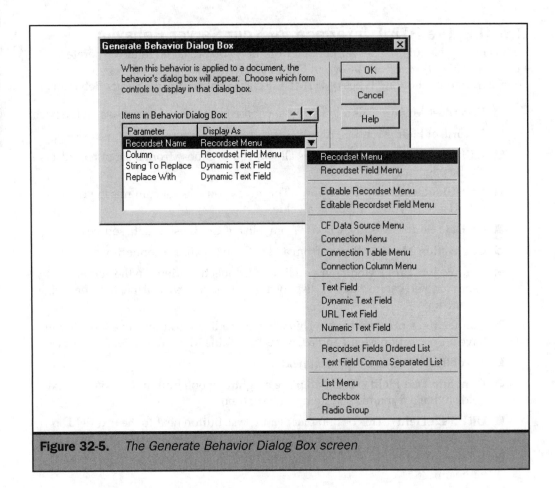

Figure 32-5. *The Generate Behavior Dialog Box screen*

Most of the Server Behavior Builder controls can be used without modification, but some of them, like the Radio Group, have to be edited manually in the Server Behavior HTML file after your Server Behavior is created.

For this behavior, choose Recordset Menu for the *Recordset Name* parameter, Recordset Field Menu for the *Column* parameter, and Dynamic Text Fields for the two remaining parameters—*String To Replace* and *Replace With*. The up and down arrows allow you to position the fields on the interface in the order you choose. Figure 32-6 shows that the list is as follows: Recordset Name is first, followed by Column Name, String to Replace, and Replace With. This order follows the logical order of the Server Behavior.

After clicking OK, you now have a new Server Behavior that you can apply to any page you choose. The behavior appears in the Server Behavior panel at the bottom of the list of behaviors.

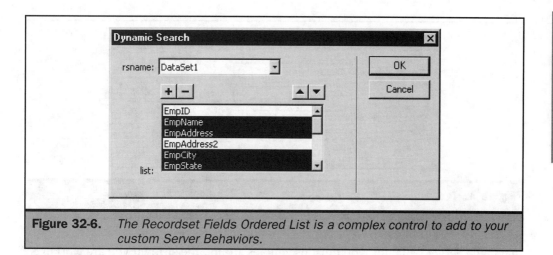

Figure 32-6.   *The Recordset Fields Ordered List is a complex control to add to your custom Server Behaviors.*

Using the Server Behavior

You can now apply this behavior. Notice that because you chose Recordset Menu for the interface, the Server Behavior actually prohibits you from using it on the page if you don't have a recordset defined already. The auto-generated interfaces have basic validation only, and you would have to hand-code any other validation you might want to do on the field. For example, if you wanted to restrict a file field in a URL text field to a certain type of file, such as GIF, you could place the input validation into the HTML file. In addition, if any fields are left blank, the behavior can still be applied, which can generate errors on your final page. You should make sure you insert the proper validation in your HTML file in the *applyServerBehavior(sbObj)* function.

If you have a page with a recordset on it, apply the behavior and select one of the columns. The view_a_resume page has several columns with line breaks in them that were hand-coded in Chapter 25. Now that you have a Server Behavior to perform the work, this functionality need not be hand-coded anymore. If you apply the behavior to the page (shown in Figure 32-7), you can use the following parameters (note that this is a C# example):

- *Recordset Name*   *rsDisplayResume*
- *Column*   *ResExperience*
- *String to Replace*   "\n"
- *Replace With*   "<br>"

The Server Behavior will appear in the Server Behavior panel along with the parameters. Figure 32-8 shows the page with three instances of the behavior. Notice

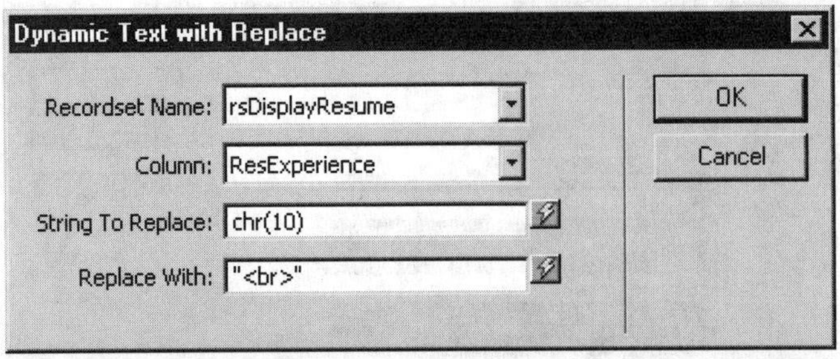

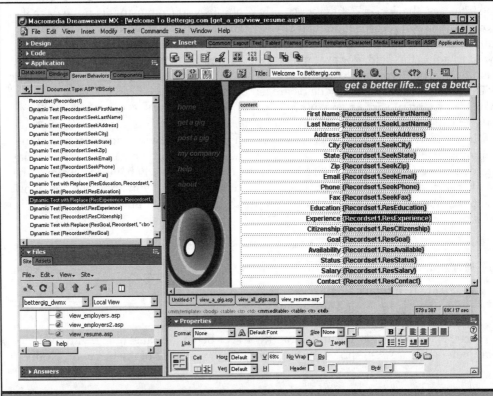

Figure 32-7.   *Applying the newly created Server Behavior to the page*

that in the Server Behavior, you must use quotes around the string if you are working with literal text. This enables you to use the behavior with any combination of possible literal or variable strings.

Figure 32-8.   *The view_resume page with three instances of the Server Behavior on it*

Creating a Server Behavior with More Than One Participant

Using the Server Behavior Builder allows you to quickly build complex Server Behaviors with as many code blocks as you may need. In many cases, there are conditions that must be met before certain parts of your page are displayed. Dreamweaver MX comes with a Show Region behavior that deals with recordsets, but, frequently, you may need to check for other conditions, such as the value of a session variable, a cookie, or whether two different values match each other. This is easy with the Server Behavior Builder because you can choose to insert a block of code before the selection and a block of code after the selection. In a situation such as this, the first block would be the IF statement, and the second block would be the END IF block. Your first block might look like this:

```
<%If (Session("AccessLevel") = "@@Access Level@@") Then %> (VBScript)
<%If (Session("AccessLevel") = "@@Access Level@@") %> (VB)
<%if (Session("AccessLevel") == "@@Access Level@@") {%> (JavaScript)
<?php if ($_Session["AccessLevel"] == "@@Access Level@@") {?> (PHP)
<%if (Session["AccessLevel"] == "@@Access Level@@") {%> (C#)
<%if (session.getValue("AccessLevel") == "@@Access Level@@"){%>
(Java)
```

and the second block might look like this:

```
<% End If %>(VBScript and VB)
<?php } ?>  (PHP)
<% } %>  (Java, C#, and JavaScript)
```

To create a Server Behavior such as this, you'll use the same methods as outlined in the preceding example, except that you would add a second participant and give the Relative Position drop-down box a value of After the Selection. You can save this Server Behavior with the name "Show If Access Level".

 Make sure you leave the box unchecked for If Code Block Is Found In Document, Display Behavior In Server Behavior Panel for the closing participant. The code block is too generic and will cause the Server Behavior to show up erroneously.

A ColdFusion user can use the special Relative Position choice of Wrap Around Selection for this example. Any time you have a tag that has a corresponding close tag, you may use this option. The ColdFusion example is as follows:

```
<cfif (Session.AccessLevel EQ "@@Access Level@@")></cfif>
```

Using a balanced set of tags like this will cause Dreamweaver MX to insert the beginning <cfif> tag before the selection and the ending </cfif> tag after the selection. However, in the previous VBScript, JavaScript, VB, C#, and Java examples, the code blocks are completely separate tag blocks, so they aren't able to use this special Wrap Around Selection feature. One of the limitations of the feature is that you can only use it once in a Server Behavior. You cannot, for example, insert a <td></td> in one block and a <tr></tr> in another block and expect them to both wrap around the selection. Doing so will actually cause the page to write out the selection twice—once with a <td> pair wrapped around it and once with a <tr> pair wrapped around it.

Creating a Translator

You may have noticed that the newly created Show If Access Level Server Behavior doesn't show anything in the design environment. You can create a new translator participant for the Show If Access Level Server Behavior by looking at the XML files that are part of the XML architecture of Dreamweaver MX.

Translators are the extensions that take care of translating the code that is inserted into the page in a user-friendly viewable item.

The Translators Folder

All the EDML files for the Server Behavior extensions created by the Server Behavior Builder are stored in the ServerBehaviors subfolder for the server model that you created the extension for. As mentioned earlier in the chapter, there is a main Group file and Participant files for each of the code blocks that were created. The Group file contains general information about the Participant files. The Participant files contain the information needed to find the code in the document so that the Server Behavior can be displayed in the Server Behavior panel. The Participant files are also the key to building a Translator for your Server Behavior.

Group Participants

Each of the participant files contains a single code block. It could be a set of server tags, HTML tags, or an attribute of a tag. If the Server Behavior was built with the Server Behavior Builder, you'll have one participant file for each code block or attribute that you assigned in the Builder. If you look at the beginning code block participant file generated for the Show If Access Level Server Behavior, you'll see the main requirements (shown here for C#):

```
<participant version="6.0">
  <insertText location="beforeSelection">
<![CDATA[<%if (Session["AccessLevel"] == "@@Access__Level@@")
{%>]]>
```

```
    </insertText>
    <searchPatterns whereToSearch="directive">
      <searchPattern paramNames="Access__Level" isOptional="false"
limitSearch="all">
<![CDATA[/if \(Session\["AccessLevel"\] == "([^\r\n]*?)"\) ¬
\{(?=\r\n|\r|\n|%>)/i]]></searchPattern>
    </searchPatterns>
    <quickSearch>(Session["AccessLevel"]</quickSearch>
</participant>
```

Depending on which server model you implemented, your own file may look a little different, but the tags will be the same. The main tag is the <participant> tag, which gives the version number of the program that the extension will work with.

Next, the <insertText> tag contains the code that is being inserted, and tells Dreamweaver MX where to put the code. The code contains a MASK string created by Dreamweaver MX that is like the MASK variables you built earlier in the chapter.

The <searchPattern> tags contain information about the regular expression pattern used to find the code in the user's document. This is similar to the PATT variables discussed earlier in the chapter. Again, with the knowledge of how these PATT variables are built, you can build your own from scratch or modify the patterns created by the Builder to make them more efficient and more powerful. The <searchPattern> tag also contains a list of the parameters that were defined in the Builder. The <searchPattern> tag is contained within a <searchPatterns> tag, allowing the use of several pattern blocks to be used by defining separate <searchPattern> tags for each one.

The <quickSearch> tag acts like a quick glance through the document to find an instance of your behavior. In the manually created Server Behaviors, you could have used a Search String comment tag at the top of the Server Behavior file to act as your quick search. If Dreamweaver MX doesn't find the <quickSearch> string in the document, it knows that a more thorough search for the Server Behavior is not required.

Translator Participants

To go along with the new EDML format for Server Behaviors, you can also write translators by using XML inside of its own EDML file. The translator participants are located in the Configuration | Translators | [server model] folder. You can create these from scratch for your own Server Behaviors, allowing you to place a user-friendly representation of your code in the design environment instead of a gold script shield that accompanies a generic server script, or nothing at all in some cases. For the Show If Access Level Server Behavior, you'll want a translator that works in a similar fashion to the Show Region translator, allowing a light, gray-colored tab to be displayed around the region. In the Show If Access Level behavior, the tab should say Show If Access Level instead of Show If.

To create the Translator participant files for the Show If Access Level Server Behavior, you can cheat a little and use the begin block and end block Participant files of the Show If Access Level Server Behavior as starting points. The translator participants must have unique names that are different from the names of the Server Behavior participants.

The following is the XML code for the ShowIfAccessLevel_Start.edml participant for ASP.NET_Csharp. The search patterns will be different for the other server models, but the tags are the same:

```
<participant version="6.0">
<translator>
  <insertText location="beforeSelection">
<![CDATA[<%if (Session["AccessLevel"] == "@@Access__Level@@") {%>]]>
  </insertText>
  <searchPatterns whereToSearch="directive">
    <searchPattern paramNames="Access__Level" isOptional="false"
     limitSearch="all">
<![CDATA[/if \(Session\["AccessLevel"\] == "([^\r\n]*?)"\) ¬
\{(?=\r\n|\r|\n|%>)/i]]>
    </searchPattern>
    <searchPattern requiredLocation="trailing" isOptional="false"
     limitSearch="all"><![CDATA[/\} (?=\r\n|\r|\n|%>)/i]]>
    </searchPattern>
  </searchPatterns>
  <translations>
    <translation whereToSearch="directive"
     translationType="tabbed region start">
      <openTag>DWMXTCR:SHOW</openTag>
      <display>Show If Access Level</display>
    </translation>
  </translations>
</translator>
</participant>
```

The first <searchPattern> tag is similar to the same tag in the Server Behavior participant files. The regular expression defined in this tag will be identical to the expression defined in the Server Behavior participant file. In fact, you can copy/paste the <searchPattern> tag from the Server Behavior participant file.

The second <searchPattern> tag in this participant is actually the same pattern that is in the end participant of the Server Behavior. Therefore, it follows that you can copy/paste the pattern from the participant and use it here. The added attribute *requiredLocation="trailing"* tells the translator that this participant is the end of the translation and that it is a required participant.

When creating translator participant files for your own Server Behaviors, it is easier to copy the Server Behavior <searchPattern> tags verbatim from the Server Behavior EDML participant files.

Next are the <translation> tags, enclosed within a pair of <translations> tags. The *whereToSearch* attribute tells the translator where the search patterns might be located. A *whereToSearch* attribute of Directive implies that it is in a section of server-side script. The *whereToSearch* attribute could contain a tag name here as well. For example, if you had a special type of table you wanted to translate, you could use an attribute of *whereToSearch="table"*. The *translationType* indicates the type of translator this is. Here, it's a tabbed region start type. Other possible types are dynamic data, dynamic image, dynamic source, tabbed region end, and custom.

The <opentag> tag is an optional tag that will actually allow you to place a tag into the translated source code of the document. The <opentag> tag can also have attributes that usually correspond to the variables defined by the user for the Server Behavior. In this case, you can leave the attributes off and use a tag name of *DWMXTCR:SHOW*.

Next is the <display> tag. This is where you place the actual text the user sees in the design environment. You can put a global variable or literal value in the display tag. In this case, use the literal value "Show If Access Level." This will cause the tab in the design environment to show the proper label.

After completing the changes and saving this file, you can do the same thing for the ShowIfAccessLevel_End.edml file. Copy the participant patterns from the Server Behavior participant files once again. The code is as follows:

```
<participant version="6.0">
<translator>
  <insertText location="beforeSelection">
<![CDATA[<%if (Session["AccessLevel"] == "@@Access__Level@@") {%>]]>
  </insertText>
  <searchPatterns whereToSearch="directive">
    <searchPattern requiredLocation="leading" paramNames="Access__Level"
    isOptional="false" limitSearch="all">
<![CDATA[/if \(Session\["AccessLevel"\] == "([^\r\n]*?)"\) ¬
\{(?=\r\n|\r|\n|%>)/i]]></searchPattern>
    <searchPattern isOptional="false" limitSearch="all">
<![CDATA[/\} (?=\r\n|\r|\n|%>)/i]]></searchPattern>
  </searchPatterns>
  <translations>
    <translation whereToSearch="directive" translationType="tabbed region end">
```

```
    <closeTag>DWMXTCR:SHOW</closeTag>
  </translation>
 </translations>
</translator>
</participant>
```

Notice that in the ShowIfAccessLevel_End file, there is a <closetag> to correspond with the <opentag> from the ShowIfAccessLevel_Start file. Also, the <searchPattern> tag has a *requiredLocation="leading"* to correspond to the pattern for the Server Behavior participant.

If you save these files and apply the Server Behavior to a selected area of code in the design environment, it should appear as in Figure 32-9, with a tabbed outline that says Show If Access Level.

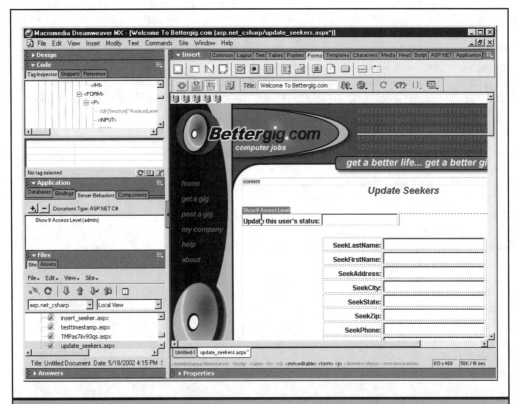

Figure 32-9.   *The Show If Access Level Server Behavior has been applied to a selected area of code, and the custom translator accents the region.*

Copying an Existing Server Behavior

If you have used the Server Behavior Builder in UltraDev 4, you know that you can copy existing Server Behaviors and create your own variations of them. With Dreamweaver MX, the Server Behaviors don't show up by default in the Server Behavior Builder. This is to prevent errors from occurring in your copies of these complex Server Behaviors, and also to prevent users from damaging the built-in Server Behaviors. Most of the built-in Server Behaviors rely on custom JavaScript for much of their functionality. Simple copies almost never work properly without you getting into the JavaScript code and tweaking it a little.

You can create your own copies, however. All you need to do is to find the Group EDML file for the Server Behavior that you want to copy and find the *hideFromBuilder* attribute. This attribute is set to true in all Server Behaviors that come with Dreamweaver MX, but you can remove the attribute to allow you to make your own copy in the Server Behavior Builder. For example, you can alter this code from the CheckNewUsername.edml Group file:

```
<group serverBehavior="Check New Username.htm"
hideFromBuilder="true">
  <groupParticipants selectParticipant="CheckNewUsername_main">
    <groupParticipant name="CheckNewUsername_main" />
  </groupParticipants>
</group>
```

After you remove *hideFromBuilder* attribute, the Server Behavior will show up in the Server Behavior Builder and you'll be able to make a copy.

Tweaking the SBB-Generated Patterns

One of the timesaving features of the Server Behavior Builder is that it generates all of the regular expression patterns that your Server Behavior needs. This saves time in the long run, but you also have to be aware of the pitfalls.

The expression that is generated is a strict translation of your code into a regular expression, with no room for code modifications by the end user. For example, if you have a Server Behavior that consists of the following code:

```
<table>
    <tr>
        <td><%=Session("@@Firstname@@")%></td>
    </tr>
</table>
```

the regular expression that will be generated looks like this:

```
/<table>\s*<tr>\s*<td>\s*<%=Session\("([^\r\n]*?)"\)%>\s* ¬
<\/td>\s*<\/tr>\s*<\/table>/I
```

The problem with the pattern is that as soon as someone modifies the table on the page, the code will look completely different, like this:

```
<table width="157">
    <tr>
        <td height="131"><%=Session("Firstname")%></td>
    </tr>
</table>
```

The pattern doesn't work any more and the Server Behavior doesn't show up in the panel. By changing the generated pattern inside of the EDML participant files, you can change the pattern so that it is more receptive to change, as in the following pattern, which will match both pieces of code:

```
/<table[^>]*>\s*<tr[^>]*>\s*<td[^>]*>\s*<%=Session\("([^\r\n]*?)"\)
%>\s* ¬
<\/td>\s*<\/tr>\s*<\/table>/I
```

By simply modifying the <table>, <tr>, and <td> tags with a [^>]* pattern to reflect "anything or everything up to the > character," you have made the pattern much more flexible in the Dreamweaver MX environment.

Where Do You Keep Your Server Behaviors?

You might be wondering how to keep track of Server Behaviors after they start to accumulate. The Server Behavior panel will become cluttered in no time if the Server Behaviors are kept in the main ServerBehaviors folder. The Server Behavior Builder will put the Server Behaviors that it creates at the root level of the ServerBehaviors > [server model] folder, making it even more cluttered. Let's take a look at how the folder is organized and where you can put your files, which can also apply to the files made with the Server Behavior Builder.

Inside the main Server Behaviors folder are several other folders—one for each server model (ASP_Vbs, ASP_Js, ASP.NET_Csharp, ASP.NET_Vb, JSP, PHP_MySQL, UD4-ColdFusion, and ColdFusion). In a Macromedia extension, the file will typically be saved as an HTML file in the main folder. Together with the HTML files in some of the larger extensions are JS files for the functions. The Server Behavior you just completed was fairly short, so it was just saved as a unit, along with the EDML Group file and the

EDML Participant file. However, you could also have removed all the JavaScript and placed it in its own file. The extensions, however, must reside in the *individual server model folders* in order for the Server Behavior panel to be able to see them.

Fortunately, Dreamweaver MX is smart enough to give a new menu item to each folder that resides in the server model folders under the ServerBehaviors root folder. Just as you did in the last chapter with Objects, you can create a Custom Extension folder, or call it by any name you choose, and put it in the ASP_Vbs, ASP_Js, ASP.NET_Csharp, ASP.NET_Vb, JSP, PHP_MySQL, UD4-ColdFusion, or ColdFusion folder for your own use. You can then put your extension into this folder.

In addition, you will need to change any references to JavaScript that include files in your main HTML Server Behavior file. These references are usually at the top of the file—you should change them to reflect the new location of the HTML file. For example, if you are moving the file into a subfolder, you would have to append ../ to the beginning of each include path, as in this example:

■ Was:

```
<SCRIPT SRC="../../Shared/Common/Scripts/dwscripts.js"></SCRIPT>
```

■ Change to:

```
<SCRIPT SRC="../../../Shared/Common/Scripts/dwscripts.js"></SCRIPT>
```

Another way to change the menus is to write commands in the MXI file that are used to create a packaged extension. These commands allow you to put your extensions virtually anywhere and point the menu items to the appropriate file.

Extending the Server Behavior Builder (SBB)

In keeping with the tradition of extensibility, Macromedia also made the Server Behavior Builder in Dreamweaver MX extensible. You can customize the look and functionality of the Server Behaviors that you build by simply changing the template that is used to generate the Server Behaviors, or by adding your own custom JavaScript controls to the Server Behavior Builder.

Extending the Server Behavior Template

You can extend the SBB by changing the ServerBehaviorTemplate.asp file located in Configuration | Shared | Controls. This template, upon examination, is actually JavaScript. If you've looked at a few Server Behaviors generated by the SBB, you'll see exactly where they came from—the ServerBehaviorTemplate.asp. Although it's beyond the scope of this book to delve too deeply into customizing this template, we show you a simple change you can make to include your own logo into the files generated by the SBB.

If you want to modify the ServerBehaviorTemplate.asp file, we strongly suggest that you make a backup copy of the original file and keep it in a safe place. If the original file is damaged, the SBB won't work anymore.

If you open up that file (ServerBehaviorTemplate.asp) and look inside the <body> tags of the document, it looks like this:

```
<BODY onLoad="initializeUI()">
<% if (numParameters > 0) { %>
<FORM NAME="theForm">
  <TABLE BORDER=0>
<% for (i = 0; i < numParameters; i++) { %>
    <TR>
      <TD ALIGN="right" VALIGN="baseline" NOWRAP>
        <%= paramLabels[i] %>:
      </TD>
      <TD VALIGN="baseline" NOWRAP>
        <%= paramControlSources[i].replace(/\n/g, "\n          ") %>
      </TD>
    </TR>
    <TR><TD HEIGHT="1"></TD></TR>
<% } %>
  </TABLE>
</FORM>
<% } %>
</BODY>
</HTML>
```

The code is easy to understand and is easily modified. First, the <body> tag is written to the Server Behavior file with an event: *initializeIU()*. Next, if there are parameters, a form and table are written to the Server Behavior. If not, the closing </body> tag is written.

Just by looking at the looping code in the code listing, you should be able to tell that the parameters are each inserted into a separate table row. You can easily sneak your own logo into a row of its own after the parameters loop has ended. Right after the closing <% } %> tag, you can insert your logo with a link to your home page in one row and a brief description in another row:

```
<tr bgcolor="#d3d3d3">
  <td align="left" valign="baseline" colspan="2">
    Insert a <%= serverBehaviorTitle %> Server Behavior on the page.
  </td>
</tr>
```

```
<tr bgcolor="#d3d3d3">
  <td align = "left">
  <input type="image"
   src="../../Shared/dwteam/images/dwteam.gif"
onClick='dreamweaver.browseDocument("http://www.dwteam.com")'>
  </td>
  <td align="right" valign="baseline" nowrap><br>
   <b>written by Tom Muck</b><br>
   http://www.dwteam.com
  </td>
</tr>
```

Most of this is self-explanatory, but the one thing that you may not have noticed is this:

```
<%= serverBehaviorTitle %>
```

As you can see, the ServerBehaviorTemplate.asp file uses the syntax of ASP JavaScript!

You can also modify this file to add functions that you need (such as *copyServerBehavior* and *pasteServerBehavior*), include your own custom JavaScript shared file references, or expand the interface even more by using a tabbed interface in place of the plain interface file that is standard.

Adding Custom Server Behavior Builder Controls

Another way you can extend the SBB is by building your own controls. The main controls for the SBB are located in Configuration | Shared | Controls | String Menu. These are the HTML files that the SBB uses to populate the drop-down list of available controls. You can easily add a new one by copying an existing control file and making changes in it.

The interface of the control is in the HTML file, but the functionality is in the JavaScript file located in Configuration | Shared | Controls | Scripts. If you add your own control to the SBB, you have to make sure you include the JS file of the new control in your Server Behavior package if you distribute it. We guide you through building an extremely simple control, based on the standard text field, which will add the Dreamweaver Color Picker control to the standard drop-down list of available SBB controls.

Because this file will be modified from the existing text field, we just highlight the changes. First, make a copy of the TextField.htm file located in Configuration | Shared | Controls | String Menu and name it "ColorField.htm." These files contain a reference to the JavaScript file that contains the functionality, as well as the entire code that will be used in the final Server Behavior. Like the ServerBehaviorTemplate.asp file that was just shown, this file has variables in it that will be filled in by the SBB. You could say that these controls extend the ServerBehaviorTemplate.asp file, not Dreamweaver MX itself.

Three changes need to be made to ColorField.htm:

```
<TITLE>Text Field</TITLE>
```

needs to be changed to:

```
<TITLE>Color Field</TITLE>
```

Next, this line:

```
    "Shared/Controls/Scripts/TextField.js");
```

needs to be changed to:

```
    "Shared/Controls/Scripts/ColorField.js");
```

Finally, the *controlSource()* function needs to replaced with the following:

```
function controlSource(name) {
  return '' +
    '<input type="mmcolorbutton" name="' + name +
    'color' onChange="dwscripts.findDOMObject(' + "'" + name +
    "'" +         ').value=this.value"><input type="text" name="' +
    name + '" style="width:150px" onBlur="dwscripts.findDOMObject(' +
    "'" + name + "color').value=this.value" + '">';
}
```

The *controlSource()* function is the actual string that you will insert in your Server Behavior when you build it with the SBB and choose the ColorField as your input source. As you can see, just as in the ServerBehaviorTemplate.asp file, there are variables in this function that are going to be replaced by the SBB. In this case, the string is returned to the SBB after the *name* variable has been replaced in this function four times and the string has been concatenated.

Now, you'll need to make a copy of the TextField.js file located in Configuration | Shared | Controls | Scripts. Name this one ColorField.js. The first thing you'll need to do to this copy of the original file is a global find/replace on all instances of the word "TextField," replacing it with "ColorField." Next, you need to add the functionality to read the *mmcolorcontrol* and return the value to the Server Behavior using this control. This is done in three separate functions:

In the *ColorField_initializeUI()* function, add this line right after the similar line for the text field:

```
this.colorControl = dwscripts.findDOMObject(this.paramName+'color');
```

In the *ColorField_inspectServerBehavior()* function, add this line right after the similar line for the text field:

```
this.colorControl.value = theValue;
```

Finally, in the *ColorField_setValue()* function, add this line right after the similar line for the text field:

```
this.colorControl.value = theValue;
```

That's all there is to it for the new ColorField Server Behavior control. The Server Behavior that you build with this control will actually read the value from the text field—the color picker is simply there to set the value of the text field. The text field also has the ability to set the value of the color picker. That is, if you change the value of the color in the text field itself, the color in the color picker will change. You can now use this control in any Server Behavior that you build that may need to have a color attribute assigned somewhere in the behavior, such as in an alternate colored row extension.

Server Models

Currently, Dreamweaver MX offers support for ASP VBScript, ASP JScript, ASP.NET VB, ASP.NET C#, ColdFusion, JSP, and PHP/MySQL. You can add a new server model fairly easily so that Dreamweaver MX could support another server type, such as PHP PostgreSQL, CF Express, ASP 3, ASP.NET JScript, or any other server-side technology. As of this writing, there is a popular PHP 4.0 Server Model available for Dreamweaver MX that was described in Chapter 18. Server Model extensions are not to be taken lightly, because you will have to implement an entire set of Server Behaviors in Dreamweaver MX for the server that you want to support.

Server models are much easier to implement in Dreamweaver MX than they were in UltraDev 4, however. Functionality for the different server models has been moved into server-specific folders within the Configuration folder. In Dreamweaver MX, you can create a server model without infringing on any of the existing Dreamweaver MX functionality.

To add a new server model, several files must be in place, and you must make several other configuration changes. To start with, the Configuration | ServerModels folder contains the main ingredients of the server model. You can start by creating a new server model definition file in this folder. It's easy to copy an existing server model file and add your own bits to it to make it work for your server model.

Next, create the document type for your server model in Configuration | DocumentTypes folder. Take a look at the existing document types in the

MMDocumentTypes.xml file for an indication of how to proceed. You can either add to that file or create your own XML file.

Next, create the Configuration | ServerBehaviors | [your server model] folder. The easiest way, once again, is to copy an existing folder that is similar to the server model that you want to add and then simply make changes to the Server Behaviors rather than create them from scratch.

Next, the Connections | [your server model] folder will contain the connection files for your server model. Once again, look at the way that existing connection files are made. This is always the best way to start rather than to try to create one from scratch.

Other folders that you will have to create are the DataSources, Translators, and ServerFormats folders. With all of these folders in place, your new server model should be functional.

Summary

In this chapter, you've learned how to create Server Behaviors in several ways. You can hand-code Server Behaviors in HTML and JavaScript, or you can create EDML participant files for the Server Behavior. In addition, the Server Behavior Builder has removed a lot of the tedious work in building basic Server Behaviors. The Builder was introduced in Dreamweaver UltraDev 4 and has some limitations, but promises to be an outstanding feature in years to come. For a full explanation of the Server Behavior EDML format, you should read the extensibility documentation that comes with Dreamweaver MX.

A Few Last Words

Dreamweaver MX is a program that deals with a multitude of different technologies. To become proficient in the use of Dreamweaver MX, you'll need to be proficient in HTML, JavaScript, SQL, graphics, database design, and one of the server technologies that Dreamweaver MX can be used with. We've tried to present the material in such a way as to give the user a complete picture of what is possible with the program. We've also tried to give enough information about each topic so that it can serve as a useful guide for related technologies, enabling the reader to delve more deeply into areas that he or she might be interested in. Web development is not a static profession that has a set of rules that everyone must follow. There are many paths you can take, and many technologies you can learn. We've tried to give you a look at those technologies through Dreamweaver MX.

Ray West and Tom Muck
June 2002

Index

References to figures and illustrations are in italics.

G

H

INTERNATIONAL CONTACT INFORMATION

AUSTRALIA
McGraw-Hill Book Company Australia Pty. Ltd.
TEL +61-2-9415-9899
FAX +61-2-9415-5687
http://www.mcgraw-hill.com.au
books-it_sydney@mcgraw-hill.com

CANADA
McGraw-Hill Ryerson Ltd.
TEL +905-430-5000
FAX +905-430-5020
http://www.mcgrawhill.ca

**GREECE, MIDDLE EAST,
NORTHERN AFRICA**
McGraw-Hill Hellas
TEL +30-1-656-0990-3-4
FAX +30-1-654-5525

MEXICO (Also serving Latin America)
McGraw-Hill Interamericana Editores S.A. de C.V.
TEL +525-117-1583
FAX +525-117-1589
http://www.mcgraw-hill.com.mx
fernando_castellanos@mcgraw-hill.com

SINGAPORE (Serving Asia)
McGraw-Hill Book Company
TEL +65-863-1580
FAX +65-862-3354
http://www.mcgraw-hill.com.sg
mghasia@mcgraw-hill.com

SOUTH AFRICA
McGraw-Hill South Africa
TEL +27-11-622-7512
FAX +27-11-622-9045
robyn_swanepoel@mcgraw-hill.com

**UNITED KINGDOM & EUROPE
(Excluding Southern Europe)**
McGraw-Hill Education Europe
TEL +44-1-628-502500
FAX +44-1-628-770224
http://www.mcgraw-hill.co.uk
computing_neurope@mcgraw-hill.com

ALL OTHER INQUIRIES Contact:
Osborne/McGraw-Hill
TEL +1-510-549-6600
FAX +1-510-883-7600
http://www.osborne.com
omg_international@mcgraw-hill.com

Complete References

Herbert Schildt
0-07-213485-2

Jeffery R. Shapiro
0-07-213381-3

Chris H. Pappas & William
H. Murray, III
0-07-212958-1

Herbert Schildt
0-07-213084-9

Ron Ben-Natan & Ori Sasson
0-07-222394-4

Arthur Griffith
0-07-222405-3

For the answers to everything related to your technology, drill as deeply as you please into our Complete Reference series. Written by topical authorities, these comprehensive resources offer a full range of knowledge, including extensive product information, theory, step-by-step tutorials, sample projects, and helpful appendixes.

OSBORNE
www.osborne.com

For more information on these and other Osborne books, visit our Web site at www.osborne.com